To Pe[illegible] 1982

THE STATE OF THE LANGUAGE

The State of the Language

EDITED BY LEONARD MICHAELS
AND CHRISTOPHER RICKS

*Published in Association with the
English-Speaking Union,
San Francisco Branch*

UNIVERSITY OF CALIFORNIA PRESS
BERKELEY · LOS ANGELES · LONDON

University of California Press
Berkeley and Los Angeles, California

University of California Press, Ltd.
London, England

ISBN 0-520-03763-4
Library of Congress Catalog Card Number: 78-62847
Printed in the United States of America

CONTENTS

Ways and Means

Societies

PREFATORY NOTE

LANGUAGE IS THE most vital instance of an undying human achievement: navigating between the rock Scylla and the whirlpool Charybdis. Scylla is the petrification of the obdurately measurable, of objectivity, and of the cult which is not science but scientism; the claim that everything which matters is a matter of fact. Charybdis is the flux of the personal, of subjectivity, of madness and solipsism; the claim that everything which matters is a matter of opinion. Hideous alternatives, the objective Scylla and the subjective Charybdis conspire to rule the waves.

Yet a language resists this collusive imperialism, resists it by being the most extraordinary and the most ordinary defiance of the seductive false claims made on behalf of immovable facts and irresistible opinions. For the meaning of a word is not a matter of fact (which is why an argument about it can't be settled by recourse to the dictionary), and it is not a matter of opinion (which is why an argument about it mustn't be unsettled by a refusal to have recourse to the dictionary). The meaning of a word is a human agreement, created within society but incapable of having meaning except to and through individuals. We may find evidence for such agreements, but we can't find proof of them. A language is a body of agreements. Some lapse; others change; new ones form. "Our language," said the creative and critical genius who was

American and then English—T. S. Eliot—"Our language, or any civilized language, is like the phoenix: it springs anew from its own ashes."

It is not only that a language has an astonishing power of renovation. For when a language creates—as it does—a community within the present, it does so only by courtesy of a community between the present and the past. We who are alive can touch each other through language only because we are touched by those who are no longer alive. Eliot was expressing his specific religious beliefs when he said that

> the communication
> Of the dead is tongued with fire beyond the language of the living.

But his words are not limited to his religious beliefs, for they depend upon the fact that the language of the living is tongued only because it communicates with the communication of the dead.

A preface is always tempted to assure others and itself that "here is no random collection of, etc., etc." But let it be said that the hope is that the diverse contributors to this book show themselves at one in this: their being alive to some of the countless ways the state of a language is one of living relationships, of its holding to a community with the past so that it may hold a community in the present and may hold open a community in the future.

C. R.
Cambridge, England
June 1979

ACKNOWLEDGMENTS

TO WRITE ABOUT the English language is to discover something about who we are and who we are not, and this is true not only in what we say but also in how we say it. The language is our most excellently revealing thing. For some it is our chief philosopher, for others our best historian. Even as we complain about its declining powers—and, as we decline, we are tempted to complain—we remember those powers, and, thereby, begin a little to redeem them. But what flourishes so well under criticism as our English language? Only our rose bushes, perhaps, which the world knows we love.

The editors are very grateful to our essayists who, in very different ways, have contributed so much energy, knowledge and time to this book. We are also indebted to the English-Speaking Union, San Francisco Branch, and especially to its Executive Director, Maryellen Himell, for initiating this project and then continuing to support it in many kind and practical ways. We give particular thanks to William J. McClung, of the University of California Press, who helped in solving problems at every stage. To Marilyn Schwartz, whose exceptional editorial skills, diplomatic persistence, patience, and angelic good humor were vital to the making of this book, we say thank you very much indeed.

L. M.
Berkeley, California
June 1979

Proprieties

RANDOLPH QUIRK

Sound Barriers and *Gangbangsprache*

THERE IS ALWAYS a temptation to think that the issues of one's own time are somehow special—maybe unique. Relativistic training then makes us lean over backwards to see that every age has been confronted by remarkably similar issues.

So it is with language. We swing between feeling (even as linguists) that things are going on today that are virtually unprecedented in linguistic history and dismissively asserting (especially as linguists) *plus ça change, plus c'est la même chose.* When the Germanic peoples were Christianized, English, Scandinavian and German became imbued with Christian lexicon which was the ready springboard for entirely new metaphors. When Japan was opened up in the nineteenth century, thought and language speedily became flooded with industrial and mechanical ideas. Within the present century, we have seen English (and virtually all other languages) responding with similar immediacy to the mental technology of Freud. In these respects nothing that we see in current English is more than *la même chose.* Different ideas are hailed as "new" with each passing generation, they are absorbed into our systems, and we excitedly match "new" language to the "new" notions.

But we may be forgiven if—even as linguists—we are tempted

to think that recent developments are a bit more than a bit more of the same old thing.

In many ways, modernism resembles in its iconoclastic impact the Renaissance and the Reformation—a new "dispersal of shared beliefs." There has been a spate of philosophical, political and critical *isms*—frequently in mutual contradiction, calling in question the entire basis of our society and its already uneasy sense of its values.

To grow up in a society where Laura Nauder (as right-minded British might say) is liable to be despised might be expected to result in an absence of firm ideas on what is to be admired. And we must recognize that this is exactly how it seems to a fairly large number of people: the type of people for whom Joseph McCarthy spoke in the fifties and for whom (on a different wavelength) Mary Whitehouse speaks today. To the silent majority (at least allegedly a majority, and actually not all that silent), liberalism begat permissiveness which in turn begat a fashionably rigid orthodoxy. One may (becoming must) be permissive about issues once decently outlawed: adultery, homosexuality, the extreme left, women's rights, blacks' rights. One may not be permissive about issues once regarded as reasonably respectable: colonialism, anti-Semitism, the extreme right, men's rights, whites' rights. Anyone might in fact be pardoned for suspecting a mindlessly perverse inversion of norms. All very confused and confusing.

But the young or at any rate the pacesetters have not been particularly confused. They have shown a rather consistent sense of direction, and clear ideological norms seem to have emerged. These can be summed up broadly as (a) a concerned sympathy for others, particularly the perceived underdog; (b) a contempt for hypocrisy; and (c) an existential determination to explore human experience to the fearless limits of individual need. This is not how everyone sees things, of course, and I shall have something to say later about the very real abuses and perversions.

The linguistic reverberations of all this are as sharply palpable as the social ones. Sensitivity to the other guy shows up in the welcome proscription of racially disparaging labels—*hun, wop, wog, yid* and the like. No little nigger boys sit upon a wall—and even the chummy *my boy* is avoided by the more discriminating if the chum is black; a British minister gets into trouble because he says he hates "welshing"; we learn to be careful about saying "a man" where a woman could justly feel excluded. Or just "you." "The thing about ball points is that they make you careless about your handwriting: not you, I mean—anyone." Here is language as it ought to be, one feels: pliably responsive to human feelings.

There is no serious antipathy to this "social concern" trend: merely some scepticism as to its value, some sneering at what are seen as its pretensions, and some raucous jesting at the wit-level of "personipulate." Nor has there been much opposition to the second trend, exposing hypocrisy: explicit opposition there could scarcely be. The idols of "participation," "open government" and the like could scarcely be worshipped without acknowledging at least the existence of homosexuals, the wife-swappers, the homeless, the censored, the tax refugees, and other groups that convention, cowardice or guilt may prompt us to ignore. Linguistically, this has meant for instance despising pussyfoot titillation by evasive euphemism accompanied by the knowing wink, the conspiratorial giggle: the smut of the music hall, Chuck Berry and his "ding-a-ling," sexual innuendoes conveyed by *it, do, thing*: it was this style of "good clean fun" that earned contempt. It came to be widely felt that linguistic concealment was itself obscene. And if all this promoted the urge to call a bowel movement a shit and a colored gentleman a black, it was just another aspect of the reluctance to call a spade a nigger.

The exploring of human experience, and using language to match, has roused more feeling: not surprisingly, since the effects have been far more remarkable; and the extent we have moved from Victorian standards is little short of startling. Dickens began *Oliver Twist* in the same year that Victoria began her reign and in his preface to the third edition (1841) he discusses public reaction to the book—reaction, at any rate, "in some very high moral quarters" where it had seemed "coarse and shocking" that "some of the characters . . . are chosen from the most criminal and degraded of London's population; . . . that the boys are pickpockets and the girl is a prostitute." In other words, offence was taken on the grounds of *content,* and in defending himself vigorously (with appeals to Gay, Hogarth, and Fielding) Dickens made the point that he had been careful to ensure propriety in respect of *expression.* "No less consulting my own taste, than the manners of the age, I endeavoured . . . to banish from the lips of the lowest character I introduced, any expression that could by possibility offend."[1]

A century later, "the manners of the age" were not vastly different. In the preface to his poetic and impressionistic memoir, *In Parenthesis* (London, 1937), David Jones regretted that in describing the horrors and obscenities of war he had been "hampered by the convention of not using impious and impolite words." He used several that Dickens denied himself (*bloody, bugger, arse, shit,* for example; *you prize Maria Hunt, effing,* and *efficacious*—elaborately annotated), and would have been happy to defend the inclusion of more (save "blasphemy in any theological sense"—a point to which we shall return) because of his conviction that they gave to the speech of his fellow victims "a kind of significance, and even at moments a dignity." Sometimes in fact their use "under poignant circumstances" could produce "real poetry."

So, still the disjunction of experience and expression. But between these two dates, 1837 and 1937, a great deal had of course happened. Notably *Ulysses* and D. H. Lawrence. The fuss over *The Rainbow* (1915) was on the grounds of content, but with *Lady Chatterley* content was obtrusively and inalienably tied to language: just how inalienably we can see by comparing the expurgated version of 1928 with the unabridged version which could achieve a London publication only in 1960—and then amid outcry and court proceedings.

For the 1950s were little more liberated than 1937 and 1837. When Herman Wouk's novel of the other "great" war, *The Caine Mutiny,* was published in 1951, the author noted in his preface (whether in apology or pride is not clear) that "the general obscenity and blasphemy of shipboard talk have gone . . . unrecorded." Interestingly, the *Sunday Times* recommended the novel explicitly because it abjured "conscientious obscenity" (the choice of *conscientious* is significant: the backlash beginning before real permissiveness had been felt), and the *Times Literary Supplement* actually praised it for the "realistic atmosphere."[2] Even travelling with Charley in 1960, John Steinbeck could find (extraordinarily) nothing more serious happening to the language than the destruction of "localness" by the "package English" delivered by the media, sad even if the result was "perhaps better English than we have ever used."

It is against this background that we can perhaps see the sixties and seventies in perspective; see how far we moved in how short a time from the agonizing over *Lolita, Lady C, Last Exit*—to Kurt Vonnegut, Erica Jong, and Martin Amis, making footsteps for his father to follow.

But we mustn't get fixated on the reception of contemporary fiction. At least as striking is the way writers have shifted their linguistic stance in a more pervasive way. "My English text is chaste," wrote Edward Gibbon autobiographically, "and all licentious passages are left in the decent obscurity of a learned language." As in the eighteenth century so in the first half of the twentieth. When I was a child, it was normal for translations of the more entertaining "classics" to leave in the original the juicily salacious bits—on the theory, I used to suppose, that for all their huffing and puffing, editors never really expected us to master the languages we were supposed to be learning. Or that those who had traded their adolescent energies for philological acolades could have no grounds for complaint—including Portnoy's.

Not long ago, I compared the commentary on the *Summoner's Tale* that we find in the 1957 Harvard edition (for university students) with the London edition of 1975 aimed at girls and boys in (high) school. The guide who takes the friar on his tour of hell says to Satan:

> Shew forth thyn ers, and lat the frere se
> Where is the nest of freres in this place!

The Harvard editor, doubtless glad to hide his blushes behind the screen of Middle English spelling, can bring himself to mention the point only periphrastically: a "repulsive conception" also represented, he says, in pictorial art of the time. The British editor of 1975 chats amiably in his notes of "Satan's arse" and grapples with the central bawdiness with frank confidence.

Sex and scatology, all right. David Jones would have defended such explicitness; but blasphemy is quite another thing. "Quite obviously," he says, "that is all I would consider" as beyond the pale. Clearly, there is still a good deal of feeling in support of this view. Witness, for one thing, Anthony Burgess's obvious awareness of daring in his concern with G. G. Belli (born in the same decade as Keats) both in *Abba Abba* and *Beard's Roman Women.* When *Gay News* published James Kirkup's poem "The Love that Dares to Speak its Name" in June 1976, a prosecution ensued, not on the grounds of the necrophily nor of the (rather mildly) obscene language but of the blasphemy involved in attributing active homosexuality to Christ. The case was successful and the verdict conferred a (suspended) prison sentence.

But if this was significant, the storm of protest over the verdict was at least equally so. It was made abundantly clear that offending God was for many thinking people a great deal less offensive than offending a woman job applicant, an Asiatic immigrant—or a writer's white-hot sense of freedom. This is the ironic climax of the Laurentian puritanism to which Richard Hoggart drew attention in the *Lady Chatterley* lawsuit, back in what now sometimes seems the Middle Ages.

The defiantly repeated attempts in our time to endow God with sexuality are strictly parallel to the age's implicit insistence on the godhood of mankind. The wheel of anthropomorphism turned full circle: the deification of *Homo sapiens* coinciding with unisex—the concept, like the word, reflecting the will to see something deeply common to man and woman. In this context the flagrant exposure—pictorial and linguistic—of sexuality is not unlike the outward display at voluptuous Hindu Konarak: the will to recognize that our thought and language have traditionally exaggerated, by hiding, what can be seen as commonplace biological facts when they are openly paraded.

Here is where I see my tripartite trend (social concern, rejection of hypocrisy, the frank exploration of experience) as essentially unitary. The three aspects can be seen coming together, for instance, in women's lib. Equal opportunity, "affirmative action," bra burning, resistance to sexploitation in advertising—with their linguistic correlates in *Ms., chairperson,* the hunting down of covert claims to male supremacy (as in *Stone Age Man* or the excess use of masculine pronouns and of male characters in children's literature) are strictly congruent with the liberation of the female as a lover: the right to orgasm by whatever agency and through whichever organ the individual pleases, the right to sexual initiative, and so on. These in turn of course have their linguistic correlates, as in the verb *fuck* being able to take a plural subject and an unexpressed reciprocal object, like *kiss* ("we kissed" equaling "we kissed each other") or even—again like *kiss*—to take a feminine subject as readily (according to Erica Jong) as a masculine.

But in any case the trend is one that is part of a quite long-established movement away from old constraints and rigidities. Democratization and a limbering up in social mores are plainly rooted in Victorianism itself, and significant linguistic reflexes are not difficult to find. They are prominent, for example, in the insistence by the Fowler brothers that simple is beautiful and that the short "Anglo-Saxon" words are to be preferred to polysyllabic classicisms.[3] This tradition, strongly developed by A. P. Herbert, Ivor Brown, Eric Partridge, Ernest Gowers and others (to mention only British exponents), has resulted in marked changes in the style of white papers, nonstatutory documents, *Times* leaders, and other traditional repositories of extreme formality. One thinks too of how far the BBC has come since the early days when announcers sat reading the news, unseen, in dinner jackets and Oxford accents. One recalls that Franklin D. Roosevelt increasingly established presidential contact with his radio "fireside chats," rather than with platform rhetoric. There has been, in fact, a rather widespread reaction against the remoter aspects of formality and the sense of rigid appropriacy. We have come to insist that the different styles of language (or dress) required for different occasions and purposes are neither immutable nor even absolutely obligatory.

Not that we have in actual fact levelled out to a "unistyle," of course, any more than to a unisex. One of the things that reduces *1985* from horror to farce is Burgess's projected linguistic engineering. We are to envisage not merely a generalizing of substandard grammar (*I've ate it*)—which can be paralleled in many languages—but also a standardizing of a single style, fit equally for idle chatter and for translating the Declaration of Independence. Here is a sample of the "Workers' English" version of Hamlet's *To be* speech:

> Is it more good to get pains in your fuckin loaf worryin about it or to get stuck into what's getting [*sic*] you worried and get it out of the way and seen off?

Such a monotone language—though not inconceivable—is inherently implausible, not least because it is not easily paralleled in observable natural languages. Certainly nothing in the linguistic changes accompanying the current social revolution leads us to expect a dissolution (as distinct from a diminution) of the distinction between "distant" (formal) and "intimate" (informal) language, however obviously the defining characteristics of both have shifted. Even those who feel most free to sport liberated slang and obscenity readily appreciate the unacceptable mixture of tones in

> "Bye-bye, Your Holiness. See you!"
>
> "Hi, John: I'm just phoning to say your sister has croaked."
>
> "Professor Crowell, I think I understand your first two points but could you explain that last fucker?"[4]

Now, of course, there are presumably folk who can say "Bye, bye" to the pope, but they are not among those who call him (in the same breath, at any rate) "Your Holiness." Professor Crowell, like his student, could well have referred to a ticklish bit of some hypothesis as "that last fucker," given the right circumstances.

And the circumstances include relations between the discourse participants.[5] The two invitations

> Patrons are requested to ascend to the next floor.
>
> Up you go, chaps!

may be paraphrases of each other but they are not interchangeable. We operate to a delicate sense of appropriacy rules, and relations between participants are not merely convention but (again) involve social concern. It may always sound brutal to refer to death as "croaking," but it is less brutal when used of a stranger's death than that of a friend's sister. Beside Grice's discourse maxims (be informative, truthful, relevant, clear, etc.),[6] it has been pointed out that "politeness and consideration for the feelings of one's addressee" can be overriding.[7]

This means, among other things, that one's addressee needs to know whom he is listening to:

> "John's drunk, it seems."
> "Who says?"

The question is not merely to demonstrate the foregoing point but to show how easily a speech act can fail to make its authority clear: *it seems* could mean "it seems to me" (in which case it is the speaker who "says," in the sense of asserting John's inebriation) or "it seems from what I can gather of other people's allegations."

Now there is a long-standing appropriacy rule in fiction such that the narrator (the third-person narrator, that is) observes a decently "distant" linguistic relation to his unseen, unknown reader, however he may "allow" his characters to speak to each other or to themselves. "Blameth not me," says Chaucer, "if you are offended by the Miller's coarse language: my job is just to repeat what he said." Just as *Umgangssprache* is of the *Umgang,* the speech of familiars, so is *Gangbangsprache* the speech of the gang: the narrator, *qua* narrator, hesitates to soil his typewriter. Ardently preserving the stance of the archetypal narrator, even the most salacity-slanted newspapers primly cover the pubic hair of their language. Even contemporary novelists would tend to regard the first of the following as discoursally ill-formed in comparison with the second:

> Smith helped Priscilla into the car and drove off to where he had fucked her the previous week.
>
> "We'll go to where I fucked you last time," Smith thought to himself, as he helped Priscilla into the car.

But the liberal and skillful use that is now made of "free indirect speech" has markedly diminished the distinction between narrator and narrative, in consequence tending to obliterate the linguistic constraints hitherto placed upon the narrator in relation to his reader, above all making more ambivalent what Benveniste has called "les indicateurs de subjectivité."[8] This is true even in first-person narratives. Does Gore Vidal himself endorse the following view of history or is it only his brilliant but far from omniscient heroine: "the time of the Beatles, the spiritual high noon of the twentieth century" (*Kalki*)? And notice that even "delocutive" verbs provide authority only for the substance, and authority for the expression is left equivocal:

> John claimed that he fucked her.

Is the narrator repeating John's choice of verb or is it his own paraphrase of John's claim?

In *Jake's Thing* (1978), a novel of some linguistic sophistication, Kingsley Amis ably illustrates ways in which the role of narrator can be superimposed on that of character. Jake is travelling by bus and the narrator looks through his character's sardonic eyes. Near Warren Street

> the stone face of a university building was spattered with rust-stains from scaffolding on which Jake had never seen anybody at work. Even Gr nville Co rt, Collin woo C urt . . . lofty structures of turd-coloured brick . . . seemed to be deserted. Even or especially.

It is Jake who sees (and *notices*) the decadently unrepaired signs, Jake who selects the epithet "turd-coloured," Jake who bleakly adds the pedantic afterthought: just as it is Jake who (in passages of "narrative") bitterly mimes other people's talk, refers to an elderly stranger as "an old bitch," and who has frequent mental-linguistic flashbacks to the tired coarseness of army days thirty years ago. And just as it is Jake (in dialogue with his wife) who feels called upon to comment on the two senses of *fucking*

> Anyway, what is this fucking Workshop? I may say that if it's a *fucking* Workshop you can all count me out

—no gangbang for him—so too it is Jake who (in narrative) plumps for the same verb, in its nonliteral sense, though the "indicateurs de subjectivité" are not explicit:

> He took a gulp. Although he much preferred drink with food he was fucked if he was going to, etc. 'I don't know,' he said a little wildly.

But although (like Burgess in *1985*) Amis is taking a bitterly jaundiced view of his times, he apparently sees little danger of our collapsing into linguistic uniformity. On the contrary, much of his satire focuses upon several of the traditional stylistic distinctions which polarize language use: for example, clinically pompous and euphemistic jargon for what is very differently expressed in the *Umgang*:

> . . . oh and by the way non-genital includes tits, excludes them rather, I should say breasts. No, mammary areas.

Changes in constraint mean not so much a new style as the use of an already established style in new environments. And this takes us back to the question raised at the beginning of this essay: how new are the linguistic forms we are discussing? A year or so ago in Bombay, I was asked by an Indian emeritus professor why the English language had changed so calamitously. He went on to contrast his experience at Oxford in the 1920s with his impressions on a visit made fifty years later. Whereas his memory had been of students' language being "correct and standard," it seemed now incomprehensible with slang, regionalisms, and coarseness. I had to tell him that in all probability everything he now heard could have been heard fifty years ago—but less publicly and less in university circles; that, whereas a couple of generations ago, students and dons suppressed any urge they might feel to speak with the vernacular frankness that they undoubtedly understood, the suppressive urges were now if anything working in the opposite direction, with the young fearing rather the sneers at mealy-mouthed euphemism and even at careful pronunciation.

Put it another way. In the 1880s, George Gissing commented that the foul language of "the nether world" had "never yet been exhibited by typography, and presumably never will be." But he must surely have been equating "typography" with the conventional and respectable press—just as my Indian professor was equating the English of the twenties with the conventional English of the conventional Oxford type. Gissing could scarcely have been unaware of the *Pearl* ("A Journal of . . . Voluptuous Reading" whose monthly issues ran for a year or so just a century ago) and the voluminous printed material of his own and previous times in which such language was very fully "exhibited" indeed. And when we look back at the style of explicitness today, there is not a great deal that seems different ("To put my prick in here—into your sweet cunt, and fuck you" [*Pearl,* October 1879]): it is rather that we are now used to encountering it in social and literary contexts from which it was once excluded. A big enough change in all conscience, but one that is in tune with the social, moral and philosophical changes I have postulated. Most notable: it is less a change in language than in its distribution, and even the changed distribution must not be exaggerated, largely being as confined as ever to very intimate talk and as absent as ever from the printed media and mass fiction.

Must not be exaggerated? Those with sensibilities recently offended by spray-gun obscenities flagrantly unignorable on walls in Chicago or London (or by poems like Kirkup's) may feel rather that I have underestimated the social and linguistic changes to the point of being dismissively complacent. I find it no easier than anyone else to view sympathetically the abuses and perversions of what I have been trying to see as broadly beneficent trends. Obscene and brutal language is certainly more audible not merely among the idealistic and "progressive" but also among the muggers, the "Paki-bashers," black hoodlums, and white backlashers, and it is not surprising if the relaxed constraints are linked in the minds of many not with an enhanced democracy but with more sinister fascistic trends, street violence, and mob rule. There is nothing liberal or "liberated" in getting a thrill out of linguistic flashing at old ladies, in the hope of shocking but with the effect "only" of terrifying. Some of the self-consciously offensive language of student revolt and the proscriptions of unfashionable subjects and speakers undoubtedly blur the distinction between the extremes of liberalism and neo-Nazism.

Nor am I unaware of the sillier extravagances and exaggerations of even the most high-minded among libbers—still less of the uneven motivation of many who have jumped on the bandwagon. Lenora Timm has drawn circumspect attention to the way enthusiasts actually damage women's lib by sloppy linguistic observation and hasty ill-considered generalizations.[9] Worse, not only have the porn racketeers predictably cashed in on the increased freedom to exploit the titillatory and surviving shock value of quadriliteralism: so have purveyors to superficially more serious and scholarly readers.[10]

I do not ignore (still less condone) such things: I am merely asserting their lack of significance and above all the lack of evidence they provide of significant linguistic change. To take just one obvious point, graffiti. We have evidence of a vigorous tradition measured not in hundreds but in thousands of years: one can scarcely get excited by the fact that felt pen and spray gun have recently made graffiti easier to write. Certainly no change in what is apprehended as "obscene" can be in question: otherwise, why bother to spray? And if they are now on outside walls rather than in (what Gibbon might have called) the "decent obscurity" of (what I have certainly called) "lewd low loos,"[11] I would be inclined to chalk (or spray) this up to the antihypocrisy trend.

The porn merchants like the poor have always been with us, as have the cruel and the brutal and the mentally retarded. We must take the roughnecks with the smoothies and accept that any major social movement will spawn its deviants. Taken as a whole, I remain convinced that the sociolinguistic health of English speakers now[12] is in better shape than when Dickens could congratulate himself on avoiding speech that might "offend the ear" or when the *TLS* could praise the tight-lipped Wouk for his "realistic" language.

Notes

1. *Oliver Twist,* ed. K. Tillotson (Oxford, 1966), pp. lxi, lxiv. Although the *Quarterly Review* in 1837 marvelled at Dickens's having captured (in *Pickwick*) the "unadulterated vernacular idioms of the lower classes," a critic in the same journal two years later more aptly praised him for the linguistic "dilution" and for wrapping up the oaths of Bill Sikes in "silver paper."

2. The two reviews nearly replicate the contradictory attitudes of the *Quarterly Review* mentioned in note 1 above.

3. H. W. and F. G. Fowler, *The King's English* (Oxford, 1906), p. 11.

4. Cf. B. K. Dumas and J. Lighter, "Is *slang* a Word for Linguists?," *American Speech* 53 (1978), and my article "Language and Tabu," *New Society* 44 (1978).

5. Cf. R. Quirk et al., *A Grammar of Contemporary English* (London and New York, 1972), pp. 23ff.

6. H. P. Grice, "Logic and Conversation" (1975), in P. Cole and J. L. Morgan, eds., *Syntax and Semantics* (New York, 1975), vol. 3.

7. J. Lyons, *Semantics* (Cambridge, 1977), vol. 2, p. 593.

8. E. Benveniste, *Problèmes de linguistique générale* (Paris, 1966); cf. R. Quirk, *The Use of English* (London, 1968), ch. 15, and A. Banfield, "Narrative Style and the Grammar of Direct and Indirect Discourse," *Foundations of Language* 10 (1973).

9. In *Lingua* 39 (1976) on R. Lakoff, *Language and Woman's Place* (San Francisco, 1975). See also C. Miller and K. Swift, *Words and Women* (London, 1977), and my review in *TLS,* 28 October 1977.

10. See the discussion by D. J. Enright in *TLS,* 25 August 1978.

11. "The Smut Smiths," *TLS,* 19 August 1977.

12. And not only English speakers, of course. The trends I have discussed in English (sometimes with America leading and Britain following after a discreet interval of a year or so; sometimes—as with the admission of tabu words in dictionaries—with Britain in the lead) can be paralleled in many if not most languages. In Sweden we have the recent "du-reform"; in Japan the immensely complex sociolinguistic constraints are weakening somewhat, with girls using certain forms traditionally the prerogative of males; in French-speaking countries, older people have had to get used to words like "bouquin" in noncolloquial contexts and to "je m'en foutisme" in quite ordinary exasperation.

ROBERT BURCHFIELD

Dictionaries and Ethnic Sensibilities

AT THE BEGINNING of *Macbeth,* a bleeding sergeant describes how brave Macbeth killed the "merciless" rebel, Macdonwald: "he unseamed him from the nave to th' chaps," that is, from the navel to the jaws, "and fixed his head upon our battlements." It may seem a far cry from the rebellious "kerns and gallow-glasses" of Macdonwald to the persevering scholarship involved in dictionary editing, but the connection will be made clear as I proceed.

The head some want to display on the battlements is that of a dictionary, or of its publishers, and, especially, any dictionary that records a meaning that is unacceptable or at best unwelcome to the person or group on the warpath. The ferocity of such assaults is almost unbelievable except as a by-product of what Professor Trevor-Roper calls the twentieth-century "epidemic fury of ideological belief." Key words are *Jew, Palestinian, Arab, Pakistan, Turk, Asiatic, Muhammadan,* and *Negro,* and there are others.

It is impossible to discover exactly when the battle cry was first heard, but certainly by the 1920s a pattern of protest existed. In the *Jewish Chronicle* of 24 October 1924, a leading article expressed "no small gratification" that, in deference to complaints that had been published in the *Jewish Chronicle,* the delegates of the Claren-

---

This essay is a modified version of a talk given on BBC Radio 3 in April 1978, the text of which was printed in *The Listener* of 13 April 1978, pp. 454–56.

don Press had decided that the "sinister meaning" attached to the word *Jew* (that is, the meaning "unscrupulous usurer or bargainer," and the corresponding verb meaning "to cheat, overreach") should be labelled to make it clear that it was a derogatory use. The *Jewish Chronicle* had maintained that users of the *Pocket Oxford Dictionary* would conclude that "every Jew is essentially the sort of person thus described." Mr. R. W. Chapman, who at that time was the head of the section of OUP which publishes dictionaries, replied that "it is no part of the duty of a lexicographer to pass judgement on the justice or propriety of current usage." The editor of the *Pocket Oxford Dictionary,* the legendary H. W. Fowler, in a letter to Chapman declared:

> The dictionary-maker has to record what people say, not what he thinks they can politely say: how will you draw the line between this insult to a nation and such others as 'Dutch courage', 'French leave', 'Punic faith', 'the Huns', 'a nation of shopkeepers', and hundreds more? The real question is not whether a phrase is rude, but whether it is current.

The *Pocket Oxford* and other Oxford dictionaries, and dictionaries elsewhere, labelled the "sinister meaning" of the word *Jew* "derogatory," "opprobrious," or the like, and an uneasy peace was established. But not for long. Some other "sinister" meanings in the *Pocket Oxford* were pointed out. "*Turk:* Member of the Ottoman race; unmanageable child." "*Tartar:* native of Tartary (etc.); intractable person or awkward customer." "*Jesuit:* member of Society of Jesus (etc.); deceitful person."

Fowler felt that he was being incited, as he said, "to assume an autocratic control of the language and put to death all the words and phrases that do not enjoy our approval." He maintained that the *POD* was not keeping the incriminated senses alive but that, unfortunately, they were not in danger of dying. In a letter to Kenneth Sisam in September 1924, he insisted: "I should like to repeat that I have neither religious, political, nor social antipathy to Jews"—nor, by implication, to Turks, Tartars, or Jesuits. The episode passed, but was not forgotten. The *Jewish Chronicle* at that time appeared to be satisfied by an assurance that the unfavorable senses would be labelled as such. They did not ask for, far less demand, the exclusion of the disapproved meanings.

In the United States in the 1920s, a parallel protest movement aimed at the compulsory capitalization of the initial letter of the word *Negro* and the abandonment, except among black inhabitants of the States, of the word *nigger.* Again, dictionaries were among the main targets, and here, too, the lexicographers replied that if writers, including the editors of newspapers, used a capital initial for *Negro,* they would themselves be happy to include this form in their dictionaries, and to give it priority if it became the dominant form in print.

A half-century later, it is easy to see that the lexicographers had "scotch'd the snake, not killed it." Resentment smoldered away in certain quarters, and the issues were brought out into the open again after the 1939-1945 war. But this time there was a difference. Dictionaries remained a prime target, but the protesters brought new assault techniques to bear, especially the threat of sanctions if the lexicographers did not come to heel. Now, dictionary editors, judged by the standards of the broad world, are a soft target. With little personal experience of the broil that forms the daily experience of, for example, politicians, newspaper editors, and psychiatrists, editors of dictionaries tend to be too unworldly and too disdainfully scholarly to recognize the severity of an assault made on them. What is this assault and what form does it take? Quite simply, it is a concerted attempt by various pressure groups to force dictionary editors to give up recording the factual unpleasantnesses of our times and to abandon the tradition of setting down the language as it is actually used, however disagreeable, regrettable, or uncongenial the use.

Two definitions in the *Concise Oxford Dictionary,* one in the early fifties and the other in 1976, exacerbated things. One concerned the word *Pakistan,* and the other, the word *Palestinian.* The editor of the *Concise Oxford Dictionary* unwisely entered the word *Pakistan* in his dictionary in 1951—unwisely, because names of countries as such do not normally qualify for an entry in Oxford dictionaries—and defined it as "a separate Moslem State in India, Moslem autonomy; (from 1947) the independent Moslem Dominion in India."

It lay apparently unnoticed until 1959, when somebody must have pointed it out. The Pakistanis, understandably, were outraged, and called for a ban on the *COD* in Pakistan and for all unsold copies in Pakistan to be confiscated. The OUP admitted that the definition was "tactless" and "locally irritating," but pointed out that the intention had been to show that Pakistan was in the familiar, triangular section of territory which had always been called India on maps and in geography books. No political motive was in question. The Karachi police raided bookstalls in the city and seized 215 copies of the fourth edition of the *COD.* They also raided the Karachi office of the OUP, and seized the only copy of the dictionary on the premises, which was, in fact, the typist's copy. Copies in government offices were commandeered by the police, and apparently hundreds of copies were collected from public offices, schools, and colleges.

After high-level discussion, the Pakistan government decided to lift its ban on the *COD* in November 1959, after receiving an undertaking by the OUP to issue a correction slip for insertion in all copies of *COD* sold in Pakistan, and to enter a new definition in the next impression of the dictionary. Later, a more permanent solution was found when the word *Pakistan* was dropped from the main-line Oxford dictionaries altogether, as a proper name with no other meanings. It remains in the semi-encyclopedic *Oxford Illustrated Dictionary,* where it is defined as "Muslim State in SE Asia, formed in 1947 from regions where Muslims predominated."

This was a striking example of the serious consequences arising from a simple error of judgement by a lexicographer. There were other minor skirmishes, for example, when it was noticed that the definition of the word *American* in some of the Oxford dictionaries failed to allow for the existence of black Americans and of Latin Americans. The dictionary editors gladly revised the definitions and brought them up to date with a minimum of fuss and with no heat generated on either side.

However, the problem of the word *Jew* kept returning in an increasingly dramatic way. Some correspondents contrasted the derogatory definitions of *Jew* with the colloquial senses of the word *Christian*. *Christian* is defined as "a human being, as distinguished from a brute," for example, in Shaftesbury (1714): "The very word Christian is, in common language, us'd for Man, in opposition to Brute-beast." It is also recorded with the colloquial sense, "a decent, respectable, or presentable person," as in Dickens (1844): "You must take your passage like a Christian; at least as like a Christian as a fore-cabin passenger can."

One correspondent, in 1956, said that she was concerned with the way in which stereotypes about groups of people became formulated, and she argued that the preservation of derogatory definitions in dictionaries did nothing to prevent the persistence of such stereotypes. Others drew attention to the cultural and scholarly achievements of Jews, for example, that thirty-eight Nobel prizes had been awarded to Jews by 1960. A representative of the American Conference of Businessmen came to the OED Department in Oxford in March 1966, and he and I discussed the problem amicably. "Men of good will," he said, "should unite to do everything possible not to give any appearance of acceptance to unfavorable applications of the word *Jew* if they exist." If they exist? But we knew from our quotation files that unfavorable applications of the word *Jew* did and do exist, both in speech and in print, deplorable though they are. All I could do was to repeat the familiar lexicographical arguments. It is the duty of lexicographers to record actual usage, as shown by collected examples, not to express moral approval or disapproval of usage; dictionaries cannot be regulative in matters of social, political, and religious attitudes; there is no question of any animus on the part of the lexicographers against the Jews, or the Arabs, or anyone else.

In 1969, a Jewish businessman from Salford came on the scene and claimed that the definitions of *Jew* were "abusive and insulting and reflected a deplorable attitude toward Jewry." He turned the screw more forcibly by releasing the text of his letters to the national newspapers, who by now realized that the matter was an issue of public controversy. He also wrote to politicians, church leaders, including the chief rabbi and the archbishop of Canterbury, to the commissioner of police, and to other instruments of the church and state.

In 1972, this Salford businessman brought an action against the Clarendon Press, claiming that the secondary definitions of the word *Jew* were "derogatory, defamatory, and deplorable." He lost the case in the High Court in July 1973. Mr. Justice Goff held that, in law, the plaintiff had no maintainable cause of action because he could not, as required by English law, show that the offending words in the dictionary entries "referred to him personally or were capable of being understood by others as referring to him."[1]

The next episode occurred on the other side of the world. Toward the end of 1976, Mr. Al Grassby, Australia's commissioner for community relations, called for the withdrawal of the *Australian Pocket Oxford Dictionary* from circulation because it contained a number of words applied in a derogatory way to ethnic or religious groups: words like *wog, wop,* and *dago.*

Knowing very little, if anything, about lexicographical policy, he thought it deplorable that there was no entry for *Italy* but one for *dago,* none for Brazil as a country but one for *Brazil nut,* and so on. This wholly simplistic notion was rejected with humor and scorn by the Australian press. A cartoon in the *Australian* showed two European migrants looking very unhappy, and the caption read: "Did you hear what those ignorant Aussie dingoes called us?" And a headline in the *Melbourne Sunday Press* made its point quite simply: "You are on a loser, pal Grassby."

The most recent example of hostility toward dictionary definitions occurred a short time ago. On this occasion, as with *Pakistan,* the criticized definition *was* inadequate, and, curiously, the concession of its inadequacy merely transferred the attack from one quarter to another. In the sixth edition of the *Concise Oxford Dictionary,* published in July 1976, the word *Palestinian* was defined as "(native or inhabitant) of Palestine; (person) seeking to displace Israelis from Palestine." Early in 1977, the definition provoked angry editorial comment in newspapers in the Middle East, and threats were made that if the Oxford University Press did not agree to amend it at once, the matter would be brought to the attention of the Arab League, with a proposal to place the OUP on the Arab boycott list.

Each day's post brought fresh evidence of what appeared to be a severe reaction throughout Arabic-speaking countries, if the newspapers were anything to go by. The sales records for the *Concise Oxford Dictionary* in Egypt showed that all of eleven copies had been sold there in the financial year 1976-1977! But, sales apart, what was clear was that the Arabs considered the definition to be partisan, and that, in my opinion, would have been the attitude of the man on the Clapham omnibus, too.

In two lines of the *COD*—because that was all the space available in such a small dictionary—we concluded that it was not possible to arrive at other than a formulaic definition of *Palestinian.* Any form of words ascribing motives to "Palestinians" simply failed by one test or another when the space available was so limited. We therefore decided to adopt another type of definition, one of the type that is used in every desk dictionary in the world, and the new definition reads as follows: "*n*. Native or inhabitant of Palestine. *a.* Of, pertaining to, or connected with Palestine."

The Arabs were satisfied ("it represents a victory for truth and objectivity," declared the *Egyptian Gazette* of 3 May 1977) and, had the matter rested there, without further publicity, that would probably have been the end of it. Not content with severing the head, however, the Arabs wished to fix it upon the battlements. A press statement was issued to British national newspapers by a London-based Arab organization, and even though this statement was factually and unemotionally expressed, it brought an instant reaction from the other side.

Letters of protest began to arrive from various Jewish organizations, and the scholarly lexicographers of the OUP had to endure the kind of concerted campaign with which politicians have always been familiar. The letters expressed "profound distress" and declared that the lexicographers "had departed from their usual standards of scholarly objectivity in yielding to pro-Arab pressure groups." The "selfsame tune and words" came from several directions. "We consider this an encroachment on traditional British integrity and on British values," "political appeasement for commercial considerations," "I wish to register the strongest protest against such abject and cowardly behaviour on the part of your organization," and so on. It dawned on us, as the letters arrived, that we were dealing with an organized petition. The individuals and groups writing to us had been urged to write to us by some central body. The same phrases occurred in several of the letters; for example: "In describing a Palestinian as a native or inhabitant of Palestine, you impliedly deny the existence of the State of Israel." That "impliedly" rather gave the game away.

This Palestinian affair is for all practical purposes over, though not without bruises on all sides. Dictionary editors are now at last aware that they must give maximum attention to sensitive words, like *Palestinian, Jap,* and so on. Politically sensitive words like *Palestine* and *Kashmir* can be entered only as geographical, and not as political entities unless there is adequate space to describe the claims and counterclaims and there are facilities for the frequent updating of the entries.

For the most part lexicographers are agreed about the necessity of recording derogatory applications of words even if some sections of the general public are not. Since the 1960s or so most dictionaries (other than the smallest ones and those prepared for the use of children) have also included most of the more commonly heard expressions used in contexts describing sexual or excretory matters. A different practice, which I believe to be mistaken, is defended in classical manner by David B. Guralnik in the foreword to his *Webster's New World Dictionary of the American Language* (Second College Edition, 1972), p. viii:

> The absence from this dictionary of a handful of old, well-known vulgate terms for sexual and excretory organs and functions is not due to a lack of citations for these words from current literature. On the contrary, the profusion of such citations in recent years would suggest that the terms in question are so well known as to require no explanation. The decision to eliminate them as part of the extensive culling process that is the inevitable task of the lexicographer was made on the practical grounds that there is still objection in many quarters to the appearance of these terms in print and that to risk keeping this dictionary out of the hands of some

> students by introducing several terms that require little if any elucidation would be unwise. In a similar vein, it was decided in the selection process that this dictionary could easily dispense with those true obscenities, the terms of racial or ethnic opprobrium, that are, in any case, encountered with diminishing frequency these days.

In respect of such vocabulary, inclusion or exclusion should be governed by the size of the dictionary or by the educational market envisaged for it. In large dictionaries like the *OED,* the *Shorter Oxford English Dictionary,* and *Webster's Third New International Dictionary,*[2] such vocabulary should be automatically included, with suitable indications of the status of each item. In desk dictionaries like the *Concise Oxford Dictionary* and *Webster's New Collegiate Dictionary* the editors normally have sufficient space to include such words: a wide range of suitable status labels is available to indicate the degree of vulgarity of words like *crap, cunt, fart, fuck, turd,* and so on; and for terms of racial abuse a special symbol meaning "regarded as offensive in varying degrees by a person to whom the word is applied" is long overdue. Such dictionaries should aim to be regulative or normative in such matters only by the use of cautionary labels and/or symbols and not by censorship. In smaller dictionaries, and in school dictionaries, the absence of such vocabulary needs no defense.

In the end, in their function as "marshallers of words,"[3] lexicographers responsible for the compilation of the larger dictionaries must aim to include vocabulary from the disputed areas of vocabulary as well as from safe or uncontroversial subject areas, words that are gracefully formed as well as those that are not, words from sets of religious, political, or social beliefs with which one has no sympathy beside those that one finds acceptable. And to the list of words that must not be excluded I should add those that are explosive and dangerous, like words of ethnic abuse, as well.

Notes

1. From newspaper reports it appears that the same businessman now proposes to approach the International Court of Justice at The Hague on the same matter, since he failed in the action he brought in 1973, and also because the Attorney General, Mr. Sam Silkin, has refused permission for him to take legal action against dictionary publishers under the Race Relations Act of 1976.

2. In the latest printing of this dictionary the word *fuck* is, unaccountably, still not listed.

3. Joseph Trapp's description of Dryden as "the best Marshaller of words" (Preface to his *Translation of Aeneis* [London, 1718], I, p. xlix) is a phrase that comes as near as possible to a description of the perfect historical lexicographer, bearing in mind the *OED* definition of *marshal* (sense 5) as "to dispose, arrange or set (things, material or immaterial) in methodical order."

KINGSLEY AMIS

Getting It Wrong

THE CONCISE OXFORD DICTIONARY (*COD*) defines malaprop(ism) as, "Ludicrous misuse of word, esp. in mistake for one resembling it," and gives the example *derangement of epitaphs* for "arrangement of epithets." A glance at Sheridan's play *The Rivals* reveals this and comparable misuses, but a second glance shows there to be others present of a rather different kind. For instance, immediately upon her first entrance, Mrs. Malaprop says of her daughter Lydia:

> There, Sir Anthony, there sits the deliberate simpleton who wants to disgrace her family, and *lavish* herself on a fellow not worth a shilling.

(I will italicize malapropisms throughout, hoping to save my readers' time without insulting their intelligence.) In the fourth act, the lady commends Captain Absolute for being full of *alacrity* and *adulation*. A distinction is soon stated. *Derangement* is nothing more or less than the wrong word, and the right one very readily suggests itself. The other three are nearly the right words, but not quite. Thus "lavish" means not "bestow" but "bestow liberally"; "alacrity" can be used of somebody's demeanor at a given moment ("he followed with alacrity") but not of his settled state; "adulation" likewise refers to what is shown a second party, not what is possessed as a characteristic, and in any case carries an inappropriate suggestion of obsequiousness. Nevertheless, the closeness to the target each time is such as to let us feel the wind of the shot, and might prompt us to say that the speaker has not so much used the wrong word as used a word in the wrong sense. Anyway, in what follows I have kept apart Wrong Word malapropisms and Wrong Sense ones, more for convenience than to suggest any deep division of principle. Note that all citations are genuine, though many are immaterially shortened or changed to save space or confusion; paraphrases, of something heard in talk, on radio, etc., or seen without possibility of copying or clipping, are prefixed *P.*

In *Modern English Usage* (1926), Fowler devotes a little over a column to "Malaprops" and a little more again to "Pairs & Snares," words often confused with each other through similar sound and appearance, like affect/effect, alternative/alternate. If he were writing today he would surely devote several pages at least to such topics. Till quite recently, perhaps about 1960, it was comparatively rare to find a misuse of words in the writings of the supposedly educated, among whom I include journalists and those who get their letters printed in the newspapers. But now, five minutes' reading almost anywhere will turn one up. No research was needed for this article, just the energy to record the examples that passed by me in the ordinary way of business over some weeks. I collected a dozen times more material than I could use. The meaning of this sudden abundance I will consider when I have displayed my collection.

To start with, then, Wrong Word malapropisms at the shallow end, simple pairs and snares. Someone *alternatively* sulks in his tent and issues out to make statements, does not wish to *distract* from another's fine sporting performance, will not *detract* from any part of his planned speech and descends vigorously on all punctuation sins—however *venal.* An actor is *derisory* about Ernest Hemingway, last week some demonstrators *laid* down in front of a police vehicle, a mixture of acting styles didn't wholly lend *credulity* to a hugely enjoyable film, an epidemic of moderation has *inflicted* ("infected" plus "afflicted") some West European communists and certain factors *mitigate* against successful treatment. A new snare-setting pair, flaunt/flout (show off/mock, insult), has arrived; it is hardly a pair any more, because one element has killed the other and taken its place. As far as I know, no one uses "flout" for "flaunt," but there is plenty of this kind of thing:

> We might call the recent performance of sterling 'obscene', not to suggest that it is lewd or indelicate [ah, but whether he likes it or

> not that is just what he is absurdly suggesting], but because it *flaunts* every rational calculation of British currency.

More shortly:

> French Communists *Flaunting* Party

(Those communists again.) But the word confusingly survives in its old sense, as I heard on the radio since starting this paragraph:

> *P* Beethoven doesn't allow the pianist to flaunt his virtuosity.

Perpetrate/perpetuate is another old pair, similar in that they often write *perpetrate* for "perpetuate," but not, or not often, the other way round:

> Small neo-Nazi and German-American groups picketed NBC in protest against the film, claiming that the holocaust was a hoax and that the television series *perpetrated* that lie.

Quite often a Wrong Word seems little more than a spelling mistake, resulting from telephoned copy or bad luck at the printers', but we must reflect that someone thought it was right. Thus a question *illicits* a reply, an unfortunate has a *fiercesome* appearance and there is the *martialling* of evidence. There is even a concert audience in a state of *psychophantic* respect. Often, too, the writer seems just to be choosing a till-then unrecorded variant of a familiar word, either perversely or in the grip of a desire to find a form of higher cultural standing than the one ordinary people use, a very common motive behind solecisms of most sorts. Thus:

> The Kremlin has been *appraised* of the President's interest.
>
> We *unreservably* apologise.
>
> I believe the pamphlet to be *inimicable* to the essential idea of a university.
>
> *P* The school-book was full of violence and *depravation.*

In roughly ascending order, an anthology of getting it wrong (alert readers will have to forgive me for jogging the memories of others):

> The sonatas are just the *anecdote* to a gloomy summer day. ("antidote")
>
> A wind-machine is used to *emulate* breathing at the start and finish of the work. ("simulate")
>
> The food and surroundings were very poor value for money and in *inexorable* taste. ("execrable")

Even those apparently *simultaneous* gestures that inspired his men were the result of careful planning. ("spontaneous")

The Council is not a *paradigm* of virtue. ("paragon"—nice example of a Wrong Word that is also what Fowler would have called a vogue-word)

Marriage was ordained for the *procuration* of children. ("procreation," but one of the actual meanings of "procuration" is "obtaining for immoral purposes")

Alice B. Toklas and Gertrude Stein, both American *ex-patriots.* ("expatriates"—after a moment's thought)

Anthony and Cleopatra, by *roisterous* William Shakespeare. ("roister" and "boisterous" run into one)

We have so *emaciated* our laws that the young hooligan is almost immune from punishment. ("emasculated" eventually suggests itself)

It was a rather elderly, staid, condescending but solicitous aunt gathering her *voluptuous* skirts. ("voluminous"—presumably)

The actress had to run the *gamut* of protesters. ("gauntlet," influenced by phrases like "run up and down the gamut")

In our course of study we covered the whole *gambit* of banking, *cashiering,* current accounts, deposits. (Two misses in four words. "Gamut," of course, and "cashing," I suppose, influenced by words like "pioneering" and by "cashiering" itself, which means only "discharging [from armed forces, etc.] with ignominy.")

Many of these young refugees may eventually *pass muster* as guerillas. ("be mustered"—U.K. or "muster in"—U.S.; influenced by "pass muster" meaning "be pronounced adequate," even perhaps partly intended)

For anyone who wants to know about the Victorian theatre this book will be a *minefield.* ("gold mine" or "mine of information," with some influence from phrases like "rich field of study"; writer not being sarcastic)

P The Americans really have a free Press; it's *incarcerated* in their constitution. ("incorporated," certainly, but only after a long struggle to establish beyond reasonable doubt that no ironical or other nuance is to be found, and perhaps the recognition of a faint influence from "enshrine" where it comes nearest to "enclose")

He brought to his job a style and verve which were refreshing and *enervating.* ("energizing" and "elevating" in as near equal proportions as could be, with what "enervating" actually means—"causing weakness"—forgotten or never known)

She is supposed to have most trust of all in the *implacable* screen of her senior adviser. (No certain meaning. How any kind of screen could ever be placated, appeased, conciliated it is impossible to say. Some influence from "impassable," "impassive," "impenetrable," "impermeable," "impregnable," etc.)

There's a lot of *ethos* about living in poor London [i.e., poor parts of London] these days. (No certain meaning. "Ethos," somebody's or some group's set of beliefs, was not what the writer meant; "kudos," glory, prestige, possibly was. Or could he have reasoned that as "pathos" is to patheticness so "ethos" is to ethnicness? He must have meant something like that. Last guess: ethnic kudos.)

His speech would not prevent an unprecedented and possibly *volatile* White backlash. (No certain meaning further than that it is gloomy or otherwise unfavorable. All the meanings of "volatile," viz. "evaporating quickly, gay, transient," are ruled out by the context or "and." Influenced by "violent," or conceivably "versatile" thought to mean something like "mercurial.")

Students of Russian and Chinese subversive activities have noted that *esurient* revolutionary movements in most parts of the non-communist world have been receiving less support from Moscow and Peking than formerly. ("Esurient," noted in *COD* as a jocular or archaic synonym for "hungry" or "greedy," out of use for almost a century, is impossibly fanciful for the businesslike flatness of the context. The word confounded itself in the writer's mind with "emergent" or "existent" or something or other.)

As far as I know, the above anthology consists entirely of novelties, of nonce-uses. For some mysterious but fortunate reason, Wrong Word malapropisms don't catch on, except for wrong members of pairs like *flaunt*. Those apart, no harm is done beyond some momentary bafflement or irritation among readers and possibly an outburst of editorial rage, and here and there amusement may be caused—no direct harm, that is. Whether it is the hankering after an up-market synonym or an over-hasty search of the memory or both that brings such a solecism to consciousness, what gets it down on paper is a lazy or defiant refusal to think twice, let alone check. No need to get it right (I imagine them mumbling), not very near is near enough, and what does it matter? That isn't harmless.

Wrong Sense malapropisms are more of a mixed bag. Some,

not always the most obviously useful, take a one-way trip into the language, others vanish from sight after a single showing. In nearly every case, their appearance is the third stage of a process which may never be as clear-cut and as conscious as I show it here.

STAGE I: A writes (let us say): He was a voracious reader, doing little else but work and sleep. (A knows that "voracious" means "greedy"; it seems a legitimate metaphor, like "devouring" books.)

STAGE II: B reads A's sentence and takes "voracious" for a learned-looking synonym of "keen, enthusiastic, constant."

STAGE III: In due time, B writes (in actual fact): This *voracious* contributor of letters to the correspondence columns of the Press. . . . (We should think ourselves lucky he didn't write *veracious,* which I once saw used in such a context: Wrong Word piled on Wrong Sense.)

Exactly the same thing has happened to "avid," producing someone "who believes *avidly* that everybody needs love" and someone else who is "an *avid* pilot." Well, those who don't know or who fail to remember what the words mean elsewhere aren't going to mind, and the rest will tend to smile rather than scowl. The effects of Wrong Sense can be much more inappropriate than that, as follows. We have a Stage I involving "pantheon," not in the root meaning of a temple to all the gods but, figuratively, of a group of admired characters as in, say, "When he was a boy his pantheon included Plato, Shakespeare, Buffalo Bill and his headmaster." In Stage II, B thinks it refers to one's favorite personifications or symbols, and in Stage III writes (in actual fact):

> Democratic Campuchea, as the country is renamed, occupies in the *pantheon* of the Right the same places [*sic*] as does Chile in that of the Left.

It is always something of a feat to come up with the least apt word in the language. The existence of "pandemonium," abode of all demons, should have warned B, but of course he would never have heard of that. No such excuse serves the writer of the next Stage III:

> The report [of alleged sightings of unidentified flying objects] is unlikely to shake hardened sceptics, but on those who already believe in such phenomena the effect will be *devastating*.

Undeflected by knowing—as he must surely have known—what is meant by utterances like "The hurricane caused great devastation," he managed to say exactly the opposite of what he intended.

Perhaps he thought cloudily that the participle and the noun were unconnected.

Briefly noted:

> He stiffened in alarm, but the look-out remained *oblivious* to his presence. (To be oblivious to something is not to be unaware of it but to be no longer aware of it.)
>
> *P* Many children leave school altogether *bereft* of mathematical skills. (To be bereft of something is not to be without it but to be deprived of it. This extract from an editorial in the London *Times*—on falling educational standards—comically suggests that many children, possessed of mathematical skills, have them taken away from them. Not even British schools of the late 1970s could do that to more than comparatively few children.)
>
> The sound of the car rose to a *crescendo.* (A crescendo is not a loud noise but is itself a noise that rises, from soft or not-loud to loud.)
>
> Compared to the 'Save Our Children' campaign, the campaign waged by the anti-repeal forces was *pristine* clean. (A pristine thing is not spotless but primeval, as in, say, "the pristine innocence of America before the white man came." Not that I admire that phrase much either.)
>
> *P* Courage is often thought of as a virtue we should try to *emulate.* (To emulate someone is to try to equal him. Trying to try to equal a quality brings nothing very definite to mind. The speaker was a professor of philosophy in a television series called "Dilemmas." These were questions like the nature of virtue. A dilemma is not a question but specifically a situation posing a choice between two equally unattractive courses, as it might be lying to save your skin and telling the truth to save your soul.)
>
> A universal *panacea* from a mixture of sulphur, lime and water. (A panacea is already, so to speak, a universal remedy.)
>
> New York City is *paranoid*—with reason—about rising crime. . . .

Enough. The result of such misuses is no more than to make us change our use of the language, each small in itself. We will perhaps go extra carefully with "avid" and "voracious," we can afford to go on using "pantheon" and "devastating" on the confident assumption that they will not lose their old meanings, but in other cases those old meanings have been extinguished or are being driven out. If we want to be sure of being completely understood, a concern that takes priority over any notions of elegance, let alone correctness, we must stop saying and writing "oblivious" and make it "no longer aware" instead, substitute something about louder and louder for "crescendo" except in musical circles, abandon "panacea" and fasten on to "cure-all," etc. At the same time, when another uses these words in an ambiguous context we must try to establish, if unavoidable by asking a question, whether he is ignorantly and trendily applying the new meaning or obstinately and uselessly sticking to the old. Or that is what we would do if we were inhumanly energetic and logical.

Let me produce my three final exhibits. The first only gets in because it is my favorite solecism of all time; it is that because of its ludicrous history, more complex than the shift from avid reader to avid pilot. To be sure, this is a reconstruction, but I regard it as certain.

STAGE I: A writes (let us say): His arguments are unoriginal and jejune. (A knows that "jejune" means "thin, unsatisfying," a rare word, admittedly, but one with a nice ring to it.)

STAGE II: B notices the nice ring. He doesn't know what the word means and of course doesn't consult the dictionary—you would be as likely to find him consulting the Doomsday Book. There is something French as well as nice about the ring to "jejune"; in fact now he comes to think of it it reminds him of "jeune," which he knows means "young." Peering at the context, he sees that "jejune" could mean, if not exactly "young," then something like "un-grown-up, immature, callow." Hooray!—he's always needing words for that, and here is a new one, one of superior quality, too.

STAGE III: B starts writing stuff like "Much of the dialogue is *jejune,* in fact downright childish." With the latest edition of *COD* giving "puerile" as a sense of "jejune," the story might be thought to be over, but there is one further stage.

STAGE IV: Having "jeune" in their heads, people who have never seen the word in print start pronouncing "jejune" not "dji*djoon*" but "zher*zhern*" (*r*'s silent), in the apparent belief that Frenchmen always give a tiny stutter when they say "jeune." (I have heard "zher*zhern*" several times in the last few years.) Finally C takes the inevitable step of writing *jejeune* (I have seen several examples), or even, just that much better:

> Although the actual arguments are a little *jéjeune,* the staging of the mass scenes are [*sic*] impressive.

Italics in original!—which with the acute accent sets the seal on the deportation of an English word into French, surely a unique event.

(For the interested, "jejune" is indeed connected with a French word, but it is "jeûne" with distinguishing circumflex. Both derive from the Latin "[dies] ieiuna" or "jejuna," a "fast [day]." Hence the familiar "déjeuner," to de-fast as we break-fast. "Jejune" then first meant "fast-like, scanty, Lenten"—like the entertainment which Rosencrantz feared the players would receive from Hamlet.)

My last two examples can be considered more briefly.

> *Hopefully* the new product will reach bars and liquor-stores by end of next month.

It is not of course the product that is hopeful but the writer. Floating *hopefully,* once German, then become English in the U.S., is now establishing itself in the U.K. Its misuse in the way illustrated is a matter of function rather than of meaning.

> *P* Is it true that you've abused your powers as President?
> I *refute* that totally and categorically. [end of interview]

(A popular misuse: I have a dozen other examples.) To refute is not to deny or to repudiate but to disprove, to overturn with facts or argument or both. A refutation on the scale required might take a millennium, involving as it would a demonstration that everything said and done by the President during his presidency was a nonabuse. He should have said "deny," but after decades of authoritarian governments denying things, and indicted criminals denying similar things, the word is irredeemably tarnished. "Refute" has both the feel of quality and the valuable covert suggestion that somehow something more than a mere denial is going on, which is what makes it a politician's word. That is the unarguable objection to floating *hopefully.* The fellow can't say "I hope" because that would imply he has surrendered control of events; he can't really use J. F. Kennedy's favorite, "I am hopeful that," without being J. F. Kennedy; he can't say "with luck" which is all he means; so he says "hopefully" and basks in a fraudulent glow of confidence.

I promised near the start to say what I thought had happened. That won't take long. Various changes, not all of them educational, have seen to it that most of the men and women who use words in public don't care any more which words they are, apart from a feeble hankering after the seemingly stylish. The concept of finding the right word, which used to be a strong influence on that of finding a good word, is being lost. How such people keep awake while they write is beyond me. Anyway, their handiwork, or handi-idleness, is all about: growing imprecision as words without a synonym, like "disinterested," become synonyms of other, less exact words; quite commonly ambiguity or sheer nonsense; and everywhere awkwardnesses that force the reader to pause without profit, even if only for an instant. This is decline.

I know, or at least am constantly being told, about languages having to change if they are not to die, though it seems to be often forgotten that death is a very important form of change. Not that I see this as imminent in the case of our language now: the biggest recent change in it—the immense expansion of its vocabulary since 1945—seems successful enough. And in one way of course there's nothing you can do about it. Floating *hopefully* was the most widely and loudly denounced import to the U.K. in living memory until Japanese motorcars came along, and now it and they are everywhere. People who use floating *hopefully* aren't the ones who read articles on good and bad English. But there is something you can do, or someone can do, as follows.

In the introduction to *COD* the editor explains what he calls his usage labels, which appear in the main body of the dictionary between a word and its definition; for instance, "(joc.): jocular, used only in humorous or playful style; (vulg.): vulgar, used only by those who have no wish to be thought either polite or educated" (this eccentric and anachronistic gloss appears, not as I originally supposed in the first edition of *COD* in 1911, but in that of 1976). What about "(illit.): illiterate, used only by those who have no wish to write accurately or vigorously"? The principle could be extended. A dictionary records usage impartially, agreed, but whatever anybody says or does (here come some italics that don't signal a malapropism) *when consulted it is taken as prescriptive too* by almost everybody who is not either a lexicographer or a linguist, and prescription is partiality. It seems harsh to deny guidance to the lonely and diminishing minority who may genuinely need and want it.

CHARLES TOMLINSON

Ritornello

WRONG HAS A twisty look like wrung misprinted
Consider! and you con the stars for meaning
Sublime comes climbing from beneath the threshold
Experience? you win it out of peril
The pirate's cognate. Where did the words arise?
Human they sublimed out of the humus
Surprised by stars into consideration
You are wrung right and put into the peril
Of feelings not yet charted lost for words
Abstraction means something pulled away from
Humus means earth place purchase and return

JOHN SIMON

The Corruption of English

"WE ARE ALL in the gutter, but some of us are looking at the stars," wrote Oscar Wilde about life. The same applies to language: we all make mistakes (somebody just wrote me to point out a badly constructed sentence in one of my columns), but some of us at least try to maintain standards. It is not easy, and the best may stumble. Thus the worthy Irving Howe writes, on the front page of the *New York Times Book Review* (April 9, 1978), about "main protagonists." Now, the protagonist is *the* main actor in something and has, since Greek times, always been in the singular. "Protagonists" is incorrect (unless you refer to the protagonists of two or more dramas), and "main protagonists" (main main actors) is redundant to boot. A double-barreled error, but even the ablest among us, harried by the exigencies of rapid-fire journalism, are not immune to lapses.

What worries me more is rock-bottom illiteracy: in the gutter and looking at the sewers. David Sheff of *New West* sent me a

---

I am indebted to the present editors of *Esquire* for allowing me to publish the columns "Pressure from Below" and "Pressure from Above" (*Esquire*, June 20 and July 18, 1978) for the first time in one piece, as originally written. This essay is part of a book on language to be published by Clarkson and Potter in early 1980.

good-size National Airlines poster the other day, depicting a charming flight attendant (formerly stewardess) and bearing this caption emblazoned in mighty letters: "Watch us shine with more flight's to Houston." Be honest: did your jaw drop when you read that "flight's"? I showed the poster to a couple of civilized friends, and it took them some time and quite a bit of prodding to notice the howler. So there you have it: half the population (I guess) thinks that any plural ending in *s* requires an apostrophe, and the other half stands idly by without squirming, if, in fact, it even notices.

Where does it all come from? Who is the chief culprit? Surely, the schools, both lower and higher, and the distemper of the times that influences them. Let me give you some horrible examples. Jim Deutsch of Greenville, Mississippi, has just sent me a Xerox of a letter published in *American Studies International* (Winter 1977), in which Toby Fulwiler protests what seems to be a fairly obvious plagiarism of a paper he wrote. But he twice misspells *plagiarize* as *plagerize,* which the editors duly note with a *sic.* If Mr. Fulwiler is that concerned with plagiarism, he might at least ascertain how it is spelled, especially since he is the Director of Freshman English at Michigan Technological University. It is clear, furthermore, that he knows neither Latin (*plagiārius:* a kidnapper) nor any major modern language in which the spelling of the word is made manifest by the pronunciation, e.g., French (*plagiat*) or German (*Plagiat*). But it may be asking too much of a contemporary director of freshman English that he know other languages: English, though, should still be part of his competency.

Or need it be? Two readers, no less (Hortense Berman and Thomas A. Long), have sent me identical clippings from *UC This Week,* a University of Cincinnati faculty and staff newspaper. The May 2 issue summarizes a talk by William Lasher, associate professor of English, chairman of the committee on linguistics, and director of undergraduate studies in English. Professor Lasher adduced two sentences—"we was at the ball game last night" and "Mary had five card"—calling them clear and logical attempts to simplify the language.

I quote: "In the first example, Lasher says, the speaker has decided that the distinction between 'was' and 'were' is insignificant and has chosen 'was,' no matter if the subject is singular or plural." Note the assumption that the speaker consciously "decided" to make a simplifying choice. How about the supposition that the speaker was an illiterate ignoramus who neither knew nor cared to know better? But to go on: "The second example is what Lasher calls Black English, a social dialect of American English. In it the speaker drops the 's' from 'cards' because the five already indicates more than one." And Lasher proceeded, at least by strong implication, to belittle those who would consider the above speakers ungrammatical just because they violate what he patronizingly called "the experts' rule." For Lasher, "the people who say 'was' for 'were' or drop the 's' have a grammar that describes the relationship between sound and meaning in their cultures."

Why should we consider some, usually poorly educated, subculture's notion of the relationship between sound and meaning? And how could a grammar—any grammar—possibly describe that relationship? Grammar exists mainly to clarify meaning. *Five* does indeed indicate plurality, but the final *s* confirms it. After all, the speaker may have said "a fine card" or "a five card," and it is the final *s* that ensures that we have not misheard him. So, too, we may be uncertain whether we heard, say, *he* or *we* until the *were* dispels our doubt concerning who was at the ball game.

There is more to it, though. Maintaining these alleged niceties links our language to that of the giants of the English tongue who preceded us, all those great writers and speakers who were—not was—in the ball game that counts: the great struggle to use English as clearly and beautifully as possible. We do not wish to dissociate ourselves from them, lose familiarity with their mode of utterance on account of ignorant, misguided, or merely lazy creatures for whom making distinctions is an unnecessary effort. When Professor Lasher invokes the lofty principle of "making things easier," he serves up a typically disingenuous historical example: the shifting of *inpossible* to *impossible* from circa 1300 on. Yes, *inp* is harder to say than *imp;* but is *were* more of a strain on the tongue than *was*? Or, to put it differently: should we destroy a beautiful old building because it has decorative elements on its facade and replace it with a square box because that is a simpler structure? Of course, there are people who tear down architectural masterpieces for just such reasons; but whatever they call themselves, *we* should call them barbarians and fight their vandalism in every way we can.

What this is, masquerading under the euphemism "descriptive linguistics" (and Lasher is far from being an isolated promulgator of it—in fact, he is part of a growing majority), is a benighted and despicable catering to mass ignorance under the supposed aegis of democracy, of being fair to underprivileged minorities, and similar irruptions of politics where it has no business being.

Black English, for example, has a perfect right to exist; it just hasn't the right to change Standard English. The Lashers of this world are being illogical. Either Black English is something different from Standard English, in which case it is no more entitled to interfere with it than Portuguese is, or it is—or means to be—part of Standard English, in which case it has to espouse the latter's rules. And it will not do for the Lashers to say that they do not pass judgment, that they merely record changes in the language that may actually make the language "better" as it "adapts to cultural needs." What kind of cultural need is it that demands *we was* for *we were*? An uncultured, indeed anticultural, need, for the supporting of which Lasher deserves five kick in the pant.

There is, I believe, a morality of language: an obligation to preserve and nurture the niceties, the fine distinctions, that have been handed down to us. And the Lashers cannot wash their dainty hands and pretend that anyone who uses the term *language deterioration* displays "ignorance of the facts of language change." Well, there may actually be some ignorance at work in that, though not as Lasher perceives it: "deterioration of language" would be better than "language deterioration."

The pressure on language to deteriorate does not, however, come merely from below, from the "democratic" levelers. It comes also from above, from the fancy jargonmongers, idle game players, fashionable coteries for second-rate intellectuals.

So far, I have discussed corrupting pressures on language from below—from misguidedly democratizing sources. Now, let me consider the attack on language from above: obfuscation in the name of some supposedly higher philosophy, academicism, linguistic or literary arcanum being foisted on language by allegedly exalted authorities. Here I do not mean simply mistakes—as when William Safire, in his commencement address at Syracuse University ("The Decline of the Written Word," May 13, 1978), declares: "We need not degenerate further from written English to verbal signals to sign language." Safire means *oral,* i.e. spoken signals; *verbal* means anything pertaining to words, written or spoken—hence "written English" is also a series of "verbal signals."

No, I refer to the so-called superior wisdom destructively inflicted on language in an effort to rise above what "lesser" people consider correct, straightforward, and self-evident. A typical and highly offensive example of this was submitted to me by Philippe Perebinossoff of Plattsburgh, New York. It is a prospectus for a summer seminar being given at Brown University under the sponsorship of the National Endowment for the Humanities.

These seminars, as my correspondent quotes, are "for college teachers . . . who are concerned primarily with increasing their knowledge of the subjects they teach."

The case in point is a seminar entitled "Theories of Reading: Fiction and Film," offered by Robert Scholes and Michael Silverman, both members of the Brown faculty. Scholes instructs "in the semiotics of fiction, in semiotic theory [etc.]—all for undergraduate students." Silverman teaches courses in "visual theory and film." The bibliography for the seminar, replete with texts by structuralists and semiologists, also features movies by Robert Altman, Bernardo Bertolucci, and Nick Ray. Lacking space for the whole prospectus, I quote its essence:

> The engagement of reader, text, and culture in the act of reading points to the constant play of two elements over the face of the third; and this play of movement we would see as semiotic activity.
>
> We intend the seminar members to read a number of examples of current theory, to read some prose passages and to see some films. . . . We do not want them to come up with "readings" of stories and films in the traditional sense; the substantive notion of "a reading" is opposed to our more participial sense of reading. . . . We will at all times read a "primary" text *through* a theoretical text. We hope in this to avoid the notion that the theory of reading and the practice of reading can be divorced. [Surely, what professors Scholes and Silverman have joined together, no man would be rash enough to put asunder!] Those not conversant with recent theory of reading will not acquire it in isolation from texts, but will at the very least be led to posit a dialectical relationship between texts. Thus a Lawrence story will be read through Todorov's *Poetics of Prose,* Bertolucci's *Before the Revolution* will be read ["Read any good movies lately?" "No, but I've seen the books."] through Althusser on Brecht.

Now, it may be that this playing of two elements over the face of the third comes down to not much more than viewing films, reading fiction, and also consulting some critical works. But note the horrible obfuscation of this "reading through other readings," these "positings of dialectical relationships between texts." Amid all that "semiotic activity" and the embargo on "readings in the traditional sense" will anyone see *through* to the books and movies? But, to go on:

> The aim is not to make the theoretical text a transparent gloss or aid [no danger of that, I daresay] to the understanding of the "pri-

> mary" text (thus inevitably producing new "readings" of the primary text), but to help us situate the text (both theoretical and "primary") within the area of something that can be read, while simultaneously undertaking to question the relationship between texts and our relation to them. Ideally, we would like at the end of eight weeks to have reached the point in our work in which a seminar member might undertake to read Todorov through Lawrence, or to theorize his own position as a reader through an examination of *Before the Revolution.*

Just as there are some people from whom I would not buy a used car, there are certain professors from whom I refuse to buy this secondhand semiology—not that it would be much better new. Even without being able to make sense out of all this tautologizing, highfalutin jargon, obnubilation, and deadwood, I am dead certain that I have nothing to gain from reading Todorov through Todorov, much less through D. H. Lawrence. And whereas I would be happy to assess the artistic value of Bertolucci's second film (in my opinion, minimal), I would not, while in the possession of a shred of sanity, wish to theorize my own position to it as a reader through Althusser. Rather than that, I would even watch the movie through a bunch of women refusing to take off their hats.

Now for a few further caveats from our pundits: "We must stress that we do intend, in any case, to stress the differences between fiction and film. . . . there is a clear difference, for example, in [*sic*] reading a novel in one's study and viewing a film in a public place." O profundity! Could one have arrived at this wisdom without viewing it through Todorov and Althusser? I seriously doubt it. But onward with Scholes and Silverman: "Since one of us is a specialist in prose narrative, the other a specialist in film, our approach to the material will not be fully congruent (this would seem to us a distinct advantage)." Perish the thought of anything so unstructuralist as congruence, so unsemiotic as clarity! Rather, the students will be expected to read Scholes through Silverman, and ideally, if one dare hope it after a mere eight weeks, even Silverman through Scholes. Note also that wonderful "We must stress that we do intend . . . to stress. . . ." I wonder: do two stresses equal one distress?

And here at last, as stressed by Scholes and Silverman, is the promised end: "(1) To establish that the reader of fiction must himself be activated in dramatistic terms, set into motion and theorized; (2) that the cinematic viewer must give over his passivity, undertake the more strenuous activity of reading, while analyzing what this does to his relation to the text; (3) that the use of a by now widespread body of semiotic material on the place [*sic*] of the reader-viewer will facilitate a re-thinking of old critical positions." So in order to view—I mean, read—an Altman movie or Hemingway story—pardon me, "primary" text—I must be dramatistically activated, set into motion, and theorized; I must read while analyzing my relationship to the text (a bit onerous for someone already spinning like a top from all that activation); and I must use a widespread body of semiotic material while dramatistically whirling about in one place—the place allotted to the reader-viewer. All this will immeasurably facilitate my rethinking (with or without a hyphen) and is sure to jolt me out of any old position as a sitter-reader or sitter-viewer that I might have eased myself into in my outmoded and benighted, dramatistically unactivated state.

If I consecrate all this space to Scholes and Silverman, it is because the woods are full of them, various endowments sponsor them, and your tax dollars and the English language have to pay for them. In the place of the three R's, the new education has posited the three S's: structuralism, semiotics, stultification.

Look now at a more obvious disaster wrought by the new higher philosophizing. Mrs. M. C. (I am deeply sorry that legal reasons forbid my naming names), of a Dade County, Florida, college, has sent me a Xerox of the memo from her division director that lists his reasons for denying her tenure as an instructor of freshman composition. I quote:

> She holds some tenets regarding her role as an English teacher which . . . does [*sic*] not lend itself to freedom of thought and exchange [of what?] for students because students are too busy looking for the right answers, i.e. the truth. For example: "Language (English) is precise. . . . I want my students to be precise when they write. They should not use one word when there is a better (more precise) word to say what they mean." This principle ignores two basic considerations: A. Denotative definitions of English words can vary from one to ten (10) or more definitions. Very few English words, usually nouns, have less [correctly: *fewer*] than two meanings. [Actually, quite a few leap to mind; for example, nincompoop, numskull, ignoramus, cretin, division director.] B. Connotative definitions are as many as there are people. They are

> functions of our perceptual field, our view of the world, and are based on our experiences and our psychological imprinting. Hardly precise. This belief is a major guiding principle for Mrs. C.

When you get into the higher reaches of semantics, epistemology, textual explication, and semiology, seven or more types of ambiguity doubtless creep into almost every statement. But while you are writing a simple freshman English composition in Dade County, there is no reason for not hitting your simple point Dade center. A teacher must be propaedeutic before turning heuristic; a student must learn precise, unambiguous expression before he can start contemplating the relativity of the universe and all its components. Or, as they used to say in my school days, you must know the rules before you can learn to break them. Breaking them, in any case, is for shrewd and sophisticated writers, usually of fiction. Otherwise, the rules are still the most practical solution.

So, you see, the language is being attacked from above by the relativists and overcomplicators, from below by the democratic levelers. And, of course, there is overlapping: demotic ignorance plays into the hands of pseudoscientific mumbo jumbo, and structural linguistics rushes to the defense of every popular distortion or misconception. Can the beleaguered middle survive? Perhaps, if you will reject the trends, and yield neither to ignorance nor to obfuscation.

JULIAN BOYD & ZELDA BOYD

Shall and Will

WE WANT TO DISCUSS some notorious grammar rules—those governing *shall* and *will*. The subject may seem at first extremely trivial and hardly the kind of thing grown-up people should worry about. After all, when to use *shall* and when to use *will* seems at best simply a question of usage and at worst a distinction both snobbish and arbitrary. Nevertheless, beyond issues of use or prescript, a very real and conceptually necessary distinction is involved—one that includes among other things two different kinds of knowledge, two different ways of representing the world and our place in it.

To take a specific case, in a dialect that doesn't distinguish between "I will" and "I shall," if I say "I will be there," it is not clear whether I am expressing an intention or making a prediction. In a dialect that does preserve such a distinction, "I will be there" can only be an expression of intention and "I shall be there," by contrast, a prediction (although there is also an emphatic use). Both "I will" and "I shall" are prospective; the difference is one of responsibility. In the one instance, I undertake to get there; in the other, I am only foretelling something I anticipate as likely.

What happens in the dialect in which "I will" is used for both intentions and predictions? How do we distinguish between the two in situations where it really matters? Fortunately, in the vast majority of instances, it doesn't really matter because most often the focus is on the prospective event itself rather than on whether or not our will is involved. In "I will be there" chances are that what is important is the result—my being there—and it is not relevant or even desirable to specify the degree to which I will take responsibility for getting there. When such a distinction does matter, "I will be there" can be qualified by something like "I promise" for the one and "I think" for the other.

For a dialect that does distinguish *shall* and *will* a summary of the handbooks would look like this (ignoring the negative and subordinate occurrences):

1. I shall—predicts, foretells, surmises, etc.
2. I will—promises, threatens, warns, etc.
3. You shall (he, she, it, they, etc.)—promises, etc.
4. You will (he, she, it, they, etc.)—predicts, etc.
5. Shall I (we)?—asks for orders
6. Will I (we)?—asks for a prediction
7. Shall you?—asks for a prediction (rare, British)
8. Will you?—makes a request
9. Shall he (she, it, they)?—asks for orders
10. Will he (she, it, they)?—asks for a prediction

Perhaps it would be useful to take a look at the paradigms for *shall* and *will*.

I. Predictive Use

I shall	We shall
You will	
He, she, it will	They will
Will I?	Will we?
Shall you?	
Will he, she, it?	Will they?

II. Volitional Use

I will	We will
You shall	
He, she, it shall	They shall
Shall I?	Shall we?
Will you?	
Shall he, she, it?	Shall they?

A glance will indicate that there are strange shifts here; nevertheless, strange shifts can be learned, as with irregular verbs (consider *be, am, is, are, was, were*). What makes these paradigms difficult is that there are conceptual perplexities as well.

In the first paradigm, the stance is that of a spectator, and while it is perfectly understandable to look at external events and say "I think it will rain" or "I expect him to leave shortly," to what extent can we take a spectator's view of our own actions? To what extent can we disentangle prediction from intention in the first person? In the second paradigm, too, we find a shift in meaning between the first person and the others. In this instance, the intention expressed is always that of the speaker, always "I," no matter what the grammatical subject. To cite just one example, "You shall have your money" is strictly my promise.

It becomes apparent that *shall* and *will* are not irregular in the same way as *sing, sang, sung.* They are irregular because the very domain of a prediction or a volition is conceptually restricted. Prediction only works in the first person insofar as we can regard ourselves as objects for speculation. Conversely, in volition, nothing besides "I" is, or can be, the true subject of intention.

The history of attempts to deal with *shall* and *will* is a long and vexed one, although it begins innocently enough. The rules for the proper use of these forms were first stated clearly in the seventeenth century by Bishop John Wallis, a distinguished British mathematician, who was nice enough, he thought, to write the rules to help non-native speakers of English get them straight once and for all. The difficulty has to do with the difference between the first person uses as opposed to the second and third person uses, and with the curious reversal of their roles in interrogative and conditional sentences.

What Wallis says is relatively simple: in the first person *shall* simply predicts while *will* does things like promise, warn, or threaten. Obversely, in the second and third person *will* simply predicts and *shall* does things like promise, warn, or threaten. Bishop Lowth, in the eighteenth century, added rules for interrogative sentences, noting that

> this [the above] must be understood of Explicative Sentences; for when the Sentence is Interrogative, just the reverse for the most part takes place: Thus "I shall go; you will go"; expresses the event only; but "Will you go?" imports intention; and "Shall I go?" refers to the will of another. But again, "He shall go," and "Shall he go?" both imply will.

For the reader who finds Wallis incomplete or Lowth confusing, William Ward (1765) provides a rhyming set:

> The Verb by *shall,* States of fixed Order shows; Or States which Chance directs, as we suppose. And *shall* those verbal Future States declares Which *for itself,* an Object hopes or Fears, Thinks *of itself,* surmises, or foresees; But which for other Objects it decrees . . .

> The Verb by *will* those Future States declares For others, which an Object hopes or fears, Of others thinks, surmises or foresees; But *for itself* decrees.

Lowth and Ward were not alone. There were countless attempts in the eighteenth century to codify and/or explain the uses of *shall* and *will*. But in every case the facts either proved too elusive or the explanations too arcane to be satisfactory. It is no wonder that Cobbett in his grammar of 1817 takes another tack. He regards the rules as intuitive and therefore scorns such painstaking elucidation.

> I need not dwell here on the uses of "will," "shall," "may," "might," "should," "would," "can," "could," and "must"; which uses, various as they are, are as well known to us all as the uses of our teeth and noses; and to misapply which words argues, not only a deficiency in the reasoning faculties, but almost a deficiency in instinctive discrimination . . . words, with regard to the use of which, if you were to commit an error in conversation, your brother Richard, who is four years old, would instantly put you right.

While the appeal here to intuition may seem refreshing after so many quasi-Cartesian attempts at clarity, grammars of the later nineteenth century often use the notion of intuitively correct usage in a far more insidious way. The proper use of *shall* and *will* becomes an index of belonging to the proper class or region. Outsiders are peculiarly unable to make the finer discriminations—indeed, they frequently don't seem to care to—and four-year-old brother Richard's infallible ear becomes the sign of an upper-middle-class child with a south of England dialect—not at all the property of all native speakers of English.

Dean Alford, the Archbishop of Canterbury, says this, in *The Queen's English* (1864), of "the use of the auxiliaries shall and will":

> Now here we are at once struck by a curious phenomenon. I never knew an Englishman who misplaced "shall" and "will." I hardly ever have known an Irishman or a Scotchman who did not misplace them sometimes. And it is strange to observe how incurable the propensity is.—It was but the other day that I asked a person sprung of Irish blood, whether he would be at a certain house to which I was going that evening. The answer was, "I'm afraid I won't." Yet my friend is a sound and accurate English scholar and I had never before, during all the years I had known him, discovered any trace of the sister island.—In attempting to give an explanation of our English usage, I may premise that it is exceedingly difficult

> to do so. We seem to proceed rather on instinct, than by any fixed rule.

Alford goes on, then, to give a very cogent account of the relations of *shall* and *will* in British English.

> The simplest example that can be given is "I will". . . . It can only be used as expressing determination; only where the will of a person speaking is concerned . . . We cannot use "I will," where a mere contingent future event is concerned. . . . "Help me, I'll fall," if strictly interpreted, would be an entreaty to be saved from an act of wilful precipitation. . . . Now, what is "I shall?" In its ordinary use, it just takes those cases of things future . . . where the things spoken of are independent of my own will. *"Next Tuesday I shall be twenty-one"*—an event quite out of my own power. . . . "You will" is used when speaking to another person of matter entirely out of the speaker's power and jurisdiction. *"You will be twenty-one next Tuesday." "If you climb that ladder, you will fall"*. . . . For all announcements of common events foreseen in the future, "will" is the word to be used. *"I think it will rain before night"*. . . . We may sometimes use "shall," but it can only be in cases where our own will, or choice, or power, exercises some influence over the events spoken of . . . Notice: You would not say *"Next Tuesday shall be my birthday;"* you must say *"Next Tuesday will be my birthday:"* because that is a matter over which you have no control; but the Queen might say, *"Next Tuesday shall be my birthday:"* because she would mean, "shall be kept as my birthday," a matter over which she has control.

Richard Grant White, an American and a Bostonian, in *Words and Their Uses* (1870), describes the situation like this:

> *Shall and Will*
>
> The distinction between these words, although very clear when it is once apprehended, is liable to be disregarded by persons who have not had the advantage of early intercourse with educated English people. I mean English in blood and breeding; for, as the traveller found that in Paris even the children could speak French, so in New England it is noteworthy that even the boys and girls use *shall* and *will* correctly; and in New York, New Jersey, and Ohio, in Virginia, Maryland, and South Carolina, fairly educated people of English stock do the same; while by Scotchmen and Irishmen, even when they are professionally men of letters, and by the great mass of the people of the Western and South-western States, the words are used without discrimination, or, if discrimination is attempted,

> *will* is given the place of *shall,* and *vice versa* . . . . Why, indeed, do we suffer a smart little verbal shock when the Irish servant says, "Will I put some more coal on the fire?" . . . But those who have genuine, well-trained English tongues and ears are shocked and do laugh.

The eminent American philologist William Dwight Whitney, in *Language and the Study of Language* (1868), makes explicit the fear that so many other writers on the subject share. He sees the loss of the form as loss of the concept itself. There is a sense that not only is the English language falling into degenerate ways but that something terrible is happening in the world as a consequence:

> A reprehensible popular inaccuracy—commencing in this country, I believe, at the South or among the Irish, but lately making very alarming progress northward, and through almost all classes of the community—is threatening to wipe out in the first person of our futures the distinction between the two auxiliaries *shall* and *will,* casting away the former, and putting the latter in its place . . . making arbitrary resolve the sole guide, is a lesson which the community ought not to learn from any section or class, in language any more than in political and social conduct.

C. T. Onions in *Modern English Syntax* (1903) says,

> The traditional idiomatic use of *shall* and *will* is one of the points that are regarded as infallible tests of the true English speaker; it offers peculiar difficulties to Scots, Irishmen, and Americans, the main difference being that these use *will* in many places where the Englishman uses *shall*.

And in Fowler's much reprinted handbook on modern English usage we find under *shall & will*:

> 'To use *will* in these cases is now a mark of Scottish, Irish, provincial, or extra-British idiom'—Dr. Henry Bradley in the OED. 'These cases' are of the type most fully illustrated below . . . & the words of so high an authority are here quoted because there is an inclination among those who are not to the manner born, to question the existence, besides denying the need, of distinctions between *sh,* & *w.* The distinctions are elaborate; they are fully set forth in the OED.

The distinctions as presented in the *OED* certainly are elaborate—there are approximately six pages on *shall,* ten on *will*—but the rules are not in fact fully set forth for all that. To take just one example, the interrogative forms are not given, although the *shall* in "shall I?" means something very different from the *shall* of "I shall." In addition, it is extremely unlikely that anyone not already familiar with the rules would come away from the abundance of the *OED* with any sense of how or when to use one form rather than another.

Fowler circumvents the problem very neatly by referring the reader to the *OED*—a wise move since attempts to pin down the simple rules too often end in terrible confusion. Instead, he proposes to offer examples "from newspapers of the better sort, in which one or other principle of idiom has been outraged. The 'Scotch, Irish, provincial, or extra-British' writer will thus have before him a conspectus of the pitfalls that are most to be feared."

Not surprisingly, Leonard Bloomfield, from a strictly empiricist perspective, singled out the *shall* and *will* rules as a perfect example of the way grammarians had tried to impose a set of arbitrary restrictions on the real language of real people. Moreover, considering the vicious, often overtly political, ends which the *shall* and *will* rules were made to serve, it is understandable that Bloomfield rejected all attempts at prescription. The only alternative he could imagine was description—gathering data which would someday yield useful inductive generalizations. He did not understand that there might be rules which were not regulative but constitutive, that what we do or do not say might be systematic, although complex, evidence for what we can or cannot conceive. On the contrary, he regarded any attempt at correlating bits of natural language with conceptual analysis as, if not totally unscientific, at least greatly premature.

But Bloomfield is only half right about rules. Some of the rules governing *shall* and *will* are indeed only regulative, and like all regulations, convenient, but easily violated. Some of the rules, however, are not. There is no point even saying "*if* these rules are violated" because they cannot be. The distinctions they preserve are so fundamental that to violate them would be to fall into nonsense.

The primary distinction in every case is one between intention or desirability on the one hand and belief or probability on the other—the difference between ought and is. This applies not only to *shall* and *will* but to the other modals as well, although the latter make do without the benefit of separate forms. For example, the following sentences can all be understood in two different ways:

He should be in his office.

He must be in his office.

You might say something.
He may stay.
He could call tonight.

"He should be in his office" means either that he has an obligation to be there or that he probably is there. "He must be in his office" works the same way. It means either that he ought to be or that he presumably is. "You might say something" is either a (qualified) recommendation or a (qualified) prediction. "He may stay" either grants permission or expresses a likelihood. "He could call tonight" means either that it's possible that he will or it's possible for him to (i.e., in his power). This is not the place to go into the many other modal expressions and their paraphrases; here we want to emphasize the deeply consistent nature of the kinds of meaning and the equally consistent way the division cuts through the whole modal system.

What we must do is separate usage both in the empirical and in the normative sense from what underlies it, although the twists and turns of usage are themselves subtle and amusing. To return to *shall* and *will,* when most Americans and Irishmen say "I will go" it is either ambiguous or doesn't make any difference. When General MacArthur said "I shall return," he was using the prophetic, or emphatic, *shall,* which is equivalent in the Wallis rules to "I will return." When an American student at Oxford asks a don "Will you be in this afternoon?" he may be considered very rude since he appears, according to the Wallis rules, to be requesting the don to be there rather than merely inquiring whether he will be. In some dialects, a schoolchild's saying "I will be late" is taken as a sign of unabashed willfulness. As Dean Alford points out, only the queen can say "Next Tuesday shall be my birthday."

The much-cited drowning man example offers a nice four-way contrast. "I shall drown; no one will help me" makes a (fearful) prediction whereas "I will drown; no one shall help me" expresses the absolute determination to drown unaided. From a strictly grammatical point of view, only an Irishman or an American, heedless of such subtleties, would jump in to save him. When David Hilliard says at an antiwar rally, "I will shoot that —— President," the Secret Service moves in and he cannot then testify that as an American he was only making a prediction which turned out to be false.

But although all this is not uninteresting, it is not precisely to the point. The point is that no dialect of English fails to make certain distinctions, no matter what the surface vagaries of *shall* and *will* are. Any schoolchild knows that "Shall we eat on the plane?" means "Do you want to?" and "Will we eat on the plane?" means "Do you know whether in fact we will?" and even if there is some schoolchild who doesn't know, it still doesn't matter because the difference can easily and quickly be made clear to him.

Now let's turn from what people do say to what they cannot say, or, more accurately, what they cannot say and actually mean. Even the queen cannot *make* next Tuesday *be* her birthday, whatever she says. Similarly, we often "promise" what we are unable to bring about, as when we guarantee a child that it won't rain on his birthday, or swear at a deathbed "I won't let you die." An eager child or a desperate patient may be willing for the moment to enter into the make-believe but they know as well as we do that such things do not lie in our power.

In the example of the Irish servant asking, "Will I put some more coal on the fire?" White meant for us only to snicker at the improper usage. Yet, the sentence as it stands is not incorrect; it is absurd. If that were what the servant really meant, White ought to have been horrified at the vision of a person so enslaved that he knew not what he did. Perhaps he was not more disturbed because he knew that the servant could not literally mean what he said since it is difficult to conceive of a human being genuinely asking someone else his or her own intentions, or even asking for a prediction about his or her own immediate actions.

The handbooks record countless instances of "will I" questions, but those that are to be understood as inquiring about volition are virtually all "echo" questions ("Will you take me home?" "Will I? I'd love to"). Even those "will I" questions that ask for a prediction are logically restricted. We can ask about what might *happen* ("Doctor, will I die?"); it is far less easy to imagine situations in which we would seriously ask another for a prediction about what we will *do*. To the extent that we can, we are no longer talking about action but behavior.

"You will" as literally expressing the intention of another is conceptually absurd in the same way. Just as "will I" cedes intimate knowledge of one's volition to another, "you will" usurps it. Nevertheless, there are examples of "you will" as a kind of imperative, which seem, in a curious way, to acknowledge the will of another and preempt it at the same time. Jespersen, in *A Modern English Grammar* (1931), notes this apparent paradox:

> *You will* is often used in a request or order, most often to a subordinate . . . and thus, while formally pre-supposing the will of the

> second person, it really eliminates that will [as in] *You will see the box into the van.*

G. Molloy, in *The Irish Difficulty* (1897), generously suggests that this form "is founded on a certain delicacy of feeling which prompts the superior to avoid the strict form of the command."

The last two examples, "will I" and "you will," are, as we noted, instances of what people cannot say and actually mean (except under the most specialized of circumstances, e.g., where the agent becomes the patient, as with the psychoanalyst or the hypnotist). What makes such sentences seem strange is the very stability of the notion of human intention from which they depart. If William Dwight Whitney were right, if the loss of *shall* really reflected a culture that conceived all future events as determined by the human will, the case would be truly frightening. We should be at least as upset as White should have been at the prospect of a will-less automaton of an Irish servant. But we are not upset. Even White, in fact, is only mildly shocked and Whitney, for all his alarm, surely knows that this invasion from the South will be no more successful than the earlier one. Finally, the loss of a form, any form, cannot entail the loss of so fundamental a distinction. The worst that can happen is that we will find other ways of saying what we mean and that, across dialects, the differences will continue to sound strange.

Philosophers, who are always good at finding "other ways," provide some illuminating examples. To cite only one, Wilfrid Sellars in *Science and Metaphysics* (1968) simply stipulates the wholesale reversal of ordinary usage.

> I am reconstructing English usage pertaining to "shall" in such a way that, in candid speech, it always expresses an intention on the part of the speaker . . . In other words I shall use "shall" and "will" in such a way that "shall" always expresses an intention, whereas "will" is always a simple future.

The significant point is less that he violates the "rules" of common speech than that he scrupulously observes the distinction they indicate.

To turn, then, to the meaning rather than the forms, Bishop Wallis, for one, simply assumed that everyone, and certainly any mathematician, could understand the difference between the *kind* of thing a promise is and the *kind* of thing a prediction is. A promise is an expression of intention and is essentially related to an action and hence thereby to deliberation. A prediction is, at least at first glance, entirely different. It has to do with believing that something in the future (or the past or present) is, or might turn out to be, true. What we are talking about is very much like the distinction Aristotle makes between demonstrative reasoning and practical (or deliberative) reasoning. The latter requires a human agent choosing to do or trying to do or trying to choose what in the world to do. Science, in the easiest cases, is interested in causes, effects, predictions, retrodictions—how something was possible, how to explain or present or subsume under the laws of nature, whether the events to be analyzed involve earthquakes or highway accidents or psychotic behavior.

The last case, namely psychotic behavior, seems to blur the agent/object line. In a truly scientific world view, the explanation for it would be chemical or neurological, or neuro-chemico-physiological, or whatever. And, no doubt, such explanations are or will be possible. But that is emphatically *not* what we want to know when we are seeking to understand human beings in the most meaningful sense. Generally, when we ask ourselves why a person, as agent, did something, we really don't want a scientific explanation. We want reasons—which are necessarily related to intention, deliberation, will, desire, and so on.

The difficulty with *shall* and *will* in relation to these two conceptual domains is that they partly reveal and partly obscure the issues. Frustrating as the variations of dialect and history may be, both the attempts to keep *shall* and *will* separate and the tendency for them to fall together tell us something, and despite Bloomfield's skepticism, the evidence can yield glimpses of those nonempirical categories which make possible the very idea of a human being.

CHRISTOPHER RICKS

Clichés

THE ONLY WAY to speak of a cliché is with a cliché. So even the best writers against clichés are awkwardly placed. When Eric Partridge amassed his *Dictionary of Clichés* in 1940 (1978 saw its fifth edition), his introduction had no choice but to use the usual clichés for clichés. Yet what, as a metaphor, could be more hackneyed than *hackneyed,* more outworn than *outworn,* more tattered than *tattered*? Is there any point left to—or in or on—saying of a cliché that its "original point has been blunted"? Hasn't this too become blunted? A cliché is "a phrase 'on tap' as it were"—but, as it is, is Partridge's "as it were" anything more than a cool pretence that when, for his purposes, he uses the cliché *on tap* it's oh so different from the usual bad habit of having those two words on tap? His indictment of "fly-blown phrases" has no buzz of insect wings, no weight of carrion.

Even George Orwell (whom William Empson, with an audacious compacting of clichés, called the eagle eye with the flat feet)—even Orwell had to use the cliché-clichés (*hackneyed, outworn*), and could say, "There is a long list of fly-blown metaphors which could similarly be got rid of if enough people would interest themselves in the job," without apparently being interested himself in whether *fly-blown* wasn't itself one of those very metaphors which could be got rid of. That was in 1946, in his famous piece "Politics and the English Language." More than thirty years later, a sociological treatise *On Clichés: The Supersedure of Meaning by Function in Modernity* (1979), by Anton C. Zijderveld, finds itself trapped as usual, but—also as usual—without wincing enough and without pondering enough the implications of this trap. Clichés "roll ever so easily over our tongues" (like those words themselves); they are "like the many coins of our inflated economic system" (itself a metaphor which has long since gone off any linguistic gold standard); they are "reach-me-downs," "off the peg"; or they are "rubbed smooth by use." This last is a cliché which the best literary critic of dead metaphors, Donald Davie, could not do without in his fine book *Purity of Diction in English Verse* (1952). But if the phrase "rubbed smooth by too much handling" hasn't itself been rubbed so smooth as not to come in handy when discussing this very matter, don't we have to think again about whether it makes sense to urge that clichés should be—in Orwell's words—scrapped, got rid of?

Partridge's blurb still says in 1978 exactly what it said in 1940, that his book "is full of the things better left *unsaid*"—but there was no way his introduction could, or can, say the things it needs to say except by saying many of these phrases better left unsaid, clichés about clichés. Instead of banishing or shunning clichés as malign, haven't we got to meet them imaginatively, to create benign possibilities for and with them?

But then Orwell's darkest urgings, in the words which end his essay, have a weirdly bright undertow.

> From time to time one can even, if one jeers loudly enough, send some worn-out and useless phrase—some *jackboot, Achilles' heel, hotbed, melting pot, acid test, veritable inferno* or other lump of verbal refuse—into the dustbin where it belongs.

For what is most alive in that sentence is not the sequence where Orwell consciously put his polemical energy—his argumentative train of serviceable clichés from "worn-out" and "useless" through "lump of verbal refuse" to "the dustbin where it belongs"—but rather the sombre glints lurking in the sequence of the scorned clichés themselves: the way in which, even while he was saying that they were useless phrases, Orwell used them so as to create a bizarre vitality of poetry. The *jackboot* has, hard on its heels, *Achilles' heel;* then the *hotbed* at once melts in the heat, into *melting pot,* and then again (a different melting) into *acid test*—with perhaps some memory of Achilles, held by the heel while he was dipped into the Styx; and then finally the *veritable inferno,* which not only consumes *hotbed* and *melting pot* but also, because of *veritable,* confronts the truth-testing *acid test.* Orwell may have set his face against those clichés, but his mind, including his cooperative subconscious, was another matter.

The feeling lately has been that we live in an unprecedented inescapability from clichés. All around us is a rising tide of them; we shall drown and no one will save us. A great poet, Pope, expected to "win my way by yielding to the tide." It is hard to know whether the gloomy sense that we are more than ever threatened by clichés is historically grounded. For it is easy to forget that there were a great many clichés in the past which are now entirely forgotten. We are conscious of our time's clichés as we can never be of past times', and one of the pleasures of reading Swift's derangedly meticulous *Polite Conversation,* a tissue of eighteenth-century clichés, is discovering how many of the moribund vacancies it records have since died away entirely from the language. Again, there is certainly a morbid propensity just now to claim that clichés are springing up to endanger us. The sociologist Zijderveld musters the predictable sense of outrage:

> Since modernization has progressed the farthest in the USA, American English and much of its *slang* has become the *lingua franca* of modernity. Thus, wherever a nation modernizes on the scale of North-America (which is called significantly, though falsely, 'Americanization'), hackneyed American words like 'jeans', 'sneakers', 'hamburgers', 'disc-jockeys', and the all-American 'hi' as a means of greeting, are liable to penetrate into the native language, just as American-based multi-nationals are liable to well-nigh invisibly sneak into the native economic system.

But even if some words (*viable,* for instance) can manage single-handed to become clichés, *jeans*—since it is an object—certainly isn't one of them. Trousers of that material which is named after Genoa aren't a product of any new Americanization; the first reference to them cited in the *Oxford English Dictionary* is from that sturdily English figure Robert Surtees (in 1843), and it describes Septimus "with his white jeans." An entry for 1846 gives us "my friend in the jeans," and as recently—so to speak—as 1923 it was John Galsworthy who remarked that "he wore, not white ducks, but blue jeans." If an American writer has to be enlisted, it shouldn't be someone from our era of multinationals, but Mark Twain just over a century ago: "They were dressed in homespun 'jeans', blue or yellow." A tiny instance, but these cries of alarm are often ridiculously late in the day, as when people speak as if rediscovered clichés like *no way* or *slush money* hadn't been around for a very long time indeed.

Yet the feeling that those valuable dangerous things, widespread literacy and the mass media, have helped to create a new torrent of clichés is unlikely to be simply mistaken. Language has its ecology and its spoliations; for every landscape being raped, there may be a language too. Conspicuous consumption and planned obsolescence are features of the linguistic as well as of the social scene (it is only aeons ago that restaurants were trying to catch an eye by calling themselves "Salad Wars"). Words and idioms are created and worked to death with a ruthless speed that would have shocked earlier ages—the process resembles one of those eerie films which speed up a flower's life from budding to withering. No sooner had President Nixon's press secretary Ronald Ziegler uttered his lying word for lying, *inoperative,* than it had itself become inoperative. No sooner minted than devalued.

Yet as is suggested by the nemesis which so soon rendered Ziegler inoperative, this obsolescence doesn't have to be a cause for gloomy indignation, for the wringing of hands or of necks. Just as there is no opportunity which cannot be abused, so there is no abuse which cannot be an opportunity. The writers against clichés tacitly recognize this, even if they don't openly acknowledge it, when they find that they themselves can illuminate clichés by—can do so only by—calling up clichés to aid them. By using clichés. But using is the nub. Not being used by them.

Marshall McLuhan is one of the few who have delighted in the opportunities presented these days by clichés. *From Cliché to Archetype* (1970) insists that a cliché can be a probe, or even that it cannot but be a probe. McLuhan deplores those who simply cry out at clichés, "Avaunt and quit my sight!" For a cliché is

> an active, structuring, probing feature of our awareness. It performs multiple functions from release of emotion to retrieval of other clichés from both the conscious and unconscious life. . . . The banishing of the cliché from serious attention was the natural gesture of literary specialists. The Theater of the Absurd has shown us some of the creative contemporary uses of cliché.

Not just the theater of the absurd either; McLuhan seizes on Hamlet's response to the clichés of the players: "It is the very cliché, or stereotype qualifying of the actor's performance, that awakens him. Such can be the function of cliché at any time for anybody."

McLuhan has an air of professional high hopes. Still, we should welcome his voice against the doom-dealing despairers. I am less sure that we should welcome Anton Zijderveld. For although he too knows that we mustn't simply suppose that we can avoid clichés, his fear of them is inordinate. Countless times he warns of their *tyranny;* he shudders at the way they are *moulds* of our consciousnesses; and he laments the simple stimulus/response way they artfully work upon us—as if stimulus/response psychology were authoritatively unimpeachable. "It is a kind of brainwashing, and in order to be successful, a rather crass kind of behaviourism has to be applied: the cliché as stimulus has to be repeated over and over again in order to achieve the thoughtless, mechanical response it set out to elicit." I doubt whether clichés do in fact work by "a rather crass kind of behaviourism," but I am sure that this argument about them does.

True, Zijderveld comes in the end to acknowledge that all is not lost. But even then he is lugubrious. The most we can hope for is "stratagems to relativize the power of clichés," and these—especially his pages about "comic sublimation"—turn out to be a dourly defensive business. "Aesthetic sublimation" too is a bitter battle. There is no feeling that a cliché may become the artist's—or the witty humane conversationalist's—delighting ally. Instead, we are in a grim world where if you don't sourly subjugate clichés they will subjugate you. A feat of imagination is the inflicting of defeat. What we must do is make sure that the brutal boot is on the right foot. Thus Brecht used clichés "cynically" (a good thing, apparently), used them "cynically in order to shatter them." Such art gains "a temporary victory over the power of clichés." For Zijderveld, the right metaphor (as is suggested by the word *stratagem,* much loved in the 1970s by armchair non-generals) is of military might. The artistic gracing of clichés, or their imaginative redemption, coarsens here into a replacing of tyranny-by-clichés with tyranny-over-clichés. Clichés are to be *attacked.* An oppressive campaign and not likely to issue in any heartfelt play of mind, whether in ordinary life or in extraordinary literature.

But it is heartfelt play of mind which the best of our recent writers elicit from a vigilant—not beady-eyed—engagement with clichés. In the poems of Geoffrey Hill, as in the songs of Bob Dylan, there is a continual creation of delight—theirs and ours—from the opportunities presented by the countless clichés of our times, clichés which are not to be scorned or expelled (your writing will only become haughty and *outré*), and not to be truckled to, but which are to be imaginatively, wittily, touchingly cooperated with. Clichés invite you not to think—but you may always decline the invitation, and what could better invite a thinking man to think?

Zijderveld is right to say that it is of the nature of a cliché that it has "a capacity to bypass reflection," but he is melodramatic when he gloomily inspissates this into "gradually making everyone immune to reflection." "One suddenly realizes how easily clichés are exchanged, how rarely we hesitate to use them in daily life, and above all how seldom we apologize for their use." Speak for yourself. (But then clichés discourage that.) For a great deal of daily conversation finds wit and humor and penetration in a conscious play with clichés. Irony, not sarcasm; irony has respect for what was once a living truth within what has become a truism, and the difference between an irony and a sarcasm is—as William Empson has said—that a worthwhile irony is to some degree true in both senses.

One serious and various way you may resist a cliché's propensity to bypass reflection is by using the cliché self-reflexively, with a sense of how the very words of a particular cliché have some relation to what makes a cliché. McLuhan's anecdote doesn't say so, but it enacts this:

> A teacher asked her class to use a familiar word in a new way. One boy read: 'The boy returned home with a cliché on his face'. Asked to explain his phrase, he said: 'The dictionary defines *cliché* as a 'worn-out expression'.

An accident? A felicity? A trouvaille, perhaps—we live in an age which delights in *objets trouvés* and in found poems and which appreciates the fine fluke which is a trouvaille.

In the art of Geoffrey Hill, one of the two best poets now writing in England, there is a supple and diverse sense of how a witty or rueful or sardonic reflexiveness may animate a cliché.[1] Hill achieves dignity by rising above cliché; he achieves truthfulness by not eschewing cliché. What fascinates him is the appalling gulf between the way we usually mutter such-and-such a phrase and how we might use it if the doors of perception were cleansed. Take the end of his sombre poem "The Guardians," which tells how the old gather the bodies of the drowned young:

> There are silences. These, too, they endure:
> Soft comings-on; soft after-shocks of calm.
> Quietly they wade the disturbed shore;
> Gather the dead as the first dead scrape home.

"Scrape home" is a triumph, though it winces at a defeat. It is unforcedly literal, "scrape" being the dead body as like a keel that runs ashore, and "home" being nothing but the truth. But in the gap between such a way of scraping home and our usual application (in American, *scrape by*?—just winning, just safe, gulping with relief)—in that gap is the appalling heartbreak of the poem, the gap between what we always hope of life and what we often get. Yet a full recognition of why the cliché here is so alive, even while it gazes upon the bodies of the dead, would have to incorporate some feeling of the cliché *scrape home* as itself here scraping home. Only just. Our relief is partly (only partly, because Hill doesn't give in to the fashionable wish that poems should have no subject other than their own workings) a matter of how the cliché itself is brought home to us. To use a cliché is to take a risk. But then nothing is more dangerous than playing safe.

In Hill's poems, as in those of Marvell and Jonson which he has praised, "the perspective requires the utterance of deliberate cliché, but cliché rinsed and restored to function as responsible speech." The deliberate and responsible use of cliché can foster critical self-consciousness; not a paralyzed self-consciousness or the narcissistic kind that disappears into itself, but the kind that properly grounds its imaginative flights in the cliché's unservile acknowledgment that it is a cliché. In "Ovid in the Third Reich," Hill has written a poem which says what can be said for those Germans who remained silent. The remarkable thing is that at the same time he says what must be said against them.

> I love my work and my children. God
> Is distant, difficult. Things happen.
> Too near the ancient troughs of blood
> Innocence is no earthly weapon.

Eloquence is saved from becoming oratory because that last line teeters on the edge of a collapse into self-pitying despair. But the (unspoken) cliché—"Innocence is no earthly good," no earthly use—does offer a faint hope that innocence may be a heavenly weapon, a heavenly good or of heavenly use. For where else did the cliché *earthly* come from, where but in a contrast of the earthly and the heavenly? Once more, though, the tragic wit is salted with a sense that in the ordinary way—if imagination were not to take its opportunity—the cliché, these very words, would be no earthly good, no earthly use.

Or there is the end of Hill's "Orpheus and Eurydice":

> Love goes, carrying compassion
>   To the rawly-difficult;
> His countenance, his hands' motion,
>   Serene even to a fault.

The shrivelled phrase blossoms wonderfully. "Even to a fault": it admits our doubts about the ideal of self-sacrificial love, yet at the same time it offers an unforgettable feeling for what true forgiveness is, "serene even to a fault." Others' faults are twined so simply with its own. But then what would ordinarily be a fault is here redeemed: the use of a cliché like *to a fault.*

Geoffrey Hill's poems are not aloof, but they are high. Yet he has his own proper accommodation with our casually down-to-earth clichés. So does an artist of a very different kind. Bob Dylan's art does not traffic in clichés, but it travels far and near by the vehicle of cliché. For what could a popular song be which scorned or snubbed cliché? Those who wish to disparage the art of Dylan ought to make sure, at least, that they go no further than did William James in his affectionate disparagement of William Shakespeare:

> He seems to me to have been a professional *amuser,* in the first instance, with a productivity like that of a Dumas, or a Scribe; but possessing what no other amuser has possessed, a lyric splendor added to his rhetorical fluencey, which has made people take him for a more essentially serious human being than he was. Neurotically and erotically, he was hyperæsthetic, with a playful graciousness of character never surpassed. He could be profoundly melancholy; but even then was controlled by his audience's needs. . . . Was there ever an author of such emotional importance whose reaction against false conventions of life was such an absolute zero as his? (To T. S. Perry, 22 May 1910)

For Shakespeare, read Dylan? But is this the best thing for an artist to do with false conventions of life, or of language: to *react against* them?

Dylan has a newly instinctive grasp of the age-old instincts which created a cliché in the first place, and this is manifest on all the occasions when he throws new light on an old cliché, or rotates a cliché so that a facet of it catches a new light. At the same time, like the very unlike Geoffrey Hill, he often grounds his wit, humor, and pathos on an intuition as to how a cliché may incite reflection, and not preclude it, by being self-reflexive.[2]

> Well, ask me why I'm drunk alla time,
> It levels my head and eases my mind.
> I just walk along and stroll and sing,
> I see better days and I do better things.
> ("I Shall Be Free")

The phrase *seen better days* has itself seen better days—that would do as the definition of a cliché. But Dylan brings it from its past into his and our present, by turning it into the present tense, "I see better days"; and by marrying it to "and I do better things," he does a far better thing with it than usual. He eases it from a dim past into a bright present. He helps us see it in a better light, so that instead of its ordinary sad backward glance, there is a step forward, the strolling of an unaggressive intoxication which refreshes the flat old phrase. Just an accident? There are too many such happy accidents in Dylan's songs for them not to be felicities. Anyway, Dylan knows perfectly well that the tired phrase *seen better days* is usually imprisoned within its exhausted meaning—you can hear him sing the glum words in someone else's song on a tape from 1961. His own "I Shall Be Free" is free from the clichéness of its clichés, without getting proudly trapped in the illusion that you can free yourself from clichés by having no truck with them.

"I see better days" has its appealingly wide-eyed hopefulness. But Dylan can narrow his eyes, suspicious of too easy a sympathy with those who are dangerously wrong. So take the cliché *see through your eyes*. Ordinarily, casually, it means putting yourself in the other man's place, seeing things through his eyes. Far harder to do than the easy saying of it would suggest. Possibly a very misguided thing to do, too. So Dylan wrests the cliché into the more stringent sense which goes with sharp-eyed suspicion: "seeing through things" as knowing their cunning and hypocrisy.

> A world war can be won
> You want me to believe
> But I see through your eyes
> And I see through your brain
> Like I see through the water
> That runs down my drain
> ("Masters of War")

For the first verse had sung "I just want you to know / I can see through your masks"—the vigilant sense of "see through"—so that when we hear "But I see through your eyes," we see that it doesn't mean the usual blandly magnanimous thing ("from your point of view"), but the stubborn opposite: I see what your eyes are trying to hide. The cliché has been alerted, and we are alerted to its clichéness, seeing the words from a new perspective, a different point of view, and seeing penetratingly through them.

A cliché begins as heartfelt, and then its heart sinks. But no song about lovers and their hearts can afford to turn away from those truths which may never get old but whose turns of phrase have got old and grey and full of sleep. The trouble with a cliché like *take it to heart* is that by now it's almost impossible to take it to heart. Yet genius with words is often a matter, as T. S. Eliot said, of being original with the minimum of alteration, and such is one of the evidences of Dylan's genius.

> So if you find someone that gives you all of her love,
> Take it to your heart, don't let it stray. . . .
>
> ("I Threw It All Away")

"Take it to heart" becomes "take it to your heart," just enough to take it into the heartfelt; *it* stands for "all of her love," and there is the tiny touching swerve from "someone" in the previous line—you'd think it was going to be "So if you find someone that gives you all of her love / Take *her* to your heart," and take her in your arms.

"Make it new," commanded Ezra Pound from the captain's tower. It goes for clichés too. Not one is irredeemable, thanks especially to the grace of that self-reflexiveness which, so long as it doesn't escalate its claim as if it were the only thing which art were ever preoccupied with, can rightly be valued as a great deal of very recent criticism has valued it: as a power for wit, humor, true acknowledgment, thought, and feeling, in the renovation of the state of the language.

Notes

1. In what I say of Geoffrey Hill, I have at times drawn on, and changed, an earlier essay of mine (*London Magazine,* November 1964). The quotations of Hill's poetry are from *For the Unfallen* (London, 1959) and *King Log* (London, 1968), collected in *Somewhere Is Such a Kingdom: Poems* (Boston, 1975).

2. The quotations from Dylan's songs are from Bob Dylan, *Writings and Drawings* (New York, 1973)."I Shall Be Free" and "Masters of War" are © 1963 by M. Witmark & Sons; "I Threw It All Away" is © 1969 by Big Sky Music.

IAN ROBINSON

Parliamentary Expressions

IN 1978, for the first time in history, there began to be some regular radio broadcasts of the proceedings of the House of Commons and the House of Lords. The prime minister's question time is broadcast live twice a week and the daily half-hour reports of parliament now include recorded extracts.

This may sound unimportant enough, especially to a nation where committees of the Senate have long been broadcast, and where even the private conversations of the president have recently been published.

The broadcasting of parliament did bring home to me, however, with some freshness, some changes in our manner of life, and did set me reflecting on some old questions with a new interest. I am not sure whether it is better to say that the English of politics is changing, or the politics of England.

The House of Commons is of course a very small chamber. It is impossible for all the members to be simultaneously seated. The smallness has always had its effect on the style of oratory practiced: the drop to the *sotto voce,* the sudden snap, the telling interjection, the groan, have always, I understand, been much heard, as well as the rhetorical crescendo, the level tone of sweet reason, the righteous anger. The House of Commons sounds about as far from its written record in *Hansard* as a good film does from its script, and so is hard to quote convincingly in print. The interruptions, formal and informal, are much more dramatic than in the printed record; the hear-hears and nonverbal noises that do not always get into the printed record show the important continuity between the high court of parliament and the nonlinguistic expressiveness of a football crowd. This is, I think, far from a cause for regret, and the immediacy of this whole element of parliament does suggest that there is life in the old place yet. It would be going a little far to say that there will always be an England so long as one member can raise as a point of order that another is attempting to speak and eat peanuts simultaneously; but I do feel that all is not lost in the House while there is so much immediately effective criticism, by way of rude noises, of the nonsense occasionally uttered, and as long as there is the judgment of good healthy laughter and applause, as well as the simulated varieties. The boisterousness of parliament is not surprising except as it always is surprising to find something very remarkable to be what one expected.

What does surprise me, quite unpleasantly, is the great speed, and the informality, of most of the speeches.

Other listeners may find the word *informal* surprising, for the House maintains many of its traditions, to the disgust of some members. The old forms of address are still used: they refer to one another as "honorable members," "the right honorable lady" (for a privy councillor), "the honorable and gallant gentleman" (for a former member of the armed forces) and so on. But the forms conflict with the generally unceremonious modes of speech. Mr. Speaker is still so addressed, but as often as not in a tone of voice to which "George" would come more appropriately.

The speed, at any rate, is beyond dispute. MPs habitually talk faster than a teacher addressing a class or a lecturer an array of notebooks, faster than a parson delivering a sermon, faster than they themselves talk when addressing a public meeting, faster perhaps than any non-private address except in some board or committee meetings.

The first bit of the Commons I ever heard, during a period of experimental broadcasts, was a personal statement by a lady who took the chance of making her reasons for resignation very well known. Out it all came in a great rush that yet seemed somehow unspontaneous. Somehow the absence of a public style meant that there was little character in the personal statement.

Some speakers, it is true, do go slower, and utter sentences that go into *Hansard* unchanged without misleading anyone. They sound like written speeches read aloud, writings in reasonable prose. But prose is not speech, and modern prose does not convey the styles that used to be thought proper for parliament. (There is a tradition that a speaker late in a debate should try to answer previous speakers: as well as ensuring attendance throughout, this is presumably to make the occasions spoken and spontaneous.) The intrusion of the written upon the spoken word is an odd inversion of the position in, say, Henry VIII's day, when many men were competent public speakers but the writing of prose was a rare accomplishment. The written language cannot at any rate supply the style necessary to the national assembly.

If the styles heard in the Commons are more suitable to the boardrooms of multinational corporations, the House of Commons has no style for the conduct of its own work and cannot do it, not even the work that has much in common with multinational corporations'.

This is a large claim to make from a small observation about style. Before giving some examples and attempting some discussion of principle, I had better make it clear that I do intend the claim. I hoped at first that the so offbeat, so unceremonious manner is after all what one expects in a state concerned only for real income and social welfare, and that it is not inappropriate for discussing the size of the annual wage increase. But in fact I do not believe that the bread-and-butter concerns of parliament are well looked to, that the economy is well managed or well criticized, or that we live in a very comfortable nation; and I intend to give one example in which, recently, a government whose dear wish is to present itself as the competent management of a large state-owned concern (namely the United Kingdom of Great Britain and Northern Ireland) allowed itself to be defeated by an opposition seeking an identical "image" after a debate where common sense was reduced to utter muddle by the style I have mentioned and by presuppositions I shall discuss.

Literary criticism, I am sometimes afraid, has not very much to say to the world; but one matter about which it may be easier for literary critics than others to be quite clear—though there are other possibilities for literary critics—is that discussion of style is often essential for the discussion of *what* is said. If you try to restate in other words what a poem says, the other words have a way of saying something else and the "what" changes with the "how." The truism can be used the other way round. Unless a style, a way of saying, is available or creatable, the thing to be said, the "what" of what is said, remains unspoken.

In both the larger and smaller matters of human life, in family and marital relations, in religion, in those connections between individuals called "politics" or "the state," the inseparability of style and content is as sure as it is in poetry. "Maners makyth man" is not a high-flown sentiment, it is a literal truth about the "grammar" of being human. What makes us human is the "how" of doing certain things, the sincere playing of a variety of roles on the stage of the human world. We discover our real selves in our re-creation of various styles. So it is that since Jane Austen's day the English novelists have been able to reveal character, the very soul of individuals, through attention to their manners. Trollope's Mrs. Proudie has to be prevented from interfering in what is no concern of hers, but her different defeats at the hands of Rev. Josiah Crawley and Rev. Dr. Mortimer Tempest are both expressible only by way of comedy of manners. If there are no styles for the young to grow into and modify, many human things become impossible. If there are no manners, in the quite ordinary sense of the word, a future Ms. Proudie will have to be felled with a blow. But really without manners her case will not arise, for there will be no bishops either.

English used to have a set of styles for dealing with public matters and another set for dealing with private life. They both seem to be vanishing much like the Cheshire Cat, and without being satisfactorily replaced.

I know that there used to be a style of political English, because it survived into my lifetime. It was not an unmixed blessing, but it did permit political self-consciousness to the nation. Words would be spoken to the tunes of traditional rhetoric, and between each well-rounded phrase there would be a pause long enough for the speaker to decide in what way to continue the sentence or for the interposition of a heckler or a point of order. To take a very minor instance which, because the polite BBC failed to notice a *double entendre,* brightened countless homes momentarily some years ago: there was once a newsreel report of Winston Churchill in his old age receiving in his capacity of Lord Warden of the Cinque Ports the gift of a golden winkle. He made a speech of thanks that I will quote complete from memory. "Thank you for giving me this winkle," said Churchill; which accurate quotation entirely misses what he said. "Thank you [pause] for giving me [pause] this [pause] winkle" is only slightly better. One needs to remember the intonations, which anyone under thirty is unlikely to do. Even to record them by phonetic markings would be little better, for unless one is familiar with the style, the tunes will be meaningless.

Churchill giving thanks for his golden winkle before, as the BBC said, waving it high in the air, spoke in a heroic style used mock-heroically. He knew he was playing with a grand style. Yet the style made that comic little occasion at least memorable. Churchill's style on more important occasions made them what they were, as well as showing what he was.

On 13 December 1978 Mr. James Callaghan's Labour government, in a minority in the Commons, was defeated and had to change its policy as a result. The Labour governments of 1974 onward had had some success in reducing wage and price inflation, whether because of their policies or because of the effect on the British economy of unemployment in excess of a million. After several "phases" of forcible wage-restraint, with the trades unions chafing for what they call "free collective bargaining" and a general election in prospect, Labour's policy was to recommend a maximum wage increase of 5 percent per annum and to enforce their recommendation by what they called "sanctions." Now as to the wisdom of a government's offering "guidelines" about pay, or the possibility of a government in a free society having much effect either by such recommendation or by legislation, I make no comment. Nor, for the most part, did the MPs on 13 December 1978. The opposition's attack was directed simply against "sanctions." It had better be explained what a sanction is. Mr. Callaghan's government declared that government orders would not be forthcoming for firms which broke the "pay guidelines." They did not publish a list of the firms affected, but the case that provoked the defeat was a large pay increase agreed for its workers by the Ford Motor Company. The government let it be known that it and the agencies it influences, including the very important nationalized industries, would not be buying Fords.

Mr. James Pryor, for the Conservative Party, characterized this as the making outlaws of honorable men. The sanctions had been imposed by "a kangaroo court" and were "a trial action for which there is no basis in law." Her Majesty's government, said Mr. Pryor, has "no right to blacklist honest companies which have broken no laws." The opposition did try to bring out and to fire off the big guns of the constitution, the rule of law. I was surprised to hear no mention of *habeas corpus* and *Magna Carta*. The big guns refused to go off.

Why any purchaser of goods is under any obligation to go to one supplier rather than another I cannot in general see; but whatever reasons might be offered (superiority of workmanship, loyalty to a tried manufacturer, cheapness, the wish to maintain employment in certain areas . . .) have nothing to do with our rights under the law. The sanctions were arguably an economic lost cause or merely silly, but not "a trial" and not "a kangaroo court" (whatever quite that is) because not a court at all.

"Why Fords and not others?" asked Sir Geoffrey Howe, the "shadow" Chancellor of the Exchequer. There are obvious reasons. The Ford decision was particularly influential, and a peculiarly clear example of a company's conceding an inflationary wage increase against its own judgment, with the obvious intention of recouping it in higher prices. Even in judicial affairs there are such things as test cases and exemplary sentences. But the proper answer to "Why Fords?" was "Why not?—as we are considering a pure exercise of discretion."

A government that uses its patronage to enforce its policy is not jeopardizing anybody's rights or privileges. A government has a perfect right to blacklist an honest company which has broken no law if the honest company defies the will of the government, as it has a perfect right to do. This is a twofold instance of freedom of action. The company makes its decision and runs its risk of losing government orders; the government in turn makes *its* decision.

The opposition parties on that little occasion, Conservative, Liberal, Scottish Nationalist (for it was Mr. Douglas Henderson, for the last-named, who found it "hard to imagine a more blatant abuse of executive power") confused the British constitution with the unimpeded operation of the capitalist "sector" of the "mixed economy." Let everything go on without too much inconvenience; let *them* have their money as long as *we,* the managerial class and shareholders, have something left over for ourselves too, or else we will froth a good deal about the rule of law and the British constitution—that, I am afraid, was my impression of the sense from which the opposition's attack derived.

Parliament seems to be losing its common sense. Style, content, and what I shall call a sense of a whole do go together. The invocation of the large matter of the rule of law, at an utterly inappropriate moment and in fairly casual tones, meant that there is no genuine sense of the importance of the rule of law available to the opposition. The inauthenticity of the government on the same occasion was rather different.

The opposition won the vote. Her Majesty's government responded with the demand for a vote of confidence next day, which they got. Sanctions, said the prime minister, were "not acceptable to the House." He also said, "We're democrats and we accept that." So much for his belief that sanctions were necessary for the national good. If he had really held to that, he had another alternative. He could have refused to give an inch on sanctions, have faced a consequent defeat on a motion of confidence and have gone to the country on the issue, taking the opportunity, at the same time, of getting rid of his own rebels. I would have found myself in some serious temptation to vote Labour in that case, a contingency which otherwise I can hardly imagine. Labour would at least have pictured all the opposition parties, convincingly, as wanting to hamstring the government in its perfectly proper efforts to exercise its authority, and also of being so afraid of strikes and of the unions as to prefer ruinous inflation to any risk of industrial disharmony. What the prime minister did was to promise anew to "try for a consensus that will keep inflation at bay." I am sorry: being a professional academic I can't help noticing mixed metaphors. In the first place, if an animal is at bay there is no point in keeping him there: the hunter has to go in for the kill. In the second place, fresh from a rereading of that spendid poem *Sir Gawain and the Green Knight,* I reflect that if you have got a wild boar frenzied, killing the hounds and with his back to a rock and his front to a stream, he is unlikely to be kept there, once he has got his breath back, by that marvellous modern cure-all, the "consensus." When the frantic boar takes on the consensus, my money will be on the boar. So I am afraid that when Mr. Callaghan, in words that could have been used by any Conservative in his position, expressed his fear that the "private sector" might, "as it has in the past," take "the soft option of buying industrial peace," he was not to be taken seriously, because he had just set these businessmen the good example of buying parliamentary peace by capitulating to their representatives. A month later, as I write this, with numbers of workers threatening strike action because three times the "guideline" is not enough, and inflation obviously set to get back to its dizzy heights of 1974–1975 before the year is out, I hope to be excused for taking Mr. Callaghan's search for the consensus that is to keep it at bay *cum grano salis.*

I chose the example of the "sanctions" business to suggest an idea about where sense in politics may come from, and how style is the mark of sense. Before stating this idea explicitly and saying why I have been aiming at a judgment more important than the criticism of one minor debate, I will offer another example, of a debate not restricted to the economy and which had indeed to do with life-and-death matters and the rule of law.

On 2 August 1978 the House of Commons debated Rhodesia, as

they have been doing with some frequency since they lost all control of that part of the world. The debate gave me the odd impression of not being about anything. A number of missionaries of the Elim Church, and their children, had just been murdered by members of what the BBC, without audible inverted commas, calls "Mr. Joshua Nkomo's Patriotic Front," in conditions of savagery unusual even to the post-imperial dark continent. Shock-horror-outrage had as usual been expressed by politicians and set in the dailies by compositors experienced in such phrases. In the Commons debate too the words were used, but I couldn't hear any shock or horror, nor yet, from the pro-terrorist party, any serious feeling that the murders were (as W. H. Auden once put it) necessary. It wasn't just that in the best club in London everyone was being clubbable. Even in the smoke-room of a club serious political discussions are said to be held. I had the feeling that in this debate nothing was being said at all.

When the so reasonable foreign secretary, Dr. Owen, declared that he would talk to anyone, "as I have always strived to do," there seemed no sense that the talk would change anything or define anything. The Conservative spokesman, Mr. John Davies, just back from a tour of the area, always sounds like a businessman because he is a businessman, and sees little difference between the House and a boardroom. On this occasion he sounded as if he were addressing possibly refractory shareholders; his sentences were carefully underplayed, with no emphases, but an occasional well-placed stumble: a style calculated to minimize any sense of occasion there might have been and to get the meeting over without undue trouble. Then came a Labour elder statesman, Mr. Michael Stewart. As a former headmaster and foreign secretary he speaks with a blandness and mildness that must have told on many a staff meeting and visiting potentate. Mr. Stewart considered the charge that in talking to what he, too, called "the Patriotic Front," we are negotiating with murderers, and did not deny it. "Unhappily," he said, "there are so many." If there is a lot of murder—at a safe distance from Westminster—it becomes a familiar and not uncomfortable feature of our world, and causes no ripple on the smooth surface. "Blood has to be forgiven and forgotten on both sides," said Mr. Stewart in his blandest tones. He might as well have been forgiving his prefects for smoking behind the gym.

How can the realities of the situation in Rhodesia be discussed? Some would want to say, if a word not heard in the debate were still usable, that Mr. Ian Smith has committed high treason; also that he practices a racial tyranny. Others, or even the same people, might say that the blood of the innocent Elim missionaries cries to heaven for revenge, and that atrocities are not to be condoned. But how can *murder, treason,* and *tyranny* have their proper force if unhappily there is enough of them about to make them unremarkable?

From that debate it would have been impossible to realize anything of what life is like in Rhodesia now, either for the "Patriotic Front" or for the white ruling classes or the black supporters of the Internal Settlement or the surviving Elim missionaries. The debate was conducted in a set of styles in which judgment cannot be formed, in which the life-and-death concerns of politics are unreal. For there is nothing natural about the significance of human death: like other significances, it has to be created and in the proper style.

If something is going wrong with the styles of our public life it might seem reasonable enough to suppose that there has been a corresponding gain in private life. If we can be more fully ourselves in private, and extend the styles of ordinariness and familiarity of private life into the public world, surely that is at least a sign of a release from the rigidity of old-fashioned private manners? I am afraid I don't think so.

I do not believe that the deliberate informality and generalized friendliness which mark the manners of our age—and which are as much manners as any other style—are conducive to true friendliness or to the full development of human beings.

> How but in custom and in ceremony
> Are innocence and beauty born?

I don't know. I do know that the efforts to extend the familiar style into professional relationships are wrongheaded.

Think of the range of relationships we have with professional men. I want to be on good friendly professional terms with my solicitor, and also with my dentist. In some cases perhaps people even make personal friends with a dentist, for those unfortunate people, known in such painful circumstances, presumably have friends like other folk. But unless we do become friends I don't want to be on first-name terms with the dentist. I would expect a familiar dentist to do harm to my teeth. And imagine first-naming the bank manager, even if you manage to discover his name at all!

In my own sphere, the academic, the question is acute, because the relationship within small tutorial groups is human and, one hopes, quite friendly. It is still a professional one, and the deliberate matiness of some academics, the pretence that we are all personal friends—as if young people of eighteen want to befriend us middle aged—seems to me to militate against any genuine warmth or personality in the relationship. I myself stick to surnames for most of a year and I find that many students like it: they like to be treated with some ceremony as adults.

Institutionalized intimacy has worse results, however, than embarrassing moments in tutorials. Students are encouraged to explain examination failures as caused by the stresses of private life, and many universities now have review bodies which keep up their numbers by deeming students who have failed examinations to have completed a part of a course if the said students can tell a convincing enough tale of woe. Since traditional standards of morality ceased to be enforced at universities and many students live in concubinage or promiscuity, the explanations of failure most often, and in detail, concern their "sex lives." "Well, there is this feller messing me about," began one girl before I could insist that we should not listen. Private lives are constantly paraded before the awful institutional sympathy of these committees, and good advice, rebukes, tips of the kind (minus morality) that used to appear in the Heart-to-Heart columns of women's weeklies, freely dispensed. Ugh!

The modern public friendliness is predictably insensitive. It is not a guarantee that persons are being recognized as such; it actually tends to deny personality by denying the distinction between public and private, the styles proper to each, on which personality depends.

It is not my case that if we speak ceremoniously at the proper times we shall necessarily confer any dignity on life. The more likely result at the present time is some kind of comical eccentricity. The opinion which I hope gives some coherence to the observations I have made, an opinion which there is space here only to report, not to argue, is that the various styles of our language are our various ways of expressing our sense of the unity of life. By saying so I propose an answer to the question which in one form or another has been troubling students of language for a long time, the question where the meaning of language comes from. I don't believe that the meaning of any utterance arises predictably from the orderly combination of the elements of language, nor from any correct imitation of style. It may be predicted that if such and such words are combined according to the rules of grammar, the result will be a well-formed sentence, and words may certainly appear as entries in dictionaries, whose business is to define them. It does not follow that the meaning of a sentence is predictable from the definitions of the words and the rules of their grammatical combinations, or from the effect of a style imitated from earlier examples. So if you ask me where the meaning of an utterance comes from I will in one mood answer "from inspiration" and in another "from whatever whole the utterance is a part of." I regret again that this is not the place to argue an opinion which is certainly to the linguists foolishness, nor to explore the relationship between the ideas of style and the whole.

If I am right, however, the absence of formality from contemporary life is neither the cause nor the effect of the decline of the styles proper to formality, and formality will not be restored by any artificial reintroduction of formal styles, any more than the divine right of kings could be restored by the return of King Charles II from his travels. Rather, the style and the thing are internally related. On the other hand, I do not mean that the part derives from the whole as temporal sequence. The whole is only suggested by the parts and does not precede them.

One may nevertheless venture a "because." The polite styles of English are in decline because the whole language, from which they derive, is losing the cohesion of which the formal is one essential evidence.

In that debate on the "guidelines sanctions," the sense the opposition attempted to make was indeed derived from a higher whole, from their sense of the British constitution. Unfortunately the sense was not genuine. The falseness was evident in the feebleness of the arguments about the rights of the executive as well as in the failure to command the ceremonious style in which such things have to be mentioned. At least once the failure was also plain in the imagery. "We cannot allow a once-great country," said Mr. Pryor, "to be relegated to the second division." Again, there is a kind of mixture in the metaphor, for if, in another constantly used image, the once-great country is at the bottom of the international league and plays by the rules, how can it avoid relegation? The United Kingdom is not, however, like a football team: it is not as if playing competitive fixtures at home or away and it has no end in view such as the league and cup double. The failure to see the ludicrousness of the image is the failure both to achieve any adequate conception of the whole nation, and to derive a style fit for discussing it.

But in the century of the common man, of the "media" and a "public opinion" definable by poll counts, the age of universal first-naming, free love, estate duty, and *The Sun* newspaper, it will be said that the unceremoniousness of parliamentary style is inevitable; and that three years after the referendum that tied us to the European Economic Community, the whole that political sense might derive from is no longer to be found in these islands.

I see some sense in both points. I think the collapse of style and the failure to grasp political reality in the Commons are indeed symptoms of a malaise widespread in our whole civilization. I nevertheless believe that by "our whole civilization" I am ordinarily referring to the U.K.—within, of course, Europe and the West. The recovery of political style will be both a sign and the means of the recovery of national identity. I do not believe it is accidental that the best political styles I hear often, those of Mr. Enoch Powell, Mr. Anthony Wedgwood-Benn, and Mr. Michael Foot, belong to men deeply opposed in their policies but all committed to working on and defending the idea of the United Kingdom.

LISEL MUELLER

The Possessive Case

YOUR FATHER'S MUSTACHE
My brother's keeper
La plume de ma tante
Le monocle de mon oncle
His Master's Voice
Son of a bitch
Charley's Aunt
Lady Chatterley's Lover
    The Prince of Wales
    The Duchess of Windsor
    The Count of Monte Cristo
    The Emperor of Ice Cream
    The Marquis de Sade
    The Queen of the Night
        Mozart's Requiem
        Beethoven's Ninth
        Bach's B-Minor Mass
        Schubert's Unfinished
        Krapp's Last Tape
        Custer's Last Stand

        Howards End
        Finnegans Wake
            The March of Time
            The Ides of March
            The Auroras of Autumn
            The winter of our discontent
            The hounds of spring
            The Hound of Heaven
        Dante's Inferno
        Vergil's Aeneid
        Homer's Iliad
    The Fall of the City
    The Decline of the West
    The Birth of a Nation
The Declaration of Independence
The ride of Paul Revere
The Pledge of Allegiance
The Spirit of '76
    The Age of Reason
    The Century of the Common Man
    The Psychopathology of Everyday Life
        Portnoy's Complaint
        Whistler's Mother
        The Sweetheart of Sigma Chi
        The whore of Babylon
        The Bride of Frankenstein
        The French Lieutenant's Woman
            A Room of One's Own
            Bluebeard's Castle
            Plato's cave
            Santa's workshop
            Noah's ark
            The House of the Seven Gables
        The Dance of the Seven Veils
        Anitra's Dance
        The Moor's Pavane
        My Papa's Waltz
    Your father's mustache

FRANCES FERGUSON

The Unfamiliarity of Familiar Letters

I HAVE BEEN TOLD that television and the telephone have conspired to ruin our epistolary habits and talents, but the ever-lengthening list of letters I ought to write persists in nagging my conscience even after I've heard that explanation of why I don't write letters. Thus, in a last-ditch effort to avoid writing letters, I decided to write an essay about why or how we don't write letters.

The option of writing a letter to Abby* for help in writing letters was, of course, not open to me, but one day as I read letters asking her advice on problems dire enough to have forced their victims to write (a letter must be as serious testimony of wanting to solve one's difficulties as payment is of being committed to psychoanalysis), I saw Abby's offer of help: for only a dollar, one could receive a "handy booklet" that would "serve as a guide for those who put off writing because they don't know 'what to say'—or 'how to say it.'" What Abby's booklet told me, however, was not "how to say it" but that Abby possesses extraordinary courage; with every page, I encountered another peril of letter writing as Abby bravely reminded me that "it" was "etiquette" even if "it" didn't make sense (for example, a much

---

*Abigail Van Buren, whose nationally syndicated advice column *Dear Abby* appears daily in newspapers all over the United States.

divorced and much married lady should retain all her husbands' names and sign herself "Bertha Britton Hawthorne Stevens Hill").

Under the heading "Getting Started," Abby announces her basic epistolary philosophy: "The important thing about letter writing is to say what you want to say, say it so you can be easily understood, and say it so it sounds like *you*" (emphasis hers). Before one can start sounding like oneself, however, one needs writing supplies, and purchasing these begins to indicate the difficulties of being oneself. When you go to order personalized stationery, you should, Abby advises, "Ask *your friendly neighborhood printer* to help you select an attractive style of type" (emphasis mine), and she soothingly informs you that "perhaps he can even help you dream up something individual and clever, such as 'News from the Hughes' or 'Slowly but Shirley' or 'Hello from Flo.' "

Letter writing is fraught with contradiction, of which the cardinal principle is that he who would sound like himself must sound like someone else. A few years ago, when a cause-oriented soap opera included in its script advice to women on how to avoid rape, it suggested that one should avoid buildings and doorways on the one hand and parked cars on the other—thus leaving oneself with nowhere to walk except where the sidewalks happen to be exceptionally broad. Advice on letter writing similarly combines injunctions to you (1) to be yourself and (2) to find out from someone else how to be yourself. While any advice on etiquette is pulled by those two contradictory urges to do what is proper (i.e., what everyone else does) and to make the social appear to be natural (i.e., what one would have done of one's own accord), accounts of letter writing particularly exacerbate the lurking suspicion that the various elements of a letter carry a freight of significance that is more than an ordinary mortal can manage. Even Abby's efforts to reassure one that the " 'Dear' in a salutation is a standard greeting in the friendly or informal letter" quickly raise the dread specter of misunderstanding when she recalls a query from a fifty-two-year-old spinster who had wanted to know if the author of a postcard had "meant anything" by addressing her as "Dear Margaret." And just as one has firmly accepted the *Dear* of a salutation as purely conventional, Abby issues a bulletin: "Caution: NEVER close with 'Love' unless you mean it."

The difficulty that quickly arises in Abby's discussion is that the famous "casual letter" is not casual at all, for the significance of every aspect of the letter continually seems to undergo a kind of escalation under the obtuse, hopeful, or suspicious glance of the imagined recipient. Thus, the whole project of writing a letter ceases to seem natural, and the conventions lose their force as helpful guidelines; in fact, they appear positively arcane in Abby's description (did you realize, for example, that the use of a colon is "a little on the formidable side" and that "it even looks like a double barreled shotgun, yes?").

Whereas the aspiring letter writer may put pen to paper with fantasies of achieving heroism, Abby's booklet suggests that one must write with the ever-diminishing hope that one is addressing someone who understands one exactly as one wishes to be understood—who also feels that gun-control laws should apply to colons and who isn't about to raise any fuss over the conventional use of *dear* in the salutation. This ideal recipient of the letter, this soulmate should share all of one's assumptions without, however, having had recourse to Abby's booklet, lest the depths of one's sincerity seem a bit shopworn. One may start out with the aim of writing lively, fascinating letters like Byron's, but the recognition that one simply can't trust the recipient to understand starts urging one in the direction of the deep cliché—the grandiloquence rather than grandeur of Donna Julia in Byron's *Don Juan,* who seizes upon the end of a one-night stand as an occasion for epistolary tragedy "written upon gilt-edged paper / With a neat little crow-quill, slight and new" (Canto I, lines 1577–78):

> 'They tell me 'tis decided you depart:
> 'Tis wise—'tis well, but not the less a pain;
> I have no further claim on your young heart,
> Mine is the victim, and would be again:
> To love too much has been the only art
> I used;—I write in haste, and if a stain
> Be on this sheet, 'tis not what it appears;
> My eyeballs burn and throb, but have no tears.'
>
> (lines 1529–36)

If concern over the reader's comprehension drives you to the safety of the recognizable cliché, however, Abby unfolds the "not uncommon" scenario in which "a naive or clean-minded person" purchases a card for a friend, "who upon receiving it is horrified." The lesson she draws is that "if you want to send a 'cute' card, be sure it's not offensive or crude." If, however, you are naive or clean-minded, how will you be able to be sure? Either you will trust to your own judgment and send out the card and horrify your friend, or you will have to consult your friendly local salesperson, who might of course be as naive and clean-minded as you (or who might lie to you for profit).

Abby is, however, a true friend to the aspiring letter writer. The situations for which she arms you are all rather tame, a fact that she accounts for by explaining that you won't need to write many letters with bad news because that commodity "travels fast, so it is usually unnecessary to inform anyone [of a broken engagement or some such catastrophe] by mail." And whereas she encourages one to write nasty letters to get "it out of one's system," she also suggests that it is best not to send "it"; the world may be such a hostile place that only bad news speeds on its way, but Abby's letter-writing followers will not compound the world's misery by reciprocating with anger or malice. As Max Beerbohm suggests in "How Shall I Word It," his brilliant parody of a letter-writing manual, one who writes letters is near sainthood in virtue if not in recognition—at least in the eyes of the ever-trusting and trustworthy letter-writing advisor. "In all of them [the sample letters that Beerbohm reads and parodies], though so many are for the use of persons placed in the most trying circumstances, and some of them are for persons writhing under a sense of intolerable injury, sweetness and light do ever reign."

Whereas Beerbohm provides models to consult if one is contemplating blackmail, Letitia Baldridge in revising *The Amy Vanderbilt Complete Book of Etiquette* goes Abby and Beerbohm one better by combining the advisor's fiction of the nobility of the aspiring letter writer with self-conscious self-interest:

> The use of the personal letter in business is an important tool, not only from the point of view of manners, but also because it can influence one's career in a most affirmative way. Since no one orders us to sit down and write a personal letter in our adult life, the mere act of writing it is creative, and the motivation is usually unselfish. A well-written letter requires sympathy or empathy on the writer's part, so it does, in fact, denote a certain amount of good character. (p. 476)

If Abby continually suggests that the letter writer can revel in the luxury of knowing that he did right *and* was unappreciated (or insufficiently appreciated), Baldridge is more of an activist. Abby's letter writer merely reacts with exactly the right (and prompt) response to others, but Baldridge's letter writer is a play-maker, one who anticipates others' reactions—in short, a Machiavel. Unlike Machiavelli, however, Baldridge quickly manages to convince herself that the greatest self-interest is not only appropriate but positively philanthropic. The very process of looking for personal advancement fosters creativity, "usually unselfish" motivation, sympathy or empathy, and "a certain amount of good character" (modesty?). In other words, thinking about how others might be useful to you at least serves the purpose of making you think of others with enough "sympathy or empathy" to play on their emotions.

The sense of the importance of the reader's reactions and of the writer's actions does, of course, increase rather dramatically in this scheme of things. Thus, one finds a sample letter for an "apology for having seriously offended someone" that begins, "There is no way I can erase the tragic error of my bumbling tongue this morning" (p. 477). But if the actions represented in these sample letters are of grand dimensions, the scope of our heroic letter writer's attention and interest is nearly divine. He bothers to congratulate a colleague on his son's having won a scholarship to Yale—"You and your wife must be bursting forth with unmitigated but understandable pride" (p. 478); thanks a colleague by mail for "a lunch invitation, even if it was strictly business" (p. 476), and becomes an instant sympathizer when an acquaintance has lost his job:

> I was shocked when I heard the news. Your company must be in real trouble to let a man of your caliber and professionalism go. It will be their tough luck and someone else's great gain. I'm sure that after the usual painful period of job hunting you will end up with a much better position in a firm that will appreciate your talents. . . .
> (p. 477)

The extraordinary confidence that wide-ranging emotion, pragmatically deployed, will find receptive readers does, however, begin to crumble when Baldridge turns from her discussion of general office manners to the personal. Business may be business, but the personal is always potential history, and the gaze of mobs of ingrates in future ages begins to dwarf the heroic figure of the letter writer:

> I often wonder when writing a letter to someone I haven't seen for a long time and to whom I have much to relate, "Will he or she possibly save this letter?" If I think the person might I tear it up and start over again, paying attention to the manner in which I express myself. . . . (I also type it, so that no one in future years will ever judge my bad handwriting!) I would hate anyone in the year 2050 to come across one of my usual hastily written, careless letters, and to judge me on its merits.
> (p. 513)

If letter writing is "the ultimate in human communication," as Baldridge says it is, because "the reflective written word" can express the entire "range of human emotions" and "our real selves," the various drafts of a letter become stages in the fashioning of "our real selves"—those selves that never have bad handwriting or write carelessly.

While Baldridge laments "how few of us communicate anything of ourselves to anyone any more" (p. 515), she is careful to keep some selves torn up in the wastebasket where they belong. After all, the recipient of a congratulatory letter may have plans for "rereading it years from now"; a letter of condolence will "probably be read by several members of the family and close friends" at the very least, and it might always "be saved and passed down through the family" (p. 519). Thus, the writer of what Baldridge calls "the impulse note" (for which she provides a few convenient models) may write in haste, but the projected audience will judge for an imagined eternity—the letter writer's nightmare of an afterlife. And if one is not alert, one can expose oneself to an eternity-sized audience within one's own lifetime by writing an excessively interesting postcard (Baldridge warns, "One must remember, however, that many pairs of eyes see a postcard, so nothing of a serious nature or requiring confidential treatment should be written on them" [p. 530]; one can only wonder how many felons have unwisely resorted to the postcard because they felt they didn't have much to say).

But even if Baldridge sees letters as "the ultimate in human communication," she also makes it clear that they aren't nearly good enough. "A letter of apology should be sincere and rather humble" (p. 522), but a face-to-face apology takes priority. The reasoning behind this, which emerges in the section called "Letters of Complaint," is that "the interreaction [*sic*] of human voices usually settles the problem more quickly than the exchange of letters," because "the written word, with emotional overtones, has too many interpretations" (pp. 527–28).

Now we all know that the written word and the spoken word both have more interpretations than we sometimes would like to admit, but the crucial difference between the two is that the written word can always be used as *evidence*. In fact, Baldridge herself has already forearmed her letter writers with that knowledge in her advice on refusing a gift:

> If you feel you should not accept a present, don't. Let your instincts be your guide. If a young girl receives a piece of jewelry from a

> man she hardly knows; if a young person is paid a large sum by a much older person for performing a simple service; if one feels there is a hint of bribery involved—send the check or gift back and say, "Thank you anyway, for being so thoughtful and kind." *Be sure to make a carbon copy of this letter for your files.*
>
> (p. 518, emphasis mine)

Since the reader of Baldridge's advice on letters is, by definition, virtuous and noble, he can preserve copies of his letters as lasting proof of his good character—and the possible evil of others.

For anyone less convinced of his inherent goodness than Baldridge's reader, the hazards of letter writing have become all too clear by this point in the discussion. The very fiction of the letter writer's heroic stature that Abby and Baldridge rely on must be painstakingly constructed for any letters to get written at all, because most of us have a strong enough sense of our inheritance of original sin—or a strong enough predisposition towards guilt—to suspect that our letters might eventually become evidence of our callowness, obtuseness, idiocy, or worse. However cheerful Ms. Baldridge may sound about the prospects of having one's letters saved for posterity, the rest of us know that what we send out in the mail can with time almost automatically become the grounds for blackmail.

Recently a Los Angeles trial offered itself as an illustration of the insidious process by which letters come back to haunt their authors. The movie star Lee Marvin was sued by one Michelle Triola Marvin for half of the money he had earned during the six years they had lived together out of wedlock, because she (who had had her name legally changed to Marvin immediately before or immediately after their relationship ended) claimed that she had in effect been his wife and should thus have the same property rights as a legal wife. Letters that Lee had written to Michelle years before figured in the case against him. On the one hand, the plaintiff's lawyer tried to interpret Lee Marvin's letters as constituting professions of love that amounted to a commitment to spend the rest of his life with Miss Marvin; on the other hand, Marvin insisted that "what he wrote her meant very little" and that "they were rather silly letters" (*San Francisco Chronicle,* 27 January 1979).

If Lee Marvin had only read *Clarissa,* he would have known better than to have written any letters to Miss Marvin in the first place. He would not then have duplicated Lovelace's foolish blunder of committing pen to paper and thus finding himself overcommitted. *Clarissa,* like the Gothic novels that follow in the wake of its inspiration, offers us the recognition that any letter all too quickly becomes the imaginative property and product of the recipient and starts to bind its author to significances he may never have dreamed of. Lee Marvin may want to think of himself as a rake and Michelle Marvin may want to imagine herself an innocent, but Richardson and the Gothic tradition suggest that letter writing is the first fatal step towards being surrounded by authority that takes one to task for having imagined that one could author a letter lightly. The Inquisition stands not far from the writing desk—definitively interpreting back to the letter writer motives rather different from any he may have recognized in himself.

Angela Davis's letters written to George Jackson during his incarceration at San Quentin may further dramatize this dilemma of meaning for letters that refuse to die. While the prosecution in Davis's trial argued that the letters proved that she had been so passionately involved with Jackson that she would have been capable of participating in the plan to spring him from prison, the defense gathered scholarly comment designed to show how the love letters presented not her love but instead her knowledge of epistolary conventions—just what one says in letters. The prosecution wanted to yoke Davis to an interpretation of the letters as evidence of passion in all its immediacy and truthfulness; the defense wanted to see the letters as so typical as to be trivial to the point of meaninglessness. As in the Marvin case, the status of the letters alternated between that of absolute veracity (on which no conventions seemed to impinge) and that of absolute emptiness (in which conventionality was the equivalent of nothing at all).

It is no mystery, when one considers it, that Richardson should have used materials from a letter-writing manual he was composing to begin the tradition of the English novel. For while Richardson's *Familiar Letters . . . on Important Occasions* is a book of model letters which directs "not only the requisite style and forms to be observed in writing familiar letters, but how to think and act prudently, in the common concerns of human life," *Pamela* (which grew from Richardson's own model letter for a serving maid whose virtue had been assailed by her master) demonstrated the extraordinary difficulty of being interpreted as one intended. Indeed, the struggle to cling to one's sense of what one meant by a letter becomes truly heroic, because a letter writer must defend himself against nothing less than a world eager to impose its rival interpretations on both letter and letter writer. Although the format of the letter-writing manual enables Abby and Baldridge to breeze from one letter to another and one character to another, Richardson's genius was to have seen that one letter is never enough. One may write one's first letter in the full consciousness of one's own virtue, but it will take letter upon letter upon letter to clarify, amend, and defend one's sense of virtue. The fiction of heroism that letter-writing manuals promulgate finds its substantiation in the fiction of *Pamela* and *Clarissa,* for what Richardson recognizes is that the task of writing enough letters to wrest one's destiny from the hands of the reader of the letters is the labor of a lifetime.

The letter-writing manuals tell you only how to write one letter to one person on one particular occasion. The glories and horrors of Richardson's novels lie in their telling you what happens when one must respond to a response to one's letter. Richardson recalled getting his start in writing at "not more than thirteen" when three young women in his neighborhood, "unknown to each other, having a high opinion of my taciturnity, revealed to me their love-secrets in order to induce me to give them copies to write after, or correct, for answers to their lovers' letters." That experience must have led to his knowledge of how hard it is to sustain the appropriate self-image when the self is sincerely compounded out of impersonation. He knows what those of us who don't write letters any more know—that one can never get away with writing on one occasion but must write for an eternity to defend one's own glamorized image of oneself once one has made the disastrous mistake of sending an example of what one thinks of as one's courtesy or virtue or thoughtfulness off in the mail.

On first reflection it may appear rather implausible that abduction, imprisonment, and rape all issue more or less directly from Clarissa's unwisely having sent letters to Lovelace when her family had forbidden her to have any communication with him. Yet that series of dramatic examples of losing self-determination and the sense of control also seems to represent Richardson's tracing out of the logic of letter writing with its naturalization of paranoia in the service of the recognition that someone else is in fact controlling whatever self one has imperfectly manifested in a letter. Lovelace and Clarissa spend what would seem by most standards an inordinate amount of time quibbling over terms in their letters, yet they never manage to agree on mutually acceptable definitions of words like *honor* and *power* and so forth. The claustrophobia of the novel finally rests not on Clarissa's imprisonment or Lovelace's seeming omnipresence; rather, it is a claustrophobia that stems from Clarissa's constantly, continually being confronted by yet further evidence that she has been misunderstood, or certainly not understood as she would have liked. It is only when Clarissa seems to register the alarming possibility that letters provide *only* misunderstanding that she regains some kind of control of the self she lost in letters:

> SIR,—I have good news to tell you. I am setting out with all diligence for my Father's House. I am bid to hope that he will receive his poor penitent with a goodness peculiar to himself. . . .
>
> I will write a letter, which shall be sent you when I am got thither and received: till when, I am, etc. / CLARISSA HARLOWE.

This note, which might—if the world of letters were ordinary—be an almost routine statement of one's plans (going on a trip, more later. . . .), is Clarissa's famous ambiguous announcement to Lovelace of her imminent death. Of course, the one thing Clarissa can count on is Lovelace's misunderstanding, and her triumph is to understand his misunderstanding: She knows he will think of her father rather than of her heavenly father. Clarissa's joy in the face of death, moreover, does not merely display her spirituality or her resentment of Lovelace. The logic of letters has simply and inexorably led her to prefer death to the endless subjection of being read, abducted, imprisoned, and raped—of being bound by others' misunderstandings of her. Clarissa's death pays the ultimate tribute to the conventionality of even letters that attempt self-explanation: death is the closest approximation to meaning nothing that she can muster.

Clarissa's composition of her own death exposes the fragility of the notion of the self in the business of letter writing; she, quite simply, wearies of the tending that her misunderstood self continually requires—as if it were a house always needing to be cleaned again. Occasional letters, written to the moment, may provide a temporary role, but they threaten to erode any confidence that the self may be more than the mere accumulation of its various roles; and the assertion of the self's transcendence in the non-occasional, self-expressive epistolary mode always runs the risk of expressing not the self but some clichéd otherness—like the "self-expression" of a Las Vegas nightclub singer insisting that "I gotta be me." In letters the self vanishes, so to speak; at least, the grand, noble self that transcends all its moments disappears. What is left is the letter writer's sense of being left with a self that is no better than its pedestrian formulations—only what the uncharitable letter reader might perceive. If letter writing begins in self-consciousness, it ends by offering an implicit rebuke to any claims for the self. Each letter may end with a closing, but the closing becomes more and more obviously "merely" conventional as one thinks of the ways in which the finality of getting "the whole soul summarized" always eludes the letter-writer's reader. Another letter and another and another will be necessary not just to explain, interpret, and clarify for the reader but also to resurrect, if only temporarily, the letter writer's sense of having a self to express—which will appear in the next letter.

JANET WHITCUT

The Language of Address

SOON AFTER HER ARRIVAL in Wonderland, Alice found herself swimming about in a pool of tears, and wished to attract the attention of a nearby mouse. "So she began: 'O Mouse, do you know the way out of this pool? I am very tired of swimming about here, O Mouse!' (Alice thought this must be the right way of speaking to a mouse: she had never done such a thing before, but she remembered having seen in her brother's Latin Grammar, 'A mouse—of a mouse—to a mouse—a mouse—O mouse!')."

Alice's problem was one that affects all of us every day. It is that of how to attract the attention of a stranger, an important function of language; and English, unlike Latin, offers no one obvious way of doing it. "Hey, you!" would have been rude. Like all of us, she could have fallen back on the safe "Excuse me" or "I say." At least she was lucky in noticing that her interlocutor was a mouse. Otherwise, there is simply nothing neutral she could have said to it. Most of the following would have obliged her to know its sex and perhaps its age, and would in addition have given away a lot about herself. She could have chosen, if she felt slangy, *chum, luv, mush, toots, stranger, friend, cock, pal, mate, old bean* (as in P. G. Wodehouse), or *old boy.* She could have pretended to be American and said *mac* or *bud*. She could have played it Australian and called the mouse *cobber* or *sport,* appealed to common political affiliations by addressing it as *comrade,* or used the respectful Cockney *guv'nor.* She could have approached a female mouse, polite Victorian little girl as she was, with *ma'am,* which would also have done if she had been a deferential young man from Virginia. A more forthright American male could have called it *babe* or *sister*; a Shakespearian gallant could have hailed it as *wench,* or a friendly Yorkshireman as *lass.*[1]

If Alice had felt fond of the mouse, or if she were a warmhearted sort of person, a lot of endearments would have been available to her. One can summon aid with cries of *beloved, cherub, chicken, darling, dear, ducky, honey* (rather American, this one), *lovey, pet, poppet, precious, sweetheart,* my *treasure.* Any of the foregoing can be spiked up by the addition of *my,* but if one were advising a foreigner on the nuances of English one should add that in the hands of an expert this usage may carry a touch of deliberate patronage. *Man* used on its own has a flavor either of the contemporary jazz scene or of Holmes in mild expostulation to Watson—"Good heavens, *man*, have you allowed the miscreants to effect their escape?"—while *my man* went out with Lady Bountiful. In *Zuleika Dobson* the Duke of Dorset has occasion to wreak vengeance.

> The sole point for him was how to administer her punishment the most poignantly. Just how should he word his letter?
>
> He rose from his chair, and "Dear Miss Dobson—no, *My* dear Miss Dobson," he murmured, pacing the room, "I am so very sorry I cannot come to see you. . . ."

If Alice had known the mouse's name, she could have called it by that. All names can be used to address people directly, although in practice there are interesting restrictions on their use.[2] In the first place, she could have used its simple first name, *Arthur* or *Tabitha,* a habit which has become enormously more common in recent decades. In many circles, though, first-naming still corresponds to the use of the intimate second-person pronoun in French or German, applying more naturally to contemporaries or juniors than to seniors. Children may be encouraged to avoid it by saying *Uncle Arthur* or *Auntie Tabitha* to their parents' friends. Many people feel a certain *frisson* at hearing progressive moppets first-name their parents, and American democratic bonhomie has been known to come unstuck if a boss's boss's American boss presses a shy young British employee to address himself and his elderly wife as Homer and Mary Lou when the youth thinks of them as Mr. and Mrs. Pennypacker. And just because the one-way use of the first name implies a somewhat stereotyped one-way relationship, a modern middle-class housewife may be shy of using it to a cleaning woman of her own age.

Alice could have called the mouse *Art* or *Tabbie,* and paradoxically today the familiar diminutive may often be used, among workmates for instance, to express less intimacy than the full first name; which is perhaps reserved for the family, as in Falstaff's "JACK FALSTAFF with my familiars, JOHN with my brothers and sisters, and SIR JOHN with all Europe." (The British may feel the excessive use of diminutives to be somewhat transatlantic, a point made by a recent advertisement for a British gin, which asserts its Britishness by claiming to be "for every Thomas, Richard, and Harold.") Alice could have said *Sir Arthur* or *Lady Tabitha, Mr. Arthur* or *Miss Tabitha* (if Alice had been an old retainer talking to a son or daughter of the boss), *Mr. Simpkins* or *Colonel Mustard.* Curiously, she could not as a female call the mouse merely *Simpkins,* though a generation ago a man might have used this form to an equal, "Elementary, my dear *Watson*"; it may still be used to or among some schoolboys; and it could once have been used by a woman to a servant of either sex.

In fact the form of address that Alice did choose was that of poetic apostrophe rather than any of the usual attention-catching devices, and one can apostrophize anybody or anything. It is a style common in poetry: "O wild west wind . . ."; at the beginning of a letter: "Dear Sir . . ."; in prayers and religious style generally: "Onward, Christian soldiers," "Awake, my soul," "Our Father, which art in Heaven . . ."; and perhaps in expletives: "Ye gods!"

Alice's fairly simple predicament was that of being alone in a pool with only one mouse. It is when we use direct address to single out one individual from a group that things get more complicated. "Hey, you!" besides being rude will make all heads turn at once, and "You in the corner with the whiskers" is more specific but no politer. If we don't mind which individual we get, we can scream "Help me, somebody!" A name can be used to single out an individual from a group, and one important reason to use a name is to show everyone else who is being singled. The compere of a panel show, for instance, especially on sound radio where the participants are invisible to the listening audience, uses this device all the time so that listeners will know who is to speak next. He says "The type of case you've just quoted, Levin . . ." or "Perhaps you'd like to comment on that, Anthony Wedgwood Benn," and we know where we are.

When it comes to getting the attention of a whole group collectively, various devices are available. We could say, effectively though not very politely, "You two," "All of you." In appropriate contexts we could use *dearly beloved, folks, fans, gentlemen, listeners, viewers.* These are forms which will only work in the plural, in contrast with the *reader* of old-fashioned fiction; the singular, so to speak, of *gentlemen* is *sir.* They can be combined in series, so we get *ladies and gentlemen; my lords and members of the House of Commons; Black and White,* unite and fight (which doesn't mean one black man and one white man). Many corporate names for a whole group are used to attract attention in direct address: *Corps,* dismiss! In political oratory, groups can be addressed rather freely in the plural: *Workers* of the world, unite! And on the telephone, in particular, we often need to single out one whole group or organization without knowing the names of the individuals who compose it: Hello, *exchange? Room Service? Du Pont?* These last may sound more like things than people, and in this they resemble the only case I have so far found of the use of a thing-word as a direct attention-getter. Any of us may ask a person *for* a thing, for instance when we say "Jam, please," at tea; but we seem to be uniquely addressing the thing itself when we rush out into a London or San Francisco street and shout *Taxi!*

We have noticed so far that we use these forms of address to gain attention or to single out an individual, but that they may also express attitude; as in Alice's choice between, say, *chum* and *poppet.* Whether or not attention is gained or there is any problem over who is being addressed, we may still wish to use a form of address of some kind, for mere civility. An enormous amount of social protocol still comes in here, which can cause agonies. People find themselves in the position of the tailor Jupien in Proust's *Le Côté de Guermantes,* who had "the air of being made as uncomfortable as a guest who arrives in morning dress at a party where everyone else is in evening dress, or as a commoner who having to speak to a Royal Personage does not know exactly how he ought to address him and gets round the difficulty by cutting down his remarks to almost nothing." If you know someone's rank or function you can often address him or her by it. Often we can address someone according to his or her rank, occupation, or relationship to ourselves.

First, there is a small set of words, of the kind that Jupien might have been agonising over, that go with *your* in direct address and with *his/her/their* when the person is referred to. These are your *Eminence,* your *Excellency,* your *Grace,* your *Highness,* your *Holi-*

ness, your *Ladyship,* your *Lordship,* your *Majesty,* your *honor* and your *reverence.* We must notice here my *lady* and my *lord*; they belong in this set by virtue of the *my* which we earlier found to be used with expressions of endearment. Without *my,* they function quite differently: *lady* alone is nowadays a somewhat fretful American address to any woman, "Hey, *lady,* you just stepped on my ear"; quite different from the Shakespearian "*Lady,* by yonder blessed moon I swear. . . ." *Lord* on its own means God.

When we leave these rarefied heights, we come to a large group of words that can be used in address with various restrictions, with or without an attached name. *Lady* and *Lord* appear here again as posher equivalents of *Mr.* and *Mrs.* They need a following name: *Lady* Tabitha, *Lord* Arthur, *Lady* Simpkins, *Lord* Simpkins, *Mr.* Arthur, and *Mrs.* Simpkins are all possible. (But not *Mrs.* Tabitha. *Mrs.* Arthur would be Arthur's wife.) Only rude little boys can really call people *Mister* or *Missus* without qualification. *Miss* appears to be different. It can stand alone, and in this resembles the set of words that we use in polite address to various sorts of foreigners: *Monsieur, Señor, Fraülein, Signora,* and so on. One can use *Miss* to a waitress, or a child can say it to a teacher.

Some words for people's functions can precede a name. Either *Colonel* Mustard or just *Colonel* is possible. We can say *Admiral* Mustard or just *Admiral, Professor* Mustard or just *Professor, Doctor* Mustard or just *Doctor* (although for me, at any rate, *Doctor* alone is more likely to be a medico than just someone with a Ph.D. in sociology). Other expressions of rank or respect, superficially similar, take no following name: *effendi, maestro, vicar.*

It is important to notice, though, that these words for human function need not necessarily carry respect, and can indeed be used *de haut en bas,* as with *corporal* when said by a general. There are people, particularly in service occupations, whom we summon or address by their jobs: *conductor, waiter, operator, nurse, driver;* or even people we address by their occupation of the moment, as with *caller.* We are approaching now the region of interlocutors defined by their relationship to ourselves, of which the most obvious are our family.

With various nuances of formality or regional distinction, we use a lot of kinship names, though not all, in direct address: *dad, daddy, mum, mom, mummy, ma, pa, papa, grannie, grandma, grandad, grandpa, auntie, uncle,* and so on. Those that anyone can have more than one of may be further specified by a following name: *Aunt* Tabitha, perhaps *Grandma* Simpkins. But certain family names are not used either in address or before a name; if they are so used, the meaning changes. *Brother* Simpkins is either a monk or a fellow union member. *Sister* Tabitha is a nun, while *sister* alone is either an important hospital nurse or another of those American forms of address to any woman. *Mother* and *father* may still be used to parents in some formal circles, but they are as likely to be nuns or priests, and *Father* Mustard is nobody's father. *Mother* and *Mother* Simpkins might be used to or of any old woman in British English. *Son,* with no following name possible, can be used either to one's son or to any male much younger than oneself, but there seems no equivalent use today of *daughter, nephew,* or *niece,* and it is doubtful whether *cousin, wife,* or *husband* still survive anywhere in this usage. There is a gradation between these words of pure relationship and those that address people by their functions. Perhaps somewhere halfway between the two is the cardplayer's or tennis player's use of *partner.*

What all this group of rank, function, and relationship terms have in common is that they identify the person addressed, rather than making an evaluative comment about him, and therefore they have an all-or-nothing quality. A person either is your *uncle* (or a *bombardier* or an *abbot*) or he isn't. It is not a matter of degree, and thus it is not possible to say "rather a *grandma*" or "you absolute *barmaid,*" as one might say "you absolute *darling.*" In this way they differ from the endearment group of words and resemble the set that follow.

Any animal word, presumably, can be used to address the appropriate animal: "Stop nibbling my typewriter, *aardvaark.*" There are namelike words, traditionally belonging to a few animals, that could be used in the same way: *Pussy, Polly, Reynard, Dobbin.* These latter seem to be the closest thing in English to the similar stylized names for certain national groups: *Paddy, Taffy,* and the British *Mac* for a Scotsman; and to the occupational names, like *Sparks* for an electrician or *Chippy* for a carpenter. Most of these names are fairly amiable in direct address, as compared to the much more offensive, more wordlike group of national or racial epithets: *wog, wop, yid.* But the point about all of them is that they are as identifying and all-or-nothing as *bombardier* or *abbot.* You don't say *aardvaark* to a raven, *Paddy* to a Frenchman, or *wop* to a German, and no creature can be "an absolute *Kraut*" or "rather a *poodle.*" In this they differ sharply, both from our earlier list of endearments (my *darlingest,* such a *ducky*) and the nasty words that come next.

One useful function of language is name-calling, which means using a nice or nasty epithet as a total utterance. Consider the following interchange, from a Victorian *Punch* cartoon of two lovers on a park bench:

EDWIN: Darling!
ANGELINA: Yes, darling?
EDWIN: Nothing, darling. Only just *darling,* darling.

Angelina, in fact, takes the opening gambit of her intended as if it were an attention-getter, but it turns out to be all he had to say on the subject. In a different frame of mind he could have called her *bonehead* or *greedy-guts.*

Both nice and nasty epithets are used for evaluative comment rather than to identify. It is only when a word has lost its use for factual identification, and become emotively evaluative, that we can name-call with it: "You *fascist*" is somehow more possible than "You *conservative,*" and *"Warmonger!"* more likely than "*Fishmonger!*" Many of the nasty words that follow seem to go naturally with *you*, while both *you* and *my* are available for words like *darling,* and neither of them could be used before a descriptive noun. Edwin could use any of these expressions, with or without *you,* as a total utterance: *bastard, beast, bighead, blackguard, bounder, bugger, butterfingers, cheat, clot, copycat, coward, crackpot, creep, crosspatch, crybaby, dimwit, dolt, fathead, fidget, fiend, fusspot, harlot, hussy, hypocrite, idiot, ignoramus, minx, monster, moron, muggins, ninny, nitwit, numbskull, oaf, pedant, racialist, rotter, scoundrel, toady, twit, windbag*—and many, many more. Expressions used in name-calling need not be words for people. They can be animal words: *ass, bitch, cow, goose, pig, rat;* or thing words: *turd, scum.* In fact, any evaluative noun can be used for name-calling, and an evaluative adjective makes it possible to use a descriptive noun in this way, as in "*Good* girl!"

It should now be beginning to appear that this whole area of language is extremely quirky and idiosyncratic. We can summon a person by calling *cock* but not *hen,* address him as *doctor* but not *dentist,* or your *honor* but not your *virtue,* show him affection with my *precious* but not my *charming,* or abuse him adjectivally with *stupid* ("Over here, *stupid!*") but not with *slow.* Some of these words function as ordinary nouns: besides calling *Nurse!* we can say "She became a nurse," and besides calling someone a *fusspot* we can say "George is an old fusspot." Other words of address function like names, besides of course the true names themselves (*Nurse* says . . . *Father* went . . . *Junior* thinks . . .). *God* is a vocative ("O *God,* our help in ages past") or a name ("*God* said 'Let Newton be . . .' ") unless we are thinking polytheistically; a *god* is

Shiva or Odin. A final class of words, including *ma'am, sir, love,* and the Liverpudlian *wack,* are vocative alone.

Some words change their meaning when they are used in direct address. *Matron* as an ordinary noun may mean a middle-aged married woman, but in the vocative, or as a name, it can mean only the head nurse of a hospital or the professional housekeeper of an institution such as a school. *Boy* as a singular noun is a young male, and can in the plural be used of one's adult male buddies (a night out with the *boys*), but in singular address is probably either one's dog or a nasty racist summons to a nonwhite waiter. *Old boy* as an ordinary noun is either a greybeard or an alumnus of a school, but can apply in direct address (old-fashioned, British) to any male. A *guy* is male, but "you *guys,* are you coming for a beer?" may be addressed to a mixed group or even perhaps to a group of women. *Lord* in the vocative means God, as opposed to its ordinary noun use in "twelve lords a-leaping." We have seen that *Son!* need not mean one's son, and that *Brother!* cannot mean one's brother.

We distinguish this attention-getting, singling out, and exclamatory function of address from the rest of our speech by various signals of intonation. A common call signal, for instance, is the falling-rising tune familiarly used with *Yŏo-hoo!* (Try it for yourself.) On the same tune we may sing out a summons like *Gĕorge!* or *Wăiter!* When we use a form of address within a sentence, we separate it off in speech by a shift of pitch level, corresponding to the way it would be separated in writing by parenthetic commas: "Sòrry, *chúm*!" "Come hère, *love.*" "Pùsh, you *bastards*!" "The fact ìs, *géneral,* we're surròunded." Phrases following a noun in grammatical apposition are distinguished by intonation according to whether they describe or evaluate: "That's Bill Smìth, the chàirman" will be uttered with two parallel falling tones, while "That's Bill Smìth, the numbskull" ends in a final low growl. The exclamations of abuse that we have been considering can end with this same final growl: "Gèorge, you numbskull!" which further distinguishes them from the identifying forms of address.

Many of us first have our attention drawn to this question of address when we begin to learn a foreign language, and are faced, say, with the choice between *vous* and *tu* in French. I hope I have said enough to show that, even with only one second-person pronoun, we manipulate every day a range of English address forms immensely more numerous, complicated, and delicate in their distinctions than we think.

Notes

1. Most of the examples in this essay come either from the Longman *Dictionary of Contemporary English* or from the corpus of the Survey of English Usage at University College, London.

2. I am indebted here, as elsewhere, to the interesting discussion of vocatives by Arnold M. Zwicky of Ohio State University, in his article "Hey, Whatsyourname!" (Chicago Linguistic Society Papers, 1974).

❧ BASIL COTTLE

Names

IN 1977, the year of Queen Elizabeth II's jubilee, a South Wales couple called Lee gave their newborn daughter three first names, of which the third was *Jubi.* Here the name happily enacts the circumstances, but namers are not always so cooperative, and there is now near Portsmouth, in the pleasant south of England, a house called Kwitcherbelyakin; I am not sure of the motive, but it is probably in line with the explanations "to spite the neighbors" or "we were fed up" given for the bestowal of the house names *Knickers* (a British word for female underpants) and the Iberian-sounding *Llamedos,* which has to be read backwards for the full effect. *Kwitcherbelyakin* impudently seeks to inflict a lesson in spelling reform; but how can one carve such a name with pride? Well, *sullen* originally meant "solitary," and there is something sturdily independent and—we like to think—British in this new type of name, where the misanthrope speaks his mind with more frankness than the house builders of a century ago, who chiselled *Grosvenor* or *Arlington* or *Montpelier* above the doors, or on the fat gateposts, of the villas that they hoped to sell to the pretentious.

I have begun with house names because this is the chief area where complete freedom of choice is allowed; for even though people occasionally coin silly first names, and an English law lecturer has adopted a new surname *Whatsisname* as a maneuver in an argument with the Law Society, and pop groups erupt into names deliberately senseless, yet house names are above all others a proprietary and possessive assertion, an epitome of social history: council-owned houses can have only numbers. It is noticeable that a small private housing estate engulfed by corporation property will gamely bear on every house a name as well as the statutory number; and even in roads where only numbers are the rule, the nostalgic type *Number Eight* will often occur.

Ungracious house names are still exceptional, which makes for suburban peace; but suburban boredom is surely stiffened by the limited range of imagination in the naming. Here even the latest fashions are already stale, especially the commemoration of one's Spanish package-holiday: *Ibiza, Costa Brava*—jocosely capped by the insular neighbor's *Costa Fortune/Packet/Lott.* He-and-she names go drearily on (*Roneth, Wilfrose*), along with the mortgaged cry of *Stilowen* or *Ard Erned,* the statement of the obvious like *The Pines* or *Stonewalls,* and the misspelt boast of a not shy retirement like *Dunromin* or *Thistledome* (that is, "This'll do me," with its ugly *do* idiom). Outstanding for its snobbish humor is *Lautrec,* for a house with two loos (the polite English slang for toilets); *Carmania* in Somerton, Somerset, sums up the love-hate status of a Briton and his automobile. I may appear fussy in seeking a standard, in hinting that there are names intrinsically apt for houses; after all, *God* and its Russian equivalent *Bog* are not intrinsically lovely words for use in religion. But since Britain has this house-naming habit, which it shares with much of the Commonwealth but which finds very slight echo in the United States, where the streets are so much longer and more systematized, it is a pity that the practice is now so often dull or foolish.

The elegant solution is a simple one: numbers only. Unless one's house is isolated, conspicuous, or high-walled, like a manor or one too fine to be flush with the line of a street, it is considered politest not to live in a named house; here, as so often in morals and in motivation, the upper and lower classes agree against the middle. But if wan dignity or an unnamed road demands a named house, to what range of reference should the genteel turn? People adequately schooled in Greek and Latin, or dependent on the older English classics, are growing fewer; the burden of living with religion or history or fiction—of longing to stand side by side with heroes of fine name at Antioch or Blenheim or Troy—now seems to many not privileged but absurd. Ordinary people, in naming their houses or their offspring, will often look no further back than their Spanish trip or their pop hero, and the only common forays into literature concern books that have been televised in serial form.

Naming of the newborn still proceeds along rather different lines in Britain and America, despite the levelling influence of film, song, and television. Some American books merely diagnose the "vibes" (especially the sexy ones) in certain names, but many otherwise unbookish people in Britain consult Miss Withycombe's *Oxford Dictionary of English Christian Names,* and Welsh patriots use an exclusive publication offering names like *Buddug* (which means Boadicea, and is pronounced less alarmingly than it looks); so although *Gary, Hayley, Rock* and *Tracy* seep in from the "media," the traditional names are still holding their place. This can be seen not only in the upper-crust tables compiled yearly from *The Times* birth announcements, where even *Nigel* seems a naughty intrusion on the recurring *John* and *Richard* and *Peter,* but in any normal wardful of babies. And it is not just that Britain almost wholly does without *Dwight, Calvin, Elmer* or *Irving* as first names; there is still some sensitiveness in the juxtaposing of chosen and inherited names. In a recent American legal document I saw names of officials that could still not occur in Britain—the Scots village and the exotic in *Houston Flournoy,* the Breton-Welsh-Scots-Robinhoodish and the Russian in *Alan D. Pasternak,* the unfamiliar first names *Milton* and *Omer* combined with English surnames, the overfamiliar first names *Hal* and (coyly, in quotes) *"Bill".* Miss Withycombe made it clear that some abbreviated names are impolite; she picked *Les, Reg* and *Bert,* hastening to add that *Reggie* and *Bertie* were all right and tactfully supposing that the monosyllables had "not yet had time to rise in the social scale." Thirty-two years later she wrote that this "was true in 1944, but is no longer so"; is she evasively saying that they have now had plenty of time, but haven't used it? Certainly they are no more acceptable in elegant society than they were, and her suggestion that occurrence in the *Radio Times* now canonizes *Des, Ron, Vic, Doug, Cliff* is pretty naive; all these, along with *Sid, Perce, Stan, Len, Fred, Alf* and other demotic fragments, are still not considered quite nice, whereas unpredictably *Tom, Dick, Harry, Bill, Bob, Frank* and *Jim* could go grouse shooting with anybody, and recent bishops have been signing "Tom Hereford" and "Freddy Malmesbury." Perhaps such forms are favored as being from names older and less assuming than adapted place names like *Clifford, Stanley, Sidney, Leslie,* or *Douglas.*

Altogether, even while American and British "media imperialism" is imposing names of a pop order on the world, the naming of children in both our countries remains pretty staunch, and for baptized children very traditional indeed. Anglican fonts are broad-minded, and turn away neither Sam nor Kate nor (as topically occurred some years ago) Yuri Nikita; for my part, I should welcome more discipline in both British and American naming, like the French rule of allowing only Christian and classical names—whence *Aristide* and *Achille*—and the German rule against neologisms. This at least would foil fathers who name a son after all eleven members of a local soccer team or by plodding through all twenty-six letters of the alphabet; these genial idiots get into the news off and on. Ignorance of associations is probably responsible for calling girls Shelley and boys Byron (why not poor Keats?), and a distasteful sequence has arisen based on Diana, a horrid deity even for the Pantheon; whence the ruthless spellings *Dyan, Dianne, Deeann, Deanna,* and other inventions. Orotund names are *out*—even Rossetti's choice of five names in *The Blessed Damozel* that "Are five sweet symphonies," for only *Margaret* is constant, *Cecily* and *Magdalen* are rare, *Rosalys* freakish, and *Gertrude* eroded by the tag "dirty Gertie"; this last casualty reminds us of the killing power of both alliteration and jingle, as in *Dismal Desmond, Dennis the Menace,* and *Elvis the Pelvis*. Again, lip service to the monarchy, whereby various towns, railway stations, pigeons, plums and carriages were called Victoria, has now ceased; if we practice such coinings now, they are rueful, as with calling the unpopular seven-sided fifty-pence piece a Harold (after H. Wilson, Prime Minister) or with a lady of my acquaintance who said when her hirsute husband came downstairs in an open-necked shirt, "Darling, you've got your Wilkinson on" (from an American hairy-chest wig which enabled the youthful purchaser to "be a man"). Perhaps the greatest scope for first-naming is now afforded by dogs, who can be no more consulted than babies; and whereas the apostolic succession of Lassie and Sooty and Rex is still being passed on, I recently heard of a lady whose large tomcat is called Rover, and in Scotland in 1976 I saw a fine Tibetan apso or Dougal-dog called Tissot because his master is a jeweller and sells Tissot watches. A pedigreed dog with a multiple name is usually called by a distinctive fragment of this title, but happy little mongrels answer to *Spot*.

With surnames we reach a nomenclature showing little that is radically new. Ugly names may be smoothed, and foreign ones altered, by deed poll, but the only little upheavals in English surnames are occasioned by the importation of European names and especially of names from the Indian subcontinent. Thus *Patel* was the forty-first commonest name in the birth registers for the first quarter of 1975, with *Kaur* and *Singh* not far behind; since the Asiatic immigrants are in general young and fertile, their figures will make inroads further up the lists, though they are still far behind the Big Five—*Smith, Jones, Williams, Brown, Taylor*—which account for about one in eighteen of the population of England and Wales, and which even in America stood first, sixth, fourth, third and tenth respectively as late as 1939. The ten commonest surnames in England now were the ten commonest in 1853; thereafter the sagging fortunes of *Wood* and *Hughes,* and the resurgence of *White* and *Thompson,* are among the changes in these 126 years, and *Kelly* and *Murphy* from Ireland are creeping up behind. Meanwhile immigrants from the West Indies are unexpectedly fortifying the stocks of seemingly insular names like *Macdonald;* and England is luckily without the American names, bizarre to her ears, of improvised type such as *Cabbagestalk* or *Turnipseed* or *Cashdollar.*

New "conurbations," which are named officially rather than by personal whim, are dully labelled in Britain nowadays, and are anyway rare: we have no outback to cut back, as in the New World, and in general our towns just bloat. In so anciently and densely settled a country, there is always a hamlet or field whose name can be reused when houses spring up, so there is no need for exotics like *Athens* or *Syracuse,* and no call for whimsies like *Tombstone;* the exclamation mark on *Westward Ho!,* the Devon resort named after Kingsley's novel, has looked absurd ever since its Victorian founding. Our few new towns are mostly called after the old nucleus, like Harlow New Town or Hatfield New Town; though when a really big development took place, over good farming land in Buckinghamshire, the long-winded *Milton Keynes* (an existing village) was pompously chosen instead of the obvious *Bletchley,* where the railway station is and where the crucial breaking of the Nazi "Enigma" cipher could have been justly eternized. Wry self-depreciating names like *Little London* are not now resorted to, or grovelling ones like *Sodom* (in North Wales); bureaucratic pomp would be hostile to the former, and humor and the new irreligion to the latter. There is no sign that double-barrelled village names are unpopular or in danger of reduction to one word—in fact, there is something undeniably elitist about those that alliterate, like *Westley Waterless* or *Flyford Flavell;* Halton Holgate has recently given its name to a hymn tune, even as someone has remarked that Gonfalon Royal could be nothing but an English hymn tune. And Britain still positively *likes* the perverse slurrings of *Woolfardisworthy* (pronounced Woolzery) or (in a snobbish film of which I forget the title) *St. John-cum-Leigh* as SINjun-COMEly. By the side of such riches, the cooked-up names of the new factitious counties seem pale and poor indeed; officially imposed on England in 1973, and still not mentioned by any normal person, they are mostly based—as never before—on river names, and an American could well be excused for seeking Stratford in the county of Avon.

There are, of course, in Britain no towns laid out on such a grid as to need a 57th Street; Whitehaven and little Winchelsea have the plan only in embryo. So new road names (*street* is now an inelegant designation) have to be found for every development. Bristol has been particularly fortunate in having for its municipal estates a brilliant archivist and an enlightened housing manager, who between them conferred very lively sets of hallowed names out of tithe maps and every sort of document. Thus historic names of farms and fields on the outskirts are preserved, along with names of citizens worthy or merely past; I recall my pleasure at seeing a Cottle Road, savoring a new whiff of my family history, and then finding that it commemorates one Charles Cottle, who in 1674 couldn't pay his hearth tax! Even when this skill and dedication has to give place to a demand for sets of painters or authors or wildflowers, Bristol tries to apply its stated rule: "The name shall be euphonious. . . . The majority of the selections are polysyllabic. . . . Probably three [syllables] is the ideal." In Wales the old street names are now subject to change, since nationalist feeling has made them bilingual; *Heol Y Frenhines* looks very handsome beside *Queen Street* in Cardiff, but the sign

DYNION
MEN

at the National Museum caused a monoglot lady, when questioned why she was descending some steps, to say, "I wanted to see what the dinny-on men were." Warning for visitors to Ireland: the words for males and females in Erse begin with *F* and *M*.

Up to now I have been dealing with names that think themselves dignified; the exceptions were the hostile house names, in whose attitude there is a link with the restless and shocking names adopted by young singers or instrumentalists for themselves and their groups. *Revolutionary* is too thoughtful a word to apply to these names, and their mark is the flouting of convention. Being wholly ignorant of the music involved, I don't know whether Jethro Tull composes or sings or bangs what it puts forth, but I'm sorry that the group equates itself with the great agriculturist who died in 1741; the surnames *Glitter* and *Stardust* could hardly be authentic, to be Screaming Lord Sutch is an odd way of aspiring to the peerage, and to change one's name to Johnny Rotten or Sid Vicious is rather arrogance than humility. Names are snatched up, as if deliberately ephemeral, and the nastier the better: *Animals, Sex Pistols, Monkees* (with a trite misspelling, and lacking even the poor pun of the Beatles). America does all this kind of thing much more and much earlier, but between the two countries spreads this common culture and its stock of droll names. There is delicate allusion in *A Taste of Honey, Lindisfarne, Earth Wind and Fire, The Grass Roots, Lynard Skynard* (which had a man almost so called as its gym teacher), *The Mothers of Invention, New Riders of the Purple Sage, Quicksilver, Steppenwolf, Uriah Heep, Village People.* There is a nice idiocy in *Led Zeppelin, Procol Harum* (pseudo-Latin), and *Bonzo Dog Doo-dah Band;* a spurious importance in *Fairport Convention, Jefferson Starship* (carefully updated from *Jefferson Airplane*), and *Tower of Power;* an unimaginable mystery in *Wishbone Ash, Tangerine Dream, Beaverteeth, Electric Flag, Whispering Giant,* and *Iron Butterfly;* an echo of G. M. Hopkins in *Widow Maker;* and by insertion of such a vocabulary as *Speed, High, Rush, Funk, Punk, Soul, Black,* or *Sabbath,* the pretence or admission of drug-addiction or necromancy or racial exclusiveness or anything else that will startle.

Well, this is presumably the way to sell yourself to your contemporaries; the sale of racy goods is sped by similar names for boutiques, and here again America sets the pace: *The Face Place* (for a beautician's); *The Mis-Haps, Foxy Lady, The Snooty Hooty, Glad Rags, Tickle Your Fancy* (for women's clothes); *The Briar Patch, Just Pants, The Rogue, The Shirt Shack* (for men's clothes); *The Athlete's Foot, High Country, The Fish Hawk* (for sportswear); *Achilles Inc.* (for shoes); *The Gap* (for jeans); *High Ol' Times* (for paraphernalia); *The Good Earth, The Golden Temple* (for health foods); *Lady Madonna* (for maternity clothes). In these and many others, the various hints of naughtiness, newness or brute force are meant to be fetching; Bristol now has a fruit and vegetable shop called *Melon-Cauli,* a clever title, but contrived and inappropriate. American hairdressers, with memories of Dan Druff put behind them, entice people in by names like *The Sassy Scissors, The Head-Shed, Canned Ego* (this is lost on me), *Guys and Dolls;* their British counterparts, once they can dismount from the high horse of Trichology, frolic with *The Hairem, Lunatic Fringe, Samson and Delilah, Elle, Sweeney Todd, Curly Barnet* (very Cockney: it's rhyming slang—*Barnet Fair* for "hair"), *Jane Eyre* (a heroine whose crowning glory was not her hair). The will to be frenchified is badly served by a spelling seen recently on a Cardiff hairdresser's, *Franćiose;* and a Newark (Notts) sports shop kept by Messrs. Grant and Green is locally known as Grunt and Groan.

English tea shops, once with names chintzy and romantic (we were the last customers at the Astolat in Guildford), have now grown brash and wanton to go with their new table licenses. American restaurants have long been franker: *Daddy's Money, The Bearded Clam, Hoolahan's Old Place, The Boston Sea Party* (for seafood), *The Tummy Tickler, Honey For The Bears Inc.,* and the Southern home cooking suggested by *Aunt Fanny's Cabin;* yet *Pittypat's Porch* is as dainty as *Petronella's Plat* on the other side of the Atlantic in Winchelsea.

The goods sold compete with one another too often by stridency rather than quality. The loud claim accompanies the loud things—cars, bras, male cosmetics (*Brut*!), engulfing paints. But there is poetry here, too: who has not thrilled to a Ruston-Bucyrus earth-mover as at the blast of a trumpet, or felt like a hawk of the tower at a Pingon Tichauer crane? Cars must be minatory and ruthless (*Avenger, Jaguar, Scimitar, Rapier, Mustang*), or must recall rich playgrounds (*Capri, Dolomite, Granada*) or privilege (*Diplomat*); but the Rolls Silver Mist had to be renamed when exported to Germany, where *Mist* = "dung." To sell a food, add *Farm;* to cleaners, add *Blue* or *Biological* ("the only flake with a hydrogen warhead") or *New,* with *Bold* as the sole name of one daring detergent; bemuse your customers with names of the polybenzedrine type, or say that the product is *Bionic.* But at least the dull old phrasal joke like *Uneeda* or *Odorono* or *Winalot* is out of favor; insidious subtlety characterizes the nail varnish called Shy Peach and perhaps the perfume Bakir ("back-ear"?—surely not).

It has always been customary for boats to be named, even London's dump barges that are towed with their freight of refuse, and this habit continues, but I am told that a regrettable spirit is entering even into *this.* It may have been the tang of spindrift in her nostrils, but my informant pursed her lips on telling me that in 1977 she had seen three little boats tied alongside one another on the Medina River, in the Isle of Wight, called Vitamin Sea, Damnsel, Current Affair; the wit, and the touch of bitterness, she felt to be out of place. But Dutch boats are still often given English names of the old healthy type. If barges and little boats can have pet names, why not what the British call lorries and cars?—yet names on these are still quite rare, though machines such as computers are commonly named, either with lucky acronyms like the star-name *Algol* or with something that has a more technical bite. Stars themselves, of course, are not new save in their brilliant demise, and nowadays, with improved observation, these mere novae are so frequently seen that they no longer get their discoverers' names like *Jonesii* but instead are assigned to their constellations, as in *Nova Vulpeculae* 1978; whereas every decent comet now has at least two Japanese personal names because their astronomers get up earlier or have a clearer sky or better lenses. And though man does not presume to name all phenomena, he has always vindictively given women's names to hurricanes—until the recent wholesome decision in the United States that the next one would be male. Elsewhere in nature the rose, being now so largely an artifact, is treated as one of the family and named, but resonant beauties like *Agnes Lady Bapchurch* are growing less common.

For thoughtful people, the ethics of naming have changed somewhat in our time, and faced with a name we instinctively want to know not just "what's in" it but whether its mere sound is deafening us to a deeper issue. The sonorous names are rolling away; churches are being starkly dedicated to Christ the Servant, verses like Milton's "Lancelot or Pelleas or Pellenore" seem easy and shallow, novels with titles like *To What Green Altar* are felt to be mawkish from their cover onwards, and we side with Jaques as to the dislikeability of the name *Rosalind* rather than with Orlando's sensible point that there was no thought of pleasing Jaques when she was christened. The traditional names which we have imposed on the world's culture are lasting well, even such an un-French word as *rugby* in France (where they play it so successfully and pronounce it so oddly), but the rootless names from the "media," especially the preposterous and defiant ones, are doomed to a short life. We have, perhaps, become obsessed with naming every gadget; even the indefinable is labelled, and no doubt some estate agent will find a generic term for the "purpose-built utility room/study/playroom with an unusual seating pit at one end" of which a friend of mine found himself the possessor. Every nuance of fashion is catered for, and the other day I passed a pub that was advertising Ploughperson's Lunches.

People sometimes start by disliking me because I can interpret their surnames: this nakedly shows the atavistic fear that in admitting one's name one is yielding up the essence of one's being. Magic, it is held, can get to work on a name even in the absence of its bearer; I am reminded of those dowsers who ply their art over maps to tell you where the metal lies hidden, and are believed.

There is now at least one periodical (called just *Nomina*) dealing with all kinds of naming; and since "Sovereigns die and Sovereignties," since whole dreaded nations like the Gepids and Petchenegs have disappeared without imprinting their names, it is as well that so many scholars are collecting in its flight the nomenclature of fields and their flowers, folk and their trivia. It is a characteristic of primitive races to have names for individual objects but no generic terms like *tree* or *hill*; thus what Carlyle caused to sound sophisticated, when he said that "Giving a name is a poetic art," may well be a fundamental and instinctive wrapping-up of the loved or dreaded object, for its protection or defusing, by means of a name.

MARGARET A. DOODY

"How Shall We Sing the Lord's Song upon an Alien Soil?": The New Episcopalian Liturgy

PRAYER is the soul's sincere desire
Uttered or unexpressed. . . .

J. Montgomery (1771–1854)

Indeed, to many of us prayer could not be otherwise, for we in this late Romantic age still believe that sincere feeling creates speech and motivates action, and that to utter words not caused by the soul's desire at the moment is damaging, a violation of the psyche. In this view prayer must be inward, private and spontaneous.

But there is a tradition, a view of human nature older than Romanticism and quite alien to modern notions of sincerity, according to which outer actions and words spoken can create the feelings and move the desires. In the context of this idea, a liturgy makes perfect sense; it isn't necessary to find yourself in the right mood before going to church. The worshipper need not, and indeed should not, anxiously expect or keep a tally of the emotions that arise as a result of his actions, for he is not waiting upon his own emotions, but serving God and accepting whatever change in himself may be the consequence. The liturgy is simply there, public, accessible, and inescapable.

There is in a sense something vulgar about any liturgy, for these prayers are known to the many. The service book is a book of *common* prayer. None of the liturgies is an individualistic expression. The work of liturgy is done by language and dramatic ritual to which the individual submits.

In this century there has been a great unease about the liturgy and an almost universal desire to change its forms. Changes in the liturgy are always promoted (from above) in reasonable and rather bland terms. The laity are informed that changes are necessitated by the need for greater intelligibility, and for the creation of a stronger sense of community in the congregation. Yet if we analyze the changes which are taking place, we see that much more fundamental alteration is involved. It is possible that the process of uneasy alteration arises from an unacknowledged fear of the nature of liturgy itself.

I am led to these meditations by contemplating the new Episcopalian prayer book, the Draft Proposed Book (DPB) which will, if accepted by the General Convention of 1979, become the standard Book of Common Prayer (BCP) for the Episcopal Church in the United States. The new Prayer Book has not escaped the traditional Anglican spirit of compromise; for the three main services of the church—the Eucharist, Morning Prayer, and Evening Prayer—it offers two rites each (Rite I and Rite II). The first of these bears a resemblance (though faint at times) to the service book of 1662. Rite II constitutes an ambitious and thoroughgoing change.[1] The Episcopalian who wants to go to church is going to have to come to terms (if he can) with Rite II, which his pastors and masters largely support, just as the English Anglican must submit to services in the new Series Two and Three. And what a change is there! It is hard to experience the shock of finding that the language of a book which survived for four centuries has gone. It is like finding that Shakespeare has been rewritten.

Well, the believer goes to church to worship God and not a book. How, indeed, can we or should we speak to God? Is there a language appropriate for speaking to God? From some points of view any language would do, either because (a) there is no such Person, and the worshippers are talking to themselves, or (b) God understands any language or tone. The cry "Oh God, help!" is a prayer. But spontaneous public prayer is a tricky business. In United Church and Presbyterian services I have attended it is quite evident that the member of the congregation giving an extempore prayer has thought it out (or even written it out) carefully beforehand. The strain is on the auditor, who waits in suspense to find out if he can approve the sentiments which are going to be uttered.

As soon as extempore prayer lasts any longer than "God be

merciful to me a sinner" (which would not be said nowadays) the going gets difficult. In modern public language prayer tends to swerve between the business style, the lecturing style, the legal or journalistic styles. Politeness also gets in the way; if we don't lecture God, we treat him in a civil manner, strangely (and proudly) at odds with our requests. In the Presbyterian church I was attending in Berkeley in 1977 (the year of the drought), the prayers for rain were made with polite casual diffidence, as if we were asking someone to please pass the cakes.

Modern Anglicans and Episcopalians aren't willing to forsake the written service and ritual, but the embarrassments of public language are much in evidence. There are changes with which one can concur, albeit regretfully; one can accept that *Thou* and *Thee* have lost an original intimacy and are unjustifiably archaic—so therefore *You* with the appropriate verb ending is to be used throughout. But when one comes to the tone and conduct of the prayers of central services, it is quite clear that tone is doctrine, and that the way we publicly speak to God offers a definition of the Person to Whom we speak, and also affects our idea of who we are.

One very noticeable thing about the new Episcopalian services (Rite II) is the lack of interest in penitence. Charles Price, author of a report of the Standing Liturgical Commission, comments:

> The Communion service of American Books hovered continually around a sense of the worshippers' unworthiness ("And although we are unworthy, through our manifold sins, to offer unto thee any sacrifice", "we are not worthy so much as to gather up the crumbs under thy table"). The tone of the resulting liturgies corresponded to a deep-seated need of late medieval and post-medieval psyches. There seems to be little doubt, however, that the language strikes many serious Christians of the twentieth century as exaggerated. . . .
>
> Successive American revisions of BCP have tended to mitigate this tone of unrelieved penitence and unworthiness. . . . Trial use carried this mitigation much further. Some critics felt that the process had gone too far. . . . Without trying to restore all the expressions of penitence characteristic of BCP, some added emphasis has been made in DPB.[2]

Although the new book is a little less antipathetic to penitence than the experimental revised versions which appeared just before it, the American book is not, one might say "into" penitence, which is presumably required only by old-fashioned people.

The prayer from which Price quotes (known as the Prayer of Humble Access), traditionally said by the priest shortly before the administration of the sacrament, moves splendidly and dramatically from the mood of humility to a mood of confidence from which pride has been deliberately cut out. It continues, "But thou art the same Lord, whose property is always to have mercy; Grant us therefore, gracious Lord, so to eat the flesh of thy dear Son Jesus Christ, and to drink his blood, that our sinful bodies may be made clean by his body, and our souls washed through his most precious blood, and that we may evermore dwell in him, and he in us." The slow cadence of the clauses forces the participant in the liturgy to follow the rhythms of feelings which are thus made known to him whether they are the original feelings he might have on his own, or not.

The DPB (Rite II) makes no such demands for publicly expressed humility. The Confession (for which one has to search) in its modernized version differs very markedly from the old one (still printed here in Rite I). The traditional form of Confession at Holy Communion contains the following:

> We acknowledge and bewail our manifold sins and wickedness, Which we from time to time most grievously have committed, By thought, word, and deed, against thy Divine Majesty, Provoking most justly thy wrath and indignation against us. We do earnestly repent, and are heartily sorry for these our misdoings; The remembrance of them is grievous unto us; The burden of them is intolerable. Have mercy upon us, Have mercy upon us, most merciful Father; for thy Son our Lord Jesus Christ's sake, forgive us all that is past; And grant that we may ever hereafter serve and please thee in newness of life. . . .

The equivalent portion of the new prayer runs thus:

> we confess that we have sinned against you
> in thought, word and deed,
> by what we have done,
> and by what we have left undone.
> We have not loved you with our whole heart;
> we have not loved our neighbours as ourselves.
> We are truly sorry and we humbly repent.
> For the sake of your Son Jesus Christ,
> have mercy on us and forgive us;
> that we may delight in your will,
> and walk in your ways. . . .

This is a mild and scanted mixture of both the old Confession at Holy Communion and the form of Confession at Morning Prayer:

> Almighty and most merciful Father; We have erred and strayed from thy ways like lost sheep. We have followed too much the devices and desires of our own hearts. We have offended against thy holy laws. We have left undone those things which we ought to have done; And we have done those things which we ought not to have done; And there is no health in us. But thou, O Lord, have mercy upon us, miserable offenders. Spare thou them, O God, which confess their faults. Restore thou them that are penitent; according to thy promises declared unto mankind in Christ Jesus our Lord. And grant, O most merciful Father, for his sake, That we may hereafter live a godly, righteous and sober life, to the glory of thy holy Name.

The old forms of the prayers of Confession, with their doublets of words and phrases, with the varied repetition combined with the building up of clauses in a tension which has to be acknowledged by a slowing of pace, make an enactment which is something more than flat statement. One cannot hurry through them—not the most careless priest or uneasy offender—and they reflect the states of being lost and ill, and of being found and healed—and the movement between those states. We ask "Spare. . . . Restore . . . and grant that we may live . . ."; we rise to a prospect of "newness of life." The speaker at the end is different from the speaker at the beginning. This is not true of the modern revised Episcopalian Confession, which gets the nasty business over as soon as possible. Our sins are no longer "intolerable"—an acknowledgment that they are truly unbearable by ourselves alone, whether we have been previously conscious of this burden or not. There is no longer the appalling sense of a dispassionate, firm and thorough diagnosis—no wounded surgeon plies the steel here. We don't say anything as shocking as "there is no health in us"; we admit that we haven't quite done our best. Without sufficient preparation, the echo of Jesus's two commandments tends to appear mere hyperbole; that we haven't quite managed to love our neighbors as ourselves means that we have merely failed as it were to get an A, not that our grade average isn't relatively respectable.

Interestingly, the modern prayer reverses the order of the old Confession at Morning Prayer; it puts "what we have done" (undefined) before "what we have left undone," thus implying that the former is more important than the latter. The old version, with much more spiritual subtlety, clearly puts what "we have left undone" ahead of "those things which we ought not to have done"—and thus avoids the doctrinal and spiritual error of considering sin merely as a matter of a few actions, and not as a debilitating condition. The sixteenth century here seems more "modern" than the moderns in comprehending that a healthy spiritual life is no matter of mere abstinence, but involves a constant exertion of creative energy. But the God to Whom we are talking in the revised Episcopalian Confession doesn't seem likely to be too interested in any particulars (in the old form it is hard to come upon the phrase "those things . . ." without thinking inwardly of a few particulars in one's own case) nor in penitence in general. His forgiveness seems dangerously easy to take for granted, along with that unstrenuous self-forgiveness which some Protestant theologians have called "cheap grace." Being loved by God means never having to say you're sorry—almost.

In dwelling so much, for the sake of illustration, upon prayers of penitence, I could be falling into a trap, since those who stand behind the new version hold, like Charles Price, that the old BCP and its admirers certainly err in expressing too much unworthiness. Such feelings are too "exaggerated" for modern Americans. But the penitential prayers are only parts of services which (in the old versions) present a great variety of attitudes and feelings, and call for the worshipper to participate in a great drama, heightened by contrast.

In the old order of the service for Holy Communion, after the instructional portion (readings from Gospel and Epistle, and sermon) there followed the prayer "for the whole state of Christ's Church militant here on earth" (in recent versions of the BCP, the word *militant* has been dropped as misleading). This is a public prayer for the public: for the universal Church, for all Christian rulers, and for justice; for the ministers of the Church, and for "all thy people." This intelligent and restrained prayer makes no hyperbolical claims for the virtues or glory of princes, priests or people; it emphasizes the need for grace, and the performance of duty: "and especially to this congregation here present, that with meek heart and due reverence they may hear and receive thy holy word, truly serving thee in holiness and righteousness all the days of their life." The petitions for help in personal troubles come only after the duty has been set forth: "And we most humbly beseech thee of thy goodness, O Lord, to comfort and succour all them who in this transitory life are in trouble, sorrow, need, sickness, or any other adversity." (It has been customary to insert petitions for particular individuals at this point.) In its context this petition has redefined the nature of our trouble and sorrow; they are a not-unexpected part of this "transitory life" and need not bow us down or fill our whole minds, for we have larger duties and desires. At the same time, this prayer for help is not perfunctory: a pause is demanded after each noun, and each noun is weighty; there is a fine pattern whereby the larger, more abstract but more emotive nouns, *trouble, sorrow,* are placed before the more particular nouns, *need, sickness,* which define states whose amelioration is more simply imaginable.

Once our more immediate worldly concerns have been dealt with, the ritual moves to the Eucharist proper. After an exhortation (which has fallen into disuse in this century) the priest invites the congregation to "take this Holy Sacrament to your comfort," and defines the spiritual state, or state of the will, which is an essential condition of the action: "Ye that do truly and earnestly repent you of your sins, and are in love and charity with your neighbours, and intend to lead a new life, following the commandments of God . . . Draw near. . . ." The focus is steadily on the conscience of each person in the congregation, and the approach to the sacrament is slow and dramatic. There follows the General Confession, in which all join: "We acknowledge and bewail our manifold sins and wickedness." This whole section of the service is sublimely disconcerting; after the serenity of the earlier instructional part, and the pleasures of listening to music or joining in the singing of hymns, the worshipper has moved from the smiling plain into a dark forest. He cannot get through all this quickly, and the words ritually enforce a concentration on the state of his life, a concentration from which self-love is removed. The emphasis is very much on the need for renewal, for rescue from the past. If there is a language which can be conceived of as the extreme opposite of psychobabble, this is it. Only after participating in the acute minutes of such concentration does the worshipper come to the release of absolution.

The absolution is followed by consolation; the discomfiting process of repentance is succeeded by the "comfortable words" which consist of a sequence of short passages from the New Testament, assuring us of Christ's love. With this assurance, the service wells up into joy, with the *Sursum corda* ("Lift up your hearts"), the introduction to the *Sanctus,* and the *Sanctus* proper. "Therefore with Angels and Archangels, and with all the company of heaven, we laud and magnify thy glorious Name; evermore praising thee, and saying, 'Holy, holy, holy Lord God of hosts, heaven and earth are full of thy glory.'" From the rational uneasiness and necessary un-happiness of repentance, the worshipper has been transformed into a creature capable of joining in the celebration of heaven. The rhythm of the service has quickened into joy and exaltation; it then becomes slower again, as the exaltation of the *Sanctus* is balanced by the humility of the Prayer of Humble Access ("We do not presume to come to this thy Table, O Lord, trusting in our own righteousness") before the central action, the Prayer of Consecration and the taking of the sacrament.

The sacrament is followed by the Lord's Prayer, and then by a prayer that God will accept this act of sacrifice which is a sacrifice of ourselves: "And here we offer and present unto thee, O Lord, our selves, our souls and bodies, to be a reasonable, holy, and lively sacrifice unto thee." The words are in poetic contrast to the description of Christ's sacrifice in the Prayer of Consecration: "Who made there (by his one oblation of himself once offered) a full, perfect and sufficient sacrifice, oblation and satisfaction for the sins of the whole world." Christ is "full, perfect, and sufficient"; our self-offering can be only "reasonable, holy and lively [i.e., living]." But this is not the end of the service; that tempered prayer is followed by the outburst of joy which is the *Gloria:* "Glory be to God on high, and in earth peace, goodwill towards men." The service ends in joy and praise. The whole congregation has participated in an act of worship which, taking them individually as well as collectively through the dark places of the soul, emerges into peace and praise and the light of glory. The language, which is a language both pithy and elaborate, both exact and comprehensive, has done its work. The words of the old BCP constitute an inescapable language.

To go from this liturgy (or from years of using it) to the new rite (The Holy Eucharist, Rite II) is to be conscious of a loss. The service often seems pleasant enough, but thin. The emphasis on penitence is no longer there: the new form of the Confession is as much of humility as we get, and the absolution is correspondingly shortened. The devisers of the new Prayer Book do not seem to have realized that cutting out the emphasis on penitence, and the solemnity, entails also a diminution of joy—although their very object is to emphasize joy, and collective social happiness. The individual conscience is less touched; throughout, there is a sense that this mildly jolly occasion is something to which we have a right. The priest's invitation to the sacrament is one line: "The Gifts of God for the People of God." There is no introduction of sacrifice, no emphasis on renewal, on "newness of life." The section before that, now labelled "The Great Thanksgiving" (the

Sursum corda and the *Sanctus*) manages, with its different wording, to lose impact. The introduction to the *Sanctus* in the old version read, "It is very meet, right and our bounden duty that we should at all times, and in all places, give thanks unto thee, O Lord, Holy Father, Almighty Everlasting God." It is now, "It is right, and a good and joyful thing, always and everywhere to give thanks to you, Father Almighty, Creator of heaven and earth." The rhythm of "It is very meet, right and our bounden duty" is lost, and of course the statement is now widely different, for it no longer seems our *duty* to praise God, just a nice thing to do. And oddly, although the fact that it is joyful is insisted upon, the earlier version seems more joyful. "At all times and in all places" is not only metrically more satisfactory, but more satisfactory and insistent as a definition: "at all times"—even when ill or anxious; "in all places"—even in hospital or in jail. "Always" and "everywhere" are vague; again an idea is passed over quickly, unemphatically. The new version continues, "Therefore we praise you, joining our voices with Angels and Archangels and with all the company of heaven, who for ever sing this hymn to proclaim the glory of your name." A poetic statement has been dismissed, partly with the introduction of a kind of heavy literalness. The old version doesn't say anything about the *voices* of the angels, as this seems to do; grammatical fastidiousness is offended by the false comparison, too—it should be "joining our voices with *those of* Angels. . . ." The implication that the angels know only one hymn is obtruded upon the consciousness, to the detriment of one's opinion of the heavenly choir's *repertoire.* The import in the new version is muted by the long clause "who for ever . . ," which lets one down after "company of heaven." A series of strong verbs ("laud," "magnify," "evermore praising . . . and saying") is exchanged for two weaker ones ("praise" and the awkward "joining our voices"). In the new version of the eucharistic ritual, the praise has been flattened out as much as the penitence.

The essential desire of the devisers of the new ritual (probably not a conscious desire) is to keep things on an even keel. The service moves in a cheerful monotone; it provides, as it were, an unchanging landscape, a plateau, without heights and depths, without darkness and light. The old service entailed and enforced a pattern of change and transformation, a movement from depths to heights:

> These are thy wonders, Lord of power,
> Killing and quickning, bringing down to hell
> And up to heaven in an houre.

The old service did—no, I will not use the past tense—it does its work through a language which combines *gravitas* with excitement. The service itself lets one know that language is important—that it is no trivial matter to find the right words, to define and redefine through double nouns, through triple adjectives, through clausal sequences—and through the relation of each of these to what went before and what comes after. Those who drafted the new Prayer Book are at times disarmingly frank about considering language as not of the first importance. In discussing the central place of the service of the Eucharist, Price says,

> Western culture today seems open to sacraments in a way that has not been true for centuries. It has been said that the printing press provided a cultural resonance for the Reformation emphasis on the Word. Television may provide cultural resonance for communication by means of visual and enacted symbols.[3]

What is missing in this feeble McLuhanism (which already seems old-fashioned) is a sense that language, words spoken aloud, can be an enactment. It is not possible to construct a religious ritual which does not use language. What one can do is change the language, and make it less intrusive on the consciousness—as with certain television shows. The essential flaw in the appeal to television as an analogy or model is that television is notoriously nonparticipatory, and makes no demands on the will. For the worshipper, a ritual is an act undertaken, not merely spectacle, not even "communication." Through the ages worshippers have been able to combine ritual actions performed with ritual words spoken. The new editors are almost conscientiously weakening the words, as if words, "the Word," were taking an unfair advantage by impinging on the consciousness too sharply. (Incidentally, Christ was spoken of as the *Logos,* the Word, long before printing provided "cultural resonance.") The new service is concerned to create—or at least not to disturb—a cheerful mood.

One thing clearly stands out about the language of the new Prayer Book. It is not a language to get by heart. Even if iteration breeds some familiarity, the phrases and clauses lack that poetic power of rhythm and statement which engraves itself upon the memory. These words will not intrude upon the public mind. They are bland, consumable words. There is no danger of their becoming proverbial phrases as did "we have left undone those things which we ought to have done," "there is no health in us," "hear what comfortable words our Saviour Christ Saith," "at all times, and in all places," "erred and strayed from thy ways like lost sheep," "newness of life." This language will not become common, in that sense. It stands in little danger of entwining itself in the language of writers. It is strange, therefore, that many of the prayers are written out in the new book as if they were poetry—with a neat rivulet of text meandering through a meadow of margin:

> Send us now into the world in peace,
> and grant us strength and courage
> to love and serve you
> with gladness and singleness of heart. . . .

It looks like poetry—but it isn't. The prayers in the old BCP appear in close prosaic paragraphs—and anyone can tell that they are poetic. Perhaps the format of this new book is a symptom of the way in which poetry is regarded by many modern people—as a something with irregular lines that catch the eye. If so, this is one of the most acidulous criticisms of modern poetry ever put forward—the more so for being so unconscious, and it might indicate that modern people have got out of the habit of hearing, and no longer seek in language on a page the excitement of sound and rhythm, or the pressure of well-wrought speech.

The flabby, prosaic qualities we find in the new Eucharist, the major ritual, can be found elsewhere in the DPB. The version of the Psalms printed in this book provides a heart-breaking disappointment for anyone brought up on the Coverdale version of the Psalms in the old Prayer Book, as well as the slightly different translation of Psalms in the King James Version. The Psalms have always been of considerable importance in Anglican and Episcopalian worship; in following the services for Morning and Evening Prayer the congregation goes through the whole book of Psalms once a year. The revisers proclaim with some pride that they have endeavored to use no word not known to Coverdale—this seems a strange piece of piety, especially considering the result.

The new version of the Psalms is fussily accurate. Of course, justice to the original demands accuracy, though one is sorry to lose the sun "like a giant to run his course" for "like a champion." But at times the alteration seems unnecessary and pedantic. "God is gone up with a merry noise; and the Lord with the sound of the trump" (Psalm 47:5) becomes "God is gone up with a shout, / the Lord with the sound of the ram's horn." One might ask if the "ram's horn" tells the modern ear more than "trump." The new version becomes particular when it might be more general (the important thing about "the ram's horn" in Psalm 47 is that it is an instrument of music), and general where it loses the impact of the particular: "He bringeth forth grass for the cattle: and green herb for the service of men" (Psalm 104:14) becomes "You make grass grow for flocks and herds / and plants to serve mankind," although "green herb" is literally more colorful. Metaphorical parallels become lists, synecdoche an almost avoidable embarrassment, and pictures become processes. "They that go down to the sea in ships: and occupy their business in great waters" (Psalm 107:23) becomes "Some went down to the sea in ships / and plied their trade in deep waters." "These men see the works of the Lord: and his wonders of the deep" becomes "They beheld the works of the Lord / and his wonders in the deep" (107:24). The old version gives us a sense of continuous wonder, but in the new version wonderful things evidently appeared only once. Sometimes tiresome words are inserted, even archaic words, as with "beheld" above, or (Psalm 104:26) "Yonder is the great and wide sea"—"yonder" in the television age? Alliteration and other poetic devices are eschewed as often as possible. The industrious avoidance of the masculine noun or pronoun is almost a fetish, and the solution is often to use a plural noun or pronoun, like *some* or *they,* even when that injures the dramatic import.

But it is when one looks at some of the most famous and best-loved of the Psalms that one realizes how working with poetry is, for these translators, a work against the grain. In Coverdale's version of Psalm 137 ("By the waters of Babylon") verse 4 is the poignant question "How shall we sing the Lord's song: in a strange land?" This is now "How shall we sing the Lord's song / upon an alien soil?" In the old version, the alliteration of *song* and *strange* points the unendurable contrast; in the new one, the alliterative and syntactic and rhythmic emphasis all falls upon the word *soil,* giving it far more than its due. It is not the fact that they are upon "soil" that bothers the questioners. The meaning seems contorted—for does one think of oneself as singing "upon a soil"? What is the connection? What is "an alien soil"—something with an inhospitable pH? or moonrock? The old version gives us a simple, emotive and central meaning—"in a strange land"—words that are by no means archaic or hard to understand. A well-known utterance is lost, for no reason at all.

And if we look at the new rendition of Psalm 126, we find that some of the best-loved and most resonant phrases in the literature of our language have disappeared. The Coverdale translation of the last three verses runs thus:

> 5 Turn our captivity, O Lord: as the rivers in the south.
>
> 6 They that sow in tears: shall reap in joy.

7 He that now goeth on his way weeping, and beareth forth good seed: shall doubtless come again with joy, and bring his sheaves with him.

We now have

5 Restore our fortunes, O Lord,
like the watercourses of the Negev.

6 Those who sowed with tears
will reap with songs of joy.

7 Those who go out weeping, carrying the seed,
will come again with joy, shouldering their sheaves.

One can accept that the south really refers to the Negev—though the appeal of the south is lost, and the uninstructed may have to hunt through atlases. But "Turn our captivity" is a much deeper utterance than "Restore our fortunes"—which irresistibly smacks of the desires of industrialists whose shares have collapsed. Any connection between the restoration of fortunes and watercourses is to seek—the language gives no clue, whereas in the old version the dramatic "turn" functions as a kind of zeugma. The change of tense from present to past in verse 6 makes the pain less pressing—though the tense shifts again arbitrarily to present tense in the next verse.

It is in verse 7 that one feels the greatest damage has been done. Coverdale's version moves from general to particular, from "they that sow" to the view of an individual sower; presumably to avoid the fashionably dislikeable masculine pronoun, the modern translation makes everything plural, and less intensely focused. The phrase "go out" is simple, but puzzling, as it usually means, colloquially, to go out of doors; "goeth on his way" is clearer. But we have lost the emphasis on the individual who suffers and rejoices; in the older version "bring his sheaves with him" is a beautiful phrase, coming after the affirmation in "doubtless"—an affirmation in the face of bitter sorrow—and the last phrase gives rhythmic emphasis to "bring . . . sheaves . . . him." The climax comes with "sheaves," but the ending "with him" gives point and poignancy; it is the weeping sower who—against reason in one sense, yet in the course of nature, in another—shall ultimately bring the sheaves. The new version gives instead of this poignant simplicity the fussy participle "shouldering" in heavy alliteration with "sheaves"; the attention is not on the fact of the sower's bringing the sheaves with him, but on a group of people's shoulders. The phrase makes reader or hearer endeavor suddenly to picture something very literally, and in doing so the triumphant emotional sense is lost. The word *shouldering* shoulders out the sheaves. Could Thackeray have adapted this verse in its new form as he did the old one in that memorable speech in *Henry Esmond*?

> "Do you know what day it is?" she continued. "It is the 29th of December—it is your birthday! But last year we did not drink it—no, no. My lord was cold, and my Harry was likely to die: and my brain was in a fever; and we had no wine. But now—now you are come again, bringing your sheaves with you, my dear." She burst into a wild flood of weeping as she spoke: she laughed and sobbed on the young man's heart, crying out wildly, "bringing your sheaves with you—your sheaves with you!"[4]

Could Thackeray have had Lady Castlemaine say "now you are come again, shouldering your sheaves"? Maybe—but he could not have used it thrice—the "shouldering" is too full of comical possibilities. The new translators dislike metaphor, and are much happier with the literalisms which release us from too much bondage to the metaphor. That is probably why so many of their translations veer towards the potentially comic, or to understatement and prosy-ness, as in the new "a day in thy courts is better than a thousand in my own room"—where the addition of the last phrase is irresistibly comic, reminiscent of bed-sitter-land—and who wouldn't rather be anywhere else than shut up in one room for a thousand days?

The secret hostility to metaphor is of a piece with the revisers' general antagonism to any language which demands too much response, and plays on the feelings of the members of the congregation. Everywhere—in the Eucharist, in the Psalms—language which is pronounced and evocative is ironed out, not just in getting rid of archaic pronouns or images, but in getting rid of language which exerts pressure. It seems to be felt that we shall be nearer to God if we are not caught by language. Our renovating editors are rather hostile to the old Prayer Book, though they pay lip service to it. Something in it strikes them as definitely inimical—the dominance of the Word, and of words, fit only for a society which was putting too much "emphasis on the Word." I believe that they suspect such language of being in some deep sense undemocratic because it is in one sense so common—so well known, so insistent, so publicly forceful that it has moved people in spite of themselves, made them think and feel in ways that they would not have thought or felt without that language. Thus, they are happy to get away from a book which takes such unfair advantage over the people.

Those who like myself are upset by the changes are often accused of being obscurantist, standing in the way of self-evident progress because of a reactionary fondness for archaic speech or a selfish pleasure in certain forms of embellishment. But we are not sighing after antique pronouns and verb forms, nor yearning for mere ornament. We are, I believe, lamenting the loss of substance and of a whole activity.

My own life would have been so much the poorer without the Book of Common Prayer that I feel a kind of horrified pity for an Anglican and Episcopalian posterity which may have to do without it. It is hard to describe my own experience in adolescence, of growing up in cramped and rather poor surroundings, without the plastic and performing arts, without nearly enough access to literature—in an environment where, with the very large exception of natural beauty of landscape, there was little to persuade one that life was not banal, and gritty, and dull. And in this circumstance I was at least once a week compelled to be moved by a public ritual which had the stature of great art (though that was not its purpose), which was not commonplace and not dull and not mean. The Book of Common Prayer gave me insistent constant contact with something much greater than myself—and unlike attendance at an artistic performance, it forced me very literally and publicly to participate in it, whether that were my immediate fancy or not. It really constituted my first and deepest acquaintance with what is classical in spirit as differentiated from Romantic. I was reached through language which shaped my own sense of language, and my own life. It has been essential to my own love of literature, and hence to my career. Much more important, ultimately, it has been essential to my life as a believer, and the development (though that is a poor and misleading word) of my Christian life, as far as I understand and try to practice Christianity. This language was a perpetual instruction about the nature of God—one knew one was speaking to a God who is very great indeed, and that it is perpetually necessary to long for and reach out to something which is greater and better than the surface satisfactions of ordinary life—something beyond contentment, beyond success, beyond cheerfulness or happiness. I knew inescapably some things which my lighter will might not have chosen to know. I knew what penitence was (even if impenitent); the liturgy told me and made me enact it. I knew what joy was, and a refreshed turning to God (even if not joyful, not returning); the language forced me to know. Although as I have said it provided me with great art, I always knew that that was not its function. It was not there to provide easy channels for adolescent or adult flickering velleities, to be a resort for the feelings. It came to me and changed me, this tough compelling language, which demands that it meanings be practiced even in the uttering of the words.

A strong liturgy perpetually communicates the relationship of man to God and God to man, and it needs a language which will include, celebrate and evoke a range of emotions and attitudes which only language can convey—until we arrive at the point of the mystics, loving God without language, a state not to be found by bypassing the use of language at the outset. There is a real danger in devising rituals which are trivial or flabby, which do not press upon the hearer's attention or ring along the nerves. The language of the old BCP is comforting in the older sense—strengthening, offering bark and steel for the mind and soul. The language of the new liturgies is comfortable in the upholsterer's sense: "To rest, the Cushion and soft Dean invite." It will never make one uncomfortable, in itself, for it is not stirring; any sense of discomfort must be brought by the individual, or any terrific sense of joy and wonder. The new liturgy does not make any palpable demands, does not shanghai anyone into drama. Indeed, if the worshipper comes into church really penitent or really joyful, the language of the service will tend rather to defuse the intenser emotions, while the inarticulate and unfocused feelings which may arise in the worshipper on weekdays will not be made articulate and concentrated for him on a Sunday. The old liturgy is being rejected not for archaism or dryness but fundamentally because it exerted too much dramatic force on the emotions. This liturgy will not make anyone feel what he is not feeling already—any emotions must be brought and dealt with by the worshipper himself, for the service withdraws from that task. It is thus ironically, for all its devisers' emphasis on community, a liturgy for a late Romantic age, a liturgy which lets the sincere desires of individual souls pretty well alone, and is not going to be so impertinent as to shape and change them.

Notes

1. The post-Restoration BCP of 1662 was an importantly modified version of the original Book of Common Prayer of 1549, and has remained the model for all subsequent Anglican and Episcopalian service books. Although there have been

certain accretions and deletions over the centuries, the Prayer Book remained fundamentally unaltered until the Anglicans produced their Series Two and Series Three (in the 1960s) and the Episcopalians produced their recent draft revisions culminating in the present DPB. The 1928 Prayer Book contained modifications and some modernizations of language, but prayers and services did not undergo essential alteration.

2. Charles P. Price, *Part of the Report of the Standing Liturgical Commission to the General Convention of 1976* (New York, 1976), p. 42. The word *medieval* as used in the above passage is deliberately dismissive. In fact, the "sense of unworthiness" is to be found in the Old Testament also, but it would be more tendentious of the modern reviser to say that it corresponded to a deep need in ancient Jewish psyches. The implied historical argument is that in a new Reformation we are restoring the tone and manner of the Early Church—pre-medieval—and that that was not colored by any sense of unworthiness. Such modernizers, however, are by no means fond of St. Paul. And do St. Augustine and St. Jerome count as medieval?

3. Price, p. 32.

4. William Makepeace Thackeray, *The History of Henry Esmond,* Bk. II, ch. vi.

D. J. ENRIGHT

Orthography

The good souls spelt it 'abhominable',
As if to man's nature such things ran contrary.
A fallacious etymology—

Scholars laughed at that vagrant 'h',
Which the vulgar habitually
Omit wrongly or supply mistakenly.

A thing of 'ill omen' and best avoided
(Though not to man's nature entirely contrary)—
It was 'abominable', properly.

Since nothing inhuman is alien to us,
We match the spelling with the derivation—
Without vain aspirate, vain aspiration.

Identities

❧ RICHARD RODRIGUEZ

An Education in Language

SOME EDUCATIONISTS have recently told me that I received a very bad education. They are proponents of bilingual schooling, that remarkable innovation—the latest scheme—to improve education. They think it is a shame, a disgrace, that my earliest teachers never encouraged me to speak Spanish, "my family language," when I entered the classroom.

Those educators who tell me such things, however, do not understand very much about the nature of classroom language. Nor do they understand the kind of dilemma I faced when I started my schooling. A socially disadvantaged child, I desperately needed to be taught that I had the obligation—the right—to speak *public* language. (Until I was nearly seven years old, I had been almost always surrounded by the sounds of my family's Spanish, which kept me safely at home and made me a stranger in public.) In school, I was initially terrified by the language of *gringos*. Silent, waiting for the bell to go home, dazed, diffident, I couldn't believe that English concerned me. The teacher in the (Catholic) school I attended kept calling out my name, anglicizing it as *Rich-heard*

An early version of this essay appeared in *College English* 40, no. 3 (November 1978).

Road-ree-guess, telling me with her sounds that I had a public identity. But I couldn't believe her. I wouldn't respond.

Classroom words were used in ways very different from family words; they were directed to a general audience. (The nun remarked in a friendly, but oddly theatrical voice, "Speak up, Richard. And tell it to the entire class, not just to me.") Classroom words, moreover, meant just what they said. (*Grammar* school.) The teacher quizzed: Why do we use that word in this sentence? Could I think of a better word to use there? Would the sentence change its meaning if the words were differently arranged? And wasn't there a much better way of saying the same thing?

I couldn't say.

Eventually my teachers connected my silence with the difficult progress my older brother and sister were making. All three of us were directed to daily tutoring sessions. I was the "slow learner" who needed a year and a half of special attention. I also needed my teachers to keep my attention from straying in class by calling out, "Richard!" And most of all I needed to hear my parents speak English at home—as my teachers had urged them to do.

The scene was inevitable: one Saturday morning, when I entered a room where my mother and father were talking, I did not realize that they were speaking in Spanish until the moment they saw me they abruptly started speaking English. The *gringo* sounds they uttered (had previously spoken only to strangers) startled me, pushed me away. In that moment of trivial misunderstanding and profound insight I felt my throat twisted by a grief I didn't sound as I left the room. But I had no place to escape to with Spanish. (My brothers were speaking English in another part of the house.) Again and again in the weeks following, increasingly angry, I would hear my parents uniting to urge, "Speak to us now, *en inglés.*" Only then did it happen, my teachers' achievement, my greatest academic success: I raised my hand in the classroom and volunteered an answer and did not think it remarkable that the entire class understood. That day I moved very far from the disadvantaged child I had been only weeks before.

But this great public success was measured at home by a feeling of loss. We remained a loving family—enormously different. No longer were we as close as we had earlier been. (No longer so desperate for the consolation of intimacy.) My brothers and I didn't rush home after school. Even our parents grew easier in public, following the Americanization of their children. My mother started referring to neighbors by name. My father continued to speak about *gringos,* but the word was no longer charged with bitterness and suspicion. Hearing it sometimes, I wasn't even sure if my father was saying the Spanish word, *gringo,* or saying, gringo, in English.

Our house was no longer noisy. And for that I blamed my mother and father, since they had encouraged our classroom success. I flaunted my second-grade knowledge as a kind of punishment. ("Two negatives make a positive!") But this anger was spent after several months, replaced by a feeling of guilt as school became more and more important to me. Increasingly successful in class, I would come home a troubled son, aware that education was making me different from my parents. Sadly I would listen as my mother or father tried unsuccessfully (laughing self-consciously) to help my brothers with homework assignments.

My teachers became the new figures of authority in my life. I began imitating their accents. I trusted their every direction. Each book they told me to read, I read and then waited for them to tell me which books I enjoyed. Their most casual opinions I adopted. I stayed after school "to help"—to get their attention. It was their encouragement that mattered to me. Memory caressed each word of their praise so that compliments teachers paid me in grammar school classes come quickly to mind even today.

Withheld from my parents was any mention of what happened at school. In late afternoon, in the midst of preparing our dinner, my mother would come up behind me while I read. Her head just above mine, her breath scented with food, she'd ask, "What are you reading?" Or: "Tell me about all your new courses." I would just barely respond. "Just the usual things, ma." (Silence. Silence! Instead of the intimate sounds which had once flowed between us, there was this silence.) After dinner, I would rush off to a bedroom with papers and books. As often as possible, I resisted parental pleas to "save lights" by staying in the kitchen to work. I kept so much, so often to myself. Nights when relatives visited and the front room was warmed by familiar Spanish sounds, I slipped out of the house.

I was a fourth-grade student when my mother asked me one day for a "nice" book to read. ("Something not too hard which you think I might like.") Carefully, I chose Willa Cather's *My Ántonia.* When, several days later, I happened to see it next to her bed, unread except for the first several pages, I felt a surge of sorrow, a need for my mother's embrace. That feeling passed by the time I had taken the novel back to my room.

"Your parents must be so proud of you. . . ." People began to say that to me about the time I was in sixth grade. I'd smile shyly, never betraying my sense of the irony.

"Why didn't you tell me about the award?" my mother scolded —although her face was softened by pride. At the grammar school ceremony, several days later, I heard my father speak to a teacher and felt ashamed of his accent. Then guilty for the shame. My teacher's words were edged sharp and clean. I admired her until I sensed that she was condescending to them. I grew resentful. Protective. I tried to move my parents away. "You both must be so proud of him," she said. They quickly responded. (They were proud.) "We are proud of all our children." Then this afterthought: "They sure didn't get their brains from us." They laughed.

Always I knew my parents wanted for my brothers and me the chances they had never had. It saddened my mother to learn of relatives who forced their children to start working right after high school. To *her* children she would say, "Get all the education you can." In schooling she recognized the key to job advancement. As a girl, new to America, she had been awarded a high school diploma by teachers too careless or busy to notice that she hardly spoke English. On her own, she determined to learn how to type. That skill got her clean office jobs in "letter shops" and nurtured her optimism about the possibility of advancement. (Each morning, when her sisters put on uniforms, she chose a bright-colored dress.) The years of young womanhood passed and her typing speed increased. Also, she became an excellent speller of words she mispronounced. ("And I've never been to college," she would say, smiling when her children asked her to spell a word they didn't want to look up in a dictionary.)

After her youngest child began high school, my mother once more got an office job. She worked for the (California) state government in civil service positions, numbered and secured by examinations. The old ambition of her youth was still bright then. Regularly she consulted bulletin boards for news of openings, further advancements. Until one day she saw mentioned something about an "anti-poverty agency." A typing job—part of the governor's staff. ("A knowledge of Spanish required.") Without hesitation she applied, and grew nervous only when the job was suddenly hers.

"Everyone comes to work all dressed up," she reported at night. And didn't need to say more than that her co-workers would not let her answer the phones. She was, after all, only a typist, though a very fast typist. And an excellent speller. One day there was a letter to be sent to a Washington cabinet officer. On the dictating tape there was reference to urban guerillas. My mother typed (the wrong word, correctly): "gorillas." The mistake horrified the anti-poverty bureaucrats. They returned her to her previous job. She would go no further. So she willed her ambition to her children.

"Get all the education you can," she would repeatedly say. "With education you can do anything." When I was a freshman in high school, I admitted to her one day that I planned to become a teacher. And that pleased her. Though I never explained that it was not the occupation of teaching I yearned for as much as something more elusive and indefinite: I wanted to know what my teachers knew; to possess their authority and their confidence.

In contrast to my mother, my father never openly encouraged the academic success of his children. Nor did he praise us. The only thing he regularly said to me was that school work wasn't *real* work. Those times when I claimed to be tired by writing and reading, he would laugh, not scornful so much as bemused. "You'll never know what real work is," he would say smiling, unsmiling. Whereas my mother saw in education the opportunity for job advancement, for my father education implied an even more startling possibility: escape from the workaday world. (After I introduced him to some of my high school friends he remarked that their hands were soft.)

His hands were calloused by a lifetime of work. In Mexico, he was orphaned when he was eight. At eight (my age when I achieved my first academic success) my father had to leave school to work for his uncle. Eighteen years later, in frustration, he left for America. There survive photos of him, in his first American years, dressed in a dandy's wardrobe. My mother remembers how he used to spend a week's salary then at the San Francisco opera on Saturday nights. And how they used to watch polo matches on Sundays.

He had great expectations of becoming an engineer. He knew a Catholic priest who had promised money to enable him to study full-time for a high school diploma. But the promises came to nothing. Instead, there was a dark succession of warehouse, factory, and cannery jobs. Nights, he went to school with my mother. A year, two passed. Nothing much changed, except that fatigue worked its way into the bone. And then suddenly everything was different. He gave away his fancy clothes. He didn't go to the opera. And he stayed outside, on the steps of the night school, while my mother went inside.

In almost my earliest memories of him, my father seems old. (He has never grown old gradually like my mother.) From boyhood to manhood, I have remembered him most powerfully in a single image: seated, asleep, on the sofa, his head thrown back in a hideous grin, the evening newspaper spread out before him. ("You'll never know what real work is. . . .")

It was my father who became angry when watching on television a Miss America contestant tell the announcer that she was going to college. ("Majoring in fine arts.") "College!" he snarled. He despised the trivialization of higher education, the inflated grades and cheapened diplomas, the half-education that increasingly passed for mass education in my generation. It was also my father who wondered why I didn't display my awards in my bedroom. He said that he liked to go to doctors' offices and see their certificates on the wall. My awards from school got left at home in closets and drawers. My father found my high school diploma as it was about to be thrown out with the trash. Without telling me, he put it away with his own things for safekeeping. ("We are proud of all our children.")

The separation which slowly unraveled (so long) between my parents and me was not the much-discussed "generation gap" caused by the tension of youth and experience. Age figured in our separation, but in a very odd way. Year after year, advancing in my studies, I would notice that my parents had not changed as much as I. They oddly measured my progress. Often I realized that my command of English was improving, for example, because at home I would hear myself simplify my diction and syntax when addressing my parents.

Too deeply troubled, I did not join my brothers when, as high school students, they toyed with our parents' opinions, devastating them frequently with superior logic and factual information. My mother and father would usually submit with sudden silence, although there were times when my mother complained that our "big ideas" were going to our heads. More acute was her complaint that the family wasn't as close as some of our relatives. It was toward me that she most often would glance when she mimicked the "yes" and "no" answers she got in response to her questions. (My father never asked.) Why was everyone "so secret," she wondered. (I never said.)

When the time came to go to college, I was the first in the family who asked to leave home. My departure only made physically apparent the separation that had occurred long before. But it was too stark a reminder. In the months preceding my departure, I heard the question my mother never asked except indirectly. In the hot kitchen, tired at the end of the workday, she demanded to know, "Why aren't the colleges around here good enough for you? They were for your brother and sister." Another time, in the car, never turning to face me, she wondered, "Why do you need to go so far away?" Late one night ironing, she said with disgust, "Why do you have to put us through this big expense? You know your scholarship will never cover it all." But when September came, there was a rush to get everything ready. In a bedroom that last night, I packed the brown valise. My mother sat nearby sewing my initials onto the clothes I would take. And she said nothing more about my leaving.

II

In pages and pages of modern educational literature nothing is written about the silence that envelops the scholarship boy and his parents; there is thus no suggestion that this silence implies a lesson important for all students.

Those social scientists who are our educational experts do not speak about the price good schooling exacts. Self-styled "radical" educators merely complain that American ghetto schools attempt to "mold" students and that they stifle native characteristics. (The bilingualists slightly vary the theme.) More moderate educators, meanwhile, busily propose ways of increasing the self-esteem and early self-confidence of students. Their prose glitters with a constellation of predictable terms like *originality* and *creativity* and *self-expression*.

Assumed by radical and moderate alike is the progressivist idea that education is largely a matter of teaching (encouraging) students to become (to give voice to) the persons they already were before they entered the classroom. It is a comforting idea, appropriately so at a time when full educational opportunity has been extended to the middle class. But the growing influence of this idea on educational policy over the last several decades has paralleled the decline in "basic" education. Today, as a result, parents are troubled by the fact that their children are being taught the value of self-expression but are not able to read and write well.

When I began to speak classroom English, my teacher encouraged me to start reading. "You'll learn to speak well, if you practice your reading," she said. And though I followed her instruction, I remember how puzzled I was by the implied connection between reading and speaking. My parents were good speakers of Spanish, but they did not read very much.

They *did* read, it is true. Spanish and English. From an early age I had watched them read. I remember seeing my father make his way through, what I suppose now, must have been income tax forms. On other occasions, I waited apprehensively while my mother learned of a relative's illness or death from letters airmailed from Mexico. For both of my parents, however, reading was something done out of necessity and as quickly as possible. Never did I see either of them read an entire book. Nor did I see them read for pleasure.

Each school year would begin with my mother's instruction: "Don't write in your books so we can sell them at the end of the year." Teachers at school echoed the comment, but only in part: "Don't write in your books, boys and girls. You must learn to treat them with care and respect."

It soon was apparent to me that in the classroom written words possessed almost sacred authority. They were key to all knowledge. "READ TO LEARN," read the poster over the teacher's desk in September. What one read in a text was unquestioned. "OPEN THE DOOR OF YOUR MIND WITH BOOKS," the sign commanded later in the year. I privately wondered: What was the connection between reading and knowing? Did an idea become an idea only when it was written down? In June, "CONSIDER BOOKS YOUR BEST FRIENDS." Friends? Reading was only a chore at the start. I needed to look up whole pages of words in a dictionary. And the sentences in the first books I read were coolly impersonal. I tried reading in a very soft voice. But, "Who is doing all that talking with his neighbor?" an instructor shouted during the afternoon reading period. Reading sessions were then arranged for me with an old nun.

At the end of each school day, for nearly six months, I would meet with her in a tiny room which served as the school's library, but was actually a storeroom for used textbooks and a vast collection of *National Geographics*. Everything about the sessions pleased me: the size of the room; the vague sounds of some children playing far away; the sound of the janitor's broom in the long hallway outside the door; the soft green of the sun lighting the wall; and the old woman's face, blurred with a white beard.

We took turns reading. I began, reading from an elementary text. ("The boys ran with the girls. The kite rose in the blue sky.") Then the old nun would read from her favorite books—usually biographies of early American presidents. She ran playfully through complex sentences, making the words sound friendly. Listening to her, I sensed for the first time some possibility of a fellowship between reader and writer and even a bond between readers—never *intimate* like the bond spoken words could convey at home, but personal nonetheless.

The nun ended the session one day by asking me why I was so reluctant to read by myself. I tried to explain my fears, said something about the way written words made me feel all by myself—almost like, I wanted to add but didn't, when I spoke in a room just emptied of furniture. She studied my face as I spoke; she seemed to be watching more than listening. Then she replied that I had nothing to fear. Didn't I realize that reading would open up whole new worlds? A book was like a magic carpet, she said. I listened respectfully, but her words were not very influential. I was thinking of another consequence of literacy, one I was too shy to admit but deeply trusted. Books were going to make me educated. That confidence enabled me, after a few more months, to overcome the initial difficulties of reading by myself.

In the third grade, I embarked on a grandiose reading program. "Give me the names of important books," I would say to my teachers. They soon discovered that I had in mind "adult books." I ignored their suggestions of anything I suspected to be written for children. (Not until I was in college did I read either *Huckleberry Finn* or *Alice in Wonderland.*) Instead, I read Franklin's *Autobiography* and Hawthorne's *Scarlet Letter.* Whatever I read, I read for "extra credit." Each time I finished a book, I was careful to report the achievement to a teacher and wait for praise. Despite my best efforts, however, there seemed to be more and more books I needed to read. At the library I would come upon whole shelves of unfamiliar titles. So I read and read and read: *Great Expectations,* the first volume (A–ANSTEY) of *The Encyclopedia Britannica, The Iliad, The Collected Novels of John O'Hara, Speak Memory, The Sermons of Bishop Sheen, War and Peace.* . . . Librarians, who worried initially when I checked out the maximum ten books at a time, started saving books they thought I might like. Teachers would say to the class, "I only wish the rest of you took reading as seriously as Richard." But at home I would hear my mother asking, "What do you see in your books?" (Was reading a hobby?

Was so much reading good for a boy? Was it a sign of fabulous intellect? Was it just an excuse for not helping around the house?) "What do you see . . . ?"

What *did* I see in my books? I had the idea that they were crucial to my academic success, though I couldn't have said how or why. In the sixth grade, I concluded that what gave a book its value was some major idea or "theme." If that essence could be found and memorized, I would become educated. I decided to record in a notebook the themes of the books I read. After finishing *Robinson Crusoe,* I wrote that its theme was "the value of learning to live by oneself." When I completed *Wuthering Heights,* I noted the "danger of letting emotions get out of control."

In spite of my earnestness, reading was a pleasurable experience. I had favorite writers—though those I enjoyed most were the writers I was least able to value. When I read William Saroyan's *Human Comedy,* for example, I was immediately pleased by the narrator's warmth and the simple charm of the story. But as quickly I became suspicious. A book so easy and enjoyable couldn't be very "important." Another summer, I determined to read all the novels of Dickens. I loved the feeling, after the first hundred pages, of being at home in a complex fictional world. I also loved the feeling of finishing a big book. I would run my fingers along the edge of the pages and marvel at how much I had achieved. I entered high school, having read hundreds of books. Reading made me a confident writer and speaker of English as my first teachers had promised. Reading also gave me a broad sense of the concerns of Western culture. I could say something about Greek tragedy and Marx and sentimental novels. But I was not a good reader. I lacked a point of view when I read. Rather *I read in order to acquire a point of view.* Merely bookish, I vacuumed books for epigrams, scraps of information, ideas, "themes"—anything which would help fill the hollow within me. When one of my teachers suggested to his drowsy tenth-grade class that a person could not have "a complicated idea" until he had read at least two thousand books, I heard the remark without detecting either its irony or its complicated truth. I decided to compile a list of all the books I ever had read. Harsh with myself, I included only those books over a hundred pages in length. (Could anything shorter be a book?)

There was yet another high school list I kept. I had read a newspaper story about the retirement of an English professor at a nearby college. The story was accompanied by a list of "the hundred most important books of Western civilization." "More than anything else," the teacher told the reporter, "these books have made me all that I am." That kind of remark I couldn't ignore. I clipped out the list and kept it for the several months it took to read all the titles. Most books, of course, I barely understood. While reading Plato's *Republic,* for instance, I needed to keep looking at the book jacket comments to remind myself what it was all about. Nevertheless, with the special patience of a scholarship boy, I looked at every sentence and, by the time I reached the last page, I was convinced that I had read the *Republic.* In a ceremony of great pride, I solemnly crossed Plato off my list.

JANE MILLER

How Do You Spell *Gujarati,* Sir?

KULVINDER IS FIVE and halfway through her first year of primary school. Her teacher sometimes feels concerned that Kulvinder doesn't speak at school, but she lets herself be reassured by the child's bright watchfulness and by the alacrity with which she always does what she is told. Besides, Kulvinder's mother and father are so keen for their daughter to speak good English that they have given up speaking Punjabi at home and speak only English now. Kulvinder doesn't say much at home either, but perhaps that will change when her parents have learned more English themselves.

Andreas lives in East London, and he goes to the nearest school, though his father worried at first about sending him there. He had heard that over half the children were black and that the school had gone downhill since it became comprehensive and some of the Jewish families round there began to send their sons to fee-paying schools. Andreas is tall for twelve, one of the tallest in the second year, and he seems to like school, though his father is never sure that he's learning anything. This week he's been teaching his class some Greek, in English lessons if you please. He began with the alphabet, writing it up on the board. Then he made the class work out the words "West Ham for the Cup," which he'd written in Greek letters. He could tell they'd got it when they jeered. His father has written a funny poem which Andreas will give them tomorrow, though he'll have to help them translate it. It's good the way Mr. Orme lets the boys be teachers sometimes. They're learning all about the history of writing and alphabets with him. Andreas finds it strange that some people hate writing, can't see the point.

Michelle is twelve too. There was a lady in her English lesson today who asked them all what languages they knew. They thought at first she meant French, which they started last year with Mrs. Brooke. But it turned out that she meant things like Indian and Brok French. Michelle was really surprised that apart from her there were five others in the class who spoke Brok French. She'd thought Nadia was Indian, but she speaks the sort of French they speak in Mauritius. By the end of the lesson they'd discovered that besides English, which everybody speaks, there were children who knew Egyptian, Greek, Urdu, Spanish and Italian, as well as Jamaican language and French Creole. The lady said that their French teacher might be interested that six of her pupils spoke French patois. Michelle nearly told her that Mrs. Brooke never seemed interested in anything much except getting your homework in on time.

Three voices, one of them inaudible, must be allowed to speak for themselves out of what is variously regarded as a Babel or a resource for teaching of unimaginable richness. A recent survey of just over three thousand children in their first year at eighteen London secondary schools turned up fifty-two languages spoken apart from English, thirty-three overseas dialects of English and nearly as many home-based ones. Among the three hundred children in their first year of just one of those schools, twenty-eight languages were spoken apart from English.[1] London schools are often in the news for doing worst in tests set for the whole country, worse even than Glasgow schools. There was a time when researchers got used to urban children doing better than rural ones.[2] Children living in towns were expected to be better off, more ambitious and sophisticated. All this has changed, and London is suffering from that worldwide complaint, the inner-city crisis. It would be easy to blame that on all those languages, but mistaken. They aren't spoken in the schools, after all. There are some English teachers who say that the children in their classes have too little language, not too much, and that what there is is usually bad, in every sense.

In Andreas's class they had a lesson last week from one of the boys, on Korean, and how you write it in different directions to show whether you're talking about the past or the future. That was amazing. Mr. Orme did Ancient Greek when he was young and he wanted to find out whether that helps at all with Modern Greek. He's impressed by all the languages his pupils speak. One boy, who speaks Urdu, Punjabi and Hindi, can read and write in Urdu and Punjabi and is learning to read Hindi at after-school classes. It has taken him only four years to sound like a native Cockney speaker and his writing is good too. Mr. Orme is rather a rarity. He has gone to the trouble of finding out what languages the boys speak at home, and because a lot of them are from Jamaican families he has learned to speak their language and can discuss in detail the differences between Kingston Jamaican, London Jamaican and the sort of English he speaks. Some teachers think he's wasting his time, that he'd have to agree that since these children live in England and will probably stay for the rest of their lives, teaching them the sort of English which helps them to pass exams and get jobs is what he's there for. Mr. Orme does agree, though he finds it harder and harder to be sure that he knows what sort of English that would actually be. When he was a boy he won a place at a grammar school in Durham. All the boys spoke with an accent, even used different words, but their English teacher saw to it that they didn't speak sloppily with him. So that for a long time Mr. Orme had believed that you couldn't expect even to spell properly if you didn't talk like the BBC. Wouldn't all those rules for doubling letters, spelling the *or* sound and silent *e*'s be much easier to get right if you talked posh? He remembered one of his mates saying that squeezing up the vowels and making a big thing of the consonants was the way to get on. Mr. Orme's ideas have changed since then. He likes the way his pupils speak and he even likes his own accent now; still "rough," as he thinks of it, after all these years in London. When he talks about these things with his friends they think he's a bit sentimental or just making the best of a bad job. It is difficult enough to explain, let alone to justify, his conviction that his being interested in the languages his pupils speak does actually help them to write English of several sorts and to speak more confidently in class. It isn't as if he knew all those languages himself, though: Yoruba, Arabic, Cantonese, Gujarati. He often wishes he did when he's teaching his examination classes. He can't even find good dictionaries for most of the languages, let alone science textbooks or novels.

For a long time research into bilingualism operated within the assumption that bilingual children were likely to have problems at school. Welsh-speaking children in Wales[3] and French-speaking children in Canada[4] did less well than their monolingual (English-speaking) counterparts. In the way of so much of that kind of research, most of it had, by the sixties, been queried and even contradicted on the grounds that the tests which were used to establish the inferior attainment of bilingual children ignored both the social factors underlying the bilingual ones and the effects on a child of speaking one language at home while learning (and being tested) in another one at school. There had, as well, always been some people in Wales who were prepared to concede that knowing Welsh as well as English might be seen as providing the benefits of a cheap classical education; benefits, by the way, which were not queried. For that is one of the anomalies about attitudes to bilingualism. Whereas learning a foreign language and even one or two dead ones as well has always been the *sine qua non* of a "good" education, and whereas a child who picks up fluent French and Italian, say, because her father has been posted abroad, is likely to be thought fortunate, at an advantage, even "finished," a child with two or three non-European languages, in some of which he may be literate, could be regarded as quite literally languageless when he arrives in an English school, where "not a word of English" can often imply "not a word." Partly, this is a matter of the history which has made of English a *lingua franca.* I should want to suggest, however, that it also has a good deal to do with the view that English as a school subject is bound to concentrate exclusively on its written form. It is not that there need be any argument with the tradition which makes schools the promoters of literacy, but that the written form and its intimate relation with Standard English speech can be made to exclude the realities of the language as it is spoken. Many children spend a larger proportion of their day in school on writing than on reading, speaking or listening. Even tests which are intended to assess oral comprehension, reading competence and response to literature are made to depend on the child's knowing how to write a certain sort of English prose. That is the sort of English Mr. Orme *should* be teaching his pupils, and it is not a form easily learned by anyone whose own speech is under suspicion. The best examples of expository or imaginative prose draw vitally upon the spoken language. The belief that a child can learn to produce even the most modest versions of such prose while his speech is dismissed, even perhaps excoriated, is likely to be doomed, and we can't, surely, be wanting children to "talk like a book."

To be genuinely multilingual or multidialectal in contemporary Britain is allowed, then, to be a drawback. It is still thought "useful" to know some Latin, while knowledge of Standard Tamil, say, and one of its dialects, is thought "confusing." There is, of course, a special kind of usefulness in knowing something of a language from which English partly derives and which has certainly mattered to English literature, just as there is another kind of usefulness in speaking your mother tongue. Other claims have been made for the learning of a second language, however, beyond these sorts of usefulness. One would be that another language embodies as it expresses another culture, and that another culture introduces the possibility of critical detachment about one's own. Another would be that there are aspects of the nature of language itself, which are often more easily learned through an encounter with a second language. Connected with this is the notion that the conscious mastery of a language is an intellectual discipline in itself. Recent research on bilingual Hebrew/English children[5] draws attention to those things which these children do better than their monolingual peers. Because they are earlier able to separate meaning from sound, they are also able to develop earlier what Margaret Donaldson has called "a reflective awareness of language as a symbolic system,"[6] which is a prerequisite for developing abstract thought. Perhaps because the learning of language has required more effort of them, these children are often more sensitive to the appropriateness of their speech and to the effect it produces on hearers of it. They also become aware earlier than most children of the structures within one particular language system which contrast with those of the other one. Even at those points where one language might be expected to interfere with the other, to overlap or create confusion, possibilities for particular insights were noticed, so that fusion rather than confusion worked to produce at an earlier age a sense of what languages generally consist of, get up to, are used for.

What, it might be asked, is the hurry? Many monolingual children will develop that kind of awareness of language too, in time. But since learning to read depends on this ability to stand back from language, to hear it and watch it function, as it were, and since learning to read quickly and successfully can determine a child's whole school experience, it is important that teachers exploit what may be real advantages for the bilingual child. There are teachers who have done so. A fifteen-year-old bilingual Turkish boy, for instance, was asked to translate into written English a story told by his mother in Turkish to her three-year-old daughter. He was able to discover for himself, and partly to solve, the problems of turning into written English an oral story in another language intended for a young child and told by a woman who was elaborating a narrative out of a real experience. Then two thirteen-year-old Jamaican girls improvised a play in patois on videotape. Because they wanted to transcribe their play, in order to develop and improve it, they decided to transcribe its present version. They found themselves having to invent an orthography and a way of representing their own speech which would allow a reader to "hear" it as far as possible. The exercise was useful on several counts, not the least important being that it introduced one of the girls, who had barely been able to read and write until then, to the nature of written language and to the purposes there might be for her in learning to write. It is the kind of exercise which would be hard to match in a language for which conventional spelling already existed.

In one sense, it is all quite simple. Where a child grows up speaking more than one language or dialect, and those languages or dialects have equivalent status in his own and in other people's eyes, and where the connections between those languages and their differences are made explicit, multilingualism can be an unqualified good. Mr. Orme's pupil, Andreas, is in that rare position. He still visits Cyprus. English people know about Greek, even hear it spoken on their holidays. Andreas speaks Greek for most of the time at home, but other members of his family speak English too; and he is not aware of making conscious decisions about which language to speak to whom, about what or where. He could read and write in Greek before he arrived in England,[7] and he learned English in a school where it was assumed, rightly, that he was competent linguistically even if he didn't know English, and where they have come to rely on and to admire his success. He was lucky too to embark on the second of his languages before he was too old to do so easily and to learn it principally through using it with children of his own age. As an example of bilingual advantages he is ideal, though hardly typical.

It is a characteristic irony that while the learning of languages can be an expensive business, nearly all those people in the world who grow up bilingual do so because their mother tongue or dialect has associations with poverty which make it likely to be thought inappropriate for education and some kinds of employment. Many of the people who have come to live in England during the last twenty-five years are in the position of speaking either a dialect of English or another language altogether, which they are encouraged, and in some cases are themselves all too ready, to relinquish. What will happen to Kulvinder between now and her first letter of application for a job? Her parents' refusal to use their own language may have implications about their view of themselves which go well beyond the danger of depriving their daughter of a language which is hers as well as theirs. Kulvinder's watchfulness has something of the look which children acquire when they are brought up by deaf parents. Modern language teaching often makes good use of a temporary outlawing of the mother tongue. It is a strategy which assumes that sheer need to communicate is sure to power the acquisition of a new language, as it has been thought, simplistically, to power the acquisition of the first. For a child in Kulvinder's circumstances the refusal to speak Punjabi is probably disastrous. Certainly she has proved that her need to communicate is not as powerful as all that.[8]

The variety of ways in which multilingualism is experienced by children is probably infinite, ranging from a kind of "anomie" at one extreme to a quite special flexibility and effectiveness as a language user at the other. Somewhere between are all those children who leave their mother tongue at home and learn "English" at school. This can produce a damaging dividedness, particularly when it is not discussed, shared or understood. A second language learned and used only in school can feel like a language for passivity, acceptance, attention, listening and Kulvinder's obedience. Its use will be constrained by rules and prohibitions, its vitality and subtleties hidden. Similarly, the home language may be relegated to the terrain of childhood, interesting only as the expression of a vestigial folk culture. The life of action and feeling, of first experiences and what is directly known can become divorced from the world where language has become an instrument for generalization, organization and the assimilating of new ideas and knowledge. There is a danger of that happening to any child, but the danger is a much greater one if the two selves, so to speak, talk different languages. Cultural values can be distorted, polarized into what is quaint, half extinguished, and what is practical, modern and remunerated. Many children are marooned between languages and between cultures, forgetting one more rapidly than they acquire another; and meanwhile they may be regarded by teachers and by other children—ultimately, perhaps, by themselves—as bereft of all the things language stands for: intelligence, humor, daring, inventiveness, enthusiasm, discrimination and curiosity. And without those qualities it is not easy to learn the new language which might enable you to regain them. A child's first sorting out of its impressions of the world, of its own place there, and of noises which are meaningful from those which are not came with a particular language, which is now forced underground, made inaudible, unintelligible. Learning a second language is bound to be a matter of attaching it to the meanings which will always adhere in a special way to the first one. The confidence which allows us to use our language to make jokes and tell stories, let alone to answer a court charge or infer something of motive and intention from another person's speech, is not gained by dismissing as irrelevant the language which both produced and expressed the child's first thoughts.

Michelle's parents came to London from St. Lucia before she was born. They still speak French patois at home, and though she thinks her parents' English absurd she herself knew some English by the time she was five and went to primary school. Most of the time she speaks like the other children in her class, a nonstandard London dialect. When she is with her West Indian friends she shifts into London Jamaican as they do. She says she has never spoken patois outside her home and that "most West Indian people say that patois is bad for young children to speak." That may be why her parents sent her to a school where there are relatively few West Indian children. That, at any rate, is what Michelle believes. When she recalls, and mimics, her first teacher at primary school telling her, "You're talking bad language, bad English," she assumes that her teacher meant that there was something wrong with her accent. She is also able fiercely to say, "You should be able to speak patois, Jamaican or English." When Michelle assents to the disapproval her speech can elicit while defending her right to speak as she wants to and needs to, she is expressing the sort of ambivalence many dialect speakers grow up with. Her English teacher has no views about her language except that her writing is "weak in sentence structure." Neither this teacher's comment nor that earlier one about "bad language" has been substantiated or explained to Michelle. She speaks, in fact, three languages:[9] French patois, non-Standard English and London Jamaican. She is fluent and effective in all three, makes easy shifts between them, stylish use of the incongruities the shifts can produce,[10] and is able, as well, to do an excellent imitation of Mrs. Thatcher. It is worth remembering, I think, that whereas all non-Standard English speakers are compelled to understand and sometimes to assume Standard speech patterns, Standard English speakers are rarely required to do the reverse. Yet in spite of this rich language repertoire, Michelle, at twelve, has already been made aware that neither her speech nor her writing will quite do.

That many of the difficulties which exist for a multilingual child also exist for a multidialectal one is due to their being the product of attitudes to languages generally, and to particular languages, rather than to their being inherent in multilingualism itself. They are especially difficult attitudes to grapple with because they are about class and race and status, though they masquerade as value judgements about language and fine (even musical) discriminations.

There is nothing new about multilingualism, or about the passions or the prejudices it provokes. Language has always been felt as a measure of identity, by individuals and by whole communities. The certainties which wiped out Gaelic in the Scottish Highlands and deplored Scots in the Lowlands have been relaxed, so that it is now respectable for plays on television to be in dialect and for novelists and poets to use the language of their childhood. It is, therefore, all the more surprising that no such welcome has been given by schools to the mother tongues and dialects of children. This may have something to do with the teacherly obsession with something called "correct" language, and with correcting, in red ink, children's writing. It is an obsession which is encouraged and applauded by many people who would themselves find it hard to say what they meant by "correct." Children are famously less responsive to the thorough sub-editing job done on their writing—which can look at times like no more than a display of credentials—than to more positive ways of suggesting how a piece of written or spoken language might be made more effective, clear or truthful. That sort of approach, to be successful, relies on a sense of language being complex and diverse and its "correctness" being no more than one aspect of what children need to know about it. Official documents are circulated, it is true, which preach the virtues of "mother tongue maintenance," without specifying how this is to happen, let alone mean very much, if the examinations which are still allowed to validate all schooling continue to rely on a definition of English so exiguous as to exclude not just dialect but speech of any kind.

In America attention is focused at the moment on the predicament of Spanish-speaking and Indian children,[11] and there have been schemes to promote mother-tongue literacy before school and the use of the mother tongue as the language of instruction in school. These are brave moves, though it is not clear that they have managed to change the attitudes which have made such schemes essential and which still undermine them. In this country, where a request for a modest central government grant towards the funding of bilingual education in Wales can still produce an angry letter to *The Times,*[12] what little mother-tongue teaching goes on is undertaken by members of particular language communities, and only in a handful of cases with help from schools or local authorities.[13] There have been, no doubt, some successes, though all the schemes are on a small scale and necessarily dependent on a voluntary commitment to them. They may also encourage minorities to feel defensive about a culture and a language which are plainly not valued by the majority if they are excluded from school. The tragedy is that schools themselves see their role here as so confined, and the English language as so inflexibly unresilient, as to reject the value of their pupils' languages to themselves, to the curriculum and to the community to which the school belongs. Kulvinder could be beginning an education which allows her to feel proud of her language and of the special knowledge she brings to the learning of English. She could as easily remain in a state of profound bewilderment, fearful of having another language snatched from her, struggling not toward an English which she can take on positively as her own but towards something which, at best, will enable her to spell her employer's letters correctly, at worst, will get her a job where speech, and indeed thought, are not required of her.

Any normal child has mastered by the age of five an elaborate symbolic system and internalized its rules. This is true for any child learning any language. Through speech, and through learning to read and write, the child will "learn to turn language and thought in upon themselves,"[14] so that he can talk about language and think about thinking. Children with more than one language are well placed to do this. Teachers in multilingual classrooms have at their disposal resources for introducing all their pupils to the nature of language, to the quality and the implications of linguistic and cultural diversity, and, thereby, to an outlook on knowledge built upon the kind of relativism which produces both intellectual rigor and intellectual openness. The best teaching always moves from a sensitive awareness of what the learner already knows to what is new; and the best users of English, speakers and writers, plunder the tensions and the variety which English has always so vigorously incorporated. If children are to become powerful users of language for their own purposes, and responsive to the subtleties and the excitements of what has been done, and can be done, with language, teachers would do well to begin from an appreciation of the strengths, the highly developed social and linguistic skills, children bring with them when they come to school. And that means all children. There is more and more evidence that children who are "weak in sentence structure" or possessed of "limited vocabularies" are encountered with unusual frequency by some teachers and most researchers.[15] Perhaps it is because such teachers and researchers are the only people given to asking children questions to which they don't really want answers, and to engaging children in conversation about matters of interest to neither party. They might try listening more to children talking their own language to their own friends about things they urgently want to talk about and find out about.

It is time to make use of language diversity; not just the diversity as between one school and another, or between one child and another, but the diversity within each individual child and within the use of language itself. This respect for diversity would, after all, make of an examination or a letter of application no more than single items in a genuine language repertoire, one for use not one up for judgment.

Notes

1. These figures are drawn from the interim report of the survey of linguistic diversity in ILEA secondary schools (1978) by Professor Harold Rosen and Tony Burgess of the English Department, University of London Institute of Education.

2. See, for example, W. R. Jones, *Bilingualism and Intelligence.* (Cardiff, 1959).

3. Jones, *Bilingualism.*

4. W. E. Lambert, "A Social Psychology of Bilingualism" (1967), in J. B. Pride and Janet Holmes, eds., *Sociolinguistics* (London, 1972).

5. Sandra Ben-Zeev, "Mechanisms by which Childhood Bilingualism Affects Understanding of Language and Cognitive Structures," in P. A. Hornby, ed., *Bilingualism: Psychological, Social and Educational Implications* (New York, 1977).

6. Margaret Donaldson, *Children's Minds* (London, 1978).

7. Chester C. Christian, "Social and Psychological Implications of Bilingual Literacy," in António Simôes, Jr., ed., *The Bilingual Child* (New York, 1976). This article describes a project undertaken in the U.S. and based on the belief that preschool literacy in the mother tongue is an advantage to the second-language learner.

8. It is now accepted that there is much more than a need to communicate involved in a child's learning to speak. For a fascinating illustration of this see A. R. Luria and F. Ia. Yudovich, *Speech and the Development of Mental Processes in the Child* (London, 1973).

9. There are drawbacks to using the word *language* for the dialect of a language. I do use it here, not because Michelle's dialect is so aberrant as to seem something quite different from English, but because it works as a complete and coherent system for her, which cannot simply be judged in terms of its divergences from Standard English. A blurring of the distinction between "language" and "dialect" is also appropriate here, in my view, because the problems they pose for the child in school have so much in common.

10. This capacity to shift between two or more dialects of English is at last being recognized; and some superb documentation is coming out of London schools at the moment. For examples of this, see John Richmond, *Brixton Blues* (London, 1976) and *Dialect* (London, 1977).

11. Muriel Saville-Troike, *Bilingual Children* (Resource Document prepared for the Centre for Applied Linguistics, Arlington, Virginia, 1973).

12. Letter from Walter Clegg, MP for North Fylde, to *The Times,* 18 August 1978.

13. John Wright, *Bilingualism and Schooling in Multilingual Britain* (London, 1978). This article gives an excellent account, and evaluation, of the successes and failures of some schemes to improve the situation in Britain.

14. Margaret Donaldson, *Children's Minds* (London, 1978). For a brilliant and elaborate discussion of this point see L. S. Vygotsky, *Thought and Language* (Cambridge, Mass., 1962).

15. Courtney B. Cazden, "How Knowledge About Language Helps the Classroom Teacher—Or Does It: A Personal Account," *Urban Review* (1976).

❧ MAXINE HONG KINGSTON

"How Are You?" "I Am Fine, Thank You. And You?"

WITH NO MAP SENSE, I took a trip by myself to San Francisco Chinatown and got lost in the Big City. Wandering in a place very different from Stockton's brown and gray Chinatown, I suddenly heard my own real aunt call my name. We screamed at each other the way our villagers do, hugged, held hands. "Have you had your rice yet?" we shouted. "I have. I have had my rice." "Me too. I've eaten too," letting the whole strange street know we had eaten, and me becoming part of the street, abruptly not a tourist, the street mine to shout in, not to worry if my accent be different. She introduced me to the group of women she'd been talking to. "This is my own actual niece," she said in a way that they would understand that I was not just somebody she called a niece out of politeness but a blood niece. "Hello, Aunt. Hello, Aunt," I said, but mumbling mumbling because there are different kinds of aunts depending on whether they're older or younger than one's mother, and both addresses familiar. And they'd tease also for being too distant, for calling them Lady or Mademoiselle, affectations. Some people feel insulted at young, low-rank titles, but there are also Americanized women who don't like being older, and me not good at ages anyway, and some not wanting to be

These excerpts are from *Gold Mountain Heroes,* a work in progress.

roped into your family, and some not liking to be excluded. "Who is this?" the women asked, one of them pointing at me with her chin, the way Chinese people point, the other with her rolled up newspaper. This talking about me in the third person, this pointing at me—I shoved the resentment down my throat; they do not mean disdain—or they *do* mean disdain, but it's their proper way of treating young people—mustn't dislike them for it. "This is my real niece come to visit me," my aunt said, as if I had planned to run into her all along. "Come see my new apartment," she said to me, turned around and entered the doorway near which we were standing.

We went up the stairs, flight after flight. I followed her along a hallway like a tunnel. But her apartment need not be dismal, I told myself; these doors could open into surprisingly large, bright, airy apartments with shag carpets. "Our apartment is very small," she warned, her voice leading the way. "Not like a regular house. Not like your mother's big house." So she noticed space; I thought perhaps people from Hong Kong didn't need room, that Chinese people preferred small spaces.

When she opened the door, it just missed the sofa and didn't open up all the way because of a table. Stuff was stored along the walls on shelves above the furniture, which had things on top and underneath. I fitted myself in among the storage. "Cake?" asked my aunt. "Pie? Chuck-who-lick? Le-mun?" She went into the one-person kitchen. There wasn't room in the space between the sink and the stove for me to help. I sat on the sofa, which could open up into a bed.

"Small, isn't it?" she said. "Please have some cake."

"I just ate," I said, which was true.

She got herself some chocolate cake and lemon pie and sat next to me. "I saw those hoppies they tell about in the newspaper," she said. "Some of them talked to me. 'Spare change?' That's what they say. 'Spare change?' I memorized it." She held out her hand to show their ways. "'Spare change?' What does 'spare change' mean?" "They're asking if you have extra money." "Oh-h, I see," she said, laughing. "'Spare change?' How witty." She was silly compared to my mother; she giggled and talked about inconsequentials. "Condo?" she asked. "Cottage cheese? Football? Foosball?"

"Are you working?" I asked because it was odd that she was home in the middle of a weekday. "Is it your day off?"

"No. I'm not working anymore."

"What happened to your hotel job? Didn't you have a hotel job?

As a maid?" I said "maid" in English, not knowing the Chinese word except for "slave." If she didn't know the word, she wouldn't hear it anyway. Languages are like that.

"I've been fired," she said.

"Oh, no. But why?"

"I've been very sick. High blood pressure," she said. "And I got dizzy working. I had to clean sixteen rooms in eight hours. I was too sick to work that fast." Something I liked about this aunt was her use of exact numbers. "Ten thousand rooms per second," my mother would have said; "Uncountable. Infinite." I did some math while she talked: half an hour per unit, including bathrooms. "People leave the rooms very messy," she said, "and I kept coughing from the ashes in the ashtrays. I was efficient until I fell sick. Once I was out for six weeks, but when I came back, the head housekeeper said I was doing a good job, and he kept me on." She said the name of the hotel; it was one of the famous ones. I had thought from the dirty work and low pay it was some flop house in Chinatown. She'd given us miniature soaps whenever she came to visit. "The head housekeeper said I was an excellent worker." My mother was the same way, caring tremendously how her employer praised her, never in so much trouble as when a boss reprimanded her, never so proud as when a forelady said she was picking cleanly or fast. ("Folaydee"; "chup-bo"—trouble; "bossu"; "day offu"—more Chinese American words.) "He said I speak English very well." She was proud of that compliment; I thought it was an insult, but it was too much trouble to try to explain to her why. When white demons said, "You speak English very well," I muttered, "It's my language too." The Japanese kids, who were always ahead of us socially, said the way to answer is, "Thank you. So do you."

"What do you do all day long now that you aren't cleaning hotel rooms?"

"The days go by very slowly. You know, in these difficult times in the Big City mothers can't leave their children alone. The kidnappers are getting two thousand dollars per child. And whoever reports a missing child to the FBI gets turned over to Immigration. So I posted ads, and one in the newspaper too, that I wanted to mind children, but I haven't gotten any customers. When the mothers see the apartment, they say No." Of course. No place to run, no yard, no trees. "I could mind four or five children," she said. "I'd make as much money as cleaning the hotel. They don't want me to watch their children because I can't speak English. My own son doesn't talk to me," she said. "What's 'nutrition'?"

"It has to do with food and what people ought to eat to keep healthy."

"You mean like cooking? He's going to college to learn how to cook?"

"Well, no. It's planning menus for big companies, like schools and hospitals and the army. They study food to see how it works. It's the science of food," but I did not feel I was giving an adequate explanation, the only word for "science" I knew was a synonym or derivative of "magic," something like "alchemy."

"You speak Chinese very well," she said. But I could talk to her. Some people dry up each other's language.

II

The first of the brother's students to go to Vietnam was Alfredo Campos, who was twenty-one years old, the age when the brother had graduated from college. Alfredo had emigrated alone to California from Puerto Rico when he was nineteen. He was going to high school to learn a job away from the grape fields. He asked the brother to help him write letters to his eleven brothers and sisters, who could practice their English and someday come to the U.S. one by one. But suddenly in the middle of the semester he dropped out and went to Vietnam, from where he wrote letters. "I send honor to you, my Teacher," he wrote. "I send congratulations to you, my Teacher, on Christmas Day."

The brother had to answer Alfredo's letters. "Dear Alfredo," he wrote, and could not think of the next thing to say. "I hope you are well," he wrote because that was the truth. He did hope he was well. "Take care of yourself," he wrote, but not "Take *good* care of yourself" because Alfredo might have to kill someone in order to do that. The brother kept writing the same letter, "I am fine. I hope you are too." He did not send any appropriate war or history books or peace pamphlets. Alfredo might let down his guard at a crucial moment and not defend himself. He did not mention religion, though he knew Alfredo had one. If he put doubt into him, maybe he would hesitate at the wrong moment and get shot. Nor did he ask if he had killed anybody yet.

He did not want him to kill.

He did not want him to get killed.

After awhile, Alfredo quit writing, and the brother joined the Navy. An officer read his records and assigned him to teach English classes on board ship, remedial reading to grown men who were so ignorant they did not know where Indochina was or

Europe or the various states. There were people who didn't know all the letters of the alphabet, or they knew them but out of order.

"What do you see when you read?" he asked. "Describe what you see." Obviously they were not seeing the stories or ideas.

"I see small, small words, and they get darker and darker." Poor boys; they must have joined the Navy to get away from school, and here they were in school again.

"I see words, and the ink runs together. Then it's dark."

"I see letters at first, but they turn into colors that jump around."

"Colors. Blue, I think. Or purple."

"The words look like they're melting in the water. They float."

"I see a mist. Like fog."

"Dark like a tunnel."

"Like in an elevator."

"Like a tight cave. And I can hardly breathe."

"Can't I stop reading now? I'm getting dizzy."

"I have a headache."

"My eyes are watering."

"I can't breathe."

"My eyes hurt."

"Dark. Claustro."

He taught writing by having them write home. They had a textbook with sample letters. "Dear Mom," the boys printed. "How are you? I am fine. I hope you are fine too. We sure have a lot to eat here. They keep you busy in the Navy. The weather has been cool/warm. Lots of love. Yours truly, Your Name." Some of the students copied it out just like that. "Your Name," they wrote.

What the brother wrote to his own parents because his Chinese vocabulary was small was "I am fine. I hope you are fine too." But when he wrote in English for the sisters and other brothers to translate, he found that in order not to worry anyone, he didn't have much to say except "How are you? I am fine."

His commanding officer asked him into his office and said that since he was a communications expert with language abilities, wouldn't he like to go to the Monterey Language School to study Chinese? "You studied French," said the C.O. "You speak Chinese too, don't you? Your records show language aptitude." A vision of Monterey leapt up like a mermaid out of the sea and lured him. He wanted that Pacific coast, that sunshine and fog, the red tile roofs among the dark trees, the fiery and white bougainvillea, the streets leading to the ocean—and school again, to be a student a luxury. "No," he said. "No, thank you," leaving quickly not to change his mind. If he learned Chinese better, or if he let on how much he already knew, the Navy would assign him to be a spy or an interrogator. The most pleasant job for interpreters was to monitor radio signals and phone calls coming from China. There was only one use the military had for Chinese language—war, the same use it had for raw materials and science. He would be assigned to gouge Viet Cong eyes, cattle prod their genitals. It wouldn't be Chinese poetry he'd be memorizing but the *Vietnamese Phrase Book* published by the Pentagon: "Welcome, Sir. Glad to meet you. How many are with you? Show me on your fingers." "Are you afraid of the enemy? Us?" "Do you place faith in America? Will the people fight for their freedom? We are here to help them in the struggle on the side of (1) the free world (2) the U.S. (3) the Allies (4) freedom (5) God." "Would they (1) support (2) join (3) fight on the side of (4) work for (5) sacrifice their lives for U.S. troops?" "Your nickname will be ——. My nickname is ——." "Do you believe in (1) U.S. victory (2) annihilation of Bolshevism?" "Open the door or we will force it." "Are you afraid? Why?" "If we cannot trust a man, (1) wink your right eye (2) place your left hand on your stomach (3) move your hand to the right, unnoticed, until we note your signal." "Is he your father? Village leader?"

The Vietnamese called their parents Ba and Ma; *phuoc* meant "happiness," "contentment," "bliss," the same as Chinese; *lan* was an orchid, the same as his mother's name; Vietnamese puns were like Chinese puns, *lettuce, life;* they probably also brought heads of lettuce home on holidays. *Study, university, love*—the important words the same in Chinese and Vietnamese. Talking Chinese and French, he'd be a persuasive interrogator-torturer. He would have to force a mother to choose between her baby with a gun at its belly and her husband hiding behind the thatch, to which she points silently with her chin. No, he would withhold his talents until America could make better use of them.

GENEVA SMITHERMAN

White English in Blackface, or Who Do I Be?

AIN NOTHIN IN a long time lit up the English teaching profession like the current hassle over Black English. One finds beaucoup sociolinguistic research studies and language projects for the "disadvantaged" on the scene in nearly every sizable black community in the country.[1] And educators from K-Grad. School bees debating whether: (1) blacks should learn and use only standard white English (hereafter referred to as WE); (2) blacks should command both dialects, i.e., be bi-dialectal (hereafter BD); (3) blacks should be allowed (??????) to use standard Black English (hereafter BE or BI). The appropriate choice having everything to do with American political reality, which is usually ignored, and nothing to do with the educational process, which is usually claimed. I say without qualification that we cannot talk about the Black Idiom apart from Black Culture and the Black Experience. Nor can we specify educational goals for blacks apart from considerations about the structure of (white) American society.

And we black folks is not gon take all that weight, for no one has empirically demonstrated that linguistic/stylistic features of BE impede educational progress in communication skills, or any other area of cognitive learning. Take reading. It's don been

Reprinted from *The Black Scholar* (May-June 1973) by permission.

charged, but not actually verified, that BE interferes with mastery of reading skills.[2] Yet beyond pointing out the gap between the young brother/sistuh's phonological and syntactical patterns and those of the usually-middle-class-WE-speaking-teacher, this claim has not been validated. The distance between the two systems is, after all, short and is illuminated only by the fact that reading is taught *orally.* (Also get to the fact that preceding generations of BE-speaking folks learned to read, despite the many classrooms in which the teacher spoke a dialect different from that of her students.)

For example, a student who reads *den* for *then* probably pronounces initial /th/ as /d/ in most words. Or the one who reads *doing* for *during* probably deletes intervocalic and final /r/ in most words. So it is not that such students can't read, they is simply employing the black phonological system. In the reading classrooms of today, what we bees needin is teachers with the proper attitudinal orientation who thus can distinguish actual reading problems from mere dialect differences. Or take the writing of an essay. The only percentage in writing a paper with WE spelling, punctuation, and usage is in maybe eliciting a positive *attitudinal* response from a prescriptivist middle-class-aspirant-teacher. Dig on the fact that sheer "correctness" does not a good writer make. And is it any point in dealing with the charge of BE speakers being "non-verbal" or "linguistically deficient" in oral communication skills—behind our many Raps who done disproved that in living, vibrant color?[3]

What linguists and educators need to do at this juncture is to take serious cognizance of the Oral Tradition in Black Culture. The uniqueness of this verbal style requires a language competence/performance model to fit the black scheme of things. Clearly BI speakers possess rich communication skills (i.e., are highly *competent* in using language), but as yet there bees no criteria (evaluative, testing, or other instrument of measurement), based on black communication patterns, wherein BI speakers can demonstrate they competence (i.e., *performance*). Hence brothers and sisters fail on language performance tests and in English classrooms. Like, to amplify on what Nikki said, that's why we always lose, not only cause we don't know the rules, but it ain't even our game.

We can devise a performance model only after an analysis of the components of BI. Now there do be linguists who supposedly done did this categorization and definition of BE.[4] But the descriptions are generally confining, limited as they are to discrete linguistic units. One finds simply ten to fifteen patterns cited, as for example, the most frequently listed one, the use of *be* as finite verb, contrasting with its deletion: (a) *The coffee be cold* contrasts with (b) *The coffee cold,* the former statement denoting a continuing state of affairs, the latter applying to the present moment only. (Like if you the cook, (a) probably get you fired, and (b) only get you talked about.) In WE no comparable grammatical distinction exists and *The coffee is cold* would be used to indicate both meanings. However, rarely does one find an investigation of the total vitality of black expressive style, a style inextricable from the Black Cultural Universe, for after all, BI connects with Black Soul and niggers is more than deleted copulas.[5]

The Black Idiom should be viewed from two important perspectives: linguistic and stylistic. The linguistic dimension is comprised of the so-called nonstandard features of phonology and syntax (patterns like *dis heah* and *The coffee be cold*), and a lexicon generally equated with "slang" or hip talk. The stylistic dimension has to do with *rapping, capping, jiving,* etc., and with features such as cadence, rhythm, resonance, gestures, and all those other elusive, difficult-to-objectify elements that make up what is considered a writer or speaker's "style." While I am separating linguistic and stylistic features, I have done so only for the purpose of simplifying the discussion since the BI speaker runs the full gamut of both dimensions in any given speech event.

I acknowledge from the bell that we's dealing with a dialect structure which is a subsystem of the English language; thus BE and WE may not appear fundamentally different. Yet, though black folks speak English, it do seem to be an entirely different lingo altogether. But wherein lies the uniqueness? Essentially in language, as in other areas of Black Culture, we have the problem of isolating those elements indigenous to black folks from those cultural aspects shared with white folks. Anthropologist Johnnetta Cole suggests that Black Culture has three dimensions: (1) those elements shared with mainstream America; (2) those elements shared with all oppressed peoples; (3) those elements peculiar to the black condition in America.[6] Applying her concepts to language,I propose the accompanying schematic representation.

Referring to the first column, contemporary BE is simply one of the many dialects of contemporary American English, and it is most likely the case that the linguistic patterns of BE differ from those of WE in surface structure only. There's no essential linguistic difference between *dis heah* and *this here,* and from a strictly

FEATURES SHARED WITH MAINSTREAM AMERICA	FEATURES SHARED WITH ALL OPPRESSED PEOPLES	FEATURES UNIQUE TO BLACK AMERICANS
Linguistic	*Linguistic*	*Linguistic*
1. British/American English lexicon	1. Superimposition of dominant culture's language on native language, yielding	Unique meanings attributed to certain English lexical items
2. Most aspects of British/American English phonology and syntax	2. Pidginized form of dominant culture's language, subject to becoming extinct, due to	*Stylistic*
	3. Historical evolution, linguistic leveling out in direction of dominant culture's dialect	Unique communication patterns and rhetorical flourishes

linguistic point of view, *God don't never change* can be written *God doesn't ever change* (though definitely not from a socio-cultural/political perspective, as Baraka quite rightly notes).[7] Perhaps we could make a case for deep structure difference in the BE use of *be* as finite verb (refer to *The coffee be cold* example above), but we be hard pressed to find any other examples, and even in this case, we could posit that the copula exists in the deep structure, and is simply deleted by some low-level phonological deletion rule, dig: The coffee is cold . . . The coffee's cold . . . The coffee cold. My conclusion at this point is that despite the claims of some highly respected Creole linguists (with special propers to bad Sistuh Beryl Bailey),[8] the argument for deep structure differences between contemporary BE and WE syntax can not pass the test of rigorous transformational analysis.

Referring to the second column, we note the psychological tendency of oppressed people to adopt the modes of behavior and expression of their oppressors (also, during the African slave trade, the functional necessity of pidginized forms of European language). Not only does the conqueror force his victims into political subjugation, he also coerces them into adopting his language and doles out special rewards to those among the oppressed who best mimic his language and cultural style. In the initial language contact stage, the victims attempt to assemble the new language into their native linguistic mold, producing a linguistic mixture that is termed *pidgin*. In the next stage, the pidgin may develop into a Creole, a highly systematic, widely used mode of communication among the oppressed, characterized by a substratum of patterns from the victim's language with an overlay of forms from the oppressor's language. As the oppressed people's identification with the victor's culture intensifies, the pidgin/Creole begins to lose its linguistic currency and naturally evolves in the direction of the victor's language. Reconstructing the linguistic history of BE, we theorize that it followed a similar pattern, but due to the radically different condition of black oppression in America, the process of *de-creolization* is nearly complete and has been for perhaps over a hundred years.

The most important features of BI are, of course, those referred to in column three, for they point us toward the linguistic uniqueness and cultural signficance of the Oral Tradition in the Black Experience. It should be clear that all along I been talkin bout that Black Experience associated with the grass-roots folks, the masses, the sho-nuff niggers—in short, all those black folks who do not aspire to white middle-class American standards.

Within this tradition, language is used as a teaching/socializing force and as a means of establishing one's reputation via his verbal competence. Black talk is never meaningless cocktail chit-chat but a functional dynamic that is simultaneously a mechanism for acculturation and information-passing and a vehicle for achieving group recognition. Black communication is highly verbal and highly stylized; it is a performance before a black audience who become both observers and participants in the speech event. Whether it be through slapping of hands ("giving five" or "giving skin"), Amen's, or Right on's, the audience influences the direction of a given rap and at the same time acknowledges or withholds its approval, depending on the linguistic skill and stylistic ingenuity of the speaker. I mean like a Brother is only as bad as his rap bees.

I

Toward a Black Language Model: Linguistic

While we concede that black people use the vocabulary of the English language, certain words are always selected out of that lexicon and given a special black semantic slant. So though we rappin bout the same language, the reality referents are different.

As one linguist has suggested, the proper question is not what do words mean but what do the users of the words mean? These words may be associated with and more frequently used in black street culture but not necessarily. *Muthafucka* has social boundaries, but not *nigger.*

Referring to the lexicon of BI, then, the following general principles obtain:

1. The words given the special black slant exist in a dynamic state. The terms are discarded when they move into the white mainstream. (Example: One no longer speaks of a "hip" brother; now he is a "togetha" brother.) This was/is necessitated by our need to have a code that was/is undecipherable by foreigners (i.e., whites).

2. In BI, the concept of denotation vs. connotation does not apply.

3. What does apply is shades of meaning along the connotative spectrum. For example, depending on contextual environment, the word *bad* can mean extraordinary; beautiful; good; versatile; or a host of other terms of positive value. Dig it: after watching a Sammy Davis performance, a BI speaker testified: "Sammy sho did some *bad* stuff," i.e., extraordinary stuff. Or upon observing a beautiful sister: "She sho is *bad,*" i.e., beautiful, pretty, or good-looking. Or, noticing how a brother is dressed: "You sho got on some *bad* shit," i.e., *good* shit = attractively dressed.

Note that the above examples are all in the category of *approbation.* It is necessary to rap bout *denigration* as well, since certain words in the black lexicon can frequently be used both ways. Consider the word *nigger,* for instance. "He's my main nigger" means my best friend (hence, approbation); "The nigger ain't shit," means he's probably lazy, trifling, scheming, wrong-doing, or a host of other *denigrative* terms, depending on the total context of the utterance.

4. Approbation and denigration relate to the semantic level; we can add two other possible functions of the same word on the grammatical level: *intensification* and *completion.* Slide back to *nigger* for a minute, and dig that often the word is void of real meaning and simply supplies the sentence with a subject. "Niggers was getting out of there left and right, then the niggers was running, and so the niggers said . . ." etc., etc., my point being that a steady stream of overuse means neither denigration nor approbation. Some excellent illustrations of this function of the word are to be found in *Manchild in the Promised Land,* where you can observe the word used in larger contexts.

To give you a most vivid illustration, consider the use of what WE labels "obscenities." From the streets of Detroit: (a) "That's a bad *muthafucka.*" Referring to a Cadillac Eldorado, obviously indicating approval. (b) "He's a no-good *muthafucka.*" Referring to a person who has just "put some game" on the speaker, obviously indicating disapproval. (c) "You *muthafuckin* right I wasn't gon let him do that." Emphasizing how correct the listener's assessment is, obviously using the term as a grammatical intensifier, modifying "right." (d) "We wasn't doin nothing, just messin round and *shit.*" Though a different "obscenity," the point is nonetheless illustrated, "shit" being used neutrally, as an expletive (filler) to complete the sentence pattern; semantically speaking, it is an empty word in this contextual environment.

Where I'm comin from is that the lexicon of BI, consisting of certain specially selected words, requires a unique scheme of analysis to account for the diverse range and multiplicity of meanings attributed to these words. While there do be some dictionaries of Afro-American "slang," they fail to get at the important question: what are the psycho-cultural processes that guide our selection of certain words out of the thousands of possible words in the Anglo-Saxon vocabulary? Like, for instance, Kochman[9] has suggested that we value action in the black community, and so those words that have action implied in them, we take and give positive meanings to, such as *swing, game, hip, hustle,* etc.; whereas words of implied stasis are taken and given negative connotations, such as *lame, square, hung-up, stiffin and jivin,* etc. At any rate, what I've tried to lay here are some suggestions in this particular linguistic dimension; the definitive word on black lexicon is yet to be given.

I shall go on to discuss the stylistic dimension of black communication patterns, where I have worked out a more definitive model.

II
Toward a Black Language Model: Stylistic

Black verbal style exists on a sacred-secular continuum, as represented by the accompanying scheme. The model allows us to account for the many individual variations in black speech, which can all be located at some point along the continuum.

The sacred style is rural and Southern. It is the style of the black preacher and that associated with the black church tradition. It

SACRED	SECULAR
Political rap style	*Political rap style*
EXAMPLES: Jesse Jackson Martin Luther King	EXAMPLES: Malcolm X Rap Brown
Political literary style	*Political literary style*
EXAMPLES: Barbara Ann Teer's National Black Theatre Nikki Giovanni's "Truth Is on Its Way"	EXAMPLES: Don Lee Last Poets

tends to be more emotive and highly charged than the secular style. It is also older in time. However, though I've called it "sacred," it abounds in secularisms. Black church service tends to be highly informal, and it ain nothin for a preacher to get up in the pulpit and, say, show off what he's wearing: "Y'all didn't notice the new suit I got on today, did y'all? Ain the Lord good to us. . . ."

The secular style is urban and Northern, but since it probably had its beginnings in black folk tales and proverbs, its *roots* are Southern and rural. This is the street culture style; the style found in barbershops and on street corners in the black ghettos of American cities. It tends to be more cool, more emotionally restrained than the sacred style. It is newer and younger in time and only fully evolved as a distinct style with the massive wave of black migration to the cities.

Both sacred and secular styles share the following characteristics:

1. Call and response. This is basic to black oral tradition. The speaker's solo voice alternates or is intermingled with the audience's response. In the sacred style, the minister is urged on by the congregation's Amen's, That's right, Reverend's, or Preach Reverend's. One also hears occasional Take your time's when the preacher is initiating his sermon, the congregation desiring to savor every little bit of this good message they bout to hear. (In both sacred and secular political rap styles, the "Preach Reverend" is transposed to "Teach Brother.") In the secular style, the response can take the form of a back-and-forth banter between the speaker and various members of the audience. Or the audience might manifest its response in giving skin (fives) when a really down verbal point is scored. Other approval responses include laughter and phrases like "Oh, you mean, nigger," "Get back, nigger," "Git down, baby," etc.

2. Rhythmic pattern. I refer to cadence, tone, and musical quality. This is a pattern that is lyrical, sonorous, and generally emphasizing sound apart from sense. It is often established through repetition, either of certain sounds or words. The preacher will get a rhythm going, conveying his message through sound rather than depending on sheer semantic import. "I-I-I-I-I-Oh-I-I-Oh, yeah, Lord-I-I-heard the voice of Jesus saying. . . ." Even though the secular style is characterized by rapidity, as in the toasts (narrative tales of bad niggers and they exploits, like Stag-O-Lee, or bad animals and they trickeration, like the Signifying Monkey), the speaker's voice tone still has that rhythmic, musical quality, just with a faster tempo.

3. Spontaneity. Generally, the speaker's performance is improvisational, with the rich interaction between speaker and audience dictating and/or directing the course and outcome of the speech event. Since the speaker does not prepare a formal document, his delivery is casual, nondeliberate, and uncontrived. He speaks in a lively, conversational tone, and with an ever-present quality of immediacy. All emphasis is on process, movement, and creativity of the moment. The preacher says "Y'all don wont to hear dat, so I'm gon leave it lone," and his audience shouts, "Naw, tell it Reverend, tell it!," and he does. Or, like, once Malcolm mentioned the fact of his being in prison, and sensing the surprise of his audience, he took advantage of the opportunity to note that all black people were in prison: "That's what America means: prison."

4. Concreteness. The speaker's imagery and ideas center around the empirical world, the world of reality, and the contemporary Here and Now. Rarely does he drift off into esoteric abstractions; his metaphors and illustrations are commonplace and grounded in everyday experience. Perhaps because of this concreteness, there is a sense of identification with the event being described or narrated, as in the secular style where the toast-teller's identity merges with that of the protagonist of his tale, and he becomes Stag-O-Lee or Shine; or when the preacher assumes the voice of God or the personality of a Biblical character. Even the experience of being saved takes on a presentness and rootedness in everyday life: "I first met God in 1925. . . ."

5. Signifying. This is a technique of talking about the entire audience or some member of the audience either to initiate verbal "war" or to make a point hit home. The interesting thang bout this rhetorical device is that the audience is not offended and realizes—naw, expects—the speaker to launch this offensive to achieve his desired effect. "Pimp, punk, prostitute, Ph.D.—all the P's— you still in slavery!" announces the Reverend Jesse Jackson. Malcolm puts down the nonviolent movement with: "In a revolution, you swinging, not singing." (Notice the characteristic rhythmic pattern in the above examples—the alliterative poetic effect of Jackson's statement and the rhyming device in Malcolm's.)

An analysis of black expressive style, such as presented here, should facilitate the construction of a performance instrument to measure the degree of command of the style of any given BI speaker. Linguists and educators sincerely interested in black education might be about the difficult, complex business of devising such a "test," rather than establishing linguistic remediation programs to correct a nonexistent remediation. Like in any other area of human activity, some BI rappers are better than others, and today's most effective black preachers, leaders, politicians, writers are those who rap in the black expressive style, appropriating the ritual framework of the Oral Tradition as vehicle for the conveyance of they political ideologies. Which brings me back to what I said from Jump Street. The real heart of this language controversy relates to/is the underlying political nature of the American educational system. Brother Frantz Fanon is highly instructive at this point. From his "Negro and Language," in *Black Skins, White Masks:*

> I ascribe a basic importance to the phenomenon of language. . . . To speak means . . . above all to assume a culture, to support the weight of a civilization. . . . Every dialect is a way of thinking. . . . And the fact that the newly returned [i.e., from white schools] Negro adopts a language different from that of the group into which he was born is evidence of a dislocation, a separation. . . .

In showing why the "Negro adopts such a position . . . with respect to European languages," Fanon continues:

> It is because he wants to emphasize the rupture that has now occurred. He is incarnating a new type of man that he imposes on his associates and his family. And so his old mother can no longer understand him when he talks to her about his *duds,* the family's *crummy joint,* the *dump* . . . all of it, of course, tricked out with the appropriate accent.

> In every country of the world, there are climbers, 'the ones who forget who they are,' and in contrast to them, 'the ones who remember where they came from.' The Antilles Negro who goes home from France expresses himself in the dialect if he wants to make it plain that nothing has changed.[10]

As black people go moving on up toward separation and cultural nationalism, the question of the moment is not which dialect, but which culture, not whose vocabulary but whose values, not *I am* vs. *I be,* but WHO DO I BE?

Notes

1. For examples of such programs, see *Non-Standard Dialect,* Board of Education of the City of New York (National Council of Teachers of English, 1968); San-Su C. Lin, *Pattern Practices in the Teaching of Standard English to Students with a Non-Standard Dialect* (USOE Project 1339, 1965); Arno Jewett, Joseph Mersand, Doris Gunderson, *Improving English Skills of Culturally Different Youth in Large Cities* (U.S.Department of Health, Education and Welfare, 1964); *Language Programs for the Disadvantaged* (NCTE, 1965).

2. See, for example, Joan Baratz and Roger Shuy, ed., *Teaching Black Children to Read* (Center for Applied Linguistics, 1969); A. L. Davis, ed., *On the Dialects of Children* (NCTE, 1968); Eldonna L. Evertts, ed., *Dimensions of Dialect* (NCTE, 1967).

3. For the most racist and glaring of these charges, see Fred Hechinger, ed., *Pre-School Education Today* (Doubleday, 1966); for an excellent rebuttal, see William Labov, *Nonstandard English* (NCTE 1970); for a complete overview of the controversy and issues involved as well as historical perspective and rebuttal to the non-verbal claim, see my "Black Idiom and White Institutions," *Negro American Literature Forum,* Fall 1971.

4. The most thorough and scholarly of these, though a bit overly technical, is Walter Wolfram, *Detroit Negro Speech* (Center for Applied Linguistics, 1969).

5. Kochman is one linguist who done gone this route; see for instance his "Rapping in the Black Ghetto," *Trans-action,* February 1969. However, he makes some black folks mad because of what one of my students called his "superfluity," and others shame cause of his exposure of our "bad" street elements. Kochman's data: jam up with muthafuckas and pussy-copping raps collected from Southside Chicago.

6. Johnnetta B. Cole, "Culture: Negro, Black and Nigger," *The Black Scholar,* June 1970.

7. Imamu Baraka, "Expressive Language," *Home,* pp. 166–172.

8. See her "Toward a New Perspective in Negro English Dialectology," *American Speech* (1965) and "Language and Communicative Styles of Afro-American Children in the United States," *Florida FL Reporter* 7 (Spring/Summer 1969).

9. See Thomas Kochman, "The Kinetic Element in Black Idiom," paper read at the American Anthropological Association Convention, Seattle, Washington, 1968; also his *Rappin' and Stylin' Out: Communication in Urban Black America.*

10. Frantz Fanon, *Black Skin, White Masks,* trans. Charles Lamm Markmann (New York, 1967), pp. 17–40.

MONROE K. SPEARS

Black English

DOES "BLACK ENGLISH"—a dialect peculiar to American blacks—exist? The connotation of the term and the issue which it raises have a curious recent history.

In the old days, before, say, 1950, it is my impression that the casual observer, or man in the street, believed in the existence of a distinctive black dialect, though he would have been unlikely to call it Black English. The representation of the dialects of various ethnic minorities was a major form of American humor (from newspaper columnists and cartoonists to *Abie's Irish Rose*), and in the South black speech was accurately rendered from Mark Twain and Joel Chandler Harris to Ambrose Gonzales, Octavus Roy Cohen, Julia Peterkin, and DuBose Heyward. Not only authors but most white Southerners prided themselves on the fluency with which they could reproduce typical black dialect. Peculiarities were, of course, exaggerated, for comic or other effects, most obviously in the language of "stage darkies" from minstrel shows to Rochester, Stepin Fetchit, Amos n' Andy, and innumerable later black comics in movies and TV shows and situational comedies. The assumption that there is a distinctive black dialect, ethnically identifiable, is essential to this kind of humor; though with the more recent black comics, at least, awareness of their bidialectalism—their equal fluency in standard English which allows them to shift dialects at will—is equally essential.

By the early 1950s, however, scholarly investigations of American regional dialects had begun to appear, all pointing to the same conclusion: that there was no significant difference between the speech of blacks and whites of the same geographical origin and economic and educational status. Analyzing the interviews that were their primary source of evidence, scholars found that differences between black and white speech, which seemed on the surface to be considerable, were essentially statistical: that is, every apparent characteristic of black speech was also to be found in white speech, but with greater frequency among the blacks.[1] (This conclusion had been anticipated by Cleanth Brooks's study of 1935, in which, comparing the language of the *Uncle Remus* stories with L. W. Payne's records of current Alabama-Georgia dialect, he found the difference to be merely one of degree: the distinguishing marks of the dialect—as of most Southern speech—are its archaism and its resemblance to the provincial dialects of southwestern England, both these features being preserved from the language of the original settlers in the seventeenth and eighteenth centuries; the blacks' dialect being more isolated and less subject to educational and other influences, had simply changed less. Brooks's point was that Southerners, black or white, had no reason to consider their language inferior or incorrect; it was merely more conservative than and somewhat different in origin from the language of other regions.)[2] The skewed statistics, or greater linguistic conservatism, of blacks were obviously related to segregation, and the conclusions of linguists were in complete accord with, and gave support to, the movement toward integration in the 1950s and 1960s. The term *Black English* was rarely used because of possible racist implications; earlier racist explanations of black speech in terms of differences in anatomy (flat noses, thick lips, clumsy tongues, thick skulls and small brains), temperament (careless, lazy, incapable of sustained attention, childlike, excitable), or climate (slow and lethargic because of the heat) were indignantly rejected. Dialectal differences between blacks and whites, it seemed clear, were culturally determined and transmitted; in the era of integration there also seemed to be no doubt that the pedagogical objective should be to eliminate these differences as rapidly as possible.

The next phase began about 1965. By this time enormous numbers of blacks had migrated to the cities and formed black ghettoes; rather than integration, Black Power was militantly asserted, and "Black Consciousness" and "Black is Beautiful" became popular slogans. Sociolinguists in the inner cities were confronted by the urgent problem of formulating programs to deal with the linguistic and other educational difficulties—often desperate—of vast numbers of black children and adolescents. In their laudable concern to avoid suggesting that black speech was simply inferior or careless standard English, they refused to label it substandard or nonstandard or even dialectal, and hence arrived at the remarkably imprecise term *Black English.* Obviously the sociolinguists had powerful motives for arguing, and believing, that regional differences were unimportant, so that their government-sponsored materials and programs would be applicable not just in Washington but also in New York, Philadelphia, Detroit, Chicago, Los Angeles, and so on. Reviewing the Urban Language Series published by the Center for Applied Linguistics in Washington from 1966 to 1974, Lee Pederson remarks that the "Great Black English Controversy" was "a pseudo-issue for linguistics, but a gut-issue for marketeering."[3]

To establish Black English as not only separate but equal and uniform throughout America, it was necessary first to ignore or discredit the work of the dialect geographers and then to provide an alternate genealogy for Black English. This genealogy was based on the rediscovery of Gullah, the strange, archaic dialect spoken on the Sea Islands and nearby coasts of South Carolina and Georgia. Gullah had not only been recognized by the dialect geographers as the single distinctive black dialect in this country[4] but was also admitted to be a genuine creole. (Creoles are pidgins that become the principal and native languages of speech communities—for example, Haitian French, or Papiamento in Curaçao.) Furthermore, the definitive study of it, *Africanisms in the Gullah Dialect,* had been produced in 1949 by a great black linguist, Lorenzo Turner. Creolists and sociolinguists proceeded to construct an elaborate hypothesis assuming not only that Black English was a separate and distinct dialect but that it always had been; and that insofar as it resembled white English, it was because blacks had influenced whites, and not the other way around. According to this hypothesis, the creole which now survives only in Gullah was once spoken by slaves all over America (Plantation Creole), and by a process of decreolization became modern Black English.[5]

At this point I must make a brief personal digression. Though not a professional linguist, I have been more than casually interested in these questions. I grew up in South Carolina not far from the Gullah area; I spent a little time in Africa; and I am acquainted with the speech of a wide variety of American blacks.

When J. L. Dillard's *Black English* appeared in 1972, therefore, I was interested enough to work up the background and write a substantial review.[6] I praised it as "the first book-length study by a qualified linguist of the speech of black Americans" and "a convincing demonstration that black English exists as a distinct and fascinating dialect and that its study and use in teaching black children is very important." As popularization I thought it somewhat unscrupulous in turning conjectures into assumptions,[7] and as polemic somewhat addicted to exaggeration and overkill. For example, Dillard sees the Academic Establishment—in a mythological drama pervading the whole book—as engaged in a conspiracy to suppress the true knowledge of Black English, denying that it is different from the white regional dialects whose origins it traces back to Britain. This ancient and evil conspiracy (which somehow takes on overtones of British snobbery as well as of power and privilege) is now being exposed and overthrown by creolists, sociolinguists, and other students of minority languages, especially the Black English of the urban ghettoes. Down with Anglo-Saxon attitudes; up with minorities!

To simplify, we may call the three principal theses of the book the ontological, the historical, and the educational. (1) Black English is different from (Southern and standard) white English not only in vocabulary but in structure. It is not a corruption of white English but probably influenced white English more than it was influenced by it. At any rate, it is a separate, distinctive, and legitimate dialect. (2) Black English originated in a West African–English Pidgin which developed into a Plantation Creole once spoken by slaves all over the United States and still spoken by the Gullahs of coastal South Carolina and Georgia; the characteristic structure of this creole is still preserved in modern Black English. (3) Bidialectalism (or biloquialism or bilingualism) should be the method and goal of language instruction. This means recognizing both the legitimacy of the black student's native speech and the special problems he has in learning standard English; in practice, it means teaching him standard English as if it were a foreign language. My own view was that Dillard was successful in establishing (1) and (3), but that (2), the historical thesis deriving Black English from a hypothetical creole perhaps like modern Gullah, while not inherently improbable, rested on a tendentious interpretation of insufficient evidence.[8]

Since that time, what new evidence I have seen and what new arguments on both sides I have read, together with my own further reflections, have inclined me to take a less positive position on (1) and (3) and to feel even greater skepticism about (2). But let us look briefly at some of the specific issues.

(1) Following William A. Stewart and others, Dillard argues that Black English differs not only in vocabulary but in structure, and that its verb system "reveals the greatest difference from white American dialects—as from British dialects—and the closest resemblance to its pidgin and creole ancestors and relatives."[9] Aspect is more important than tense. Tense can be omitted in Black English, provided the necessary time cues are given elsewhere: *He go yesterday.* Distinctions of meaning are shown most clearly in the various negative forms. "When *he ain' go* is the negative of *he go,* the verb base marks a point-of-time category. This, again, is a creole language characteristic, and is very different from Standard English" (p. 42). "*He ain' go* is the negative for a momentary action, whether or not in the past. *He ain' goin'* is the negative of a progressive action, whether or not in the past" (p. 43). Thus forms such as *He stood there and he thinkin'* are possible. Verbs in the Aspect category "are marked for the ongoing, continuous, or intermittent quality of an action rather than for the time of its occurrence. . . . This is perhaps the most basic difference from Standard English, since a speaker of Standard English must mark tense but can choose to indicate or to ignore the ongoing or static quality of an action. Black English gives the speaker an option with regard to tense, but its rules demand that he commit himself as to whether the action was continuous or momentary" (pp. 43–44). These categories express important differences in meaning. "If one says of a workman, *He workin' when de boss come in* he is paying the worker no compliment; the work is coterminous with the presence of the boss. . . . On the other hand, *He be workin' when de boss come in* means that the work went on before and after the boss's entry. . . . One might also say to a scorned acquaintance's rare intelligent remark, *You makin' sense, but you don't be makin' sense* meaning something like 'You've blundered into making an intelligent statement for once . . .'" (pp. 45–46). *Been* marks an action which is decidedly in the past; it can be called Perfective Aspect; like West African languages, Black English has also a contrasting Immediate Perfective Aspect, for which the preverbal form is *done: I done go, I done went, I done been gone.* The auxiliary *have* is replaced by *been, done,* and *is:* thus for standard English "Have you seen him?" there is Black *Is you see(n) him?* The contrast between *be* and zero as copula markers is significant: *My*

brother sick means that the sickness is currently in effect, but of short-term duration; *My brother be sick* indicates a long-term illness (pp. 46–48, 52).

Dillard, by this kind of analysis, certainly makes the point very effectively that Black English is a legitimate dialect, not just an inferior or corrupt form of standard English. (No linguist would need to be convinced of this, but lay readers might.) On the other hand, the most authoritative scholars say that there is no feature of the verb system to be found among blacks that does not also occur among whites, though they are more common among blacks.[10] The examples given by Dillard of *be* as marker of habituative aspect have been shown to have parallels in Irish, Welsh, and Anglo-Irish;[11] it is not peculiar to Black English, and may well have arrived in it through the influence of Irish or Welsh settlers, of whom there were many in the South. The urban sociolinguists are ignorant of white Southern speech and especially of the speech of poor whites, say the linguistic geographers;[12] they do not compare the speech of their ghetto blacks to that of poor white migrants to the cities.

Analyzing numerous studies of the linguistic features of black speech, David Shores finds the most frequently mentioned of them to be: the uninflected plural (*five girl*), the uninflected possessive (*the boy hat*), the uninflected third person singular (*he think*), the uninflected past tense and participle (*he play, he has play*), the absence of the copula (*he here*), the uninflected *be* (*it be*), overinflection (*I knows*), final consonant reduction (*firs*), the existential *it* (*it is a man there*), and question inversion (*I want to know can he go*). But all these are also to be found in white Southern speech, and those who know most about regional dialects agree in finding the difference to be statistical only.[13] A particularly striking case is that of Beryl Bailey, a Jamaican creolist who, in a famous article of 1965, suggested "that the Southern Negro 'dialect' differs from other Southern speech because its deep structure is different, having its origins as it undoubtedly does in some proto-creole grammatical structure."[14] Using as her material the speech of the narrator in Warren Miller's *The Cool World,* she selected four structures as distinctively black: "the absence of the copula (zero copula), the marked forms which are 'past and future,' the negation markers *ain't* and *don't,* and the treatment of *there* and 'possessive *their.*'" In an equally famous article of 1970, Juanita Williamson, herself a black and an experienced student of Southern dialects, analyzed numerous examples of Southern white speech in terms of these four "distinctively Negro" structures, and found the structures occurring frequently in them all. (The examples included an article by a white "redneck" klansman, the speech of white characters in a wide variety of recent Southern novels, and samples of Southern white speech quoted in various travel books, articles, and newspapers, with a final collection from Ms. Williamson's first-hand observation.)[15] In another brief but significant article, Ms. Williamson demolished the notion that "existential *it*" is peculiar to the black ghetto, tracing its honorable lineage not only to white Southerners but to Shakespeare and *Cursor Mundi.*[16] And in another she proves that the sociolinguists are wrong in saying that whites always invert word order in questions, while blacks do not. "Descriptions of the black American's speech which indicate that the omission of *be, do,* or *have* in the direct question is found in the speech of the black person but not in standard English do not take into consideration actual American usage."[17]

(2) A few final words on the creolist hypothesis. Lorenzo Turner, in his great study, stressed the uniqueness of Gullah and the impossibility of extrapolating from it to other black dialects. Gullah was a very special case, a language spoken by slaves who lived for centuries in almost total isolation on the Sea Island rice plantations, developing their own combination of archaic English and African languages. Only a few words of Gullah penetrated the surrounding region, and in my own experience black as well as white speakers in this region found Gullah fascinating but almost wholly unintelligible. To prove that Black English is a decreolization of Gullah would require far more evidence than has yet been forthcoming.[18]

Logically, there is no need to prove that Black English has a creole deep structure or substratum in order to establish its distinctiveness as a dialect. Whatever *dialect* means (and linguists do not agree), recognizability is a sufficient practical criterion; and this may be based on statistical incidence of vocabulary and pronunciation just as well as on grammatical structure. Why, then, so much emphasis on an argument so hypothetical and supported by so little evidence? Partly, I suspect, to justify a monolithic concept of Black English; partly to assert black identity and independence, turning the tables on the white man by proving that black influenced white linguistically; and perhaps most of all, to satisfy the yearning to find black roots in Africa. (The parallel with Alex Haley's *Roots* and the two enormously popular TV series based on it is, in fact, striking: the appeal is based on motives any decent person must find sympathetic, but in both cases, they lead to a highly simplistic version of history and a highly emotional concept of evidence.)

My own opinion is that history interpreted in terms of affirmative action or radical chic is not going to help blacks; there is no black history any more than there is black truth or black justice. For human beings, black or white, there is no escape from the constant struggle to keep in touch with reality; to abandon blacks to fantasies is to patronize and ultimately to betray them.

(3) No genealogy or pedigree is required to demonstrate the legitimacy of black dialect. Everyone needs to respect and take pride in his native way of speaking, which should never be dismissed by teachers as merely careless or incorrect. Leonard Bloomfield stated the principle well in 1933:

> For the native speaker of sub-standard or dialectal English the acquisition of standard English is a real problem, akin to that of speaking a foreign language. To be told that one's habits are due to "ignorance" or "carelessness" and are "not English," is by no means helpful. Our schools sin greatly in this regard.[19]

But Bloomfield had no doubt that the objective should be the prescriptive teaching of standard English. Only Black Power militants, extreme linguistic relativists, and holders of other paradoxical positions would be likely to deny that bidialectalism is a useful pedagogical device in elementary school, though I gather there is some disenchantment with teaching English as a foreign language, the methods used for teaching foreign languages not being notably successful for their original purposes either. Interestingly enough, those who are most suspicious of bidialectalism as an educational aim are black college educators. In an article based on evidence from hundreds of black educators from more than sixty traditionally black colleges, David Shores found that "they refuse to accept Black English as a separate dialect independent of American White English."[20] What bothers them most is "that people in the Black English business give the impression that these features are in the speech of all Blacks and that all Blacks, regardless of age, region, and social class, speak alike. Furthermore, they view with suspicion . . . the whole enterprising nature (and I use the word advisedly, for Blacks have recognized that Black English is a booming business) of the investigation of Black speech. They are especially put off by the linguists who say that it was they who have studied, described, and have struggled to get Black English accepted as a legitimate language" (p. 184). They "consider the best policy as that of trying to eliminate nonstandard features from the speaking and writing of their students, insofar as that is possible" (p. 185), recognizing that the public does not judge speech with the same tolerance that linguists do.

Some may consider these black educators to be excessively concerned with getting ahead as a goal for their students; but they are shrewd, practical people, and their attitude is understandable. They are certainly right in objecting to the notion of Black English as a monolithic entity and in their feeling that anyone who encourages students to believe Black English is acceptable at the top levels of our society is perpetrating a cruel hoax. Whites, whatever their native dialect, have exactly the same educational problem, though often in lesser degree. Everyone has to learn the basic difference between spoken and written language, and then the kinds of language, oral or written, appropriate to many different situations and contexts. To purify the dialect of the tribe, as Eliot and Mallarmé put it unforgettably, is a task worthy of a lifetime for us as for our dead masters; trying to learn to use words requires all the knowledge, cultivation of taste, and subtlety of discrimination we can manage to acquire. The way a man speaks—his idiolect, in linguistic jargon—is one of his most individual and revealing characteristics, and different in each person; hence the study of language is infinitely complex. Dialect geography will remain perennially fascinating because the relation of people to places is important to their individual and collective histories, and language is a cherished part of their heritage. In this light, the simplistic concept of Black English is not helpful; and Dillard's later vision of All-American English, consisting of Network Standard (pure, nonregional offspring of Colonial Koiné, itself descendant of Plantation Creole), surrounded from sea to shining sea by International English, is not an inspiring one. Let us hope instead for the continued flourishing of many black dialects—some, of course, indistinguishable from white—and rejoice that they have been accurately represented by novelists of both races (Ellison, Wright, Baldwin; Faulkner, O'Connor, Welty) and that some of their special flavor and rhythm, with their exceptional vitality and flair for imaginative metaphor, may be seen in the poetry of Gwendolyn Brooks, Ishmael Reed, Philip Levine, and many others.

Notes

1. Raven I. McDavid, Jr., and Lawrence M. Davis, "The Dialects of Negro Americans," in M. Estellie Smith, ed., *Studies in Linguistics in Honor of George L. Trager* (The Hague, 1972), pp. 303–312; David L. Shores, "Black English and Black Attitudes," in David L. Shores and Carole P. Hines, eds., *Papers in Language Variation* (Alabama, 1977), pp. 177–187.

2. Cleanth Brooks, *The Relation of the Alabama-Georgia Dialect to the Provincial Dialects of Great Britain* (Baton Rouge, 1935) and "The English Language of the South" (1937) in Juanita Williamson and Virginia Burke, eds., *A Various Language: Perspectives on American Dialects* (New York, 1971), pp. 136–142.

3. Lee Pederson, "The Urban Language Series," *American Speech* 50 (1975): 106.

4. Riley B. Smith, "Research Perspectives on American Black English: A Brief Historical Sketch," *American Speech* 49 (1974): 24–39; Thomas Pyles, "Early American Speech Adoptions from Foreign Tongues," in Williamson and Burke, *A Various Language*, p. 77.

5. Though suggested as early as 1941 by Melville J. Herskovits, the "Creolist Hypothesis" was first proposed in 1965 by Beryl Bailey, "Towards a New Perspective in Negro English Dialectology," reprinted in Harold Allen and Gary Underwood, eds., *Readings in American Dialectology* (New York, 1971), pp. 421–427. It was then developed by William A. Stewart in 1968, "Continuity and Change in American Negro Dialects," reprinted in J. L. Dillard, ed., *Perspectives on Black English* (The Hague, 1975), pp. 233–247, and elsewhere; and most extensively expounded by J. L. Dillard in his *Black English* (New York, 1972) and *All-American English* (New York, 1975).

6. *New York Review of Books,* 16 Nov. 1972.

7. Stewart, for example, calls for further work on the two questions, the relationship between Gullah and other black dialects, and the relationship between black dialects other than Gullah and white dialects. Dillard seems to feel no need of confirmation. William Labov, in his *Social Stratification of English in New York City* (1966) and *Language in the Inner City* (1972), is careful to specify the exact nature and applicability of his evidence; the latter book, for example, deals with the speech (which he prefers to call Black English Vernacular) of "black youth from 8 to 19 years old who participate fully in the street culture of the inner cities." Dillard tends to ignore such specifications.

8. I am here quoting my review of Dillard's later book, *All-American English,* which appeared in the *New York Review of Books,* 17 July 1975.

9. *Black English,* p. 40. Subsequent page references are given in the text.

10. McDavid and Davis, "The Dialects of Negro Americans," pp. 306–307.

11. William A. Stewart was apparently the first to note this usage, in his 1967 article, "Sociolinguistic Factors in the History of American Negro Dialects," reprinted in Dillard, *Perspectives on Black English,* p. 231: "On various occasions, I have pointed out that many speakers of non-standard American Negro dialects make a grammatical and semantic distinction by means of *be,* illustrated by such constructions as *he busy* 'He is busy (momentarily)' or *he workin'* 'he is working (right now)' as opposed to *he be busy* 'he is (habitually) busy' or *he be workin'* 'he is working (steadily)', which the grammar of standard English is unable to make." William Labov noted that this "provides no strong argument for a Creole origin; the closest analogy is with the Anglo-Irish *be,* stemming from the Celtic 'consuetudinal' or habitual copula" (*Language in the Inner City,* p. 51). The Anglo-Irish, Irish, and Welsh forms are cited in *American Speech* 48 (1973): 144–146 and 50 (1975): 323–325.

12. See McDavid and Davis, "The Dialects of Negro Americans"; McDavid and G. J. Forgue, *La Langue des Américains* (Paris, 1972), pp. 242–250.

13. See Shores in Shores and Hines, *Papers in Language Variation,* and McDavid and Davis, "The Dialects of Negro Americans."

14. Bailey, "Towards a New Perspective," p. 422.

15. Juanita Williamson, "Selected Features of Speech: Black and White," in Williamson and Burke, *A Various Language,* pp. 496–507.

16. Williamson and Burke, *A Various Language,* pp. 434–436.

17. Juanita Williamson, "A Look at the Direct Question," in Lawrence M. Davis, ed., *Studies in Linguistics in Honor of Raven I. McDavid, Jr.* (Alabama, 1972), pp. 207–214.

18. The movie *Conrack* gave an accurate impression of the Gullah region, though with the commercialization of Hilton Head and St. Simon's Island, acculturation may take place with terrifying speed. Whatever one's doubts about decreolization, McDavid has well said that a process of neocreolization seems to be taking place in the urban ghettoes.

19. Leonard Bloomfield, *Language* (New York, 1933), p. 499.

20. Shores, in Shores and Hines, *Papers in Language Variation,* p. 183. Naturally enough, a great many blacks (and whites, too) have rushed to enlist under the banner of Black English. For example, Deborah Harrison and Tom Trabasso, eds., *Black English: A Seminar* (Hillsdale, N.J., 1976), based on a seminar given at Princeton in 1973; Thomas Kochman, ed., *Rappin' and Stylin' Out* (Urbana, 1972); and Geneva Smitherman, *Talkin and Testifyin* (Boston, 1977).

ISHMAEL REED

How Not to Get the Infidel to Talk the King's Talk

"HOW WILL WE eradicate Black English?" Dick Cavett, public television's resident Anglo-lover, asked a group of linguists and John Simon. "You'd have to eradicate the Black people," a linguist answered. Chilling thought, considering the fact that there are historical precedents for people being exterminated because they didn't speak and write the way others thought they should.

When his arguments failed to convince the linguists of the existence of a "standard English," guest John Simon said that Blacks should speak "'standard English' in order to get ahead," or as William Prashker wrote in the *New York Times* magazine section, "Black culture doesn't mean zip" when you're trying to impress "the man downtown." The Man downtown.

Of course, neither Prashker nor Simon and Cavett could explain the successes of Gerald Ford, or of New York City's Mayor Koch, who confuses "each other" with "one another." Nor did they explain the triumphs of Dwight Eisenhower, who introduced the word *finalize* and whose press conference transcripts do not obey the rules of good grammar.

Nelson Rockefeller, the late governor of New York, was a wealthy man, yet this man thought that the word *horrendous* was a word of praise. Really. The president of the United States says "fahm" for what we call "farm."

If people who make these errors are "idiots" as Simon says, then many of our elected officials, industrialists, and writers are idiots: "As I Lay Dying."

Did the powerful people who "rule" America—all white males according to the April 16, 1979, issue of *U.S. News and World Report*—"get ahead" by speaking like characters in a Henry James novel? Did oilmen? Did Teamster presidents? I doubt it.

You not gone make me give up Black English. When you ask me to give up my Black English you askin me to give up my soul. But for reasons of commerce, transportation hassleless mobility in everyday life, I will talk to 411 in a language both the operator and I can understand. I will answer the highway patrolman who stops me, for having a broken rear light, in words he and I both know. The highway patrolman, who grew up on Elvis Presley, might speak Black English at home, because Black English has influenced not only Blacks but whites too.

So when trying to get the infidel to talk so that the British Tea Company can keep an eye on the infidel, they should instruct the missionaries that appeals to "getting ahead" will be seen through by the millions of Black English followers both overt and covert. The phantom legions.

Don't blame the mass defections from "standard English" on them; their rulers were the first to surrender.

KATHRYN HELLERSTEIN

Yiddish Voices in American English

IN HER PREFACE to *Bloodshed and Three Novellas (1977),* Cynthia Ozick complains about constraints she felt in writing her peculiarly Jewish story, "Usurpation":

> It came to me that if only I had been able to write "Usurpation" in a Jewish language—Hebrew or Yiddish, or, say the Ladino spoken by Ibn Gabriol's descendants—it would have been understood instantly. No one would suppose it to be a story that leads nowhere, with no point.[1]

Indeed, if Ozick had been able to write the story in a Jewish language—Yiddish—it might have made more sense to its audience; but, in America, the audience for Yiddish is dwindling, along with the number of writers who feel compelled to use it. This makes Ozick's complaint no less serious, but, ironically, her need for a Jewish language reverses a trend begun nearly a century ago by East European Jews immigrating to America. Their language, Yiddish, thrived for about fifty years while its speakers tried to acculturate, especially by learning American English. The contrafluence of American English and Yiddish produced a dialect which is still spoken in communities of aging Jewish immigrants[2] and which is used by contemporary Jewish writers in prose where language itself is a crucial issue.

Yiddish speakers at the turn of the century exhibit in their writing an intense yearning for American English. The immigrant writers who chose to write English, such as Alexander Harkavy in his *American Letter-Writer and Speller* (1902) and Abraham Cahan in his novel *The Rise of David Levinsky* (1917), allowed (or were helpless against allowing) Yiddish to influence their prose. In the next generation, which has acquired American English, some Jewish writers express a yearning for Jewishness by the use, to varying degrees, of Yiddish words and syntax, from Philip Roth's vulgarly Americanized Yiddish clichés, to Bernard Malamud's ambivalently sentimental "Yinglish," to Saul Bellow's lyrical quotations from the "mamaloshen." Over the decades, the appearance of Yiddish in the works of these writers traces a development of American English, in which the language absorbs the East European Jewish immigration. Such linguistic appropriation is analogous to the social process of assimilation, in which aspects of the old culture survive in new forms. But, like assimilation, the linguistic incorporation of Yiddish into American English eliminates fundamental elements of the Jewish language. Thus, Cynthia Ozick, a writer of considerable power, wonders how "English, this Christian tongue" can "release" a story that is conceptually Jewish. The conflict between the writer's American vernacular and his/her Jewish identity results in a transformation of both language and the experience portrayed.

The Jewish immigrants at the turn of the century learned English at night schools, on the street, and from bilingual books compiled specifically for that purpose, such as Alexander Harkavy's *Amerikanisher Briefen-Shteler Un Speller—English un Yidish,* published in New York in 1892, revised and reissued in 1902. The 1902 edition includes, according to its title page, "business letters, family letters, love letters, inquiries, telegrams for birthdays and weddings. Also rules of reading and separate section for learning how to write." Harkavy's *American Letter-Writer and Speller* records the first step of the transition from Yiddish to English by the East European Jewish immigrants mainly in sample letters which appear on facing pages in Yiddish and English.

The paragraph introducing "the language of letters" reads (in translation):

> In the writing of letters one must be clear in the sense of the points one intends to write about, and these points must be put in an appropriate order: more important things must come earlier, and less important things must come later. The language of the letter

must be clear and exact; one must never use more words than is necessary to express what one has to write. (p. 46)

Harkavy's rule of "clear and exact language" presumes that conventional phrases or clichés are the exact way of expressing an idea, request, or sentiment in English. The Yiddish versions are also formulaic and formal, due in part to the Germanic spelling and numerous Germanisms then considered high style by enlightened Yiddish speakers. While he uses many clichés in English, Harkavy avoids Yiddish idioms, including Hebraic and Slavic words. A letter expressing "New Year's Wishes to a Friend," reads, "May fortune continue to smile upon you. May some favorable star light up the path you have selected, and guide you safely to the goal of your wishes" (p. 117). The Germanic *guter shtern,* "good star," is used instead of the more idiomatic Yiddish *mazl,* a Hebraic word which means fortune, or star, in the sense of a lucky star. Another letter portrays a father's response to his son's conventional birthday wish as "May you live 120 years," the lifespan of the patriarch Abraham. In colloquial Yiddish it would read "biz hundert un tzvantzik!" Harkavy avoids this idiom and chooses the abstract phrase "That your life may be a long one" or, in his Yiddish, "dos ayer zolt hobn lange yor" (pp. 104–105). Thus, Harkavy's Yiddish reflects the tendency of immigrant Jews to move away from traditional lore and religion of the Old Country. In a letter "to a friend at the death of his sister," the correspondent writes, "Her death is the more melancholy, as her youth and blooming health entitled her to a long and happy life. But the ways of nature are hidden and it was not in your power to prevent it to come" (p. 133). A religious Jew would comfort the bereaved not with reference to "the ways of nature," but rather to "the ways of the Lord."

On formal occasions—"from an ardent lover to a lady," "from a young workman to his sweetheart," "from a lady to a gentleman accusing him of infidelity and demanding the return of her letters"—Harkavy's conventional English chills even the most passionate ardor:

My Dear Miss Gordon:—

I write to you because the burning love which consumes my heart must find some expression. In your presence I am dumb, not daring to pour out to you the ardent devotion which consumes me. I hear that oftentimes you have thought me stupid and dull, while I was only intoxicated with your loveliness, and listening with eager delight to the music of your voice.

> That I love you with all the ardor and devotion of a first true love, I think you must have seen, but I pine for a smile to bid me hope, a word of encouragement to save me from despair.
>
> Will you grant that smile? Will you speak that word? I anxiously await your answer. (p. 145)

Harkavy thinks such phrases as "burning love," "the music of your voice," and "ardent devotion" suitable to the feelings of refined people. The immigrant's urge to become an American included the desire to become respectable and, for Harkavy, respectability means conventional, even hackneyed, phraseology.

Only one letter in the book resounds with the particulars of an actual voice: "From a Young Workman to his Sweetheart."

> Dear Tillie:—
>
> I have been long in love with you, but I was afraid to tell you. When I go with you to the theatre or park I am almost like a fool, and altogether unfit for company. I think of you all day, and at night I dream of my Tillie. I am well settled in work, and my wages are nine dollars a week. You and I can live comfortably on that. I hope, my dear, you will not be angry, for I am really in love. I cannot be happy unless you are mine. I was afraid to mention this to you, but if you will leave an answer at my lodgings, I will meet you next Sunday after dinner, at the park, where we will take a walk and have some coffee and cake. How happy shall I be to hear from you, but a thousand times more to think you will be mine. I am, my dear, your real lover. (p. 151)

We see Yiddish syntax in the English prose, such as "I have been long in love with you," resembling Harkavy's Germanic Yiddish, "ikh lib dikh shoin lang," and "I am almost like a fool," echoing the Yiddish construction literally, "bin ikh epes azoi vi a nar." The Yiddish-speaking immigrants learned American English to discover forms in which to fit their lives. Harkavy's letters display the range of this new language, from the ornate and hackneyed figures of speech, appropriate for formal or cultured communications, to the plainness and particularity of the workman's expression.

Abraham Cahan (1860–1951), one of the founders and the editor of the *Jewish Daily Forward,* wrote his second novel, *The Rise of David Levinsky,* in English. Although it has many characteristics of Harkavy's letters, Cahan's style incorporates formal and colloquial English, and tries to retain the flavor of Yiddish. While the process of learning English dominates the novel thematically, David also has to acquire the manner, mannerisms, and values of his new country. Here he is learning from his English teacher, Bender, ". . . watching intently not only his enunciation, but also his gestures, manners, and mannerisms, and accepting it all as part and parcel of the American way of speaking."[3] Throughout the book, Levinsky studies American mannerisms as "part and parcel" of the American language.

To achieve an effect of the idiomatic in his characters' conversations in both Yiddish and in English, Cahan inserts British colloquialisms. Often, to avoid the problem of direct quotation, he narrates what was said and how it was said:

> The most ignorant "man of the earth" among our people can read holy tongue (Hebrew), although he may not understand the meaning of the words. This was the case with Gitelson. "Saying, 'bless the Lord, O my soul'?" he asked reverently. "Why this chapter of all others?" "Because—why, just listen." With which I took to translating the Hebrew text into Yiddish for him. (p. 88)

When we do hear conversations which occur in Yiddish, but which the narrator translates for our benefit, they often sound like this: "'Cheer up, old man!' I said with bravado. 'America is not the place to be a ninny in. Come, pull yourself together'" (p. 89). And when Levinsky tries to speak English, as here, where he converses with his teacher, Bender, we hear this:

> "What do you mean by '*real* difference'?" he demanded. "I have told you, haven't I, that 'I wrote' is the perfect tense, while 'I have written' is the imperfect tense." This was in accordance with the grammatical terminology of those days.
>
> "I know," I replied in my wretched English, "but what is the difference between these two tenses? That's just what bothers me." (p. 134)

Although we are told that Bender speaks English as a native speaker should, and that David Levinsky speaks brokenly, we actually hear both voices speaking the same acceptable "wretched" English.

On occasion we hear the cadence of Yiddish syntax in Cahan's English, as when Nodelman's mother responds in Yiddish to her newly clean-shaven son:

> "I don't want to look like a man-dog," he explained, gaily to his mother, who was unpleasantly surprised by the change.
>
> "Man-dog nothing," she protested, addressing herself to me. "He was as handsome as gold in those whiskers. He looked like a

> regular monarch in them." And then to him: "I suppose it was that treasure of a wife you have who told you to have them taken off. It's a lucky thing she does not order you to have your foolish head taken off."
>
> "You better shut up, mama," he said sternly. And she did. (p. 179)

Nodelman's mama shuts up—she stops the flow of Yiddish idiom translated for us by the narrator as "handsome as gold," "regular monarch," "treasure of a wife." These expressions depend on exaggerated analogies for their humor and flavor, particularly the final joke where the wife's tendency to clip whiskers is extended to the whole head. In Cahan's prose we rarely hear this voice of Yiddish humor, and only in one instance is the English dialect of Yiddish speakers transcribed: "'Is that the vay to talk to a gentleman? Shame! Vere you lea'n up to be such a pig? Not by your mamma!'" (p. 230).

Cahan does not consistently control the levels of language from colloquial to formal, from dialogue to description, although he differentiates between voices and moods with more finesse than did Harkavy in his *Letter-Writer* of fifteen years earlier. It was up to the next generation, the children of immigrants or those who had themselves immigrated as very young children, to develop a style in American English which reflected the Yiddish origins of the author, yet which had the control of language required by novelistic art. Henry Roth's *Call It Sleep* (1934) is a case in point.

Roth portrays the psychological and perceptual development of an immigrant child, using various styles to dramatize David Shearl's growing comprehension of the contrast between his orderly home, the world of his mother Genya; and the heterogeneous, alien street, the world in which his father Albert precariously exists.

Immediately, Roth establishes the terms of his style through a dialogue. Though some of it is in English and some in Yiddish, all of it, in the context of the fiction, is in Yiddish. In this dialogue colloquial English represents spoken Yiddish:

> The harsh voice, the wrathful glare, the hand flung toward the child frightened him. Without knowing the cause, he knew that the stranger's anger was directed at himself. He burst into tears and pressed closer to his mother.
>
> "Quiet!" the voice above him snapped. Cowering, the child wept all the louder.

> "Hush, darling!" His mother's protecting hands settled on his shoulders.
>
> "Just when we're about to land!" her husband said furiously. "He begins this! This howling! And now we'll have it all the way home, I suppose! Quiet! You hear?"
>
> "It's you who are frightening him, Albert!" she protested.[4]

A page later, the conversation is recorded in incorrect Yiddish:

> This was that vast incredible land, the land of freedom, of immense opportunity, that Golden Land. Again she tried to smile.
>
> "Albert," she said timidly, "Albert."
>
> "Hm?"
>
> "Gehen vir voinen du? In Nev York?" [sic]
>
> "Nein. Bronzeville. Ich hud dir shoin geschriben." [sic] She nodded uncertainly, sighed. (p. 16)

By establishing this equivalence between colloquial English and Yiddish, Roth takes into account not only the levels of correspondence between fiction and fact, but also his American audience. Thus, through linguistic analogy, he reproduces the immigrant's experience of language in America. Roth writes idiomatic English to represent the Yiddish of the Jewish home and family, while broken English represents David's relationship to the outside world:

> In the street David spoke English.
>
> "Kentcha see? Id's coz id's a machine."
>
> "Oh!"
>
> "It wakes op mine fodder in de mawning."
>
> "It wakes op mine fodder too." (p. 21)

The challenge of the street is, for David, the challenge of forsaking Yiddish.

Unlike Cahan's awkward mixing of Yiddish idiom with a supposedly colloquial slang, Roth uses hardly any actual Yiddish words, idioms, or syntax. Nevertheless, Roth retains the sense that his characters speak Yiddish to each other and the dialogue seems as natural to American readers as it would have seemed in Yiddish to Yiddish speakers. For example, here David and his mother converse about a calendar numbered in black and red:

> He held back. "Show me where my birthday is."
>
> "Woe is me!" she exclaimed with an impatient chuckle. "I've shown it to you every day for weeks now."
>
> "Show me again."

> She rumpled the pad, lifting a thin plaque of leaves. "July"—she murmured, "July 12th . . . There!" She found it. "July 12th, 1911. You'll be six then."
>
> David regarded the strange figures gravely. "Lots of pages still," he informed her.
>
> "Yes."
>
> "And a black day too."
>
> "On the calendar," she laughed, "only on the calendar. Now do come down." (p. 19)

Two idiomatic phrases from Yiddish work their way naturally into the English prose. "Woe is me" (in Yiddish, "Vey iz mir") and David's observation about the color of the calendar number, "And a black day too," which echoes the idiom, "Geyn tzum schvartzn yor," or "go to the devil" (to the black year). In Yiddish, a "Schvartze tog" signifies a bad day, bearing bad tidings. Henry Roth's prose style alludes delicately to its Yiddish source, while the substance of his paragraphs evokes the immigrant's difficult transition from Yiddish to English.

After the Second World War, American Jewish writers depict immigrant characters who learned to speak English in America. In the fiction of Bernard Malamud, Saul Bellow, Philip Roth, and Cynthia Ozick, Yiddish-speaking Jews grow old, isolated from their *landsleit* (countrymen) and from their American-born children. Many of them speak a caricature of the Yiddish-English dialect, "Yinglish," to their children, the *Amerikaner-geborene,* who answer them in American English. Even when these old people converse with immigrants of their own generation, they speak this broken English as if they have forgotten the old language, Yiddish, and have not mastered the new one. They are caught between cultures, between languages.

In *The Magic Barrel* (1958), Bernard Malamud creates Yiddish speakers who converse in a stereotyped dialect of English. For example, in "The First Seven Years," Feld speaks the dialect to his daughter Miriam, who responds in American English:

> "So where did you go?" Feld asked pleasantly.
>
> "For a walk," she said, not looking up.
>
> "I advised him," Feld said, clearing his throat, "that he shouldn't spend so much money."
>
> "I didn't care."
>
> The shoemaker boiled up some water for tea and sat down at the table with a cupful and a thick slice of lemon.
>
> "So how," he sighed after a sip, "did you enjoy?"[5]

Malamud achieves the effect of the dialect beginning sentences with *so,* more or less equivalent in English to the Yiddish *Nu,* by leaving out conjunctions such as *that,* by using intensifiers just a shade off the idiomatic, such as *so* instead of *very much,* by omitting pronoun objects, by leaving out or adding auxiliary verbs, and by reversing the order of a sentence.

Feld speaks dialectal English not only to his American-born daughter, but also to Sobel, his helper in the shoe repair shop, "this Polish refugee . . . a landsman." Sobel confronts Feld with his feelings for Miriam in this passage:

> "What do you want from me, Sobel?"
> "Nothing."
> "I always treated you like you was my son."
> Sobel vehemently denied it. "So why you look for strange boys in the street they should go out with Miriam? Why don't you think of me?"
> "So what has my daughter got to do with a shoemaker thirty-five years old who works for me?" (pp. 13–14)

Both Polish immigrants communicate not in their native Yiddish, but in the awkward English dialect of their new home. Sometimes the dialect enters Malamud's narrative voice, especially when it represents a Yiddish speaker's point of view. In this sentence the object of the verb *discovered* is delayed to the end: "Ashamed to go in, Manischevitz gazed through the neon-lit window, and when the dancing couples had parted and drifted away, he discovered at a table on the side, towards the rear, Levine" (p. 50).

But Malamud uses very few actual Yiddish words in his characters' dialect, the exceptions being *schnorrer* (beggar) in *The Magic Barrel* and *Yiddishe kinder* (Jewish children) in "The Last of the Mohicans." However, he occasionally implies a Yiddish word. For instance, the character Susskind fills the role of the Yiddish businessman who seems to live on air, the *luftmentsch* (literally, person made of air). Fidelman asks Susskind,

> "Under such circumstances . . . how do you live?"
> "How do I live?" He chomped with his teeth. "I eat air."
> "Seriously?"
> "Seriously, on air. I also peddle. . . ." (p. 164)

Malamud uses the dialect to suggest comical pathos in his immigrant characters, but unlike Cahan and Roth, he doesn't dramatize the tension between the languages. All Malamud's Yiddish speakers are elderly, static, or declining. They assert themselves against their circumstances and their approaching demise by conning or manipulating people. The one younger character who knows Yiddish, Fidelman, prefers not to speak it. In *The Magic Barrel,* Yiddish has merged partway into English, and has hardened there, powerless, except through the sour pathos of old voices, to affect the world.

Saul Bellow views Yiddish differently. In his oft-quoted "Introduction" to the Dell paperback edition of *Great Jewish Short Stories* (1963), Bellow states, "Jews have been writing in languages other than Hebrew for more than 2,000 years."[6] He dismisses the *angst* of writing in American English—

> But I, American-born, . . . I am out of place in America. . . . An artist must be a perfect unit of time and place, at home with himself, unextraneous. . . . Who am I? Where do I come from? I am an accident. What right have I to scribble in the American language that comes no more naturally to me than it does to the laundry Chinaman? (p. 15)

—with this counterstatement:

> We are all such accidents. We do not make up history and culture. We simply appear, not by our own choice. We make what we can of our condition with the means available. We must accept the mixture as we find it—the impurity of it, the tragedy of it, the hope of it. (p. 16)

Bellow's acceptance of "the impurity of it," of the artist's condition, particularly the Jewish artist's condition, allows him a style enriched not only by the dialect of English spoken by immigrant Jews, but by whole phrases and passages of Yiddish.

In Bellow's *Herzog* (1964), Valentine Gersbach comforts Herzog, whom he is cuckolding, in a comically affected and misused Yiddish:

> "Hell with that. *Hob es in drerd.* I know Mady is a bitch. And maybe you think I never wanted to kick Phoebe in the ass. That *klippa!* But that's the female nature. . . . You've taken care of her for some time, okay, I know. But if she's got a disgusting father and a *kvetsch* of a mother, what else should a man do? And expect nothing in return. . . . The bitch is testing you. You're an ignorant professor. . . . She wants you to admit her importance. You're a *ferimmter mentsch.*"
>
> Moses, to save his soul, could not let this pass. He said quietly, "*Berimmter.*"

> "*Fe—be,* who cares. Maybe it's not so much your reputation as your egotism. You could be a real *mentsch*. You've got it in you."[7]

On the page before, Herzog has commented that

> Valentine loved to use Yiddish expressions, to misuse them, rather. Herzog's Yiddish background was genteel. He heard with instinctive snobbery Valentine's butcher's, teamster's, commoner's accent, and he put himself down for it—My God! those ancient family prejudices, absurdities from a lost world. (pp. 78–79)

For Herzog, good, high-class Yiddish is associated with childhood, with a world that no longer exists. He visits his Tante Taube, his stepmother and the widow of his father, who speaks a pathetically ungrammatical Yinglish:

> "Ach, Moshe, you changed."
>
> He limited his answer to a nod. "And how are you?"
>
> "You see. The living dead."
>
> "You live alone?"
>
> "I had a woman—Bella Ockinoff from the fish store. You knowed her. But she was not clean."
>
> "Come, Tante, sit down."
>
> "Oh, Moshe," she said, "I can't stand, can't lay. Better already, next to Pa. Pa is better off than me." (p. 301)

Tante Taube is one of "the living dead." Yiddish thrives only in Herzog's memory as, for example, in this remembered speech, in Yiddish, by his father:

> "I need my money. Who'll provide for me—you? I may bribe the Angel of Death a long time yet." Then he bent his knees a little—Moses read that old signal; he had a lifetime of skill in interpreting his father's gestures: those bent knees meant that something of great subtlety was about to be revealed. "I don't know when I'll be delivered," Father Herzog whispered. He used the old Yiddish term for a woman's confinement—*kimpet.* (p. 304)

In the world contemporaneous with Herzog, Yiddish takes the ludicrous form of Valentine Gersbach's mispronunciation, or the vaudeville voice of Simkin, the divorce lawyer:

> In conversation his voice was very small, meek, almost faint, but when he answered his secretary's signal and switched on the intercom, it suddenly expanded. He said loudly and sternly, "Yah?"
>
> "Mr. Dienstag on the phone."
>
> "Who? That schmuck? I'm waiting for that affidavit. Tell him

plaintiff will kick his ass if he can't produce it. He better get it in this afternoon, that ludicrous schmegeggy!" (pp. 41–42)

Sometimes Herzog expresses things to himself in Yiddish. When his brother Will meets him in his Ludeyville home in the Berkshires, the scene of his marital demise, Herzog observes his brother's reaction:

> Only his eyes were quietly and firmly shrewd, not dreaming. Moses, however, saw without the slightest of difficulty what Will was thinking. He expressed it to himself in Yiddish. *In drerd aufn deck. The edge of nowhere. Out on the lid of hell.* (p. 401)

Bellow translates the expression first idiomatically, then literally. In this setting of past destruction and future repair, Herzog uses the immigrants' language, replete with hope and despair.

In *Portnoy's Complaint* (1969), Philip Roth reduces the complex issues of cultural assimilation and language to an analogy between language and sex; the latter is a means by which the immigrant Jew's offspring assimilate into American culture. Indeed, Alexander Portnoy self-consciously asserts his ethnic identity against the American world by sleeping with gentile women: "What I'm saying . . . is that I don't seem to stick my dick up these girls, as much as I stick it up their backgrounds—as though through fucking I will discover America."[8] Portnoy connects his sexual experiences and his desire to acculturate precisely in terms of language when he recalls his efforts as an adolescent to pick up a *shikse* ice-skating. What makes gentile girls so attractive is, in part, the language their parents speak:

> Their fathers are men with white hair and deep voices who never use double negatives, and their mothers the ladies with the kindly smiles and the wonderful manners who say things like, "I do believe, Mary, that we sold thirty-five cakes at the Bake Sale." (p. 163)

But Portnoy's efforts toward discovering America are made difficult by language:

> I am afraid to open my mouth for fear that if I do no words will come out—or the wrong words. "Portnoy, yes, it's an old French name, a corruption of *porte noir,* meaning black door or gate. Apparently in the Middle Ages in France the door to our family manor house was painted . . ." et cetera and so forth. No, no, they will hear the *oy* at the end, and the jig will be up. (pp. 167–168)

In this example sexual union obliterates Portnoy's linguistic ethnicity:

> . . . and then this amazing creature—to whom no one has ever said "Shah" or "I only hope your children will do the same to you someday!"—this perfect, perfect stranger, who is as smooth and shiny and cool as custard, will kiss me—raising up one shapely calf behind her—and my nose and my name will have become as nothing. (p. 170)

First Portnoy envisions the pick-up—

> So after her—when she is safely out of sight—I madly begin to skate. "Excuse me," I will say, "but would you mind if I *walked* you home?" If I walked or if I walk—which is more correct? Because I have to speak absolutely perfect English. Not a word of Jew in it. (p. 184)

But the result is a broken leg: "For skating after *shikses,* under an alias, I would be a cripple for the rest of my days" (p. 186). Thus, trying to seduce America, Portnoy ends up crippled.

The true language, spoken by Portnoy's parents, consists of an American dialect, occasionally flavored with Yiddish words and phrases, often jolted by Yiddish-like sentence structures and inconsistent verb tenses. For example, Alexander's mother reprimands him at age thirteen, "'Alex, why are you getting like this, give me some clue? Tell me please what horrible things we have done to you all our lives that this should be our reward?'" (p. 26). Both questions are joined with an imperative statement. In proper English, these questions would be statements each containing an indirect question. By punctuating these statements as questions, Roth suggests that Mrs. Portnoy inflects her voice in the Yiddish manner. When Alexander kicks his mother in the shins, his father queries, "'—a little boy you want to be who kicks his own mother in the shins?'" (p. 136). Normal English syntactical order is inverted by putting the object *little boy* before the verb and omitting the question marker *do.* Occasionally, Portnoy's parents use Yiddish terms:

> "*Hamburgers,*" she said bitterly, just as she might say *Hitler,* "where they can put anything in the world in that they want—and *he* eats them. Jack, make him promise, before he gives himself a terrible *tsura,* and it's too late." (p. 35)

Tsura, a dialectical pronunciation of *tsore,* means trouble or calamity: another such term occurs, in Portnoy's narrative voice, as he rails to his psychiatrist about the constraints of Judaism on his psyche: "Oh, the *milchiks* and *flaishiks* besides; all those *meshuggeneh* rules and regulations on top of their own private craziness!" (p. 37). Though Portnoy sprinkles Yiddish words in his speech, and even quotes a supposedly Yiddish proverb ("Ven der putz shtet ligt der sechel in drerd"), he doesn't really know Yiddish: "Talk Yiddish? *How?* I've got twenty-five words to my name—half of them dirty, and the rest mispronounced" (p. 253). Yet, the influence of Yiddish is present even in this statement. One does not "talk" a language, one "speaks" it.

This Yiddish-English dialect, for Portnoy, is associated with screaming and debating, as well as certain syntactic patterns. For him, American English is a more civilized form of communication which he discovers when he visits the Iowa home of his college girl friend:

> My God! The English language is a *form of communication!* Conversation isn't just crossfire where you shoot and get shot at! Where you've got to duck for your life and aim to kill! Words aren't only bombs and bullets—no, they're little gifts, containing *meanings!* (p. 250)

Also unlike pure English, the Yiddish-English of Portnoy's home is a form of masturbation. At home, speaking the dialect and masturbating, Portnoy ritualistically engages in fantasy and dream. When he tells of breaking his leg ice-skating, having failed in his sexual and linguistic assault on a *shikse,* Portnoy asks his psychiatrist, "With a life like mine, Doctor, who needs dreams?" (p. 186).

In Portnoy's voice the Yiddish-inflected culture has hardened into neurotic family relations and a stereotyped dialect retaining the oddities of literal translation and none of the richness of Yiddish. The American culture and language remain inaccessible to him despite his efforts to attain them through sexual conquest. Within Yiddish-inflected culture, Portnoy masturbates, stimulating himself with the fantasy of the "other," the American. But no real communication, or intercourse, occurs. When Portnoy initially tries to enter American culture, by dreaming of relationships with gentile women, he attempts to learn the American language. Later, ironically, he finds himself "teaching these girls how to talk right, me with my five-hundred word New Jersey vocabulary" (p. 263). The grammatical ideal, personified in Portnoy's several gentile women friends, is not as gratifying or instructive as he had imagined it. Masturbation, his imagined means of communication, seems his only option. The one time he attempts intercourse with a Jewish woman, the *sabra* in Israel, Portnoy fails because the Jewish dialects of English, whether Yiddish or Hebrew, connote incest.

Language frustrates Portnoy, whether it be the dialect of his parents or the talk of the outside world. In his final statement— "It makes me want to *scream,* the ridiculous proportion of the guilt. . . . Because maybe that's what I need most of all, to howl. A pure howl, without any more words between me and it!" (p. 309)—Portnoy wants to assert himself vocally, not verbally. The psychiatrist—dispassionate observer of society—has the last word in the book, ironically, in the dialect and the accent of the old world: "So (*said the doctor*). Now vee may perhaps to begin Yes?" (p. 309).

For Philip Roth and Malamud, Yiddish figures as a spectral presence of the constraining, delimited, stultified past. For Roth, Yiddish has frozen halfway to English. The characters who speak the resulting dialect are caught between cultures. These characters, and Roth's prose, lack all sense of what Yiddish is as a language, of the culture behind it. Yiddish shows through the English prose as a flat, comical jargon spoken by caricatured types. Portnoy, who uses the voice of his id, who wants to put "the id back in Yid," takes the spirit and life out of Yiddish.

Cynthia Ozick allows a greater range of Yiddish to echo in her prose. In her story, "Envy; or, Yiddish in America" (1976), Ozick creates an effect of the multiplicity of Yiddish with several levels of dialect and idiom. The story itself concerns the isolated position of the Yiddish poet in America, Edelshtein. Lacking a translator, he envies the Yiddish fiction writer Ostrover, who has a large following of American readers because his work is translated. The question arises whether this story concerns the envy of one writer for another's readership—the envy of ego and reputation—or whether it concerns the death of Yiddish in America and Europe:

> Of what other language can it be said that it died a sudden and definite death, in a given decade on a given piece of soil? . . . Yiddish, a littleness, a tiny light—oh little holy light-dead, vanished, perished. Sent into darkness.[9]

Ozick uses Yiddish words and phrases to establish Edelshtein's point of view, as, for example, in the opening paragraph of the story:

> Edelshtein, an American for forty years, was a ravenous reader of novels by writers "of"—he said this with a snarl—"Jewish extrac-

> tion." He found them puerile, vicious, pitiable, ignorant, contemptible, above all stupid. In judging them he dug for his deepest vituperation—they were, he said, "*Amerikaner-geboren.*" Spawned in America, pogroms a rumor, *mamaloshen* a stranger, history a vacuum. Also many of them were still young, and had black eyes, black hair, red beards. A few were blue-eyed like the *cheder-yinglach* of his youth. School boys. He was certain he did not envy them, but he read them like a sickness. They were reviewed and praised and meanwhile they were considered Jews, and knew nothing. (p. 41)

By using the Yiddish words *Amerikaner-geboren, mamaloshen,* and *cheder-yinglach,* Ozick keeps them alive in the consciousness of the American reader. She translates—"Amerikaner-geboren. Spawned in America"—to let the American reader into the Yiddish language. Ozick translates Yiddish phrases into her English text in order to create the idiomatic voice of the character Edelshtein. Edelshtein describes Avremeleh, a boy he recalls from his youth: "Avremeleh had a knack of getting things by heart. He had a golden head" (p. 42). "A golden head" is the English rendition of the Yiddish idiom *a goldene kop.* In the passage previously quoted, Edelshtein calls Yiddish "a littleness, a tiny light." In Yiddish, adjectives often are made into nouns: a *kleynikayt,* littleness, or trifle, comes from *kleyn,* meaning little. In this same passage the list of verbs meaning "to die" parallels the Yiddish tendency to euphemize death by avoiding the literal expression *gevoren toit,* to die. When Edelshtein wanders in the snowstorm, searching for Hannah, the young girl who he hopes will be his translator, his arms and legs numb with cold, and he feels as though he has lost them:

> He lurched from the booth into rushing daylight. The depth of snow sucked off one of his shoes. The serpent too prospers without feet, so he cast off his and weaved on. His arms, particularly his hands, particularly those partners of mind his fingers, he was sorry to lose. . . . He wanted to stand then, but without legs could not. Indolently he permitted himself to rise. (pp. 87–88)

Here Ozick puns on the Yiddish idiom *on hent un on fis,* which literally translates as "without arms and without legs." The idiom means, in context, "without sense, without skill."[10] Ozick renders the idiom literally: by making Edelshtein lose feeling in his arms and legs, he seems to lose the limbs themselves. Hence, he has trouble walking in search of a translator. His search becomes "without sense, without skill," impossible.

Ozick presents Yiddish conversation in English, and makes it sound like Yiddish, by transposing Yiddish syntax into her prose:

> Baumzweig's lethargic wife was intelligent. She told Edelshtein he too had a child, also a son. "Yourself, yourself," she said. "You remember yourself when you were a little boy, and *that* little boy is the one you love, *him* you trust, *him* you bless, *him* you bring up in hope to a good manhood." She spoke a rich Yiddish, but high-pitched. (p. 59)

The actual Yiddish version of this sentence would read something like this:

> Du aleyn, du aleyn. Gedenkst aleyn ven du bist geven a yingele, un ot dos yingele, is dem vos du host lib, im getroitstu, im benshstu, im dertziestu hofendik tzu a guter desvaksnkayt.

The syntax in the English reproduces the emphatic structure of the Yiddish, in which the direct object of the verbs *bless, bring up,* and *trust*—*him*—precedes the subject and the predicate.

Ozick occasionally writes a kind of dialect intended to mock a character and stereotype him. In Ostrover's story, which he reads to his audience at the YMHA on Lexington and 92nd Street, the popular author ridicules Edelshtein's envy: "'Feh,' says the poet, 'what do you expect from a people that kept colonies, they should know what's good in the poetry line?'" (p. 59). The exclamatory *Feh,* the use of *that* for *who,* the interrogative construction of "they should know," are all elements of the "Yinglish" dialect in which Yiddish speakers are stereotyped and made comical. This dialect is the language the Portnoys speak, the idiom of Salzman the matchmaker, the language of the greenhorn. By implication, Ostrover is no longer a greenhorn. He has translators. His works reach the American audience, and feed them the stereotypes that they expect.

Ozick uses yet a third dialect, in English, to distinguish Edelshtein's stilted efforts to write English from his idiomatic and idiosyncratic Yiddish. He begins two letters to Hannah, the *Amerikaner-geboren* who knows Yiddish, whom he hopes will be his translator:

> Dear Niece of Vorovsky:
>
> It is very strange to me to feel I become a Smasher, I who was born to being humane and filled with love for our darling Human Race.

> But nausea for his shadowy English, which he pursued in dread, passion, bewilderment, feebleness, overcame him. He started again in his own tongue—
>
> Unknown Hannah:
>
> I am a man writing to you in a room of the house of another man. He and I are secret enemies, so under his roof it is difficult to write the truth. Yet I swear to you I will speak these words with my heart's whole honesty. I do not remember either your face or your body. Vaguely your angry voice. To me you are an abstraction. . . . Writing to the Future one does not expect an answer. (pp. 73–74)

The first letter, Edelshtein's attempt to write in English, is ungrammatical. As in the mocking "Yinglish" dialect of Ostrover's story, this sentence omits the subordinate conjunction and the auxiliary verb: "It is very strange to me to feel (that) I (have) become a Smasher." But in the second letter, Edelshtein writes Yiddish, which resonates in Ozick's English prose. This passage is grammatical, unlike the first passage. But its grammar has a flavor all its own. It is acceptable English, but it is not "correct." Ozick structures English sentences as though they were Yiddish sentences: "He and I are secret enemies, so under his roof it is difficult to write the truth." A "correct" English construction would read, perhaps: "Because he and I are secret enemies, it is difficult for me to write the truth under his roof." In places, too, the phrasing rings of the Yiddish. "My heart's whole honesty" echoes the Yiddish *gantz,* which means "all, entire, whole." The Yiddish idiom *mitn gantzn hartz* means "with my whole heart." Ozick also uses devices in the prose which have no direct relationship to Yiddish, but which give the passage its foreign flavor. To contrast with the first letter's repeatedly misused preposition *to* Ozick repeats *of* twice in the first sentence of the second letter: "I am a man writing you in a room of the house of another man." Ozick strives here to rectify the awkward rhythm of the first letter by repeating it in a more graceful form. The sentence achieves a lyric intensity, aided by internal vowel rhymes in "roof" and "truth," and alliteration, in "heart's whole honesty" and "vaguely your voice."

In contrast to Philip Roth, and like Henry Roth, Ozick creates several levels of dialect, in order to convey the multiple strata of language formed when Yiddish speakers speak English. She succeeds in reproducing in English the feeling of Yiddish that Philip Roth loses in his prose.

Bernard Malamud's story "The Talking Horse" (1974) is a parable on one level for the place of Yiddish in contemporary Jewish writing.[11] A horse named Abramovitz, who narrates the story in a Yiddish English dialect, wonders whether he is "a man in a horse (or) just a horse that happens to be able to talk."[12] Abramovitz is owned by a deaf-mute, Goldberg, who makes him perform in a circus by asking him questions in Morse code, which Abramovitz answers aloud. When Abramovitz attempts to ask his own questions, Goldberg becomes infuriated, beats him, and threatens him. Abramovitz says, ". . . in fact the blow hurts less than the threat" (p. 165). But for Abramovitz, "the true pain . . . is when you don't know what you have to know" (p. 166). Abramovitz "has to know" what he is and where he came from. He concludes: "Goldberg is afraid of questions because a question could show he's afraid people will find out who he is. Somebody who all he does is repeat his fate" (p. 166). Abramovitz, attempting to escape from "the horse he was in," cries to his audience at the circus for help: "Gevalt! Get me out of here! I am one of you! This is slavery! I wish to be free!" (p. 185). Some years later, he attacks Goldberg with his hooves and Goldberg grabs Abramovitz by the ears,

> and the horse's head and neck, up to the wound, came off in his hands. Amid the stench of blood and bowel a man's pale head popped out of the hole in the horse. He was in his early forties, with fogged pince-nez, intense dark eyes, and a black mustache. Pulling his arms free, he grabbed Goldberg around the neck with both bare arms and held on for dear life. As they tugged and struggled, Abramovitz . . . slowly pulled himself out of the horse up to his navel. (pp. 189–190)

The story concludes with Abramovitz's departure from the circus grounds, "across a grassy soft field into a dark wood, a free centaur" (p. 190).

The man in horse can be interpreted as Yiddish trapped in English. The horse's name, Abramovitz, is very close, coincidentally or not, to the name of the "grandfather of Yiddish literature," Shalom Y. Abramovitsh, better known by his pseudonym, Mendele Moikhr Sforim, Mendele the Bookseller. The deaf-mute master Goldberg is afraid to know, afraid to answer questions. He can be read as the assimilated, ignorant Jew, "Somebody who all he does is repeat his fate." The metamorphosis of the horse into the centaur is analogous to the emergence of Yiddish from American English prose, into its own form, the dialect and intonation of Malamud's prose and the prose of his contemporaries. The metamorphosis figures as the blossoming of Jewish letters in America in the 1960s and 1970s. Yiddish, trapped and repressed in English—the man in the horse—pulls itself only part way out. What we have is a hybrid, half-man, half-beast, a new creature, galloping "into a dark wood, a free centaur."

Notes

1. Cynthia Ozick, *Bloodshed and Three Novellas* (New York, 1977), p. 11.

2. See J. R. Rayfield, *The Languages of a Bilingual Community* (The Hague, 1970).

3. Abraham Cahan, *The Rise of David Levinsky* (New York, 1960), pp. 129–130. Cahan first wrote this novel as a purportedly autobiographical piece, which was serialized in *McClure's Magazine* in 1913, in four installments entitled "The Autobiography of an American Jew." He revised, expanded, and published the work as a novel with Harper Brothers in 1917.

4. Henry Roth, *Call It Sleep* (New York, 1962), p. 15.

5. Bernard Malamud, *The Magic Barrel* (1958; New York, 1960), p. 10.

6. Saul Bellow, ed., *Great Jewish Short Stories* (1963; New York, 1975), p. 15.

7. Saul Bellow, *Herzog* (New York, 1964), p. 79.

8. Philip Roth, *Portnoy's Complaint* (New York, 1972), p. 265.

9. Cynthia Ozick, "Envy; or, Yiddish in America," in *The Pagan Rabbi and Other Stories* (New York, 1976), p. 42.

10. Alexander Harkavy, *Yiddish-English-Hebrew Dictionary* (New York, 1928), p. 184.

11. This reading was suggested to me by Leonard Michaels's review "Sliding into English," *New York Review of Books,* 20 September 1973, p. 37.

12. Bernard Malamud, "The Talking Horse," in *Rembrandt's Hat* (New York, 1974), p. 181.

JUDY DUNN

Playing in Speech

'I'VE SAID TO HIM, you know, 'That's never happened, you're imagining things!' I've told him, I've said 'Now, that's *wrong*—you've got a vivid imagination.'"

"He'd make up stories. . . . It got so bad that I tried to stop it, because I didn't want him to go from an imaginary story to a downright lie—because there's not much difference between the two."

"He's got a . . . I'll tell you what it is—it worries me sometimes—he's got a vivid imagination; and it goes on and on and on until he *lives* it; and sometimes, these imaginary people, you have to *feed* them with him, do you see what I mean? It worries me."[1]

Three mothers—two miners' wives and a fitter's wife—in Nottingham back in 1968 were clearly disturbed by and distrustful of their four-year-olds' imaginations, which they believed might lead to "plain dishonesty." Is this reaction unusual? Is it likely to affect the children's imaginative use of language, their play with words and ideas? How do English-speaking mothers today differ in the ways they respond to their children's verbal play?

As soon as they begin to speak, children show a fascination with the properties and possibilities of words. They play with sounds and with the shapes of words, with rhymes and rhythms, with grammatical operations, with puns and metaphors, and distortions of the conversational conventions of English, and they do so while they are still fresh to the "right" way of using the language. As they master each new skill in using the language it becomes a new resource for play. As soon as a rule or convention is understood, breaking it becomes a source of delight.

Liam, two years old, scratches rhythmically with a chalk on his blackboard: "That's a seagull. Beegull. Beegull. That says beegull. Megull. Megull." Tamsin, going into the backyard of her terrace house with me: "The eagle's gone. It may be here. Another one in my garden."

JUDY: The eagle?
TAMSIN: Yes the eagle. I have eagles in my garden. Like a dog.

Tom, aged five, asks: "If that's the head of the table, where's its face?"

Some of this play is essentially private. Ruth Weir's son Anthony, another two-year-old, alone in his bed at night followed sequences of private word associations, as well as "practicing" counting, listing, naming, substituting words, addressing himself, and endlessly varying the properties of words in sequences both of sense and nonsense.[2]

Bobo's not throwing.
Bobo can throw.
Bobo can throw it.
Oh. Oh.
Go. Go. Go.

When young children talk together they often cooperate with great zest and invention in exploiting these distinctive linguistic possibilities, varying stress, pitch, and the sounds of words, violating conversational rules, playing with metaphor, with fantasy or nonsense far less inhibitedly and narrowly than would ever occur in conversations between child and adult. There is, naturally, a particular pleasure in nonsense names and rhymes, in the adoption of blatantly inappropriate identities and roles, and in scatological overtones.

GIRL: (*five years*)
I'll have to be grandmomma grandmomma grandmomma.
BOY: (*five years*)
Grandmother grandmother grandmother.

GIRL: Grandmomma grandmomma grandmomma.
BOY: Grandmother grandmother grandmother.
GIRL: Grandmomma grandmomma grandmomma.
BOY: Momma.
GIRL: Momma I . . . my mommy momma. Mother humpf.
BOY: Hey.
GIRL: Mother mear (*laugh*). Mother smear.
BOY: (*laugh*)
GIRL: I said mother smear mother near mother tear mother dear (*laugh*).
BOY: Peer.
GIRL: Fear.
BOY: Pooper.
GIRL: What?
BOY: Pooper. Now that's a . . . that's a good name.[3]

Some play involves systematic operations such as forming adjectives from nouns: *fish* to *fishy, spark* to *sparky, rain* to *rainy:*

BOY: (*five years*)
'Cause it's fishy too. 'Cause it has fishes.
GIRL: (*five years*)
And it's snakey too 'cause it has snakes, and it's beary too 'cause it has bears.
BOY: And it's . . . and it's hatty too 'cause it has hats.[4]

Together or alone, children play with noises, rhymes, with the invention of words, with alliteration and assonance. There is a particular intimate excitement in the shared pleasure of forbidden words: with *bum, knicker, silly bugger,* or *poo poo* the conversation dissolves into giggles. But there are also much more elaborately orchestrated games which exploit conversational conventions such as question and answer, or request and refusal, often developing ritualized chains of repetitions.

GIRL: (*three years*)
Come and play cooking.
GIRL: (*three years*)
No.
FIRST GIRL: Come and play cooking.
SECOND GIRL: No.
FIRST GIRL: Come and play cooking.
SECOND GIRL: No.

What marks off the ritual from an adult-child exchange is not simply the perseverance of the children, the number of rounds in the sequence, but rather the precise timing and regularity of the turns which sometimes develop into a type of sing-song chanting.

Catherine Garvey has shown that there is a striking regularity to the timing of these rituals, with the rhythm of pauses between each utterance matching down to precise seconds and tenths of seconds.

CHILD 1: (*five years*)
I'm going to work.
CHILD 2: You're already at work.
CHILD 1: No I'm not.
CHILD 2: (*pause*)
CHILD 1: I'm going to school.
CHILD 2: You're already at school.
CHILD 1: No I'm not.
CHILD 2: (*pause*)
CHILD 1: I'm going to the party.
CHILD 2: You're already at the party.
CHILD 1: No I'm not.
CHILD 2: (*pause*)[5]

The patterns, sequencing and timing of these exchanges reflect a much subtler attention and adaptation to the partner than a psychologist like Piaget, with a conception of the child as essentially "egocentric," would have considered possible.

One of the dominant aspects of the speech of young children in England and America, whether on their own or in the company of adults or other children, is verbal fantasy. The character of the fantasy, naturally, varies greatly according to its context, from the solitary and unconstrained to the very different styles of conversational partnership with other children or with adults. A child will often pick up a metaphor or simile used quite casually by an adult and respond with delight to the magnificence of its possibilities.

MOTHER: (*surveying wet draining board*)
Ugh it's like a swimming pool in here.
STEWART: (*aged two*)
Like swimming pool! A pool! A pool! A swimming pool! Spoons swimming!

How do parents respond to these fancies and to the child-child rituals which parallel a Beckett dialogue in their timing and repetitive pattern? Studying the conversation of mothers and children in an English provincial town, we find at one extreme mothers who, like the three Nottingham mothers already quoted, so disapprove of their children's imaginative life that they flatly refuse to join in the fantasy. The hostility of these parents to fantasy could well extend beyond disapproval of children's verbal play. Resentment and suspicion of what appears to be infantile exchanges between adults, presented as art, may indeed be part of the same pattern of response.

Nigel, two-and-a-half years, plays with two combs slotted together to make a plane:

NIGEL: Look there. Plane coming.
MOTHER: You don't want to play with dirty combs. They want washing.
NIGEL: Plane wants washing.
MOTHER: Eh?
NIGEL: Plane wants washing.
MOTHER: Plane wants washing? Them *combs* want washing.
NIGEL: Plane broken. Plane broken. Crash.
MOTHER: Look. Come and throw out all them broken toys.

In contrast, another mother for two and a half hours one morning engaged in a continuous series of elaborate, if repetitive, verbal adventures with her daughter who for the moment (in fact for about two weeks) was a particular Welsh railway engine.

Many mothers do greet their children's fantasy with some enthusiasm, but the ways in which they respond differ strikingly from the ways in which other children respond. The mother's interest is very much in drawing the child's attention to *how it is* in real life, rather than in elaborating on the child's particular flight of fancy. With the mother, the theme of the fantasy is explored in terms of its adequacy to reality. Is that what would really happen? Is that what would follow in everyday life? Is that how it *is* at work, at nursery, at the shops? The parental concern with reality means that their contributions are very often along domestic lines:

MOTHER: Are you going to the shops for me?
FRANCES: (*three years*)
No. I'm going to the shops for Judy first. I got some. They're fish. Now I'm getting some for Mummy. My scooter fall down.
MOTHER: Did it? Never mind. I should go and find somewhere to park it while you are at the shops. Go and find a parking place.
FRANCES: I did.
MOTHER: You did park? Oh.
FRANCES: There wasn't any people.

MOTHER: There wasn't any people? Oh well, you can go and look in the car park and see if you can find a space to park the scooter, then you can go and find me some fish in the market.

FRANCES: I *got* some fish. It's in the cupboard.

MOTHER: Oh. I don't think that that's a very good place for it. Can you put it in the fridge for me.

FRANCES: Oh dear! It's gone! I've eaten it! And Father Christmas eaten it too.

Anthony, two years, shows his mother a tractor:

ANTHONY: It going to spray Anthony.
MOTHER: Is it going to spray Anthony?
ANTHONY: It got little big wheels.
MOTHER: Has it got big little wheels?
ANTHONY: It got big little wheels. Big wheels.
MOTHER: Is it going to plough, do you think?
ANTHONY: It going to hide. Who can get it?
MOTHER: Who can get it?
ANTHONY: It like a tiger.
MOTHER: Mmm?
ANTHONY: It like a tiger. It got a spray here.
MOTHER: That's nice Anthony.
ANTHONY: It go through a bridge here.
MOTHER: Did it go through a bridge? Do you think you get bridges on fields? I don't remember seeing bridges out there on the field, do you?
ANTHONY: Oh. Making big noise. Raaa! Raaa! Raaa!
(*Tractor continued as tiger for rest of monologue. Mother did not join in.*)

Tamsin, three years, refers to her dolls:

TAMSIN: The babies are crying.
MOTHER: Are they all right, your babies?
TAMSIN: Crying.
MOTHER: Oh.
TAMSIN: Can't sleep. The babies. She always cries in her pram. I mean 'cause Teddy kicks her feet. In the afternoon. When it's 4 o'clock he kicks her feets. In the afternoon. He always kicks her very hard. I mean when she was born he always kicks in bed. When they are upstairs in the afternoon. When I put them in the bedroom they always cries. Really.

MOTHER: Are they all right your babies?
TAMSIN: Yes they go in my bedroom.
MOTHER: Have you not left them in the nice sunshine?

There is a clear contrast between the development of the fantasy of a child playing alone, or with a second child, and what usually happens when a mother joins in. The mother in the next example joined in with enthusiasm at the hint of a fairy story theme in her three-year-old son's solitary play, but her son's fantasy went in a very different direction from that suggested by her own conventional contributions.

GARRY: (*playing with a teddy bear*)
He's got to have a rest. He feels much better now, Ted does. He's eating it up. He's gone to sleep now. He's got his pillow for his head. Night night.
MOTHER: Have you read him a story?
GARRY: No he doesn't want a story.
MOTHER: He doesn't want a story? Ooh, you have a story when you go to bed. Why don't you get your caterpillar book and read him that?
GARRY: He doesn't want a story. He's asleep now. . . . Now he's sitting on the chair. 'Cause he's one of the three bears.
MOTHER: One of the three bears? And there's Mother Bear. And there's Father Bear. Where's their porridge? Here's Goldilocks. Look.
GARRY: This is . . . Goldilocks. She went for a walk. And sat down there. And went for a walk. And Big Father see that (*growls*). And he went to bed with him. And he went to Goldilocks. And he . . . went in that bed. And it was too little for him so's he could go in it (*growls*). So Daddy Bear tried Baby Bear's. Daddy tried Baby Bear's. Now he's in Baby Bear's. Baby Bear's tired. Who's this he says (*growls*). I'm going to wake her up. And he smacks Little Ted. Waw Waw Waw. Smack smack. . . . He doesn't want to go to bed any more. He wants to go to the toilet. He's doing weewee on the floor.
MOTHER: He'd better not. Go and sit him on the potty.
GARRY: He's done it. Naughty Bear. . . . He's done weewee in his bed. He's weeing on the floor. He's weeing on the floor again. He's done it again and again and again. He's done it on the floor. He's done it on the sofa. . . . There's Father Bear coming. And Baby wakes up.

Smack him! Smacked his father! And he goes and. . . .
And Father says That's my chair! (*growls*) And smack!
Smack! Smack!

(*continues on theme of smack, wee, father*)

While many working-class mothers are unlikely to join in the fantasy at all, with middle-class mothers the conversation often becomes an exchange with a strongly educational tone; the fantasy becomes an instructional discussion where intellectual operations are demanded of the child. To emphasize the insistence of the adult on everyday realities, or on the conventional theme of stories with which both adult and child are familiar, and to contrast the quality of the fantasy that the child engages in alone with that which the mother enjoys, is *not* to urge that fantasy playing and the grasp of reality are incompatible. On the contrary, it is precisely because the two are necessarily related, and because the delight of fantasy depends on its adventurous and enquiring relationship to reality, that differences between social classes in the response of adults to children's fantasy are potentially disturbing. If fantasy is a mode of thought, a vital aspect of a child's exploration and apprehension of the properties of other human beings and of nature, then the ways in which a mother perceives and reacts to the expression of her child's fantasies may be of enormous importance in shaping his subsequent understanding. There is good evidence, certainly, that the beginnings of verbal fantasy are closely bound up with adults or older children suggesting, modelling or encouraging the make-believe.[6] But it is striking that children as young as three or four years old demonstrate a remarkable intellectual and imaginative independence in verbal play—*the* distinctively human form of play, and the form which most depends on a mastery of specifically human skills. Do we then have good reason to believe that the dramatic variation between English-speaking mothers in their interest in verbal fantasy has any real impact upon children's later use of imaginative language, and upon the vividness and complexity of their fantasy life?

This is a very sensitive issue, since it is in engaging in verbal play that social class differences are particularly marked in the conversation between mothers and children in Britain.[7] (To refer to differences between the members of different social classes does not of course imply that all members of a social class much resemble each other. It is essentially a statistical reference; it is not possible to generalize about social actions except by using categories of this kind.) The disapproval by the two miners' wives and the fitter's wife of their children's imaginative stories was characteristic of a substantial number of the working-class mothers studied by the Newsons in Nottingham, but *not* of the middle-class mothers. Only 14 percent of the working-class mothers reported that their children discussed verbal fantasies with them, whereas half the middle-class mothers commented that their children did so. It is possible that some of the differences between mothers in different social classes in the ways they respond to fantasy are changing: in Britain now we are busy "popularizing" the ideas of psychologists on television and in magazines, and in America pediatricians and psychologists have a wide audience. The notion that it is good for children to imagine and pretend may well spread quite quickly, although whether this will affect the way mothers *talk* to their children is more debatable. And *where* people pick up the ideas of psychologists is sometimes unexpected:

> We used to sit there stroking this [imaginary] cat, and I really thought that she was going up the pole! But then I saw this film with Peter Sellers in it, and *he* had a little girl that was always imagining things; so of course I took it in. It's just one of those developments—you know, *developing.*[8]

At present, however, these differences in parental response are marked. (How different matters used to be here, or are in other countries and cultures, we have as yet no means of knowing.) And we know that there are marked social class differences in the quality of verbal fantasy and imaginative play of young children, both when they are alone, and when they are talking to other people. Compare the following responses from three children in Leeds, looking at a line drawing of a stick man walking up a slope:

DAVID: It's a man I think, walking up a hill but I don't know why or where he's going.

OBSERVER: What might he see from the top?

DAVID: Well . . . he might be setting out on an adventure. He'll get to the top of the hill and he might see a castle down in the valley and perhaps houses and trees and a river.

OBSERVER: Mmm?

DAVID: And they'll all look small because they're so far away. Perhaps he's looking for someone and he'll go down to the castle to find him.

OBSERVER:	What do you think he might see when he gets to the top?
LYNNE:	A cottage.
OBSERVER:	Yes . . . anything else?
LYNNE:	Snow.
OBSERVER:	Yes snow . . . what else might he see?
LYNNE:	No . . . nothing.

OBSERVER:	What do you think he might see when he gets to the top?
DAVID 2:	A slope.
OBSERVER:	Yes . . . anything else?
DAVID 2:	No.
OBSERVER:	What else might he see?
DAVID 2:	Grass.
OBSERVER:	Anything else?
DAVID 2:	I don't know anything else.[9]

The first David's response was typical of the children of professional parents studied by Joan Tough; each extended his or her own ideas of what the man saw—shepherds, mountaineers, bridges or boats. The brief answers of the other two children were characteristic of the "disadvantaged" working class children in the group.

Studies which show us differences in the conversations between mothers and young children, and later differences in the children's powers of imagination, do not as yet provide evidence of a clear or conclusive kind on the causal mechanisms involved. But the practical difficulty of identifying precisely what is happening to a child's imaginative and intellectual life, and of understanding precisely why it is happening, and the political and social sensitivity of the issues of the reproduction of class cultures are no reason for ignoring this question. Perhaps all that the findings of these studies imply is a certain variation in the richness of the imaginative life of very young children in Britain today. But it is also possible that what is at stake is the formation of decisive differences in the capacity to use language imaginatively in adult life, not simply in the capacity to talk elaborately, but in the capacity to understand the social and natural world and the place of oneself and others within it. It is not only an extraordinary linguistic feat, a remarkably sophisticated exploration of the different functions of language, that a three or four-year-old demonstrates as he exploits and experiments with conversational skills in monologues on his own or in conversation with friends. When he engages in fantasies that involve the tones and speech styles of others, he is also in part at least seeing the world their way, and making an imaginative leap of enormous significance in doing so.

James, aged five years, plays two different parts with ease when he is alone:

> Are you better Mrs. Borg Boop?
> I'm not a Mrs. you know. I'm a Mr.
> You are a Mrs. I saw you wearing ear rings once.
> Ah ha. You are silly. I've never weared ear rings.
> You have. I saw you. I put them on for you.
>
> Where shall I go? I'll pop in here.
> No you mustn't. Someone has to drive. And you don't know how to work it do you?
> No I forgot.[10]

Listening to the conversations of mothers and young children in England today, you can certainly hear the different styles of English speech now being passed on to another generation. But it is at least possible, if you can only learn to listen sensitively and intelligently enough, that you can hear something more awesome: the imaginative grammar of a differentiated society's understanding of and attitude toward itself being laid down solidly in a new generation, as the improvisatory panache of young children's speech is shaped, more or less bluntly and firmly, to the adoption of varying class cultures.

Notes

1. J. Newson and E. Newson, *Four Years Old in an Urban Community* (Harmondsworth, 1968).
2. R. Weir, *Language in the Crib* (The Hague, 1972).
3. C. Garvey, *Play* (Cambridge, Mass., 1977), p. 68.
4. Garvey, *Play*, p. 70.
5. Garvey, *Play*, p. 116.
6. D. El'konin, "Symbolics and Its Functions in the Play of Children," *Soviet Education* 8 (1966); J. Dunn and C. Wooding, "Play in the Home and Its Implications for Learning," in B. Tizard and D. Harvey, eds., *The Biology of Play* (London, 1977); L. V. Vygotsky, *Mind in Society* (Cambridge, Mass., 1977).
7. Dunn and Wooding, *The Biology of Play*; J. Tough, *The Development of Meaning* (London, 1977).
8. Newson and Newson, *Four Years Old in an Urban Community.*
9. Tough, *The Development of Meaning.*
10. M. Martlew, K. Connolly, and C. McCloed, "Language Use, Role, and Context in a Five Year Old," *Journal of Child Language* 5 (1978): 93.

KARLA KUSKIN

The Language of Children's Literature

"ONCE UPON A TIME in an old town, in an old street, there stood a very old house. Such a house as you could hardly find nowadays, however you searched, for it belonged to a gone-by time—a time now quite passed away." Those lines open *The Cuckoo Clock and The Tapestry Room,* a book for children by Mrs. Molesworth (with pictures by Walter Crane), published in Edinburgh in 1877.

And this dialogue begins *A Bargain for Frances,* an "I Can Read" book by Russell Hoban, illustrated by Lillian Hoban and published in New York City in 1970:

It was a fine summer day,
and after breakfast Frances said,
"I am going to play with Thelma."
"Be careful," said Mother.
"Why do I have to be careful?"
said Frances.
"Remember the last time?" said Mother.
"Which time was that?" said Frances.
"That was the time you played catch
with Thelma's new boomerang,"
said Mother. "Thelma did all the
throwing, and you came home
with lumps on your head."
"I remember that time now,"
said Frances.

Both Mrs. Molesworth and Mr. Hoban have written very well for children. In different times. Should Mrs. Molesworth's prose be dismissed as that of a "gone-by time—a time now quite passed away"? Since she described that old house with its "quaintly terraced garden" and "parliaments" of rooks, how has the language of children's literature changed? The question before that question is, how does one define children's literature?

The term itself is relatively new. Among the folk, fairy, and authored tales and the poetry and nonsense now thought of as belonging to children, much was originally intended for an audience of any age at all. But as more and more books were printed, a borderline between adult and children's literature began to appear. For a long time it was very hazy.

Pilgrim's Progress is a good example of a book written for adults and appropriated by children. On the other hand there is a lullaby composed by Thomas Dekker in 1599 which eventually became adult fare. The lyric goes "Golden Slumbers kiss your eyes, / Smiles awake you when you rise. / Sleep, pretty wantons, do not cry, /And I will sing a lullaby." In the 1960s John Lennon and Paul McCartney changed a word or two—*wantons* became *darling* (perhaps to protect the guilty)—and Dekker's cradle song was transformed into a love lyric belted out between two throbbing choruses on the record *Abbey Road.*

Both young and old of the seventeenth century were delighted by Charles Perrault's versions of French fairy stories. In Italy the collected tales of the *Pentamarone* had an equally wide-ranging audience. In the early nineteenth century, when Wilhelm and Jacob Grimm undertook the enormous job of collecting German folk tales, they had the "firm intention that the book be regarded as an educational book" that parents could read to their children "little by little." Reviewing some of these same stories in *The Borzoi Book of French Tales* in 1957, W. H. Auden wrote, "Children enjoy them, it is true, but that is no reason that grownups, for whom they were primarily intended, should assume they are childish." Dickens, Washington Irving, Mark Twain, Kipling, Emily Dickinson, Robert Frost, and Crockett Johnson are just a few of those read by many of all ages.

With the enormous growth of publishing in the twentieth century, books became much more firmly categorized. To help publishers and purchasers make order out of abundance, the approximately 2,000 books printed each year for children are generally separated into picture books (ages 2–8), story books (ages 7–12), and young adult novels (ages 11–37, depending on the youth of the adult). In order to examine the language of these books, it will help here to limit a definition of children's literature to picture and story books, present and past, that have either been expressly created for a young audience or have been adopted by the young over time.

When the *Orbis Pictus* was published in 1657, it was the first of its kind: an illustrated book especially for children. Before its publication there had been chapbooks and broadsides, undecorated but conceived for the edification of the young. Paintings of the period show the young these works must have been meant for. Dressed in imitation of their parents, their small heads set on small bodies, they look like scaled-down adults. That is the way they were seen and treated, their books as stiffly tailored as their suits and frocks.

A popular chapbook theme was "the Godly dying young." The Reverend James Janeway took it when he wrote a "token for children, being an Exact Account of the Conversion, Holy and Exemplary Lives and Joyous Deaths of Several Young Children." The youthful heroes and heroines of such works were "as pure as the snow before it's driven" (in the deathless words of Lorenz Hart) and they were knowing beyond their tender years like the "sage enfaunt" in the *Wyse Three Year Olde,* who answered with virtue and alacrity such questions as who made the sky and why it was blue. Another example of the species, printed in America in 1648, had a frontispiece that read "Spiritual milk for Boston Babies, in either England: drawn out of the breasts of both testaments for their soul's nourishment but may be of like use to any children."

The formal sermonizing of these tales prevailed into the nineteenth century. It dramatized not only society's concept of its children, but a gulf between written and spoken language that has narrowed steadily over time, most notably in recent years. It is not a coincidence that as children began to be thought of as interesting young people, instead of the short adults or idealized innocents of other centuries, the stilted phrasing of the old tracts and moral tales fell into disuse and the written word became more playful, more direct and very much more conversational.

However, long before the earliest written and printed words, in striking contrast to the sternly formal tone of those early works, there was always the voice of the storyteller. Deep in the past it wove the stories and poetry of different peoples in different ages, around richly laid tables and rough firesides, worldwide. Blending gossip with superstition and imagination, it made magic rituals of the rhythms and repetitions of familiar speech. Folklorist Katharine Briggs describes a Highland *ceilidh,* or storytelling session. In a house crowded with listeners, the houseman is asked for a story. It "is full of incident, action and pathos. It is told simply, yet graphically, and at times dramatically—compelling the undivided attention of the listeners . . . men, women, boys and girls." The voice held them all.

It still does. The tales passed from teller to teller are passed from book to book. Recorded in collections for hundreds of years, they also now stand alone as the foundations for countless picture books. In many of these versions the rhythms and idioms of the storyteller's speech echo with life. They have contributed significantly to diminishing the historical separation between written and spoken language.

Times without number, the illustrative and literary styles of a particular era have shaped and reshaped the old tales. During those periods when children (and perhaps their parents) were considered either too pure or too easily corrupted to be exposed to the horrors of their own psyches or the terrors of the world, numerous murders, rapes, and incests were relegated to the cutting-room floor. Recently, in a conscious attempt to tell it like it was, much of this material has been, to borrow a Dickensian phrase, recalled to life. And translations of a more literary kind, popular in past times, have been replaced by those closer in spirit and speech to the old tellings.

When *Snow White* was first published in England in 1823, a few details were excised—among these the Wicked Stepmother's directions to the hunter that he bring back Snow White's heart after disposing of the child, so that the Queen could dine on that delicacy. The story's ending was also softened. Years later that bowdlerized version was restored to Grimm reality. In Randall Jarrell's 1962 translation the queen makes her final exit just as the Hassenpflug sisters of Cassel told it to the brothers Grimm: ". . . they had already put iron slippers over a fire of coals, and they brought them in with tongs and set them before her. Then she had to put on the red-hot slippers and dance till she dropped down dead." But through all the variations and modifications certain conventions of phrasing and form have remained basically the same.

"This is a story of how the moon began. Once upon a time there was no moon . . ."; "There was once a king who had three sons . . ."; "A poor woodcutter once lived by the edge of a forest with his two children and their stepmother . . ."; "Once there was a mother and the goblins had stolen her child out of the cradle." Those are sentences that have been spoken and written for hundreds of years. Read them aloud. Each has its own sound and simplicity. Each declares, Here is a story and here is what it is about.

Differentiating between folk fiction and folk legend, Katharine Briggs isolates "once upon a time," or a similar "formula," as proclaiming fiction. But a legend, which "is an account of something that was believed to have happened . . .", is more apt to open anecdotally, "Well it's a queer thing, but as my grandfather was . . . going past the churchyard one night. . . ."

It does seem that the word *once* is sufficient to place the reader somewhere in the magical past that serves as the landscape of a story. "Once it was the middle of winter and the snowflakes fell from the sky like feathers. . . ." Thus you are drawn into the story of *Snow White.* Illustrating the Randall Jarrell translation, Nancy Ekholm Burkert crystallized the power of that single word. The initial *O* in *Once* stands in decorative isolation on the large, snowy page. Within its frame and rising around it is a barebranched tree and the slightest indication of a wintery vista that melts into the whiteness of the paper. A hunter and his dog step through the *O* and into this scene and the story, while the reader, almost literally, follows the picture into the words. Where a human voice once supplied the invitation to the listener to sit still and listen by bringing nuance and color to an otherwise unembellished narrative, the invitation, color, and nuance are now, in large degree, visible, borne by the illustrations of a book.

When words and pictures were first combined in illuminated manuscripts, only a few reproductions of such treasures could be made. To produce hundreds or thousands of copies of a book illustrated with color required a series of interrelated inventions only developed over the last 150 years.

In 1865 Lewis Carroll's Alice "peeped into the book her sister was reading" and saw nothing but a desert of description; ". . . what is the use of a book," thought Alice, "without pictures or conversation?" Alice's own book had pictures in it thanks to John Tenniel, who drew them, and George Dalziel, who cut the woodblocks from which electrotypes were made. However, at around this same time a much more revolutionary printing technology was being developed. Joseph Nicéphore Niépce had made the first photograph in 1826, and with that new process all the succeeding steps became possible. Photoengraving was patented in 1852. A method for black-and-white halftone reproduction was introduced in 1873. Toward the end of the nineteenth century increasing numbers of wonderful illustrators turned to illustrating books, but it was not until the twentieth century that photo-offset made feasible the production of full-color books at costs that were not prohibitive to printer, publisher, and buyer. And it was only about twenty-five years ago that the new techniques and a rapidly growing, child-oriented market discovered each other's potential and the picture book as we are familiar with it began to proliferate.

The additional importance of this new role assumed by pictures affected the language of children's books in a number of ways. In part it led to simpler, more concise writing.

A storybook with some illustrations is not a picture book. In the latter, words and pictures are of almost equal importance. Together they carry the story. The form is constantly changing. It has dramatic range, exacting requirements, and it occupies an enclave of its own somewhere between comic strips and opera. Although the words must lead the way in a picture book, the pictures need to be wedded to the rhythm and meaning of the words, like perfect dance partners, so that the audience is only conscious of their partnership, the *pas de deux.* Thus words are illuminated and augmented by the pictures, which fill in visually what may be left out verbally.

In his introduction to the *Anchor Book of Stories* Jarrell wrote, "Stories can be as short as a sentence." Identifying these as the basic stories of life he went on, "When we try to make . . . works of art of comparable concision, we almost always put them into verse." And into picture books.

Clever Bill, a picture book first published in England in 1926, is the work of William Nicholson, an excellent artist and designer, who constructed it around one elongated sentence. It begins with some deliberated speed: "One day the postman brought Mary a letter from her [*turn the page*] Aunt [*next page*] which said [*here we see the Aunt's letter*] Mary replied [*here we see Mary's letter*]. . . ." The words, written by hand, are perfectly paced to the pictures. They tell you that Mary is invited to visit her aunt so she packs her toy horse, trumpet, doll, and some other necessaries in "the box her Father gave her." In order to get everything into the box, she has to repack several times and finally (the pages almost seem to turn themselves as the action speeds faster and faster) she hurries to catch the train, forgetting her favorite toy soldier Bill Davis. At once the toy runs after her, down the stairs, along the road, through the pages that separate them so that when Mary's train arrives at Dover station Bill Davis is there. "He was just in time to meet her. . . ." Her arms go out to him and (turn to the last page) as she hands him a bouquet he bows. The crowning, final line? "Clever Bill." The author-artist never missed a beat. Words and pictures are joined in a skillful display of invisible weaving; neither would be complete without the other.

Another important influence on the language in picture books arises from the fact that they are designed for very young children and are therefore written to be read aloud, much as poetry is. Because the voice of the live reader, like the voice of the original storyteller, becomes part of the story, simple phrasing works most effectively, as it does working in tandem with pictures.

Margaret Wise Brown, who wrote over ninety picture books from the late 1930s to the early 1950s, found a tone that many other writers adopted. It was that of a friendly adult talking to a child. She called some of her stories "interludes" and described that form as "not a story with a plot, it isn't very long. It is somewhere between a story and a poem . . . a recreation of some experience. Whether this is a good form for children's writing I am not sure. I think, because it is a quiet and simple form it might be, if it is read to a child at the right time."

In *Goodnight Moon,* published in 1947, this quiet, comforting tone is so palpable that the book seems incomplete when it is not read aloud. The verse is neither intricate nor playful, but absolutely to the point. It starts with what are in effect stage directions: "In the great green room / There was a telephone / and a red balloon / And a picture of / The cow jumping over the moon. . . ." Each homely detail enumerated to set a complete scene is pictured in the same direct, unmannered fashion by artist Clement Hurd. When everything is named and placed visually, the goodnights begin. The voice goes around the room once more and each object already named is now bade goodnight "Goodnight room / Goodnight moon / Goodnight cow jumping over the moon." The linking of name and object, the accumulation of pictured details to be searched for and found, the gentle swing of the lines (as if they were timed to the slow rocking of the chair in which the "quiet old lady" sits knitting), the repetition of words and phrases—all are used to engage the young listener in the mood and movement of the story. Read by a familiar voice the words take on the sound and weight of a lulling incantation. In this uncomplicated verse, as in difficult poetry, the reader is helped to read the lines rhythmically as the writer intends them by the way they are set on the page, line for line and from one page to the next.

Using simple rhythmic verse and prose, Margaret Wise Brown conveyed emotions and images relevant to childhood experiences. Ruth Krauss concentrated on children's language patterns and feelings in books which incorporated her studies of their speech. *A Hole Is To Dig* is a book of definitions written from a child's perspective.

A sea shell is to hear the sea
A wave is to wave bye-bye
Big shells are to put little shells in.

Bears sounds like a song a child would be proud to have composed:

Bears, bears, bears, bears, bears.
On the stairs
Under chairs
Washing hairs
Giving stares. . . .

An emphasis on rhythms, word sounds, rhyme, and mood is a natural way to address the generation particularly tuned to just these elements in stories, verse, tongue twisters, song lyrics, commercial jingles, and assorted nonsense. New perceptions, popularized by psychiatry and education, of children as important, unique individuals influenced those writing for them. And that child who had for so long been hardly seen and certainly not heard became a star, the audible, visible axis of proliferating children's books.

Clever Bill is one example of how the slenderest story can be turned into a complete picture book by an imaginative artist. Maurice Sendak performed a comparable alchemy with apparent nonsense. Taking two Mother Goose verses, twelve lines in all, he built them into fifty-four pages of absolutely logical silliness in *Hector Protector and As I Went over The Water.* Line one of verse one goes "Hector Protector was dressed all in green." That inspires four full pages starring a worried but insistent mother frilled to the gills and just as furbelowed in her overblown eighteenth-century finery, who is struggling to dress her rebellious son in his own fine greenery. The artist permits the characters a few monosyllabic comments on the proceedings, "NO! . . . so! ho! NO NO NO!" etc., which float in early American word balloons. The pictures which were initially the fruit of the words have produced words of their own. Sendak, who comprehends picture books both intellectually and intuitively, makes each one a drama. Consequently, the words in many of his books become dialogue or narration served by and serving the pictures. For him every title page is the credits before the action, every set of margins a proscenium arch.

Among the people who understand the power of a picture coupled with a few words are good cartoonists. It seems natural that a number of them have done picture books. Misha Richter is one of these. In *Quack* the words are very few indeed. They don't even make up a sentence but are, rather, a dialogue of animal sounds which goes, in part: "Quack? Quack? Quack? Quack? Croak. Quack? Eeeeek? Quack? Bzzzzzzzzzzz. Quack? Tweet Tweet. . . ." The words without pictures are nonsense. The pictures without the words don't make a lot of sense either. But match the many quacks et cetera with the many ducks et cetera and before the reader's eyes a classic quest unfolds. It is the ages old search for friendship or very possibly love.

Pare a story down to its core and what is left, drama or mood or a mixture of the two, has the strength and at times the poetry of a distillate. But simplification is an art, and when it is poorly conceived, instead of a tight, linear tale, the result is a collection of empty words in search of an author with an idea. In the last ten or fifteen years there have been more empty children's books. Vibrantly colored, handsomely printed, designed and drawn in the latest award-winning styles, they sit on shelves like starlets of the forties: very glamorous but dumb.

On the other hand, there are some wordless books that have a lot to say. In these one-hundred-percent picture books the language has been so simplified it exists only by implication. *Anno's Alphabet,* by Mitsumaso Anno, is one of these. Like a good silent film, it speaks volumes in images (and images in volumes). Each of the twenty-six well-known letters that make a cameo appearance, one to a double-page spread, is painted as a *trompe l'oeil* wood construction in which some pictorial sleight of hand has been worked. The painting of *M* is constructed by leaning one half an *M* against a mirror. Reality added to its reflection make the whole. *O,* a tube of orange oil paint materializes, Magritte-like, from the pallette. Or is it just disappearing? Across the page from a rainy village street, vignetted in the shape of an umbrella with a *U* for a handle, the wooden *U* is grained with rain. Like many good picture books and story books, Anno's can be understood on successive levels by a growing reader. It is silent but it is subtle.

Nonsense is the special language of children. Although it is seldom silent, it does have subtleties that can be appreciated at different ages. *Alice in Wonderland* is a classic example. If nonsense is bisected, Mother Goose, with its political and cultural roots, exemplifies historical nonsense. This arises, in part, from the natural development of language; changes in spelling and pronunciation, misinterpretations of antiquated words, use of rhyming slang, those cases in which the original meanings of words are lost and they are used as abstract sound. Deliberate nonsense includes many stories that appeal to a child's triumph at seeing someone else get things wrong for a change. Much of Edward Lear, some of Lewis Carroll, the works of many other serious practitioners of the absurd are deliberately nonsensical.

Very young children learning to speak sentences are fascinated by the sounds of words. They tend to pronounce with great care, to savor syllables for sense and nonsense. Lyrics and limericks are their meat. Because of this there are always aspiring lyricists trying to borrow Mother Goose's quill. Often it is a mistake. The semi-new stuff is rarely as fine or funny as the old. It sounds tired: ". . . Down with sneezles, / Coughs and wheezles, / Measles, mumps and chicken pox" owes whatever lilt it has to A. A. Milne's Christopher Robin, who had measles, sneezles, and wheezles back in the twenties. As for "Rub-a-dub-dub / Fishy in a tub / Swimming for the deep blue sea / Dig for the oyster / Dive for the clam / And then come back to me," it doesn't measure up either to the nursery rhyme or to the folk song from which it was garnered. The lexicon of prose and poetry, the rhythms and rhymes, must grow out of the times and alter as they do. Lear created his own kind of nonsense. Lewis Carroll mingled reality, absurdity, and dreams in a scenario that has influenced many but remains inimitable.

In the late 1930s Theodore Seuss Geisel, alias Dr. Seuss, wound up an interior metronome and began to write like the wind. He used words that, by the standards of the day, were unrefined and not literary. And he drew a nutty, smirking zoo of farfetched fauna in flat, bright colors with a careening pen that dared anything. Some adults were not amused but it didn't matter; by following his own rules of versifying and by making up a vocabulary as he went along, Seuss was able to rhyme and usually scan whatever he had in mind. His brand of nonsense didn't need complex rhyme schemes or intricate rhythms. It was short and snappy. It was funny and it flew.

In the 1950s, when an editor and friend persuaded Seuss to try writing an elementary school reader, his rhyming muse was in luck. The two words that winked at him from the prescribed list were *cat* and *hat*.

The Cat in the Hat and Else Minarik's *Little Bear,* illustrated by Maurice Sendak, were both published in 1957. Each was conceived as an answer to the dull-looking, dull-reading readers that had been handed down, with very little alteration or inspiration, from one generation to the next. Here were new patterns of simplified language developed to meet educational goals. Because both books were intended as beginning readers, they were limited to the short sentences and elementary vocabulary that four, five, and six-year-olds could conquer. At first some publishers were guided by restrictive word lists. Others relied on the writer's intuition. Arnold Lobel found the perfect voice for his books by using dialogue as the prime ingredient in the amusing mini-adventures of a charismatic frog and toad.

One of the first books to use pure dialogue for young children was Else Minarik's *No Fighting No Biting* in 1958. It was a harbinger of prose to come. Dialogue, it is thought perhaps rightly, has an immediacy that involves readers directly in a story. It is a natural form of expression for writers whose work is growing increasingly conversational and concerned with a child's concerns, fears, fantasies, emotional problems, everyday life. Tales told in the first person, present tense, have burgeoned in the last fifteen or twenty years. For a while there seemed to be a small army of second-string, coed Holden Caulfields speaking their minds. Ethnic books with ethnic voices emerged from long-held silences, and syntax was broken up in ways that had not been common in children's books. There were echoing re-echoes of Gertrude Stein and E. E. Cummings.

> 9:00 this morning 133 street is awake.
> men and ladies talk and sing on the stoops.
> men and ladies are talking rainbows in the street . . .
> chocolate children on the sidewalk skip and play.

or

> where wild
> willie
> with
> the
> whisper
> in
> feet
> willie
> wild
> willie
> street
> feet

And in another ethnic key: "'Thank you, Aunt Shirley,' said Trudy. 'Say "thank you for the nice bucket, Jacob!"' But Jacob said, 'I already got a bucket,' and Jacob's father said, 'Shush, Jacob. Why don't we all go for a nice walk in the park?' "

If the diversities in speech are confusing to some and the accents of one area don't travel easily to another, those are the breaks of the moment. After all, voices that have not been heard now are heard, which is good. And being different has been publicly acknowledged, on an elementary school level, to be positive. That's good too.

To reiterate for a moment. The language of children's books has been manipulated, woefully and well, by time's trends. It has consistently grown closer to spoken language. It has been altered and often streamlined by the increasing importance of illustrations, which can assume much of a story's detail and drama. "Read-alone" books have done their share in emphasizing dialogue and simplified language, as have writers who, like poets, are writing work intended to be read aloud. Influenced by modern concepts of each individual's importance, many children's books attempt to embody the viewpoints and language of their readers. This stress on the child's unique self has unveiled a multitude of unique selves speaking in ethnic and poetic voices. Among them all, only superficially changed, one very old voice remains strong. It is that of the storyteller, still compelling, still giving life to so much of the literature that continues to survive passing fashions, because in those books best beloved by children, style is never all. Old or new, worn or chic, what the best books have in their marrow is a good story.

"Ladies and Gentlemen, there are 500 reasons why I began to write for children, but to save time I will mention only ten of them," Isaac Bashevis Singer announced in a speech after he had accepted the Nobel Prize for literature. Just two of those reasons will suffice here. The first: children "still believe in God, the family, angels, devils, witches, goblins, logic, clarity, punctuation . . ."; and two: "they love interesting stories. . . ."

Those who write interesting stories for children, stories that last, have a common answer to a single question, "Who are you writing for?" The answer is "myself," followed possibly by the qualification, "a part of myself." That part is the well-remembered child. Some forget childhood as they grow out of it, others push it away, but for still others it remains close and clear throughout life.

Hans Christian Andersen, Kenneth Grahame, Beatrix Potter, E. B. White, Richard Kennedy, Paula Fox, Natalie Babbitt—writers who have already been named here and others who have not lead a list of storytellers who fuse a sharp consciousness of childhood with imaginative thought, language and one other element: truth.

The Tailor of Gloucester, first printed in England in 1902, was Beatrix Potter's favorite of her own books. It is prefaced by this letter:

> My Dear Freda:
> Because you are fond of fairy-
> tales, and have been ill, I have
> made you a story all for yourself—
> a new one that nobody has read before.
> And the queerest thing about it is—
> that I heard it in Gloucester, and that
> it is true. . . .

All the best stories are. True to their fantasies or mysteries. Each true in its own context. Myths are anchored and sustained by truth. These "bones of stories," to use Randall Jarrell's phrase, are fundamental in much the same way that names are.

When a child connects a word to a thing he begins the process of naming. That is the point at which one acquires language. At first, according to Jean Piaget, children may not differentiate between the name and the thing, they may even practice a kind of word magic in which the name controls the thing. In the same way that a word is a symbol of a thing, the myth is a symbol, more complex than a word, but nonetheless a symbol naming the primary relationships and emotions of our lives. This quality of naming truths may explain the strength of those stories that have crossed the lines separating cultures and survived to the present from the depths of the past.

Abel's Island is a storybook that beats with the heart of a myth. It is by William Steig, an artist who writes like a writer in language of his own: courtly, touching, filled with humor and a lifelong love of words. Like Robinson Crusoe, Gulliver, or Jacob, Abel is lost, passes through many trials and finally returns to love and "Home! He grasped the graceful railing and bounded up the steps. He still had the keys in his ragged pants. He opened the door. It was all exactly as he had left it, as he had remembered it so often during his exile. . . . He went into the kitchen, looked in a pot on the stove, tasted the soup." Steig's story is about the loneliness of art and the triumph of love that lasts. There are extended monologues, unexpected words, and it is full of thought and feeling. The hero is a mouse in a smoking jacket. The book is for children. But that is beside the point, which is for everyone.

ANGELA CARTER

The Language of Sisterhood

A GOOD DEAL of harmless fun has been poked at certain neologisms coined by the Women's Movement in its sexually egalitarian or sometimes even female supremacist zeal. The militant who wanted to change her name to "Personchester." Ho ho ho. *S/he* to replace the offensively sectarian yet ubiquitous use of *he* as an impersonal pronoun? What? Have the girls no sense of proportion? (Yet, if the reader consults the manner in which his buttons do up, he might, to his surprise, discover he is a woman.) *Herstory. That* always provokes the big belly laugh.

It should be said here and now that the motive behind some at least of these innovations and attempted innovations is to make apparent, by means of absurdism (always a tricky thing to handle) the patriarchal bias of the English language, a bias created and maintained by the historic socio-economic institutions of Western European culture since the time the Greeks, for gynopathic reasons of their own, transformed the myth of Oedipus from a positive, creative, matriarchal one (s/he who sleeps with its mother gets on in the world; how else did Oedipus become king, after all) to a negative, destructive, patriarchal one (if you murder your father, it's tears before bedtime and nobody is going to bother to ask Jocasta what *her* line on the messy business was).

Now, this digression contains several implicit points which relate to Women's Lib newspeak. Note that in it jargon derived from the social sciences has been crossed with the metaphysics of the "think positive" therapies and then freely utilized in the revision of myth. The Women's Movement has a number of interesting conceptual roots besides what some of it might term the "narrow, legalistic" demand for equal constitutional rights for women and the same pay for the same jobs. Many of my sisters studied the social sciences before they were "freaked out" by the authoritarian, patriarchal bias of the methodology of sociology and "got into" personal growth, itself a conceptually vague area that has bastardized a good deal of its own jargon out of the vocabulary of the sociology of interpersonal relations. (Please note that I do not use the verb *bastardize* in a way that suggests there is anything wrong with bastards. The use of the legal fact of bastardy is just one more piece of evidence of patriarchal bias, and a particularly farcical one; "it's a wise child that knows its own father," as my grandmother gnomically opined over every childbed in her village and, certainly, nobody in that village was ever *quite* sure.)

Forgive me; a digression within a digression! A characteristically feminine mode of discourse, if you don't mind my saying so; think of Scheherazade, mother of digressions. (But, if an inability to keep to the point be indeed evidence of a sex-linked gene, where does that leave Laurence Sterne?)

The sisterhood tends toward the social sciences because we not only want to know, we feel we *need* to know why the world is as it is; why undergraduates in arts faculties tend to be female and postgraduate students male, why the "brotherhood of man" is moving idealism but the "sisterhood of man" a grotesque paradox and so on. We tend to go in for "personal growth" cults of all types when we find that nobody but ourselves will consent to love us on our own terms, since we do not have the self-confidence to make of this a *modus vivendi,* as did, e.g., Benvenuto Cellini. And we tend toward a study of myth because of the paucity of historical references to that statistically rather more than half the human race to which we belong. It is still possible for an academic monograph on the Rastafarian religion of Jamaica (Leonard E. Barrett, *The Rastafarians* [London, 1977]) to make no explicit references at all to the official status of women in that newborn patriarchal faith, when one of the most interesting things about the Rastas (at least, to me) is their emergence as a politico-religious system with a male supremacy platform out of a predominantly matrifocal culture. Post-Oedipal revisionism in our own lifetimes, yet.

Women, then, tend to disappear in the abyss of time unless they were born male, that is, a king in all but gender. Those of us whose kin never hit the power-political high spots therefore feel more at home—as who, in the circumstances, wouldn't; indeed, the Rastas themselves prove it—in the misty but emotive area of those myths that reflect society as much as they create them. And we feel a compulsive need to rewrite those myths, since myth is more malleable than history, in order to accommodate ourselves in the past. In this way, cross-disciplinary bastards are born.

Therefore a book like Adrienne Rich's *Of Woman Born* looks, at first sight, like some monstrous hybrid, a legendary obstetrical autobiography which, because of its impurity of form, its lateral interpretation of the chronology of gynecology, necessitates a new area of speculation to accommodate it: so the nascent discipline of women's studies accretes its set texts. It is, after all, very rarely possible for new ideas to find adequate expression in old forms.

This also applies to language use.

Certain legislation about the official status of all women has begun to affect the patriarchal bias of English over the last ten years, though it will take rather longer than that to make English fit women as well as it fits men because women haven't been around much in official life for the last fifteen hundred years and it is in churches and law courts and trade union meetings and other places where men gather together that official speech is made. However, nice men now scrupulously use "chairperson" rather than "chairman" and can get an official rap over the knuckles if they don't when they advertise for one; yet they still stick to "chairman" in informal conversation among their peers because, while it is perfectly okay for a woman to be mistaken for a man, it is *not* perfectly okay the other way around.

The use of *Ms.* proceeds more or less apace, although in England, at least, it has already acquired a curious life of its own, not as a nonaligned form of address for all women everywhere but as a convenient appellation for divorcées or unmarried women of a certain age who aren't fish or fowl, i.e., probably *not* without some kind of sexual experience, and may, in this way, be officially shown to be good red herring. If *Miss* means respectably unmarried, and *Mrs.* respectably married, then *Ms.* means nudge, nudge, wink, wink.

The very word *liberated,* when applied to women, speedily acquired an erotic connotation in the early days of the Women's Movement, when it was known as the Women's Liberation Movement and coincided, probably not fortuitously, with the widespread use of new, foolproof methods of contraception. It took about three seconds flat for *liberated* to acquire the sub-meaning of "promiscuous." "Ms. Jane Doe, a very liberated lady"; there following a positive spasm of nudging and winking. As the movement purged itself of the ideologically impure—which turned out to mean the heterosexually inclined, because of the revolutionary puritanism that saw the relaxation of sexual mores that took place in the late sixties as a diabolical plot for the furtherance of the heterosexual exploitation of women by men—the adverb dropped out of use among my sisters at roughly the same time that the contraceptive pill dramatically waned in popularity. However, because of the increasingly radical ideology of the most hysterically publicized Women's Libbers, the very word *feminist* itself became eroticized in a curious way. It acquired an active sub-meaning, both proudly among sisters and spitefully against them, as a euphemism for *lesbian.*

This is an extreme example of the way that words with a particular application to the condition of women attract to themselves a "women only" quality, a precision of reference that limits their use to a notional "world of women" with which men need not concern themselves. In the recent past, this "world of women" had a perfectly real existence; it consisted of the kitchen, the nursery, not necessarily one's own kitchen and nursery, and certain forms of labor such as prostitution in which men involved themselves only at the higher executive profit-sharing level, as pimps. In this "world of women," one may find a kind of ur-language of sisterhood—clues as to the origins of its specific grammar and syntax, though not its vocabulary.

The traditional language system of the "world of women" can often transcend class, race, and creed because it is used by woman as a dependent subgroup when they are speaking of their relations to men as a dominant group. This produces the possibility of a certain free-masonry of all women, everywhere, in itself a subversive factor; perhaps the motto of the "world of women" has always been "it's a wise child that knows its own father," except among those anthropological curios, the aborginal Australian tribes where the relation between sexual intercourse and human reproduction is not acknowledged because people get on very well as they are.

This free-masonry exists because of certain basic similarities between the experience of all, or almost all, women *as* women. Indeed, anywhere I go in the world, I can, given a few basic words in common, have perfectly splendid conversations with other women about babies, cooking, sex, and what dolts men are. (I personally have had such conversations with Japanese fisherwomen; Lancashire mill operatives; doctors of philosophy; Soviet construction workers; and, among others, an itinerant vendor of paw-paw, she claimed, in Bangkok.) These conversations easily persuade us to indulge in sentimental wishful thinking, thus: if I and my sisters, with our firm grasp on eternal verities, ran things instead of our husbands (or elder brothers), we would never let our sons go off to fight one another, or perpetrate the nuclear megadeath, or pollute the rivers with industrial effluvia or club to death baby seals, etc. This is the utopian aspect of traditional feminism; in mythic terms, it is Kali, the mother goddess of destruction, in her benign aspect, or, in Kleinian terms, it is Good Breast. It is imaginative compensation for historical powerlessness yet is rooted in a perfectly real sense of a camaraderie of impotent yet sensitive condition.

There is a curious paradox, here, which is at the root of all speech that describes emotions or conflicts within widely differing cultures in terms that appeal directly to personal experience, as though that experience had not been modified by the culture in which it took place. It creates a sense of universality that is both true and false at the same time. Inflated with hot air, this kind of speech becomes the rhetoric of populism: "Women Unite" is not a feminist slogan but a populist slogan of the same order as "Power to the People," or "I'm Backing Britain," or "America—love it or leave it"—appeals that beg all the questions implicit in them. (Women unite against what? What kind of power to what kind of people?) The language of the heart, which is the ur-language of sisterhood, can exist as a mode of communication because it "speaks directly," and therefore grossly oversimplifies the world.

Because of this ur-language of sisterhood, many middle-class women have infinitely more intimate and satisfying relationships of communication with their cleaning ladies than they do with their husbands; both can speak as woman to woman, with a concentration on the particularity of female experience that is especially necessary to conceal from themselves the real, economic nature of their bond. Indeed, they talk to one another about their wombs, their affairs, their problems with their children precisely because they have nothing else in common; anything else is divisive. On the other hand, only a deeply cynical or frivolous person could call conversations about birth, love, and death trivial. And, with their husbands, both cleaning lady and employee may well have nothing in common at all except a fiscal symbiosis. Unfortunately, it is the relative social status of these husbands that keeps the women "sisters under the skin," that is, not overtly friends. They're not going to take one another out to lunch, are they. So there is a fictive quality about the notion of a universality of "women only" experience.

The sense of an emotional bond is created by ignoring the disparate circumstances of social reality; and this is an improper use of language since social reality may only be perceived through, and is in part created by, language. This improper use of language is, alas, a characteristic of the language of sisterhood.

Nevertheless, the areas in which traditional "women only" language is used most often define the traditional social reality of women. Many men excuse themselves entirely from the vocabulary of childcare, unless they are professional pediatricians, in which case they use a "men only" occupational jargon which women have to reinterpret for themselves. The vocabulary of housework, "to do the lounge," for example, shocks men by its typically feminine allusive vagueness. The language of the domestic kitchen may be a closed book to a professional chef, accustomed as he is to the "men only" jargon of the male-dominated profession of "haute cuisine." Conversely, this jargon is one that the rare women who themselves become professional chefs must learn to use before they are taken seriously in the trade. "Haute cuisine" is accomplished in a technical language, a public language, the language of work and therefore of the objective, male world. In the female kitchen, cooking is a commonplace, everyday activity and is performed in the private language of the subjective, "women only" world in which catering is not a painfully acquired skill but (as we say) part of our heritage as women. At work, our female chef might create a "boeuf en daube" with a "jardinière" garnish, be she never so English, or Hungarian, or of mixed Chinese/Uruguayan extraction. (There's a cultural hegemony to "haute cuisine"; it's always in French.) At home, the same dish would be called a "nice stew," or whatever the Hungarian, Chinese, or Spanish demotic for a stew is. (In the Anglo-Saxon domestic kitchen, a stew is always made of beef unless it is explicitly stated otherwise. In Islamic countries, all stew is lamb; in Scandinavia, fish. Or elk. Women's language unites and confuses simultaneously.)

It is the private quality of this kind of women's language that allows its high degree of unspecificity, because just this subjective privacy is, in fact, what is common to our experience as women. We live in a shared privacy of oblique reference, perhaps originally designed to keep whatever is going on from the masters. Arcane allusion is handed on from mother to daughter; at "difficult times of the month," we nod sympathetically. We *know* what she means. We know that a child who looks "a bit peaky" doesn't need a doctor yet. We use nebulous measurements, such as a "bit of meat." Men who deal with women in the service industries pick up this system of measurement quickly; any butcher knows how big a bit of meat will do for "just me and the kids." Any daughter sent out by her mother for a "piece of cheese" will return with roughly the same amount (about half a pound). In fact, we all know what we mean by virtue of praxis, pure and simple; any fool ought to be able to work out how much butter, how many eggs, given a knowledge of the number of mouths there are to feed. (Men always insist on shopping lists itemized down to the last microgram and milliliter.) This is, of course, the key to the rigorous logic behind female linguistic imprecision, a logic of relativity and ad hoc-ism and using your eyes.

It is just this lateral logic, in which all the middle terms of the syllogism are suppressed because it is a waste of breath to state them, that has produced the myth of female intuition. For example: man comes home late, drunk, kicks the cat, falls into chair, weeps. She: you've lost your job. He: how did you know? In a society where the sexes are polarized, much of the behavior of either seems mysterious to the other precisely because they do not spend enough time together to learn to understand their little ways, let alone their socially determined modes of speech. In the advanced, industrialized countries of East and West, the sexes are being depolarized and are depolarizing themselves very rapidly indeed; on all sides, women quit the "women only" world in droves for good and those who sometimes return there do so only intermittently. It is a characteristic of the "man's world," with its hard-edged, public speech, a language that is a tool for the clarification rather than the speedy negotiation of circumstances, that women are allowed into it to the extent to which they are prepared to conform to its linguistic usage. This means that often women develop two distinct forms of speech, just as people who come from areas with dialectal peculiarities do. When we go home, that is, to mother, we fall back into the primordial usage of all women everywhere, even if we don't like her very much. Women active in the "man's world" of public activity unconsciously accept male speech patterns except in moments of absence of mind, when they can lose their jobs.

One of the qualities of the language of sisterhood, the language spoken by the newly self-conscious "women only" world created by the Women's Movement, is that it will often posit allusiveness as a valid alternative method of expression to concrete "men only" language in public discourse. This is an attempt to bring the traditional "world of women" language, and the methodology of thought behind it, out of the closet. Sisterhood, therefore, has a certain self-confidence about dismissing structured, patriarchal, authoritarian devices like syntax, grammar, and artistic form with a supercilious smile; they are part of the conspiracy to stifle Woman's Voice in its uniqueness. (In a sense, they are part of a wider conspiracy to stifle everybody's voice in its uniqueness for the sake of our understanding one another more easily, if less profoundly, but that's another story.) On the other hand, we also jettison centuries of female evasive vocabulary vis-à-vis our sexual organs in favor of the most affrontingly brutal terms we can find. Feminists have "tits" and "cunts," although we scrupulously excise these terms, and, indeed, all sexual abuse, from the language of imprecation.

Given the heritage of an archaic private language system among women based on common experience and guesswork, together with a new injection of terminology from the social sciences, the final contribution to the language of sisterhood of the late twentieth century came from the hippy radicalese of the sixties, when feminism was reborn, a strange phoenix from the ashes of the suffragettes. This can already give a quaint, period quality to the conversation of sisters. They "freak out"; they are "hassled," especially by lascivious taxi drivers and unsympathetic "pigs." They often live in "communal" or "group situations," and have great difficulty, when moving into monogamous relationships, in finding appropriate terms for cohabitors. These slang phrases are used to consciously informalize language, out of a desire to get rid of all the shit and speak spontaneously, directly from the heart, an organ which, correctly or incorrectly, we believe to be at least partially atrophied in the greater part of the male sex. And if the heart can oversimplify, then does not the intellect overelaborate? Verbal discourse and debate are often seen as themselves an intellectual overelaboration of spontaneous feeling. At some sisterhood get-togethers, the attempt at verbal intercourse is abandoned altogether in favor of "touching rituals," tactile exchanges that bring those who engage in them closer together than words can. The hippy penchant for play survives in the way sisters enjoy "bopping" and "looning" together, that is, dancing and clowning around for fun. "Bopping" and "looning" can often create a "really high energy situation" in which women are released from their traditional passivity. This aspect of sisterhood fun is really important.

Really is an interesting word. It is sisterhood's favorite affirmatory adverb; "it was really nice" is the highest possible commendation, as if authenticity—the very fact of being real—is the highest qualification. Which, with so much "alienating" (a social science bastardization) experience around, it is indeed. This kind of anti-eloquence certainly has the air of a stultifying newspeak, yet anti-eloquence is the rhetoric of privatization, as those who try to write love poetry these days find out when they soon fall silent. Sisterhood has inherited anti-eloquence from hippy radicalese, which honored authenticity of experience, and of being, as the highest value; and the verbal stuttering, the use of ugly shorthand forms, results from the attempt to communicate aspects of being which are, perhaps, essentially incommunicable. The lust for the real thwarted by the necessary artifice of language.

Therefore the ability to provoke reader or audience identification is one of the most highly valued qualities of a feminist writer, performer, or filmmaker. "I really identified with her," "I could totally identify with that situation," is proof positive of an artistic integrity which transcends language in the creation of a shared authenticity, a metaphysical recreation of a universal truth.

Totally almost vies with *really* in adverbial popularity and may be used with it, e.g., "really totally gripping." *Incredible* and *fantastic* are used both in adjectival and adverbial forms as accolades, which suggests an unconscious awareness that the metaphysic of universal truth is a fantasy. Yet a performer such as Patti Smith may be described in a perfectly respectable sisterhood journal as "really totally incredibly moving." An analysis of the semantics of this piece of sisterhood newspeak reveals a forlorn conclusion: for what else can it mean, however clumsily it is expressed, than that there has been an attempt at the communication of an authentic wholeness of experience which, in the context of contemporary society, it is impossible to believe to be true.

As to the effect of the anti-eloquent and allusive language of sisterhood on the evolution of the English language toward the end of the century, I leave the reader to draw his own conclusions. Please observe, from the above sentence, that the English language does indeed assume everybody to be male unless they are proved to be otherwise; and this kind of usage is, simply, silly, because it does not adequately reflect social reality, which is the very least one can expect language to do. The language of my militant sisters reflects reality in the way that the language of any politico-religious subgroup does, partially, with its own polemical, subversive bias.

EDMUND WHITE

The Political Vocabulary of Homosexuality

GAY LIBERATION is a new phenomenon, yet it has already transformed attitudes among homosexuals and modified the ways in which they speak. In June 1969 a group of lesbians and gay men resisted a routine police raid on the Stonewall, a popular dance bar in Greenwich Village. Opposition to police harrassment was unusual enough to signal a quickening sense of solidarity. Soon after the Stonewall Resistance gay organizations and publications were springing up across the country and, by now, gay liberation has become both a national and an international movement.

I was present at that original event and can recall how the participants cast about for political and linguistic models. Black power, feminism, resistance to the war in Vietnam and the New Left were all available, and each contributed to the emerging gay style and vocabulary. Discussing the beginning of the movement in this way, however, makes it sound too solemn and deliberate. Our recognition that we formed an oppressed minority struck us as *humorous* at first; only later did we come to take ourselves seriously.

I can remember that after the cops cleared us out of the bar we clustered in Christopher Street around the entrance to the Stonewall. The customers were not being arrested, but a paddy wagon had already hauled off several of the bartenders. Two or three policemen stayed behind, locked inside with the remaining members of the staff, waiting for the return of the paddy wagon. During that interval someone in the defiant crowd outside called out, "Gay Power," which caused us all to laugh. The notion that gays might become militant after the manner of blacks seemed amusing for two reasons—first because we gay men were used to thinking of ourselves as too effeminate to protest anything and secondly because most of us did not consider ourselves to be a legitimate minority.

At that time we perceived ourselves as separate individuals at odds with society because we were "sick" (the medical model), "sinful" (the religious model), "deviant" (the sociological model) or "criminal" (the legal model). Some of these words we might have said lightly, satirically, but no amount of wit could convince us that our grievances should be remedied or our status defended. We might ask for compassion but we could not demand justice. Many gays either were in therapy or felt they should be, and the words *gay liberation* would have seemed as preposterous to us as *neurotic liberation* (now, of course, Thomas S. Szasz in the United States, R. D. Laing in England and Felix Guattari on the Continent have, in their different ways, made even that phrase plausible enough).

What I want to stress is that before 1969 only a small (though courageous and articulate) number of gays had much pride in their homosexuality or a conviction that their predilections were legitimate. The rest of us defined our homosexuality in negative terms, and those terms isolated us from one another. We might claim Plato and Michelangelo as homosexuals and revere them for their supposed affinities to us, but we could just as readily dismiss, even despise, a living thinker or artist for being gay. Rich gays may have derived pleasure from their wealth, educated gays from their knowledge, talented gays from their gifts, but few felt anything but regret about their homosexuality as such. To be sure, particular sexual encounters, and especially particular love relationships, were gratifying then as now, but they were explained as happy accidents rather than as expected results.

Moreover, the very idea that sexual identity might demarcate a political entity was still fairly novel. Minority status seemed to be vouchsafed by birth, to be involuntary. One was born into a race or religion or nationality or social class—that was the way to become a member of a *real* minority. One could also be born a woman, though the large claims advanced by feminists still struck many people then as preposterous. Women, after all, formed a majority and they scarcely seemed to have much in common. Did an upper-class WASP woman from Boston share a perspective with a poor chicano Catholic woman from Waco? The same question could be asked about gays: what was our common bond? This "category confusion" assailed us and may have been one source of our laughter upon hearing the phrase *gay power.*

Then there was the problem about how people become gay. If they're born that way, they may represent, depending on the point of view, a genetic mistake or an evolutionary advance or a normal variation. If, on the other hand, they choose to be gay, then their rights seem less defensible; what has been chosen can be rejected. A third possibility is that the environment makes people gay against their will—but this etiology, because of conventional associations if not logical arguments, again smacks of pathology and suggests gays should seek to be "cured."

I raise these issues not because I propose answers (the whole discussion strikes me as politically retrograde, since at this point any etiology would disguise a program for prevention). I bring up the matter only because I want to demonstrate what a strange sort of "minority" homosexuals belong to and why we were reluctant to embrace the political vocabulary (and stance) that had been useful in securing the civil rights of other groups.

Nevertheless, because the black movement was highly vocal and visible at the time of Stonewall, slogans such as "black is beautiful" were easily translated into "gay is good" and "black power" became "gay power." Some of the resistants even dubbed themselves "pink panthers," but that name did not catch on. These derivations, I should hasten to point out, were not approved of by black militants who, like most young white leftists, regarded homosexuality as "decadent" and "bourgeois." In 1971, I believe, H. Rap Brown did propose a coalition between blacks and gays, but that suggestion was not very popular among his constituents.

A less obvious imitation of the black movement by gays was the elevation of the word *gay* itself. Just as *Negro* had been rejected as something contaminated because it had been used by (supposedly hypocritical) liberals and the seemingly more neutral *black* was brought into currency, in the same way *homosexual,* with its medical textbook ring, was dismissed in favor of the more informal and seemingly more innocuous *gay* (I say "seemingly" because these words, *black* and *gay,* do have complex etymologies).

No one I know has any real information about the origins of the word *gay;* the research all remains to be done. Those who dislike the word assume that it is synonymous with *happy* or *lighthearted* and that its use implies that homosexuals regard heterosexuals, by contrast, as "grim." But *gay* has had many meanings, including "loose" and "immoral," especially in reference to a prostitute (a whorehouse was once called a "gay house"). In the past one asked if a woman was "gay," much as today one might ask if she "swings." The identification of *gay* with "immoral" is further strengthened by the fact that *queen* (a male homosexual) is almost certainly derived from *quean* (the Elizabethan word for prostitute).

In American slang at the turn of the century, a "gay cat" was a younger, less experienced man who attached himself to an older, more seasoned vagrant or hobo; implicit in the relationship between gay cat and hobo was a sexual liaison. Yet another slang meaning of *gay* is "fresh," "impertinent," "saucy" (not so very distant from "immoral"). In French *gai* can mean "spicy" or "ribald." My hunch (and it's only a hunch) is that the word may turn out to be very old, to have originated in France, worked its way to England in the eighteenth century and thence to the colonies in America. It has died out in Europe and England and is now being reintroduced as a new word from the United States. But this is only speculation.

If the exact etymology is vague, no wonder; the word served for years as a shibboleth, and the function of a shibboleth is to exclude outsiders. Undoubtedly it has had until recently its greatest vogue among Americans. In England, the standard slang word has been *queer.* In Bloomsbury *bugger* was the preferred term, presumably because it was salty and vulgar enough to send those rarefied souls into convulsions of laughter. One pictures Virginia Woolf discussing "buggery" with Lytton Strachey; how they must have relished the word's public school, criminal and eighteenth-century connotations.

Today heterosexuals commonly object to *gay* on the grounds that it has ruined for them the ordinary festive sense of the word; one can no longer say, "How gay I feel!" It seems frivolous, however, to discuss this semantic loss beside the political gain the word represents for American homosexuals. An English novelist visiting the States, after boring everyone by saying she felt gay life was actually sad (an observation she presented as though it were original), proceeded to call gay men "queer," which I presume is less offensive in England than in America (a few older Americans use the word).

Many homosexuals object to *gay* on other grounds, arguing that it's too silly to designate a life-style, a minority or a political movement. But, as the critic Seymour Kleinberg has mentioned in his introduction to *The Other Persuasion: Short Fiction about Gay Men and Women,* "For all its limitations, 'gay' is the only unpompous, unpsychological term acceptable to most men and women, one already widely used and available to heterosexuals without suggesting something pejorative." *Gay* is, moreover, one of the few words that does not refer explicitly to sexual activity. One of the problems that has beleaguered gays is that their identity has always been linked to sexual activity rather than to affectional preference. The word *gay* (whatever its etymology) at least does not *sound* sexual.

In any event, *gay* is so workable a word that in the last ten years it has shifted from being just an adjective to being both an adjective and a noun. One now says, "Several gays were present," though such a construction sounds awkward to older American homosexuals. Just as Fowler in *A Guide to Modern English Usage* objects to *human* as a noun and prefers *human being,* so many homosexuals still prefer *gay person* or *gay man.*

The connection between feminism and gay liberation has been strong for a decade, though now it has broken down. Because of this break, the word *gay* now generally refers to homosexual men alone. Homosexual women prefer to be called *lesbians,* pure and simple. Most lesbian radicals feel they have more in common with the feminist movement than with gay liberation. Since political lesbians tend to resent a male spokesman, I have confined most of my remarks in this essay to the gay male experience which, in any event, is more within my range of competance and understanding.

This fairly recent rupture, however, should not obscure the debt that gay liberation owes to feminism. The members of both movements, for instance, regard their inner experiences as political, and for both gays and feminists the function of consciousness-raising sessions has been to trace the exact contours of their oppression. Women and gay men, as the argument goes, have been socialized into adopting restricting roles that are viewed with contempt by heterosexual men (despite the fact that these very roles reinforce the values of a virilist society). Accordingly, at least one aspect of feminism and gay liberation has been to end the tyranny of stereotyped behavior. Much of this stereotyping, of course, is perpetuated by the victimized themselves. Many women have a low opinion of other women, and many gays are quick to ridicule other gays.

For example, political gays have fought the use of the feminine gender when employed by one homosexual man of another. In the past a regular feature of gay male speech was the production of such sentences as: "Oh, *her*! She'd do anything to catch a husband. . . ." in which the "she" is Bob or Jim. This routine gender substitution is rapidly dying out, and many gay men under twenty-five fail to practice it or even to understand it. This linguistic game has been attacked for two reasons: first, because it supposedly perpetuates female role playing among some gay men; and second, because it is regarded in some quarters as hostile to women. Since one man generally calls another "she" in an (at least mildly) insulting context, the inference is that the underlying attitude must be sexist: to be a woman is to be inferior.

Following the same line, a large segment of the lesbian and gay male population frowns on drag queens, who are seen as mocking women, all the more so because they get themselves up in the most *retardataire* female guises (show girls, prostitutes, sex kittens, Hollywood starlets).

This rejection of transvestites has been harsh and perhaps not well thought out. As long ago as 1970 Kate Millett in *Sexual Politics* saw the drag queen in quite another light—as a useful subversive:

> . . . as she minces along a street in the Village, the storm of outrage an insouciant queen in drag may call down is due to the fact that she is both masculine and feminine at once—or male, but feminine. She has made gender identity more than frighteningly easy to lose, she has questioned its reality at a time when it has attained the status of a moral absolute and a social imperative. She has defied it and actually suggested its negation. She has dared obloquy, and in doing so has challenged more than the taboo on homosexuality, she has uncovered what the source of this contempt implies—the fact that sex role is sex rank.

Anyone familiar with drag knows that it is an *art* of impersonation, not an act of deception, still less of ridicule. The drag queen performing in a night club, for instance, is often careful to reveal his true masculinity (deep voice, flat chest, short hair) at some point in his performance; such a revelation underscores the achievements of artifice. Since, in addition, most gay transvestites are from the working class and many are either black or Puerto Rican, discrimination against them may be both snobbish and racist. The greatest irony is that the Stonewall Resistance itself and many other gay "street actions" were led by transvestites.

As for why drag queens have singled out prostitutes and show girls to imitate, the explanation may be at least partially historical. In Jonathan Katz's *Gay American History,* one discovers a clue.

Testimony given to the New York police in 1899 has this to say of male prostitutes: "These men that conduct themselves there—well, they act effeminately; most of them are painted and powdered; they are called Princess this and Lady So and So and the Duchess of Marlboro, and get up and sing as women, and dance; ape the female character; call each other sisters and take people out for immoral purposes."

Obviously, then, many of the early drag queens actually were prostitutes. Others may have found that the world of the theater and prostitution was the only one where overt homosexuals were welcome. Or perhaps the assertive make-believe of such women, purveyors of sex and fantasy, seemed naturally related to the forbidden pleasures of gay men. Or perhaps the assault on convention staged by prostitutes and performers appealed to gay men because it was a gaudy if ambiguous expression of anger. In any event, this legacy can still be faintly heard in gay speech today, though less and less often ("Don't be such a cunt," "Look, bitch, don't cross me," "Go, girl, shake that money-maker" and in a vagueness about proper names and the substitution of the generic *darling* or *Mary*). Much more hardy is a small but essential vocabulary derived from prostitute's slang, including: *trick* (a casual sex partner as a noun, to have quickie sex as a verb); *box* (the crotch); *trade* (one-sided sex); *number* (a sex partner); *john* (a paying customer); *to hustle* (to sell sex); *to score* or *to make out* (to find sex) and so on. Few young gays, however, know the origins of these words, and certain locutions borrowed from prostitutes have been modified in order to obscure their mercenary connotations. For instance, few homosexuals still say, "I'd like to turn that trick." Instead, they say, "I'd like to trick with him." That homosexual slang should be patterned after the slang of prostitutes suggests that in the past the only homosexual men who dared talk about their sexual tastes and practices either were prostitutes themselves or lived in that milieu. Curiously, that vocabulary has flourished among gay men who have never dreamed of selling sex.

In the past, feminization, at least to a small and symbolic degree, seemed a necessary initiation into gay life; we all thought we had to be a bit *nelly* (effeminate) in order to be truly gay. Today almost the opposite seems to be true. In any crowd it is the homosexual men who are wearing beards, army fatigues, checked lumberjack shirts, work boots and T-shirts and whose bodies are conspicuously built up. Ironically, at a time when many young heterosexual men are exploring their androgeny by living with women in platonic amicability and by stripping away their masculine stoicism and toughness, young gays are busy arraying themselves in these castoffs and becoming cowboys, truckers, telephone linemen, football players (in appearance and sometimes also in reality).

This masculinization of gay life is now nearly universal. Flamboyance has been traded in for a sober, restrained manner. Voices are lowered, jewelry is shed, cologne is banished and, in the decor of houses, velvet and chandeliers have been exchanged for functional carpet and industrial lights. The campy queen who screams in falsetto, *dishes* (playfully insults) her friends, swishes by in drag is an anachronism; in her place is an updated Paul Bunyan.

Personal advertisements for lovers or sex partners in gay publications call for men who are "macho," "butch," "masculine" or who have a "straight appearance." The advertisements insist that "no femmes need apply." So extreme is this masculinization that it has been termed "macho fascism" by its critics. They point out that the true social mission of liberated homosexuals should be to break down, not reinforce, role-playing stereotypes. Gay men should exemplify the dizzying rewards of living beyond gender. But they have betrayed this promise and ended up by aping the most banal images of conventionally "rugged" men—or so the anti-macho line would have it.

In the heady early days of gay liberation, certainly, apologists foresaw the speedy arrival of a unisex paradise in which gay angels, dressed in flowing garments and glorying in shoulder-length, silken hair, would instruct heterosexual men in how to discard their cumbersome masculinity and ascend to the heights of androgyny. Paradoxically, today it is the young straights who wear their hair long and style it daily, who deck themselves out in luxurious fabrics and gold filaments, who cover their bodies with unguents, dive into a padded conversation pit and squirm about in "group gropes" (in which, mind you, lesbianism may be encouraged for its entertainment value to male spectators but never the swains shall meet). Simultaneously but elsewhere, crew-cut gays, garbed in denim and rawhide, are manfully swilling beer at a country and western bar and, each alone in the crowd, tapping a scuffed boot to Johnny Cash's latest.

Another objection to the masculinization of gay life is that it has changed a motley crew of eccentrics into a highly conformist army of clones. Whereas gays in the past could be slobs or bohemians or Beau Brummels or aesthetes striking "stained glass attitudes" or tightly closeted businessmen in gray flannel suits, today this range of possibility has been narrowed to a uniform look and manner that is uninspiredly butch. The flamboyance and seediness and troubling variety of gay life (a variety that once embraced all the outcasts of society, including those who were not gay) have given way to a militant sameness.

This argument, I think, ignores our historical moment. In the past gay men embraced the bias of the oppressor that identified homosexuality with effeminacy, degeneracy, failure. To have discovered that this link is not necessary has released many homosexuals into a forceful assertion of their masculinity, normality, success—an inevitable and perhaps salutary response. Moreover, the conformism of gay life, I suspect, is more on the level of appearance than reality. The butch look is such a successful get-up for cruising that some sort of "natural selection" in mating has made it prevail over all other costumes. But this look does not preclude the expression of individuality, of tenderness and zaniness, in conversation and private behavior.

Yet another thought occurs to me. In the past many homosexuals despised each other and yearned for even the most fleeting and unsatisfactory sexual (or even social) contact with straight men. Some gays considered sex with other homosexuals pointless and pitiable, a poor second best, and thirsted for the font of all value and authenticity, a "real" (i.e., straight) man. Today, fortified by gay liberation, homosexuals have become those very men they once envied and admired from afar.

The apotheosis of the adult macho man has meant that the current heart-throb in gay pornography—and in actual gay cruising situations—is no longer the lithe youth of nineteen but rather the prepossessing stud of thirty-five. The ephebe with hyacinthine curls has given way to the bald marine drill sergeant, and Donatello's *David* demurs to Bernini's.

The change has affected the language of approbation. In the past one admired a "boy" who was "beautiful" or "pretty" or "cute." Now one admires a man who is "tough" or "virile" or "hot." Perhaps no other word so aptly signals the new gay attitudes as *hot.* Whereas *beautiful* in gay parlance characterizes the face first and the body only secondarily, *hot* describes the whole man, but especially his physique. One may have a lantern jaw or an assymmetrical nose or pockmarked skin and still be "hot," whereas the signs of the "beautiful" face are regular features, smooth skin, suave coloring—and youth. The "hot" man may even fail to have an attractive body; his appeal may lie instead in his wardrobe, his manner, his style. In this way "hotness" is roughly equivalent to "presence" with an accent on the sexy rather than the magisterial sense of that word. In addition, "hot" can, like the Italian *simpatico,* modify everything from people to discos, from cars to clothing. Gay chartered cruises promise a "hot" vacation and designers strive after a "hot" look. If an attractive man strolls by, someone will murmur, "That's hot." The "that" in place of "he" may be an acknowledgment that the person is as much a package as a human being, though more likely the impersonal pronoun is a last echo of the old practice (now virtually abandoned) of referring to a one-time-only sex partner as an "it" (as in, "The trick was fine in bed, but I had to throw it out this morning—couldn't get it to shut up").

Gay male culture, as though in flight from its effeminate past, is more and more gravitating towards the trappings of sado-masochism. The big-city gay man of today no longer clusters with friends around a piano at a bar to sing songs from musicals; now he goes to a leather and western bar to play pool and swill beer. Gay men belong to motorcycle clubs or engage in anonymous sex in backrooms, those dimly lit penetralia behind the normally sociable bar.

The popularity of sado-masochistic sex has introduced new words into the gay vocabulary—as well as their domesticated, more casual variants. The original terms, such as *slave* and *master,* must have seemed too absurd, too theatrical, not quite plausible, too . . . well, *embarrassing.* It is socially awkward to ask a stranger if he wants to be your "slave" for the night. The word invokes dungeons, chains, pornographic novels of the eighteenth century—a sort of period claptrap. As a result, nearly every word in the original vocabulary has found its more conversational, more up-to-date euphemism. "Sado-masochism" itself has thus become "S and M" or, more recently and innocuously, "rough stuff." Bondage and discipline is now "B and D." "Sadist" and "masochist" have become "top man" and "bottom man." The way to ask someone to be your slave, therefore, is "Are you into a bottom scene?" Similarly, sexual aggression kept on the level of fantasy is a "head trip," whereas to want physical abuse is to be "into pain." And the "dungeon" has become the "game room."

Interestingly, gay men, usually so fastidious about staying *au courant,* are willing to utter outmoded hippy words from the drug culture of the sixties such as *scene, trip* and *into* if those words enable periphrases that stand in for the still more ludicrous vocabulary of classical sadism.

I have tried to point out that gay male culture and language have registered a shift in taste away from effeminacy to masculinity and from youth to maturity. But now a larger question might be posed: has the status of—and the need for—a private language itself become less important to homosexuals?

I think it has. In the past homosexuality was regarded with such opprobrium and homosexuals remained so inconspicuous that we faced some difficulty in detecting one another. A familiar game was to introduce into an otherwise normal conversation a single word that might seem innocent enough except to the initiated ("I went to a very lively and gay party last night"). If that risk was greeted with words from the same vocabulary ("I'm afraid the party I went to was a real drag; everyone acted like royalty," i.e., "queens"), a contact was established. Two businessmen could thus identify themselves to one another in the midst of a heterosexual gathering.

But the value of a private language was not merely practical. It also allowed gays to name everything anew, to appropriate experience in terms that made sense only to the few. Sailors became "sea food," "chicken" (always singular) were teenage boys and so on—there is a whole book, *The Queen's Vernacular,* that lists these words. Equally amusing and subversive was the pleasure of referring to a revered public leader as "Miss Eisenhower," or to oneself (as Auden does at the end of an otherwise serious poem) as "Miss Me." When gay frustration had no outlet in action it could find expression only in language. But even in language the impulse had become sour and self-destructive through long suppression; its target was more often other gays than straights or in the fiction that respectable straights were actually outrageous queens. In self-satire lies the reflexive power of thwarted anger. Gay identity, now rehearsed nightly in thronged discos and in a myriad of gay bars, was once much more tenuous. It was an illegitimate existence that took refuge in language, the one system that could swiftly, magically, topple values and convert a golf-playing general into a co-conspirator in a gingham frock and turn a timid waiter into a queen for a night—or at least into the Duchess of Marlboro.

Now that homosexuals have no need for indirection, now that their suffering has been eased and their place in society adumbrated if not secured, the suggestion has been made that they will no longer produce great art. There will be no liberated Prousts, the argument goes, an idea demonstrated by pointing to the failure of *Maurice* in contrast to Forester's heterosexual novels. A review of my novel, *Nocturnes for the King of Naples,* claimed that it was not as strong as my earlier, "straight" *Forgetting Elena* precisely because I no longer need to resort to the pretense of heterosexuality.

This position strikes me as strange and unexamined. Proust, of course, *did* write at length about homosexual characters—in fact, one of the complaints against his novel is that so many characters implausibly turn out to be homosexual. *Maurice,* I suspect, is a failure not because it is homosexual but because it is a rather exalted, sentimentalized masturbation fantasy. When he wrote *Maurice,* Forester had even less knowledge of the homosexual than of the heterosexual world, and he was forced back on his day-dreams rather than on his observations from life. It is not for me to judge the merits of my own books, but what strikes me as most "homosexual" about *Nocturnes* is not the content so much as the technique, one that uses endless dissolves of time and geography, as though the same party were being reassembled over decades and on different continents, something like that "marvellous party" in the Noel Coward song. Anyone who has experienced the enduring and international links of gay life will recognize how the technique is a formal equivalent to the experience.

Unless one accepts the dreary (and unproved) Freudian notion that art is a product of sublimated neuroses, one would not predict that gay liberation would bring an end to the valuable art made by homosexuals. On the contrary, liberation should free gays from tediously repetitious works that end in madness or suicide, that dwell on the "etiology" of the characters' homosexuality (shadowy Dad, suffocating Mom, beloved, doomed, effeminate Cousin Bill) and that feature long, static scenes in which Roger gently weeps over Hank's mislaid hiking boot. Now a new range of subject matter has opened up to gays, much of it comic; Feydeau, after all, would have loved gay life, since every character can cheat with every other and the mathematical possibilities of who may be hiding under the bed (if not in the closet) have been raised geometrically. Still more importantly, gay liberation means that not so many talentless souls need to continue lingering about in the sacred precincts (i.e., the gay ghetto) of high culture. Finally they are free to pursue all those other occupations they once feared to enter—electrical engineering, riding the range, plumbing. The association between homosexuals and the arts, I suspect, suited some of us but not most; the great majority of gays are as reassuringly philistine as the bulk of straights.

ALICIA OSTRIKER

Body Language: Imagery of the Body in Women's Poetry

BEGIN WITH three passages: an observation about women writers; an explanation for that observation, in the form of a little poetic fable; and the voice of a woman poet advising her daughter.

> The American artist has sometimes avoided [her femininity] by getting her mental hysterectomy early. She will often not speak for female experience even when the men do. She will be the angel-artist, with celestially muted lower parts. Sometimes, in any of the arts, where women's work remains beautifully mandarin or minor, it may be not because of their womanhood but from their lack of it.
>
> (Hortense Calisher, "No Important Woman Writer")

> We sat across the table.
> he said, cut off your hands.
> they are always poking at things.
> they might touch me.
> I said yes.
>
> Food grew cold on the table.
> he said, burn your body,
> it is not clean and smells like sex.
> it rubs my mind sore.
> I said yes.
>
> I love you, I said.
> that's very nice, he said.

I like to be loved,
that makes me happy.
Have you cut off your hands yet?

(Marge Piercy, "The Friend")

Oh, darling, let your body in,
let it tie you in,
in comfort. . . .
What I want to say, Linda,
is that there is nothing in your body that lies.

(Anne Sexton, "Little Girl, My String Bean,
My Lovely Woman")

Muted lower parts. Burn your body. Nothing that lies. One of the ways we recognize a "poetess" is that she steers clear of anatomy. One of the ways we recognize a woman poet, these days, is that her muted parts start explaining themselves.

During the last two decades, American women poets have been employing anatomical imagery both more frequently and more intimately than their male counterparts.[1] Their female audiences enjoy this. Male readers, unsurprisingly, tend to be made uncomfortable by female candor and to feel that it is inartistic. It is of course difficult for any of us to evade the mental yardstick which seems to have been let down from heaven like Jacob's ladder, governing thousands of years of religion, philosophy, and literature, according to which the mortal and corruptible flesh imprisons the immortal and incorruptible soul, the body is base and the mind is exalted. If anatomy is destiny, we all want to escape it. From Plato to Freud, and beyond Freud to Simone de Beauvoir, civilization means vertical mobility: one transcends the body in order to achieve anything of public worth.[2] As to woman: woman in our mythology *is* the flesh, when men write about her; she has not been required to write about the flesh herself. *E puor,* as Galileo remarked of her earthy prototype, *il muove.*

I propose to examine three sorts of representative attitudes discernable in women poets who explore female bodily experience,[3] associated with three sorts of verbal strategies. In the work to which I refer the familiar vertical standard has disappeared; body is not assumed to be inferior to some higher principle. The attitudes are rejection, ambivalence, and affirmation; the verbal devices are irony, comedy, and revisionist symbolism. I am interested in the emotions, the forms employed, and the reinterpretations of other matters which follow from interpreting the body.

I

What a trash
To annihilate each decade.
What a million filaments.

SYLVIA PLATH, "Lady Lazarus"

Poets who despise the flesh traditionally do so for two associated reasons. The flesh is both corrupt and corruptible; that is, both inherently sinful and inherently subject to change and death. The former grievance is expressed morally, the latter lyrically—and with the understanding that in the youth and prime of life, the flesh is a source of pleasure.

A large number of women poets since the 1960s appear to view the body as a source essentially of pain, not pleasure. Poems about abortion, poems about breast surgery, poems about rape have become part of women's poetic repertoire. There exists a subgenre of poems in which a woman's flesh and blood are manipulated by a condescending doctor figure. The damaged bodies of war victims, the hungry bodies of famine victims, are important images in the work of Adrienne Rich, Muriel Rukeyser, Denise Levertov. Women also seem drawn to describe psychic hurt in somatic terms:

He tells me I am boring.
He hollows out a space inside my chest
as a whittler would do it,
carefully, coolly,
whistling a tune
everyone knows and likes.

(Lynn Sukenick, "The Poster")[4]

My first sister is sewing her costume for the procession.
She is going as the Transparent Lady
and all her nerves will be visible.

My second sister is also sewing
at the seam over her heart which has never healed entirely.
At last, she hopes, this tightness in her chest will cease.

(Adrienne Rich, "Women")[5]

Stop bleeding   said the knife.
I would if I   could said the cut.
Stop bleeding   you make me messy with this blood.
I'm sorry   said the cut.

(May Swenson, "Bleeding")[6]

The normal as well as the abnormal in a woman's life may feel like imprisonment, as in Lisel Mueller's "Life of a Queen," which summarizes the biological cycle of a cognate species ("They build a pendulous chamber / for her, and stuff her with sweets. . . . A crew disassembles / her royal cell") or the opening of Anne Sexton's "Snow White":

> No matter what life you lead
> the virgin is a lovely number,
> cheeks fragile as cigarette paper,
> arms and legs made of Limoges,
> lips like Vin du Rhone,
> rolling her china-blue eyes
> open and shut.[7]

To understand the connection between physical vulnerability and ironic self-rejection in women poets, we may consider Sylvia Plath.[8] Plath's work is filled with body images both internal and external: skin, blood, skulls, feet, mouths and tongues, wounds, bone, lungs, heart and veins, legs and arms. She writes of both male and female bodies. She also projects human anatomy into the natural world. The moon is "a face in its own right, / White as a knuckle and terribly upset." Goldfish ponds being drained "collapse like lungs." An elm speaks like a woman pregnant, or cancer-ridden—one cannot tell the difference:

> Terrified by this dark thing
> That sleeps in me;
> All day I feel its soft, feathery turnings, its malignity.

Tulips, when the poet is hospitalized, breathe

> Lightly through their swaddlings, like an awful baby.
> Their redness talks to my wound, it corresponds. . . .
> They are opening like the mouth of some great African cat.

The organic, for Plath, is approximately identical with suffering. Her poetry offers fragments of beings, not whole persons. A critic observes:

> The living flesh is felt as . . . a prey to axes, doctor's needles, butchers' and surgeons' knives, poison, snakes and tentacles, acids, vampires, leeches and bats, jails and brutal boots. Small animals are butchered and eaten, man's flesh can undergo the final indignity of being cut to pieces and used as an object. . . . Subjects and metaphors include a cut, a contusion, the tragedy of thalidomide, fever, an accident, a wound, paralysis, a burial, animal and human sacrifice, the burning of heretics, lands devastated by wars, exter-

> mination camps: her poetry is a "garden of tortures" in which mutilation and annihilation take nightmarishly protean forms.[9]

A number of the persistent motifs are particularly feminine. Plath's imagery of strangulation implies in extreme form the woman fatally imprisoned and stifled by her own body. Attacks by miniature enemies evoke the idea of a woman's body as parasite, feeding from her life. Children are hooks sticking in one's skin, and placenta and umbilical cord threaten the poet in "Medusa." Most painfully, her imagery of laceration suggests woman's essential anatomical condition, shameful to endure, difficult to confess—as in "Cut," where the poet runs through a series of brilliant metaphors for the thumb she has just sliced with a kitchen knife "instead of an onion." All the metaphors are masculine and military, "Little pilgrim . . . Redcoats . . . Homunculus . . . Kamikaze man," before the final

> How you jump—
> Trepanned veteran,
> Dirty girl,
> Thumb stump.

What, after all, is more humiliating in our culture than being a bleeding, dirty girl? At the same time, the landscape of war and mutilation in a poem like "Getting There," the references to Jews and Nazis in "Daddy" and "Lady Lazarus," the "Hiroshima ash" of "Fever 103" and even the sour commercial comedy of "The Applicant," in which a wife is sold like a household appliance and only the mutilated man can be normal enough to marry, reinforce Plath's vision of worldly existence as at worst holocaust, at best tawdry sideshow. The drama of social and political life plays out, on a nightmarishly large scale, the victimization of the body.

Plath demonstrates a will toward detachment from body and world in two ways, of which the first is Art—the distancing of experience through poetic manipulation. Her early verse employs tight formal structures, bookish diction, an armory of allusions to sanctioned works of art and literature, and a consistently ironic impersonality of tone, which has everything to do with rising above experience, little to do with dwelling in it. The looser, less traditional forms of her late work rather intensify than relax our sense of the poet's control. She manipulates rhyme and off-rhyme, regular and irregular meter, with the casualness of a juggler tossing knives, and her mature mastery of colloquial idiom illustrates her contempt for the vulgar and cruel social relations which generate such idiom. She becomes a mocker of the vernacular, using language against itself:

> The peanut-crunching crowd shoves in to see
> Them unwrap me hand and foot—
> The big strip tease.
>
> ("Lady Lazarus")

> Every woman adores a Fascist,
> The boot in the face.
>
> ("Daddy")

But "Dying / Is an art, like everything else." The implicit equation is clear as early as "Two Views of a Cadaver Room," which places a real-life scene with corpses next to the "panorama of smoke and slaughter" in a Breughel painting. In "The Disquieting Muses," Plath rejects her mother's cheery songs and stories for the three bald and faceless figures she accepts as artistic guides. And in *Ariel,* as in poem after poem, the poet "unpeels" herself from her body, lets it "flake" away, annihilates the "trash" of flesh which disgusts her because it would make her kin to the ogling peanut-crunching crowd—as she transforms herself from gross matter to "a pure acetylene virgin" rising toward heaven, or to dew evaporating in the sunrise—transcendence always means death. And if she fears and scorns death's perfection ("Perfection is terrible. It cannot have children." "This is what it means to be complete. It is horrible."), self-annihilation is nevertheless the ultimately artistic, ultimately ironic response to humiliation.

Plath is an extreme example. We may view her work aesthetically as a radical extension of the mode of disenchanted alienation in the Eliot-Auden-Lowell line. We may view it morally as a capitulation to weakness, a self-indulgence. Perhaps it is both. In any case, the identification of woman and body, body and vulnerability, vulnerability and irony—which in effect responds to the implacable indifference or cruelty of the external world by internalizing it—is a common phenomenon in women's poetry of the last twenty years.

II

Our Masks, Always in Peril

CAROLYN KIZER, "Pro Femina"

As W. B. Yeats has his "beautiful mild woman" (actually Maude Gonne's sister) observe in "Adam's Curse,"

To be born woman is to know—
Although they do not speak of it at school—
Women must labour to be beautiful.

In reply, one may imagine a chorus of not-so-mild women poets remarking: you said it. The labors of loveliness have not been traditionally spoken of in poetry, beyond mysogynist attacks on the foulness of the painted woman, like Swift's "Celia." But they are now, commonly to hilarious effect. Honor Moore's poem "My Mother's Mustache" gives a wry and detailed account of adolescence with and without depilatories. Karen Swenson tells of a bosom which never attains movie star amplitude, and hopes (with oral metaphors in the Spenser-to-Keats tradition) to find a man who will settle for dumplings at the feast of life. Kathleen Fraser writes a "Poem in Which My Legs Are Accepted." The opening poem of Diane Wakoski's *Motorcycle Betrayal Poems* complains about "this ridiculous face / of lemon rinds / and vinegar cruets."[10] Grumbling with the voice of multitudes in "Woman Poem," Nikki Giovanni summarizes:

it's a sex object if you're pretty
and no love
or love and no sex if you're fat[11]

Beauty, when a woman stops to think about it, means bondage. In "A Work of Artifice" Marge Piercy compares the feminine fate with that of a bonsai tree, artificially miniature:

It is your nature
to be small and cosy,
domestic and weak;
how lucky, little tree. . . .
with living creatures
one must begin very early
to dwarf their growth:
the bound feet,
the crippled brain,
the hair in curlers,
the hands you
love to touch.[12]

The adaptation of advertising language in the final lines grimly indicates both commercial-economic and emotional reasons for woman's bondage. Her face is someone else's fortune. But what can she do? She needs to be loved. Only slightly less bitter, Carolyn Kizer in "Pro Femina" talks "about women of letters, for I'm in the racket," and addresses the unique dilemma of the lady with brains and ambition:

> Our masks, always in peril of smearing or cracking,
> In need of continuous check in the mirror or silverware,
> Keep us in thrall to ourselves, concerned with our surfaces.

Men, says Kizer, do not have this problem. Male fashions are "hard-fibered . . . designed to achieve self-forgetfulness":

> So, sister, forget yourself a few times, and see where it gets you:
> Up the creek, alone with your talent, sans everything else.
> You can wait for the menopause, and catch up on your reading.[13]

While quizzical poems on the topic of beauty versus truth as applied to cosmetics will admittedly weigh lightly in most literary scales, they typically embody two interesting stylistic decisions. First, the poems are not only openly autobiographical and factual, but anti-literary, even anti-aesthetic, in the sense that they refuse, rather than cultivate, formal distance.[14] No persona, no gloss of verbal refinement, intervenes between the poet and her sense of personal inadequacy, or between herself and her audience. There is no "extinction of personality" here. As readers, we are asked to participate in the predicament of someone who wants to be beautiful while challenging, implicitly or explicitly, the standards or value of beauty for a woman, and who does not pretend to transcend the situation. It would be inappropriate to make the poem itself too beautiful.

But the poem must be comic. Comedy enables writer and reader to agree that the predicament is, after all, innately absurd. Not a life-or-death matter, is it? Clowning shows that we have perspective. Or perhaps we laugh that we may not show the frown lines to the mirror? The rollicking meter and jaunty-to-blustery tone of "Pro Femina," unlike Kizer's more usual lyric style, serve the same function as a woman's preening: they make a disguise for a naked emotion, as paint for a woman's naked face.

Possibly the funniest, certainly the most outrageous poem of this subgenre is Erica Jong's tour de force "Aging," subtitled "Balm for a 27th Birthday," published in 1968.[15] Jong at the outset presents herself as

> Hooked for two years now on wrinkle creams   creams for
> crowsfeet   ugly lines (if only there were one!)

any perfumed grease which promises youth beauty
not truth but all I need on earth
I've been studying how women age
how

it starts around the eyes so you can tell
a woman of 22 from one of 28 merely by
a faint scribbling near the lids a subtle crinkle. . . .

She imagines through several stanzas the advancing track of the wrinkles, as "ruin proceeds downwards" and the face begins to resemble "the tragic mask." Her tone grows increasingly nervous. But the poem is undergoing a transformation of its own, from self-mocking panic to self-loving acceptance. Though "the neck will give you away" and the chin in spite of face-lifts "will never quite love your bones as it once did,"

the belly may be kept firm through numerous pregnancies
by means of sit-ups jogging dancing (think of Russian
ballerinas) & the cunt
as far as I know is ageless possibly immortal becoming simply
more open more quick to understand more dry-eyed than at 22
which

after all is what you were dying for (as you ravaged
islands of turtles beehives oysterbeds the udders of cows)
desperate to censor changes which you simply might have let play
over you lying back listening opening yourself
letting the years make love the only way (poor blunderers)
they know

If a woman is naturally narcissistic, she might as well go the whole hog. Beauty is, Jong reminds us, as beauty does. Incidental amusements like the play on "lines" and "plotting" in a woman's face or her writing (both of which show "promise" of "deepening") occupy the reader through the first part of the poem. The four-letter term at the poem's crux has been cunningly prepared for by suggestions that decline in one aspect may bring ascendance in another. The close gracefully offers the pun on "what you were dying for," and concludes with a deft inversion of a centuries-old poetic convention. Time, the enemy of love in lyric poetry since the Greek *Anthologia,* has become a sequence of lovers—blundering, presumably young and inexperienced lovers at that—to whom a woman, ripe with herself, can condescend.

Jong writes less successfully when she attempts to make narcissism look sublime rather than ridiculous, and poems of self-examination in this surface sense do not easily survive the comic mode. Because humor can effectively spotlight problems and conflicts which are naggingly real if ostensibly trivial, the comic-autobiographical mode has become a major option in women's writing.

III

It is that dream world Anais speaks of
that dark watery place
where everything is female
where you open the door of the house
and she waits upstairs
the way you knew she would
and her hair floats over the world. . . .
Until she rises as though from the sea
not on the half-shell this time
and not as delicate as he imaged her,
a woman big-hipped, beautiful, and fierce.

SHARON BARBA, "A Cycle of Women"[16]

When women write to praise the body, rather than attack or joke about it, their most significant technique is symbolism. Water, moon, earth and living things, the natural as opposed to the artificial, provide the strongest sources of imagery for women poets engaged in commending the basic physical self, just as they always have for men describing women.

Nevertheless, there are differences. The identification of woman with flowers, for example, is at least as old as the *Roman de la Rose.* Elizabethan poets agreed that "Beauty is but a flower / Which wrinkles will devour." Keats urged the melancholy lover to glut his sorrow on a rose, a wealth of globed peonies, or his mistress's peerless eyes, all of which dwell with beauty that must die. Poets have seen both woman and flower from without, whether in erotic poetry, poetry of witty seduction, or poetry of reflection on the transience and mutability of life. But when Diane Wakoski in 1968 compares an armful of roses first with skin and then with internal organs, the focus changes:

The full roses with all their petals like the wrinkles of laughter
on your face as you bend to kiss someone
are bursting on the bush,

spotting my arm, as I carry a bundle of them
to my friends;
they seem to have come out of my skin
on this hot fragrant night,
and I imagine the inside of my body
glowing, phosphorescent, with strange flower faces
looking out from the duodenum
or the soft liver,
white as my belly, the eyes always disbelieving
the ugly processes that make a living body.[17]

In their particularized detail—color, texture—as well as dramatic quality, these flowers resemble Plath's poppies and tulips. We experience not "beauty" but an overwhelming vividness, energy, and terror in the sense of self as living organism. The rapid and radical alterations of focus in Wakoski's lines blur spatial distinctions between night and roses, face, arm, and the inside of the body, until everything seems equally bursting, hot, fragrant, and in flux. The extreme vitality of flowers and body approaches the obscene, as in Plath it approaches the predatory. Though wrinkled, there is nothing frail or weak in the blossoms of either poet.[18]

Again, when Adrienne Rich writes of diving into the wreck, or Sharon Barba of entering "that dark watery place," both poets accept a woman-water identification held in common with Shakespeare's Cleopatra, identified with the fertile and capricious Nile, or with Milton's Eve—whose first act in *Paradise Lost* is to kneel and behold her own image in water, where Adam at the moment of his creation sprang upright and looked at the sky. We recall the sea-mother in Whitman's "Out of the Cradle," and the mermaids of Prufrock's plunge into memory, into fantasy, into that brief moment of womblike ease before he wakes and chokes on mortal air. Throughout western tradition, descent into water signifies danger or death, consistently associated with the feminine. If a Conrad recommends "in the destructive element immerse," he does not mean to minimize its alien quality.

Women who make the same plunge also evoke the dangerous and the unknown, but they tend to evoke at the same time a sense of trust. The destructive element is *their* element. It is alien, and yet it is home, where one will not be hurt. Rich notes that relaxation rather than force is required to maneuver here, and she is confident of finding treasure as well as devastation. At the deepest point in the poem she becomes her deepest self, the androgyne: "I am she . . . I am he." Barba anticipates, from these waves, the birth of a new Venus, closer to nature than Botticelli's.

Still again, if our most celebrated and compendious symbol for woman is earth, adored as mother, revered as virgin, Earth is of course always "other" than the celebrant; she is always the principle of passive material life divided from the mental or spiritual; and she is always subject to conquest. Women who identify with earth, however, include Margaret Atwood who in her "Circe/Mud" poems taunts Odysseus: "Don't you get tired of saying Onward?"[19] and Yosana Akiko who in "Mountain Moving Day" makes the mountain a symbol both of women's bodies and of their awakening consciousness.[20] The idea of a consciousness indivisible from the earthy body appears in Anne Sexton's notorious "In Celebration of My Uterus," written on the occasion of a medical reprieve which has defied rational diagnosis.[21] Sexton's opening is euphoric, buoyant, hyperbolic:

> They wanted to cut you out
> but they will not. . . .
> They said you were sick unto dying
> but they were wrong.
> You are singing like a school girl.

The poem's central portion compares the uterus with "soil of the fields . . . roots," and the poet announces, in an engaging combination of insouciant self-confidence and generosity:

> Each cell has a life.
> There is enough here to feed a nation.
> It is enough that the populace own these goods.
> Any person, any commonwealth would say of it,
> "It is good this year that we may plant again,
> and think forward to a harvest."

Then comes another shift, as the poet announces that

> Many women are singing together of this:
> one is in a shoe factory cursing the machine,
> one is at the aquarium tending a seal,
> one is dull at the wheel of her Ford,
> one is at the toll gate collecting,
> one is tying the cord of a calf in Arizona,
> one is straddling a cello in Russia,
> one is shifting pots on the stove in Egypt,
> one is painting her bedroom walls moon color,
> one is dying but remembering a breakfast,
> one is stretching on her mat in Thailand,
> one is wiping the ass of her child,

one is staring out the window of a train
in the middle of Wyoming and one is
anywhere and some are everywhere and all
seem to be singing, although some can not
sing a note.

The abundance and fertility of the poet's imagination in inventing her group of women of all types, from all regions of the globe, must be understood as parallel to, or an extension of, her uterine health. Moreover, this chorale of far-flung women cannot be perceived from without, precisely as the continued vitality and fertility of the womb has evaded external discernment. As matter, so spirit. Both, according to this poem, lie within, in the realm of the immanent rather than the transcendent. The function of spirit is to celebrate matter, not to subdue or escape it, and women become mutually connected beings by the participation of spirit in the principle of flesh they commonly share. Sexton has used a conventional fertility-and-harvest symbolism to lure us into a set of convictions—here presented as perceptions—entirely opposed to those of the vertical standard.

For a woman, perhaps the most decisively difficult act is to think of herself as powerful, or as more powerful than a man, and capable of influencing the outward world without sacrificing femaleness. One poet who has asserted that female biology equals power, and has found a set of symbols to state its nature, is Robin Morgan.

In the series of poems entitled "The Network of the Imaginary Mother," Morgan describes a conversion from flesh-loathing to flesh-affirmation while nursing her dying mother, and defines her biological capacities in terms of goddess-figures—Kali, Demeter, Isis, African and pre-Columbian madonnas—representing a triumphant will to love and nurture. Her husband in this poem is Osiris, a "consort," and her son teaches "the simple secret" of delight. For Morgan it is not the god-man of the Gospels, but a nursing woman who says to her own son, and by extension all children, envisioning a world unthreatened by violence and famine:

Take. Eat. This is my body,
this real milk, thin, sweet, bluish,
which I give for the life of the world . . .
an honest nourishment
alone able to sustain you.[22]

Biological fact and spiritual interpretation here become indistinguishable. The poet's fantasy of a maternal politics would eliminate the burden of conflict between humanity and nature, between individual and species, between woman's body and social change.

IV

Don't you get tired of wanting to live forever?
Don't you get tired of saying Onward?

MARGARET ATWOOD, "Circle/Mud Poems"

Poets have perennially occupied themselves with discovering analogies between the macrocosm of the world and the microcosm of the self. For many women poets at present, the microcosm means, emphatically, a physical self from which it is neither possible nor desirable to divide mental or emotional existence. A particular endeavor of twentieth-century thought has involved a questioning of distinctions between private and public life, in order to understand how each influences and reflects the other. Here too, women poets seem inclined to insist that we begin with the body to understand the body politic. None of these poets seems disposed to celebrate a world of "transcendent" public action at the cost of minimizing the given physical self. For some, the dominant experience of life in the flesh is suffering. We can scarcely deny the public validity of such an apprehension in the light of history. For other writers, the relation between private and public means a conflict between what used to be called appearance and reality. To cosmetize or not to cosmetize? This is a battle fought on the fields of the skin, as well as on more dignified terrain. For still others, the body is felt as a strength, a kind of connective tissue uniting human beings at a level beneath the particularities of individual ego or circumstance, a set of capacities both socially and personally valuable.

Compared with the variety and richness of work by women in this area, that of most male poets in the 1970s appears inhibited and unoriginal. The exceptions—a Ginsberg, a Bly, a Kinnell—make the general polarization clear. If we may say that women have contrived to make a continental landscape out of the secret gardens to which they have been forcefully confined, we may say by the same token that men have endured a certain self-imposed exile. "Distance" remains a virtue in the male poetic establishment, almost like a corollary of the training which defines the masculine body exclusively as tool or weapon, forbids it to acknowledge weakness or pain, and deprives it accordingly of much potential sensitivity to pleasure—a sensuous man is an "effeminate" man—apart from the pleasures associated with combat or conquest. The discourse of male bonding may derive from big and little game hunting and the tennis court, or from allusions to the responses of women in bed. These are the safe, sane, blushproof topics.

Men also look in mirrors, experience troublesome and delicious sensations, contribute to the generation of species, and ride throughout life the tide of emotions influenced by glandular secretions. They too get ill, grow old and withered, and are, in sum, precisely as rooted in nature as women. Will they in due time acknowledge this condition? Will women begin comparing the bodies of men to flowers? Confronting old age, Yeats divided himself into two beings: an old man craving fiery purification from the flesh and an old woman—Crazy Jane—raucously declaring her satisfaction with it. We must assume that the discoveries women poets are making about bodily experience, and the verbal tactics employed to name their discoveries, will enter common usage and become readily available to men as well as women. Crazy Jane stands at the foot of the tower, inviting the man to come down.

Notes

1. A thousand lines from male poets in Stephen Berg and Robert Mezey's *Naked Poetry* (1969) and Donald Hall's *Contemporary American Poetry* (1963) contain 127 references to human (or animal) bodies. A thousand lines from women poets in Barbara Segnitz and Carol Rainey's *Psyche* (1973) and Laura Chester and Sharon Barba's *Rising Tides* (1973) contain 236 body images. Heads, faces, eyes, and hands commonly appear in the work of both sexes, and there is overlapping usage of many other terms. Terms used by male poets but not females were *saliva, snouts, gills, loins, knees, all fours, lover's nuts, brains, skull, pubic beards, torsos, cock, balls, eyeball, fistbones, wishbones, funnybone, sacrum, luz-bone, ribcages, feather, tongue-bone, bruises, foot, left shoulder, right foot, palate, jaws, ends of fingers, nipples, forearms, eyebrows, corpse.* Terms used by women poets but not men were *lid, lids, nape, foetus, scalp, braincap, throat, scales, shoulders, ears, belly, finger, fingers, knucklebone, forehead, eyelashes, tit, fro* (for *afro*, the hairdo), *armfuls, abdomen, guts, muscle, muscles, skullplates, left ear, toes, fists, hairs, teeth, instep, orifice, wrinkles, lines, breast, breasts, wings of the nose, corners of the mouth, chin, earlobes, cunt, udders, duodenum, liver, membrane, scar, scars, scalp, legs, mustache, screwcurls, lap, cheeks, palm, legs, arm, arms, thumb, epiderm, valves, nerves, vein, pore, cells, ligaments, tissue, bladder, spit, sweat, fingernails, jelly* (of an eye, during a lynching), *pulse, little toe, hips* (of the poet's father), *ovaries,* and *sperm sac* (of a queen bee). The women thus employed a greater range as well as a larger number of body images, and included more "internal" parts; specificity of observation may be indicated by the fact, e.g., that while poets of both sexes mentioned hair, the term was unmodified in the male poets but appeared variously in the women poets as "sticky gold hair," "eelgrass hair," "yellow hair," "acanthine hair," "fro," and

"screwcurls." But the largest discrepancy between the sexes appears in the fact that the women poets wrote both about their own bodies and about external figures, while the men's work included no more than a dozen references to the poets' own bodies.

The twenty male poets included in my count (50 lines each, taken from the opening of the anthology selection for each one) were Roethke, Patchen, Stafford, Kees, Berryman, Lowell, Bly, Creeley, Ginsberg, Kinnell, Merwin, Wright, Levine, Snyder, and Berg (in *Naked Poetry*); Duncan, Nemerov, Dickey, Justice, and Ashbery (in *Contemporary American Poetry*). The twenty female poets were May Swenson, Levertov, Kizer, Sexton, Rich, Plath, Piercy, Owens, Wakoski, Atwood, Lifshin, Jong, and Giovanni (in *Psyche*); Van Duyn, Mueller, Kumin, Sanchez, Clifton, Pastan, and Jordan (in *Rising Tides*). A different selection might of course have produced slightly different figures, but if the selection were made from poems published only in the 1970s, the gap between masculine reticence and feminine expressiveness about the body would appear still more pronounced.

The passage by Hortense Calisher that opens this essay is quoted in *Rising Tides;* Marge Piercy's poem is from *Hard Loving* (Wesleyen University Press, 1968); Anne Sexton's from *Live or Die* (Boston, 1966).

2. Simone de Beauvoir in *The Second Sex* develops this idea more explicitly than any other writer, in the course of an argument designed to show that male biology, because its strength and independence encourage masculine deeds of control, acts relatively to man's advantage, while female biology, because it is organized to serve "the iron grasp of the species" (i.e., the ends of procreation) rather than the individual, is a handicap. For de Beauvoir, the inferior life of "immanence" associated with the body must become the superior life of "transcendence" willed by the striving individual ego; this, she believes, will improve the lives of individuals of both sexes, and the quality of civilized life.

3. This is a relatively narrow topic. It excludes, for example, poems descriptive of the bodies of others, the great range of erotic poetry by women, surrealist work such as that of Rochelle Owens, or nature poetry such as that of May Swenson, which finds anatomical images everywhere.

4. Lynn Suckenick, "The Poster," in Laura Chester and Sharon Barba, eds., *Rising Tides: 20th Century American Women Poets* (New York, 1973).

5. Adrienne Rich, *Poems Selected and New, 1950-1974* (New York, 1975).

6. May Swenson, *Things Taking Place: Poems Selected and New* (Boston, 1978).

7. Anne Sexton, *Transformations* (Boston, 1971).

8. Passages by Sylvia Plath are quoted from *The Colossus* (New York, 1960), and *Ariel* (New York, 1965).

9. Annette Lavers, "The World as Icon: On Sylvia Plath's Themes," in Charles Newman, ed., *The Art of Sylvia Plath* (Bloomington, Indiana, 1970), pp. 104–105.

10. Diane Wakoski, "I Have Had to Learn to Live with My Face," *The Motorcycle Betrayal Poems* (New York, 1971).

11. Nikki Giovanni, "Woman Poem," *Black Feeling, Black Talk / Black Judgement* (New York, 1970).

12. Marge Piercy, *To Be of Use* (New York, 1973).

13. Carolyn Kizer, *Knock upon Silence* (New York, 1963).

14. The "personalism and particularism" of women writers can provoke both disapproval and approval (the phrase is from Sherry Ortner, "Is Female to Male as Nature Is to Culture?" in Michele Zimbalist Rosaldo and Louise Lamphere,

eds., *Women, Culture, and Society* [Stanford, 1974], p. 81). Suzanne Juhasz, writing on modern women poets, quotes both a woman psychologist who believes that the female tendency to define the self in terms of relationships with others is a defect and a woman critic who believes that it is a virtue and that "relationship, communication, and identification" are primary devices for women writers. See Juhasz, *Naked and Fiery Forms: Modern American Poetry by Women* (New York, 1975), pp. 140–141.

15. Erica Jong, *Fruits and Vegetables* (New York, 1968).

16. Sharon Barba, "A Cycle of Women," in *Rising Tides* (New York, 1973), pp. 356–357.

17. Diane Wakoski, "In Gratitude to Beethoven," *Inside the Blood Factory* (New York, 1968).

18. A recent small-press volume of women's poetry (*Making the Park* [Berkeley, 1976]) contains the following, by Marina La Palma, on the woman-flower theme:

> In a shop there are dark red
> and purple flowers growing from a pot.
> My fingers hesitate, then press against their
> folds—which yield only a little
> and give no sign that they've been touched.
> "Like intestines" the woman says.
> To me they are inside
> vagina convoluted folds.
> I hesitate before I say it
> thinking it might shock her
> obvious and careful point of view
> ("Holding Fast")

19. Margaret Atwood, "Circe/Mud Poems," *You Are Happy* (New York, 1974).

20. Yosano Akiko, "Mountain Moving Day," in Elaine Gill, ed., *Mountain Moving Day: Poems by Women* (Trumansburg, N.Y., 1973).

21. Anne Sexton, *Love Poems* (New York, 1967).

22. Robin Morgan, *Lady of the Beasts* (New York, 1977).

VERNON SCANNELL

Protest Poem

IT WAS A good word once, a little sparkler,
Simple, innocent even, like a hedgerow flower,
And irreplaceable. None of its family
Can properly take over: *merry* and *jolly*
Both carry too much weight; *jocund* and *blithe*
Were pensioned off when grandpa was alive;
Vivacious is a flirt; she's lived too long
With journalists and advertising men.
Spritely and *spry,* both have a nervous tic.
There is no satisfactory substitute.
It's down the drain and we are going to miss it.
No good advising me to go ahead
And use the word as ever. If I did
We know that someone's bound to smirk or snigger,
Of all the epithets why pick on this one?
Some deep self-mocking irony?
Or blindfold stab into the lexicon?
All right. Then let's call heterosexuals *sad,*
Dainty for rapists, *shy* for busy flashers,
Numinous for necrophiles, *quaint* for stranglers;
The words and world are mad: I must protest
Although I know my cause is lost.
A good word once, and I'm disconsolate
And angered by this simple syllable's fate:
A small innocence gone, a little Fall.
I grieve the loss. I am not gay at all.

Reprinted from *New Statesman* (9 June 1978) by permission.

Media and the Arts

M. F. K. FISHER

As the Lingo Languishes

HUNGER IS, to describe it most simply, an urgent need for food. It is a craving, a desire. It is, I would guess, much older than man as we now think of him, and probably synonymous with the beginnings of sex. It is strange that we feel that anything as intrinsic as this must continually be wooed and excited, as if it were an unwilling and capricious part of us. If someone is not hungry, it indicates that his body does not, for a time and a reason, want to be fed. The logical thing, then, is to let him rest. He will either die, which he may have been meant to do, or he will once more feel the craving, the desire, the urgency to *eat.* He will have to do that before he can satisfy most of his other needs. Then he will revive again, which apparently he was meant to do.

It is hard to understand why this instinct to eat must be importuned, since it is so strong in all relatively healthy bodies. But in our present Western world, we face a literal bombardment of cajolery from all the media, to eat this or that. It is as if we had been born without appetite, and must be led gently into an introduction to oral satisfaction and its increasingly dubious results, the way nubile maidens in past centuries were prepared for marriage proposals and then their legitimate defloration.

The language that is developing, in this game of making us *want* to eat, is far from subtle. To begin with, we must be made to feel that we really find the whole atavistic process difficult, or embarrassing or boring. We must be coaxed and cajoled to crave one advertised product rather than another, one taste, one presentation of something that we might have chosen anyway if let alone.

The truth is that we are born hungry and in our own ways will die so. But modern food advertising assumes that we are by nature bewildered and listless. As a matter of fact, we come into the world howling for Mother's Milk. We leave it, given a reasonable length of time, satisfied with much the same bland if lusty precursor of "pap and pabulum," tempered perhaps with a brush of wine on our lips to ease the parting of body and spirit. And in between, today, now, we are assaulted with the most insulting distortion of our sensory linguistics that I can imagine. We are treated like innocents and idiots by the advertisers, here in America and in Western Europe. (These are the only two regions I know, even slightly, but I feel sure that this same attack on our innate common sense is going on in the Orient, in India, in Brazil . . .)

We are told, on radio and television and in widely distributed publications, not only how but what to eat, and when, and where. The pictures are colorful. The prose, often written by famous people, is deliberately persuasive, if often supercilious in a way that makes us out as clumsy louts, gastronomical oafs badly in need of guidance toward the satisfaction of appetites we are unaware of. And by now, with this constant attack on innate desires, an attack that can be either overt or subliminal, we apparently feel fogged-out, bombed, bewildered about whether we really crave some peanut butter on crackers as a post-amour snack, or want to sleep forever. And first, before varied forms of physical dalliance, should we share with our partner a French aperitif that keeps telling us to, or should we lead up to our accomplishments by sipping a tiny glass of a Sicilian love potion?

The language for this liquid aphro-cut is familiar to most of us, thanks to lush ads in all the media. It becomes even stronger as we go into solid foods. Sexually the ads are aimed at two main groups: the Doers and the Dones. Either the reader/viewer/listener is out to woo a lover, or has married and acquired at least two children and needs help to keep the machismo-level high. Either way, one person is supposed to feed another so as to get the partner into bed and then, if possible, to pay domestic maintenance—that is, foot the bills.

One full-page color ad, for instance, shows six shots of repellently mingled vegetables, and claims boldly that these combinations "will do almost anything to get a husband's attentions."

They will "catch his passing fancy . . . on the first vegetables he might even notice." In short, the ad goes on with skilled persuasion, "they're vegetables your husband can't ignore." This almost promises that he may not ignore the cook either, a heartening if vaguely lewd thought if the pictures in the ad are any intimation of his tastes.

It is plain that if a man must be kept satisfied at table, so must his progeny, and advertisers know how to woo mothers as well as plain sexual companions. Most of their nutritional bids imply somewhat unruly family life, that only food can ease: "No more fights over who gets what," one ad proposes, as it suggests buying not one but three different types of frozen but "crisp hot fried chicken at a price that take-out can't beat": thighs and drumsticks, breast portions, and wings, all coated with the same oven-crunchy-golden skin, and fresh from freezer to stove in minutes. In the last quarter of this family ad there is a garishly bright new proposal, the "no-fire, sure-fire, barbecue-sauced" chicken. Personal experience frowns on this daring departure from the national "finger-lickin'" syndrome: with children who fight over who gets what, it would be very messy . . .

It is easy to continue such ever-loving family-style meals, as suggested by current advertising, all in deceptively alluring color in almost any home-oriented magazine one finds. How about enjoying a "good family western," whatever that may be, by serving a mixture of "redy-rice" and leftover chicken topped with a blenderized sauce of ripe avocado? This is called "love food from California," and it will make us "taste how the West was won." The avocado, the ad goes on, will "open new frontiers of wholesome family enjoyment." And of course the pre-spiced-already-seasoned "instant" rice, combined with cooked chicken, will look yummy packed into the hollowed fruit shells and covered with nutlike green stuff. All this will help greatly to keep the kids from hitting each other about who gets what.

The way to a man's heart is through his stomach, we have been assured for a couple of centuries, and for much longer than that, good wives as well as noted courtesans have given their time and thought to keeping the male belly full (and the male liver equally if innocently enlarged). By now this precarious mixture of sex and gastronomy has come out of the pantry, so to speak, and ordinary cookbook shelves show *Cuisine d'amour* and *Venus in the Kitchen* alongside Mrs. Rombauer and Julia Child.

In order to become a classic, which I consider the last two to be, any creation, from a potato soufflé to a marble bust or a skyscraper, must be honest, and that is why most cooks, as well as their methods, are never known. It is also why dishonesty in the kitchen is driving us so fast and successfully to the world of convenience foods and franchised eateries.

If we look at a few of the so-called cookbooks now providing a kind of armchair gastronomy (to read while we wait for the wife and kids to get ready to pile in the car for supper at the nearest drive-in), we understand without either amazement or active nausea some such "homemade" treat as I was brought lately by a generous neighbor. The recipe she proudly passed along to me, as if it were her great-grandmother's secret way to many a heart, was from a best-selling new cookbook, and it included a large package of sweet chocolate bits, a box of "Butter Fudge" chocolate cake mix, a package of instant vanilla pudding, and a cup of imitation mayonnaise. It was to be served with synthetic whipped cream sprayed from an aerosol can. It was called *Old-Fashion Fudge Torte.*

This distortion of values, this insidious numbing of what we once knew without question as either True or False, can be blamed, in part anyway, on the language we hear and read every day and night, about the satisfying of such a basic need as hunger. Advertising, especially in magazines and books devoted to such animal satisfaction, twists us deftly into acceptance of the new lingo of gastronomical seduction.

A good example: an impossibly juicy-looking pork chop lies like a Matisse odalisque in an open microwave oven, cooked until "fall-from-the-bone-tender." This is a new word. It still says that the meat is so overcooked that it will fall off its bone (a dubious virtue!), but it is supposed to beguile the reader into thinking that he or she (1) speaks a special streamlined language and (2) deserves to buy an oven to match, and (3) appreciates all such finer things in life. It takes *know-how,* the ad assures us subliminally, to understand all that "fall-from-the-bone-tender" really means!

This strange need to turn plain descriptive English into hyphenated hyperbole can be found even in the best gastronomical reviews and articles, as well as magazine copy. How about "fresh-from-the-oven apple cobbler," as described by one of the more reputable food writers of today? What would be wrong, especially for someone who actually knows syntax and grammar, in saying "apple cobbler, fresh from the oven"? A contemporary answer is that the multiple adjective is more . . . uh . . . contemporary. This implies that it should reach the conditioned brain cells of today's reader in a more understandable, coherent way—or does it?

II

The vocabulary of our kitchen comes from every part of the planet, sooner or later, because as we live, so we speak. After the Norman Conquest in 1066, England learned countless French nouns and verbs that are now part of both British and American cooking language: *appetite, dinner, salmon, sausage, lemon, fig, almond,* and on and on. We all say *roast, fry, boil,* and we make *sauces* and put them in *bowls* or on *plates.* And the German kitchen, the Aztecan: they too gave us words like *cookie* and *chocolate.* We say *borscht* easily (Russian before it was Yiddish). From slave-time Africa there is the word *gumbo,* for okra, and in *benne* biscuits there is the black man's sesame. Some people say that *alcohol* came from the nonalcoholic Arabs.

But what about the new culinary language of the media, the kind we now hear and view and read? What can "freezer-fresh" mean? *Fresh* used to imply new, pure, lively. Now it means, at best, that when a food was packaged, it would qualify as ready to be eaten: "oven-fresh" cookies a year on the shelf, "farm-fresh" eggs laid last spring, "corn-on-the-cob fresh" dehydrated vegetable soup-mix . . .

Personal feelings and opinions and prejudices (sometimes called skunners) have a lot to do with our reactions to gastronomical words, and other kinds. I know a man who finally divorced his wife because, even by indirection, he could not cure her of "calling up." She called up people, and to her it meant that she used the telephone—that is, she was not calling across a garden or over a fence, but was calling up when she could not *see* her friends. Calling and calling up are entirely different, she and a lot of interested amateur semanticists told her husband. He refused to admit this. "Why not simply *telephone* them? To telephone you don't say telephone *up,*" he would say. Her phrase continued to set his inner teeth, the ones rooted directly in his spiritual jaw, on such an edge that he finally fled. She called up to tell me.

This domestic calamity made me aware, over many years but never with such anguish, how *up* can dangle in our language. And experience has shown me that if a word starts dangling, it is an easy mark for the careless users and the overt rapists of syntax and meaning who write copy for mass-media outlets connected, for instance, with hunger and its current quasi-satisfactions. Sometimes the grammatical approach is fairly conventional and old-fashioned, and the *up* is tacked onto a verb in a fairly comprehensible way. "Perk up your dinner," one magazine headline begs us, with vaguely disgusting suggestions about how to do it.

"Brighten up a burger," a full-page lesson in salad making with an instant powder tells us. (This ad sneaks in another call on home unity with its "unusually delicious . . . bright . . . tasty" offering: "Sit back and listen to the cheers," it says. "Your family will give them to this tasty-zesty easy-to-make salad!")

Of course *up* gets into the adjectives as well as the verbs: *souped up chicken* and *souped up dip* are modish in advertising for canned pudding-like concoctions that fall in their original shapes from tin to saucepan or mixing bowl, to be blended with liquids to make fairly edible "soups," or to serve in prefab sauces as handy vehicles for clams or peanuts or whatever is added to the can-shaped glob to tantalize drinkers to want one more Bloody Mary. They dip up the mixture on specially stiffened packaged "chips" made of imitation tortillas or even imitation reconditioned potatoes, guaranteed not to crumble, shatter, or otherwise mess up the landscape . . .

Verbs are more fun than adjectives, in this game of upmanship. And one of the best/worst of them is creeping into our vocabularies in a thoroughly unsubtle way. It is *to gourmet up*. By now the word *gourmet* has been so distorted, and so overloaded, that to people who know its real meaning it is meaningless. They have never misused it and they refuse to now. To them a gourmet is a person, and perforce the word is a noun. Probably it turned irrevocably into an adjective with descriptive terms like *gourmet-style* and *gourmet-type*. I am not sure. But it has come to mean fancy rather than fastidious. It means expensive, or exotic, or pseudo-elegant and classy and pricey. It rarely describes a person, the gourmet who knows how to eat with discreet enjoyment. It describes a style, at best, and at worst a cheap imitation of once-stylish and always costly affectation.

There is gourmet food. There are gourmet restaurants, or gourmet-style eating places. There are packaged frozen cubes of comestibles called gourmet that cost three times as much as plain fast foods because, the cunningly succulent mouth-watering ads propose, their sauces are made by world-famous chefs, whose magical blends of spices and herbs have been touched off by a personalized fillip of rare old Madeira. In other words, at triple the price, they are worth it because they have been gourmeted up. Not long ago I heard a young woman in a supermarket say to a friend who looked almost as gaunt and harried as she, "Oh god . . . why am I here? You ask! Harry calls to say his sales manager is coming to dinner, and I've got to gourmet up the pot roast!"

I slow my trundle down the pushcart aisle.

"I could slice some olives into it, maybe? Pitted. Or maybe dump in a can of mushrooms. Sliced. It's got to be more expensive."

The friend says, "A cup of wine? Red. Or sour cream . . . a kind of Stroganoff . . . ?"

I worm my way past them, feeling vaguely worried. I long to tell them something—perhaps not to worry.

There are, of course, even more personal language shocks than the one that drove a man to leave his dear girl because she had to call people up. Each of us has his own, actively or dimly connected with hunger (which only an adamant Freudian could call his!). It becomes a real embarrassment, for example, when a friend or a responsible critic of cookbooks or restaurants uses words like *yummy,* or *scrumptious.* There is no dignity in such infantile evasions of plain words like *good*—or even *delicious* or *excellent.*

My own word aversion is longstanding, and several decades from the first time I heard it I still pull back, like the flanges of a freshly opened oyster. It is the verb *to drool,* when applied to written prose, and especially to anything I myself have written. Very nice people have told me, for a long time now, that some things they have read of mine, in books or magazines, have made them drool. I know they mean to compliment me. They are saying that my use of words makes them oversalivate, like hapless dogs waiting for a bell to say "Meat!" to them. It has made them more alive than they were, more active. They are grateful to me, perhaps, for being reminded that they are still functioning, still aware of some of their hungers.

I too should be grateful, and even humble, that I have reminded people of what fun it is, vicariously or not, to eat/live. Instead I am revolted. I see a slavering slobbering maw. It dribbles helplessly, in a Pavlovian response. It *drools.* And drooling, not over a meaty bone or a warm bowl of slops, is what some people have done over my printed words. This has long worried me. I feel grateful but repelled. They are nice people, and I like them and I like dogs, but dogs *must* drool when they are excited by the prospect of the satisfaction of alerted tastebuds, and two-legged people do not need to, and in general I know that my reaction to the fact that some people slobber like conditioned animals is a personal skunner, and that I should accept it as such instead of meeting it like a stiff-upper-lipped Anglo-Saxon (and conditioned!) nanny.

I continue, however, to be regretfully disgusted by the word *drool* in connection with all writing about food, as well as my own. And a few fans loyal enough to resist being hurt by this statement may possibly call me up!

III

It is too easy to be malicious, but certainly the self-styled food experts of our current media sometimes seem overtly silly enough to be fair game. For anyone with half an ear for the English-American language we write and speak, it is almost impossible not to chuckle over the unending flow of insults to our syntax and grammar, not to mention our several levels of intelligence.

How are we supposed to react to descriptive phrases like "crisply crunchy, to snap in your mouth"? We know this was written, and for pay, by one or another of the country's best gastronomical hacks. We should not titter. He is a good fellow. Why then does he permit himself to say that some corn on the cob is so tender that "it dribbles milk down your chin"? He seems, whether or not he means well, to lose a little of the innate dignity that we want from our gourmet-judges. He is like a comedian who with one extra grimace becomes coarse instead of funny, or like an otherwise sensitive reader who says that certain writing makes him drool.

Not all our food critics, of course, are as aware of language as the well-known culinary experts who sign magazine articles and syndicated columns. And for one of them, there are a hundred struggling copywriters who care less about mouth-watering prose than about filling ad space with folksy propaganda for "kwik" puddings and suchlike. They say shamelessly, to keep their jobs, that Mom has just told them how to make instant homemade gravy taste "like I could never make before! *Believe* me," they beg, "those other gravies just aren't the same! This has a real homemade flavor and a rich brown color. Just add it to your pan drippings." And so on.

Often these unsung kitchen psalmists turn, with probable desperation, to puns and other word games. They write, for instance, that frozen batter-fried fish are so delicious that "one crunch and you're hooked!" Oh, hohoho ha ha. And these same miserable slaves produce millions of words, if they are fortunate enough to find and keep their jobs, about things like synthetic dough that is "pre-formed" into "old-fashioned shapes that taste cooky-fresh and crunchy" in just fifteen minutes from freezer to oven to the kiddies' eager paws and maws.

When the hacks have proved that they can sling such culinary lingo, they are promoted to a special division that deals even more directly with oral satisfaction. They write full-page ads in juicy color, about cocktail nibbles with "a fried-chicken taste that's lip-lickin' good." This, not too indirectly, is aimed to appeal to hungry readers familiar with a franchised fried chicken that is of course known worldwide as finger-lickin good, and even packaged Kitty Krums that are whisker-lickin good. (It is interesting and reassuring, although we must drop a few *g*'s to understand it, that modern gastronomy still encourages us to indulge in public tongueplay.)

Prose by the copywriters usually stays coy, but is somewhat more serious about pet foods than humanoid provender. Perhaps it is assumed that most people who buy kibbles do not bother to read the printed information on all four sides of their sacks, but simply pour the formula into bowls on the floor and hope for the best. Or perhaps animal-food companies recognize that some of their slaves are incurably dedicated to correct word usage. Often the script on a bag of dry pet food is better written than most paperback novels. Possibly some renegade English instructor has been allowed to explain "Why Your Cat Will Enjoy This." He is permitted tiny professorial jokes, now and then: "As Nutritious As It Is Delicious," one caption says, and another section is called "Some Reading on Feeding," and then the prose goes all out, almost euphorically, with "Some Raving on Saving." The lost academician does have to toss in a few words like *munchy* to keep his job, but in general there is an enjoyably relaxed air about the unread prose on pet-food packages, as opposed to the stressful cuteness of most fashionable critics of our dining habits.

Of course the important thing is to stay abreast of the lingo, it seems. Stylish restaurants go through their phases, with beef Wellington and chocolate mousse high in favor one year and strictly for Oskaloossa, Missouri, the next. We need private dining-out guides as well as smart monthly magazines to tell us what we are eating tonight, as well as what we are paying for it.

A lot of our most modish edibles are dictated by their scarcity, as always in the long history of gastronomy. In 1979, for instance, it became *de rigueur* in California to serve caviar in some guise, usually with baked or boiled potatoes, because shipments from Iran grew almost as limited as they had long been from Russia. (Chilled caviar, regal fare, was paired with the quaintly plebeian potato many years ago, in Switzerland I think, but by 1979 its extravagant whimsy had reached Hollywood and the upper West Coast by way of New York, so that desperate hostesses were buying and even trying to "homemake" caviar from the Sacramento River sturgeons. Results: usually lamentable, but well meant.)

All this shifting of gustatory snobbism should probably have more influence on our language than it does. Writers for both elegant magazines and "in" guides use much the same word-appeal as do the copywriters for popular brands of convenience foods. They may not say "lip-smackin" or "de-lish," but they manage to imply what their words will make readers do. They use their own posh patter, which like the humbler variety seldom bears any kind of scrutiny, whether for original meaning or plain syntax.

How about "unbelievably succulent luscious scallops which boast a nectar-of-the-sea freshness"? Or "a *beurre blanc,* that ethereally light, grandmotherly sauce"? Or "an onion soup, baked *naturellement,* melting its knee-deep crust of cheese and croutons"? Dressings are "teasingly-tart," not teasing or tart or even teasingly tart. They have "breathtakingly visual appeal," instead of looking yummy, and some of them, perhaps fortunately, are "almost too beautiful to describe," "framed in a picture-perfect garnish of utter perfection and exquisiteness," "a pinnacle of gastronomical delight." (Any of these experiences can be found, credit card on the ready, in the bistrots-of-the-moment.)

It is somewhat hard to keep one's balance, caught between the three stools of folksy lure, stylish gushing, and a dictionary of word usage. How does one *parse,* as my grandfather would say, a complete sentence like, "The very pinkness it was, of mini-slices"? Or "A richly eggy and spiritous Zabaglione, edged in its serving dish with tiny dots of grenadine"? These are not sentences, at least to my grandfather and to me, and I think *spirituous* is a better word in this setting, and I wonder whether the dots of grenadine were wee drops of the sweet syrup made from pomegranates or the glowing seeds of the fruit itself, and how and why anyone would preserve them for a chic restaurant. And were those pink mini-slices from a lamb, a calf? Then there are always verbs to ponder on, in such seductive reports on what and where to dine. One soup "packs chunks" of something or other, to prove its masculine heartiness in a stylish lunchtime brasserie. "Don't forget to special-order!" Is this a verb, a split infinitive, an attempt of the reporter to sound down-to-earth?

Plainly it is as easy to carp, criticize, even dismiss such unworthy verbiage as it is to quibble and shudder about what the other media dictate, that we may subsist. And we continue to carp, criticize, dismiss—and to *eat,* not always as we are told to, and not always well, either! But we were born *hungry* . . .

DAVID REID

At Home in the Abyss: Jonestown and the Language of Enormity

On 18 November 1978, shortly after 5:00 P.M., 913 members of the Peoples Temple died at Jonestown, Guyana, in what the press called "a mass murder and suicide ritual." The event became one of the most thoroughly and widely reported of the century. In time a recording of the "ritual" was found and aired on television and radio.

Photographs of Jonestown show that the Reverend Jim Jones addressed his flock from a chair above which was posted: "Those who do not remember the past are condemned to repeat it." The irony of Santayana's words appearing in that place is frequently remarked in news reports of Jonestown, but what in the past was it Jones and his followers failed to remember? The world press turned up many instances of mass self-destruction—Masada, Albigensians who starved themselves to death in the thirteenth century, Russian Old Believers who immolated themselves in the seventeenth, the *Maji-Maji* movement in German East Tanganyika before the First World War, the several hundred Japanese civilians who threw themselves from cliffs in Saipan in 1944; but none of these really furnishes an exact precedent or parallel for Jonestown, nor is it clear why anyone there should have been expected to remember them.

It was "ironic" that Jim Jones quoted Santayana, but then as the reporter for *Rolling Stone* wrote after seeing the bodies, "Everything was ironic."[1] Put another way, Jonestown was an event peculiarly adapted to the modern imagination of disaster, which is in the ironic mode.[2] The purpose of this essay is to inquire into the language in which this exemplary disaster—"an emblematic, identifying moment of the decade," in *Time*'s phrase[3]—was reported and explained.

Jonestown inspired worldwide reportage and commentary, including the "instant" books, *Guyana Massacre: The Eyewitness Account* by Charles A. Krause, Laurence M. Stern, Richard Harwood, and the staff of the *Washington Post* (New York, 1978) and *The Suicide Cult: The Inside Story of the Peoples Temple and the Massacre in Guyana* by Marshall Kilduff and Ron Javers of the *San Francisco Chronicle* (New York, 1978). Reviewing the accounts of Jonestown, one finds how often reporters in Guyana and commentators in New York, London, San Francisco, and Washington, D.C., detected the same ironies, found the same words and phrases, turned to the same compact body of historical references and literary allusions. The words they found comprise, if not the language of enormity, a language for enormity; but, as it happens, the words are mostly hand-me-down psychologese and sociologese and the range of literary allusion is claustrophobically small (Joseph Conrad, Eugene O'Neill, Dostoevsky).

News accounts of Jonestown are neither inhibited nor squeamish. They dwell with medieval relish on details of decomposition, the "infestations of maggots" and "smell of rotten flesh" (*Guyana Massacre,* p. 150). Yet we are told (the phrase is Herb Caen's in the epilogue to *The Suicide Cult*)[4] Jonestown proves that "the vocabulary of horror stretches only so far": why?

The history of Jonestown begins with the rhetorical success story of Jim Jones, which belongs in any discussion of Jonestown and language. Jones was, obviously, a skillful practical rhetorician, and he manipulated magazine and newspaper reporting of Peoples Temple with notable success, but his downfall came from a morbid sensitivity to criticism in the very medium he thought he had mastered. The 913 victims were at Jonestown in the first place because of a detailed exposé in *New West* magazine. Accused of brainwashing and otherwise coercing his disciples, and reasonably fearing that San Francisco would become inhospitable, Jones retired to his jungle outpost.

Herb Caen encapsulates Jones's rise and fall in media language, and, for contrast, in his own catchy style. "In the early days of Peoples Temple, the media found him to be 'a charismatic figure' who exerted 'considerable clout' in politics. He became the 'madman' of Guyana only in the dark, dying days of his dynasty. By the same token, his followers turned 'fanatical,' in the estimation of the media, as they crumpled in the convulsions of cyanide. Until then they had been 'dedicated followers,' perhaps misguided but seeking a better life and hence deserving of sympathy" (*The Suicide Cult,* pp. 192–193).

In San Francisco, as Jones predicted, his sect made it to the big time.[5] His ability to swell rallies with the racially integrated ranks of his followers, to organize overnight letter-writing campaigns, and to get out a dependable bloc vote recommended Jones to the late Mayor George Moscone, who appointed him chairman of the city Housing Authority, and to many other local and national political figures, including Rosalynn Carter. Their support in turn enabled him to mobilize progressive opinion for the purpose of killing unfavorable stories about Peoples Temple in magazines and newspapers. When defectors sought help from Ralph Nader, the letter was turned over to a Jones aide.

Jones's appeal was very much a matter of language, especially his facility with those "power-to-the-people slogans left over from the sixties," as *New West* put it,[6] which by the mid-1970s had become the standard idiom of political life in San Francisco. Steve Gavin, a former city editor of the *San Francisco Chronicle,* remembers how Jones "said all the right things."[7] What sort of "right things"? Caen, who publicized and defended Jones in his influential newspaper column, recalls a lunch at which Jones was distant, "becoming voluble only on the subject of 'helping those who cannot help themselves.'" He quotes from a letter Jones wrote him from Guyana: "Many of the young people who came here were alienated, angry, and frustrated. They were tired of the hypocrisy that cried over 'human rights' while they were being buried alive. . . . The society we are building in Guyana has given people who were considered the refuse of urban America a new sense of pride, self-worth, and dignity" (*The Suicide Cult,* pp. 194–195, 199).

With fine impartiality Jones appealed to credulity wherever he found it, and in whatever language the occasion demanded. As his wife Marceline confided to the *New York Times* in September 1977, he was a Marxist who "used religion to try to get some people out of the opiate of religion" (*Guyana Massacre,* p. 33). With the theatrical assistance of his leadership cadre, the "planning commission" (mostly young, white, and affluent in a congregation predominantly old, black, and poor), Jones raised the dead and relieved sufferers of their tumors. Al Mills, a defector who was drawn to Peoples Temple by its "progressive politics," says, "Jones was so charismatic that he could talk at one meeting to very religious people about healings and at another to very political people about justice. . . . I knew that some of the healings were phony and staged. But if that's the level people are at and it gets them to work for social justice, then that's fine."[8]

By the time he reached Guyana, however, Jones was impatiently trampling on his Bible during church services ("Too many people are looking at this instead of looking at me!") and instructing his congregation in an old-fashioned Stalinist idiom. Or so one judges from the letters to "Dad" discovered after the slaughter. Kecia Baisy, eleven, wrote, "I fell gillty because i had money in the state and i did not turn it in. I am an andareech [anarchist] and I think i am a eleist [elitist]" (I take the emendations from *Time,* where the letters were reproduced [11 December 1978, p. 6]). A young man wrote, "I don't respect Dad the way I should. I respect Dad out of fear of getting in trouble. Rather than respecting him for what he is, a Marxist Leninist." The talismanic use of the vocabulary of the Old Left, slightly updated, survived Jonestown in the case of a follower who said that the only dissatisfied communards were "parasites" and "bourgeois city folk" unable to accept "structure."

A pastoral letter Jones sent from Guyana to followers in San Francisco contains no scriptural references or allusions, but social scientific clichés, such as "the regimentation and extreme tension of a highly technological society," appear in almost every paragraph (*Guyana Massacre,* p. 205). There are touches that reflect the style of the welfare bureaucracy, for example "seniors" used to mean old people.

One of many letters of reference from notable Americans that Jones handed over to the government of Guyana was an encomium from the U.S. Secretary of Health, Education, and Welfare, Joseph Califano, which reads in part, "Knowing your commitment and compassion, your humanitarian principles and your interest in protecting individual liberty and freedom have made an outstanding contribution to furthering the cause of human dignity." As the *New Republic* indignantly observed, this is not even a sentence.[9] But it does repay Jones for his political efforts in his own rhetorical coin. In Guyana the camp brig was the "extended care unit."

An early commentary on Jonestown in the *Economist* (25 November 1978, pp. 12–13) staked out what soon appeared to be an eccentric and lonely position. The gruesome cover carries the headline, "Is Satan Dead?" Inside the editors reflect that in searching for God in a secular world, "it is all too easy to blunder into the arms of Satan instead" and "if Satan, in some sense, is not dead, that implies that God is not either."

Unexpectedly, the point turns out to be that the West is maybe at the beginning of a new "development of human consciousness" and "If the search is to follow any sort of scientific principle, as it should, the aberrations will be examined and their causes noted. . . . The early and popular reaction to the horror at Jonestown, which was to ask, 'Is Satan not dead after all?', may be a start of that process."

However, Jonestown did not inspire many long thoughts about the evolution of human consciousness, nor was it widely viewed as presenting new evidence for the existence of God. If other press commentaries were indicative of public reaction, it did not often lead to reflections along the lines of "Is Satan not dead after all?" Apart from the *Wall Street Journal,* which editorialized about "the fathomless human beast," commentary on Jonestown was almost completely untinged by religious or moral interpretation. According to *Time,* even theologians shared the general reluctance to apply such categories; or as Barbara Hargrove, an instructor at Yale Divinity School, remarked, "In other ages, what happened to Jim Jones would have been referred to very clearly as coming under the influence of evil forces—'the devil got in him.' But I haven't heard any people using that kind of language."[10]

Rather than being used diagnostically, religious and moral language appears in writing about Jonestown as a decorative or intensifying device to bring out the event's "unspeakable" horror. It possesses no more (perhaps less) intrinsic authority than the references to Conrad, O'Neill, and Dostoevsky. In *Time* we read that Jonestown was "an appalling demonstration of the way in which a charismatic leader can bend the minds of his followers with a devilish blend of professed altruism and psychological tyranny" (p. 16). The elucidative intent of "charismatic" is apparent, but "devilish," which these days ordinarily suggests mischievous charm, seems unfelt, all but unmeant. The problem of evil becomes very distant. When *Time* asks, "How could such idealistic, if naive, people set out to build an idyllic haven from modern society's many pressures and turn it into a hellish colony of death?" (p. 18), one begins to suspect that the explanation will have more to do with those "pressures" (which we will soon encounter again) than with the devil.

Confident analysis conducted in psychological and sociological terms, accompanied by an odd reluctance to use what the social scientists call value judgments, is a striking feature of commentaries on Jonestown. As Diane Johnson observes in a review of the instant books in the *New York Review of Books* (19 April 1979, p. 3), "Temperate press comment indicts abstractions: 'society,' 'poverty,' 'ignorance,' 'alienation.' Psychiatrists name 'hunger for transcendence,' or even '*la grande crise libidinale . . . le nouveau mal du siècle.*' The rest of the country likes to think it's California that brings out these weird crimes, and the foreign press blames America itself, or capitalism." These tendencies corroborate one another. (No gulf separates the confident psychiatrists from the temperate journalists.) Commentaries on Jonestown are also almost always preceded by the observation that there has been a lot of commentary (mine is not the exception), and there is often a show of unwillingness, always overcome needless to say, about engaging in the same enterprise. *New West,* which did so much to expose Jones, furnishes an overwrought example in a note from the editors (18 December 1978, p. 45): "The mind rebels. Too much death; too much madness; too many grotesque details. The punditry mills grind on. . . ."[11]

An explicit disdain for "judgmental" language is palpable in the chapters of *Guyana Massacre* that were written by Laurence M. Stern and Richard Harwood. "But long before the last infant or adult had been placed in a body bag, tagged, counted and airlifted to the United States," we are told, "recriminations had begun and the search for scapegoats had begun" (p. 147). By "recriminations" and "the search for scapegoats," Stern and Harwood mean any attempt to fix blame for anything that happened at Jonestown on anyone who is still around to suffer from it. They regard that kind of enterprise, and the moral language in which it is comprehensible, as intellectually bankrupt. "For the dead," they conclude in a startling *non sequitur,* the question of responsibility "signified nothing. The problem at Jonestown was not who was to blame or why it happened. It was a question of logistics. What was to be done with those bodies rotting in the tropical heat?" (p. 148).

The only commentator to satisfy their austere standard turns out to be the *Washington Post* columnist, William Raspberry, who is applauded for wondering if "maybe we would be better off simply accepting the fact that some tragedies cannot be prevented. . . . I don't mean that there should be no effort to understand the dynamics of cultism, of alienation, or of group suicide. . . . But I do make a distinction between scientific inquiry aimed at discovering truth and ritual questioning calculated to restore our sense of equilibrium" (p. 156).

Ritual is itself a word that often appears in writing about Jonestown, used descriptively as in "mass suicide ritual" and, as here, pejoratively to mean moral inquiry (as opposed to scientific probings into the "dynamics of cultism," etc.). The distinction reflects a particular linguistic style. For Raspberry such terms as *dynamics of cultism* are the language of science and as such intrinsically valuable. Still, if ritual questioning really could restore our equilibrium, why not engage in it? But as Raspberry uses it, *ritual* means something like a mental twitch; that is why Harwood and Stern can endorse his distinction while remaining gloomily doubtful that even science will ever furnish society with any "prescriptive wisdom" derived from the study of Peoples Temple. (Like Stern and Harwood's "recriminations," *ritual* in this sense has a specific provenance in the 1960s. An "orgy of recrimination," like that sponsored by Senator Joseph McCarthy after the "loss" of China, is what Lyndon Johnson and Dean Rusk, Richard Nixon and Henry Kissinger, used to argue would infallibly follow an American defeat in Vietnam. "Ritual questionings" are what Americans accused themselves of after the guilty postmortems of the assassinations and race riots.) "In the end," write Stern and Harwood, "we will have to accept what happened in Guyana as the dark spasm of history that it was, a tragedy in which fates were assigned both by chance and by inevitable circumstance, beyond the control of any government agency or political party" (p. 157). A toughly reasonable conclusion that absolves everybody except the dead.

But how easily the embargo on moral language and the "dark spasm of history" theory coexist with psychological and sociological analysis. Another chapter in *Guyana Massacre,* "Cults: The Battle for the Mind" by Henry Allen, includes a compendious summary of these analyses, virtually all of which the author ecumenically endorses by way of supporting his own explanation—there are no "simple answers," but Jonestown shows "how the madness of one man could converge with the spirit of an age in upheaval to weave a doomed nexus of strands ranging from the most ancient of human instincts and customs to the physiology of the human brain" (p. 112). You see?

"In an age in which everything was permitted, yet little seemed real," we learn, "the Reverend Jim Jones promised a refuge." How? By offering his followers "the terrible charm of absolutism—or paranoia." The charm held even when Jones ordered the mass suicide; everybody died happy (according to Mark Lane). But the victims were "literate, adult Americans supposedly immunized against such madness by 20th century education and science." These "children of the Enlightenment" had "everything, by conventional wisdom, to live for." Unfortunately, "conventional American wisdom has never come to terms with the spiritual upheavals and cult phenomena that started growing out of the disarray of American society a decade ago. As a secular society, we've ignored the power of messianic personalities and their persuasive techniques . . ." (pp. 111–113). Like so much temperate press comment, Allen's essay identifies the quest for certainties with unreason and paranoia, only to indict society for depriving people of certainties, thereby alienating them and making the simple vulnerable to mystagogues. The "*Time* Essay" by Lance Morrow makes the point more elegantly: "At their worst, the cults acquire a psychosis of millenialism. . . . In their terrific surrender, cultists reduce a multiform, contradictory world to cant formulas, and thus they become as dangerous as anyone whose head resounds with certainties" (p. 30).

Allen's essay remembers Dostoevsky and Nietzsche. *Time* quotes Dostoevsky. Dostoevsky, Nietzsche, Eugene O'Neill (many references to *The Emperor Jones*), and Conrad appear and reappear in writing about Jonestown. *Time:* "The Jonestown story, like some Joseph Conrad drama of fanaticism and moral emptiness, has gone directly into popular myth." Diane Johnson's review is titled "Heart of Darkness." Herb Caen's epilogue to *The Suicide Cult* evokes "the unforgettable grotesquerie of mass suicide by Kool-Aid laced with cyanide: the summer drink and the winter death, presided over by the Emperor Jones of the Jungle" (pp. 200–201).

F. R. Leavis's famous objection to the theme of the "unspeakable" in *Heart of Darkness*—Conrad's "adjectival and worse than superogatory insistence"—may suggest why it is appropriate that Conrad turns up so frequently in writing about Jonestown. Jonestown seemed merely to answer to the standard themes of modern ironic literature, and these themes were evoked very insistently. Johnson: "Jones is no mystery, only a kind of antinomian victim, playing the part of deranged demagogue with scrupulous attention to tradition. In the course of his deterioration he omitted no detail we have come, from our experience of Mr. Kurtz, Emperor Jones, Idi Amin, to expect . . ." (p. 3). Rather than concentrating our perplexities, the allusions, which place real enormities on the same plane with familiar imaginary ones, ironically intend to domesticate the horror. "Just as we knew Jones, we recognize the place itself in these accounts from its prefiguration in other books. People have always imagined Guyana: it is the heart of darkness" (p. 3). (Bertrand Russell once rationalized Lenin's tyranny, telling Lady Ottoline Morrell, "If you ask yourself how Dostoevsky's characters should be governed, you will understand.")[12]

When myth and symbol collide with fact in writing about Jonestown, fact is compromised. The commentators who insist on our facing the spectacle of "children of the Enlightenment" cheerfully slaughtering themselves at the behest of a crazed Conradian mystagogue forget that most of the victims were poor, ill-educated old people or children, and that perhaps as many as 150 children were at Jonestown because their custody had been granted to Peoples Temple by courts of the state of California.

Returning now to the questions that launched this essay: What language did the commentators on Jonestown find for enormity? Why was it said enormity exhausted language's resources?

To begin with, writing about Jonestown confirms the triumph of what Hannah Arendt in *The Human Condition* calls "the all-comprehensive pretensions of the social sciences."[13] The only explanations that are considered belong to psychology or sociology, a fact reflected or rather embodied in a common vocabulary whose salient terms range in increasingly comprehensive pretension from the humble *pressures* to *psychosis of millennialism*.

The editors of *New West* write (18 December 1978, p. 45):

> Some quick and dirty analysts have tried to blame the various tragedies [Jonestown and the killings of San Francisco Mayor George Moscone and Councilman Harvey Milk] on some specifically California malaise, some disease of permissiveness, some half-formed notion that tolerance destroys other values and reaps its own ghastly inevitable rewards. This is media foolishness, of course, the slick and slippery generalization. . . . And yet . . . [their ellipsis] we do seem to have more than our share of paranoid personality cults.

"Malaise," "some disease of permissiveness," "paranoid personality cults." The error of the quick and dirty analysts laboring away in the punditry mills was to apply a psycho-sociological paradigm so as to implicate California, where reside the readers of *New West*. Jim Jones, we are told a few sentences later, was not merely affected by "pressures" but "motivated" by them. Parenthetically, the article that follows these observations, Phil Tracy's "Jim Jones: The Making of a Madman," ingenuously remarks: "Perhaps his ideas were more idealistic than most, but they contained nothing that hadn't been preached in one form or another somewhere in California for at least 40 years" (p. 47).

That Jim Jones used the same psychological and sociological terms to explain his mission, that he indicted the same abstractions that would be adduced by sociologues to explain the nightmare he authored, is ironic perhaps but not surprising or paradoxical. He simply didn't have much originality or imagination. His "Marxism" seems to have grown out of some village atheist instinct of perversity; one suspects he embraced it because "Communism" was hobgoblinized in the United States during the 1950s. But he was adaptable enough, even near the end, to spice his sermons and letters with the psychobabble to which, one imagines, he was introduced by his younger and more affluent disciples. "For those who would be concerned about our eventual fate, you should know we have found fulfillment," he writes in his pastoral letter from Guyana. "We have gotten ourselves together" (*Guyana Massacre,* p. 207).

How is it possible to be morally severe these days, a celebrated critic recently wondered, "when we have a sense of evil but no longer the religious or philosophical language to talk intelligently about evil"?[14] In a similar vein, Geoffrey Hill writes in his poem, "History as Poetry," of "the tongue's atrocities" and the damage language does when it inadequately engages enormity.[15] But Hill's own poems confirm, as in a different way do such testimonies as Nadezhda Mandelstam's *Hope Against Hope* and Primo Levi's *Survival in Auschwitz,* that poetry is possible after Auschwitz, that literature can be made even out of enormity, and that "intelligent" writing about evil is possible, despite the collapse of the great philosophical systems and the waning of religious faith. Hill's "Ovid in the Third Reich" is eerily pertinent to Jonestown and the reaction to it, especially the lines:

> I have learned one thing: not to look down
> So much upon the damned. They, in their sphere,
> Harmonize strangely with the divine
> Love. I, in mine, celebrate the love-choir.

The emptiness of so much writing about Jonestown does not point to the limits of language, but rather to the horrible ease with which we find categories for enormity. Jonestown was said to elude moral definition, but not the ghostlier demarcations of the social sciences, and if it was called "unspeakable" or said to exhaust the vocabulary of horror, it was because, as Paul Fussell has noted, we have agreed that *unspeakable* means indescribable when "it really means *nasty*."[16] The word usefully wards off the old-fashioned language of the value judgment; of "scapegoating."

Certainly the "unspeakable," the "grotesque," the "absurd"—all terms that have been applied to Jonestown—are categories of experience with which we imagine ourselves thoroughly familiar; and familiarity breeds familiarity. Almost twenty years ago, Lionel Trilling remarked on

> the readiness of . . . students to engage in the process that we might call the socialization of the anti-social, or the legitimization of the subversive. . . . the minds that give me the A papers and the B papers and even the C+ papers, move through the terrors and mysteries of modern literature like so many Parsifals, asking no questions at the behest of wonder and fear. Or like so many seminarists who have been instructed in the constitution of Hell and the ways of damnation. Or like so many *readers,* entertained by moral horror stories. I asked them to look into the Abyss, and, both dutifully and gladly, they have looked into the Abyss, and the Abyss has greeted them with the grave courtesy of all objects of serious study, saying, "Interesting, am I not? And *exciting,* if you consider how deep I am and what dread beasts lie at my bottom. Have it well in mind that a knowledge of me contributes materially to your being whole, or well rounded, men."[17]

The speed with which *Jonestown* found a place in the language confirms the ease with which it was understood and placed as an exemplary moral horror story, just as the language in which it was analyzed confirms that, far from straining the resources of language, enormity accommodated itself to the leading preoccupations of the age and to the wretched language in which they are usually embodied. The deaths occurred in late November, and before the year was out, political columnists were talking about how unimpressed voters had "done a Jonestown" on some defeated candidates for Congress. Or as *Guyana Massacre* concludes, "Today it [Jonestown] simply haunts us . . . with its reminder that 'the jungle is only a few yards away.' "[18] The solemnity with which that untroubling and untroubled commonplace is quoted must haunt us with its reminder of how at home in the abyss we have become.

Notes

1. Tim Cahill, "In the Valley of the Shadow of Death: An On-the-Scene Report from Guyana," *Rolling Stone,* 25 January 1978, p. 52.

2. Cf. Paul Fussell, *The Great War and Modern Memory* (New York, 1975), p. 35. See also Northrop Frye, *Anatomy of Criticism: Four Essays* (Princeton, N.J., 1957), pp. 223–239. In Frye's terms Jonestown would be a "demonic epiphany."

3. *Time,* 4 December 1978, p. 16. Unless otherwise noted, all quotations attributed to *Time* are taken from this issue.

4. Kilduff and Javers, *The Suicide Cult,* p. 191.

5. Jeanie Kasindorf, "The Seduction of San Francisco," *New West,* 18 December 1978, p. 49.

6. Kasindorf, p. 49.

7. Kasindorf, p. 52.

8. Krause et al., p. 55.

9. "The Age of Credulity," an unsigned editorial in the *New Republic,* 2 December 1978, p. 6. In a letter to the *New Republic,* 16 December 1978, Secretary Califano denies any recollection of signing such a letter.

10. *Time,* 18 December 1978, p. 51.

11. These observations apply most directly to the American and English news magazines and the instant books. These were the first publications that could even pretend to take a considered view.

12. Quoted in Aileen Kelly, "Introduction: A Complex Vision," in Isaiah Berlin, *Russian Thinkers,* ed. Henry Hardy and Aileen Kelly (New York, 1978), p. xiii.

13. Hannah Arendt, *The Human Condition* (New York, 1959), p. 41.

14. Susan Sontag, *Illness as Metaphor* (New York, 1979), p. 82.

15. Cf. Christopher Ricks, "Geoffrey Hill and 'The Tongue's Atrocities,'" *Times Literary Supplement,* 30 June 1978, p. 743. "A poem by Geoffrey Hill speaks of 'The tongue's atrocities' ('History as Poetry'), compacting or colluding the atrocities of which the tongue must speak with the atrocities which — unless it is graced with unusually creative vigilance — it is all too likely to commit when it speaks of atrocities."

16. Fussell, *The Great War and Modern Memory,* p. 175.

17. Lionel Trilling, "The Teaching of Modern Literature," in *Beyond Culture: Essays on Literature and Learning* (New York, 1968), pp. 26–27.

18. Krause et al., p. 158. The quotation is attributed to Meg Greenfield.

FELIX POLLAK

Aesthetics

THERE ARE SUCH beautiful
exotic
words in the dictionary,
euphonic songs that taste good
in the mouth—salmonella,
glaucoma, catatonia, ataxia,
words like the names of
legendary heroines or goddesses
—Acne, Hysterectomy,
Emphysema, Peritonitis, or thunderous
appellations reminiscent of old
warriors and lovers—Tetanus,
Staphilococcus, Stupor,
Cyanide, Carbuncle—

it is a joy like savoring the
hues & abstract shapes in
the medical atlas—those green
gangrenes and scarlet carcinomas,
the intricate pink & silver patterns of
psoriasis like islands on a yellow sea
of skin, Rubenesque hernias or the
Seurat-like pointillisms of atherosclerosis,
not to speak of the Japanese landscapes drawn by
cirrhosis of the liver, and the sculptures
created by certain amputations, rivalling even
the exquisite armstumps of
the Venus of Milo.

Reprinted from *Ginkgo* (New Rochelle, New York: Elizabeth Press, 1973) by permission of Felix Pollak.

RONALD HARWOOD

The Language of Screenwriting

THE LANGUAGE OF FILM is a language composed of dialects, each clearly identifying the region inhabited by the user. Producers, directors, technicians all have their own jargon; the screenwriter is no exception. The screenplay dialect is individual and capable of infinite variety. No one, as far as I know, has yet attempted to set down rules for the screenplay; no standard work exists to express unchallengeable opinions; no Fowler to insist "words used must nowadays actually yield on scrutiny the desired sense." A screenplay, like a novel or a play, is personal to the writer; the accent he employs will depend on one deceptively simple test: is the reader able to obtain from the written document a visual impression of the film? The question, therefore, which follows is, who then reads screenplays?

We may begin by discounting the general reader. The commercial publication of screenplays is rare; those which do find their way into print are invariably written by authors more distinguished in other fields of literary endeavor. Two instances are worth mentioning and both are fine examples of the screenwriter's art: *Baby Doll* by Tennessee Williams (London: Secker and Warburg, 1957) and *A la Recherche du Temps Perdu: The Proust Screenplay* by Harold Pinter (New York: Grove Press, 1978), which was not, to the cinema's loss, translated into film. An answer, however, is to be found in the nature of the screenplay itself, which is written primarily to serve the needs of all those who work in the film industry, for it is read by everyone who is concerned with the financing and making of the intended film.

The problem is instantly apparent: the screenplay has to instruct technicians of many diverse skills, cameramen, sound recordists and the like; it has to satisfy the artistic enquiry of director, actors, art directors—all those who need to understand the narrative, the interplay of characters, the atmosphere and style; it must contain information to enable the producer, accountants and production manager to cost and schedule the making of the film. But before any of the foregoing set eyes on the document, the screenplay must inspire lunatic enthusiasm and passion in those who are to be persuaded to make available several million pounds, but usually dollars, by putting their signatures in the bottom righthand corners of checks. The screenplay must communicate to so diverse an audience as to make the hopes of those who promote Esperanto seem positively parochial.

The making of films is a collective enterprise, although the director has, finally, the responsibility and authority for what appears on the screen. The screenwriter's voice is, however, the first to be heard. He or she has the prime task of dramatizing and visualizing the subject matter: what narrative style will be employed? in what order will the events be told? who will say what to whom? These questions, and others of lesser importance, must be answered in a single document which is both readable in the way a novel is readable, and instructive in the way a blueprint is instructive. It is this initial attempt with which I am here concerned, for the screenplay undergoes a series of transformations, stages of development called drafts, each draft becoming increasingly technical until a final "shooting script" is agreed upon. The director certainly, the financiers, the producer, even the clapperboy may contribute to the final version; but it is the writer, invariably after long and detailed consultation with the director, who is responsible for what is called The First Draft, and these words, alarming to writers who are accustomed to delivering their finished works of art to publishers, appear on the title page of the document.

The technical jargon, like all jargon, is easily acquired. The very form of a screenplay is designed to assist those who read it for technical information rather than for any other reason; a vocabulary, often reduced to abbreviations, has been developed which enables the writer to employ a sort of shorthand for complex instructions. The art of screenplay writing is to overcome the barriers erected by form and jargon, to transcend the limitations of a mere blueprint by conveying what E. M. Forster called in the context of the novel, "the mystery."

I give an example, at least of conventional form, from my own screenplay based on Alexander Solzhenitsyn's *One Day in the Life of Ivan Denisovich* (London: Sphere Books, 1971).

FADE IN:

1. EXT. THE CAMP—HIGH ANGLE (HELICOPTER SHOT) BEFORE DAWN

From a distance the camp looks like a solitary star in the cosmos: it glows a sickly yellow; its circles of light are no more than a luminous blur. Beyond the star, as far as the eye can see, is snow.
It seems like the middle of the night.
It is intensely cold.
THE CAMERA MOVES IN VERY SLOWLY.
SUPERIMPOSE MAIN CREDITS AND TITLES.
Gradually it becomes possible to distinguish more of the area of the camp: two powerful searchlights sweeping from watchtowers on the perimeter; a circle of border lights marks the barbed wire fences; other lights are dotted about the camp. Now, slowly, the shapes of the huts and other buildings become discernible: the gates, the near watchtowers with their guards and machine guns, the prison block, the mess hall, the staff quarters.
END CREDITS AND TITLES.
A Russian SOLDIER, wearing the regulation long winter overcoat and fur cap, emerges from the staff quarters, pierced by the cold. He makes his way to where a length of frosted rail hangs. THE SOLDIER takes up a hammer in his gloved hands and beats on the rail: a grating, clanging sound—

CUT TO:

2. INT. HUT 9 BEFORE DAWN

Under a blanket and coat lies IVAN DENISOVICH, bathed in sweat etc.

Contained in the foregoing is a mass of information, for the language of the screenplay is always economical and often subtle; and there is to the screenplay an intricate calligraphy, almost as ornate as Chinese, which governs the placing of instructions, descriptions and dialogue. My task is now to decipher.

The words FADE IN are not obligatory but traditional: they mark the opening of the film and indicate the way the first image will appear, not some sudden visual shock, but a more gradual effect.

The laboratory that will eventually process the final product has been told what to do, but the words serve, I believe, another purpose: they prepare the reader for the required state of mind, the demand, from the outset, to read not for the vocables, but for the necessity to visualize.

All scenes are numbered. In a more detailed script every shot is numbered. (The word *shot,* incidentally, describes the picture recorded by the camera in one continuous or uninterrupted run, also known as a set-up.) The rule is that the numbers, the scene or shot divisions, indicate the change of camera positions. The preference seems to be to break up a scene as much as possible on the printed page in order to reproduce the effect of the film itself. But since the opening of *Ivan Denisovich* was conceived as one long camera movement in the hope that the audience would be seduced into the monstrous atmosphere of a solitary islet in the Gulag Archipelago, no such divisions were necessary.

The abbreviations EXT. and INT. stand for Exterior and Interior, vital information for almost everyone concerned. The description of place—THE CAMP—may be as detailed or general as the writer deems necessary. HIGH ANGLE not only gives a technical instruction to the camera crew, but also prods the reader's imagination into the required point of view, yet it is the parenthetical helicopter which obliges him to look down. This is not the only reason for mentioning the helicopter: those responsible for the budget and the schedule will also want to know that it is needed. The description BEFORE DAWN is unusually precise on my part; most screenplays would settle for either NIGHT or DAY, but I wanted to communicate the essential element of extreme cold as quickly as possible.

The first authentic accent of film revealed in the extract is the instruction to the camera. The movement of the camera need not be a major concern of the writer unless such movement is to him essential to the telling of the story or to the style he is hoping to create. A vocabulary, however, exists that is both traditional and almost intelligible. The camera can be told to TRACK IN or OUT, to DOLLY, to ZOOM, to PAN, to CRANE, to TILT—words for which a long and accurate glossary would be needed. But the contemporary taste is, when instructing the camera, to employ personification. The camera becomes an eye or a person, a living observer rather than a complex machine. Thus, the camera MOVES IN or APPROACHES or LOOKS AT or FOLLOWS or PULLS BACK or SWINGS SHARPLY, any phrase, indeed, which enables the reader to visualize what will eventually be seen on the screen.

The superimposition of CREDITS—the names of the stars, technicians, director, producer, etc.—and the TITLES—the name of the film, the work or works upon which it is based—play a part in the introduction. Where they begin and end must be noted, for only then can the opening sequence be timed. Agreements exist both with individuals and unions which legislate for the amount of time a name will appear on the screen; the director, therefore, will know that he must allow x number of minutes from the moment the first credit appears to the last, and he must plan his pictures accordingly.

Near the righthand margin appear the words CUT TO, and they denote the method of passing from one scene, or one shot, to the next. CUT TO implies a sharpness, a speed of movement and is very much in demand in contemporary films. The sudden, jangled juxtaposition of images which is now the vogue requires the frequent use of CUT TO. DISSOLVE TO, an alternative method of making the division between scenes and sequences, suggests a more leisurely approach. The fact is, however, that neither instruction is strictly necessary. After the film is realized on celluloid, the editor will bring into play a different set of judgments and skills; his appreciation of the film will be derived from the reality of the pictures, and that reality may, and invariably does, alter the manner in which the story is told. But to the reader these signals are important aids to comprehending rhythm and pace.

In passing from the exterior of the camp to the interior of the hut, I hoped to create a dramatic introduction for Ivan Denisovich himself. I could have emphasized the moment by indicating CLOSE SHOT IVAN DENISOVICH or EXTREME CLOSE SHOT or CLOSE UP or reduced these demands to the abbreviations C.S. or E.C.U. These possibilities in turn reveal an obsession common to many screenwriters: the need to describe accurately the distance of the camera from the object to be photographed, a need, I suggest, not entirely rational. In the majority of screenplays one will read of LONG SHOTS, EXTREME LONG SHOTS, CLOSE SHOTS or CLOSE UPS, MEDIUM CLOSE SHOTS, EXTREME CLOSE SHOTS, MEDIUM THREE SHOTS (a picture of three characters photographed from neither too close nor too far away), FULL SHOTS and a host of concomitant variations. The contemporary screenplay, however, so far as one can generalize at all, favors a more literary and, therefore, more stylish approach. Instead of

1. EXT. ELSINORE CASTLE—E.C.S. HAMLET'S EYES DAY

one may read

1. HAMLET'S EYES.

No grammar of screenplay writing would be acceptable without mention of the necessity to indicate, from time to time, the point of view from which a scene or a moment in the scene is perceived, but it should only be indicated in the screenplay when absolutely necessary to the telling of the story. Since a film depends to a great extent on point of view, the abbreviation POV litters most screenplays. For example, Hamlet draws aside the arras and

CUT TO

167. HAMLET'S POV—POLONIUS DEAD.

Another frequently used word is ANGLE, which describes loosely the camera's position. To break up a scene in which the characters do nothing but talk, one may read ANOTHER ANGLE: this does not necessarily mean the director will move the camera at that precise moment; it may simply be a device to give the impression of an edited film.

Descriptive passages in the screenplay do not provide a reliable insight into the writer's true prose style, for brevity is always too much demanded. No lengthy Shavian descriptions of rooms or characters; no lyrical passages to conjure up the countryside. The evocation of place or person must be plain, factual and economical. The urge to paint a landscape or flesh out a character must be ruthlessly resisted. A mentor of mine once told me that he knew of a long, colorful passage describing the Nevada desert, the blazing heat, the appearance of a horseman on the horizon which had finally been reduced to

1. EXT. THE DESERT DAY
The sun, a distant horse, a glinting gun.

The instructions to actors borrow heavily from the theatre and are, indeed, called in the screenplay stage directions. But the dialect has added nuances of its own: a character ENTERS SHOT or TURNS TO CAMERA; for the need to pause briefly one may, unfortunately, sometimes read A BEAT. But "thrift, thrift, Horatio" is the best advice to screenwriters. The theatre is a medium in which the spoken word is paramount; in the cinema the visual image dominates. The reader's receptivity is hindered by too much description, the audience's by too much dialogue.

The trend now developing is to use technical jargon as little as possible on the premise that if the language restricts it must be loosened. No vocabulary should inhibit the freedom to express, nor should it come between the visual imagination of either writer or reader. I have read scripts in which the traditional numbering of scenes and shots is abandoned in favor of a more flowing form. Accountants, after all, are better equipped to number scenes. One is, therefore, presented with a screenplay which concentrates on giving the wide range of readers the experience of the film and by so doing neglects the provision of data. Borrowing from the style of an American screenplay recently brought to my attention, I give the following and somewhat extreme case as a final example:

A moon, racing clouds, a mist. Hold, then

CUT TO

A man's eyes, narrowed, alert, watchful. A noise.
He spins round and

CUT TO

The man, sword drawn, tense, challenging—

THE MAN: Who's there?

He's terrified and

CUT TO

What he sees: a figure coming out of the mist, also with sword drawn. We're on the battlements of a castle.

THE SECOND MAN: Nay, answer me: stand, and unfold yourself.

He's also frightened and

CUT TO

The two men, facing each other in the swirling mist.

FIRST MAN: Long live the King!

SECOND MAN: Bernardo?

FIRST MAN: He.

A screenplay cannot be judged by form and technique, or by the abandonment of either. In his attempt to realize in its initial form a story which is, in the end, to be told in pictures, the writer must discover or invent a language which is both personal and effective, and which, above all, stimulates the mind's eye.

FADE OUT.

ANTHONY BURGESS

Dubbing

EARLY TALKING FILMS were made the hard way. Microphones were insinuated onto the set, hidden in flower bowls, corsages, hats, or else placed frankly dangling from a boom, with the constant danger of boom shadow. If the camera was frightened of the microphone, the microphone was resentful of the camera, which made too much noise while it was being turned and had, in consequence, to be muffled with blankets or sequestered in a soundproof chamber. The process of adding dialogue and sound effects after the shooting of the action, a convenient and timesaving technique, was fairly slow to be discovered. A whole constellation of terms is applied to the artifice whereby synchronic sound and action are achieved by diachronic means, and the commonest term is *dubbing*.

Strictly, *dubbing* implies not just the addition of sound to film shot silently. It presupposes an original sound track to be modified either partially or totally. In fact, *dub* can be given three definitions: (a) to make a new recording out of an original tape or record or track in order to accommodate changes, cuts or additions; (b) to insert a totally new sound track, often a synchronized translation of the original dialogue; (c) to insert sound into a film or tape. A film can be entirely dubbed. Sounds can be dubbed in.

There are two ways of hearing a foreign film. The first and, these days, commonest, is to suffer the illusion that the actors on the screen are actually speaking the language of the audience. The other, probably still the better of the two, is to hear the original dialogue and to have this translated on the screen in the form of subtitles. In multilingual communities like Malaysia, the second method is the only practicable one, though half the frame must be filled up with Malay, Chinese, and Hindi. In Scandinavia subtitling is the rule, and it is adduced as one explanation of the admirable English, usually with an American accent, spoken by young Danes, Norwegians and Swedes. From an aesthetic point of view, it is very hard to defend dubbing, since the way in which an actor uses his voice is an important part of his artistic equipment. Humphrey Bogart not only had a distinctive vocal style but also slight labial paralysis which imparted a lisping quality to his lip consonants. This idiosyncrasy is never carried over into dubbed versions of his films, and there is a consequent loss of a highly individual flavor. Sometimes actors have foreign voices imposed on them which result in a mythic image quite at variance with the original. Thus, in Italy Stan Laurel and Oliver Hardy (called there Stanlio and Olio) are made to speak the kind of Anglicized Tuscan a tin-eared British public school boy might use though, at the same time, a wholly Italian passion for *spaghetti alle vongole* is imposed on Stanlio. Occasionally, though, dubbing can be inspired. The alley cat of Walt Disney's *The Aristocats (Gli Aristogatti)* is turned into one of the nick-eared denizens of the cat colony of the Roman Colosseum and speaks very rich Roman dialect.

Total dubbing is least applicable to musical films, where the original song lyrics, and sometimes recitative-like dialogue preceding, or contained in, "production numbers" are frequently permitted to intrude implausibly into the stream of translated speech. But dubbing has become a very fine art, especially in France and Italy, and an important musical film like *My Fair Lady* is deemed worthy of wholemeal translation. The ingenuity of the Italian version is worth remarking on. The basic *Pygmalion* situation has no applicability in Italy, where one dialect is as good as another, but there is a phonetic eccentricity in Bari—the raising of *a* to *e*—which became the staple of Eliza Doolittle's idiolect. Though there is no aspirate in Italian, the process of teaching the girl to pronounce correctly phrases like "In Hertford, Hereford, and Hampshire hurricanes hardly ever happen" was justified by her need to look ahead and accommodate British patrons of her flower shop. "Bloody," the climactic expletive of the original play, is replaced by "arse" in the musical version. Italians use *culo* on all possible occasions, but the *culo* of Eliza's speech at Ascot had as devastating effect on Italian audiences as the British equivalent on British. The situation of an idiomatic Italian comedy being played in a totally British environment is, when one comes to think of it, bizarre, but the goodwill of an audience ready to be diverted can bridge the dizziest gaps. It is a kind of Elizabethan situation, with striking clocks and doublets in ancient Rome.

Culo may mean "arse," but it does not look like it. A disyllable opening with a velar stop and containing two rounded vowels is opposed to a monosyllable with an open spread vowel. No amount of goodwill in an audience can bridge the gap between what the eye sees and what the ear hears. Very few people can lip-read, but most people are aware of the consonance between the movements of the mouth and the sounds these movements produce. My present concern is with the difficulties that have to be surmounted at the post-synchronizing stage in the making of a dubbed film. In other words, how can a mouth making one set of sounds be made to appear as if it were making another?

The problems do not arise only when a film is being dubbed into a foreign language. Excruciating *gaffes* are sometimes perpetrated by actors when recording on the set, unnoticed or uncorrected by the director—whose knowledge of the language in which the film is being made may be less than perfect. When run in the cutting-room, these errors can often, with trickery, be put right. The actor will be available for sessions of post-synchronization or "looping"—so called because a loop of film is run and rerun to familiarize the actor with his own lip-movements, enabling him to achieve an exact synchronization—but sometimes, for a variety of reasons, there has to be a drastic act of surgery on the body of the film itself. The error is most frequently discerned by the scriptwriter, and it can be a linguistic solecism or a serious deviation from the scenario. A good, or infuriating, example of the former occurred in the making of an "epic" film based on the life of Moses. Aaron, played by Anthony Quayle, was permitted by the Italian director to say "God has chosen people like you and I." A former director of the Royal Shakespeare Company should have known better. The offending *I* was uttered in close-up and could not easily be plucked out. The expense of reshooting the scene to accommodate the correction *me* would have been prohibitive. Looping to put right a single grammatical error would be dear enough. A piece of film was taken from a different scene, in which Aaron presented his back to the camera, and this was cut in to cover the "me." The pronoun itself was uttered and recorded by a mere cutting-room technician, and nobody seemed any the wiser.

The elocutionary skill of actors often belies their limited mastery of the language they speak. Errors are common—*contemptuous* for *contemptible* is the general favorite—but confidence in knowing better than the scriptwriter can lead to expensive and time-consuming restorations of the lines originally written. Only an Orson Welles can, with his "cuckoo-clock" improvisation in *The Third Man,* improve on a Graham Greene. Burt Lancaster, playing Moses, made a radical alteration in the following passage: "You will not hear from me again, Pharaoh."—"Why not, cousin Moses?"—"I am slow of speech." That last line became "Because I am uncircumcised of lips," with an appropriate circular gesture of the fingers around the labia. There was no "cover" in the form of back-views or reverse-shots to accommodate a restoration of the original line. The lips had to remain uncircumcised. The scriptwriter is usually blamed, in such circumstances, for giving the actor poor material.

Foreign actors without knowledge of the language of the film, who nevertheless have the professionalism to learn their unintelligible lines parrot-fashion to ease the eventual work of the dubber, are a great blessing to scriptwriters. They do not know what the words mean and hence are not tempted to try to improve them.

The coming of the day of the international film, with Cinecittà a Babel of monoglot actors, raised dubbing to a precise art and a major cottage industry (domestic in the sense that dubbers form syndicates or families who become used to working together). It is fascinating to visit a film set when such a film is being made (like, for instance, Fellini's *Casanova*) and hear an American actor and a German actress conducting a scene in their own languages, frequently a scene in which precision of verbal communication is essential to the narrative: the illusion of perfect mutual understanding is an aspect of histrionic skill. Bedroom scenes, of course, present no linguistic problems. Since dubbing is a major part of the whole operation with such films, it may legitimately be asked why the films are shot, which they are, with sound. Why not return to the silent days of before 1929 and construct a mute artifact, regarding the adding of sound as a separate process under a separate director? There are various reasons why not. Since 1929 actors expect to participate in a total acting process, being dually recorded by cameraman and sound engineer, even if dubbing has to occur later. The post-synchronization of speech is recognized, anyway, as a necessary evil, one submitted to because of difficulties in recording speech in the open air or in swift or violent action. But the scenes that can be shot with sound—indoor confrontations, for example—should be so shot, exhibiting the total art of the performer. And whatever the language the actor uses, it will be intelligible in one of the versions of the film.

Fellini shoots his films with sound, but is never greatly concerned about what is actually said. Indeed, he sometimes specifies that actors shall justify the use of their vocal organs by reciting sequences of cardinal numbers. Passionate performers in *Satyricon* prove to have been counting rigorously. Fellini is able to say, like an orchestral conductor, "Let us return to Number 94."

Awareness that dubbing is going to take place has influenced the director's approach to the visual aspects of his craft. Close-ups are dangerous, since they display the whole anatomy of speech. In passages of stichomythia, traditionally rendered by reverse shots, or cutting from speaker to speaker, increasingly we are shown the listener rather than the speaker, the words disembodied, the effect of the words. The symbols *VO* (voice over) and *OS* (out of shot) appear more and more frequently in shooting scripts. It is theoretically possible to make a film in which the lips of the speakers are never seen at all. Precision of lip-synchronization is often decreed by the editors at International Recording Studios in Rome or one of the workshops in Wardour Street, Soho, London. The scriptwriter is usually called in to give plausible words to rhubarbing extras in the background: this is rather like Sarah Bernhardt's making up those parts of her body that would not be seen on the stage. When this vital business of equipping a film with a sound track is being conducted by nameless men in shirt-sleeves among plastic coffee cups and half-eaten sandwiches, the director is basking somewhere in expensive sunshine.

The technicians responsible for preparing a script for dubbing have a fair knowledge of organic phonetics: at least they are aware of the relationship between sounds as acoustic entities and the oral athletics of their production. If the translation of literature is both an art and a craft, the same may be said of this other mode of translation, but, as we rarely know the names of the translators of great books (with a few exceptions like Sir Thomas Urqhart and Scott Moncrieff), so we practically never know who creates the most skilled of the dub-scripts. In practice a good deal of dubbing is worked out collectively and empirically. Men and women who edit films acquire a sensitivity to what is being silently mouthed on the editing tables, and they can at least suggest sequences of gibberish which fit exactly. Indeed, many deathless lines of translated script begin as gibberish: take care of the sounds and let the sense come later.

The most difficult elements to render from one language to another when dubbing are, as might be expected, the commonest in both. *Yes* can easily become *ja,* especially when the speaker is a slack-lipped American, but it is hard to turn it into *igen* or *kyllä* or *naam* or *ne* or *evet.* A cowboy saying *yah* or *yeah* might just about be saying *ouais,* if not *oui,* but Sir John Gielgud affirming with precise actor's diction in close-up is excruciating to dub. Greek *ne* sounds like *no,* and *o'chi,* which means no, can never be made to fit a naying mouth. A common statement in films is "I love you." Actors with unathletic lips cause little trouble when the phrase is rendered into French. The vowels of *aime* and *love* are both open and unrounded, and the lip-rounding for the *you* will serve for a syllabic *-me* at the end of *aime. Ich liebe dich* will not fit loving anglophone lips, however. "To be or not to be" does not look like *"sein oder nicht sein"* but *"essere o non essere"* matches the original by having lip-spreading for the key word and lip-rounding for the structural ones: *not to—o non.*

A typical dubber's nightmare would occur if, say, one of the key episodes in a French film consisted of the hero's reciting the first stanza of Baudelaire's *L'Albatros* in a close shot:

> Souvent, pour s'amuser, les hommes d'équipage
> Prennent des albatros, vastes oiseaux des mers. . . .

The script in straight translation would give: "Sometimes, to amuse themselves, the men of a ship's crew grab albatrosses, huge seabirds." Would any of these words fit the mouth of the reciter? Only *albatrosses,* singularized to a vocable virtually identical with the original. What phrase could contain it—"grab a tame albatross"? The labial at the beginning of *prennent* is highly visible, as is the one at the end of *tame.* Try "dazed albatross." Try, taking the last syllables of *équipage,* "play pranks on a dazed albatross." Complete the second line: "vast-winged hoverer." The *i* and the second *v* do not match the French lip-positions. Try "vast white lord of the air." There is nothing in the English to explain the pout on *mers.* "Vast white-eyed dreamer" is eccentric but seems to fit. To put Baudelaire into a film is eccentric anyway. The whole thing might be rendered as:

> At sea, for pastime, sea sailors who brutally play
> Pranks on a dazed albatross, vast wide-eyed dreamer.

This explains nearly all the mouth-positions of the French, but the problems of making the words sound like poetry and, when the next two lines come, finding rhymes, are as devastating as the reader will imagine—also time-consuming. It is not surprising that most dubbing represents a mere approximation to matching exotic mouth-positions with native phonemes: speed of utterance, labial slackness (very common with Americans, especially male actors), and the listener-viewer's own ignorance are among the dubber's best friends.(*Play* will rhyme with *way* or *day, dreamer* with *steamer:* the thing becomes obsessive. And should not that *wide-eyed* be *wide-orbed* or *white-oared?*)

Yet the sheer difficulty of a task like the hypothetical one above should serve to warn us of the fundamental unwholesomeness of dubbing—which means, in effect, the international film, its neutral idiom, its rootlessness. Fellini recently expressed his longing to return to the flavorsome regionalism of early films like *I Vitteloni,* but, so long as film financing comes from international corporations, the plastic picturesque, with its plastic dubbed dialogue, must prevail. If a Western, spaghetti or sukiyaki or authentic son-of-a-bitch-stoo, is to be dubbed into Parisian French or Roman Italian, why should it not also be dubbed into Lancashire or Cockney? It is illogical to invoke a special linguistic relationship. The dubbing into British English of Fellini's *La Dolce Vita* was a tour de force, but it was absurd to hear a Roman prostitute speaking debased Notting Hill with all that all-too-visible Roman townscape. Moreover, the Anglicization was totally unacceptable to American audiences.

Dubbing, like murder, is a craft; one can deplore the end while admiring the means. Any film-watcher is entitled to take in the sonic as well as the visual totality of the original. There was a time when a character in a French film saying "Tout, tout, tout" would bring a Wolverhampton or Poughkeepsie house down, but the mass audiences for foreign films no longer exist in Anglo-America and there is no further need to coddle the uncouth with dubbing. Subtitles are better, if they are done well. A Hindi version of *Hamlet* (ten songs for Ophelia and a dance of gravediggers) did badly with "Shall I live or do myself in? I do not know," and only the other day an American war film translated the line "Tanks?" as *merci,* but such hazards are preferable to dubber's plastic. Dubbing should be reserved to the Royal Honours List.

FREDERIC RAPHAEL

The Language of Television

LET US SUPPOSE that someone is talking about a "serious book" on the subject of television. How are we disposed to envisage its contents? Certainly they would be different from those of a serious book about literature: we should scarcely expect, for example, an analysis of the Great Tradition of television fiction. Could we hope (or want) to find a chapter on the ways in which television had extended the range of metaphor or the vocabulary of love? How many clinching quotations could be offered to prove the distinction or the grandeur of the medium? Our serious book, whatever it was serious about, would hardly contain sections of critical exegesis calculated, by their ingenious fervor, to announce the apocalypse of some new D. H. Lawrence (or even to claim the office of his unique interpreter). The television critic, whatever his pretensions, does not labor in the same vineyard as those he criticizes; his grapes are all sour. By contrast, even the most unmelodious literary critic works in print and is, in that sense, foursquare with those on whom he fastens his attention. The television critic is typically a wit. He approaches the medium as film critics used to approach movies when the cinema was widely despised by sophisticates. He neither makes nor breaks: he is there to score off the daily offerings and, the more mordant his comment, the better his editor and his readers will be pleased. If he has written our serious book, it will almost certainly deal with the sociology of the medium, not with the intrinsic qualities of the programs. There is no necessary scandal here: television is the most social as well as the most fugitive of the media. How can we distinguish its meaning from its uses? It cannot be said to exist in a pure, autonomous condition. Its gabbled language is derived from its neighboring states, for its roots lie in older, if waning, cultural categories: America is perhaps its inevitable Mecca. The great networks are there to prove that ideas can be canned like spaghetti. If everything ends up by tasting like everything else, is that not the evidence that it has been properly cooked?

Television, like all new arts, when they are new, is having to work its passage to respectability. The BBC still calls its weekly program guide the *Radio Times,* thus acknowledging that for many years the higher management—especially those who joined the corporation when TV was still a blur in its inventor's eye—regarded the wireless as broadcasting's true engine. (The title *TV Times* has been adopted by the "independent" networks: they have no noble descent to commemorate.) The cultists of radio held that there was a purity in their medium absent in television. Nor is their claim foolish: radio drama was, and remains, unlike anything else; the wireless liberated poets and writers to an imaginative articulation which does not quite resemble, yet can sometimes give rise to, literature. (*Under Milk Wood* is the most famous instance.) The radio listener is provoked to a fruitful participation, as a good reader is: the pauses in radio drama are, or can be, truly pregnant. One need but cite the early plays of Harold Pinter, who seemed to write in a dark script of "negative meaning" which lurked in the silences between his lines. Words, isolated in the velvet of radio, took on a jewelled particularity. Television has quite the opposite effect: words are drowned in the visual soup in which they are obliged to be served. One of the systematic oddities of television drama is how unsuccessfully it makes use of silent sequences: the viewer craves sound. Film, it will be recalled, was regarded by many of the best of its early practitioners, including especially Chaplin, as having fallen from grace with the arrival of the talkies. The true language of film, they said, was contained in silent pictures, their arrangement and sequence. The films even of today, certain orthodox sentimentalists would claim, should be understandable and "rewarding" without their sound tracks: a film's quality may still be judged, by such parsimonious purists at least, by looking at an in-flight movie without hiring the earphones. Television, viewed mute, lacks this approximation to a condition of primitive purity. In this sense it is more like radio than most people in the business are willing to admit: the words dominate; hence the relatively elevated social status of the writer, who is much less highly regarded in the cinema. TV is a borrower from radio, from journalism and from film, from which its first generation of executives and program makers emigrated either through opportunism or displacement. Its language owes much to the old worlds from which they derived, but this need not imply that it lacks a certain aggressive vigor—a characteristic "voice" at least—of its own. A television play is said to "mix" from one scene to the next, when the transition is a slow one (film is said to "dissolve"). *Mixing* is an ur-television term and television itself may be said metaphorically to have been mixed out of its antecedent genres: it emerges, but the exact moment when the transition has taken place is hard to spot. Lady into Fox!

Is television an art? Aesthetic essentialism has always been more or less an assumption in higher criticism: we have the idea that to be an artist one must practice an autonomous activity with a precise province. There are, no doubt, traditional reasons why "artists" feel dignified by the annunciation of vocational uniqueness: the Muse cares only for her own and we care only for the Muse. Of course, it is part of the comedy of the evolution of the arts that each, as it emerges in the wake of some banausic innovation, is regarded as unworthy of the Muses' tutelage. Plato's disdain for painting (he regarded it as a poor carbon copy of reality) can be contrasted with the solemnity with which Art (by which we now tend to mean essentially fine art—painting and sculpture) is now treated: writers of cant catalogues at least find precisely in Art the reality of which life itself is but a smudged counterfeit. Nor is the situation in literature all that different: the novel was, in no very distant days, held to be the lowest of literary genres. It was assumed to be written from a vulgar desire for fame and fortune. Graham Greene, whom everyone has now agreed to regard as a paradigm of the serious English novelist, actually maintains that he would have renounced fiction, had his third novel not proved successful. If we are disinclined to believe him, it is because we like to think that he didn't *really* write for such vulgar reasons. It would be hard to be similarly sentimental about a television writer, for one assumes that such people work for no other reason than the desire for "success" or at least acceptance: they are journalists and journeymen, not artists. The novel, meanwhile, has become the dying monarch of our prosaic glen: leading articles lament its passing, bursaries preserve the waning species. What was once the province of mere scribblers has been recommissioned the national park of true "creative" writers. Leave it and, as Byron once said, you leave your reputation behind you.

I am not, I may say, greatly dismayed by the upward revaluation of printed fiction, not least because I do not propose to abandon it. It remains true, however, that the novel is no longer a form from which one may plausibly expect to make a living. From television can one expect to do anything else? If money remains a distasteful topic in the higher reaches of aesthetic analysis (at least when conducted by academics with tenure), one certainly cannot ignore the economic structure in which any of the mechanical arts functions, if we are to understand its conceptual armature. (Even the Church as patron was, in Show Biz language, the "producer" and grammarian of that art which aestheticians have often preferred to consider as manifestations of individual sensibility.) Television cannot be practiced without the machinery of the business. It can never be—certainly has not *yet* been—a cottage industry. One may be a novelist or a poet without ever having published one's work; one cannot work in television without working in television.

There is a very close connection then, in every case we can conceive of discussing, between the means and system of production and the product; this connection is far closer than that between fiction and the reading public or between literature and print. (There was plenty of literature before Gutenberg; no television before television.) Television, one might say, is the perfect artistic medium for positivists: it is less an art than an activity. It makes "programs" rather than art objects, as even filmmakers are now said to do (and say they do). Its menu lacks a gourmet section: it is all *table d'hôte,* you take it or you leave it, it takes you or you leave.

French television, which caters above all for those who lack the *bachot,* sometimes flatters those who work in it by allowing its classier directors to sign their programs "*un film de* . . . ," the cinematic style by which *auteurs* sought to announce their affectations, if not always their achievements. (I have alluded to it elsewhere as "the *hauteur* theory.") Thus the condescending "artist" can console himself that, even when seconded to the slums of TV, he is really doing "*cinéma*." Anglo-Saxon television executives, and critics, are less willing to indulge the pretensions of the television program maker and one often finds films obstinately described as "plays" on English TV. The reasons are not necessarily derogatory: the BBC, being a correct institution, despite the matey rictus which convulses its countenance as it seeks to find the common touch, continues to think of the theatre as the most dignified dramatic medium. When it first transmitted plays on television, there was even an interval, and a warning bell to signify its impending end, as if dinner-jacketed viewers were imagined to have repaired to their private bars for inter-act refreshment. The vestiges of this leisurely time have almost entirely vanished, but the theatrical bias remains in the belief that dignity is added to a program by describing it as Play of the Week, of the Month, or whatever. Even ITV divides its "plays" into "acts," thus making possible and proper the "natural breaks" in which its revenues are earned.

There remains an almost unanalyzable difference between TV drama and movies (though American networks prefer to call a play Movie of the Week, thus seeking kudos from a different national piety). Even when filming—rather than using tape—in order to make a TV program, the director can sense that the piece has a different logic when it is destined solely for the box. The pace is not the same as that required for a "theatrical" film, i.e., one destined for a cinema. The dialogue can be far more protracted: scenes can last much longer without losing their hold on the putative audience's attention. Thus one could argue that *extension* is a feature of television's specific language: newsreels even, and programs of "actuality," can last far longer than they could in the cinema or even on the radio. Anything goes, and goes on and on. For this reason it is tempting to believe that television has almost unlimited cultural and educational potential. If so, that potency has yet to be translated into any very virile manifestations. For the paradox is a commonplace: one can watch hours and hours of TV without actually losing interest, but, as with Chinese food, one is rarely left with much residue of nourishment. One feeds in order to go on feeding; we may thus become a planet of closeted cows forever chewing audio-visual cud.

Is this a feature of the form itself or only of the forms of it available to us? I suspect that the very completeness of television numbs the viewer: there are few "spaces," I mean, into which he is incited to read meaning (here the "languages" of print, the radio and even the cinema—with its opportunities for editorial "wit"—are systematically homogenized and devitalized). The television viewer is invited to be passive. Since he sits (nearly always) at home, even his laughter is often supplied for him, should the program seem to demand it, by a studio audience—real or cynically dubbed on the tape—so that he is spared the social nicety of proving himself alert to the jokes. An American television trailer which I happened to see recently asked its audience to watch an upcoming soap opera and promised that if they did so, they would "learn how it really feels." Plato might have been amused at the idea of shadows instructing men how to have sensations, but the modern cave is better lit than the outside world: men sit outside in darkness and gaze into its seductive light. The defense of television commercials and commercialism which argues that they give people a glimpse of a better world, an ideal world even, is not entirely cynical. George Steiner has argued that the concentration camp is a mundane version of hell; television, on the other hand, offers a banal version of heaven, especially when it is as heavily commercialized as the American networks. (In the States, *educational TV* means simply those programs, admittedly sometimes with cultural affectations, which are transmitted without commercials: the rational man, not subscribing to the common credulities, substitutes the compensations of refinement for the common "heaven" of the consumer society which he is insufficiently sociable to desire.)

Television is not the "dream factory" which Hollywood was once said to be by dour sociologists: it is a reality factory. It is truer to life than life is. I am inclined to believe that confession is its essential mode. One thinks of Nixon (there is no guarantee that anyone will confess the *truth,* of course) and also of the literally countless interviews and chat-shows: television is more *convincing* than any other medium, though it is also the least persuasive (the systematic futility of Party Political Broadcasts lies in the inept importation of *rhetoric* into an unrhetorical medium). Television convinces us by immediacy and by repetition, not by structured argument or oratorical exposition. A lack of articulacy is the badge of sincerity; grammar smacks of premeditation. "Series" dominate all program planning. What has been said before—"characters" we have seen before, advertisements we "love"—may well be the evidence that originality (what has never been said before) has scant future on the box. Malcolm Muggeridge has spoken of the numbing effect of the plethora of news, especially on American television, which he has wittily dubbed "Newsak." (In the same manner, the series *Holocaust* dramatically reduced Hitler's war against the Jews to Jewsak.) By hosing us with "information" the networks affect to keep us fully up to date with the world, yet the segmentation and "personalization" of the "news," not to mention the manipulative selectivity displayed by the networks—you wouldn't like us to *bore* you with complexities would you?—actually confuse us with their discontinuous gush, so that we are less set free by the "truth" than addicted to it, not least because it seems always about to tell us something. Frustration accompanies even our most emotional responses: the eyes fill with tears, the lump engorges the throat, as victims or survivors appear on our screens, but catharsis does not follow, nor (in almost all cases) does any active response, in political or social terms. The reward of being a viewer depends on staying passive—if we are moved to leave the viewing chair we may miss the next program. Such movement then is rarely any part of a newscaster's program: "stay tuned" is the eleventh and commanding commandment.

Now it occurs to me that I must seem to be burking the real subject: what is the language of television? But it is (as they always say) no accident that I find myself more inclined to discuss either the techniques of putting together programs or the effects of them than I am the syntax of the medium, examined in isolation. The truth is that it cannot be isolated, for if I am right, television is a voracious recycler and mixer of a confluence of concepts. "Basic television" has no *distinct* vocabulary: it eavesdrops and cadges with relentless parasitism, but like the Belgians it has no specific dictionary, merely a character, or characters. It is the very instance of cultural ribbon development. Indeed, the medium normally used for program making is called tape and television proves itself the insatiably edacious worm in the gut of modern civilization.

Well, such glum denunciation—if that is what it is—is certainly part of the story. The practical consequences are not, however, always so depressing as the large diagnosis. Things *can* be said on television. No politician can duck a question without being *seen* to do so: thus a vast amount of influence can be wielded by those who ask the questions. The interviewer, unlike the journalist whom, in guild terms, he closely resembles, becomes a celebrity rather than a pundit; the new moralist is known for his questions, not his answers: Cronkite not Lippmann. Indeed the rhetorical question is an almost habitual ending to television actuality programs: thus do they meet the demand for impartiality imposed by business or political interests concerned to find that consensus—the largest possible constituency for votes or sales—which the Western democracies (i.e., democracies) regard as necessary to a public service. However, within the supposed monoliths there are, of course, many contending *prises de position:* certain programs will be the fiefdoms of strong personalities, whose political views will be seen to tilt the balance. In general, especially in England, where political views (like religious) are still, to some extent, regarded as a man's *personal* business, only cases of flagrant bias tend to be blacked out, though the steady weight of threatened disapproval will, of course, predispose the program maker to self-censorship. I do not have time here to give examples of what I take to be the many ways in which a good or a bad complexion may be added to an apparently neutral interview or newsreel clip by matching incongruous commentary or voice-over dialogue to "factual" visual images. Only naive directors will show sheep jumping over a fence when an insomniac potentate declares that he counts sheep: a militant may show the man, if he is a capitalist, counting workers through a factory gate, while an apostle of freedom might portray a commissar thrusting dissidents into a camp. One has but to adjust the electronics slightly in order to make a politician, or anyone else, seem bombastic or incomprehensible.

The games which can be played with the machinery of television are, perhaps, what distinguish the medium significantly from other forms of expression: electronics also have their nuances, and how. Television seems at once to give us a matchless opportunity for access to reality and to offer endless opportunities for its distortion and misrepresentation: the camera cannot lie / the camera cannot but lie. The Steinerian analogy between concentration camps and hell need not be applied only to the heaven of the commercial, which insists that if you buy enough, heaven can wait. Television not only gives us an airborne celestial city this side of the clouds, it also promises a program of resurrection. The action replay has become so expected a part of watching sport, for instance, that when one actually goes to a game of football one experiences a sense of deprivation when one cannot see the goal again. Television is better than the real thing: in California there are hotels where, on closed circuit TV, one can watch people making love while making love oneself. Educational TV indeed! (Cf. my novel *California Time.*) The prospect of a life after death is bettered by the promise of undying life on earth: the cult of the endless rerun. With the right equipment, one may embalm one's own life (the fastidious doubtless prefer to watch pictures of *themselves* making love, a common practice we are promised, in certain swinging homes, thus never "losing it") so that one can have the illusion of immortality right up until the day of one's death. One thus becomes one's own guardian angel, one's own God, able at any time to number the hairs on one's own head—or anywhere else—without divine accountancy. The whole metaphysical dimension of human aspiration can, with television, become literally mundane. In the graveyards of the future, the dear departed will prove not to have left: we shall hear them speak and see them move whenever we want to. It will not be what they say which will matter, but merely that they are saying it: content without form is the heartless heart of the new ethics and the new aesthetics. "Ordinary life" endlessly replayed is the machinery of its salvation. Being true to life will soon be better (more authentic) than life itself. Television, in fact, suggests that it is already: even television drama, with its almost inescapable naturalism, is more quotidian, so to say, than everyday life. The regularity of its series provides a clock and a monitor by which reality itself is calibrated. "Time for Kojak" becomes a normal way of announcing where we are in the day, while Kojak himself, at the peak of his powers and popularity, gave policemen—as do and did other realistic programs—an indication of how they should behave (and how the public would expect them to behave) if they were to maintain credibility. "As seen on TV" thus becomes a guarantee of quality, not only in advertised products, but in human behavior at large.

Mass communication communicates massively: its language lacks precise articulation and avoids demanding terms; it argues for the kind of behavior in life which will make a "good program": ethics equals showbiz. Thus it is no longer impressive or intimidating to shout; yelling is a social ineptitude because it is electronic sin; it gives rise to "howl" and is thus "unprofessional." A modern row may be savage and it will certainly contain a good deal of overlapping dialogue and tellingly controlled sarcasm: television writes our scripts and it thus gives us back our language in a verisimilitudinous recension, docked of amateurish or embarrassing passions or obsessions which might cause our audience to switch off. If, lacking a TV, you want a phrase book of the prevailing television cant, why not simply turn on a friend?

MARY-KAY WILMERS

The Language of Novel Reviewing

HOW DO NOVEL REVIEWS begin? Just like novels very often:

> Motherless boys may be pitied by mothers but are not infrequently envied by other boys.
>
> For the friends of the Piontek family, 31 August 1939 was a red-letter day.
>
> All her life Jean Hawkins was obedient.

It looks as though the writers of these reviews have set out not to summarize the plot but to tell the story, with the drawback, from the novelist's point of view, that readers may content themselves with the reviewer's version. Other reviews begin with a different sort of story—the reviewer's:

> Halfway through Beryl Bainbridge's new novel I found I was laughing until the tears ran down my cheeks.

Some start by characterizing the novel:

> An aura of death, despair, madness and futility hangs over the late James Jones's posthumous novel.

Others by characterizing the reviewer: "Count me among the Philistines," says Jerome Charyn, inauspiciously, at the start of a review in the *New York Times.* Some begin with a paragraph on the novel now; some begin by addressing the reader:

> You might not think there would be much wit or lyricism to the story of a subnormal wall-eyed Balkan peasant who spends 13 years masturbating in a pigsty. . . .

Some kick off at the end:

> *Final Payments* is a well-made, realistic novel of refined sensibility and moral scruple;

and others at the beginning: "The five writers under review have been browsing. . . ."

Different openings suggest different attitudes, both to the novel and to the practice of reviewing novels. There are ideologies of the novel and ideologies of the novel review, fictional conventions and reviewing conventions. They don't necessarily overlap. A regular reviewer, confident of his own constituency, may describe a novel in terms of his own responses to it: he wouldn't for that reason applaud a novelist for writing in a similarly personal vein. What reviews have in common is that they must all in some degree be re-creations: reshapings of what the novelist has already shaped. The writer's fortunes depend on the reviews he gets but the reviewer depends on the book to see that his account of it—his "story," to use the language of the newspaper composing room—is interesting. Dull novels don't elicit interesting reviews: not unless a reviewer decides to be amusing at the novel's expense or tactfully confines himself to some incidental aspect of it. A generous reviewer may also invent for the novel the qualities it might have had but hasn't got.

The most brusque reviews occur in the most marginal newspapers: "The new novel by Camden author Beryl Bainbridge," said the *Camden Journal,* "took just a few hours to read yet cost £3·95. . . . The story is fairly interesting, mildly amusing and a little sad." A hundred years ago the most brutal things were said about novelists and their works (cf. Henry James on *Our Mutual Friend:* "It is poor with the poverty not of momentary embarrassment, but of permanent exhaustion"). Today many literary editors, alert to the fact that the novel is under pressure, ask their reviewers to be kind and most of them are. Kind to the old novelist because he is old; kind to the young novelist because he is young; to the English writer because he is English ("all quiet, wry precision about manners and oddities") and not American or German; to others because they are black (or white) or women (or men) or refugees from the Soviet Union. Every liberal and illiberal orthodoxy has its champions. Failings are seen to be bound up with virtues ("there are rough edges to his serious simplicity"); even turned into them ("though inelegant and sometimes blurred, their heaviness and urgency create their own order of precision"); but seldom passionately denounced, and although every novelist has had bad reviews to complain of, it sometimes seems as if novel reviewing were a branch of the welfare state.

The reasons have a lot to do with the economics of publishing. In the 1920s Cyril Connolly described the reviewing of novels as "the white man's grave of journalism": "for each scant clearing made wearily among the springing vegetation," he sighed, "the jungle overnight encroaches twice as far."[1] The jungle has now dwindled to something more like a botanic garden ("it is a knockdown miracle that publishers continue to put out first novels," noted a reviewer in *The Times*),[2] and far from having to hack his way through the springing vegetation, the critic is required to give the kiss of life to each week's precarious flowering. "SAVE THE NOVEL," implored the novelist Angus Wolfe Murray addressing reviewers.[3] Only in the case of such writers as Harold Robbins or Sidney Sheldon, whose fortunes or morale he cannot affect, does the reviewer have the freedom to write as he pleases.

Given that the novel is to be saved, what claims do reviewers make for it? John Gardner in his book *On Moral Fiction* (1978) complains of the flimsiness of "our serious fiction":

> The emphasis, among younger artists, on surface and novelty of effect is merely symptomatic. The sickness goes deeper, to an almost total loss of faith in—or perhaps understanding of—how true art works. True art, by specific technical means now commonly forgotten, clarifies life, establishes models of human action, casts nets towards the future, carefully judges our right and wrong directions, celebrates and mourns.

But it is clear from the exhilarated comments they make that many reviewers regularly find in the novels they have been reading the kind of guidance and instruction Gardner has in mind:

> In the vaunted creative process, he has transcended himself and given us an access to liberty.
>
> Her book is full of lessons about the art of creative literature, and about life, and how each reflects and enhances and deepens the meaning of the other.
>
> Its indignation is blazingly imaginative, furiously vital and gives us hope.
>
> A truer and deeper perception of the world's agony comes from the . . . stories . . . about her native land.

There is no suggestion here that novelists are suffering from diminished responsibility or reviewers from any cramping of their responses. But it depends which reviewers one reads. Hope, agony, the meaning of life and of art, a transcending of the self: for every critic who finds these in the novels sent to him for review—and a critic who finds them once tends to find them once a week—there are more who see confusion, ambivalence, ambiguity—and count themselves well pleased:

> The best English novelists are getting more ambiguous all the time.
>
> I suppose this is what Iris Murdoch means when she distinguishes between philosophy and fiction—that what the novel does superlatively is mirror our continuing confusion and muddle.

Gardner is not eccentric in detecting among both novelists and critics an active commitment to uncertainty; as a reviewer in the *Times Literary Supplement* observed apropos of a novel involving a mystery and its detection: "Once upon a time novels and readers and detectives discovered things; now they fail to discover them."[4] An achieved character is a mixed-up character: "his grief and obsession lack ambiguity and don't feel real"; he "is confused but by that token the more convincing." Gardner finds repugnant the notion that confusion may be the most appropriate response to a confusing world, but on countless occasions novels are praised for making it clear that nothing is clear, that a trouble-free verisimilitude can no longer be expected:

> The book is convincingly comic, and at the same time ambiguous and nervy enough to suggest that nothing is as solid as it seems.
>
> His theatrical memoir-scribbling existence is the best (i.e., most problematic) metaphor for how most of us function.

The brackets here reinforce the point, assuming as they do a coincidence of meaning between "best" and "most problematic." In another review Frank Tuohy's stories of English life are said to have a "grim predictability" but when he writes about Englishmen abroad his "subtle talent emerges":

> The barriers of language and culture give rise to a slightly baffled and tentative querying of reality; perspectives shift and blur, appearances bemuse and all our certainties suddenly lack foundation.

The writer should not merely baffle but himself be baffled: a way perhaps of acknowledging, and absorbing into a naturalistic tradition, the more exigent dubieties of such post modernist writers as

Borges, Sarraute, or Robbe-Grillet, whose ritual dismemberings of plot and character, especially when mimicked by native writers, have not gone down well among either reviewers or the public.

The baffled writer has various ways of disclaiming verisimilitude. In Renata Adler's *Speedboat,* for instance, the narrative is fragmented into a series of discrete events, anecdotes, perceptions. Elizabeth Hardwick writing about the book in the *New York Review* showed her respect for it by adopting in her review the novel's own fragmentary procedures. Likening it to some of the work of Barthelme, Pynchon and Vonnegut, she claimed for all of them an "honorable" attempt to deploy "the intelligence that questions the shape of life and wonders what we can really act upon"; but then added:

> It is important to concede the honor, the nerve, the ambition — important even if it is hard to believe anyone in the world could be happier reading *Gravity's Rainbow* than reading *Dead Souls.*

The old, unreconstructed pleasures of reading sometimes slip the reviewer's mind but a conflict between enjoyment and the "honourable" measures writers take to accommodate doubt and perplexity has to be acknowledged. Take Robert Nye's *Merlin.* Instead of a plot, it offers, as many nonconventional novels now conventionally do, a sprawling of plots, lists, jokes, and retellings of old stories. A prospective reader may be more grateful for a review which tells him what it is like to read such a novel ("In the end, it is just too much . . . rather like finding a hotel that serves you a Christmas dinner three times a day") than for one written in the spirit of the novel itself and dedicated to teasing out its many "implications about art and reality."

The most frequent recourse of the baffled writer is to offer himself as part of his fiction, stepping into the novel either in person (Margaret Drabble in *The Realms of Gold*) or in the guise of another novel writer purportedly engaged in writing this novel or another novel contingent on it, so that the novel tells two stories concurrently, its own and the novelist's, thereby foreshadowing, and in some cases forestalling, its own reviews. Two recent instances have been *The World According to Garp* by John Irving and John Wain's *The Pardoner's Tale.* The latter links a conventional account of a novelist's life with the equally conventional novel he is currently writing. Malcolm Bradbury, a critic committed to the notion of the text that doubts itself, praised it as being "among [Wain's] best novels, realism modestly considering itself." Reviewers often talk about realism as if it were something tangible

(Tim O'Brien's *Going After Cacciato* contained, according to the *New Statesman,* "a strange and impressive balance of realisms"), the idea being that where intention and meaning are in doubt, literary styles and devices have a life of their own. *The World According to Garp* is a much more complicated book, baroque, labyrinthine, full of internal fictions and comments upon those fictions. One reviewer remarked that "there is little one can say about the book or its author that Irving has not in some way anticipated in his own text." The baffled writer, it turns out, has this advantage over his critics: he can tell them what is wrong with his novel before they tell him.

Just as some novels supply their own reviews, so many reviews supply their own novels. It isn't so much a matter of different interpretations (which are unavoidable: one reviewer saw in *The Pardoner's Tale* "the lineaments of gratified desire . . . persuasively drawn . . . an amorous haze spreading delight," another "a man who has evaded what real love requires") as of giving a novelistic account of the novel. For instance:

> William Trevor's characters . . . seem to live perpetually in an afternoon sun which filters through the Georgian fanlight on to a balding carpet.

Or:

> Whether "she" is Nell or Julie or Ellen there's always the same tear-stained voice, stuffing old love letters into the mouth to hold back the sob at parting.

That Beryl Bainbridge has a quirky way of doing things may be put straightforwardly:

> She views life from so odd an angle that normal proportions and emphases are disconcertingly altered

or, if you like, mimetically:

> The characters proclaim their loves and loathings dimpled with breadcrumbs, adorned with swellings, fiddling with troublesome socks.

One danger is that the reviewer's novel may stand in the way of the author's. Sometimes the two are incompatible: when the Canadian writer Marian Engel describes the adulterous hero of *Injury Time* as having been "instructed to clean up his act," another, mid-Atlantic Beryl Bainbridge is brought to mind. A further danger is that mimicry may become parody (one of the standard ways of dismissing a bad novel is of course to ape its mannerisms), and a reviewer adopting the manner of the novelist may do the novel an injustice where no injustice was intended.

When a reviewer mimics a novel simply as a way of describing it (without, that is, any pejorative intentions) he is in some sense taking it over, as if he too could predict how the characters might behave. Those contemporary novels that disclaim verisimilitude make it difficult for the reader to enter their world; indeed, by making an issue of their own fictiveness they deliberately set up barriers against it. In their more extreme, Sarrautian forms they may invite him to participate in the invention but that in itself is a way of pointing up what would in these cases be seen as the fallacy that fiction imitates life. More realistic novels by contrast offer the reader a whole new world with new friends (or enemies) and new places to go to. "We follow the life of her heroine," a grateful reviewer reports, "through a circuitous route where we meet a plethora of well-drawn characters and visit a number of interesting places." But reviewers in discussing this world are inclined to be overeager:

> Perfectly observed details—a steaming mug of tea in a transport café, a misfired blind date in a lurid pub—make you feel you're living Desmond's life.

It may be that the best fiction has a reality that reality itself hasn't got (however well we know the detail of other people's lives we don't often feel we're living them), but the examples here don't support the claim that is made for them, and the reviewer, mistaking familiarity for something better, has been hasty in casting aside her own life in favor of Desmond's. It's the same with characters' emotions which too readily become the emotions of the reviewer:

> I relaxed as much as the hero and his wife do when she burns her ovulation charts.

It's hard to believe in that degree of empathy.

A critic who professes to share all the characters' ups and downs tells us too much about his own responses. David Lodge reviewed Mary Gordon's *Final Payments.* He thought it a good novel and one of its qualities, he said, was that it engaged the reader's sympathies on the heroine's behalf: "It says much for the power of Ms Gordon's writing that the reader feels a genuine sense of dismay at the spectacle of the heroine's mental and physical breakdown." The point he is making is very like the one being made by the reviewer who said she relaxed when the hero's wife burnt her ovulation charts, but he is putting the emphasis on Ms. Gordon's writing rather than his own sensibilities.

Generally speaking, the more highbrow the publication the more self-effacing—or apparently self-effacing—the reviewer. A critic in a popular paper may, rightly, claim that but for him a whole section of the literate public might never hear of certain writers and that this enjoins upon him the necessity to be forthright and uncomplicated. Auberon Waugh, who reviews novels in the *Evening Standard,* is such a writer. One of his habits is to complain of personal suffering—excruciating boredom, a pain in the ass—on reading novels he doesn't like; another to award prizes—"my gold medal . . . a peerage or some luncheon vouchers to go with it"—to those he does. Waugh sees himself as deploying the common sense of the common man: a reviewer in a more serious journal or newspaper has to suggest expertise, give evidence of special qualifications (though even here there are some who choose to make their comments personal as an excuse for slipping out of responsibility—to say "I enjoyed it" is sometimes a way of saying "little me I enjoyed it").

Whatever the publication, it is probably fair to say that most readers of reviews do not go on to read the novels themselves: in that sense reviews act as substitutes for the novels, incorporating as a further dimension the experience of the reviewer in reading them. Hence perhaps the documentary interest reviewers show in the lives that are led in novels (the more sociologically particular the world that is described, the more confident the praise: "exactly conveys the tone and feel of a theatre"; "quite faultless in its delineation of every aspect of the cinema"). Experiment, symbols, allegory: reviewers don't often like them ("there may be an allegorical meaning here that I've missed; if there is, Mr Keating isn't pushing it, and I'm all for that"), and novels that have a grand plan or an easily detected message are rarely well received. Time and again a book is praised for understating its intentions:

> *Getting Through* leaves so much unsaid that what is left—the story itself, pared down—becomes the reflection of great things.
>
> The purpose of their encounter is never formulated by authorial commentary or by the intrusive use of imagery.
>
> The book never loses its distant innocence of expression—as if the full surface of the world can only be conveyed by a prose that neither moralizes nor obtrudes.

Authorial unobtrusiveness ("clear spare sentences," "direct factual observation," "clear but unemphatic patterns"); modesty of effect and affect—these are the qualities reviewers speak well of. What is wanted is not "hectic" plotting but "a meticulous circumstantiality," "not clashing symbols but uninsisted juxtapositions."

On the other hand, it is the reviewer's business to make explicit what the author has been commended for rendering inexplicit; to spell out ("in their interaction they retrace the patterns of social intercourse familiar to us all") and to extrapolate ("Violence, Bainbridge seems to be saying, is as casual, as impersonal as the shadows we know"). Novelists may not be allowed to moralize but reviewers do it all the time:

> To him, the conquest of pride is ultimately more important than the conquest of Prague. It takes a lot of courage to suggest this, but the only real antidote to the think-alike, talk-alike herd instinct of Marxism is the liberation of your own soul from second-hand thinking and borrowed feelings.
>
> I don't accept any form of racism and I applaud Mr Brink's honest novel.

And if writers don't moralize, or are told that they ought not to, they are nonetheless praised in moral currency: "Where [the characters]—and Miss Sagan—truly shine is in the sections that describe their acknowledgment of a colleague's cancer."

Praising is the reviewer's most difficult task. Allocated, in most newspapers, a thousand words in which to give his views of three or four novels of average merit, he hasn't the space to build up the case for each one and must therefore resort to an encomiastic shorthand. In what is usually the first part of a review, where we are told what sort of novel it is and what happens to whom, the novel itself does much of the work; and if a reviewer gives a coherent account of it and makes the characters seem interesting, he has already done a great deal to commend the book to the reader's attention. A skillful reviewer will also interweave judgment and description. "Bernice Rubens's new novel is convincing about the need for people to see plots in their lives": that "convincing" carries conviction because of what follows it; if it had been placed at the end of the review—in the phrase "a convincing novel," for instance—one would scarcely have heard it.

Since the vocabulary of praise is limited, the same words occur again and again, while some acquire emblematic loadings. *Truth,* for example. When a reviewer says a novel has "an overall ring of truth," he may just be talking about "plausibility" and making it sound like something more important. But it is the final adjectival blast that offends. *Marvellous, delightful, brilliant:* it is hard for a reviewer eager to say good things about a novel to avoid such words, yet they have been used so often in connection with novels which, when compared, say, with *Our Mutual Friend,* are merely mediocre that readers may find some difficulty in giving them credence. It's true they are important to publishers, who use them in their advertisements, and a reviewer anxious to promote a novel will be sure to include a few for the publisher to quote, just as many literary editors, alert to the danger of one novel review sounding very like any other novel review, will want to cut them out.

Reviewers are varyingly responsive to these embarrassments, but the stratagems they may resort to for avoiding the clichés used by their less self-conscious colleagues quickly become clichés themselves. One doesn't often come across the simple phrase "a marvellous novel" nowadays: the fashion is for triads of adjectives ("exact, piquant and comical," "rich, mysterious and energetic") or for adjectives coupled with adverbs—"hauntingly pervasive," "lethally pithy," "deftly economic"—in relationships whose significance would not be materially altered if the two partners swapped roles—pervasively haunting, pithily lethal, etc. The praise is made to sound less bland by the use of negatives ("a completely unponderous story" or of oppositions indicating that a novel hasn't made too much of its virtues ("stylish but troubling," "unforced yet painful"); and by various minor syntactic devices: one novel "is saved by energy from pretension," another is rescued from overfamiliarity "by the author's evocation of certain oblique and mysterious states of consciousness"; one "gives us a feel for our own loony culture that is so recognizable we blink with shame and embarrassment," another produces "shocks so true to life that they hardly seem paradoxical."

Some reviewers, it's obvious, are better writers than others, but even among good writers there are recurrent mannerisms. Wordplay is one: "Amid stern actualities, Kundera gamely concocts (like Sterne, and hence unsternly) stories about people playing games." Verbs are preferred to adjectives: a "story spurts and fizzes," a "sense of humour crackles"; and so sometimes are nouns, usually in their plural form—*intricacies, acutenesses,* and so on. The abstract and the concrete may be unexpectedly juxtaposed: "details slither rat-like into their lairs"; and rather than speak directly of a novelist's talents, reviewers have lately been much inclined to anthropomorphize the novel: "grinding on like that is, Hanley's fiction knows, the hardest of all feats." The desire to avoid clichés is strong and commendable, but leads to some perplexing formulations: "Through all such knots and breaks of time, a rare aptitude for patience is the unassuming form of Trevor's irreplaceable imagination."

Novel reviews don't of course end like novels: novelists seldom finish off their work by praising or scolding their characters, though they may (or may not) award them happy lives. But what is wanted of a reviewer is much the same as what is wanted by the reviewer: a modest, unemphatic originality, a meticulously circumstantial account of the novel's merits, and a plausible (or should I say truthful?) response to them.

Notes

1. "Ninety Years of Novel-Reviewing," August 1929, reprinted in Cyril Connolly, *The Condemned Playground* (London, 1945).
2. 2 November 1978.
3. *New Fiction,* No. 18 (1978).
4. 7 April 1978.

NATHAN SILVER

Architect Talk

ARCHITECTURE is a group endeavor, so architects need to build with words first. Explaining things to their clients, planners, critics, and each other, they talk far more than they draw. They conduct regular and irregular group criticisms among themselves without hesitation or special encouragement. Slightly reminiscent of the consultations of the Pre-Raphaelite Brotherhood or of Hollywood story conferences, these reflect and support a community of interest. They occur not only in actual collaboration, but routinely through the ordinary fellowship of workers within the common profession and, perhaps, style.

Noteworthy first is that architects use verbal language a good deal as a substitute for visual language, because in the infinite ways of building windows or roofs, for example, most explanation arises from the need to describe different looks, not different construction, and has to be dealt with. There is a *mainly unmet* need for words evoking looks as there is a need for twenty words for *snow* in a northern language: "I like the zorchy shape above the door," someone might say in a drafting studio. Second, architects'

In accumulating examples of architect talk, I am indebted to several knowledgeable friends in London, and Robert Silver and Helen Walker in Cambridge, Massachusetts.

verbal language is principally in the form of talk, because memos are rare and other significant writing, such as criticism, comes much later.

This combination characteristically results in a quick pounce on available verbiage with an assured presentation, as in junk sculpture. An architect typically faced with simultaneous problems of function, construction, scale, theory, and consumer appeal may have to deal with all of them adequately in talking up a proposed design to perhaps six colleagues on his team, forestalling their counter-criticisms—so any appeals and references to those ends will do, as long as they work. Whatever is lying around could be put to use ad hoc. Consequently, the words and phrases architects use are as if winnowed from a magazine rack which holds the Sunday papers, the *Radio Times,* a couple of architectural magazines, and a pop anthropology or literary criticism paperback. Or, as if dug out from a kitchen midden of contemporary jargon, ideological polemic, historical reference, and some overcolored scenic description. Architect talk doesn't have to be accurate. Since it is primarily descriptive of looks, frequently it can't be. It achieves its results by using the language of the moment that signals certain things, and by going on at three times the necessary length. In fact, the deplorable prevalence of trendiness and overkill in architect talk may explain why architectural theory and criticism—usually outgrowths of design talk, and by the same people—are generally sloppy, jargon-ridden, and long-winded. But whether so or not, architect talk is efficient for its main task: debating something that doesn't exist yet, and evoking its visual form.

Take a current word like *high-tech,* or *hi-tech,* as it is more often written. At first it seems only a rather unnecessary abbreviation for high technology. In architect talk though, one might overhear someone saying, "We should reference hi-tech at the main entrance, so that becomes the vernacular." In this sentence, *hi-tech* clearly means more than high technology. It really means the slick *looks* of technology. (In the effort of written architect language to keep pace with and to capture nuances that arise purely in speech—in this case, the slightly ironic tone in the speaker's voice when he says "hi-tech"—one critic has recently devised the phrase *the slick-tech look* to be an adequate comparable.)

As architect talk is catchall lingo, or junk lingo, as well as a means of "referencing" something very different and abstract, namely visual language, it also follows that it is a good instrument for contending ideologies. Imprecision offers scope. A review of all current theoretical positions would bear this out, but one critic alone names six major "traditions" behind contemporary architecture, each with a multitude of *isms* adherent (including *Intuitive:* naturalist, expressionist, etc.; *Self-conscious:* academic, classicist, etc.; *Activist:* futurist, utopian, etc.; *Logical:* structural, geometric, etc.), so the possibilities for contention abound. At the moment there is a specific stylistic switch afoot, from the modern movement (a phrase too old and well known to deserve quotes or capitals any longer) to "Post-Modernism," which more or less derives from the *Self-conscious* tradition noted above. Between the two may (or may not) be "Late Modernism" (which displays the defects of both with the advantages of neither, the bewildered may feel). The term *Post-Modernism* was borrowed from literary criticism—or perhaps *lit-crit* is the slick form there.

Literary criticism has to answer for many of the words and phrases that have crept into architectural theoretical writing by respected current figures such as Robert Stern, Colin Rowe, Robert Venturi, and Charles Jencks. That these writers aren't dull art historians but remain vitally in touch with architect talk (i.e., junk lingo) is reassuringly signalled by odd spelling and meaning mistakes. Jencks, the biggest junk lingo freak (and thereby, as it could well signal, the best delineator of current architectural trends), for example, thinks *hermeneutic* is a synonym of *restricted* (hermetic?), and he spells it wrong. What matters is for the reader to suspect he scavenged the word from the likes of Frank Kermode. In other writers, *contextual* is often innocently interchanged with *contextural.* If the meanings are different, that isn't crucial in architect talk where the final contexture is only the impression to be taken away, whatever the context. *Typology, epistemology, historiography, morphology,* and *holistic*—all words reasonably to be found in an educated designer's vocabulary—are frequently misused and even confused, usually without damage, for the same reason: architect talk isn't an orderly string of words, but a field. It's a landscape. One hardly needs to notice a little junk under a hedge. The proof is in the built form, not in the sweeping and approximate rhetoric.

It's contingent, too. Architect talk reveals what architects are interested in now, so it is usually more profitable if one assesses it for sources rather than carps over solecisms. Coming across a full range of terms out of linguistics, for instance, one can note their useful application to the polyvalent, expressive architecture that Post-Modernism is trying to be, along with their trendiness. Previously Saussure and Lévi-Strauss were sources for architect talk, and before them Arendt. The Bauhaus theorists of the 1910s and 1920s copiously "referenced" Marx, and sometimes Freud. At least these show that architects don't have their heads in the sand, and were undoubtedly so intended.

The École des Beaux-Arts in Paris had a profound influence on the teaching of architecture in America, an influence that lasted through the thirties. Architects formerly had an allergy to the system, which represented everything the modern movement rebelled against, but it has been cured in the last few years, and the Beaux-Arts is enjoying rebound prestige. Prestige applies to any French or even French-sounding words and phrases in architecture, whether or not actually in currency at the École. A condensed collection of a few might be heard thus:

> At first I thought I'd go for a *bricolage* rhetoric because that's certainly contextural in the site's *quartier.* But it makes the *marche* too complicated. I finally decided to celebrate the circulation instead, and I came up with this *enfilade* plan.

Bricolage means an assembly of odd juxtapositions, and derives closely from its dictionary meaning; such a concept certainly had no stylistic status at the Beaux-Arts during its eclectic heyday. Since there are adequate English equivalents its appearance is probably a response to the Beaux-Arts vogue and/or some current French writing on architecture. Ditto *quartier,* which means no more than quarter, i.e., a self-contained neighborhood. The *marche* is the route or journey through the surrounding landscape and the building; the *promenade architecturale,* one might say. While celebrating the circulation instead of celebrating the walls or doorknobs, this speaker refers to an *enfilade* plan, which would probably amount to lining up the doors of a series of rooms so one could sight down them.

Pocher is a French word meaning "to fill in, as in a stencil; to blacken." In American schools of architecture prior to the mid-seventies, "please poché in the walls" meant, simply, "go darken the area between the parallel lines representing walls on the plan." Now, at the Harvard Graduate School of Design in the late seventies, there is a "poché plan." This refers to a type of design where the inside and outside don't correspond—one of the simplest examples is an octagonal room within a square exterior. But poché plans become very complicated. In a poché plan, the very thick walls which are thrown-away areas are referred to as "the poché space" (i.e., the non-spaces, perhaps devised for the Poché Man who can move only within the thickness of walls). In other words, an aesthetic factor capable of appreciation occurs in the negative space too, as why shouldn't it? Poché plan problems are given as exercises, because the term has been adapted to vitalize a current preoccupation with complex and contradictory forms. Egyptian pyramids with their huge masses and tiny burial chambers would seem the ultimate poché solutions, but "good" solutions at Harvard usually achieve daffier surprises.

A lot of architect talk naturally has to do with reasons for liking things when reasons are hard to state. The boss or a client can merely say "I like it," but a flunky architect needs arguments. These can be hard to find in matters of preferring one light fixture to another, or placing one legitimate priority above another. It follows that some of the most endearing words and phrases are merely new ways of saying "I like it" to forestall objections if possible. Hence, the speaker above wasn't just *promoting* the design's circulation, but *celebrating* it—a few years ago *featuring* would have been the selling word. It's a bit like advertising, with ideals and cultural pretensions added.

Identifications of main motifs are often sold in such a manner that you might suppose you were listening to short story writers:

> What happens in the front hall is the thematic. I've cut the master bedroom entirely out of my narrative.

"Referencing," of course, is the prelude to a "claim." An architect references something so he can claim it for his own, like giving his chrome tubing the outline of a Palladian window. Not that references need to be so aggressively territorial. One can also flirt, or choose to have a conversation, or not:

> The upper levels have no conversation with the ground floor.
>
> His building decisively addresses the street. [And vice versa, naturally.]

As can be seen, a common means of forming architect words is simply to change verbs to nouns—*a merge, a surround* (as in "a Gibbs surround"). Robert Venturi went to greater lengths in a 1966 book by inventing or popularizing *inflection,* which came to mean almost anything before it vanished, and also *superadjacency* (meaning "superimposition"). But novelty words generally have longer appeal, since strangeness is no stranger in a professional language where dentils, annulets, modillions and mutules used to be everyday items. A recent novelty is *aedicule.* Almost exactly according to the dictionary, a contemporary aedicule is a miniature building which represents the whole solution. At Harvard sometimes this turns up as a porch or vestibule at the entrance, a doghouse nearby, or a dovecot down the drive: "Meet me at the aedicule," instead of meet me under the clock.

Architect talk is the richest of the new languages in design. Plenty of new language is about in the fine arts, graphic design, architecture, and urban planning, but a mere list of neologisms, slang, and typical jargon doesn't necessarily offer insights. Urban planning is full of fine-sounding words for largely bombastic purposes: *Kakotopia, Eutopia* (you'd have to spell it), *palaeotechnical* cities. Even Sir Patrick Geddes, a plain man for a planning pioneer, produced *conurbation,* his own neologism, because *city* and *built-up area* evidently were not sufficient. In the fine arts, whose language is it? Artists seem happy to adopt new terms invented by critics like *hard-edge, minimalist,* or *conceptual art,* but they are imposed from above. If some months there seem more new movements than artists, it is a sign of probable hyperactivity among the critics rather than the practitioners.

A game played by architects and architectural critics escapes fine arts seriousness: influence-identifying, which is a joke about art history talk. The "Queen Anne" Style, in quotes because it occurred long after Queen Anne, was the possible jumping-off point for Schlock Classicism, Levittown Quatorze, and others anyone can think of. In a recent book called *Daydream Houses of Los Angeles* (1978), Charles Jencks turns the joke back into serious criticism by insisting that the stylistic visual references tacked onto many of the ordinary but individualistic houses of Los Angeles deserve names; that, in effect, the names secure the hybrid meanings which would otherwise remain elusive and uncomprehended. So photos are labelled "Spreadwing Cadillac," "Ronchamp Ski-jump with Mushroom Overtones," "Topiary Fascist." It is enlightening indeed, at least considered as a fair way of selling semiology (which is as Jencks would no doubt wish it).

Though orthodox modernism has been under serious attack for over fifteen years, Post-Modernism is the latest stylistic assault, and the first with all the ingredients of professional, popular, critical, and intellectual support (in America; to a lesser extent in Japan, Italy, France; to a small extent so far in Britain). The case for Post-Modernism is that it is unabashed about looks and even references. It is "inclusivist" in presenting hybrid, complex, impure design, as opposed to the purist, "exclusivist" design of the modern. Post-Modernism vs. the modern movement offers an occasion for polemics that scarcely occurs more than once a generation in art and design, and hasn't happened in architecture for at least sixty years. The infighting needn't detain us, but some of the descriptive terms for various camps are characteristic of the emergent vitality: there are the New York Five, otherwise known as the Whites; the New Haven–Philadelphia Axis (sometimes now the Charles Moore–Robert Venturi Axis) called also the Grays; the West Coast Curtain Wall architects, best represented by César Pelli, or the Silvers; also the Rationalists, or Rats, who as followers of Giuseppe Terragni, an Italian architect of the thirties, promote a formalist revival of the International Style. "It's all coming back," as the farsighted Louis Sullivan probably once said.

But rivalry between contending styles of architecture is nothing compared to the contending languages of the verbal and the visual. For all its color, weight, and obduracy, architecture even at its best offers only the *occasion* for thought. We now understand that thought depends, rather unfairly, but decisively, upon verbal language. Architect talk therefore isn't merely for conjuring up what doesn't exist yet, it is to influence the outcome. A recent term like *Art Deco* advanced the appeal of one style; *Gothic* was intended to retard another; the Greek, Roman, and Renaissance *orders* of architecture were transformed by Vitruvius and his followers who, with verbal design, turned simple systems of decorated architectural detail into an entire philosophy centered on decorum and fitness. Sir John Summerson was judicious in calling his 1963 BBC broadcasts on the cultural force of the orders "The Classical Language of Architecture" because it was established by argument, it became a nomenclature, and it ended in ontological contemplation via the references to nature and human proportion, all of which required verbal language to interpret and extend the visual.

Between the contending languages there is always a space: either a credibility gap, a misunderstanding, a descriptive shortcoming—or better, an auspicious discrepancy. What starts as a sort of Poché Exercise of peculiar nonaccord can end by multiplying meanings, complementing a design with parallel and unparallel resonances. Within the space architecture is sold, or sold short. In architecture now, both words and looks are advanced by rich current variations, in a dialectic between new talk and new form.

MARINA VAIZEY

Art Language

As T. S. Eliot has so succinctly told us, naming is a difficult matter, hardly a holiday game. In the recent history of art, and in art now, naming has become of primary importance. Not only is there a torrent of language about art, past and present; but language, written and spoken language, is used by visual artists in and as art.

For from the nineteenth century the processes by which the visual arts have become institutionalized in Western industrialized societies have accelerated rapidly. Two concurrent, related developments are also visible: the dramatic, unprecedented expansion of education and the growth of a broadly based international art market, both backed by the mass media. These factors influence both the production of art and the ways in which it is discussed. These activities must be further seen in the context of an art education and apprenticeship which has continued to the present, in which copying, imitation, and quotation—Art into Art—are seen as exercises, or as skills not inappropriate to the making of art.

The history of art itself is a relatively new discipline, invented—as so much of academe—in Germany. The English and the Americans came to it late, their acquaintance much improved by numbers of German visitors, later refugees from Hitler's Germany.

Quantitatively, America must now possess more art historians and departments for the study of the history of art than any other country in the world. It is probably in America, in the 1970s, that contemporary art, the self-conscious avant-garde, has become most academicized. Many a professor has become an art critic. The rise of art history as a serious study in its own right may be seen as parallel to the acknowledgment of conscious innovation in the visual arts (thereby would hang another essay). These innovations have almost instantly been slotted into art history. No contemporary artist worth buying or criticizing comes out for view without a substantial bibliography, included in any catalogue of his work with pretensions to importance.

The method by which these innovations have been identified suggests the natural and social sciences rather than what used to be called the humanities. It is a method of classification, of description, and of labelling. What is distinct for the modern period—for convenience dated from 1874, the year of the first Impressionist exhibition in Paris, that label itself emerging from a critical snort by a journalist—is that the labelling, the identification of the new, has taken place as the new occurred. Labelling is part and parcel of the identification of art; and commercial pressures have further encouraged the fact that in some way this labelling must take cognizance of the newness, hence originality, hence worth, both intellectual and monetary, of contemporary art. What has happened is that, particularly now, art can be accredited only when a label is invented and accepted. *The Renaissance* is a vague elastic term covering centuries, although in itself so expressive of worth and goodwill, so emotive, that the term is widely borrowed. But *Minimal Art, the mobile, Cubism, art nouveau, Expressionism* are all specific as to time, place, and artists.

This is a process that has become dominant in the postwar period. It may well be influenced by the need to market art, for in order to do so, descriptions are required which reflect the importance of the art being created, and hence its desirability. The market is a mixture of public and private patronage. Both kinds of buyers may need reassurance as to the worth of the goods, which in shorthand terms may be compressed into a handy label.

Tom Wolfe's *The Painted Word,* both in glossy magazine and book form, an extended essay published in 1975, declared with *faux-naïf* but still burning indignation that this process was intellectually suspect. Furthermore, he implied that art was (wickedly) in the service of fashion and theory. This breathtaking discovery most happily ignored the fact that art—all art—is by definition the embodiment of an idea, and more often than we might suppose, of a theory.

Tom Wolfe assumed that the point of the label, or of the exegesis, was to persuade us into seeing something that was not there, to lend significance to the signifier. In Wolfe's laudable efforts to puncture pretensions or pomposity, he left himself open to justified charges of Philistinism.

Yet we should remember that London's satirical magazine *Private Eye* (the editors and contributors, art haters to a man) provides every fortnight a column called Pseud's Corner. *Pseud* itself has entered the language as a juicy syllable meaning pompous pretension, odious waffle, general intellectual fakery, drivel, and the like. Pseud's Corner is a column made up of sentences and paragraphs lifted in the main from the higher or lower reaches of art criticism. It is art criticism which leads, for the visual arts seem to call for the highest level of pseudery.

Yet it is the artists, not the critics, who quite naturally began the explanations of their art. While the critics label, the artists delve into theory: the Bauhaus books, Malevich's *The Non-Objective World,* Kandinsky's *On the Spiritual in Art,* the manifestoes of Futurism, Wyndham Lewis's BLAST.

In *Concepts of Modern Art* (1974), an anthology edited by Nikos Stangos and Tony Richardson, no fewer than sixteen *isms* and labels are described. The course of modern art winds from Fauvism (a label, as was Impressionism, which originated from a derisive phrase) to Kinetic, Pop, Op, and Minimal Art. We have been engulfed by words on the varieties of modern art, and hundreds of new phrases and labels have emerged to describe the nearly indescribable. So large has this new vocabulary or language become—with English, on both sides of the Atlantic, and even in Continental Europe, its most common vehicle—that dictionaries specializing in the subject have come to be written. Concurrently, while the historians and other academics play games with phraseology, artists who once used physical materials like paint and stone now use words. Galleries fill with words as artists too play the game of labels. A postwar artist like Saul Steinberg progresses from the covers of the *New Yorker,* armed with a validating essay by Harold Rosenberg, into the precincts of the Whitney Museum. The actual look of words—not to mention diagrams, graphic conventions, and maps—is the very substance of his art, themes and variations on the coding and communication of language (written).

The search for the name takes many forms. Everybody is familiar with the art gallery swoop: the visitor, the tourist, enters a big white room hung with paintings. The visitor moves swiftly toward a selected painting. Then there is a darting sideways or downward duck of the whole body, or swivelling movement of the head. The actual movement depends on the state of the visitor's eyesight, the size of print, and the placement of the identifying label. The artist's name and the title of the work have to be ascertained before the appreciation of the art can begin. In the Middle Ages and the Early Renaissance, donors often got into the act by being depicted in the art work itself. Now the donors don't commission the art work so much as buy it, and when they give it away, their names are to be found incorporated on the label. One of my favorites is Fuseli's *The Nightmare* (now there's a sensual painting of an idea for you) which must always be acknowledged as the property of The Detroit Institute of Arts: Gift of Mr. and Mrs. Bert L. Smokler and Mrs. Lawrence A. Fleischman. Owners and donors take up more room than the painting's title and author.

Identification may well precede understanding, naturally, but the plaintive quality of the cries Where am I? in the thickets of modern art has been growing in volume of late. Here are two firsthand stories. As a London-based reviewer I naturally often visit the Tate Gallery. Some years ago, on a local radio program about the delights of London, we extended an invitation to listeners who might want to visit, in my company, a public art gallery of their choice, their reactions to be recorded and later broadcast. One museum thus visited was the Tate. Now these visitors had little actual knowledge of art; nor were they accustomed to knowing by hearsay what was good and bad, or used to reading labels. They confessed to a dislike as to what they had heard (not seen) about modern art, and to never having visited the Tate before. We decided to go round and see what caught their fancy, after which we would talk about it, rather than my leading them to what they ought to see. So we came to the Turner galleries, where there were hung some Turner watercolors, amorphous in form. Since our visit preceded by several years the bicentennial exhibition of Turner at the Royal Academy, which ensured media coverage of the artist, Turner meant nothing to these visitors. And without the benefit of art categories, they dismissed the Turners with disarming, disconcerting frankness as trendy, modern rubbish, were frankly disbelieving when I informed them he was dead by 1851, said they couldn't see why he had three rooms to himself. One did indeed deliver herself of the classic line, hitherto not heard by me in real life, that her three-year-old could do as well; then they requested that we pass on, averting their eyes as we did so. A minority view though was expressed by a lady, confident of her own eyes, who averred that Turner's colors were pretty. So I saw that these Turner watercolors (study notes, experiments, and full-fledged paintings) could not be seen, let alone comprehended without a historical sense, especially by a group of women more accustomed to clearing up messes than admiring them, and also perhaps not accustomed to enjoyment for its own sake. For them there were no labels, and explanations did not have enough to hook into to become convincing. What they liked, incidentally, without benefit of labels was Salvador Dali. They thought his paintings were clever, they could see that a lot of work had gone into them, and my own interpretation would be too that the idiom was familiar, due to photography, film, and advertising.

On another day I came across a middle-aged pair doing the art-gallery swoop. Only what they were bending down to look at was an electrical fitting, a complex of wires and plugs (remember how complicated and old-fashioned and just downright alarming English electricity used to look: here was real presence), and what they were searching for was the label. So disoriented had this couple become, so uncertain as to what was art and what wasn't, that their eyes were taking in the sculptural possibilities of electrical plugs and wires while looking for the label that would validate their perceptions. "I can't see what this is called," said one to the other as I passed by.

The postwar period has led to a multiplicity of art styles, idioms, modes, and manners. One of the most useful (and entertaining: not always deliberately) books I possess is John A. Walker's *Glossary of Art, Architecture and Design Since 1945,* published in 1973. The author is a librarian at an art college. The blurb on the dust jacket introduces the subject:

> The rapid turnover of art movements and styles since 1945 has been accompanied by a matching growth in the number of art terms, or labels, attempting to encompass new developments. For anyone wishing to negotiate the intricacies of modern art criticism found in art books, journals and exhibition catalogues, a knowledge of this nomenclature is required.

Further, we are told,

> All terms included are derived from the published literature on art, and concentration is upon the main conceptual and theoretical notions which are so often neglected by art dictionary compilers.

Here is the beginning of a typical entry:

> EARTH ART and Land Art (also called Earthworks, Dirt Art, Site Art, Topological Art, Field Art): An international movement which emerged in the middle 1960's, developing out of *Minimal Art* and closely related to *Art Povera* and *Conceptual Art*. . . .

There are 378 items listed and defined in Mr. Walker's glossary, from *Absolute Architecture* to *West Coast School*. Mr. Walker also tells us that, at a conservative estimate, during the twenty-seven years after the war some two thousand catalogues, articles, and books per year were published concerning contemporary art. Since 1970, in my own estimate, that number would have markedly increased. Labelling keeps up, too.

My own vision is of images searching forlornly for the words that will give them their support system. The artists who wrote—and their fellow poets—explained to themselves and to a handful of interested people what they were trying to do, and why, as far as they understood it. The postwar period has seen an explosion of theory and explanation; it's a mood which asks that everything can and should be explained. This feeling may be because of the expansion of education and of arts subsidy. (Art should be understood by the people who pay for it.)

This mood is compounded by popular books which purport to explain exceedingly difficult subjects. Paintings of the past, whose meaning is not fully understood by scholars, may be expected to have their meanings made accessible to a public that may never have looked at paintings in the flesh, let alone know anything about—say—the history of Florence, the court of François I, the idea of melancholy in the seventeenth century. In such publications the language is cosy, friendly, intimate, with a sprinkling of words familiar from advertising—notably laudatory adjectives, and certainly colorful. "The dramatic handling of color, the theatrical effects, and the choice of contemporary themes made the work of Gros very important . . ." is a typical use of language from one of the many pocket dictionaries of art available on the market.[1] *Important* is naturally the most overused word in these compendia, which are now easily available in museum bookshops all over the Western world. From the same source on a fifteenth-century Italian: "His innovations in the handling of light were enormously important for the development of painting; he endows his works with a calm majesty and timelessness quite different from those of contemporary Florentine painters." As the writer not of these words but of many similar phrases, I know how difficult it can be to pinpoint (and how many angels on the head of a pin are there, then?)—for the mass market which publishers are convinced (and some writers hope) is longing for the digested and sanitized culture-packets—the reasons some artists are important and others not. In a dictionary entry for the Italian Renaissance, Michelangelo is "volcanic," Brunelleschi is "serene." The Florentines exhibit a "sculptural clarity" which is "poles apart" from the "melting forms and shimmering surfaces of Venetian painting." All of us, however well-meaning, use a shorthand of this kind. However, many of these dictionaries are in a sense promotional exercises. The result is art propaganda, for the entries do not criticize their subjects so much as praise them. The lives of the artists have become the lives of the saints. Art is good for you and not to be taken with caution.

We are not so far away from some of the impulses of—say—medieval theology. Some contemporary artists invoke Thomistic philosophy with as much zeal as Marxist ideology. The urge to classify, categorize and list is as profound and deep-rooted as ever. However, the divorce of history from practice has led to certain kinds of vocabulary, in which technical effects and changes in style are merged for the benefit of scholars. Perhaps one of the most famous of art-words is *painterly,* first used in one particular sense, in opposition to *linear,* by Heinrich Wölfflin in *Principles of Art History* (1915). Wölfflin was of course German; the word was *malerisch,* which, as Erwin Panofsky has pointed out in his essay "Three Decades of Art History in the United States," can in context have as many as seven or eight different meanings.[2] Panofsky reminds us that the native tongue of art history is German, and he regarded the transplantation of so many German-speaking scholars to the United States as a benefit for art history because thereafter its main burden had to be carried on in English, and often addressed to "non-professional and unfamiliar" audiences, when even an art historian had more or less to "know what he means and mean what he says."

But I wonder if even Erwin Panofsky could have imagined what was going to happen in the art magazines, and to contemporary art, willing and unwilling, when the collaboration between the insights of some social and behavioral scientists, not to mention the linguistic philosophers, began to work upon art students, art critics, artists, and journalists. For example, the American sculptor Donald Judd has worked as a critic, both on assignment and by his own suggestion, and a collection of his writings (*Complete Writings, 1959–1975*) was published in 1975. Judd's collected writings bear the subtitle *Gallery Reviews Book Reviews Articles Letters to the Editor Reports Statements Complaints,* which may help to indicate the many ways a contemporary artist may work with written language in support of contemporary art. About his own sculpture he declared that "occasionally new terms have to be invented. I discarded 'order' and 'structure.' . . ." Judd wrote in the years 1968 to 1974 on some living New York artists and on work seen in New York. His own use of language is a simplified version of the highly abstruse, cryptic, and inordinately lengthy sentences that characterize many other contributors to the New York scene. In writing about abstract paintings of the New York School, for instance, Judd refers to a group of them, telling us simply that

> the rectangle is emphasized. The elements inside the rectangle are broad and simple and correspond closely to the rectangle. The shapes and surface are only those which can occur plausibly within and on a rectangular plane.

(Incidentally, a critic discussing Judd's sculpture in 1979 tells us that when looking at it, "No single reading is secure." Analogies with reading, the actual physical act of reading, physical directions, are now very common in art criticism.)

Spatial, plane, discrete, hermetic, surface, primary image, ground, field, presence, situation: these are all examples of words and phrases ("the integrity of the picture plane") used in a manner somewhat technical, understandable to the initiates. A kind of professional writing, even jargon, has emerged. Art needs an audience; increasingly it uses public money and middlemen; yet the art world, the *scene* (another word with a now quite specific meaning) is self-enclosed and self-referential, like so much art. The language responds to certain needs of the art world. Claims have to be made for contemporary art; exclusivity and originality are among those claims. Judd, for instance, tells us, when discussing a certain sculptor's work, that the artist's main fault is not inherent: simply that "there are too many sculptors working this way."

Artforum is an American magazine that perhaps in the late 1970s best exemplifies the interplay between academic disciplines that is influencing the language of art. Thus, an artist named Ian Wallace is described in an article by Eric Cameron:

> Wallace came to art as an art history student. . . . He now teaches art history. . . . Along the way there was a brief stint as a critic. . . . As an artist he has been an earthworker, Minimal sculptor, political propagandist and painter before settling on his present line of photographic work.[3]

The commentator begins this article with a declaration of faith—or nonfaith: "I find that I no longer believe in semiology." The names of Barthes and Lacan are invoked. In conclusion the author tells us of his own difficulties in assessing the honesty of his response to the work he is discussing:

> The mind boggles at the diversity of his source material, and where I can follow his theoretical premises I still have to question the logic of the argument. Yet my intuition tells me that this is deeply meaningful work.

Incidentally, the reproductions of Wallace's photographs that accompany this article look just like stills from French films; these are based it seems on Wallace's understanding of the writings of Lacan, who attempts a "union of linguistics and psychoanalysis."

Another article in *Artforum,* Ross Neher's "Mentalism versus Painting" (February 1979) is headed by two quotations. One is from the artist Robert Morris:

> Julian Jaynes suggests that mental space is the fundamental analogue-metaphor of the world, and that it was only with the linguistic development of terms for spatial interiority occurring around the second millennium BC that subjective consciousness as such can be said to begin.

The other is from the behavioral scientist B. F. Skinner.

What is happening is, I think, twofold: artists have access to a wide variety of support from public and private sources, and most artists are also now exceedingly educated and have spent much time in colleges, universities, and academies of various sorts as students or teachers. They often quite naturally congregate in institutions of this kind and in certain geographical locations. A lot of discussion goes on, which may be international in character. At the same time the growth of certain kinds of support, in which the artist may not make his work directly for, and to please, an individual patron, but for other artists, for the art world, and for the world of committees, makes him seriously question his role. The torrent of language borrowed from other disciplines is used as a method of accrediting, in a search for credibility and credentials.

Of course this is a drastic simplification. But any museum visitor will have noticed that in almost any kind of exhibition or display there is an increasing urge, manifested physically, to explain. Public art galleries have increasing departments and staff commitments under the headings *Public Relations, Information,* and

Communication. At the entrance to the great Cézanne exhibition in New York's Museum of Modern Art in 1977, the visitor was first processed through a static display of panels of reproductions, photographs and text that chronologically discussed the life and art of Cézanne, followed by a side-loop visit, if desired, to a film which did more of the same, before seeing the paintings themselves. Artists feel a similar urge to tell us now what is behind their work.

Finally, many artists are working directly with written language. We have come a long way from early twentieth-century collage, in which printed ephemera were simply incorporated into their compositions by artists as diverse as Braque and Schwitters. In the 1972 exhibition The New Art, for instance, at London's Hayward Gallery, the group Art-Language exhibited as their work an elaborate filing system in some handsome steel-grey filing cabinets. In the Artist's Section of the catalogue *The New Art* (in which each artist was given space—that is, pages—to use as he/they saw fit) the statement of Art-Language followed under their own heading, "Mapping and Filing." The declaration began, "The Art-Language association is characterised by the desire and ability of its members to talk to each other." Further, "The filing system is a mimetic means of retrieval of the 'talking-to-each-other' modus operandi as seen over a period of time." Indexing has also fascinated the group. Their statements and writings involve footnotes. When using the phrase *conceptual priority* one member of Art-Language informs us via a footnote that this wording is "a Wollheimism. The context is no doubt illegitimate in his terms." Richard Wollheim is the Grote Professor of Mind and Logic at University College, London, and is credited with the original nomination of a certain tendency in contemporary work as "minimal" art. He himself has written that it is "beyond the bounds of sense, even to entertain the idea that a form of art could maintain life outside a society of language-users."[4]

Method, progress, and *process* are also words used now to give added import to artists' work. Exhibitions are entitled *Work in Progress.* New theories of progress are also evolved: these concepts have overtaken the earlier post-Darwinian concepts of revolution and evolution. Suzi Gablik's book, *Progress in Art (*1976*),* is subtitled *A radical and challenging view of art based on the ideas of Jean Piaget, Claude Lévi-Strauss and Thomas Kuhn.* Yet another book may also serve us with a clue: Lucy Lippard's *Six Years* (London, 1973), the full title of which is

> *The dematerialization of the art object from 1966 to 1972: a cross-reference book of information on some esthetic boundaries: consisting of a bibliography into which are inserted a fragmented text, art works, documents, interviews, and symposia, arranged chronologically and focused on so-called conceptual or information or idea art with mentions of such vaguely designated areas as minimal, anti-form, systems, earth or process art, occurring now in the Americas, Europe, England, Australia and Asia (with occasional political overtones),* edited and annotated by Lucy R. Lippard

Indeed there have been "important" exhibitions with such titles as *Text as Art Work, Information, When Attitudes Become Form.*

Perhaps an extreme example is the 1974 exhibition at the Rowan Gallery, London, by Michael Craig-Martin (educated at Yale, among other places, and an artist who has taught extensively, especially at Goldsmiths' College, London, a leading art college). The exhibit was a glass of water standing on a glass shelf in an otherwise empty art gallery. This was accompanied by an interview the artist had conducted with himself: "What I've done is change a glass of water into a full-grown oak tree without altering the accidents of the glass of water." His intention, he tells us, precipitated the change. What he had also done of course is not only to tease us into thinking in a certain way about the nature of art, and the transformations its nature implies (a published piece by Craig-Martin appeared in the periodical *Studio International* in 1971 under the title "A Procedural Proposition: Selection, Repetition, Extension Exchange"), but devise with himself an argument which had for long been a preoccupation of the Christian church—the argument between consubstantiation and transubstantiation.

There are new labels coming up for consideration every day, it seems. *Artists' Books* now does not mean the production of a text with integrated illustrations, as in Matisse's exemplary *Jazz,* but Book as Art Work, in which the text is the art, and by the artist. Stubbornly enough, painting itself will not be left out. A new, even attractive style recently identified in New York, and looking like nothing so much as wonderfully demented wallpaper, is—naturally enough—Pattern Painting.

Notes

1. E. S. Greenhill, *Dictionary of Art* (New York, 1974).
2. E. Panofsky, "The History of Art," in W. R. Crawford, ed., *The Cultural*

Migration: The European Scholar in America (Philadelphia, 1953), reprinted as "Epilogue: Three Decades of Art History in the United States: Impressions of a Transplanted European," in Erwin Panovsky, *Meaning in the Visual Arts* (Middlesex, England, 1970).

3. E. Cameron, "Semiology, Sensuousness and Ian Wallace," *Artforum* (February 1979).

4. R. Wollheim quoted in "Introduction," *Art Language* (May 1969).

LEON BOTSTEIN

Outside In: Music on Language

IF ONE WERE to look at the current state and future of English in America from the perspective of music, also in its current state and facing its own future, what could one learn about our language today? The following, in the spirit of Einstein, is a "soft" *Gedankenexperiment,* a thought experiment. It is entirely speculative and suggestive; the reader will be left to complete the argument, for this essay ends with more in it about music than about language.[1]

Before I embark on the thought experiment of using music to enlighten language, a consideration of the traditional reverse procedure and its implications is in order.[2] Three dimensions of discussion—philosophical, anthropological, and sociological—seem to have emerged during the last 150 years. They reflect the impact on music of a linguistic attitude—that is, the way practitioners and consumers of music interpret its nature and enterprise, including music theory and criticism, has been decisively affected by a tradition of talking about music as language, seeking in music some significance beyond itself. This quest for extra-musical meaning in music is a quest from outside, for musicians seem satisfied with the idea that music is just music, that its content and structure are self-contained and it works without identifiable social and cultural meanings.

The philosophic dimension of the music-as-language tradition, which suggests that through the organization of its elements music communicates something nonmusical, transforms the problem of music into one of translation—already a word which concedes that music is a language. One should therefore know first what sort of language music is or is not, and how it may work, so that the extra-musical meaning claimed for music can be verified. A linguistic analogy seems particularly necessary because neither in music's elements (rhythm, pitch, timbre), nor in its larger units (motifs, themes, melodies, patterns), nor in its dynamic structure (harmony and harmonic rhythm), is there any demonstrable meaning relating to an external world. Yet these elements of music are organized to make some kind of sense, like a language.

Visual art, because of a direct descriptive potential, can deftly circumvent the need for a translating mechanism. Art can make its point by altering and giving distinctive character to the very act of seeing. As Kandinsky observed simply in 1938, art functions only on a plane, whereas music, as a performing art, functions in time. Language, in its spoken form, also functions in time, and only in its printed form on a plane as well. This "plane" dimension also exists in music, but invites the consideration of (a) music or language separate from, before, and after written notation, and (b) the interchange between written notation and music or language. This distinction between music and language and their written forms raises the issue of literacy in both language and music. The comparative affinity of language and music, as opposed to language and art, is evident in the awkwardness encountered in talking about "visual literacy." The phrase means something, but not the clear notion of literacy as the ability to read language or music. These are measurable skills.

Plain music theory expresses the conception of music as language among theorists who view music as just music, without a universal, objective, or even commonplace significance with respect to nonmusical matters. Such theory describes style, form, and procedures for constructing coherence within music in much the way one would seek to explain the grammar of a language. Theorists who view music as having extra-musical significance, on the other hand, argue that music tells us about humanity and life; they use different aspects of the idea of language to shed light on music.

Aristotle, in the *Politics,* speaks of music as being mimetic of the language of emotions, so much so as to "hardly fall short" of the "affections themselves." Rhythm and melody can imitate anger and gentleness. The power of music to transcend mere representation and pierce the subject/object distinction allows it to be manipulated as an instrument of education. The "affinity of musical modes and rhythms" to the soul provides the inner dynamics of the emotions with a linguistic parallel in music. The different forms and configurations of musical speech (*modes* in Aristotle's time) evoke and correspond to differing emotions. By commanding the logic of the language of music in early stages of maturation—in an almost Piagetian manner, if one considers the cognitive linguistic parallel—an individual can tutor the emotions and morals through music.

Solving the riddle of music using the idea of language finds expression in Hegel, where art in general does not have the logical clarity of language or its power of intellectual representation. As presentation, rather than *re*presentation, music, for Hegel, falls short of being a language. It has no object, it refers to nothing externally. The constituent elements of music, the tones, "merely resound in the depth of the soul." Music gives a "resonant reflection" to the "most intimate self of the soul." Music grasps the subjective approach of the inner life of man to itself. In other words, music for Hegel requires no linguistic explanation, for its expressive nature defies actual clarification or even the grammar of clarification. Thus, defining speech and language as the instruments of objectivity, Hegel separates music from language and allows music only a limited use as a communicative instrument in man's development. The contrast with the philosophic utility, if not essentiality, of language—Hegel's notion of language—is the basis for the consideration of music and, in Hegel's case, of art in general.

The late nineteenth-century philosopher and historian Wilhelm Dilthey went beyond the Aristotelian and Hegelian approaches to music. Following a tradition (which includes Aristotle, Hegel, and Schopenhauer) that music somehow expresses part of man's inner being, the question became this: how can one decode music to assist the understanding of man's historical development, both within a specific time frame and over the longer course of time? Dilthey asked a question beyond Aristotle, who sought only specific external correspondences to something "other" in music beyond personal inwardness *per se.* In music Dilthey saw a route to understanding the meaning of life itself; and, in contrast to Hegel, Dilthey thought that music offered insights that no other mode of expression or language could. For example, the religious experience of Lutheranism, for Dilthey, was more understandable through Bach than through Luther. Rhythm, pitch, and harmony all worked in a piece of music to reveal the soul of the composer, of experience, and of life itself.

Aristotle's correspondences between music and feelings are supplanted by a correspondence of music and life in its holistic entirety. Dilthey sought to penetrate people's reactions to music and the music itself to achieve an almost metaphysical understanding of musical language which could tell us something about the coherence of life. For Dilthey music provided the general impression of an experience (*Eindruck*), the highest form of the penetration of the meaning of life in its continuum of past, present, and future, rather than its specific form (*Ausdruck*). Thus Dilthey understands historical meaning the way one understands the logic and significance of a piece of music. Understanding depends on the fact that one's memory retains that which has just passed and projects it into the perception of that which follows next. Here the language of musical composition is analogous to the formation of an understandable past.

Beyond Dilthey, more contemporary forms of the music-as-language tradition extend the basic idea of music as language to music as made up of signs, offering meaning which can be interpreted—ultimately to a "semiology" of music whose complexity and popularity merit discussion, but not by this writer here.

Claude Lévi-Strauss has made the most of this, the anthropological dimension of the music-as-language discussion, but in his writing the issue is structural. Lévi-Strauss accepts the idea of music as a language made up of signs, but the special character of music is that it reveals an active reformulation of the significance of physiology and nature as well as culture. Unlike painting, music is not tied to nature and its materials as man encounters it. Music, like mythology, works off and transcends everyday temporal experience and goes beyond articulate expression in a way which has decisive significance in a culture.

For Lévi-Strauss music is a language somehow both intelligible and untranslatable, self-contained, its own peculiar vehicle. It is unlike speech, which is clearly tied into human activity and one's constant perception of nonverbal meanings and actions. Lévi-Strauss, while rejecting any notion that music is a "natural" organization of sounds, assumes that given the infinite possibilities, the choices necessary in making music hint at the fact that music is based, in some essential way, on man's sense experience in life. Organizing that experience in music involves jumping well beyond that experience—without passivity—for the sounds of music do not exist in nature—only noises do.

Man must establish a structure and a vocabulary of signs which are mysterious but coherent and which communicate, without direct references to a visible or tangible reality *out there.* Hence, considering the significance of myth by analogy to music opens up a way of perceiving, without written evidence, how man develops cultural forms and meanings. Decoding music suggests how one can decode man's behavior as a cultural, cognitive being, for "culture is already present in it."

While Aristotle and Hegel provided limited perceptions of music as language, Dilthey and Lévi-Strauss suggest that music as a language was extraordinary in its expression and meaning. Despite Dilthey's metaphysical exaggerations and Lévi-Strauss's stress on the universal meaningfulness of the structure of music, both see it as transcending what ordinary language seems to tell us about ourselves. Although a linguistic analogy is retained, it is transcended, leaving music as a separate, powerful analytical instrument for the understanding of man. The difficulty then still remains: how does one actually decode this powerful music? Dilthey's answer is in the tradition of Goethe and the nineteenth-century Kantians: a mix of logic and intuition, *Verstehen,* arguable perception. Lévi-Strauss's method depends on a correspondence with mythology in societies which lend themselves to anthropological study.

These two traditions support the principle of looking through music for insights about language today in America's complex industrial society. Besides the philosophical and the anthropological, a third dimension further assists the effort to understand music as a language. Georg Simmel and Max Weber maintained peripheral interests in the sociology of music, in music as a revealing mode of human activity. The focus was partially on the changing nature of style and technique of music composition and performance. The scope of the inquiry, however, extended to the evolution of musical instruments, musical forms, the changing nature of the players and the listeners, and the evolution of the places and occasions of music making. The most comprehensive and significant effort to study music in this way was the work of the Frankfurt School philosopher Theodor W. Adorno. His analyses of jazz, the contrasts between Schoenberg and Stravinsky, of the way Bach is played and listened to, and of the impact of reproduction in music have had the greatest success in integrating music into the specific empirical and philosophical discussion of the history and evolution of society. The focus was on the significance of the evolution of style, performance, and modes of hearing—changing forms of music making within given historical moments.

In all the dimensions of the music-as-language tradition, one suspects that any conclusions are dependent on prior extra-musical terms, concepts, and insights. Without them can a decoding of music reveal something special about the extra-musical world? If one assumed that music, like English, is a language that works in time, in discrete units with its own structure and rules of construction and communication (apart from transferring preconceived meanings onto the elements of musical language, as Adorno and others do), could insights about culture greater than those we might derive from looking at written texts, paintings, and our oral and visual artifacts be gleaned? Of the three aspects of music—composing, performing, and listening—I will concentrate on the first and last, where the issues of the creative intention and the final reactions can be discerned. The discussion is fragmentary. It avoids the complex issues of performance practice, of the impact of the actual manner and condition of the delivery of the composer's intentions. I discuss only what composers assume and seek and what listeners are prepared to bring to their hearing.

The trends and changes in musical language in modern history—and the very recent modern history of musical style change—will be used. Composers are assumed to be working within a narrow context (their heritage and contemporary world in music writing, to which they respond negatively or positively) and within a broad one (that they translate the meaning of their own lives within a particular culture into musical terms). By reversing the process, by looking at language through music, a hypothesis emerges: that in contemporary America the twentieth-century evolution of music anticipates the future development of language, literature, and the other arts.

The sequence of historical change in the arts before the twentieth century has placed music often behind other arts. Romanticism, for example, as we understand it as a literary movement (e.g., Schlegel, Novalis), preceded real romanticism in music (Schubert, Schumann, Chopin, Berlioz) despite the fact that continental romantics regarded music as the quintessentially romantic art. What Jean Paul considered romantic music we might consider more classical in style. The historical gap was fifteen years or more, even though a musical phenomenon coincident with very early German romanticism within the classical tradition of music can be cited. Realism and nationalism, literary and political movements, preceded their closest instrumental musical counterparts, program music and the wholesale integration of folk material into the mainstream of late nineteenth-century composition.

However, at the beginning of this century composers began to shed tonality in a period parallel to the decline of strict realism and the growth of artistic abstraction in the visual arts. From that point on music began a separate historical process. Although the break with tonality, the most revolutionary, innovative step in composition, including serial composition, was born in the early years of this century, it never became the dominant mode of broad musical discourse or of all serious composition in the twentieth century, with the partial exception of an avant-garde period after the Second World War. The decisive modernist revolution in music was almost stillborn, unlike any previous dramatic historical change in compositional style. In contrast, abstraction, the innovative modern attitude in plastic arts, after its revolutionary phase, became a dominant mode of artistic expression. The most serious innovations in the English language, by Joyce and modern poets, have had a significant impact on the dominant forms of serious writing and less serious efforts at literature in this century. In contrast, radical modern innovations in music such as serial composition did not become generalized except in a closed circle of composers and their followers. The innovations of atonality were not even bastardized in an unrecognizable form into more popular art forms. Yet the impact of the work of Mondrian, Cézanne, and Rauschenberg can be seen in the cheapest interior design, architecture, and industrial design, let alone serious art. The influence of Schoenberg—even of the less innovative Stravinsky—while part of a very limited continuing world of serious composition, is not audible in the television or movie soundtracks, nor in the Musak, popular or semipopular forms of music (show tunes, advertising jingles), consumed by the public.

The issue is that the *Rite of Spring* (1913) sounds, even to the generally well-educated person, still quite modern today, whereas a Klee, Picasso, or even much later abstract expressionist work appears clichéd and historic to the same audience. In literature, Gertrude Stein and James Joyce, like Robert Musil and Karl Kraus in German literature, have become aspects of the mainstream even though the quality and daring of their efforts may not have been surpassed. In poetry (although this is from an untutored observer) that which was considered highly modern or avant-garde in form and style has lost its initial appearance of stark unfamiliarity.

The key to this historical evolution is that new music, unlike literature or art, lost its listening audience precisely at a key moment of historical change in the development of its language, its style and form. New music lost its bourgeois, educated audience, not a mythical mass audience, in the late years of European industrial and imperial expansion. Art and literature, in their serious new manifestations, have maintained an audience until now. One might argue that the initial audience for music was smaller, but that is not demonstrable. The turn-of-century audience for music in the concert hall and in the home was probably larger and more significant as a group in setting behavioral and cultural standards in society than is the contemporary audience. Today's musical audience, although large and significant, is constituted of consumers whose patterns of consumption are significantly different. First, it much more extensively consumes music of the past. The post-World War II revival of older music—Baroque, Renaissance, and Classical—was a historic acceleration of a process of rendering music a retrospective art, an art of tradition and not new production. Second, the musical audience today consumes a popular music which, unlike that of the era when Johann Strauss and Johannes Brahms were friends and mutual admirers and wrote for the same audience, is divorced from the serious tradition of modern composition. Except for some recent commercial aberrations (*Star Wars* concerts, hip young classical performers) and a flirtation with jazz and folk tunes, popular music is separate from classical music in the minds of the concert-going and record-collecting population. In contrast, the audience of the turn of the century, at the birth of modernism, expected a far more balanced fare of contemporary and past compositions and delighted in a popular music whose form and language were not in such contrast with "serious" music, in either style, subtlety, or complexity.

In the late nineteenth century, at the birth of modernism in music, audiences listened to contemporary music (e.g., Mahler, Bruckner, Debussy)—although to a lesser extent than in the early nineteenth century. The performance and writing of music were socially and culturally significant. Furthermore, the division of labor and ensuing tension between composer and virtuoso performer had not taken place. Until around 1900 these roles were usually combined in the same person. The turn of the century was also a boom time for concert tours, piano purchases, sheet music companies. Newspaper attention to music making, especially in Europe, was greater than it is now, comparable at least to the attention devoted to literature and painting. Yet in the aftermath of significant change in artistic language in painting and literature, modern literature and painting have kept an audience and extended it. The language of modernism in the other arts has seeped into the everyday environment well beyond the original efforts. In contrast, the audience and influence of new music on the twentieth century have been minimal. In previous eras, high culture music helped generalize radical changes and either influenced or maintained a minimal distance from popular music. Perhaps the fate of music—its dominant presence as a retrospective communal hobby or as popular entertainment—however extreme and rapid, will become that of the other arts for the remainder of the century in an increasingly visible and obvious way.

The origin of the special fate of music lies in mechanical reproduction. In the spirit of a leading sector of economic growth, or a leading nation in the spread of innovation in the modes of production, music has undergone an evolution of which language and art are now in the earlier stages. The mechanization and mass reproducibility of music provided it with the means of its antimodern historical evolution. These mechanized means are not the equivalents of the evolution of economical modes of mass printing and distribution which contributed to literacy, to the novelistic form, and the development of a mass audience in the nineteenth century. What differentiates the radio and the phonograph as instruments of reproduction from printing and its distribution is that these new devices interposed themselves between the individual and the work or event of art. Mass distribution of a Dickens novel, in serial or standard book form, still required a direct encounter between reader and text.[3] Music, as a performing art, requires one of two participatory acts, singing or playing, even if in rudimentary form. The late nineteenth century was replete with singing societies from all sectors of society; mass purchases of pianos at all price levels, including by the English working classes; and the sale of all manner of sheet music, including arrangements of highbrow music. The second means of encountering music, mere listening, also demanded active intention, physical motion to a special place, and the conscious investment of time as an audience member at a concert or some other public or private gathering involving music making by others. The individual actually had to arrange to listen, and was in contact with the human source of music, the authentic origin of music making. The nature of printed language, despite the mechanical, industrial nature of printing, is such that no matter its form, it retains the authenticity of an original and human creation, and requires active participation from the individual. In anticipation of objections from antielitist readers, it should be noted that the potential that mechanized reproduction holds for the democratization of the consumption and production of culture is not at issue. The desirable decimation of a bourgeois or quasi-aristocratic attachment to the refined "real" singular artistic act or artifact does not *necessitate* the consequences of the historical development of music described in this essay.

Radio and records, prototypes of the recent mechanization, altered the active human dimension of the modes of musical encounter. Active playing by the individual could be replaced by passive listening (putting a record on) without doing, and without using the anticipatory mental processes of hearing or reading music prior to playing it. Hearing music without playing it oneself could now be made possible not as an occasion, but as an afterthought, as background ambiance requiring no concerted effort at all. Furthermore, in the case of records, the initial encounter with music can be without reference to the living being or a particular human occasion. Music comes through a disk and a machine. The disk itself is a composite construct, not simply a documentary record of a live performance like a snapshot. Records are spliced, edited, doctored with disparate "takes" and elements. People now *initially* become familiar with music through the new mechanical devices, through records. If they go to concerts, they do so with a critical perspective which refers them back not to a live occasion, to their memory of a prior hearing, or their own personal encounter with the musical score, but to a mechanical recording. This modern mode of perception and consumption of music became possible and evolved at the precise moment of the stylistic revolution of modernism at the start of the century.

This mechanization of production in music has fostered the alienation of the individual from the original human facts of music making. Consequently music has become less an active human responsive art in the sense understood by Dilthey or Lévi-Strauss. From the point of view of its audience, music has been separated from the personae of its making and from the human ritual, the human occasion of its creation. For example, much pop and rock music exists only as records, for many musical effects cannot be accomplished for live audiences by live performers. The tape is the maker and the original in music, for both rock and the newest Berlioz recording. The extent of this dehumanization of music as an art is partially the result of the mechanical devices becoming part of an extensive commercial network of music based on advanced capitalism.

The new mechanical means of musical production have influenced the remnants of the older, now vestigial, forms of music making. That which gains the highest praise in the classical arena of live performance is a new level of technical virtuosity, one which rivals a machine, as demonstrated by today's great young pianists and violinists. The machine has become the creator of standards for human performance. The radio, the cassette, and the record have replaced the traditional symbols of music—sheet music, the instrument, the ticket. Music listening has become, through the dependence on machines, more an isolated individual act, less a social, public, communal act. It is perceived personally, in a living room, bedroom, or car, not publicly in a concert hall, a group gathering (with the exception of dancing places), in the home or outdoors in planned or impromptu public occasions.

The result has been a decline in musical literacy, a weakened musical memory and a regressive, stunted, static set of musical tastes, among the otherwise sensitive and highly educated. The level of the musical audience today in hearing, reading, and playing music is low, the growth in numbers of superb professionals notwithstanding. The twentieth century has obliterated the skilled amateur and widened the gap between the technical professional and the layperson. If the piano was the dominant middle-class instrument of a century ago, and a moderate acquaintanceship with it the bourgeois norm of musical literacy, the surrogate, reflected in the common possession of the guitar, represents a decline. The literacy implied by the current use of the guitar is of more primitive variety. The level of musical literacy in the hundreds of adolescent rock groups is marginal.

Real musical memory has become routinized as a result of its cultivation by exact repetition, by mechanical reproduction. The memory hears tape. Prior to that, memory in music required more imagination (e.g., retention of sounds after a few live hearings, learning of a score, or the mental expansion of piano versions of nonpiano music into the original instrumental or vocal form).

Last, mechanical reproduction has accelerated a nineteenth-century trend toward the tyranny of an eclectic historical musical taste. Habit, in its industrial sense, that of the routine assembly line, is hard to break, especially if it involves alienation, the human spiritual separation from the productive act. Jarring sounds, novel forms, new instruments or stylistic innovations in music suffer increased resistance as extreme familiarity through repetition of older repertoires becomes habitual. New music can remind the listener of a suppressed human dimension to music making in a painful, disturbing fashion. Innovation in sound and style can be seen or heard as error, as a mistake, a malfunction, since music resembles the mechanically accurate and predictable. Since the intensity of exposure to identical repeated hearings of technologically reproduced music breeds greater intolerance for the new, it is therefore no coincidence that Musak and the background music to television and films are still written in the musical language of late romanticism, of Mahler and Bruckner and early Stravinsky, the age in which mechanical reproduction became accessible on a mass scale. The taste and tolerance of the audience (perhaps the patterns of style change as well) were arrested at the time of the mass distribution of mechanical, standardized reproductions of music.[4]

The most curious recent reaction to this historical development is today's effort by serious composers to regain an audience. In America, the avant-garde composers, those who are in the tradition of Schoenberg and Webern or who followed Varèse into fields of new music, have supported themselves not by their work or performances of their work, but through the university. Some nonacademic romantic and neoclassical writing has survived throughout this century, as have a whole range of eclectic, less self-consciously original styles of music writing.

Although the avant-garde flourished in the 1960s and early 1970s, it did so without a major audience. Composer Pierre Boulez became widely known only for his work as a conductor of a primarily older repertoire. He tried, without success, to integrate newer music into the music-consuming rituals of the modern day, those dominated by an older repertoire. The audience intolerance to the new became visibly manifest among the subscribers and concert-goers at the New York Philharmonic during Boulez's tenure. That audience, by any reasonable standard, is quite sophisticated, and probably inclined to modernism in literary and artistic terms. In this context of a lost or potentially hostile audience, several serious, previously self-consciously contemporary, composers have begun to write in older styles and genres. While they have defended their "new" style as a part of a personal evolution, asserting the ultimate stylistic eclecticism of all musical writing, one which eschews dogmatic allegiances, the strikingly regressive and old-fashioned quality of their work is as unavoidable as it is significant.

Two composers merit brief mention, for their efforts may anticipate future parallels in contemporary language and literature. George Rochberg wrote a violin concerto in 1974, and a series of quartets for the Concord String Quartet in the late 1970s.[5] Rochberg had been a modernist, employing an austere but well-crafted language of musical composition which was not tonal.

While it was lyrical it did not evoke recognition of a tonal, pre-twentieth-century compositional style. These more recent works of the mid and late 1970s, the concerto and the quartets, are dominated by eerie, clear throwbacks to the forms and the actual style of previous eras. One can hear Mahler, Schubert, Beethoven, and Brahms. Whole movements of the quartets are written in the manner of these composers, with thematic material that approaches the craft and authenticity of the original. Often direct quotes are used, but primarily there is an effort on Rochberg's part to infuse new life into older romantic styles, to let his expressive self flow out in a historical language. These works initially appear beautiful, intense, and startling, not because they defy the date or the composer's name. However heartfelt, precisely because of the skill with which the imitation is carried out, there lingers a demonic quality of false artistic mimesis.

After years of being successful, but without audience, within academe, in a musical environment dominated by a pre-1915 language in popular and ambient music, Rochberg seems to have broken out of his prison by concession. It is as if the evolution of styles from one to the next (baroque to classical to romantic) was an arbitrary process and not part of the passage of time and of historical change. Can one achieve drastic reversals without generating nostalgic illusions? Yet Rochberg is responding to a drastically altered context for the modern composer, a world in which music has evolved into an advanced stage of mechanization with all its attendant resistances and alienations. The composer has been shut out and cannot pursue, if he wishes an audience, a continuous line in the evolution of style. By going back to the eras of mechanization and before, to their style of writing, perhaps Rochberg thinks he can reassert the human dimension of writing music and can reclaim an audience by writing intentionally in a familiar manner. Rochberg startles the audience with a new music that resembles the old but contains several unexpected authentic original elements. Yet the obvious problem remains, that in all other ways today cannot be the turn of the century. Curiously, Schoenberg is said to have admitted a constant temptation to return to older styles. He yielded rarely. Rochberg's resistance to the very same feeling has, in contrast, entirely collapsed.

Rochberg's new work displays the trap the contemporary composer is in, one unthinkable to Mozart or Chopin. The audience prefers familiarity to newness, the routines to the unexpected. In order to establish one's individuality as a composer, one must write in the style of a previous era. One speaks the musical language of a distant past, plays archaeologist, so as to be able to exist as a composer. Triumph rests not in stylistic modernity or originality but in the glorification and imitative idealization of the past.

A second composer, Frederic Rzewski, has recently gone through a comparable stylistic evolution, but for different reasons, with different consequences. Rzewski was part of the European electronic experimental avant-garde in the 1960s. The work of Stockhausen and others in that time period was an outgrowth of successive stylistic developments since 1915. It was self-consciously modern music corresponding to a new active cultural moment. Rzewski seems to have rejected that writing and turned to writing nineteenth-century virtuoso piano pieces, using folk melodies as material and employing tonal and well-worn pianistic clichés.[6] The result is dramatic and flashy piano music, seemingly informed by a political ideology reminiscent of socialist realism. Modernism appears rejected because it sets serious music on an elite, inaccessible plane. It addresses only a narrow group of cognoscenti. Music should reach a mass audience, and the only way to do so is to employ the popular material of the masses (in the spirit of folk music) and subject it to transformations which will rouse a large audience much the way Liszt roused his audiences with his variations and improvisations on famous operatic materials.

Unlike Rochberg, Rzewski seems to have more than a personal agenda for self-expression as a composer. Unlike Rochberg, Rzewski does not employ rarefied material, overtly sophisticated structural devices and forms. Rzewski's work is more discursive, accessible, direct, and brilliant. It seeks to make an extroverted contact with the audience. Rochberg strikes a nostalgic, inner, even bittersweet, feeling. Rzewski seeks rousing affirmation. Both have resorted to reworking past habits and modes of musical discourse. Rzewski's populist political message notwithstanding, he too has rejected the idea of a clearly modern language of musical discourse. He too recognizes the loss of audience and seeks to redress it by coming at the audience with the language of the moment when the audience became lost, the language of the era of the start of mechanized reproduction, the turn of the century.

If one takes this description of the evolution of music since 1900 and the response of certain contemporary composers of serious music, a response which is here regarded as significant, and applies it to language and literature in contemporary America, what emerges? Is a comparable historical process now underway for language and literature? Is real literacy and the command of language increasingly the province of a professional intelligentsia? Is there an end to stylistic innovation and a nostalgic regression to earlier forms and usages? Is mechanization having an impact on the character of language and literary style?

First, one can perceive a decline in the degree of literacy achieved by those completing formal schooling at both high school and college levels. This decline in literacy has been nearly universally felt and is reflected in the capacity of individuals to exercise the active human habits of reading and writing. Second, the character of colloquial conversation has taken on an increasingly vague and standardized form. "Getting it together," "doing one's own thing," and other phrases have expanded rather than contracted the development of idiomatic phrases which collapse words and provide facile, seemingly sufficient meanings. Our new idioms have a tendency to denote vagueness, and have the character increasingly of filler. The imagery of conversation is perhaps more routine. The habit of extended conversation, including oral argument, is less common. Is sentence structure becoming less complex and is vocabulary becoming impoverished? Rhetoric and the art of public speaking have fewer able practitioners. Public official language has developed a harsh and unwieldy character. New original surrogates for these atrophied practices are not in evidence.

One might argue, by analogy to music, that much of this is the result of mechanization quite different from the invention of printing. Telephone, and before it telegraph, have had a decisive impact on the use of language. The need to shorten written communication in the latter is a case in point. Brief oral conversation has substantially replaced letter writing, but the new character of the conversation is between two disembodied voices through telephone receivers. One can only speculate upon the gradual subconscious impact of the telephone on language, but that some sort of impact is demonstrable and worthy of study can be acknowledged as likely without resorting to a nostalgia for a pre-telephone world.

Other mechanical reproducing technologies have had an impact on the evolution of language. Television is a primary instrument of change. The issue here is not the usual pro or anti argument. Rather television has interposed a passive standardized mode of entertainment and expression, replacing the cheap magazine and novel. Today's magazine is increasingly visual, and the cultivation of the visual has been at the expense of the mixed visual and cognitive concentration required of reading. Reading and speaking are rendered optional by television as components of mass leisure and play. Television has also replaced the printed word as the transmitter of vital information, regarding the weather, politics, economics, death and disaster. The need to be able to read and write beyond a rudimentary level is increasingly optional politically, since vital aspects of the individual's orientation in society no longer require high literacy. Television, in its current economic condition, displays strong elements of national standardization in programming and advertisements, and provides the basic background for casual conversation among individuals. Such conversation depends less therefore on the verbal translation of one individual's exclusive experience to another. The communication of exclusively private experiences requires facility of language. If an increasing part of one's common experience is a shared exposure to standardized entertainment, the accomplishment of communication between people requires less linguistic skill. Finally, the nature of colloquial language mimics the simplicity of rock music. They both consist of a small shared set of formulae which simplify communication the way mechanical innovations and the division of labor routinize the human element in production.

On a more speculative note, consider the increasing rapidity with which books are dependent on visual presentations on television and in films (*Holocaust, Love Story*); or books are written with structural characteristics intentionally devised for television formats. The word becomes reliant on visual supports. Language becomes subordinated to other modes of communication. Some publishing firms are experimentally developing children's books with electronic devices which make the printed words on the page speak in an audible voice, so that the book reads itself aloud. This clearly could alter the way children learn to read. More profound technologies, comparable to radios, tapes, and records, face language and literature: computers, information retrieval and printout devices capable of mass home installation, and advanced photocopy and transmittal devices for communication over large distances. These shall further transform written and spoken language.

Language and literature in contemporary America may be following the fate of music. Language acquisition may become standardized and may reflect the impact of passive repetition, the dependence on technologically based presentations of language through television and comparable computer and electronic devices. The audience for serious literature may decline, even though the audience for mass entertainment, magazines with some basic writing, and the consumption of formulaic popular novels for television grows. Whether serious literature will, like music, experience an abrupt end to stylistic innovation in this period of increasing mechanization remains to be seen. Perhaps nostalgic regressive stylistic tendencies in literature like those of Rochberg and Rzewski may occur in an eventual effort to reclaim an audience in the future. Ironically, it could be argued that modern fiction now has a larger audience than traditional classic literature. The current situation of modern literature vis-à-vis tradition and innovation may be the exact opposite of music today, certainly music in, let us say, Beethoven's time, before the revival of older music in the mid-nineteenth century.

The dilution of language and literature may occur as composite forms of communication become dominant, or as nonwritten forms of communication become increasingly the only modes of connecting a body politic.

The original speaker and the writer (if there still are texts) may become separated from the audience as fiction on television continues to replace the book as primary entertainment. An aura of anonymity may begin to surround the creation of the written word. One might envisage a time when only a video-taped performance of *Hamlet* would be popularly known and available, thereby interposing a medium between the reader and the author, even though dramatic performance was the intended initial means of recognition. In the case of a dramatized novel, then, the text is obliterated altogether.

Perhaps the past career of music suggests a dismal future for the English language and for written English. The *Gedankenexperiment* predicts a decline in literacy; an alienation in the audience from the acts of writing and reading; a dependence on the habits of passive learning without written language; a reliance on mechanization; the truncating of spoken language into pat formulae; the shrinkage of a serious audience for writing in the sense of the tradition of literary production; and the interposition of mechanized gadgets with social significance in lieu of direct speech and the printed text. Literary taste may become regressive, resistant to any continuing effort at modernism within the art of literature. A gulf may be created comparable to that between serious and popular music. Speakers of literate English will become rarer and more noticeable. Those in command of skills in reading and writing a language will be increasingly isolated from the mass. The "serious" audience will continually shrink.

Here the thought experiment ceases to be attractive. The key difference between language and music is the essential nature of the former and the optional character of the latter in political, social, and cultural terms. Literacy has political implications which musical literacy never can have. The close connection between spoken and notated language, between spoken and written English, is not matched by the relation of music played and sung and music written down. The simplification of music, its devaluation and stunted growth despite an explosive consumer evolution in the twentieth century, is of some cultural significance. However, the consequences of a comparable real decline in our language are cataclysmic, for they could include the voluntary suicide of a culture and of a political order based on autonomy, active participation, the capacity of individuals to speak and to write. Our culture depends on the ability of society to respond to the coherence, the logic, and the emotion of language.

Some attention needs to be paid the future of language if its career in our technological industrial context bears any similarity to that of music. If Dilthey was right, and the experience of life is like a melody, and its meaning constructed like the structure of melody, then our life is unfolding from the past in dangerous ways, requiring courageous intervention. If the pieces of analogous musical evidence include Rochberg and Rzewski, then perhaps we should expect backward-looking efforts in language and literature, rather than new political and cultural phenomena associated with language. Perhaps we shall soon try, in desperation, to express ourselves, in language and literature, in older idioms and older forms, seeking new meaning and the rebirth of language for our own time and for the future in the ruins of a more cultivated literate past.

Notes

1. The word *language* is being used in this essay in a commonsense way. By language is meant speech and literacy and sometimes language in literature as the carrier of culture. Students of linguistics might take issue with this use of the word. Since this is a piece of speculation by a nonexpert, it might be useful for the reader to have access to the discussions about music which inform the argument of this essay. For Aristotle, see *Politics,* book 8; Hegel, *Vorlesungen ueber die Aesthetik,* vol. 3, ch. 2; W. Dilthey, *Gesammelte Schiften,* vol. 2, *Der Aufbau der geschichtlichen Welt in den Geisteswissenschaften;* G. Lukacs, *Aesthetik,* vol. 3 (abridged ed.), ch. 2; T. W. Adorno, "On the Fetish Character in Music and the Regression of Listening," in A. Arato and E. Gebhardt, *The Essential Frankfurt School Reader;* T. W. Adorno, *The Philosophy of Modern Music* and *The Sociology of Music;* S. Langer, *Philosophy in a New Key: A Study in the Symbolism of Reason, Rite and Art;* V. Zuckerkandl, *Man the Musician,* vol. 2, *Sound and Symbol;* L. Meyer, *Music, the Arts and Ideas;* W. Coker, *Music and Meaning;* J. Attali, *Bruits;*

S. Cavell, "Music Discomposed" and "A Matter of Meaning It," in his *Must We Mean What We Say?;* C. Lévi-Strauss, "Overture," in his *The Raw and the Cooked,* vol. 1.

2. There is another dimension of this thought experiment whereby music can be used to cast light on language. This dimension is the use of musical characteristics which invite new ways of thinking about language. For example, one rarely talks of timbre in language, or of rhythm and harmony. How a piece of prose works in relation to time, to silence, to variation, to formal considerations in, for example, sonata allegro form, as exposition, development or recapitulation, or in variation form, all might be suggestive. How notation affects musical perception and performance might have analogies in the way literature is placed on the printed page, or how poetry is visually presented. This kind of approach to language through music, especially in a discussion of current musical composition in relation to current fiction and poetry, requires more expertise than this writer possesses.

3. It should be remembered that photography might be used as an example to counter an argument with respect to mechanization's impact. But photography, as Walter Benjamin recognized, is the best example of the humane democratization of art, one which empowers each individual to do art. Its historical equivalent is not the radio or phonograph, but rather the piano in the late nineteenth and early twentieth centuries, when the industrial means of manufacturing pianos drove their prices, availability, and distribution into a mass market which cut across social class lines. Given this comparison, the decline of piano sales and distribution in homes over the past fifty years only supports my main argument.

4. It could be argued that the piano potentially could function as a reproducing standardized mechanical interposition between music and the audience even though it requires active manipulation. The player piano and the pianola were turn-of-the-century forerunners of other more lasting modes of mechanical reproduction and did play upon, so to speak, inherent negative potentials in the mass distribution of the piano over the years of the late nineteenth century.

5. The quartets which form the basis of this discussion are the String Quartet No. 4 (1977), String Quartet No. 5 (1978), and String Quartet No. 6 (1978).

6. The works of Frederic Rzewski which formed the basis of this discussion are the *Four Pieces,* written for Ursula Oppens in 1977; and the longer work *The People United Will Never Be Defeated!,* a set of thirty-six variations on the well-known song "El pueble unio jamas sera vencido!" by the Chilean composer Sergio Ortega.

❧ JOSEPHINE MILES

Values in Language; or, Where Have *Goodness, Truth,* and *Beauty* Gone?

WHEN I FIRST STARTED asking questions about poetry, I was mainly concerned with defining individuality, trying to recognize the special usages, words, rhythms, or sentence structures, by which one could instantly recognize one individual as different from the rest. Soon I learned, as you might have commonsensically expected, that it is not so much individual items as individual ways of combining them, complexes of traits in themselves general and familiar, which lead to a special poet's way of thought or expression. Poets may use little distinctive material as such, but are distinctive in the ways they draw upon and combine the resources available to them in the language of their time.[1]

Of their time is an important phrase because it suggests that usages are not available perennially, rather that they shift, as values in the society and the language shift. Yet if individuals do not do the innovating of new material in sound and sense, how does it get done? By the society as a whole? Sociologists tell us not; they find little correlation between politics, economics, ideologies, and the natural language. The language seems in a sense to go its own

---

This essay was the Faculty Research Lecture at the University of California, Berkeley, for 1976. Reprinted from *Critical Inquiry* 3 (Autumn 1976) by permission of The University of Chicago Press.

way, parallel to but not entailed by the social order. The articulate users of the language, prose writers as well as poets, seem to have their own sense of what has been overused and oversaid, what needs to be dropped, what needs now to be introduced or reintroduced into the mainstream, and what in the middle should be sustained in continuity of expression. During five hundred years of English and American writing, this process of selection and revision has been so steady that we can even describe it in regular proportions. It is possible to say that as half of the chief material of major agreed-upon language remains steady over a generation or two, so the other two quarters are respectively discarded as outworn and artificial and, on the other hand, brought in with enthusiasm by many writers all at once as the newly expressive material to be agreed upon. That is, the fifty or so terms most used in his work by any one poet are partly in sequence with tradition, and partly a weakening of tradition, and partly an innovating of new material. The mysteries of such continuities of change may suggest some sort of autonomy in language, and in art.

As you might guess, the words *goodness, truth,* and *beauty* are not of heavy poetic value today. Terms of concept may be stressed again someday, and maybe soon, but at the moment have gone out of poetry in favor of more concreteness, more imagery, more connotative suggestion, less effect of the naming and labeling virtues, which Ezra Pound and other twentieth-century leaders have told us not to use. But actually these terms of abstract concept were lessened in major usage in poetry long before the twentieth century. They had flourished in a setting of kings and courts. The love poetry, the political poetry, the philosophic poetry not only dealt directly with truth and goodness but used them constantly for evaluative commentary of other subjects. People, as well as moral issues, were *good;* lovers, as well as propositions, were *true.* So a characteristic popular poem by Wyatt ran in largely abstract language:

> What should I say,
> Since faith is dead,
> And truth away
> From you is fled?
> Should I be led
> With doubleness?
> Nay, nay, Mistress!

And Sir Walter Raleigh's "Petition":

O had truth power, then gentleness could not fall,
Malice win glory, or revenge triumph;
But truth alone cannot encounter all.

John Donne played over meanings in "Communitie":

Good we must love, and must hate ill,
For ill is ill and good, good still,
But there are things indifferent,
Which we may neither hate nor love,
But one, and then another prove.

Remember the popular abstraction of message in Richard Lovelace's poem on going off to war?

I could not love thee, dear, so much
Loved I not honor more.

Love and *honor, good* and *true,* these were terms of value in which poetry worked so strongly that a large proportion of its reference was limited to these alone, and so thoroughly that there was not a poet in the sixteenth and seventeenth centuries who did not share in this emphasis.

As for the term *beauty,* its major use came a little later, in the eighteenth and nineteenth centuries, as a result of one love of goodness and truth, that is the love of the God of nature. It was the Protestant belief that the goodness of God expressed itself especially through the world of nature, through mountains, seas, skies, receivable as images directly through man's senses and therefore an aesthetic as well as an ethical message. Protestants scorned the intrusive human endeavor in the art of stained glass in church windows for example; they wanted their windows to be pure clear glass to reveal the aesthetic sensory truth of the universe outside. Though the triad of values including beauty had been familiar since Plato, increasingly the scenes and shapes and colors of nature had something to do with God's meaning for man, and words like *light* and *dark, green* and *golden* in their abundance supported the sensory meaning of beauty. So *good* and *true* began to be subordinated.

As the revolutionary poet of the eighteenth century, James Thomson, wrote in an early preface to his patroness, the countess of Hereford, about his new and revolutionary descriptive poem *The Seasons:* "I know no subject more elevating, more amazing, more ready to the poetical enthusiasm, the philosophical reflection, and the moral sentiment than the works of nature. Where can we meet such variety, such beauty, such magnificence?" So he begins his first poem "Winter" with this scope:

> See, Winter comes to rule the varied year,
> Sullen and sad, with all his rising train—
> Vapours, and clouds, and storms. Be these my theme;
> These, that exalt the soul to solemn thought
> And heavenly musing. Welcome, kindred glooms!
> Congenial horrors, hail! With frequent foot,
> Pleased have I, in my cheerful morn of life,
> When nursed by careless solitude I lived
> And sung of Nature with unceasing joy,
> Pleased have I wandered through your rough domain;
> Trod the pure virgin-snows, myself as pure;
> Heard the winds roar, and the big torrent burst;
> Or seen the deep-fermenting tempest brewed
> In the grim evening-sky.

It is characteristic of poets that they are not content merely to make big changes, as from human nature to external nature, and from concept to observation, and from abstraction to imagery as Thomson is doing here; each time they denigrate what has gone before, suggesting that poetry before theirs was not only dull and wrong but especially artificial and falsely poetic. The negative epithet "poetic diction" tends always to be applied to the poetry preceding one's own. So Wordsworth would in turn call Thomson artificial, praising him for looking at the natural scene, but blaming him for the generality with which he viewed it.

If you would like a sense of the great difference between say, Renaissance and Romantic poets, or the poetry of truth and goodness versus the poetry of beauty, think of two standard American anthems, the first traditionally English, the second more noticeably American; note the essential terms of concept in the first, and the royal setting:

> My country 'tis of thee
> Sweet land of liberty
> Of thee I sing.
> Long may thy land be bright
> With freedom's holy light
> Protect us by thy might
> Great God our king.

By metaphor we take liberty back to English kingship. In the other, the language description of nature, of beauty in Katherine Lee Bates:

> Oh beautiful for spacious skies,
> For amber waves of grain,
> For purple mountains' majesties
> Above the fruited plain!
> America, America, God shed his grace on thee
> And crown thy good with brotherhood
> From sea to shining sea.

Here skies, fields, mountains, and seas are the stuff of the poet's beauty and pride; they are the words, *liberty* and *freedom,* by which the nineteenth century praised God's truth and goodness.

When with even-headed predictability the later nineteenth century wearied of these sweeping scenes of nature, where could they turn for another variety of values? The concepts of Renaissance man they now considered too "intellectual," the glories of eighteenth-century scenery they now considered too "sentimental." What other field of substance, of experience, was open to them? They turned inward, to their own consciousness, in new major poetic words like *dream;* they turned to *children,* they turned from *air* and *earth* to *water* with its intimations of immortality, and from *seas* more specifically to *rivers* and *rain,* and to human *tears.* Whenever they had the chance to reduce generality to particularity, they took that poetic way; the most used *bird* became *wing; land* became *rock* or *stone; tree* became *leaf; man* became *child.* We see the changing sense of poetic value as symbolic, implying more than it can possibly say, and leaving an air of mystery about the dreamy cry of the poem. Think of Coleridge, for example, or the pre-Raphaelite ballads, or George Moore's book on pure poetry, or Hardy's thrush, or Yeats's red roses, or the evanescent refrain-like lyrics of Matthew Arnold:

> Come, dear children, come away down.
> Call no more.
> One last look at the white-wall'd town,
> And the little grey church on the windy shore.
> Then come down.
> She will not come though you call all day.
> Come away, come away.

This is lyricism many of us can still remember being born into, where certain words and intonations carried riches of implication from image to symbol of personal relevance.

The imagists then, and most of the great generation of the first half of the twentieth century, set out to refine their particularity even further, to remove the dreams, clouds, shadows of nineteenth-century suggestion and get down to clean edges, Wallace Stevens's dish of pears, William Carlos Williams's red wheelbarrow. Never in five hundred years of English poetry had the agreed-upon major terms been so objective and minute. Colors of green and gold washed away to black and white. Bodily terms were more and more specific: not *hand, head,* or *heart* but *finger, lip, hair, skin.* Innovation became a matter of intense refining and discriminating within traditional materials.

It would seem hard to guess in the mid-twentieth century where poetry would take its next step. After stages of concept and description and symbol, did it not seem to be running into a ground of specialization too minute to be retrievable, for all its brilliance of real and surreal reflection? The basic words which had persisted through the centuries, of action, feeling, time-telling, scene-setting, anatomizing, had despite certain losses and gains moved steadily in directions of particularity that would make it hard to see what the next generation would want to do. MacLeish's "Ars Poetica" of "For all the history of grief/an empty doorway/and a maple leaf" raised the question of how much a leaf could keep saying to us about grief, *or* about goodness, for that matter. What truth *did* depend on Williams's red wheelbarrow? Here was T. S. Eliot down to the sands of the desert, and the younger generation to its fingers and toenails. What had they now to reject, what to accept?

I stress the question because as you know it has often been said of our time that we've become very fragmented, aren't moving in concert or continuity anymore, and might well be expected not to present a distinguishable new era in poetry at all. Things fall apart, the center does not hold, many people since Yeats have told us. Why then should we count on steadily continuing design in our language of values? For highly conservative elders, goodness, truth, and beauty may still be voiced by general concepts like *liberty* and *freedom.* For the young they may be voiced by the rich four-lettered words of anatomy. But what about the poets in between, and how as a whole do we hang together enough to support any new language of poetry for our time? Yet we do.

The mid-twentieth-century poets, born and writing since

nineteen-thirty, and so now perhaps twenty, thirty, or forty years old, follow the procedures of all the generations before them, in their sustaining of agreement on certain major terms, the abandoning of others, and the innovation of still others toward the future. As I have said, I can't offer a sociological explanation for this steadiness of pattern. But poetically it is a delight. Because poetically it shows us not only a bond between poets, although they may never have met or heard of each other, but also a bond between poets and their audiences both as receivers and resources, both as listeners to and as contributors to the language of values we speak. The poet, John Williams, gives a good sense of the poet's participation in a set of choices larger than he is aware of.

> I decide to make a poem when I am compelled by some strong feeling to do so—but I won't until the feeling hardens into a resolve; then I conceive an end, as simple as I can make it, toward which the feeling might progress, though I often cannot see how it will do so. And then I compose my poem, using whatever means are at my command. I borrow from others if I have to—no matter. I use the language that I know, and I work within its limits. But the point is this: the end that I discover at last is not the end that I conceived at first. For every choice made poses new problems to which solutions must be found, and so on and on. Deep in his heart, the poet is always surprised at where his poem has gone.

So the poets of our newest generation, Gary Snyder, Michael McClure, LeRoi Jones, James Tate, Victor Cruz, and others, born as they are in different parts of the country, and educated in different schools and traditions, bring in, when they begin to publish, a new set of agreements, established as if without their conscious consideration, yet full of awareness of values for each of them. Their terms of abstraction have decreased; their terms of natural symbol have decreased; they have sustained and even added to their sense of man's action in the world, his moving, calling, touching, or making. And their newly added terms of agreement are of a new sort: the terms of human construction in a humanly constructed scene.

So the words *street* and *road* are central to their usage, the terms *house* and *home* and *room,* the *walls, doors, windows,* even *glass* and *mirrors* of that room. The poetry moves inside in a new way. New sentence structures support these references which emphasize spatial forms; new connections like *through, toward, out of, under,* and new adjectives like *warm* and *cold, closed* and *open.* An early example is Robert Hayden's:

THOSE WINTRY SUNDAYS

Sundays too my father got up early
and put his clothes on in the blueblack cold,
then with cracked hands that ached
from labor in the weekday weather made
banked fires blaze. No one ever thanked him.

I'd wake and hear the cold splintering, breaking.
When the rooms were warm, he'd call,
and slowly I would rise and dress,
fearing the chronic angers of that house.

Speaking indifferently to him,
who had driven out the cold
and polished my good shoes as well.
What did I know, what did I know
of love's austere and lonely offices?[2]

Which brings us to where we are. And where we are in the twentieth century is supposed to be an era of confusion, of attenuation of traditions. Yet we have followed some of the steps from the seventeenth to eighteenth to nineteenth centuries by seeing how the major agreements of the poets in one era gradually shift to become the agreements of the next: by following the values of the time, using the language of the time, gradually abandoning old poetic usages while slowly taking on new ones, and steadily maintaining a clear line of persistence of certain traditional emphases throughout the changes. As no poet is wholly different from another, no poet is wholly like, and the pace of their changing agreements seems to be steadied by the steadily moving values of the times. So we may observe for a moment more closely the substance of the present, and its contexts.

If we look, for example, at the very new work in our day, of poets born in the mid-twentieth century and so only now beginning widely to appear in print, experimental as they are or beat as they are, followers of *Howl* as they may be, of Robert Creeley or of Gary Snyder, we see in their work the Yeatsian verbs, the Poundian nouns in the continuities of the past, and then also the new shared emphasis on construction.

Partly positive, partly negative—in Ann Stanford's trying to hold up the wall of her house:

Nothing else moved. I could hold on no longer.
I took my foot down. Carefully one hand
And then the other, I drew gently down

And lifted up my head and saw a door
And I went out and breathed under the trees.
I looked back at the walls. They stood alone

A cubicle of dryness on the lawn.
I watched the slow dust as they toppled one by one.

In David Antin's:

suppose a man travelling in a right line any distance
turning through any angle whatsoever travelling the same
distance likewise in a right line and repeating this process
any number of times encounters a wall he must step back

In Al Young's:

I sit in a white kitchen
next to the young walls
yellow paper spread on yellow tablecloth
& scratch helplessly
wanting to take leave
of the present
which was a gift,
longing to have known everything
& to have been everywhere . . .

and:

my prison is the room of myself
& my rejection of both is my solution,
the way out being the way in,
the freeway that expands to my true touch.

Notice how for Al Young truth does come back again, in the form of an adjective of value. So too for Nathaniel Whiting's "Buffalo Poem."

A window today
is the air I want in.
It's filled by the snow, yes,
and a few leaves.
Look at me
down at me . . .

The best random noise (not a bird now notice)
has sections so pure / and predictable
as an entire one minute and
with music. And when that is turned off

one more window darkens
and I feel that more strongly
than a rumor that was true,
not false.

And Michael Heller's:

Didn't you say you loved me?
under what conditions
under what
under what
under what

under the air
@ 15 lbs per square inch on the roof
on the safety-factored I-beams
slipping down through curtain walls

to the ground
to gravitational bedrock
accidental center: home.

This is where we find goodness, truth, and beauty today, at home. At home in the language of bodies and houses as it adapts itself to the tradition of concepts, scenes, feelings, and objects, a language of structures and centers, of traditional *man* and *woman,* in *life* and *death,* in *eye* and *heart* and *love,* in *time* and *day* and *night* and *world,* in *word* and *thing,* to *come* and *go,* to *hear* and *see* and *make* and *think.* The terms of the natural world persist, though in lesser abundance, with *waters, streams, rivers, rain* the most frequent now of their forces, and with *trees* and *stones* still strong. And beside these, the bodies and buildings of present value, not necessarily called *good, true,* or *beautiful,* as these abstract terms have faded, but shown to be so by the constructed centers of care in which they are presented.

Not merely words change within the interest of the times, but structures also. Certain alternatives of sentence forms open to choice in English have received, as words have, different emphases at different times. The conceptual Renaissance emphasized causal constructions and highly subordinated clausal forms requiring more verbs, as we have seen. The romantic sublime Enlightenment shifted along with its scenery, as one might expect, to highly phrasal and adjectival constructions, qualifying by epithets instead of stating by verbs, suspending time in space. The present combines these two modes in a curious balance, retrieving the Renaissance verb constructions, but not their logical connectives;

sustaining the eighteenth-century phrasal forms to such a degree that certain specific participial adjectives have become dominant, suspending time in space still further.

Now you may well say, "But these are all words and structures of poetry, not of prose." They may represent, therefore, only a very limited and special set of values, those shared by the few interested in setting ideas to measures of rhythm, lines, and patterns, not those actively speaking the language of the world. But actually the distinction does not work this way. The major words of poetry are the major words of the common spelling books. They are for prose also. We may learn by tracing through history that the chief words and the chief structures for poetry held also for prose through the Renaissance, the eighteenth and nineteenth centuries, to the present day. Indeed prose often followed in picking up values in language which poetry had already established: the strong present-participial construction, for example. The major difference between them is that prose uses a far greater variety of topical nouns; where it agrees on adjectival and verbal and even conjunctive values, it settles down less concentratedly on certain specific objects of concern. Nevertheless the main agreements hold strong. It would seem that both poetry and prose are part of a language which functions as a resource of power on which the formalizing patterns of literature may draw, and to which they may give weight, with a steady sensitivity to social concerns both changing and enduring.

Some may feel troubled as well that the artistry of authors be so generalized about, that one may talk about trends of usage within the forms of language as if they were partly determined by the developments of the language itself and the culture expressed in it, as well as by the creative intuitions of the artist as individual. But remember that the relation is *as well as* not *rather than*. Each poem I have cited to show likeness and agreement of major usage in time is also different from every other, the singular product of its author. But to believe in singularity is not to deny generality; one would not be discernable without the other. So distinguished a colleague as Fredric Jameson is able to write about what he calls "the prison-house of language," as if individuality were bound and tied by its limited resources of expression. But at the same time Jonathan Culler reminds us that as our resources are cultural as well as personal, so we find a personal competence within the powers of shared structures, a potency in a word not only by our love of it but by our fellows' love of it, our friends both literary and nonliterary who speak and relish it and what it stands for. So poetry has not only its own autonomy, moving from satiation of some values toward duration of others and exploration of new ones within the literary tradition, but poetry also participates as a function of common language, in the common changes of values which develop in the culture as a whole and in its thought processes.

In any one time, most poets are apt to be sensitive to and adopt new lines of thought in new subject matters, at the same time they consciously cut away from old modes, less consciously maintain much of traditional substance and structure. It is surprising to note, perhaps, that the so-called great poets as we recognize them are not really the innovators; but if you stop to think about it, they shouldn't be. Rather they are the sustainers, the most deeply immersed in tradition, the most fully capable of making use of the current language available to them. When they do innovate, it is within a change begun by others, already taking place. Or their major idiosyncracies do not become innovations because they are not taken up by other poets.

Rather, chief new words and structures are initiated by so-called minor poets, and often very slowly, before we perceive the direction of their emphasis. For example, in the Victorian era there were many hints of the doors and windows of the present, but they were used simply by one or two poets in special ways. It was a step forward when poetic *road* became poetic *street,* a citifying of the scene, say, from Utrillo to Chirico. It was a step when *window, glass,* and *mirror* came together as a cluster of concepts, perhaps of self-concern, or of self-knowledge, or of searching from without and within. We may remember familiar phrases from earlier eras which could have suggested to us the tendencies in a direction, had we not been focused on other directions. MacLeish's famous phrase in example seemed to pull all one way. "For all the history of grief / an empty doorway / and a maple leaf" took our attention to the leaf, the kind of natural symbol we were then intent upon—while all the time that other phrase of *empty doorway* boded the future. Perhaps loyal readers of Thomas Wolfe will remember his much quoted triad "a stone, a leaf, a door"; there the familiar selective poetics, of stone and leaf, followed by a *door* which we thought at that time relatively little of. Hart Crane in his *Bridge,* Charles Olson in his tower, and many others presaged these builded structures. But theirs was a selective interest quite different from the general concerns in day-to-day usage which we find in the new generation. For these, the construction terms provide not so much central topics as an underlying assumption, the means rather than the subjects of the poets, the ways for conveying values other than themselves.

It's probably safe to believe that a poem, a play, a picture are always trying to embody, convey something of goodness, truth, or beauty, something they make for its action or its fact or its form or all of these in all, and that to embody they don't just declare, but represent through the materials of language, which are already rich with the shared values of their time. Who would have guessed that our values today lie in the terms of building? Our poets, scarcely aware themselves of what they have found. They know that abstract terms have come to them to seem outworn, that cosmic natural terms seem too sweeping, that the minute details of the physical world seem too precious and impersonal. So they turn, with the general agreement of artists in the material of their art, to a different set of structures in the modern world, the rooms and windows of their houses. Note that these are not urbanizations, not skyscrapers or traffic barriers, or the photographic familiarities of cities. Rather they comprise a group of words more personal, around a center of personal use. At their most isolated they may represent a kind of withdrawal, a new figure of interiority and self-isolation. At their most constructive they may represent a new poetics of making and building in which facts, forms, and actions take their value from conscious human responsibility, jerry-built or no, yet man-made, as little of major poetic concern has been labeled to be since the courts of the kings.

Deep in our hearts we may be surprised at where the poetry of our day has gone—away from the abstract terms of *goodness, truth,* and *beauty,* yet into new words for them; no more into rebellion or chaos or fragmentation or even so-called tradition than ever before, but with just the same steadiness of procedure in change that we have seen over five centuries. And if we listen to the current poetries of other countries today, of France, Spain, Italy, Germany, Poland, Russia, Israel, India, China, we will hear them speaking much the same language of values in their own tongues and measures, so that we may come to take the more substantial forms and constructs, in the human body and human physical creations. As we have moved from the poetry of social orders, to the poetry of cosmic scenes, to inner feelings and their correspondences in natural objects of sense and sight, perhaps now we have come to a poetry of choice strong enough to build on words like *house* and *room* as well as *tree;* verbs like *make* and *touch* as well as *see;* human *will* as well as human *sight.* Rainer Maria Rilke has written an epitome of this poem for us, his *Eingang* or *Prelude,* in which the very process by which we have described poetic choice making is given also to an individual, whoever he may be, in his house and community, the imaginative willing and creating, not merely receiving, of the world.

> Whoever you are: at evening step forth
> out of your room, where all is known to you;
> last thing before the distance lies your house;
> whoever you are.
> With your eyes, which wearily
> scarce from the much-worn threshold free themselves,
> you lift quite slowly a black tree
> and place it against the sky: slender, alone.
> And you have made the world . . .

As man has more and more taken responsibility for making his own world, even creating his own tree, even constructing his own good, true, and beautiful objects in his own backyard, a lot of trouble has set in for him. But there may be happier possibilities also. The existentialist and the structuralist critics tell us so today, with their emphasis on the making of choices, the effort to create a whole life for oneself. Even environmentalists would be willing to reconcile the streets with the trees. So this new substance of values in poetry seems to be lived with in a very potential way. Even more than the specific answer, the general one seems to me worth pursuing: that our language provides a continuity of values for our poets to build upon. The steadiness of change which can be described so regularly, if one is not imposing one's own interests and limitations, is a fine cultural phenomenon. The agreement between talent and talent, and between each talent and each reader, in terms of time and the substances of value as they can be built into art, are at once, as we have tried to trace, good, true, and beautiful to behold. And they can be made by you: your tree, your house, against your sky. Whoever you are. In the agreements of time.

Notes

1. The material for this essay has been drawn from my studies of language in poetry, including *The Vocabulary of Poetry: Three Studies* (Berkeley and Los Angeles, 1946), *The Continuity of Poetic Language: Studies in English Poetry from the 1540's to the 1940's* (Berkeley and Los Angeles, 1951), *Eras and Modes in English Poetry*, 2d ed. rev. (Berkeley and Los Angeles, 1964), *Style and Proportion: The Language of Prose and Poetry* (Boston, 1967), and *Poetry and Change: Donne, Milton, Wordsworth, and the Equilibrium of the Present* (Berkeley and Los Angeles, 1974).

2. Poems quoted from: Robert Hayden, *Poems* (New York, 1969); Ann Stanford, *The Descent* (New York, 1970); Al Young, in *Dices on Black Bones,* ed. Adam D. Miller (Boston, 1970); David Antin, Nathaniel Whiting, and Michael Heller, in *Inside Outer Space,* ed. Robert Vas Dias (Garden City, N.Y., 1970); Rainer Maria Rilke, *Das Buch der Bilder* (Wiesbaden, 1954).

Ways and Means

DWIGHT BOLINGER

Fire in a Wooden Stove: On Being Aware in Language

AFTER THE SERPENT had tempted Eve, and Eve had tempted Adam, and the two had partaken of the fruit of the tree of knowledge, "the eyes of them both were opened, and they knew that they were naked" (Genesis 3:7).

There has always been something forbidden and forbidding about knowledge turned inward upon the self, as if our inner temples were not to be violated by the inquiring mind. To bare what is most intimate is to be naked indeed, and the more intimate the part, the more our natures rebel against revealing it. It is no accident that astronomy was the first exact science and the study of the brain the last, and that today's psychology was yesterday's witchcraft.

Understanding comes most easily with what can be easily objectified. Michael Silverstein, in his "Limits of Awareness,"[1] tells how he tried to elicit information about certain aspects of the Wasco-Wishram language that were not immediately obvious to the native speakers themselves. Though a trained linguist could discern the patterns of certain augmentative and diminutive affixes, the Wasco-Wishram were unable to associate the meanings directly with the features that conveyed them, but could only talk about the full meanings of the larger forms in which the features occurred. Ask the average native speaker of English what the meaning of *be* + ——*ing* is, and you will not get anything approaching "It means that the action is in progress at the time" but something more on the order of "It means, like, he is doing it, it hasn't already been done." The answer comes not as a definition mentioning such abstractions as action and progression, but in the form of an example sentence, something in which the form to be defined is used. *Be* + ——*ing* is obscured by the fact that it does not refer to something easily identified in our experience (such as the action "to walk," which might occur in combination with *be* + ——*ing:* "I am walking"), and it is not a single continuous element itself, but is cut in half by the verb. In Silverstein's terms, the native speaker lacks metapragmatic awareness of the point of your question—he can manipulate the progressive, but does not relate it to its meaning as a separate signal. This inhibits him from talking about it.

Talking about talk is the *meta-* side of language, *metalanguage.* Children learn to do it early, though their first attempts are halting—ask a young child to tell you what *dig* means, and you are apt to get either a pantomime or an example, "You dig a hole." It takes some sophistication even to talk about easily separable words and come up with definitions or synonyms. Most people eventually learn to manage this with concrete nouns, but even individual words, the more abstract and relational they become, get progressively harder to talk about (can you define the preposition *from*?), to say nothing of prefixes and suffixes and distinctive sounds and rises and falls of pitch. The solider the unit, the easier it is to focus on and the more secure it is. To some extent the ability to focus is reflected in the history of a language. Take the *-ess* ending in such words as *duress, largess,* and *prowess.* It is hard to pull loose from the words that enclose it. So speakers long ago took *richess(e)* and changed it to something with a more familiar ring, the fancied plural *riches,* though they never really got it pluralized to the point of saying "She has five riches"—it is still collective "wealth."

The linguist of course is the metaperson par excellence. His business is perpetual feasting on the forbidden fruit, to expose language in all its nakedness. How does he do it? His native endowment is the same as that of everyone else, so he has no special key. Furthermore, as a scientist he shares in the highest degree the handicap of all science which is expressed in the title of this essay and is variously likened to a physician's healing himself, to repairing a boat while remaining afloat in it, and to lifting oneself by one's own bootstraps. The true nature of objects is inaccessible, for to be investigated they must be interfered with.

To describe language we must use language—and this poses a conflict of interest.

It is clearly not a fatal conflict, for if it were, linguistics could not have enriched our knowledge as it has. Language must not be quite the coherent, unitary, and singular thing that it appears to be at first glance. It is not an inflexible object like a microscope, which is incapable of turning around and observing itself. It is a thing of many parts and many manifestations; in fact, there is some question as to whether it is a thing at all, rather than a loose collection of entities some of which may well be capable of serving as a platform to observe the rest. It exists in time and space—here can observe there, and today can observe yesterday. Even introspection, once despised as a source of knowledge, comes into its own as we realize that our personalities, like our brains, are divided and one half can observe the other, that part of us consists of others' views of us which we have internalized, and that subjective data become less subjective when returned to over a period of time and when checked against data from outside. In spite of the difficulties, it seems that by observing and analyzing we can approximate the realities, and put our description in a language designed for the purpose, a metalanguage.

Or simply in *another* language—and this was doubtless the first rude awakening of our primitive ancestors to the nature of their inherited speech—when, forced by trade or conquest, they had to acquire a new language. There is no incentive for the monolingual to examine the conjugation of his verbs. But if his life depends on conveying in another tongue some distinction that is embodied in one of those forms, he must learn to match them, and that means dragging them into consciousness. The multiplicity of languages is the motive for not taking the subtleties of our own language for granted. An accurate translation of a paragraph of French into a paragraph of Chinese is a metalinguistic statement about that French paragraph with Chinese as the metalanguage, for each of its nuances has had to be interpreted. Not a theoretical statement, of course, but a preliminary to one: by successive translations we come to understand the regularities in the languages that are compared and contrasted.

But nothing quite so drastic is needed for the native speaker to gain *some* understanding of the nature of his own language, because of the heterogeneity already noted. A translation often needs to be made from one part to another, and if the explicating part is more obvious, it will help in understanding the obscure part. Silverstein noted the problem with affixes; they are hard to focus on.

But the child learning English soon realizes that he is not permitted to say such things as "My stick is benter than yours." The proportion *more* : *bent* :: *-er* : *bent* yields an interpretation for the suffix *-er,* one that a child is sure to know already—*more* is one of the earliest concepts and earliest words, even in the linguistic and perceptual world of the signing chimpanzees. For an example a little less direct, take the "translation" of a question into an answer—effectively, we translate whenever we respond explicitly to a question. Though "asking a question" is something that inheres in the relationship between a speaker and a hearer and is not an objectifiable thing, nevertheless it is the meaning of a fairly obvious operation in English, the inversion of subject and auxiliary, as in the question-response pair "Would he?"—"He would." It takes no great deductive power to assign the meaning "asking a question" to this inversion. Or to assign the meaning "person" to *who* as distinguished from *what,* if whenever the question "who?" is asked, the response indicates a person rather than a thing.

Whenever such a comparison is drawn, whether between one language and another or between parts of the same language, a step is taken toward analysis and a metalanguage of sorts is used. The history of linguistics is one of greater and greater refinement of meaning and the elements that carry it. The average native speaker is not the only one who is tempted to give a concrete and superficially obvious answer to an abstract question. At every stage we find linguists making the same mistake. The meaning of the word *there* in "There's no time" is not obvious. So we limit our attention to larger structures such as "A man was at the corner" and "There was a man at the corner," and pair them off as a mere reshuffling, with *there* a kind of redundant signal that the reshuffling has taken place. Our theory here is attempting to say that a word we use is semantically empty—surely a waste of resources. Instead of taking that tack we can ask ourselves why a sentence like "Across the street was a fight in full progress" sounds so much better than "Across the street had been a fight in full progress," and why the latter is improved by adding *there:* "Across the street there had been a fight in full progress." If we already know that the perfect tenses (those with *have, has,* and *had*) do not show the ongoing scenes of a narrative but rather give a peripheral view of events, like something offstage, and if we also know that when *there* is used with an initial phrase of location such as "across the street" the result does not compel some impression of the vividly here-and-now, it is plain that the two are in harmony—the peripheralness of the perfect and the non-here-and-nowness of *there*. *There* presents things to our minds, whether or not they are also presented to our eyes.[2]

Thus linguists too at times try to operate with tools too dull to split the grain. (Or so sharp that they cut through it. A tool that analyzes "Leave me alone" expressing a desire for solitude is too sharp to deal with "Leave me alone" uttered as a command to stop bothering me. Idioms in most respects are best treated as indivisible.) This does not prove that linguists are inept, only that they have a long way to go, and that the layman's road is even longer.

The question is, should the layman take it? Is he perhaps better off not knowing he is naked? Is ignorance of language bliss? And if so, are linguists only pursuing a hobby, reaching conclusions that they had best keep to themselves?

With predators on the loose, nakedness is not a safe condition. If one is naked, it is better to know it, to put on some protective covering. Much that linguists have brought and are bringing into the open is knowledge that the public desperately needs to see and understand. The walls of our citadels are seldom assaulted these days; instead, they are sapped. "Fraud comes to replace violence as the means to success and privilege," writes Marvin E. Wolfgang; "minds are raped in subtle ways."[3] The rapist works through symbolic systems—money, computer networks, language. The victims are those who do not know how the systems function, how to read their output and tell the true coin from the bogus. What makes their victimization easier is the fact that the symbolic stream, in language especially, flows in only one direction. We are consumers of words, overwhelmed by the flood of messages, unable to talk back to the barrage that comes from the—perish the word—media. But we *can* learn to examine it critically, with the help of those whose business it is to understand language in all its complexity.

And linguists of late have improved their means of helping, for they are looking more and more at the kinds of phenomena in language that can be used for manipulation. They are less concerned with subjects and predicates and more with topics and comments—with how information is presented to lead to inferences of truth and falsity and evaluations of the important and the unimportant. After a long period of neglect, they have come back to *words* as carriers of implications as well as meanings, and are studying contexts and speaker-to-speaker interactions with the same zeal they formerly reserved for sentences.

Consider some of the typical deceptions, which are found

mostly in what is not said but implied, what is said crookedly, and what is said suffocatingly.

Many words are euphemisms or dysphemisms in disguise: they beguile as well as inform. Take *crafted.* Its use as a substitute for *manufactured,* says Kenneth Hudson, "is an attempt to delude the public into believing that something has been made by hand, in a carefully old-fashioned way."[4] It does not *say* this, it only smuggles it in. Constructions too may serve the smuggler, by implying what they do not say directly. A notorious example is the passive voice, which can refer to an action without naming the agent. During the troubles in Zaire in 1978, a newspaper reporting on the words and actions of certain African leaders referred to "the respected President Leopold Senghor of Senegal," and under a picture of President Julius Nyerere included the line "Called a Soviet Puppet?"[5] The reader, if he is unwary, swallows the bait and fails to ask, "Respected by whom? Called by whom?"

While the passive voice optionally leaves out the agent, certain other constructions leave out the verb. They are neither true nor false because they do not actually assert anything, though they may imply a great deal. A study of Danish advertising points out the difference between a complete clause and an apposition: "*Politiken* is the best newspaper" can be challenged, but "*Politiken*—the best newspaper" leaves no opening for denial; it is like a simple name.[6] These examples from syntax reveal a weakness in language that is part of its strength. We cannot say explicitly all we need to say—it would take forever, and there would not be enough words to go around. Much has to be taken on trust, and that leaves nicks and crannies that vermin can use as hideouts.

Crooked speech is ambiguous speech. Its message is two-faced. One face is what the speaker would like you to infer, the other is a mask behind which he can retreat if you corner him. The slogan "No heat costs less than oil heat" means that heating with oil is the cheapest way to heat—or that it is cheaper to do no heating at all than to heat with oil, which is a truism. A phenomenon well known to linguists is the tendency of hearers to try to make sense out of nonsense, giving the speaker the advantage of the doubt. Some crooked speech is literally nonsensical, but with a slight change it makes sense, and we impose that interpretation on what we hear. As there is no law against nonsense, this becomes a safe form of insinuation. A candy ad used to read "People eat more McDonald's than anybody," which trades on confusing two comparative constructions: "People eat more X than they eat Y," and

"X people eat more Z than Y people do." As listeners we look kindly upon nonsense because we are so often guilty of it ourselves and leave it to others to straighten out our mistakes. For example, we readily shift things around in a sentence, putting modifiers in some more accustomed place rather than where they logically belong, like an amateur splashing paint on a canvas and expecting the viewer to get the general idea—"Wait until the Assembly finally makes up its mind" becomes "Wait until the Assembly makes up its final mind,"[7] "The group most severely hit by unemployment" becomes "The severest group hit by unemployment,"[8] "Getting all the way to the bottom of it" becomes "Getting to the whole bottom of it."[9] And we have "January white sales," which are not sales that are white but sales of white goods. Since we are accustomed to reshuffle sentences like these and don't even realize when we are doing it, a foxy advertiser, official spokesman, or other artful dodger can use it to put across an idea without being guilty of literal misrepresentation. Dolly Madison promotes her "all natural flavor" ice milk—we are free, in the context of being told about a product, to conclude that it is an all natural *product.*[10] Dr. Charles Waite, Medical Director of the Tobacco Institute, assures us that he sees an "absence of total scientific facts" that would lead him to discourage smoking in general,[11] a piece of nonsense unless we oblige him by taking it as "a total absence of scientific facts."

Suffocating speech is the kind of language abuse that the public is most aware of, thanks to the complaints of editors, officials, and others who must try to make sense of it. *Jargon, gobbledegook,* and *doublespeak* are names for the same thing. Every week some new monstrosity is registered along with its "translation" to simple English, such as the following, in a letter to the *Guardian,* 18 January 1978, quoted from a social services report:

> This elderly geriatric female has multiple joint problems which limit perambulation. Absence of verbal intercourse aggravates her detachment from reality and reinforces isolationism. She is unable to relate to events at this point in time. Psychogeriatric consideration in the context of conceptual distortion and paranoia is also a parameter in the total dimensions of her problems.[12]

The letter-writer translates:

> This (83 year) old lady has arthritis, cannot get about and is lonely, confused and frightened.

"Covered, obscure, turgid, ponderous, and overblown" are Edwin Newman's terms for this kind of language.[13] It gets that way by excess: not so much by what as by how much it draws from certain departments of the common store:

buzzwords: *relate, parameter, dimensions, point in time*

abstractions: *geriatric* for *elderly lady*

compounds: *conceptual distortion*

scientific and pseudo-scientific terms: *paranoia, psychogeriatric*

nouns modifying nouns: *joint problems* ("trouble with one's joints," or simply "rheumatism")

unusual prepositions: *in the context of* for *along with*

nominal style (nouns used instead of verbs): *perambulation* for *get about*

heavy subjects (normally a subject is a topic and should do little more than orient the listener—the real weight belongs in the predicate): *Psychogeriatric consideration in the context of conceptual distortion and paranoia*

passive voice (no examples in the passage quoted): *it is believed that* for *I believe that*

Straight linguistic analysis has less to tell us here than linguistic philosophy. Jargon violates almost all the maxims of the Cooperative Principle enunciated by H. P. Grice, which are supposed to be observed when people enter into a conversation:

> The maxim of Quantity . . . require[s] the cooperative speaker to say as much but no more than is required for his particular purposes in the "talk exchange."
>
> The maxim of Quality . . . demands that the speaker say only what he believes to be true and that for which he has sufficient evidence.
>
> The maxim of Relation urges the speaker to make his contribution relevant.
>
> The maxim of Manner cautions the speaker to be methodical and to avoid ambiguity, prolixity, and obscurity.[14]

The maxims are violated simply because it is not the intention of the speaker or writer to be cooperative. "The more determined a person is to conceal his thinking, the wordier he becomes," writes Russell Baker,[15] and Edwin Newman adds, "It serves as a fence that keeps others outside and respectful, or leads them to ignore what is going on because it is too much trouble to find out."[16]

The typical jargonaut is the bureaucrat compelled to make a public statement about something he would rather keep to himself or within his professional circle. All governments try to conceal the activities for which they fear criticism, and they hide behind a smoke screen of obscure language whose density corresponds to how embarrassing the truths are that have to be concealed. This explains why the Pentagon, whose business secrets have to do with killing, and the intelligence agencies, where concealment is a way of life, are the richest sources of jargon. The rare glimpse behind the veil may even show jargon being deliberately concocted. Earl Clinton Bolton, former executive vice president of the University of California, wrote a memo to the CIA in 1968 which has recently been declassified (*classified* is itself a precious bit of doubletalk for "secret"—people do not like secrets being kept from them, but who objects to classification?). In it he offered advice on how academics under attack for assisting the agency might defend themselves "with full use of the jargon of the academy," for example by appealing to some ostensibly impartial entity: "Such an independent corporation should of course have a ringing name (e.g., Institute for a Free Society). . . ."[17]

All of which means that to keep informed—even to stay alive—our citizens and voters must demand that linguistic knowledge become public knowledge far more than ever before. Nouns, participles, parsings, and the rest of the apparatus of the grammar class are fine, but today's society needs to learn the subtleties of language that lend themselves to exploitation. Self-preservation requires that we build that fire—and spread it as a backfire to protect our sanctuary.

The time is here when all communicators, public ones especially, should be held accountable for how they use the coin of daily communication. To hold them accountable, we need to know the kinds of verbal and grammatical shelters they are most apt to retreat to when they want to give us the slip. It should be as natural for the potential victim of a verbal scam to confront the charlatan as for the victim of a financial scam to confront the cheat. "Explain your use of this passive" should cause no more surprise than "Explain your use of this percentage rate." If people are bright enough to learn the language of money—as they must if they are to pay their taxes and buy their goods without falling prey to legal and illegal con artists—they are bright enough to learn the language of language—with a bit of help from linguists who have acquired a sense of their social responsibilities.

Notes

1. Lecture at Harvard anthropology seminar, 1 November 1977.
2. See Dwight Bolinger, *Meaning and Form,* (London, 1977), pp. 90–123.
3. "Real and Perceived Changes of Crime and Punishment," *Daedalus* (Winter 1978), pp. 143–157, especially p. 147.
4. *A Dictionary of Diseased English* (London, 1977), quoted by John Cunningham in the *Guardian,* October 1977.
5. *San Francisco Examiner and Chronicle,* 11 June 1978, sec. A, p. 18.
6. E. Hansen, *Reklamesprog* (Copenhagen, 1965), p. 40; cited by Rolf Sandell, *Linguistic Style and Persuasion* (New York, 1977), p. 130.
7. Radio broadcast. Example thanks to Mary Key.
8. KGO radio, San Francisco, California, November 1974.
9. KGO radio, San Francisco, California, 25 November 1978.
10. *San Francisco Chronicle,* 15 May 1978, p. 4, reporting on the Food Marketing Convention in Dallas.
11. UPI dispatch, *Palo Alto Times,* 11 January 1979, p. 4.
12. Example thanks to Mrs. Peggy Drinkwater.
13. *A Civil Tongue* (Indianapolis, 1976), p. 6.
14. As summarized by Jerrold M. Sadock, "On Testing for Conversational Implicature," in Peter Cole, ed., *Syntax and Semantics,* Vol. 9, *Pragmatics* (New York, 1978), pp. 281–297; 285.
15. *Washington Star,* 12 August 1974, sec. A, p. 10.
16. Newman, *A Civil Tongue,* p. 146.
17. Quoted by *Public Doublespeak Newsletter* 4, no. 5 (1979): 1.

LOUIS B. LUNDBORG

The Voices of Business

BUSINESS DOES NOT have *a* language. The corporation is a Tower of Babel.

A more accurate metaphor might be that business is a modern typewriter on which interchangeable elements can be inserted to produce different type faces. Business has the added feature, not yet part of any typewriter, of being able to write in many different voices. Using the same alphabet and spelling out the same words, the same set of facts, it can convey one message differently to different audiences by a slight rearrangement of words for a different tone.

In one sense, there is no such thing as "business," or "the corporation." There are more than fourteen million companies in America, no two exactly alike. Within any one company, there may be one hundred employees, or one hundred thousand—again no two exactly alike. While occasionally an association representing a portion of these companies exhorts its members to "speak with a common voice"—or itself purports to speak as "the voice of business"—that is usually on a single public issue: a pending piece of legislation or a disputed government regulation. That business rarely speaks with a single voice would not be bad if more people in business spoke up at all, and spoke plainly enough to make the issues stand out boldly. Too often that does not happen.

Meanwhile, not only does a different voice come from each company when it does speak, but many different voices from within the same company. The language of external pronouncements is not the same as the language of internal communication. It is a little like the old practice of using Latin for formal occasions and the local patois for daily intercourse. Today, in business as in government, bureaucracy has invented a third language, a jargon of its own, for its procedural and transactional documents. (The very words *procedural* and *transactional* are bureaucratic.) Internal communication would be far better if bureaucrats used something closer to village patois, too; and progressive managements try hard to spread the Art of Plain Talk. But stilted language is as natural and inevitable a hallmark of bureaucracy as garlic is of an Italian restaurant.

At none of these levels is there one constant language, one standard tongue spoken or written under all circumstances. The annual report at the end of a good year will be explicit about the company's record performance; but when the year's earnings have been flat—or worse—and there is no hope for a dividend increase, the president's message in the annual report may have quite a different tone. A few chief executives will be as blunt and forthright about their failures as they are about their successes; but in a typical message after a bad year the only thing that is plain and clear will be that the company has been the victim of economic conditions over which it has had no control. From that point on, the obscure language about the company's strategy and deployment of resources will leave the impression that the company has handled itself so masterfully in this crisis that it has emerged stronger than ever. It is in a position to take advantage of the unprecedented opportunities of the period ahead.

If the shareholders who read those rosy-tinted words could hear this same chief executive officer addressing his division heads at their annual management meeting, they might wonder if it was the same person—or even the same company. He might be spelling out in words of one or two syllables just how badly the company has performed, and how hard it is going to be to pull the company back up to its pre-slump trend line.

Inconsistent? Insincere? Dishonest? Not necessarily—and certainly not in the mind of the chief executive officer himself. He would insist (and believe) that he has told both groups the same truth about the same set of facts; but that he has told each group in the language appropriate to that group and that occasion. He probably has never thought of the question in these terms, but in each case he has chosen his words to create an emotional effect.

With the shareholders he wants a calming, reassuring emotion; with his "troops" he wants quite a different emotion—probably a succession of several. First he wants to produce a shock, along with a trace of fear. Some executives (those I think of as the Old School) would try to maintain the fear all the way through their address to division heads and use it as their main motivational device. Others would rescue the troops from their despair and fear by injecting a mood of hope; then they would try to send everybody out of the meeting charged with zeal to wipe out last year's humiliating record and redeem the company's honor by setting a new record of sales and profits.

An even sharper contrast in the use of language could be found in a single conversation: picture a manager or supervisor who is given to chewing out anyone in his unit who fails to perform up to par. He has called onto the carpet a subordinate who never likes to work very hard, who always has excuses for his mistakes, but who this time has really fouled things up. The boss first delivers himself of a string of expletives that communicate very little substance except his general opinion of this wretch, his ancestors, and his miserable personal history. Having thus set the tone of the interview, he proceeds in quite explicit terms to recite the details of the man's misfeasance.

The response of the accused is a model of contrast: where the boss was blustery, he is soft-spoken; where the boss was abusive, he is meek and conciliatory; but above all, where the boss was finally precise and pinpointed, he is vague, evasive, and full of alibis—all of them in broad-brush generalizations about events and conditions, not of his making, that got in his way.

Then there are times when someone in the company decides that morale is bad among employees. It is time, the boss is told, that he should get out a warm, friendly message to all employees in the company to let them know how much they are appreciated. A soft-soap letter, this is sometimes called. It is addressed to "Dear Co-Workers" or "My Colleagues" or "My Fellow Workers." In an earlier day, a founder-executive might have referred in the letter to "my boys and girls"; today even the most sycophantic employee would warn him that he could not get away with that. But he will still talk about the Acme Widget family and the many interests they share; his earnest desire that management always be aware of any problems or concerns, whether official or personal, that may be troubling anyone in the company; and his assurance, therefore, that there will always be an open line of communication, right up to his office if need be, to be sure that no questions or concerns go unattended.

The fact that half the people who receive the letter have had the opposite experience with their immediate supervisors is something that even the boss may not know. But he should know it before he writes such a letter.

In another area, the company that has to deal with an unhappy customer may speak—or write—in any of several voices. The customer with a valid complaint may meet the stony face of a clerk who says, in effect, "You must have done something wrong. We never make mistakes. So don't bother me unless you can prove you have something to complain about." Or the response may be, "Let's see what your problem is and how we can help you." Those two attitudes come through just as clearly in written responses. The exact words may vary, but the tone of the letter will inevitably reveal the attitude of the writer, which may or may not represent the attitude of the company. Many company service representatives who seem negative and unfriendly may be afraid they will make a mistake, afraid they will be criticized by their supervisor, or that the complaint is an attack on themselves. So they become defensive. These failures to communicate with customers really reflect a failure of management. Even though the stated policy of the company may be positive, a management is all too rarely aware of the key elements missing: thorough training, monitoring, and demonstration of the company's policy by the example of supervisors themselves.

None of these examples should be taken as typical. But all of them happen often enough to illustrate the infinite variety of language and moods—the "words and music" that make up the real-life opera we call business.

Modern management has come to realize that communication—the use of language—is virtually the central nervous system of business that makes it function and keeps it under rational control. Sophisticated executives have learned that communication of any kind always performs two functions: it transmits facts and it conveys an attitude. What they are growing to appreciate is that the attitude may have as much impact as the facts — if not more. Yet this awareness has developed after business has already grown to gargantuan, worldwide proportions; and the spread of the awareness has not kept pace with the continuing organic growth. The result is that the vast majority of business communication is still being done by people who use language as their mood might strike them, with no thought of the secondary consequences of what they say or how they say it.

So it is not surprising that this great new central nervous

system—the network of business language—develops some neuroses and causes some apparently irrational behavior. It is also not surprising that executives who have not given much thought to the communication process do not appreciate how many of their problems—with employees, with customers, with the press, with government, with their communities, with public-interest groups—stem not from the substance of what their company is doing, but from how it communicates with each of those publics.

The most hopeful sign is that this problem is beginning to be dealt with as a major corporate concern. In one after another of the largest American companies (and in many smaller ones), "communications" is being structured as a central staff function, ranking along with other high-priority staff departments. The title, of course, can mean different things in different companies; but most of these departments aim at some, or all, of these objectives: to help everyone inside the company to have a better understanding (and the *same* understanding) of the structure of the company, its policies, practices, and goals; to make sure that any changes in company policies or programs are so announced and explained that they will be clearly understood; to help all supervisors and trainers give instructions in language that will be clearly and quickly understood—thus avoiding great losses in time and money through delays and mistakes; to coordinate and guide public pronouncements of all kinds, to the end that the company will present one clear image to the public.

These departments have to approach their chore on many different fronts, because they are dealing as counsellors with such a variety of lifelong habits. Some executives earnestly try to use language in order to be understood; they need only to be helped to use it better, so as to be understood better. But an equal number deliberately use language in order *not* to be understood. This latter group includes people at all levels, from chief executive officers to the heads of some of the most subordinate sections of a company. At times, particularly with the chief executive officers, the motive of evasive language is to protect company plans from premature disclosure, for competitive reasons. But more often, at all levels, the reason for the "weasel words" is pure fear: the fear of taking a position for which the writer might later be held accountable.

One economist I know always delivers economic forecasts that are circular: he starts with one assumption of one set of conditions and bases one prediction on that. Then he proceeds, "but if"—but if the conditions change in one direction, his forecast is a little different. If they change in another direction, still different. Before he finishes, he has gone around a complete circle. So no matter what happens a year later, he can say that he predicted it. He reminds me of Harry Truman after his first experience with White House economic advisors. He heard so many "on the one hand . . . on the other hand" comments he finally turned to his executive assistant in exasperation and said, "Would somebody please find me a one-armed economist!"

Economists are not the only ones who "hedge their bets." Bureaucratic gobbledygook has many sources; but one is the fear of being found wrong. Subordinates making proposals to their bosses (and this can apply to the very top echelon) often are so afraid to commit themselves that they cloud their language with fuzzy jargon.

While bureaucracy and its language can occasionally show up even in smaller companies, they are more typical of the larger ones. When face-to-face, oral communication has to be replaced by the written memorandum, bureaucracy raises its stiff-necked head. A company that prospered for four generations under family ownership and management was recently sold to one of the large conglomerates. Most of the key members of the old management are still there, doing what they have always done. But an added duty is taking most of the fun out of their jobs: filling out new report forms required by corporate headquarters. They are used to the bundles of forms they have had to fill out for government agencies; but most of these are statistical or quantitative: they can be answered by supplying numbers. Now they are getting questions that can be answered only by writing an essay: "Describe your accountabilities"; "What are the objectives of your section for the current fiscal year? For the next five years?" One of the executives of this company has confided to me that after a lifetime of learning to write and speak simply and straightforwardly, he is now having to retrain himself to use gobbledygook. The simplest of questions now come to him couched, as he says, "in long words strung together into long sentences." He is expected to answer them in the same coin.

Departments of communication will never by themselves stamp out bureaucratic jargon and gobbledygook. Those are the inevitable products of the rigid, inflexible mind of the bureaucrat. The bureaucrat struts his power by pontificating—and pontificating is virtually a synonym for polysyllabic language. Bad as this is, his language is the lesser of evils: the power to obstruct, exercised by self-important people, is the real bureaucratic evil. Every chief executive should take as one of his constant priorities to control this evil; the Plain Talk benefits will follow.

When everything possible has been done to improve the clarity of the language used in business—and tremendous progress is being made—the job is still only half done. I said earlier that communication always performs two functions: to transmit facts and to convey an attitude. Most of the emphasis and most of the progress have been in transmitting the message. That is not real communication, which by definition is a two-way process. Transmitting messages is one-way, usually downward. So-called downward communication never works, because it conveys only what the sender wants to get across, not what the receiver is interested in hearing—or even able to perceive and understand.

Companies that have succeeded in developing real communication, whether internal or external, have started by listening to what people are interested in, what they want to know, and how much they understand and are prepared to absorb. But they will have to go one step further before the "language of business" will be accepted as part of the broader language of the human family. They must learn to communicate their concern. If business and its executives are hearing everything told them, it is not yet apparent in the words of their response. When people are interviewed or queried in business surveys, they tell about the problems that concern them: the problems of society, of communities, of the environment. The companies acknowledge these concerns, but often only in terms of their *economic* effects. This language block has helped to create a feeling that business does not care about anything *but* profits.

If when a businessman speaks of minority employment, or air pollution, or poverty, he speaks in the language of a certified public accountant analyzing a corporate balance sheet, who is to know that he understands the human problems behind the statistical ones? If the businessman would stop talking like a computer printout or a page from the corporate annual report, other people would stop thinking he had a cash register for a heart. It is as simple as that—but that isn't simple.

He talks that way, I suspect, in part because, in managing a business in a complex world, his life becomes preoccupied by business and he hears only its language. Meanwhile his human concern is expressed in deeds if not in words. But there is still a need to take the next step. He must learn to use words that properly reflect his concern. Then he will be communicating.

DIANE JOHNSON

Doctor Talk

IN AFRICA OR the Amazon, the witch doctor on your case has a magic language to say his spells in. You listen, trembling, full of hope and dread and mystification; and presently you feel better or die, depending on how things come out. In England and America too, until recent times, doctors talked a magic language, usually Latin, and its mystery was part of your cure. But modern doctors are rather in the situation of modern priests; having lost their magic languages, they run the risk of losing the magic powers too.

For us, this means that the doctor may lose his ability to heal us by our faith; and doctors, sensing powerlessness, have been casting about for new languages in which to conceal the nature of our afflictions and the ingredients of cures. They have devised two main dialects, but neither seems quite to serve for every purpose—this is a time of transition and trial for them, marked by various strategies, of which the well-known illegible handwriting on your prescription is but one. For doctors themselves seem to have lost faith too, in themselves and in the old mysteries and arts. They have been taught to think of themselves as scientists, and so it is first of all to the language of science that they turn, to control and confuse us.

Most of the time scientific language can do this perfectly. We are terrified, of course, to learn that we have "prolapse of the mitral valve"—we promise to take our medicine and stay on our diet, even though these words describe a usually innocuous finding in the investigation of an innocent heart murmur. Or we can be lulled into a false sense of security when the doctor avoids a scientific term: "you have a little spot on your lung"—even when what he puts on the chart is "probable bronchogenic carcinoma."

With patients, doctors can use either scientific or vernacular speech but with each other they speak Science, a strange argot of Latin terms, new words, and acronyms, that yearly becomes farther removed from everyday speech and is sometimes comprised almost entirely of numbers and letters: "His pO_2 is 45; pCO_2, 40; and pH 7.4." Sometimes it is made up of peculiar verbs originating from the apparatus with which they treat people: "Well, we've bronched him, tubed him, bagged him, cathed him, and PEEPed him," the intern tells the attending physician. ("We've explored his airways with a bronchoscope, inserted an endotrachial tube, provided assisted ventilation with a resuscitation bag, positioned a catheter in his bladder to monitor his urinary output, and used positive end-expiratory pressure to improve oxygenation.") Even when discussing things that can be expressed in ordinary words, doctors will prefer to say "he had a pneumonectomy" to saying "he had a lung removed."

One physician remembers being systematically instructed, during the 1950s, in scientific-sounding euphemisms to be used in the presence of patients. If a party of interns were examining an alcoholic patient, the wondering victim might hear them say that he was "suffering from hyperingestation of ethynol." In front of a cancer victim they would discuss his "mitosis." But in recent years such discussions are not conducted in front of the patient at all, because, since Sputnik, laymen's understanding of scientific language has itself increased so greatly that widespread ignorance cannot be assumed.

Space exploration has had its influence, especially on the *sound* of medical language. A CAT-scanner (computerized automated tomography), *de rigueur* in an up-to-date diagnostic unit, might be something to look at the surface of Mars with. The resonance of physical, rather than biological, science has doubtless been fostered by doctors themselves, who, mindful of the extent to which their science is really luck and art, would like to sound astronomically precise, calculable and exact, even if they cannot be so.

Acronyms and abbreviations play the same part in medical language that they do in other walks of modern life: We might be irritated to read on our chart that "this SOB patient complained of

DOE five days PTA." (It means "this Short Of Breath patient complained of Dyspnea On Exertion five days Prior To Admission.") To translate certain syllables, the doctor must have yet more esoteric knowledge. Doctor A, reading Dr. B's note that a patient has TTP, must know whether Doctor B is a hematologist or a chest specialist in order to know whether the patient has thrombotic thrombocytopoenic puerpura, or traumatic tension pneumothorax. That pert little word *ID* means identification to us, but Intradermal to the dermatologist, Inside Diameter to the physiologist, Infective Dose to the bacteriologist; it can stand for our inner self, it can mean *idem* (the same), or it can signify a kind of rash.

But sometimes doctors must speak vernacular English, and this is apparently difficult for them. People are always being told to discuss their problems with their doctors, which, considering the general inability of doctors to reply except in a given number of reliable phrases, must be some of the worst advice ever given. Most people, trying to talk to the doctor—trying to pry or to wrest meaning from his evasive remarks ("I'd say you're coming along just fine")—have been maddened by the vague and slightly inconsequential nature of statements which, meaning everything to you, ought in themselves to have meaning but do not, are noncommittal, or unengaged, have a slightly rote or rehearsed quality, sometimes a slight inappropriateness in the context ("it's nothing to worry about really"). This is the doctor's alternative dialect, phrases so general and bland as to communicate virtually nothing.

This dialect originates from the emotional situation of the doctor. In the way passers-by avert their eyes from the drunk in the gutter or the village idiot, so the doctor must avoid the personality, the individuality, any involvement with the destiny, of his patients. He must not let himself think and feel with them. This shows in the habit doctors have of calling patients by the names of their diseases: "put the pancreatitis in the other ward and bring the chronic lunger in here." In order to retain objective professional judgment, the doctor has long since learned to withdraw his emotions from the plight of the patient and has replaced his own ability to imagine them and empathize with them, with a formula language—the social lie and the understatement—usually delivered with the odd jocularity common to all gloomy professions.

"Well, Mrs. Jones, Henry is pretty sick. We're going to run a couple of tests, have a look at that pump of his." ("Henry is in shock. We're taking him to the Radiology Department to put a catheter in his aorta and inject contrast material. If he has what I think he has, he has a forty-two percent chance of surviving.") We might note an apparent difference of style in English and American doctors, with the English inclined to drollery in such situations. One woman I know reported that her London gynecologist said to her, of her hysterectomy, "We're taking out the cradle, but we're leaving in the playpen!" Americans on the other hand often affect tough talk: "Henry is sick as hell."

The doctor's *we,* by the way, is of especial interest. Medical pronouns are used in special ways that ensure that the doctor is never out alone on any limb. The referents are cleverly vague. The statement "we see a lot of that" designates him as a member of a knowledgeable elite, "we doctors"; while "how are we today" means you, or him and you, if he is trying to pass himself off as a sympathetic alter ego. Rarely does he stand up as an *I.* Rarely does he even permit his name to stand alone as Smith, but affixes syllables before and after—the powerful abbreviation *Dr.* itself, which can even be found on his golf bags or skis; or the letters *M.D.* after, or sometimes the two buttressing his name from both sides, like bookends: "Dr. Smart Smith, M.D."; in England a little train of other letters may trail behind: *F.R.C.P.* In America another fashionable suffix has been observed recently: *Inc.* Dr. Smart Smith, M.D., Inc. This stands for Incorporated, and indicates that the doctor has made himself into a corporation, to minimize his income taxes. A matrix of economic terms already evident in the vocabulary of some doctors is expected to become more pervasive as time goes on.

We may complain even of how the doctor talks to us; doctors will say, on the other hand, that it is we who do not listen. Very likely this is true. Our ears thunder with hope and dread. We cannot hear the doctor. He says "bone marrow test," we think he says "bow and arrow test." We have all been struck with disbelief, listening to an account by a friend or family member of his trip to the doctor; the doctor cannot possibly have said it was okay to go on smoking, that she doesn't need to lose weight, that he must never eat carrots. This is the case. According to doctors, patients hear themselves. The patient says, "I can't even look at a carrot," and then imagines the doctor has interdicted them. Doctors' sense of our inability to understand things may increase their tendency to talk in simple terms to us, or not to speak at all. Nonetheless, we all hear them talking, saying things they say they never say.

DAVID S. LEVINE

"My Client Has Discussed Your Proposal to Fill the Drainage Ditch with His Partners": Legal Language

LAW IS NOT so different from other professions in its use of language. There is a core vocabulary of impenetrable jargon, and a collection of words in common use that are imbued with subtleties and nuances peculiar to the legal context.[1] Viewed from outside the profession, however, lawyers appear to inflict especially cruel and unusual punishment on the mother tongue through jargon, archaic words, endless repetition, passive constructions, overkill by synonym, and deliberate turgidity. I am a relative newcomer to the trade—in practice a mere five months as of this writing—but already I have encountered some of the factors that shape the language of our profession. With no claim to great scholarship or experience, then, permit me to report from the heart of the beast.[2]

One major determinant of legal language is the nature of legal cases. For example, I find I am unable to imagine any graceful phrasing in a "Petition for Reassessment of Railroad Unitary Property Values" which is directed at California's State Board of Equalization, criticizing the appraisal methods used to value the operating portion of a railroad for property tax purposes. The subject matter chokes my muse.

Most of the time, lawyers are burdened with technical problems in fields other than law, and must concentrate on mastering these other fields and then demonstrate their mastery to a naive judge or jury. Little opportunity remains for improving legalese, which, to us, looks relatively simple and clear when compared to the technical language of other professions.

To be sure, lawyers try to write well, but this effort is defeated in part by the very processes of the common-law system, imported from England to the New World by the colonists. Essentially, the common law is the accumulation of judicial pronouncements upon statutory and nonstatutory rights, along with the procedures for interpolating a judicial result in a new situation for which there is no exact equivalent but only numerous instructive parallels or analogies. Through legal research, the lawyer firmly establishes the relevant universe of decisional and statutory law, and then, by pushing and pulling the facts and concepts immediately at hand,[3] sidles up to the interpretation which most favors his client.[4] Thus the common-law system is capable of generating answers to questions never asked and not previously contemplated by reference to questions and solutions etched in tradition or logged in the legislated statutory law.

An overly simple example: In California, when married couples dissolve their legally sanctified union there is a division of assets they have accumulated during their marriage ("community property"). Suppose a couple—call them Lee and Michelle—are not married but act much like couples who are, and want to separate. Should the law divide this couple's assets at the point of their "dissolution," or enforce an agreement between Lee and Michelle for a division, or should it disregard the substance of their relationship and instead focus on the lack of legal status? How is this *ménage* similar to a formal marriage? How is it different? The court sifts out the substance of this relationship and finds within it a possible contractual relationship not unlike the marriage contract. Once comfortably within contract law, lawyers are on solid and well-charted ground. Unmarried couples may now seek to prove the existence of a contract (written, oral, or implied by their conduct) to treat the assets accumulated during their relationship much like community property, subject to court-enforced or prescribed division at breakup. If the partners are unable to reach agreement on the presence or terms of such a contract, the matter is now subject to scrutiny by the court, which will examine the facts and, if it finds a contract buried in the detritus, will measure the property and split it among the partners—and their attorneys.[5]

In the example given, the court embraced decisional authority ranging from 1891 to 1976. Because lawyers are constantly searching for the leading edge of the law, of necessity they face backward to cases already decided in order to determine where the edge came from and where it trails off into the ether. As a result, lawyers quote their ancestors to establish the "precedent" closest to the unique factual and legal circumstance presently contested. Ideally, they quote contemporaries, but the goal of finding for every assertion a judicial characterization which supports the desired result very often requires ancient wisdom.

Since as lawyers we spend our days finding other people's words to describe problems before us, we have a tendency to use the words of others even when our problem is not so much legal as linguistic. For example, since custom plays a large part in a court's decision, in the absence of other guiding principles we must often argue that "it has always been this way and there is no compelling reason to change it." A lawyer arguing this view or a judge supporting it could write: "It has always been this way." In one modern decision, the judge wonderfully wrote: "The mind of man runneth not to the contrary." I have no doubt that within my lifetime it will be given fresh vitality by some other lawyer arguing water rights law on the basis of the "precedent" in the cited case.[6]

Because of the value of precedent, contemporary lawyering often involves searching out and stitching together unmatched swatches of archaic judicial expression. If the courageous advocate wishes to recast these archaisms, themselves often borrowed from even earlier cases, into modern English, the client may lose the case, since in recasting the ancestral prose the lawyer presents the judge with something new and perhaps threatening. Prudence wins most cases. Prudence is not innovative.[7]

A lawyer's paragraph may contain words or phrases borrowed from so many sources and centuries that the clashing styles create a kind of grotesque technocratic poetry. Thus, one hardly ever buys "land" without buying "herididaments and tenements" too. There are differences among the three words, but most literate people (and most literate lawyers) would be hard pressed to appreciate them when forced to penetrate an attorney's version of a real estate sales contract. Equally familiar, in the language of wills we leave the "rest, residue, and remainder" of our worldly possessions to our "heirs, successors, and assigns." This "Rule of Threes" has a distinguished ancestry in the law.[8] On the wall of my office, a hand-lettered-on-parchment lease agreement for property located in the City of London, dated 26 August 1842, contains the following:

covenants, conditions and agreements
executors, administrators and assigns
paid, observed and performed
for and during and unto
leave, surrender and yield up
enter and come into and upon
carry on or permit or suffer to be carried on
retain, reposses and enjoy
observing, performing and keeping
have, hold, use, occupy, possess and enjoy
signed, sealed and delivered.

Some of these triplets contain words of subtly different meaning; others contain pyramiding words (one contained inside the second, and both contained inside the third); some are inserted because of the form and procedural requirements of a lease agreement; all may be found in twentieth-century legal instruments and guidebooks. This is our verbal heritage.

In law, the dictionary is not much use in searching out the meaning of "terms of art" (legal jargon for "jargon"), since words take their meaning from the cases construing them. Thus, there is often no convention as to the meaning of crucial legal terms, since the context of their use inevitably, and often dramatically, alters their content. For example, the lofty expression *equal protection of the law* means one degree of equality and protection when the rights of pregnant New Yorkers are at stake and another when the rights of pregnant Virginians are at issue.[9] Perhaps this is a positive thing. I can see good reasons for having degrees of meaning in the phrase *equal protection*. The term should perhaps appear precise in one use, or abstract and vague in another, depending on the accompanying details.

Professor Wydick distinguishes abstract vagueness from the "intentional and artful vagueness" sometimes employed by judges "to provide a general compass heading when it is not possible [or desirable?] to map the trail in detail."[10] As an example he cites *Bates v. State Bar of Arizona,* in which the United States Supreme Court tackled the slippery problem of lawyer advertising without really knowing where to draw the line on state restrictions of this traditionally forbidden activity. The court permitted states to impose *"reasonable restrictions* on the time, place and manner" of lawyer advertising.[11] By using terms of art which are intentionally vague, the court has provided general guidance while reserving for itself and other courts the opportunity to review, post-*Bates,* specific examples of questionable conduct. Here, imprecision permits the court to decide the issue in gross now, to let the states experiment with different standards, and to treat specific abuses as experience later demands. But such "artful vagueness" makes it exceedingly difficult to have a useful, intelligent, and precise conversation with another lawyer unless you can dash to the recorded cases and determine the meaning of the critical terms in contexts which establish the degrees of difference.

Of course, for every instance of "artful vagueness" there are many examples of "artless vagueness," some of it deliberate. A real estate contract printed by a local brokerage office demands of the seller that he deliver the premises with appliances in "working order." A colleague of mine defended this phrase in a case in which the plaintiff-buyer alleged the heating system didn't heat the house. The trial court in an unpublished opinion determined that a heating system which provided *some heat,* though *not enough,* was in "working order," while a heating system which provided *enough heat* was in "good working order." Thus, the lawyer who thoughtfully left out "good" was rewarded with a victory for his client, while the one who failed to demand an amendment to the sales contract specifying "*good* working order" was left with an expensive loss. The art of making and closing loopholes, as this example demonstrates, is at the heart of every client's expectations for his lawyers, and at the heart of every lawyer's life as a draftsman. The goal is to insure that the loopholes will let your client out without letting your opponent's client in. Since both parties are pursuing the same goal, and since their efforts are, in theory, supposed to result in the perfect agreement, no one wants to change the rules of the game too much. Accordingly, no one wishes to experiment with readable language for fear that the chutes and ladders of a written instrument will appear all too clearly to the party asked to subscribe to it.

If contracts, briefs, and opinions are made difficult by language abuse, the mere reading of our statutes can cause severe distress and disorientation.[12] Having a law degree helps, but even those with an advanced degree in tax law have trouble wading through the federal tax code without praying for periods, paragraphs, and other signs of conventional style. Notably, the tax laws are most criticized for loopholes, and yet this is where the loopholes are most manifest, formalized, and intentional. The tax lawyer's problem is in determining whether there are loopholes in the loopholes. Tax lawyers and government tax law drafters engage in a continuing game of linguistic cat and mouse.

All lawyers are familiar with "practice manuals." These are collections of working wisdom, which contain pre-cast arguments, fill-in-the-blanks sample forms, and canned analyses of common legal problems to guide lawyers in their search for the leading edge. The good collections are supplemented regularly, so that from a legal standpoint they are at most only a few months behind the latest developments. Without them, lawyers would spend countless (billable) hours reinventing the legal wheel. With them, lawyers can weave a lawsuit or an agreement quickly, tailoring the standard form only insofar as required by unique circumstances of particular cases. Thus, while all lawyers spend time searching for judicial precedent, most begin the hunt in these sourcebooks. The result is a tyranny of words and phrases canned by the compilers at some point in the past, and updated only for recent case authority or new statutory law.

An innovation in the great tradition of the practice manual is the law firm's form-and-style manual. In many larger firms the senior attorneys have developed in-house manuals which standardize certain types of relatively simple but critical legal documents paragraph by paragraph, so that an attorney in need merely passes to the clerical staff a list of numbers and receives the next day a nearly complete custom tailored reply to a lawsuit. This then is pruned and manicured to more nearly resemble the desired response. One can sometimes recognize a firm's production by its characteristic format and word order. This is *Time*-style legal writing: research is fed to a small band of stylistic robots who produce standardized prose. It saves a lot of time and clients' money, and it may prevent a substantial amount of legal malpractice, but it takes all personal vitality out of written instruments and represents an important trend toward assembly-line legal writing.

The most powerful recent development in the world of legal language is word-processing technology, in which the typewriter, computer, and television are merged to create a mechanical secretary capable of storing, retrieving, regurgitating and printing canned text.[13] In effect, lawyers can redraft documents infinitely without imposing cruel labor on their secretaries. At first glance, such a machine appears to promise improvement in language use. After all, the most verbally gifted lawyers can always benefit from another draft, and the least gifted among us absolutely need a day's rest between the *n*th draft and the next one. In fact, however, the redrafting process tends to hone documents for their adversarial thrust, not for literary or linguistic excellence. Furthermore, many lawyers now collaborate on one writing, each reworking the other's draft from a clean copy. Though the new technology gives us opportunities for thoughtful language and style, the result tends to be prose that is both over-manicured and, as always, turgid.

Almost all legal documents are designed to give the drafter the adversarial advantage at some unknown, perhaps unforeseen, future date. Thus, advocacy demands a language and style opposed to complete clarity since it seeks to bury troublesome points and raise helpful ones to the level of gospel. Theoretically, adversaries illuminate each other's legal drafting by discovering the evidence of burials; but in fact, they intensify each other's abuse of language, since each attempts to raise the other's dead and to bury the living points. Because judges are too busy to dwell on most written submissions, most journeyman lawyers avoid complex imagery. For many lawyers, "white space" is the ultimate ruler of legal language. It permits a judge to focus on an idea (frequently underlined to spare the judge pages of explication in order to find the naked conclusion).

Contrary to the popular idea derived from film and television, most lawyers do not speak for their fees, but instead they read and write.[14] Even trial attorneys spend many hours in silence, reading and writing, prior to exercising their oratorical skills before a judge and/or jury. Most judges reach their decisions on the basis of a lawyer's written submission, attending to the oral presentations mainly to clarify or to challenge points at the margin of uncertainty. As for the myth that lawyers speak with grace and power, one need only examine the verbatim transcript of an oral exchange among lawyers and judge, or an examination of a witness, to know how inarticulate most lawyers seem when forced to utter intelligible sentences without benefit of a second draft.

As with all professions, there are factors inside and, especially, outside the profession which promise to force changes in the way lawyers use language. For example, organized consumer groups have forced clarity and simplicity into the language of preprinted contracts, especially those used by banks and insurance companies. I have not yet met an attorney who could wade through a typical insurance contract in a single sitting. Happily, banks and insurance companies are now bragging about their readable contracts as if this were a special service accorded customers above and beyond the exchange of money for indebtedness. One can imagine the bloodshed at the drafting tables during the process of translating these monsters.[15]

Another hopeful element is the introduction of a modicum of legal education into other fields (business, public health, environmental monitoring). Although this trend may lead to corruption among otherwise innocent populations, it could force lawyers to modify their language for consumption by informed non-lawyers, and might inspire other non-lawyers to put pressure on the legal fraternity to tame its language excesses.[16]

A companion trend is the democratization of the profession. Law school now appears to be the preferred post-college alternative for the English major who has no prospect of a teaching position. This could send us a flock of new lawyers bringing a fresh, clear, flexible vocabulary to the profession, perhaps spiced with poetic modifiers, colorful imagery, or even subtle stylistic devices for imparting meaning without words.[17]

In fairness to our trade, I should note that most lawyers recognize better than the lay public the problems of impoverished and abused language. We should. We labor through many dozens of pages of it daily.[18] But even at the pinnacle of our profession, language use and abuse is a significant problem. For example, the late and distinguished justice of the United States Supreme Court, Felix Frankfurter, in an effort to write ordinary English, composed the following letter to a twelve-year-old who sought advice on preparing for a law career at an early age:[19]

> My dear Paul:
>
> No one can be a truly competent lawyer unless he is a cultivated man. If I were you, I would forget about any technical preparation for the law. The best way to prepare for the law is to come to the study of law as a well-read person. Thus alone can one acquire the capacity to use the English language on paper and in speech and with the habits of clear thinking which only a truly liberal education can give. No less important for a lawyer is the cultivation of the imaginative faculties by reading poetry, seeing great paintings . . . and listening to great music. Stock your mind with the deposit of much good reading, and widen and deepen your feelings by experiencing vicariously as much as possible the wonderful mysteries of the universe, and forget all about your future career.
>
> With good wishes,
> Sincerely yours,
> Felix Frankfurter

Wisdom for the young, surely, even if a touch repetitious, stilted, and ambiguous.

Notes

1. See, for instance, *Frigaliment Importing Co. v. B. N. S. International Sales Corp.*, 190 F. Supp. 116, 117–118 (S.D.N.Y. 1960), a contracts opinion which opens with that poignant age-old question: "What is chicken?" Seems the contract wasn't specific enough, "[s]ince the word 'chicken' standing alone is ambiguous."

2. If scholarship is your preferred diet, try David Mellinkoff, *The Language of the Law* (Boston, 1963), which addresses the historical development of legal language with admirable skill. Richard C. Wydick, "Plain English for Lawyers," *California Law Review* 66 (1978), provides much useful advice on improving the typical lawyer's language. The quotation in the title of this essay comes from Wydick's article (p. 749) and is an example of placing modifying words too far from the word being modified.

3. "Lawyers use the law as shoemakers use leather; rubbing it, pressing it, and stretching it with their teeth, all to the end of making it fit their purposes" (Louis XII , quoted by Tuli Kupferberg in "An Insulting Look at Lawyers Through the Ages," *Juris Doctor,* October/November 1978, p. 62).

4. "*Attorney* comes remotely from classical Latin *torno* (to turn on a lathe) . . ." (Mellinkoff, *The Language of the Law,* p. 80). Commonly, an "attorney" is a member of a state bar and thus licensed to practice law in that state, while a "lawyer" may not have passed the licensing exam. This is a distinction which only lawyers make among themselves, and one which I do not observe in this essay. Instead, the word *lawyer* is used here as an all-purpose noun describing those who peddle their legal training in one forum or another.

5. See *Marvin v. Marvin,* 18 Cal. 3d 660 (1976) [Marvin (I)]. In *Marvin v. Marvin* (II), which played in Front Page USA during the winter of 1979, the trial court determined that no such contract existed, but awarded Michelle a relatively modest amount of money to enable her to retrain herself for a career abandoned in favor of a relationship with Lee. The principle enunciated in *Marvin (I)* stands despite the Solomonic result reached in *Marvin (II).*

6. "Precedent was piled high on precedent, flattening out not only earlier precedent but sometimes principle as well. . . . [The] weight [of precedent] effectively squeezed the remaining literary juices out of the language of the law" (Mellinkoff, *The Language of the Law,* p. 104).

7. Prudence does not imply care in all circumstances. A colleague who formerly served as in-house counsel to a major American manufacturing concern reports spending a slow day reading the company's preprinted form contract for purchases. He noted the following gems (emphasis added):

> (a) Nothing herein shall be *doomed* to create the relationship of employer and employee . . . between the parties hereto.
> (b) In witness whereof *the parties hereto shall be executed* on the date first above written.

He reports that his file contained numerous completed versions of this standard contract, signed by in-house counsel for such mom-and-pop operations as IBM, Xerox, and General Motors. Were these forms ever read by the attorneys approving them? Perhaps the answer lies in the ease with which a tired attorney's eye flits across the trade terms and filler to the price tag.

8. Mellinkoff, *The Language of the Law,* pp. 120–122, writes of "doubling." The profusion of source languages in the development of the English legal tradi-

tion left lawyers with "bilingual synonyms," such as *devise* (French) and *bequeath* (English), which at one time served similar purposes and now are frequently used together and defined so narrowly as to produce different meanings.

On the role of "three" as a pattern number beyond the law, see Alan Dundes, "The Number Three in American Culture," in his *Analytic Essays in Folklore* (The Hague, 1975), pp. 206–225.

9. See and compare *Brooklyn Union Gas Co. v. Appeal Board,* 41 N.Y. 2d 84,359 N.E. 2d 393 (1976) with *General Electric Co. v. Gilbert,* 429 U.S. 125, 136 (1976).

10. Wydick, "Plain English for Lawyers," p. 738.

11. 433 U.S. 350, 384 (1977); emphasis added.

12. For the truly masochistic linguist, Wydick, "Plain English for Lawyers," p. 741, n. 20, nominates section 341 (e) (1) of the Internal Revenue Code (26 U.S.C. § 341 [e] [1]). The section contains a 522-word sentence which few lawyers could wade through, even for a fee.

13. "Man has, as it were, become a kind of prosthetic God. When he puts on all his auxiliary organs he is truly magnificent. . . ." Sigmund Freud, *Civilization and Its Discontents* (1961), at 38–39.

14. "Lawyers make a living out of trying to figure out what other lawyers have written" (Will Rogers, quoted in Kupferberg, "An Insulting Look at Lawyers," p. 62. I am advised that in ancient days, lawyers were paid by the word—an incentive arrangement which may have contributed to our profession's tendency toward repetition.

15. This knife cuts both ways. Consumers still don't read lengthy and formidable credit or insurance agreements, though in theory the agreements are now accessible to the untrained reader. As a result, consumers are still unaware of their legal rights and responsibilities under the contracts they have signed. Perversely, the improvements in (unread) language could undercut a consumer's traditional defense of a lack of understanding of the legal language.

16. The term *non-lawyers* is a peculiar one. I am unfamiliar with the inner secrets of other professions, but I confess to never hearing a person described as a "non-architect" or "non-doctor."

17. But note: "The law is not the place for the artist or poet. The law is the calling of thinkers" (Justice Oliver Wendell Holmes, quoted in the margin of *Case & Comment,* March/April 1979, p. 16).

18. Abraham Lincoln said of a fellow lawyer, "He can compress the most words into the smallest idea of any man I ever met" (Kupferberg, "An Insulting Look at Lawyers," p. 62).

19. Felix Frankfurter, "Advice to a Young Man Interested in Going into Law," in Ephraim London, ed., *The Law as Literature* (New York, 1960), p. 725.

WALTER BENN MICHAELS

Against Formalism: Chickens and Rocks

THE FORMALISM I want to discuss is not so much an issue in literary criticism or legal theory, though I concentrate on such matters, as it is a general view of meaning. And it is a view held not only by confessed formalists but by many critics who are far from thinking of themselves as formalists, and indeed by many who are not critics at all but who are nevertheless concerned with the nature of language and the proper interpretation of texts. In fact, one might even say that it is a view so deeply embedded in the tradition of Anglo-American empiricism and in our ways of thinking that it hardly seems to us a "view" at all; it's just a commonsense account of the way language works.

Let me begin with two quotations, both about meaning and intention. The first is from W. K. Wimsatt's defense (1968) of his and Monroe Beardsley's seminal essay, "The Intentional Fallacy" (1946): ". . . the intention of a literary artist *qua* intention is neither a valid ground for arguing the presence of a quality or meaning in a given instance of his literary work nor a valid criterion for judging the value of that work." The second is from an opinion by Judge Learned Hand, written in 1911:

> A contract has, strictly speaking, nothing to do with the personal, or individual, intent of the parties. A contract is an obligation attached by the mere force of law to certain acts of the parties, usually

> words, which ordinarily accompany and represent a known intent. If, however, it were proved by twenty bishops that either party, when he used the words, intended something else than the usual meanings which the law imposes upon them, he would still be held, unless there were some mutual mistake, or something else of the sort. (*Hotchkiss v. National City Bank,* 200 F287, 293 [S.D.N.Y. 1911])

Now in both instances it is important to note what is *not* being asserted. In the case of "The Intentional Fallacy," for example, debate has usually taken the form of arguments for or against the proposition that knowledge of the author's intention is relevant to determination of what his poem or novel means. But as constant as Wimsatt and Beardsley were in denying the relevance of authorial intention, they were at least equally constant in denying one aspect of their denial. As "Mr. Beardsley and I were careful to point out . . . ," Wimsatt wrote in 1968, "interpretation apparently based upon an author's 'intention' often in fact refers to an intention as it is found in, or inferred from, the work itself. Obviously the argument about intention . . . is not directed against such instances." Thus the central thrust of his position was not completely to deny the relevance of authorial intention but to limit what would be allowed to count as *evidence* of that intention. The polemic against intention can be seen as part of the more broadly formalist polemic against discussion of the aesthetic object in what were perceived as fundamentally nonaesthetic terms (historical, biographical, psychological, etc.). The poem was to be regarded as an autonomous object and to be studied, in the famous phrase, "as a poem and not another thing."

Seen in this light it is, of course, very tempting to equate American formalism with a kind of high-minded aestheticism, but the quotation from Learned Hand shows very clearly that the modern insistence on the determinate and autonomous status of the text has been by no means confined to aesthetics. The point in law has, of course, nothing to do with the aesthetic status of contracts. It was rather an attempt to guarantee the objectivity of the contract by ensuring that both parties would be bound to what the words themselves said and not to anyone's "subjective" or "private" interpretation of what the words meant. What is interesting is that the same theory of meaning should seem essential to the interests of lawyers and critics both. The primary tenet of literary formalism—that study be confined to *the text itself*—is anticipated in a context utterly removed from any aesthetic concerns and associated not with a New Critical retreat to the Ivory Tower but with the interpretive demands of the marketplace.

In contract law, one of the primary ways in which the integrity of the text is protected is by something called the parol evidence rule, which in the *Restatement of Contracts* reads as follows: "The integration of an agreement makes inoperative to add to or to vary the agreement all contemporaneous oral agreements relating to the same subject matter; and also . . . all prior written or oral agreements relating thereto." The force of this rule is clear enough; it is designed to ensure objectivity by providing a public standard of accountability. Since, as Justice Holmes wrote in *The Path of the Law,* "the making of a contract depends . . . not on the parties having *meant* the same thing but on their having *said* the same thing," the parol evidence rule ensures that evidence of one party's subjective intent will not be introduced in order to alter the objective meaning of the contract itself, what the contract says. There are, however, exceptions to this rule. Extrinsic evidence is not admissible "if the written words are themselves plain and clear and unambiguous," but if the contract is itself vague or ambiguous, then extrinsic evidence will often be admitted to clear up the vagueness or resolve the ambiguity. The evidence serves not to vary the contract but to help the judge in interpreting it.

This interpretive scenario sounds reasonable enough, but, in fact, as the late Arthur L. Corbin argued (in "The Interpretation of Words and the Parole Evidence Rule," *Cornell Law Quarterly* 50 [1965]: 161–190), it is highly misleading, depending as it does on the implicit and in Corbin's view mistaken assumption that qualities like ambiguity and clarity are intrinsic properties of texts. A judge's decision as to whether or not a contract is ambiguous must inevitably be itself based on extrinsic evidence, Corbin argued, because "no man can determine the meaning of written words by merely gluing his eyes within the four corners of a square paper. . . . When a judge refuses to consider relevant extrinsic evidence on the ground that the meaning of the words is to him plain and clear, his decision is formed by and wholly based upon the completely extrinsic evidence of his own personal education and experience." In support of this view, Corbin cited the example of *Frigaliment Importing Co. v. B. N. S. International Sales Corp* (190 F. Supp. 116 [S.D.N.Y. 1960]).

The question in this case was the meaning of a contract in which a New York company called B. N. S. (the defendant) undertook to sell to a Swiss company called Frigaliment (the plaintiff) among other things seventy-five thousand pounds of U.S. Fresh Frozen

Chicken at a price of thirty-three dollars per one hundred pounds. When the chickens arrived in Switzerland, the plaintiff was dismayed and outraged to discover that they were not the young "fryers" and "roasters" he had anticipated but were instead old "stewing chickens" or "fowl." According to the plaintiff and to witnesses on his behalf, the word *chicken* had a particular trade usage; it could mean a "broiler, a fryer or a roaster," but not a stewing chicken. Hence, the plaintiff claimed, he had every right to expect, according to the terms of the contract, that he would be sent fryers and/or roasters, not stewing chickens. The defendant maintained, however, that being new to the chicken business he was not familiar with such usage and that, furthermore, such usage was by no means universal even in the trade. Among the witnesses called on behalf of the defendant was a Mr. Weininger, the operator of a chicken eviscerating plant in New Jersey, who testified, "Chicken is everything except a goose, a duck, and a turkey. Everything is a chicken but then you have to say, you have to specify which category you want or that you are talking about." The defendant thus maintained that it had every right to understand "chicken" to mean, among other things, stewing chicken and so contended that it had complied with the terms of the contract.

The question was thus, as the judge put it, "What is chicken?" And, he wrote, "Since the word 'chicken' standing alone is ambiguous," it was clearly relevant to admit extrinsic evidence as an aid to interpretation. From the theoretical standpoint, then, this case is a clear illustration of the parol evidence rule. The written word (*chicken*) is not "plain and clear and unambiguous," hence extrinsic evidence is appropriate. But what is it about the word that is ambiguous? *Chicken* is not, after all, an example of lexical ambiguity; in fact, from the standpoint of the dictionary, it seems a more than usually precise word. If, to take a common example, someone tells you that he has spent the morning at the bank, you might reasonably (from a lexical standpoint) wonder whether he means the river or the First National. But if he tells you that he likes or doesn't like chicken you are likely to feel, and with reason, that you have some fairly concrete information about his dietary habits. If, then, the word *chicken* "standing alone" is ambiguous, it is not because *chicken* is a particularly ambiguous word.

In fact—and this is Corbin's central point—the judge's sense that *chicken* is ambiguous derives not from the word as it stands alone, but from the extrinsic evidence of conflicting meanings. The word *chicken* itself is neither ambiguous nor vague (nor clear nor precise) and the contract isn't either. To see this clearly, we have only to imagine some alternative sets of circumstances: suppose the defendant had been an old hand at the chicken business and had, like the plaintiff, regularly employed the trade usage in question; or suppose the plaintiff had been a newcomer also and, like the defendant, ignorant of trade usage, understanding by chicken just a kind of fowl. In both cases, the meaning of the contract would have been plain and clear, with its clarity deriving not from less ambiguous or more explicit language (since the language in both cases is identical) but from shared understandings or what Corbin calls "undisputed contexts." And, of course, the meaning of the contract made by the neophytes would have been plainly and clearly different from the meaning of the contract made by the old chicken hands, although again the words would have been the same.

The moral Corbin draws from this story is essentially that the parol evidence rule must be liberally understood. "All rules of interpretation . . . ," he writes, "are mere aids to the court . . . in ascertaining and enforcing the intention of the parties." Evidence of these intentions can, therefore, never be irrelevant. But this does not mean that extrinsic evidence is always admissible. For "the courts are always correct when they say that they must not by interpretation alter or pervert the meaning and intention of the parties," hence,

> When two parties have made a contract and have expressed it in a writing to which they have both assented as the complete and accurate integration of that contract, evidence, whether parol or otherwise, of antecedent understandings and negotiations will not be admitted for the purpose of varying or contradicting the writing.

Thus, where the *Restatement* admits extrinsic evidence only in the case of an ambiguity in the contract itself, Corbin would have required no such *prima facie* ambiguity. He insisted rather that ambiguity is itself a product of extrinsic evidence, and so would have allowed extrinsic evidence at all times so long as it was for the purpose of interpretation and not contradiction or variation (perversion).

As a revision of the *Restatement,* this formulation seems once again reasonable enough but in fact it founders on almost exactly the same terms. For it is reasonable to insist that we allow extrinsic evidence for the purpose of interpreting but not for the purpose of varying a contract only if we can make some neutral distinction between "interpreting" and "varying," some distinction which does not already involve a commitment to a particular interpretation. But this, as Corbin himself had shown, is what we can never do. We can decide whether or not extrinsic evidence will *vary* the writing only after we have decided what the writing means, and our decision about what the writing means is itself dependent on some form of extrinsic evidence, if only that of our own experience. We cannot, therefore, refuse to admit extrinsic evidence on the grounds that it will tend to vary the meaning of the contract without having already admitted extrinsic evidence in deciding what that meaning is. The distinction between interpretation and variation cannot be understood as the neutral and principled distinction Corbin wanted it to be. Interpreting and varying both involve extrinsic categories—the only difference between them is that evidence which according to the judge tends to serve "the purpose of varying or contradicting the writing" will be evidence for an interpretation the judge does not share—which is why it seems to him to vary or contradict the writing. Corbin's insistence that judges refuse to admit evidence that will vary the text thus becomes an exhortation to interpret correctly instead of incorrectly and, as such, has no methodological significance whatsoever.

That Corbin could have been unaware of this contradiction may seem implausible, but actually this kind of blindness on this particular issue is by no means uncommon. In another celebrated case, *Pacific Gas and Electric Co. v. G. W. Thomas Drayage and R. Co.* (442 P. 2d 641), an opinion by Chief Justice Traynor of the California Supreme Court reversed a lower court decision on the grounds that it illegitimately excluded relevant extrinsic evidence. "Although," Traynor wrote, "extrinsic evidence is not admissible to add to, detract from, or vary the terms of a written contract, these terms must first be determined before it can be decided whether or not extrinsic evidence is being offered for a prohibited purpose." This sentence sits squarely on both sides of Corbin's fence. On the one hand, it asserts that the terms of a contract must not be altered by evidence which is extrinsic to the contract; on the other hand, it asserts that what the terms of a contract are can only be discovered by the use of evidence extrinsic to the contract. The implication is that while we must recognize the importance of extrinsic evidence (since to interpret a text is always to invoke some form of extrinsic evidence), we must still insist on a principled way of distinguishing between relevant extrinsic evidence (which will help us toward a correct interpretation) and irrelevant extrinsic evidence (which will serve to vary the contract). But, on Traynor's own terms, there can in principle be no such principle. Relevant evidence will be evidence that supports the interpretation we hold. Irrelevant evidence will be evidence that supports an interpretation with which we disagree.

Literary criticism, needless to say, has no parol evidence rule to guarantee the text's autonomy, but the text has managed quite nicely on its own. The major thrust of "The Intentional Fallacy" was, as we have seen, to establish the priority of the text, insisting simultaneously on the intrinsic and objective character of meaning. The formal study of "the text itself," wrote Wimsatt and Beardsley, "is the true and objective way of criticism." And, in fact, even some of the strongest arguments against Wimsatt and Beardsley have turned out to share some of their most important assumptions. A neat example of this phenomenon is E. D. Hirsch's 1960 essay "Objective Interpretation" (reprinted in his book *Validity in Interpretation*), an argument against what Hirsch saw (in 1960) as the inevitable relativism of formalist criticism and in support of the proposition that meaning is "permanent" and "self-identical" and that "this permanent meaning is, and can be, nothing other than the author's meaning." One of Hirsch's more persuasive examples of the relevance of authorial intention and of the necessity to go outside the text in the effort to discover that intention is the critical controversy over Wordsworth's "A Slumber did my spirit seal." The poem reads as follows:

A slumber did my spirit seal;
  I had no human fears:
She seemed a thing that could not feel
  The touch of earthly years.

No motion has she now, no force;
  She neither hears nor sees;
Rolled round in earth's diurnal course,
  With rocks, and stones, and trees.

Hirsch cites two conflicting interpretations. One emphasizes the poet's " 'agonized shock' " at Lucy's death, his horrified " 'sense of the girl's falling back into the clutter of things . . . chained like a tree to one particular spot, or . . . completely inanimate like rocks and stones.' " The other suggests that the poem climaxes not in horror but in two lines of " 'pantheistic magnificence.' " Lucy's fate is consoling, not shocking, because she " 'is actually more alive now that she is dead . . . she is now a part of the life of nature.' "

These two critics, Cleanth Brooks and F. W. Bateson, agree that Lucy is one with the rocks and stones but they disagree on what exactly is implied by oneness with rocks. The issue, as the judge in *Frigaliment v. B. N. S.* might have said, is "what is a rock?" To a pantheist, of course, rocks are living things, participants, as Bateson says, in "the sublime processes of nature," and if Lucy is rolling around with them she is fairly well off. To almost everyone else, however, rocks are, in Brooks's words, "completely inanimate," and Lucy's kinship with them is indeed unfortunate. The question "what is a rock?" can thus only be answered convincingly once we know whether or not Wordsworth was a pantheist. It cannot be answered by the text itself because the text, as Hirsch notes, permits both interpretations. The available historical evidence, however, seems to indicate that in 1799 (when the poem was written) Wordsworth probably regarded rocks not, according to Hirsch, as "inert objects," but as "deeply alive, as part of the immortal life of nature." Thus, he concludes, until and unless we uncover "some presently unknown data," we are entitled to conclude that Bateson's optimistic reading of the poem is more correct than Brooks's pessimistic one.

This interpretive procedure is clearly similar to the legal procedure in cases which are understood to fall within the province of the parol evidence rule. The text itself is ambiguous (Hirsch prefers the term *indeterminate,* pointing out quite rightly that in literary criticism *ambiguity* tends to signify not the reader's inability to decide what the text means but the author's intention to have it mean more than one thing)—no matter how carefully we read, we cannot decide whether chicken means fryers or stewing chicken or both, whether rocks are alive or dead. Thus we turn to extrinsic evidence to make explicit which of the text's implicit meanings is correct. But to formulate the problem and its solution in these terms is also, I think, to point toward what is wrong with this account. For one thing, as we have already seen, the decision that a text is ambiguous cannot be made prior to the introduction of extrinsic evidence. And for another thing, while seeming to recognize and take into account the difficulty of interpreting a text on its own terms, Hirsch in fact demonstrates exactly the same kind of confidence with regard to intrinsically meaningful extrinsic evidence that the formalist has with regard to the text.

This sounds more paradoxical than it is. Imagine, for example, that rummaging through Dove Cottage, some diligent researcher were to come up with a letter dated February 1799 from Wordsworth to Coleridge, ending with the customary salutations, wish you were here, etc., and then a P.S.—"I have definitely become a pantheist." Such a discovery of "new data" would seem on the face of it to end the matter. Bateson would be proven right; Brooks, if he were in a generous mood, might send him a congratulatory telegram. But it requires little more than a glancing familiarity with the academic (or any other) world to recognize the Utopian character of this scenario. Rather we can imagine supporters of the "dead rocks" thesis maintaining that the postscript was not evidence of Wordsworth's pantheism but was in fact ironic, and hence was evidence of his scepticism in regard to the fundamental sentimentality of the pantheistic view of nature. The whole Lucy cycle, they might claim, insists on the inevitability of loss, on an "asceticism" which is the very denial of pantheistic "mysticism." How then could any critic take seriously such a disingenuously naive declaration of faith? In short, not only would the argument over the poem be simply reproduced in an argument over the postscript, but now the poem would be cited as extrinsic evidence to clear up the ambiguity of the text itself, the postscript.

The point of this example is not to suggest that even in the face of incontrovertible evidence, people will stubbornly maintain their own positions but rather to call into question the notion of incontrovertible evidence. Or, in the terms we have been using, to suggest that explicitness is a function not of language but of agreement. The problem with *rock,* like the problem with *chicken,* is not that it is vague or ambiguous but that it is in dispute. Such a problem cannot be resolved by an appeal to words which are in themselves less vague or ambiguous (there are no such words); it can only be resolved by an appeal to words which are not in dispute. If we agree that "I am a pantheist" meant that Wordsworth was indeed a pantheist, then our dispute over the meaning he attached to the word *rock* will be at an end. If we don't, it won't. The process of adjudication thus depends not on words which have plain meanings and can be used as touchstones against which to measure words whose meanings are not so plain. It depends instead on what Corbin calls "undisputed contexts," agreement on the meaning of one piece of language which can then compel agreement on the meaning of another. No text by itself can enforce such an agreement, because a "text by itself" is no text at all.

To claim, then, as I do, that the phrase *the text itself* is oxymoronic is to argue not that formalism is undesirable and that we should stop being formalists but that formalism is impossible and that no one ever has been a formalist. To read is always already to have invoked the category of the extrinsic, an invocation that is denied, as I suggested earlier, not only by avowedly formalist critics but by all those who think of textual meaning as in any sense intrinsic. Many contemporary legal and literary theorists, for example, are accustomed to thinking of language as inherently "ambiguous" or "undecidable," a position that at least appears to be more responsive to the complexities of contracts and poems than any doctrine of plain meanings. But the trouble with this account is that it simply replaces clarity and precision as properties of language with ambiguity and undecidability. In fact, although some texts are ambiguous, no texts are inherently ambiguous, and although some texts are precise, no texts are inherently precise either. That is the point of chickens and rocks—no text is inherently anything. The properties we attribute to texts are in fact functions of situations, of the contexts in which texts are read.

But, it might be objected at this point, poems are not contracts. Isn't our response to poetic language quite different from our response to legal language, and doesn't this difference manifest itself very clearly in cases like the ones we have been talking about? In *Frigaliment v. B. N. S.,* after all, people stand to win or lose thousands of dollars whereas the values of "A Slumber did my spirit seal" must be calculated quite differently. Aren't chickens and rocks, like apples and oranges, incomparable? Isn't it a fundamental mistake to treat the two texts as if they were the same when they so clearly aren't?

The response to this objection is that while there are indeed differences between poems and contracts, they are institutional, not formal, differences. We can, for example, easily imagine a certain brand of literary critic maintaining that the whole point of "A Slumber did my spirit seal" was the ambiguity of "rocks and stones," emblemizing the poet's and the reader's uncertainty as to what exactly Lucy's absence means. To insist on either reading at the expense of the other, such a critic might maintain, would be to attribute to the poem a sense of resolution that the poet is precisely concerned to deny. Etc. If, on the other hand, the judge in *Frigaliment v. B. N. S.* were to begin this decision by praising the art of the contract makers, their subtle refusal to simplify experience by specifying fryers or stewing chickens, their recognition of the ultimately problematic character of the chicken itself, etc., we would know that something had gone radically wrong. Judges cannot decide that contracts are ambiguous in the same way and for the same reasons that literary critics can. But this is not because legal *language* is less tolerant of ambiguity than poetic language is;

it is because the institution of the law is less tolerant of ambiguity than the institution of literary criticism is. Judges don't read the same way literary critics do.

These differences should not, however, be allowed to obscure some basic similarities. Legal and literary theorists both have been concerned with objectivity, they have attempted to guarantee that objectivity by a theoretical insistence on the primacy of the text, and their theoretical model had broken down when faced with what should, on their own terms, be easy questions—what are chickens? what are rocks? They should be easy because the formalist model assumes that texts have some intrinsic, plain, or literal meaning, a lexical function of the language itself, not of the situations in which the language is being used. And we may have trouble defining *good* or *beautiful,* but we know what *chicken* means and we know what *rock* means. They are hard because our lexicon won't tell us if chickens are fryers or if rocks are dead. Which doesn't mean that *chicken* and *rock* have no plain meanings, but that plain meanings are functions not of texts, but of the situations in which we read them. And which reminds us that the lexicon itself ("chicken: a common domestic fowl," "rock: a concreted mass of stony material") has meaning itself only against a background of assumptions and information which it too can never contain.

J. R. POLE

The Language of American Presidents

AMERICAN POLITICAL SPEECH resembles a low murmur in many dialects of a single language. Above it all, catching the occasional attention of a vast and extraordinarily heterogeneous population, the voice of the president engages with it in a dialogue unlike that of any other nation, and unlike that of any other head of government.

Events affect the language in which they are described. Since the inauguration of Woodrow Wilson in 1913, the Americans have fought four wars; they were the first people to experience the wide diffusion of the products of consumer industries and, in communications, of radio and television; and since the ending of mass immigration they have come to recognize themselves, to a degree which may have been implicit but was hardly anticipated in Wilson's time, as a nation of one law but varied cultures. All these transformations have been reflected, sometimes subtly, sometimes clearly, in the speech of political leadership.

In public life as in private, speech is not always spoken. Wilson adopted the practice, abandoned by Jefferson in 1800, of presenting his messages to Congress in person; later, facing obstacles in Congress, he took the case for the Versailles Treaty to the people

I would like to thank Mr. James Fallows for comments on presidential speech writing and Professor Samuel P. Hays for reading a draft of this essay.

on a back-breaking tour which crippled his health. And Franklin Roosevelt acted in direct continuation of his former chief's style when he went in person to accept his party's nomination and, moreover, made the journey to Chicago by air. As governor of New York, Roosevelt had talked to his constituents on the radio. This practice he developed into the fireside chats by which, for the first time, a president was immediately able to reach the whole of his vast constituency. These gestures were acts of speech which are better remembered now than the contents of the speeches.

Wilson brought to the presidency an innate propensity to moralize, overlaid by a professional training in academic exposition. His first inaugural address would have been an excellent inaugural lecture. "There has been a change of government," he began by observing. "It began two years ago, when the House of Representatives became Democratic by a decisive majority. It has now been completed. . . . What does the change mean? That is the question that is uppermost in our minds to-day. That is the question that I am going to try to answer, in order, if I may, to interpret the occasion." Although he owed his election largely to the Republican split, he did not hesitate to explain it as an expression of the national will. There is an almost Hegelian conviction that the nation possesses a will of which political institutions are mere agencies: "The success of a party means little more than that the Nation is using the party for a large and definite purpose. . . . It seeks to use and interpret a change in its own plans and point of view." In a special message to Congress on trusts and monopolies (January 20, 1914) he speaks again of "the thought and desire of the country." These expressions convey more than the usual politicians' cant phrases about electoral mandates; but Wilson did not command the political power to compel the nation's political representatives, or the electorate itself, to fulfill the details of the message which he interpreted as the thought and desire of the nation. Four years later he went to bed on election night believing that he had lost, to find himself saved next day only by the unexpected swing of California.

Wilson could be comfortably witty when he relaxed with political friends—"The trouble with the Republican party is that it has not had a new idea for thirty years. I am not speaking as a politician; I am speaking as a historian"—but surely he was the only president who would have attacked his opponents for not having new *ideas!* "I would not speak with disrespect of the Republican party," he went on; "I always speak with great respect of the past. . . ." He could also lecture the nation imperiously on its moral shortcomings, as again in his first inaugural: "There has been something crude and heartless and unfeeling in our haste to succeed and be great. Our thought has been 'Let every man look out for himself, let every generation look out for itself,' while we reared giant machinery which made it impossible that any but those who stood at the levers of control should have any chance to look out for themselves."

The intense moral conviction which Wilson brought to the advocacy of his policies was not only conveyed in classically constructed prose; it assisted in converting a style which owed much to the classroom and behind that perhaps something to the Presbyterian pulpit, into a powerful medium of political discourse. Yet Wilson made little if any concession to the concept of a mass audience; his paragraphs and sentences need have differed not at all if he had been writing for academic publication.

In the end, however, Wilson's ironclad moral sense, conveyed in such brilliant and often powerful prose, unhedged by circumlocutions, reservations or doubts, was to founder on the murky shoals of European nationalism; on reality. The disposition not to compromise which made him such an unyielding and eventually such an unsatisfactory negotiator could have been discerned in the faultless certainty with which he eliminated opposition from the political realities with which he had to deal at home.

Wilson was far more keenly aware than his political enemies of the social costs of American industrial progress; and he vetoed immigration bills that were promoted on ill-concealed grounds of racial prejudice. But Wilson and his Republican successors were leaders who reflected and operated through an inherited stratum of social and even racial leadership; none of them spoke or wrote as though they were much aware of addressing a population of the profoundly mixed racial, national, linguistic, religious and educational composition that in fact made up the United States.

It would be difficult to put one's finger on the precise elements of Franklin Roosevelt's diction that convinced so many Americans from all these varied backgrounds that he was *their* president as no former president had ever been. It was partly a matter of a personality that people sensed, as it might later be said that people all over the world sensed the quality of Pope John XXIII without knowing a word of Italian. Roosevelt's directness of speech was quite as clear as Wilson's, but Wilson spoke of suffering seen, Roosevelt of suffering shared. "Then came the crash," he said in his acceptance speech in 1932; and, after enumerating the bald economic facts, "Translate that into human terms. . . ."

Roosevelt never failed to translate statistics and economic facts into human terms and in talking to the people he never condescended to them. Later in the same speech he attacked the Republicans for their economic inactivity: "But while they prate of economic laws, men and women are starving. We must lay hold of the fact that economic laws are not made by nature. They are made by human beings." Nearly six years later, in a fireside chat on economic conditions, he gave a detailed account of the state and problems of the economy. It was not in all respects a completely honest account, since it made no mention of his own resumption of hard money policies in 1937, but it was an intellectually serious exercise, which invited an intelligent response from its audience.

Roosevelt liked to use homely images (a well-dressed gentleman has fallen into the water; a neighbor's house is on fire) but he did so because they were his own familiar style, and it was the authentic translation of this quality into political dialogue that gave him his type of humane eloquence. Roosevelt transformed the relationship between the American presidency and the people. Later presidents could speak in many different styles but they could not revert to the personal seclusion and moral distance of former times. Nixon, in a curious way, came closest to doing so, and disastrously failed.

From the year 1940 a gigantic shadow began to fall across the public speech of America. For Americans, receiving the words but out of earshot of the guns, it was almost as though Winston Churchill had saved the world for freedom by oratory alone. FDR's advisers were even worried about the contrast with their chief's more homely speech. But he knew better. One has only to look at the unadorned power of Roosevelt's campaign language to see that his choice of words, his cumulative short sentences, carried a charge that Americans would not miss or misunderstand.

It was fortunate that Harry Truman had his own brand of straightness that suggested no comparison and ran into no sort of competition with either Churchill or Roosevelt. Truman's very strength lay in the fact that he had no conception of himself as a stylist. "But as for style in speaking or writing, I never had any," he candidly says in *Mr. President.* "Whatever style I had just came naturally, just a natural outgrowth. But I love the style of the Bible, the King James version of the Bible. It is the finest and most stately brand of English there is." But Truman read widely, especially in history, and this shrewdly plain, blunt man also admired Demosthenes and had tried his hand at translating Cicero.

The postwar period brought certain trends which are easier to identify in the country's social and political history but which were reflected in its political language as well. Consensus America, particularly after the ravages of McCarthyism had begun to subside, was increasingly tolerant of its own genuinely pluralistic character, which was only accentuated by the white South's fierce, misguided resistance to desegregation. There may have been no intrinsic need for this social trend to take any particular linguistic direction. But other influences were at work on the language. One of the most potent was the slick and superficial style introduced by *Time* magazine, which rendered ideas palatable by trapping them, denatured, in transparent capsules; another was the insistent and pervasive language of the salesman and, as Adlai Stevenson once put it, the litany of the singing commercial. (The intellectuals' devotion to Stevenson was certainly in part a grateful response to his own style, his insistence on the value of fine distinctions and his unfashionable willingness to use irony.)

George Orwell, in his essay, "Politics and the English Language," written shortly after the Second World War, observed that the whole tendency of modern prose was away from concreteness (and also that in our time most political speech was the defense of the indefensible). Orwell's genius was for interpreting portents, and what he foresaw was perhaps to grow even worse in America than in England.

An infiltration of bureaucratic speech, deriving partly from the war, partly from the actually increasing bureaucracy and partly from an increasingly Germanic sociology, demoralized and disarmed large parts of the academic and journalistic worlds, and entered deeply into the realm of public communication. The audience was increasingly assumed to be either semiliterate or of subnormal intelligence. Tenses got out of alignment, descriptive designations were used as though they were personal titles, conditionals and subjunctives mistook each other's identity, and Orwell's perception was finding its mark in the new verbal democracy. What mattered was no longer the precise meaning (which might be a sign of overeducation) but the general idea, which could be conveyed as much by the packaging as by the content. It was perhaps a significant product of the same period that the third edition of Webster's *Dictionary of the American Language* (1961), under preparation during these years, departed from the conventional principle that each word had a correct usage, upon which others were either variants, or were incorrect, and took the novel stand that all current usage was to all intents and purposes correct usage. All words are created equal.

Not all of these trends revealed themselves at once in presidential speech, and the nation over which Dwight Eisenhower presided from 1953 to 1961 was increasingly prosperous, increasingly pleased with itself and correspondingly unself-critical. Although Eisenhower himself was not a loose thinker (and he was a sharp reader of proofs, too) he conveyed an impression of ease which almost amounted to negligence. He probably wrote very little of what passed in his name, but nearly all of his press conference answers began with "Well . . ." and many of them continued by disclaiming whatever expertise the question seemed to require. Reporters enjoyed their sense of superiority over the presidential syntax, but the nation, or large parts of it, got the impression that there was nothing much to worry about, which was no doubt exactly what their president intended. The procedure could be carried too far, however. Over the crisis of Little Rock the president gave the impression of being only dimly concerned, and he left it to others to convey his administration's guidance on the nation's one central issue of civil rights.

The contrast between Eisenhower's informal style and Truman's is striking. Eisenhower talked as though speech had been an awkwardly acquired capability; Truman was prompt, blunt and often entertaining, not so much from verbal wit as from an undisguised relish in the situation. His remarks contained few memorable phrases, and their force—which survives the passage of years—derives from their immediacy, and from a distinct sense of sharing the whole situation with the reporters, an attitude that was completely alien to his successor.

Truman's utterances, even on the more formal occasions, tended to be lacking in cadence. Eisenhower's (with rare exceptions) were lacking in the more important attribute of that emotional force which gives conviction to ordinary language. His indifference to intellectual precision became notorious, and many intellectuals resented the apparent flabbiness of the Eisenhower era—which had not been improved by such coinages as *finalize,* and from which the term *Eisenhoverian* has been derived for inelegant and unnecessary neologisms. Eisenhower was not responsible for the drift of his time, but his style reflected it with a nonchalant fidelity which encouraged loose writing and soft thinking in others; a president is closely watched, and as Stevenson as the leader of a major party showed, has it in his power to set a tone to which others must at least reply. In politics it was principally the style of Stevenson, and in more general literature the recognition of such rare stylists as Richard Hofstadter, that saved the reading public from sinking into a soapy euphoria in which the way things were said was no longer considered to matter: from which stage it is but a short step to the things themselves.

Irony was a significant case. Politicians and other public speakers, including university lecturers, seemed afraid of it, as though they feared the risk, either of being taken at face value or, if correctly understood, of being regarded as snobs. Such fears did not inhibit Stevenson, who spoke of the Republicans as having to be "dragged kicking and screaming into the twentieth century" and who offered them the bargain, "If you stop telling lies about us we'll stop telling the truth about you." During the New Deal years, FDR had known how to be fiercely ironical. "Some of these people," he told a campaign rally in 1936, "really forget how sick they were. But I know how sick they were. I have their fever charts. I know how the knees of all the rugged individualists trembled four years ago and how their hearts fluttered. They came to Washington in great numbers. Washington did not look like a dangerous bureaucracy to them then. Oh, no! It looked like an emergency hospital. . . . And now most of the patients seem to be doing very nicely. Some of them are even well enough to throw their crutches at the doctor." Coming from Roosevelt, who was in no position to do the same thing, the effect has to be imagined.

After the Eisenhower era, John Kennedy made a deliberate return to conscious literary standards of public discourse, and some of his public statements begin to show signs of the strain. He liked to achieve his effects by tight constructions, which often posed alternatives in close apposition. "Ask not what your country can do for you—ask what you can do for your country" (in which *country* is the only word of more than one syllable) has become trite with quotation, but remains an obvious example—and one which had political significance from the leader of the party which had engineered America's welfare state. Kennedy knew the force of strong, short words: "But peace in space will help us naught once peace on earth is gone." ("Short words are best and old words best of all"—Churchill.) In this sentence an effect of monosyllabic austerity is modified by the archaism of *naught*. But Kennedy, who scrutinized these questions with his speech writers, knew that rhetorical eloquence is no substitute for meaning what you say. When his use of language comes to be studied the thing to be looked for in his effects is not so much rhythm (which Nixon claimed to value above everything else) as economy.

Kennedy understood exactly what, unfortunately, Richard Nixon could not afford to acknowledge. No president in recent times has contributed so much of his own to his public statements as Nixon, an admirer of Woodrow Wilson, who was also—too consciously perhaps—influenced by Churchill. The influence he would not have wished to admit was that of the TV commercial. But here is Nixon in 1952, fighting for his political life in the "Checkers" speech: "And remember, folks, Eisenhower is a great man. Folks, he is a great man. . . ." This was early Nixon, and he later eliminated such crudities, but he never eliminated, because it was part of his character, the search for applause and the repeated exhibition of a curiously piteous form of self-dramatization.

Nixon had learnt the importance of linguistic architecture, no doubt primarily from Wilson and Churchill, but the trouble was that the frame showed through the plaster. His acceptance speech in 1968 exemplified Orwell's prediction; all the visions of the future he offered his party and the American people were inflated abstractions, so devoid of specific content that they committed no one to anything—and led to considerable subsequent doubts about where he stood on civil rights. Nixon used here a simple Rooseveltian device, that of emphatic repetition. "I see a day when Americans are once again proud . . . I see a day when every child in this land . . . I see a day when life in rural America attracts . . . I see a day when [but this required an uncomfortable wrench of the neck] we can look back on massive breakthroughs. . . ." When FDR used that technique, he did it to arouse the too easily satisfied American conscience: "I see one-third of a nation, ill-clad, ill-housed, ill-nourished." And this he used again and again.

Nixon's address to the nation on the Vietnam War, on 3 November 1969, is said to have been almost entirely his own work, and correspondingly characteristic. The structure of the argument is clear, the weighing of issues is solemn, but that effect is qualified by the extraordinary bathos of his implicit appeals for personal sympathy. Less than ten months after taking office, he is already openly thinking of the next election—which, he rightly assures the voters, is less important than the search for a satisfactory peace. Is Johnson's war to become Nixon's war? That is the question that weighs on the president's too plainly revealed, although furtive, consciousness; and he gives as a *personal* reason for wanting to end the war that he has to write letters of sympathy to bereaved families.

Nixon betrayed the fact that he did not respect the people to whom he had to appeal, which may (we can at least conjecture) have derived from some profoundly buried lack of self-respect. He dismissed the suggestion of going on TV to use (risk?) his own popularity to fight congressional tax cutting with, "No. You can't explain economics to the American people." This dismissal of the intellectual competence of the American people was a significant departure from the expectations of Wilson, or of Roosevelt or Truman. Presidents sometimes reveal themselves among friends, and also among enemies. When Nixon took the apparently bold step of addressing the AFL-CIO convention in November 1972, he admitted to them that he had been advised not to go. "I'll tell you why I came here," he then said. "Because while some of you may be against me politically and some of you may be against my party I know from experience from the last three years that when the chips are down organized labor's for America and that's why I'm here before this convention today." This strange *non sequitur* was not only irrelevant but downright insulting. Organized labor did not require to be told that it was "for America," of which, after all, it formed a very large and indispensable part, and George Meany restored the meeting's humor and accurately reflected the theatrical nature of the performance after the president's departure by saying, "We will now go on to Act Two."

Nixon used the English language with care and not without scholarship. He could and sometimes did mount an argument of considerable power. But like his contemporary Sir Harold Wilson, he lacked the power of looking as though he was telling the truth, and perhaps for similar reasons: that too many thoughts, other than the content of the speech, were running through his scanning mechanism at the same time. Yet Nixon deserves credit for the invocation of "the great silent majority," a phrase worked into his speech of 3 November 1969 with the unobtrusive skill of a craftsman, which he is. He could also be unexpectedly witty, as when, on a formal social occasion, he overcame the awkwardness of the appointment as British ambassador of John Freeman, former editor of the *New Statesman,* who had denounced him abusively: "He's the new diplomat and I'm the new statesman."

Nixon and Johnson both suffered from a novel difficulty among American presidents: half of the country at least did not believe they were telling the truth. Neither of them could overcome this, and the strain told increasingly though in different ways. Johnson, who had no formal eloquence, liked to itemize his points after a brief general statement, and as a practical politician among professionals he could argue with considerable power. His way of expounding his decision to go on with the war on 29 September 1967 was extremely skillful. He admitted the difficulty of being sure of the right course, mentioned evidence for either view, but then invited his audience to weigh the reasons for believing that withdrawal would lead to further and greater dangers. His method was to leave the opposition with the right to their own views but to leave with them also the responsibility for the consequences of following those views: for his own part he accepted the full responsibility of going on with the war. Lyndon Johnson failed to convince the American public, and eventually recognized the loss of authority—literally reflected by the vogue word *credibility*—by his dignified decision not to seek reelection in 1968.

It is perfectly possible to tell lies in flawless English, as many presidents and prime ministers have shown, but it is much more difficult to speak persuasively on matters of great technical complexity or moral difficulty in defective English. Mr. Carter, who is by training an engineer, and who possesses possibly the most analytically competent mind to have occupied the White House in this century, talks a language that owes much to the procedures of technical exposition. He seems to eschew deliberated eloquence, and although he finds time for reading, it would be difficult to find in his pronouncements any clear sense of continuity with political literature. He often seems satisfied to be understood almost exactly as the writer of a technical manual means to be understood, and is seldom concerned to arouse sentiment which will help to convince his audience. This style clearly reflects his rapid and thorough but basically mechanical grasp of complex problems.

On occasions, however, when he does want to convey his own feelings the effect varies immensely with his audience. His inaugural address was very bad; it was suffused with images of rebirth and dreamery, it recognized with a modest, practical humility the limitations of what could be achieved, but concluded by invoking "an undiminished, ever-expanding American dream." Whatever might be the effects of an expanding dream spreading over the American people, it was not the stuff that politics are made on, or with which he was going to confront the nation or Congress. He did far better when he began his first "fireside chat" on energy by telling his audience with almost Churchillian bluntness, "Tonight I want to have an unpleasant talk with you about a problem unprecedented in our history. With the exception of preventing war, this is the greatest challenge our country will face in our lifetimes. The energy crisis has not yet overwhelmed us, but it will do if we do not act quickly." The long shadow reached down to 24 October 1978 when in his national address on inflation, Mr. Carter accepted—rather reluctantly—a wartime quotation from Winston Churchill: "What sort of people do they think we are?" In this speech, Mr. Carter took a cautious step toward mixing moral persuasion with economic analysis.

When talking to groups with whom he feels at home—"at ease," he might say, as it seems to be one of his preferred phrases—he can be transformed into an old-style Southern preacher from whom language flows with his breath. He created an astounding sensation in a meeting with the congressional black caucus in September 1978 by addressing them as no former president could ever have done, as "brothers and sisters," and his speech, which began with St. Matthew, actually developed into a call-and-response style sermon. Calling on Rosa Parks, who by refusing to stand up precipitated the great bus boycott in Montgomery, Alabama, in 1957, he quoted her own words and concluded, "Well, we've got a long way to walk in the future. We'll walk together. Our feet may be tired, but when we get through our soul will be rested."

In this setting Mr. Carter, who has too much respect for the people to talk down to them, was able to transcend the distance between himself and his audience, but most of the time he has seemed to fear any sense of distance at all. A president, however, must stand somewhat apart, as all great presidents have known instinctively. Then the language which has the power to survive its own utterance is the most likely to move those to whom it is immediately spoken.

J. ENOCH POWELL

The Language of Politics

TO SIT DOWN to write about "the English of politics now" is to be appalled by the difficulty of finding any objective instruments which would prevent description from being mere whimsy or subjective guesswork.

It is possible certainly to identify *a priori* some of the influences which might have made the English of politics in 1980 different from what it was in 1880—different, that is to say, in ways additional to those in which all or any English of 1980 is different from the English of 1880. Even at the outset, however, unanswerable queries arise. How, for instance, are the standard differences, so to speak, to be distinguished from those specific to political English? Where does one go to find an analysis of the vocabulary gained and lost, the constructions invented and abandoned, the meanings altered, the changes in sentence form and structure which occurred during the century? Even if such an analysis were procurable, it would have had to be founded upon a comprehensive survey of all kinds and purposes of speech, including that of politics.

To press the same point further by posing one particular case, it is surely to be assumed that the extensions of the franchise between 1880 and 1980 must have tended to replace the sort of diction addressed by educated gentlemen to others of the same background by language calculated to be attractive and intelligible to mass audiences of widely diverse attainments and knowledge. One might go further and point to the near elimination from the education of the average Englishman of two great formative influences, acquaintance with at least the Latin classics and knowledge of the King James Bible, from which it would follow that both the conscious and the unconscious echo of those originals must have almost disappeared. These general and harmlessly uncontentious observations having been made, however, how is it possible to disentangle the consequent changes which are specific from those which are general? How far would the disappearance of latinity and Jacobean English from political harangues be due to the change in the electorate rather than to changes in education and religion generally?

The mere reference to "political harangues" opens up another vista of incurable uncertainty: where does political English begin and end? Is it restricted to speech in Parliament or does it include speech at political public meetings and on the hustings? Is it restricted to that used by politicians themselves or does it include leading articles in *The Times* and the *Daily Express* when they are on political topics? I could point to numerous influences which in my opinion might have altered parliamentary English—the increasing demand for brevity in speeches, the alteration in the class composition of the two houses, the increasing professionalism attempted or pretended by politicians themselves, even the altered racial composition of the House of Commons through the disappearance of the Irish component—but I have no reason to suppose that these have affected political English outside Parliament. In short, what sorts of changes are common to all forms of political speech without being also common to English speech in general?

Fresh embarrassments present themselves at every turn. Changes in fashion, in scientific knowledge, in popular prejudices are almost bound to produce their effects upon vocabulary and diction; and because politics is peculiarly a realm where what is fashionable holds sway, these changes will often be luxuriantly exemplified in political speech. Yet it would be a falsification to present as characteristic of political English something which is only the impress of current modes of thought and expression. There is a particular degeneration of speech, which has flourished during the last ten or fifteen years, consisting in periphrases formed with the word *situation*. Thus a war becomes "a war situation," two rival mobs are not fighting but "in a conflict situation," a firm losing money has "moved into a loss situation," partly due perhaps to having been "*involved*" (a related periphrastic word) "in strike situations." I have little doubt that the quite pathological popularity of this periphrasis, which has wreaked havoc in political English, derives from the current popularity of the environmentalist theory of human behavior: people are supposed to behave as they do because of the situations in which they find themselves, and to be the creatures, not to say the victims, of their circumstances.

Finally—to make an end of the tedious accumulation of difficulties—about *which* politician's English are we talking? In every respect—vocabulary, syntax, sentence structure, rhetoric—one politician probably differs more from another politician than all politicians collectively, if we could make a composite photograph, differ from nonpoliticians collectively. Ernest Bevin seldom finished a sentence, though *Hansard* finished a good many for him. Michael Foot on the other hand has rarely left a sentence unfinished. Which, if either of them, represents the English of politics now?

I am not arguing that it is impossible to record and characterize the English of politics now in a strict sense of the terms. What I am saying is that to do so in any objective or scientific manner would require a massive processing of material which only a computer could cope with. No doubt some university which is better endowed with computer time than with fruitful subjects for research will set a team to work on first establishing a record of standard English today, by way of control and then comparing it with a balanced sample of political English. Not having a computer or a university to hand and suspecting that, if I had, I would not employ them in that way, I propose to do something infinitely more modest and grossly arbitrary. I am going to take four speeches made in the House of Commons, seventy and ninety years ago, and two made there in the last thirty years. In the past and in the present samples I shall include one speech by an acknowledged outstanding orator on a great occasion, and one, albeit on an important occasion, by a speaker whom no one ever accused of being an orator. I intend to examine them closely to see what, if anything, comes out of so limited and random a sample. The four are Gladstone introducing the first Irish Home Rule Bill in 1886; Campbell-Bannerman speaking to the Address on becoming prime minister in 1906; Aneurin Bevan moving the Second Reading of the National Health Service Bill in 1946; and Edward Heath concluding the debate of principle in 1971 on British entry into the European Economic Community. It is convenient to attempt to characterize first the contemporary specimens, and then to treat the earlier ones as a "control."

Though introducing a measure of great comprehensiveness and complexity Aneurin Bevan did so in much under 9,000 words, including brief responses to a few brief interruptions; he got them off in 73 minutes, which, at 123 words a minute, is fast by oratorical standards—I personally find it safe with a platform speech to assume an average of no more than a hundred. Yet Bevan was evidently sensitive to the length of his speech and twice apologized for it. The average length of a sentence was 18 words and of a word 4.9 letters. As to vocabulary, *situation,* though not yet sociological, had made its appearance: "the actual situation as it exists" (tautology and trite at that); "one of the tragedies of the situation"; "it will not affect the existing situation." So had the verb *involved,* which in later years was to become, not least in Edward Heath's mouth, the prince of periphrases, against much the same background as *situation;* "a person ought to be able to receive medical help without being involved in financial anxiety"—where the words *being involved in* could be omitted altogether. There is also one sociological *ism:* "defend the very small hospital on the ground of its *localism.*"

A good deal of verbal attrition is noticeable, from the overfrequent intensive *very* to such terms as *carry out* ("carrying out all these principles and services"), *quite frankly,* "the best *solution of the difficulty,*" or the overuse of *field* (another sociologism?): "consultations have taken place over a very wide field," "they cover a very wide field indeed," "when we come to the general practitioners, we are of course in an entirely different field." This attrition sometimes descends to slovenly colloquialism: "the whole thing is the wrong way round"; the voluntary hospitals "came along" (i.e., arose); "problems that I was up against"; "to go along for a consultation."

Bevan had his own personal favorite words, *priority, frivolously, instrument,* and *fructify* (the last no doubt from Gladstone). But the most striking feature of his diction is the number of expressions, especially metaphorical, which are slightly misused through insensitivity to their exact or etymological meaning: *denigrate* in the sense of "depreciate"; *repulsion* instead of "revulsion"; "*repugnant* to a civilised community for hospitals to have to rely upon private charity"; "*communal* interests" instead of "common" or "general"; "achieve reasonable and *efficient* homogeneity"; "the health services are to be *articulated* to the health centre"; "endowments *waived* by Scottish Acts" (in the sense of "diverted"); "an *elastic, resilient* service" (which? not both?); "this is a *field* in which *idiosyncracies* are *prevalent,*" meaning that individual preferences vary.

I noted only one quotation (implicit): "the *vaulting ambitions* of those in charge"—and that, without particular point—and several slightly off-beam metaphors: "hope before long to build up a high tradition"; "a young man gets a load of debt around his neck"; "I am astonished that such a charge should lie in the mouth of any Member" (meaning simply "be made by"); "freedom of movement inside a budget." However, it would be churlish not to end with a splendid Bevanism, which illustrates his way of using metaphor with ironic humor: "I would rather be kept alive in the efficient if cold altruism of a large hospital than expire in a gush of warm sympathy in a small one."

Edward Heath's windup of the debate on British entry into the European Community was compressed by the convention of the house into the last half hour before the vote—4,000 words at 136 a minute. The average length of a sentence was nearly 23 words, and of a word 4.4 letters.

The most marked feature of the language is the quantity of metaphor eroded to the point of cliché: "to set this against a world *canvas*"; "move along the *path* to real unity"; "the position *facing* the western world"; "fit into the *framework* of European unity"; "should any of the apprehensions . . . materialise, then the *machinery* exists to deal with them." Perhaps the bureaucratic clichés "*play* an increasing *part*" and "*vitally* affect the *balance* of forces" (though mixed) are no longer metaphors at all; but the only live metaphor in the speech was "no one is sitting there waiting to have an amicable cup of tea with the leader of the Opposition."

There is a profusion of situational periphrases: "in the *situation* which I have described, the United States is bound to *find itself involved* more and more with the large economic powers"; "new institutions have been invented to meet the realities of the new *situation*"; "the position in Europe today is that . . . the *situation* has been transformed by China." The interesting periphrastic verbs are *dealing with* and *handle,* which I suggest are not merely characteristic of Edward Heath personally but denote the modern view of politics as a sort of engineering. "When it comes to *dealing with* the major economic powers in creating what has now to be a changed policy"; "we must see how these *problems* can best be *handled* by Britain"; "these matters are being *handled* the whole time"; "we differ on how best this can be *handled*"; "the necessary and appropriate means for *dealing with* the problems of its members." More prominent than *problem* as a nonword is *question:* "the *questions* of larger firms, technology, capital investment and rate of growth are of immense importance"—so they may be, if only we were asked them; "what is important is the *question* of being in the best possible position to influence economic decisions," where *the question of being* merely means "to be."

Of single vocables the most significantly prominent is *world*. "A *world* canvas" has already been quoted; "the *world* was watching New York . . . tonight the *world* is watching Westminster"; "the balance of forces in the *modern world*"; "the position facing the *western world* today"; "on the *world* scene against which we must set this debate"; "an outward-looking aspect towards *the developing world;* our influence in Europe and the *world*"; those parts of the *world* which still lie in the shadow of want"; "many millions of people right across the *world* will rejoice." The significance is not of course purely verbal—that the abstraction *world* has been talked into a part of speech—but that its prevalence marks the extent to which external systems of thought and values have come to dominate political action.

Quotations or conscious allusions do not occur at all in the speech; and the one slightly allusive term turns out to be a malapropism: "by some strange *permutation of history* in this very short span all these changes have come together," where *permutation* is used, in defiance of etymology, in the sense of "coincidence" or "conjuncture."

Turning back almost ninety years to Gladstone's introduction of the first Home Rule Bill on 8 April 1886, it is hard not to be overwhelmed by the sheer magnificence of an oration of over 19,000 words, pronounced (so far as the Official Report goes) without interruption at a speed of under 100 words a minute in nearly 3½ hours. "I sometimes thought," he wrote in his diary, "it could never end." Nevertheless some objective contrasts can be identified which may be typical rather than Gladstonian. The average length of words is lower—as low as 4.3—but the length of average sentence is high, at 30 words, covering an enormous range, modulated on a wavelike pattern, from 90 words or more to half a dozen. A characteristic *diminuendo* is the following sequence: 40, 37, 14, 22, 27, 9, 7; or again 86, 47, 23, 17, 6. In sentence construction the prevalence of the rhetorical trick of *anaphora* is impressive. It takes the form both of iteration ("it must be *different, differently* maintained and maintained with a *different* spirit, courage and consistency"—a marvellous sentence, with its balancing triplets, and subtle use of assonance) and of repeating the beginning of a sentence after a parenthetical self-interruption.

Despite its rhetoric, the speech has an intimacy like that of chamber music, the intimacy of a speaker playing with an audience he knows and who know him: "it may not seem much to say, but wait for what is coming" (note the effect of the monosyllables). A fully political use is made of circumlocution: "we have arrived at a point where it is necessary that we should take a careful and searching survey of our position"—a modern "situation"-monger need not blush too deeply after reading that. Metaphor is modest, and mingles the trite ("look this problem in the face") with the noble: "Stripping law of its foreign garb and investing it with a domestic character," where a consciousness of the etymology of *invest* is necessary to full enjoyment. Equally rare, perhaps surprisingly so, is quotation or allusion: in the first half of the gigantic speech I have noted one only: "There is the head and fruit of our offending," and even that both misquotes and, in its context, misapplies *Othello* 1.3.81.

The vocabulary is less impregnated with the language of contemporary political notions than would have been expected—unless indeed the modern reader is tone-deaf to them. The word *world* already noted as a myth word today, was colorless and literal then ("that manufacturing industry which overshadows the whole world"), while *empire*—shimmering between U.K. and British Empire—was already irrationally emotive ("this great, noble and world-wide empire"). If there is an overworked adverb, it is probably *infinitely;* but there is a remarkable absence of cheap emphasis. Even high Victorian sentiment and self-righteousness have to be looked for with a lantern before a few mild specimens can be turned up: "advanced in the career of liberal principles and actions"; "our ineffectual and spurious coercion is morally worn out."

I confess that when I came to Campbell-Bannerman's prime ministerial speech, the last of my four chosen specimens, I was dismayed; for it turned out to be a speech presenting no apprehensible characteristics of vocabulary, diction or construction whatever. But the dice must be allowed to lie where they fall: it is as well to be reminded that political speech can—at least could—be perfectly colorless in the mouth of a practitioner who by then had had nearly forty years in the collar.

The statistical count is unremarkable: average sentence length almost 28 words, substantial but behind Gladstone; average word length 4.6 letters. The only quotation or allusion in the whole speech was simply a continuation of the use which the preceding speaker, Joseph Chamberlain, had made of a passage from Sydney

Smith. At most a certain tendency to pleonasm, not unpleasant if a trifle pompous, can be detected: "he shrinks *in some measure* from a *public* appearance in the House" is really absurd, since a member—especially a foreign secretary (as here)—either does or does not appear in the house, and if he does is bound to do so publicly. Orotund, too, is a certain fondness for not leaving a noun without an adjective: "extraordinary circumstances," "strenuous observations," "lamentable circumstances," "perfect amity." Metaphor is well worn, too worn: "temperance is the keystone, or the cornerstone, of the edifice of the prosperity of this country"; "the late Government wished to have a pistol in their hands in order to terrify foreign nations"; "last session there was no disclosure: we knocked at every door that we could find."

When all is done, one is forced to admit that the attempt to find anything specifically political in the selected specimens has ended in a negative. Whether "ancient" or "modern," whether great oratory or run-of-the-mill discourse, the English remains undifferentiated, the English of the day, such as would have been spoken by contemporaries, or by the speakers themselves, on any other subject or in any other walk of life. Politics on one side, the changes are less over the course of ninety years than would probably have been expected. There is now a certain tendency to greater brevity, a certain increased susceptibility to the infection of cliché; but it would be hard to argue that the change is from the speech of more educated to that of less educated men, or from the expectations of a smaller audience of gentlemen to those of a wider audience of plebeians. The language in short has remained remarkably standard: in terms of a century, in the mouth of politicians, English now is hardly to be distinguished from English then.

ROBIN TOLMACH LAKOFF

When Talk Is Not Cheap: Psychotherapy as Conversation

As competent speakers of English we know the pronunciation of words, what they mean, their preferable order in sentences, and what combinations of words are permissible. But to be really competent we must have information of a more abstract and implicit kind. We must know what constitutes a conversation, and what is appropriate at any particular part of one. There are general principles that hold for all types of discourse, for all languages; but there are also particular constraints, some restricted to speakers of English, and, even more specialized, to members of a single ethnic group or social class. Research in conversational analysis has shown that the competent speaker respects these principles and constraints, at an unconscious level most often, and therefore can distinguish between appropriate and inappropriate utterances.[1]

However, to determine what constitutes an appropriate utterance, we need to explore the nature of conversation, and we cannot do this without specifying the various contexts in which it occurs. What is suitable for a two-person informal conversation would be strange in a lecture. As children we learn a set of rules for proper participation in conversation, and, more generally, for the production of discourse, by observation, imitation, correction, and, at the same time, by engagement in what Gregory Bateson calls "deutero learning" of conversational strategy[2]—that is, learning how to learn new and different rules. So when a child who has known only how to talk to parents goes off to school, he or she is able to figure out the different system required for conversation with the teacher. The teacher may lecture, the child not. The kinds of questions asked and answers given also differ between teacher and child. But the child has already learned that conversation is divisible into two broad types: reciprocal and nonreciprocal. In a reciprocal conversation, between peers, both participants may produce the same kinds of utterances: both may question, and respond; both may make personal statements and may be equally inquisitive about the other's personal life. Both may give and receive instructions and injunctions. But in nonreciprocal discourse, as between child and parent, the options for both are limited. Parents may question children deeply about their personal activities; children may not so question their parents. Parents may give orders, children may not. Parents may explain; children may indicate a lack of knowledge. Traditionally, these roles may not be reversed, just as, traditionally, parents call children by first names or nicknames; while children address parents by title, rather than name.

How does this discourse-learning take place, and until what age does it go on? Are adults capable of learning new kinds of conversational strategies? Under what circumstances will they submit to such learning? What is entailed in the learning of a new conversational system? Are all the old assumptions cast off, or is it merely the perspective that is changed? If we could find a type of discourse that is typically learned by adults, we would have an interesting case to study, within which to explore these questions. The existence of such a case would imply that there is at least one type of discourse to which children are not exposed, and only adults are apt to want to learn; and, further, that learning new forms of conversational interaction continues into adulthood. The conversational strategy learned by participants in psychotherapeutic encounters appears to be just such a case, specifically those types of therapy in which verbal interchange is crucial to the process—from traditional psychoanalytic therapy through the more recent developments of the so-called human potential movement.

It should be no surprise that these various therapeutic systems have left their imprint on the English language: the way we talk, along with the way we think and feel, has been deeply influenced by our discovery that conversation both reveals and influences the workings of the psyche—the basic justification for verbal psychotherapy.

The most obvious imprint has been on our vocabulary. From classical psychoanalytic theory alone, we have adopted or given old words new meanings: *complex, object, repression, identity*—to give a mere handful. (If we considered the contributions of newer therapies this list would be increased exponentially.) More subtly, and very significantly, the abstract elements of our linguistic repertoire have been profoundly altered by psychotherapy. Our ideas about what constitutes a person's character and how behavior is talked about have been irretrievably altered; and, most important, yet least observable of all, our notions about how to hold a conversation, what is necessary or permissible in ordinary discourse, have been given new form under the influence of the psychotherapeutic model.

Psychotherapy developed by borrowing (intuitively) the model of the ordinary conversation; and its rules became the basis of psychotherapeutic conversation, as Freud first (1911–1915) pointed out.[3] Now we see ordinary conversation repaying the loan with interest: psychotherapy has utilized possibilities inherent, but unrealized, in ordinary conversation, stretching those possibilities to its limits and beyond; and now we take psychotherapeutic discoveries and make them a part of our everyday discourse.

In utilizing the mechanisms and assumptions of ordinary conversation, psychotherapeutic conversation recontextualizes them so that they have a different meaning. It is not that we learn new rules in the therapeutic process, but rather we learn new applications for the old rules. So, learning to be in therapy is not like learning French; that is, not like learning a new grammar, only a new way of looking at a familiar grammar.

For instance, in any conversation, the participants must feel that they are getting some benefit from it, or they will not continue to engage in it or resume it later. This benefit is sometimes purely informative: if I ask street directions of you, I will be satisfied with that information alone. But more often, in social settings, we require emotional benefit: the sense that others like conversing with us and are doing it gladly. In such conversations, information is of course often exchanged, but it serves largely as an excuse for the real purpose of the discourse—emotional satisfaction. We give signals, overt or covert, that this need is being met.

We can do this by maintaining an appearance of spontaneity, which implies that the participants are engaging in the discourse of their own free will. We must not look as if we are conversing under compulsion—so making appointments strictly to talk is normally avoided ("Let's meet for lunch"); or, if essential, it is mitigated by an effusion of small talk and shows of camaraderie at the outset. Similarly, leave-taking must never appear to be pleasurable or desired. One departs from a conversation by pleading a commitment elsewhere: "I have to get back," not "I want to go somewhere else now." It is significant too that beginnings and endings of conversations—the stickiest points in attesting to the spontaneity of the desire to talk to someone else—are ritualized; there are socially sanctioned forms that must be followed for these parts of the conversation and not the middle part. This helps soften the awkwardness of establishing contact and breaking it.

Not only the form, but the permissible topics and the way they are dealt with are calculated for the purpose of achieving emotional benefit. The participants must feel that they are equals in the discourse, and that their participation is reciprocal. Each has equal need of the other's contributions. For this reason, the conversation itself is sufficient as recompense for holding it; to offer or accept money from others for talking to them is inconceivable ordinarily. For the same reason, each participant has the same conversational obligations and opportunities. If one can ask questions and expect answers, so can the other. And if one can ask questions about personal matters and expect straight answers rather than indignation—"none of your business!"—so can the other. It is rude for one person to ask another about, say, his or her income, be answered directly, and then, asked the same question in turn, refuse to reply or hedge the reply. Participants in informal conversation must all follow the same rules. In this respect the informal conversation is different from, say, the lecture, where reciprocity is not assumed to be in effect. There the benefit to nonspeakers is assumed to be intellectual rather than emotional. No need to worry about emotional satisfaction.

One compliment we are expected to pay to other participants is that their utterances make sense to us; they are rational. To suggest that another is speaking nonsense or cannot be understood is to risk grave insult. Hence, interpretation has generally not been considered a permissible option in conversation between adults: to say "What you meant when you said *X* was *Y*" is to suggest that the other person did not know what he or she meant, and therefore was not in control of his or her behavior.

Psychotherapeutic conversation ignores all of these assumptions about permissible discourse and it is neither intellectually nor emotionally gratifying *per se* to the participants, at least not as we normally perceive conversational gratification. Further, the discourse is not reciprocal in either topic or form. The patient soon learns that each partner may perform only one particular subset of possible conversational actions: the relationship is symbiotic rather than reciprocal.

Symbiosis, in the therapeutic setting, means: though the two partners do different things, their roles are distinguished precisely to benefit both of them. So, while in ordinary conversation it is reciprocity that confers benefit, in therapy it is the clear-cut division of roles, the symbiosis. In the many therapeutic frameworks devised over the last century, this division of roles has been variously perceived and realized. The classical psychoanalytical model makes the distinction between the roles and powers of the participants most clearly—by physical position, terms of address, and types of permissible contribution, for example—but all therapeutic systems in one way or another make it clear that the therapist has the power and the patient or client the need, that the rules are determined by the therapist, and that the therapist decides what is permissible or necessary. Meetings are held in the therapist's territory, begun and ended at the therapist's convenience.[4]

In some ways classical analysis resembles the lecture more than the conversation. One person holds the floor; the other may intervene with a brief question or comment, but no more—usually when the first indicates a readiness for such a contribution. What is strange—bizarre, even—is that while in the lecture the holder of authority also holds the floor (an intuitively reasonable position), in analysis these roles are split.

In newer types of therapy, we find a style more closely resembling normal conversational turn-taking: each participant speaks and listens, in more or less equal measure. But this similarity to ordinary conversation is deceptive, since the roles assigned to participants—implicitly rather than overtly—differ. Patients soon learn that there are questions they may ask, and others they may not; that there are questions directed to the therapists that the latter are expected to answer, others they need not answer. So patients may be asked—with the expectation of a direct response—questions about their intimate lives, while therapists may not; therapists may be asked practical questions about what patients are to do in real life; depending on the type of therapy and the therapists' personal beliefs, these may be answered directly or not. As long as differences of these kinds exist, and they do in any kind of therapy, no external appearance of reciprocity—such as the maintenance by both participants of upright posture, eye contact, and first-name address—changes the fact that the interchange is nonreciprocal. The virtue of the classical analytical model is precisely that it makes the nonreciprocity apparent.

The fact that the therapist receives a fee from the patient is clear evidence that reciprocity is not expected within the conversation itself. The fee is the therapist's benefit in the encounter. The patient's is, presumably, the "getting well" or whatever equivalent phrase may be substituted in the various models. But this is a long-term goal, and a rather vague one. How can we understand the willingness of patients to continue—sometimes for years—in conversational encounters that continually deprive them of the emotional satisfactions expected of conversation?

In explanation, we have to invoke again the nonspontaneity of therapeutic discourse, and the consequent absence of reciprocity. Some writers on the therapeutic process have found these departures from the norm a burden and an abomination.[5] But in fact, the overt denial of spontaneity is what makes therapeutic discourse efficacious—precisely because it is different from normal conversational strategy.

The initiation and termination of the therapeutic relationship have been treated extensively in the literature: there are discussions of forms and means of effecting both. The bulk of the process, on the other hand, remains up to the participants. This general framework for the entire course—weeks, months, or years—of therapy is surprisingly like the structure of the single ordinary conversation, in which beginnings and endings have been ritualized, but the middle parts, the major parts of the discourse, are expected to be, or, at the very least to seem, spontaneous. What this comparison suggests is that the entire series of therapeutic interviews is to be taken as the equivalent of the single ordinary conversation. And just as we determine the satisfaction and the emotional benefit of a single ordinary conversation from its entirety, so we determine the benefit of the therapeutic discourse from the efficacy of the entire series—not session-by-session, from some of which the patient necessarily emerges feeling discouragement or pain rather than pleasure or enlightenment. Because in therapy we are engaged in one-to-one conversation, we apply the rules for such discourse that we have known since childhood; but we apply them in a different context, in which the series is equated with the single conversation.

Learning the rules of a new language is painful and difficult; and even learning to apply our usual rules in a new context is arduous. So we may ask whether it is necessary: cannot therapy be done as a conversation between friends, equals and confidantes? Is there any reason for the imposition of the burden of learning a new format on the patient, who has much to learn besides?

Conversations between friends, even for the pursuit of therapeutic goals, are but ordinary conversations based on the normal application of rules. Friendly conversation is reciprocal, or at least must look that way. It also must be understood as beneficial to both parties, in itself. It must appear spontaneous: even if we make appointments to see friends, we make them with our mutual convenience in mind; meetings may be arranged on the territory of either one, or a neutral place; we must assume that the possibility of future meetings will be decided as the need arises, rather than by prearrangement; the topics we select are at the discretion of both, and neither may unilaterally make interpretations. Hence we cannot make the assumptions that are a part of the therapeutic framework, nor engage in the reevaluation of the applicability of our ordinary rules for a new situation.

And it is the learning of new conditions for the application of rules that, in all probability, has therapeutic effect. If it were something else, one therapeutic system would be more efficacious than another, or one would work for particular kinds of people, others for others. But, in fact, all therapies seem to be effective for anyone approximately two-thirds of the time.[6]

One can even argue that it is the surprise value of the new system that is effective: the contrast between old and new communicative strategies, and success in learning the new, suggests to the patient that other tried-and-true ways of organizing the world and determining responses to it are not the only ones, and that new ways are safe to attempt. If the linguistic reorganization—done in an atmosphere free from recrimination—can be put into successful practice, then so can these and other new strategies elsewhere. The more patients are presented with possibilities of restructuring, reevaluating, and redefining the environment, the more they can make changes in behavior and interpretation in the real world.

What therapy teaches by linguistic precept and example is that the same phenomenon can be perceived in more than one way at once. This is what therapeutic theorists like Gregory Bateson and Jay Haley refer to as learning to metacommunicate, to communicate about communication, to see an utterance at once as both itself and a statement about itself. The allusive nature that therapeutic theory attributes to all discourse helps make understandable another peculiarity of therapeutic discourse: its fondness for metaphor and parable.

A great deal of psychotherapeutic theoretical writing of all schools is expressed in metaphorical terms. This is partly because no one has ever seen a human mind working and we can only visualize this process in terms of what we *have* seen. But more pertinent is the fact that stating something as a metaphor or an allusion is a form of reframing or recontextualizing. Metaphor often consists in placing a familiar idea in a new context. So we find metaphor on all levels of therapeutic discourse: Freud talks about the ego as a rider trying to control a horse that is the id; of psychological processes as transfers of mechanical or electrical energy. More recently, as substitutes for these physicalizations or concretizations of highly abstract processes, we find mental processes described in terms derived from information theory, decision theory, or computational theory. And replacing Freud's metapsychological metaphors—the horse and rider, or armies advancing and retreating—we find images of game playing, of parent-child relationships, of concrete spatial relations, prevalent in the speech of graduates of the human potential movement (represented, albeit parodically, in Cyra McFadden's *The Serial*): people are "uptight," "up front," "laid back," or "with it"; they can or can't get "behind things"; people "feel" or "experience" rather than think things. A different class of metaphor, certainly: but what is unchanging is the representation of abstract psychological states and processes as concrete, physical realizations.

Interestingly, recent work by Ron Schafer, within a quite orthodox psychoanalytic model, has criticized this fondness for metaphor and urged the use of literal description on the grounds that the use of metaphor prevents the patient from acquiring a sense of responsibility for his or her actions.[7] The suggestion is, then, that the allusive conventions, implicitly a part of traditional therapeutic discourse, are infantilizing; they keep patients from achieving maturity. And yet—infantilizing or no—recontextualization is a necessary part of therapy through the agency of transference, a necessarily regressive relation developed between therapist and patient, in which the patient comes to respond to the therapist as to earlier figures in his or her past. Transference is not only an inevitable concomitant of prolonged therapeutic encounters—it is a crucial element.

It is never clearly discussed in the therapeutic literature why transference is present in any prolonged therapeutic contact. One reason might be linguistic as much as psychological: through metaphor and metacommunication, the patient is being taught a new language, or rather a new form of communication, by the therapist. There is but one earlier model for this shared activity: the learning of a first language in early childhood. In therapy, as at the parent's knee, the process is implicit and unself-conscious as it never will be later. Transference *is* the reactivation of that first linguistic relationship, and by reexperiencing that earliest relationship in a benign setting, the patient can undo the accretions of the past that persist into the present. So it is precisely the peculiarities and complexities of therapeutic conversation that achieve therapeutic effect, and their removal would preclude therapeutic change.

What psychotherapeutic conversation or discourse teaches the patient is new conversational possibilities in ordinary life. In turn, through the many people who have been exposed to some form of the process, therapeutic conversation has become part of the equipment of English speakers generally.

Notes

1. To enumerate and describe, however briefly, a reasonable subset of relevant recent work in conversational analysis would occupy an inordinate amount of space. To summarize briefly, contributions in this area have been made from the vantage points of several fields: formal and informal linguistic pragmatics (of which this paper is an example); ordinary-language philosophy, of which the work of Grice (1975) is of especial importance here; and ethnomethodology, of which the work of H. Sacks, E. Schegloff, and G. Jefferson is exemplary ("A Simplest Systematics for the Organization of Turn-Taking for Conversation," *Language* 50 [1974]: 696–735).

2. G. Bateson, *Steps to an Ecology of Mind* (New York, 1972).

3. S. Freud, *Papers on Technique,* vol. 12, *Standard Edition of the Complete Psychological Works of Sigmund Freud* (London, 1958).

4. Jay Haley (*Strategies of Psychotherapy* [New York, 1963]) in particular has discussed psychotherapy as a sort of struggle for power by the participants, with the therapist necessarily holding the "one-up" position. It is also arguable that the therapeutic process can be described as a kind of game in which the therapist starts out in the "one-up" position, and the progress of the therapy can be gauged by the gradual equalization of positions of the participants.

5. For example, T. Szasz, *The Ethics of Psychoanalysis* (New York, 1965).

6. The survey of Luborsky, Singer, and Luborsky is evidence for this claim. See L. Luborsky, B. Singer, and L. Luborsky, "Comparative Studies of Psychotherapies: Is It True That 'Everyone Must Win and All Must Have Prizes'?" *Archives of General Psychiatry* 32 (1975): 995–1008.

7. R. Schafer, *A New Language for Psychoanalysis* (New Haven, 1975).

❧ LIAM HUDSON

Language, Truth, and Psychology

A SIZEABLE PERCENTAGE of the English now written is the work of psychologists, psychoanalysts, sociologists, anthropologists—and most of us, sad to say, are not much good at it. The professionally literate cast glances over their various fences at our efforts, note that what we write is often slovenly or pretentious, and take it for granted that we mangle language because we know no better.

But this diagnosis, I think, is too simple. I want to argue here that while many of our garblings do arise from ignorance or indifference, others flow from a separate source. Among those concerned to discover truths about human nature, there exists a problem of style that no one yet knows how to resolve; and this problem of style is indicative in its turn of a pervasive uncertainty about how such truths are to be reached. The answer, I want to suggest, may prove to lie not in deep thoughts about scientific method but in a clearer understanding of how and what we write. In other words, it is writing itself that holds the key.

The traditional belief among British academics is that the truth can best be grasped by means of prose that is itself vigorous, disciplined, plain. The more slippery the fish to be handled, the greater the need for plain language becomes. A model might be Professor A. J. Ayer's way with a sentence in that formative work of the mid-thirties, *Language, Truth and Logic* (1935). When Ayer routs the metaphysicians, persuades us that all propositions are matters of fact, matters of definition, or nonsense, and presses on until he has turned philosophy into an outhouse of science, he does so in prose that is a joy to read:

> . . . But this belief is a delusion.
>
> There is no field of experience which cannot, in principle, be brought under some form of scientific law, and no type of speculative knowledge about the world which it is, in principle, beyond the power of science to give. We have already gone some way to substantiate this proposition by demolishing metaphysics; and we shall justify it to the full in the course of this book.

Of mythical creatures like the unicorn—and by implication of all other thoughts that do not correspond to an identifiable object in the external world:

> The realist view that such imaginary objects "have real being", even though they do not exist, has already been shown to be metaphysical, and need not be further discussed.

On the last page but one, he even spares a thought for us psychologists: it seems that we have failed to create a coherent discipline for ourselves because we have failed to emancipate ourselves from metaphysics, and have used symbols like *intelligence, empathy,* and *subconscious self* in ways which are not precisely defined.

It is a rousing text, but in many respects a shallow one. This is inevitably so, the counter-argument runs, because Ayer's thought is couched in a language in which a spurious clarity is sovereign. People and their thoughts are elusive and multi-faceted—each of us, Ludwig Pursewarden tells us, an "ant-hill of opposed predispositions." Hence it is a prime function of a prose style like Ayer's to misrepresent: to persuade us that the world is a commonsensical place; that what seems political is really apolitical, and what seems a matter for inquiry or fruitful speculation is really one for analysis.

This objection to Ayerian prose is being advanced with special energy at the moment by devotees of Jacques Lacan and Roland Barthes, and of the Frankfurt School. It bears with particular force on those human attributes that intrigue the psychologist: people's beliefs, perceptions, needs, motives, fantasies, dreams; and it invites us to execute a shift in language—away from academic English and toward French and German. This alternative "paradigm," it is hinted, gives the mysteries of the human mind their due; but in so doing, leads us—or so it seems to me—into one form or another of willful obscurity. (Barthes's recent *A Lover's Discourse* is a case in point, allusive to a perplexing degree.)

It is of course an error to suggest that difficult topics can only be discussed in language that is itself difficult. On this argument, notoriously, books about Cassius must be lean books, books about politics must be dishonest, and so on. Prose does not mirror its subject matter in order to be veridical; and the whole notion that words must somehow picture nature is confused. The insufficiency of plain words is inescapable, nonetheless; and this is nowhere more obvious than when they are used as an instrument of autobiographical reconstruction—for example, by a master of the style, Bertrand Russell:

> About the time that these lectures finished, when we were living with the Whiteheads at the Mill House in Grantchester, a more serious blow fell than those that had preceded it. I went out bicycling one afternoon, and suddenly, as I was riding along a country road, I realised that I no longer loved Alys. I had had no idea until this moment that my love for her was even lessening. The problem presented by this discovery was very grave. . . .
>
> So long as I lived in the same house with Alys she would every now and then come down to me in her dressing gown after she had gone to bed, and beseech me to spend the night with her. Sometimes I did so, but the result was utterly unsatisfactory. For nine years this stage of affairs continued.[1]

Russell seems under a compulsion to write crisply; and his sense of syntactical *comme il faut* becomes part and parcel of a failure of kindliness and intimate perception. His fastidiousness with the rhythm and balance of his sentences is not matched by the fastidiousness of his account of Alys in her dressing gown. He remarks (in the context of Whitehead's wife's illness) that "the loneliness of the human soul is unendurable"; but his own loneliness is in part avoidable, being that of someone imprisoned within the requirements of a well-turned prose.

It is only occasionally that a psychologist writes as well as Russell or Ayer. William James comes to mind; and in our own time, Roger Brown of Harvard. Norman O. Brown, too, has written about Freud with a fertile vigor; and what Brown urges on us, as it happens, is precisely the abandonment of the view of people implicit in Russell's and Ayer's prose, and the pursuit, instead, of the meaning that lies "not in the words but between the words . . . beyond the reach, the rape, of literal-minded explication." It is the dead hand of science that Brown wishes to throw off. But his advocacy has been ignored, and a tide of righteous obscurity has for the time being closed over any such effort at eloquence.[2] We are now ensnared in the wily convolutions of Lacan; immersed in the mud of Habermasian systematics—and a special chic now attaches itself, in Anglo-Saxon circles, to writing sentences that have the air of inept translations from some Continental tongue. Without question, the issues addressed by men like Lacan, Jurgen Habermas, and Barthes are of significance to the psychologist; but it now seems a point of honor among the forward-looking that they should express themselves in ways that are puzzling, even mysterious, to all but the initiated few.

This crisis of intelligibility is one that would not have arisen, though, had the philosophers of language paid closer attention to their own program. For what psychologists and social scientists really do need is not a technical language, nor—Heaven forbid!—the philosophers' help in defining our concepts, but some assistance in assembling a framework within which to scrutinize the sorts of language we actually use; the sorts of truth we try to grasp. Here the contribution of the philosopher of language could have been genuinely liberating rather than merely prophylactic, for, patently, plain words and the scientific method are only one of the routes open to us if we wish to understand human nature. Other paths offer themselves: the novel, poetry, theatre, film—and even within psychology itself, we have more options than the outsider may suspect. At one extreme, we can set up an experiment; at another, we can conduct a "clinical" inquiry—that is, we can talk to someone else and pay heed to what they say.

There is a philistine and self-deceptive assumption among the scientifically inclined that all avenues other than their own amount to "anecdote." But if a psychologist, however self-consciously scientific, is in need of personal insight—if his marriage has collapsed or his children hate him—he does not turn to the professional journals in search of it. He goes to Donne or Chekhov, Freud or Laing. As receptacles of our knowledge about people, in other words, both literary and clinical modes at present show every sign of being superior to science; and it must in principle be the case, I think, that each of these rival routes of access to knowledge about people is valid after its fashion. What we do not know is how their respective merits can be weighed, nor what hostages we give as we choose to follow one route as opposed to another. To put the matter in crudely economic terms, there are patterns of cost and benefit associated with the experiment, the clinical inquiry, the novel, the poem—and, of course, the play and film too. But we do not yet know what these are.

Scientific psychology, then, is one mode of inquiry among many. But this state of wholesome plurality is one we have been reluctant to recognize—and through this reluctance have fallen into dire ways. A recent edition of the *Bulletin of the British Psychological Society* quotes, among others, these translations from "A Glossary of Research Language":

> "It has long been known. . . ."—*I have not bothered to look up the original reference.*
>
> "Three of the samples were chosen for detailed study. . . ."—*The results of the others did not make sense.*
>
> "Typical results are shown. . . ."—*The best results are shown.*
>
> "The most reliable values are those of Jones (1967). . . ."—*He was a student of mine.*
>
> "It is believed that. . . ."—*I think.*
>
> "It is generally believed that. . . ."—*A couple of other guys think so, too.*
>
> "Correct within an order of magnitude. . . ."—*Wrong.*[3]

The effect is comic, but the implication more lugubrious: such jokes in a trade paper are only possible if the apparent dispassion of scientific writing has become a vehicle not just for carelessness but for altogether more squalid maneuverings.

Looking around, you suddenly realize how pervasive these extraneous functions of technical English have become. Impersonal sentences like "It will be seen that the above tables are not without significance" help to protect us from the pain of precise inference. But they also assert our professionalism. Through the very extravagance of their imprecision, they imply that the real burden of our paper or speech is not its words, but its graphs and tables. This implication in its turn aligns us with the great corpus of natural science, where it can sometimes seem that data really can be left to speak for themselves. To a very considerable extent, in other words, the aspiring scientist can use the language of science as an instrument of legitimation. It must follow that the air of impersonal authority that reigns over such writing is often bogus.

As a group, we sometimes comfort ourselves in our disability with the knowledge that our neighbors, the sociologists, are in the same boat, at least to the extent that we each suffer from our own form of semantic delapidation. For we now have on our hands a generation of social scientists who are scarcely able to utter a sentence that does not include the key words *situation, interaction,* and *role;* and who seem convinced that, by the very use of these words, some measure of explanation has been achieved. But such comforts are ephemeral. It is here, I think, that the scientific community in its entirety sheltered itself behind a simple-minded misunderstanding about the nature of the arts—one, unfortunately, that literary critics and commentators have done their inadvertent best to fortify.

The scientist assumes, more or less explicitly, that a novel or poem is a species of entertainment: that it is "made up." Support for this misconception comes from the literary world itself, sometimes in old-fashioned forms, sometimes in a guise that is more modern. In his *The Art of Versification and the Technicalities of Poetry* (1962), for example, R. F. Brewer describes the poetic sentence as, "nervous, terse and euphonious," and says that "every kind of inversion, elision, and departure from ordinary rule" is tolerated in order to make it so. "Though bound to be musical, and to excite pleasure, the poet is a chartered libertine in most other respects." To be musical, to excite pleasure, to be a chartered libertine: these are ideas categorically remote from the scientist's perception of himself and his own work. Such a gulf is consolidated by those up-to-the-mark critics who take it for granted that each novel, each poem, creates its own rules, its own landscape, and that it is an error to explain it in terms of the world that lies outside. (In his article on the novel as research, Michel Butor launches the notion that we can use the novel as a "laboratory" in which we examine the role of narrative—an idea as pertinent to psychologists, beset with the need to "tell a good story," as it is to novelists themselves. But he too seems to make this dangerously solipsistic assumption.)[4]

While it is easy to follow Brewer's line of thought, and exciting to follow Butor's, it remains a fact (often overlooked by scientists) that the business of writing a novel or poem is one of highly wrought discipline. It also remains a fact (often overlooked by critics) that this discipline is one that succeeds inasmuch as it recreates some aspect of the world "out there" in symbolic form, and does so in an enduringly satisfactory way. As in science and in psychology, so in art: the crucial relationship is that between what is imagined and what is observed.

The poet, the novelist, then *are* our licensed libertines; but only to the extent that jazz musicians are, improvising within the constraints of a firmly established genre. The conditional nature of the freedom they enjoy is demonstrated by William Gass, the only commentator I have read who has helped me to understand how a novelist writes. In *On Being Blue,* his memorable book about the routes a novelist can exploit when introducing sexual material into his work, Gass, a philosopher as well as a novelist, makes it clear that the fashioning of sentences—"containers for consciousness"—is a feat of meticulous skill: a skill whereby the writer invades the privacy of those he writes about. But Gass goes on to offer us two sorts of warning. "It is not simple, not a matter for amateurs, making sentences sexual; it is not easy to structure the consciousness of the reader with the real thing, to use one wonder to speak of another, until in the place of the voyeur who reads we have fashioned the reader who sings; but the secret lies in seeing sentences as containers of consciousness, as constructions whose purpose it is to create conceptual perceptions—blue in every area and range. . . . " It is difficult, Gass points out; but it is also engrossing. It takes you over: "So to the wretched writer I should like to say that there's one body only whose request for your caresses is not vulgar, is not unchaste, untoward, or impolite: the body of your work itself. . . . you must remember that your attention will not merely celebrate a beauty but create one and that you should therefore give up the blue things of this world in favor of the words which say them."[5]

The poet can easily drift into isolation, locked inside his own words, his own imaginings. If his work is to remain worth reading, this drift is one, presumably, that he ought to resist. For the psychologist, though, if he wants to remain a psychologist, there is no such leeway. Resistance becomes imperative. It is one of the defining characteristics of his genre that his re-creations must be rooted in description: in his best estimate of what is actually going on "out there," in the world that lies beyond his own head. Beyond blind convention, though, we have at the moment no idea of how to proceed. Is it sensible, for example, to envisage a whole school of psychologists writing as Gass writes—or Norman Brown? As a profession ought we to innovate stylistically, operating somewhere in the mid-ground between natural history and poetry and autobiographical memoir, say, as R. D. Laing has done in *Knots* (1972) and *The Facts of Life* (1976)? At present, we are adrift, clinging to the stale, old ways of assembling our words, for no better reason than the lack of a standard whereby to judge something new.

We began to construct such a standard, I believe, when we came to terms with the constraints, ethical as well as technical, that are an inescapable part of a chosen mode. I have found a curious reversal of the constraints under which you operate if you move from writing as a psychologist to writing as a novelist—one I have never seen remarked on, still less discussed.[6] In the collection of his data, and in assembling his results, the psychologist is tightly constrained; and this constraint is ethical. To fudge or misrepresent at this stage, however tempting, is seen throughout the profession of science as heinous. Such cheating as does occur, in my experience, is restricted to research students, to the occasional bandit of more mature years, and—more awkwardly—to all of us when we use statistical procedures the assumptions of which we do not quite understand.

Yet once our data base is assembled, once the tables and graphs are in place, we are to a remarkable extent free. His rehearsal of his evidence behind him, the psychologist is at liberty in the discussion section of his paper, to mount more or less whatever hobbyhorse takes his fancy. What is not encouraged and only rarely attempted, is a detailed exposition of the logical purchase that our evidence actually exerts. When it does appear in the professional literature, tight argument of this sort is almost invariably associated with an attempt to destroy a theory put forward by someone else.

In writing a novel, though, this pattern is neatly reversed. You are required to invent characters and plot, and are subject only to the constraint that these should be very approximately lifelike. But once launched, your characters begin to dictate their own terms; and if you write with any seriousness of intent, you are forced to "consult" them—as Thackeray pointed out. Will Jill accept a particular overture from Jack? The answer cannot be capricious. The novelist must *unearth* it as he polishes and revises, and do so not just as a broad approximation, as is so often the case in science, but accurate to the smallest nuance. Often, before he has done, he will have on his hands characters more vivid to him than almost anyone else he knows. The thought of fudging their reactions is as distant from him as it would be for an experienced scientist to think of fudging his data base.

In choosing one form of language rather than another, one genre rather than another, the psychologist commits himself epistemologically. He commits himself to one of several sorts of relationship to knowledge about the people he is trying to understand. It is precisely this kind of choice, I would have thought, that the philosophers of language should have illuminated. The choices, after all, are ones which carry with them hidden implications about the kinds of evidence we can use, the extent to which we can generalize on the basis of our evidence, and the criteria whereby we judge one reading of that evidence superior to another. Instead of creating puzzles for themselves around the Great Imponderables, or irritating physical scientists with prescriptions about how to do physical science, the philosophers could surely have made themselves useful by codifying, taxonomizing, uses of language that someone like a psychologist can legitimately entertain. To paraphrase Norman Brown, there lies behind the scientific prose of psychology the repressed problem of how the psychologist can gain access to the lives he wants to comprehend.

The gist of my argument, then, is that what lies at present between the psychologist and his subject matter is an inadequate grasp of the English language. The language lies there not as a medium of understanding, but as an obstacle. Traditionally "clear" English subverts his inquiry; and its replacement, technical English, undermines it comprehensively. Currently fashionable echoes of academic French and German—the vehicle for our "alternative paradigm"—make matters worse, not better. My fond hope is that by doing for ourselves the job that the philosophers of language should have done for us—by examining the various routes of access to knowledge about people, and rendering their costs and benefits explicit—we shall take the necessary first step toward forms of English for psychologists that are genuinely clear or pure, in that they convey what they ought to convey and nothing more. Forms, that is, that are stripped of their cargoes of mystification, posturing, and innuendo, and enable us to shape propositions about people that we can substantiate and believe to be true.

Notes

1. Bertrand Russell, *The Autobiography of Bertrand Russell, 1872–1914* (London, 1967), pp. 147–151.
2. Norman O. Brown, *Life Against Death* (London, 1959), and *Love's Body* (New York, 1966), p. 264.
3. Kemble Widmer, "A Glossary of Research Language," quoted in *Bulletin of the British Psychological Society,* August 1978, p. 297.
4. Michel Butor, "The Novel as Research," in Malcolm Bradbury, ed., *The Novel Today* (London, 1977).
5. William Gass, *On Being Blue* (Boston, 1977), pp. 86–90.
6. For recent efforts of my own in these two modes, see *Human Beings* (London, 1975) and *The Nympholepts* (London, 1978).

MICHAEL TANNER

The Language of Philosophy

THE PREVALENT MODE of writing in Anglo-American philosophy is such that adequate discussion of some of the most serious traditional issues has become extraordinarily difficult. To understand how this has come about it is necessary to realize that philosophy is, among the serious intellectual disciplines, probably the most fashion-prone, and to see what the fashions, as manifested in the idioms and techniques of philosophers, have been since the end of the Second World War. The one generally known truth about English-speaking philosophers and their output during the last thirty years is their unprecedented concern with language. For approximately the first half of that time this preoccupation was considered by the majority of interested nonphilosophers as something to be regretted, an indication that the time-honored devotion of philosophers to ultimate issues had been replaced by a narrow, purely academic concern with "mere words." In the last fifteen years, however, regret and hostility seem to have been replaced either by indifference—to philosophy rather than to ultimate issues; by respect, since the burgeoning branches of linguistics have effected the usual intimidation that people feel in the presence of something that can plausibly be called a science; or by resignation in the face of the inevitable: in a world of increasing fragmentation of knowledge, it is not to be expected that philosophy, any more than any other academic discipline, should be understood by nonprofessionals. Something very similar has happened in literary criticism.

To give some force to, even if not to demonstrate, the universal truth of my opening statement before coming to see how philosophy has arrived at where it is, I shall quote at some length from an article published in 1973, as one of a collection of reflections by contemporary Anglo-Americans—that it should be by such a group was the point of the enterprise—entitled *Philosophy and Personal Relations:* the kind of topic that would have been considered taboo twenty years ago by up-to-date philosophers. The article is called "A Conceptual Investigation of Love," and begins by lamenting the fact that such a subject as love receives so little attention from philosophers in the writer's tradition. The analysis proceeds:

> Having defined the field of investigation, we can now sketch the concepts analytically presupposed in our use of 'love'. An idea of these concepts can be gained by sketching a sequence of relations, the members of which we take as relevant in deciding whether or not some relationship between persons A and B is one of love. These are not relevant in the sense of being evidence for some further relation 'love' but as being, in part at least, the material of which love consists. The sequence would include at least the following:
>
> (1) A knows B (or at least knows something of B)
>
> (2) A cares (is concerned) about B
> A likes B
>
> (3) A respects B
> A is attracted to B
> A feels affection for B
>
> (4) A is committed to B
> A wishes to see B's welfare promoted
>
> The connection between these relations which we will call 'love-comprising relations' or 'LCRs' is not, except for 'knowing about' and possibly 'Feels affection for' as tight as strict entailment.[1]

The analysis continues in the same vein, prompting the question: How has such comically solemn ineptitude become possible? For it isn't as if this comes out of the blue; the philosophical climate is such that if one chooses to write on such a topic as love—more the kind of thing that Iberians are expected to do—there are strong forces leading one to do it in the style of the quoted passage.

What preoccupied philosophers during the forties and fifties was the felt necessity of contracting the traditional subject matter of philosophy, simply because philosophers didn't have the right kind of equipment—no one, perhaps, could have, or the only equipment worth bothering with was that to be found in laboratories—to deal with the big old issues. The amount of resentment that this contraction gave rise to was remarkable, if not surprising, and reached its peak in a book by Ernest Gellner, published in 1959 by the ever-canny Victor Gollancz (who twenty-three years earlier had published the supreme work of polemicizing contraction, A. J. Ayer's *Language, Truth and Logic*), with an introduction by Bertrand Russell, for whom philosophy still had, as he said in a book of his own published the same year, "the grave and important task of understanding the world." Gellner's book, called challengingly *Words and Things,* immediately became notorious because Gilbert Ryle, one of the most influential post-war Oxford philosophers and the editor of the then important journal *Mind,* informed the publisher that he would not have the book reviewed in *Mind* because it contained abusive passages about contemporary philosophers. This led Russell to write a letter to *The Times* in which he deplored the fact that *Mind* had become a coterie-organ. For three weeks the correspondence columns of *The Times* remained animated by letters about contemporary philosophy, mainly from nonphilosophers and mainly showing how much hostility was felt in the intellectual world to philosophy as it was then thought to be practiced. The proceedings were wound up with a leading article of appropriate vacuity and solemnity.

The burden of Gellner's book and Russell's introduction was that British philosophy—American philosophy had not then gained the ascendancy which it now overpoweringly has—under the sway of Ludwig Wittgenstein in Cambridge, and of Ryle and J. L. Austin in Oxford, had come to have a concern for no more than "the silly things that silly people say" (Russell's phrase), and an unhealthy obsession with its own nature: so that the prevalent Cambridge view, at least, was that philosophy was, as Karl Kraus succinctly expressed his view of psychoanalysis, "the disease of which it was the cure"—or vice versa. According to such philosophers, as Gellner and Russell claimed, among whom the differences seemed to outsiders to be insignificant, the traditional torments of philosophy, including such issues as the relationship between mind and body, the freedom of the will, the objectivity of values, and the possibility of nonempirical factual knowledge, originate in a disregard for the "logic of our (ordinary) language." Wittgenstein insisted that the complaints of philosophers were, or began from, "deep disquietudes" brought about by "the bewitchment of our intelligence by language," the result of "language going on holiday." For Wittgenstein (this all refers to Wittgenstein's second phase of philosophizing, the work of the man who returned to Cambridge and philosophy in 1929 after a decade of widely varying activities), we must see how language is ordinarily used and not attempt, as philosophers customarily have, to straitjacket our language and thus our thought in accordance with the kind of demands typical of philosophers to make—for instance, to seek for the necessary and sufficient conditions for the use of a term, or to operate with standards of alleged rigor which can result only in the temporarily illuminating but rapidly frustrating and ultimately paralyzing impasse of skepticism.

Wittgenstein never showed or thought that philosophers should show a concern with the nuances of language. By contrast J. L. Austin established his reputation by dauntingly intensive if unsystematic forays into the minutiae of everyday and colloquial usage, distinguishing between "Clumsily he trod on a snail," "He trod clumsily on a snail," and "He trod on a snail clumsily," as a possible contribution to dealing with the problems of responsibility and thus ultimately of free will. In the nearest thing to an apologia that he wrote for his style of philosophizing, he stated that "our common stock of words embodies all the distinctions men have found worth marking, in the lifetimes of many generations: these surely are likely to be more numerous, more sound, since they have stood up to the long test of the survival of the fittest, and more subtle, at least in all ordinary and reasonably practical matters, than any that you or I are likely to think up of an afternoon—the most favoured alternative method."[2] But this might well be thought to beg several questions, such as whether the aims of "many generations" are the same as those of philosophers who make new or different distinctions from the ordinary ones, or again whether the most favored alternative method has been thinking up distinctions in armchairs "of an afternoon."

Most seriously, the method employed by Austin, and also the widely different but apparently easily confused methods of Wittgenstein, much copied as these immediately were, could seem to traditionally-oriented philosophers such as Russell and C. D. Broad to have no serious bearing on the substantial issues (concerning "things"), which clearly couldn't be resolved by newfangled investigations (concerning "words"). So the antagonism to the most fashionable British philosophers of the fifties was predominantly an antagonism to the way they viewed language, and as a corollary, to the way they used it. For with their views about the etiology of philosophical problems in language went an intense concern with such matters as the use of technical terms by philosophers, and the adoption of the idiom of the man in the street as that was conceived by Oxbridge dons. So far as technical terms were concerned, philosophers felt that they had special reasons for suspecting their legitimacy, apart from those already given in the quotation from Austin. For they are too readily construed as necessitated by philosophers' having discovered some new class of entity, which actually, *qua* philosophers, they never can. Thus a term such as *sense-datum,* which had originated in about 1912 with G. E. Moore and Russell, had been thought to denote a class of objects—the immediate objects of sensation or perception—which had not previously been noticed, and Moore even gives recipes for having sense-datum experiences if you haven't knowingly had them already. All such "discoveries" made by philosophers are in fact misplaced inventions—so ran the view of Wittgenstein and of Ryle and Austin. The conclusion was often naturally drawn that philosophers should completely eschew technical language.

Since for Wittgenstein the genuine philosophical endeavor was wholly negative—antitheoretical, antigeneral, antisystematic—and was merely involved in restoring everything to the place that it had had before philosophers had disturbed "ordinary language," clearly he could think of technical terminology only as mischievous. However, since Wittgenstein was a very great philosopher who held many pronounced and idiosyncratic philosophical views, though he repeatedly and emphatically denied doing so, his practice was to use technical terms in some profusion and to deny that he was doing so. The inevitable consequence has been a growth industry devoted to the explication of such frequently used Wittgensteinian terms as *criterion, language-game,* and *form of life.* They may not sound as intimidating as many specimens of philosophical jargon, but they are actually used by Wittgenstein in a confusing variety of ways, and have been taken over by some of his disciples for monstrous purposes. Furthermore, his style (he wrote in German, and has been fortunate in having as his chief translator G. E. M. Anscombe, who catches his tone in English to a remarkable extent) in his late work is discursive but also epigrammatic, sometimes vatic, quite often portentous. For a time his characteristic flavor—a combination of informality with periodic suggestions of alarming depths—had a widespread influence on philosophers, and has led in extreme cases, e.g., the American Stanley Cavell, to extremes of narcissistic archness. In his well-known collection of essays *Must We Mean What We Say?*, Cavell has a thematic index, including such expected topics as Belief, Language, Fact, and Metaphor. But he also has there, with three-page references provided, "Sitting quietly in a room," and checking up on one of them, in his chapter on *Endgame,* we find

> it is simply crazy that there should ever have come into being a world with such a sin in it, in which a man is set apart because of his color—*the* superficial fact about a human being. Who could *want* such a world? For an American, fighting for his love of country, that the last hope of the world should from its beginning have swallowed slavery, is an irony so withering, a justice so intimate in its rebuke of pride, as to measure only with God. The question is whether enough men can afford the knowledge that the way the world is comes down in the end to what each son is doing now, *sitting within his ordinary walls* [my italics], making his everyday demands. And whether enough men can divine the difference, and choose, between wanting this world to stop itself, and wanting all worlds to end.[3]

It isn't easy to imagine prose drawing attention to its own sensitivity more insistently, while actually presenting a blend of the banal and the unintelligible which would surely have temporarily united Wittgenstein and Austin in contempt for what the latter called the "ivresse des grands profondeurs." But on the whole, utterances of Wittgenstein's, such as "The real discovery is the one which enables me to stop doing philosophy when I want to.—The one that gives philosophy peace, so that it is no longer tormented by questions which bring *itself* into question,"[4] were not so much imitated as taken inspirationally, the inspiration manifesting itself in many very sweeping characterizations—but in more homely English terms—of what philosophy might and might not accomplish. This informality, feigned freedom from technicality, and occasional peremptoriness of Wittgenstein's style were actually inimitable, the rash few who tried to imitate the style sounding now (it's hard to imagine that they ever sounded different) comically pretentious, as when one of the closest disciples ended a gnomic paper with the one-sentence paragraph: "Language is something that is spoken."

Informality was also the keynote of the Oxford style exemplified by Austin, who begins his best article "Ifs and Cans," with the question "Are cans constitutionally iffy?", where *cans* comes from the verb, not the noun. He clearly delighted in being shockingly unprofessorial, though actually his writings, for all their addiction to colloquialisms and fifth-form jokes, are extraordinarily pedantic in distinction drawing, often seemingly for its own sake. But oddly for a philosopher who remonstrated with his colleagues for ignoring the distinctions built up by many generations of ordinary folk, Austin probably introduced more technical terms into philosophy than any other twentieth-century figure except Heidegger; or rather, not so much into philosophy as into his own homespun branch of descriptive linguistics.

What Wittgenstein and Austin shared, despite marked disparities in temperament and outlook, was a conviction that traditional philosophy was almost wholly mistaken, that it needed to be brought down to earth, that generalities should be eschewed . . . except, of course, for such generalities as those. Their methods of puncturing traditional philosophical pretensions were frequently to take obvious but overlooked quotidian counter-examples to glamorous, large-scale philosophical theses; to ask mock and mocking questions; and, most importantly and characteristically, to get tough.

It is the quality of intellectual machismo that unites the philosophical style of the fifties with that of the seventies. Though there is an enormous change in the philosophical climate to be registered between 1955 and 1975, at least from ground level, nothing has been the same since—nineteen years before the first of those dates—Ayer began his first book with the superb matter-of-fact swagger of "The traditional disputes of philosophers are, for the most part, as unwarranted as they are unfruitful." Since then, unless one has been determinedly eccentric or able to endure the stigma of effeteness, tough-mindedness has been a *sine qua non* of academic philosophy. Until the mid-fifties, it was a matter primarily of the philosophy of meaning and of logic—theory of knowledge and destructive criticism of past philosophy being at the safely tough end of the spectrum, ethics suspect, and aesthetics and philosophy of religion out of the question. Then, thanks to a movement towards the primacy of methodology, any subject was considered in principle admissible, though aesthetics was still considered, famously, "dreary." What was most important was the attitude one adopted toward one's subject matter, and to *some* extent one's stance within it. Thus subjectivist ethical theories were considered tougher than those associated with intuitionism; a philosopher who found the concept of God incoherent was tougher than one who found it intelligible, let alone one who thought that it had application—i.e., that God existed. This may all sound like parody, but alas it isn't. My opening claim about the fashion-proneness of philosophers is confirmed by the fact that any philosopher who has been around for thirty years will be able to tell from the titles of most articles in the journals, or from a few sentences in them, when they were written, to within five years. So if you come across a friendly-sounding article called "On Buttering Parsnips," and find that it is wholly devoted to pretty intimidating semantic analysis, you can be confident that it is of approximately 1970 vintage. What makes the phenomenon more dismaying is that it's not as if a consensus of opinion is ever reached on any philosophical topic, however insignificant; it merely seems to be that philosophers get tired of discussing a particular topic in a particular way and move on.

A final gloom-laden consideration: more than half the Western philosophers who have ever lived are at present teaching in English and American universities. Since many of them are striving for tenure, the number of publications, chiefly in journals, is huge, and it is imperative that articles show, more than anything, that one is up to the minute. So the way philosophers write or converse at conferences and paper readings is predictable: a superabundance of jargon indicative of distinction-drawing expertise; a very pronounced tendency to formalize any English sentence just uttered in terms of the apparatus afforded by symbolic logic—a tendency amounting to a nervous tic on the part of some philosophers who can scarcely speak unless they are near enough to a blackboard to precisify what they have just said by rendering it into their preferred symbolism. And even if they don't do that, they feel the need to indulge in the kind of pseudo-rigor of which I produced a sad example at the beginning of this article. Anglo-American philosophy, that is, is at present—and the signs are all that it will continue to move in the same direction—wedded to an ideal of quasi-scientific precision, though lacking many of the facilities and habits of scientists, and manifesting no especial desire for them. For example, philosophers incessantly confer, but rarely collaborate. Joint enterprises are virtually unknown; but with the enormous amount of technical apparatus, the prodigious amount of argumentation, and the sophisticated nature of the most canvassed areas, above all those concerned with the philosophy of language, the possibility of being in command of all the requisite material scarcely exists. And the nature of the philosophical enterprise—or its various natures—is still sufficiently puzzling to leave it uncertain to what extent one can afford to be a moderately minute specialist, in the way that scientists can be, and that literary critics can't be (although of course many are).

To conclude by amplifying slightly my first point: the mode in which contemporary philosophy is conducted in English makes all but impossible the serious discussion of concepts, world views, attitudes, and feelings which are not susceptible of analysis of the prevailing kind. My quotation from Cavell only serves to reinforce this point. For, admirably intent as he is on dealing with questions largely neglected by his contemporaries, he finds it necessary to take refuge in a style which has its own kind of dauntingness without the compensations of rigor or enhanced insight. If one isn't to capitulate to the usual mode, one has to show oneself to be aggressively different, and it is noteworthy that Cavell doesn't get going in his collection until he has justified his idiosyncracies at considerable length in an introduction that gives a gruesome foretaste of what lies ahead. The fear, as in literary criticism, is that one will lapse, or will be accused of lapsing, back into the old belle-lettristic mode, than which it is rightly felt that nothing could be more deadly—though other things can be as bad. What is needed is a recognition that there are other modes of rigor and precision than quasi-formal ones, and ways of being profound that do not require near-unintelligibility. In the history of philosophy there have been great figures who combined imaginativeness and discursiveness with economy and powerful insight, and it should be obvious to philosophers by now that some aspects of the subject require the *kind* of gifts that Nietzsche and William James manifested, whatever one may think of their actual performances. If this platitude (as it seems to me) doesn't gain recognition, then a good deal of the obloquy directed against contemporary philosophers will be seen to be thoroughly deserved.

Notes

1. W. Newton-Smith, "A Conceptual Investigation of Love," in Alan Montefiore, ed., *Philosophy and Personal Relations* (London, 1973), pp. 118–119. It should in fairness be added that the author's specialty is space and time, where there is no doubt still ample room for him to function.

2. J. L. Austin, *Philosophical Papers*, 2nd ed. (Oxford, 1970), p. 205.

3. Stanley Cavell, *Must We Mean What We Say?* (New York, 1969), p. 141.

4. Ludwig Wittgenstein, *Philosophical Investigations* (Oxford, 1953), pt. 1, sec. 133.

HUGH KENNER

Machinespeak

Ah the creatures, the creatures,
everything has to be explained to them.
Samuel Beckett

THAT WHICH A TIME truly venerates, its reserved knowledge, the lore not for the laity (who are defined, precisely, by their nonpossession of it); the formulae which will conjure the god to speak and enable their human possessors to think as largely as gods: such arcane stuff goes into a language apart, to have learned which (since no one grows up speaking it) is by definition to have become learned; and it was at one time Hieroglyphic, and at another time Scholastic Latin, but in our time is fragmented into dialects called FORTRAN and LISP and COBOL and even BASIC, variants of the authentic speech of the thunder which is called Machine Language, and is very elegant but barely comprehended save by veritable machines, and looks like this:

```
00000000    00111010
00000001    00001000
00000010    00000000
. . .
```

This austerity is in 0's and 1's because—come on, you know that much—and its words are eight characters long because 8 is 2 × 2 × 2 and we are in a domain where all goes by twos, and as to what it means, that depends on the reader: INTEL 8080? Motorola

6800? Unlike you and me, partially shaped by our reading, that reader was fully defined before the language was. To write Machine Language your primary need is to know *all* about your reader (as you can; there is a little booklet).

Like Cuneiform, Machine Language is made of many identical elements, tedious to write and easily miswritten. There was a time when programmers wrote zeroes and ones all day long, and a few neoclassicists still do, but in these late days the Higher Level Languages are ubiquitous. They allow you to write something another human being can follow, and with less likelihood of error, in part because you can reread it yourself, in part because you need bestow less attention—ideally, none—on what is going on inside the machine. Since machines can't understand Higher Level Languages, another program called Interpreter or Compiler stands between. (Interpreter and Compiler are not quite the same, but equivalent for our purposes.) The Compiler-writers are the true High Priests, since it is they who must encode the conventions and skirt the ambiguities of the language in which the programmer is going to write. The programmer in turn is at the service of someone who wants a job done, and the whole arcane art is both necessary and possible because we have blundered into a culture abristle with jobs that entail much exact repetition. A Higher Level Language is a system of abbreviations that works by defining repeated portions exactly.

Suppose you run an office whose sole business is to produce typed copies of messages like the following:

The farmer in the dell
The farmer in the dell
Heigh ho the merry o
The farmer in the dell.

The farmer takes a wife
The farmer takes a wife
Heigh ho the merry o
The farmer takes a wife.

The wife takes a child
The wife takes a child
Heigh ho the merry o
The wife takes a child.

—and so on, as the dog takes a cat, the cat a rat, the rat a cheese; whereupon

The cheese stands alone
The cheese stands alone
Heigh ho the merry o
The cheese stands alone.

This will be recognized as a reasonable model of secretarial output; form letters are not otherwise structured.

In the early years you gave the typist written copies to copy, but all that changed with Miss Quickwit, whose flying fingers could generate anything in the office repertoire once you'd prompted her with a few hints on "how it goes." The nature of these hints is obvious from the way we abbreviated three stanzas in the example above. "The Farmer in the Dell" is characterized by a tune, a little sequence of variables, and some rules of combination, and out of her sense of these Miss Quickwit could generate it afresh whenever it was wanted.

But Miss Quickwit one day put trivial occupations behind her, having met a typewriter salesman whose socks she aspired to wash; whereupon Personnel sent up Dora, who could neither carry a tune nor remember whether the cheese came after the rat or before the dog. Dora needed explicit written instructions, which soon got longer than the ditty itself and to no avail because she kept misreading them; indeed a complete prose specification for producing "The Farmer in the Dell" is apt to sound like an excerpt from *The Golden Bowl,* a book Dora couldn't follow either.

Dora was accordingly replaced by a computer, even dumber than she but unflappable. Its neurons never flag, its iron fingers never tangle, but it can neither carry a tune nor begin a new line without being told. So it needs totally unambiguous instructions, for which the Higher Level Language called MACROGENERATOR seems suitable. They look like this:[1]

```
§DEF, VERSE, <~1~1
Hey ho the merry o ~1
>;
§DEF, LINE, <
The ~1 wants a ~2>;
§DEF, FORM, <§VERSE,§LINE,~1,~2;;>;
§VERSE,
The farmer in the dell;
§FORM, farmer, wife;
§FORM, wife, child;
§FORM, child, dog;
§FORM, dog, cat;
```

§FORM, cat, rat;
§FORM, rat, cheese;
§VERSE,
The cheese stands alone;

The swing, the beat, the bucolic lilt are gone; but if what you want is a typed copy, that will get it typed, and no customer need ever know that transistors have disposed the words he reads.

One can puzzle out how it works. A little study suggests that the symbol § marks the beginning of a new unit of attention, something analogous to a sentence, terminated by a semicolon. It also seems that "DEF," (= "definition") heads something the machine is to stash away for future reference. There are three of these, and they may be regarded as lexical definitions, for use in a convention like the following: "When you come upon the defined term, e.g. VERSE, substitute its definition." Within a definition, -1 marks a place where a further substitution will be made; such instances are serially numbered, -1, -2, etc.

When the machine encounters a statement unpreceded by "DEF," it takes its cue to be up and doing. So it deals with

§VERSE,
The farmer in the dell;

by substituting the supplied words for each -1 in the definition of VERSE, and types out stanza one. The next task,

§FORM, farmer, wife;

is a little more complicated. "FORM" has been defined as a VERSE in which the place of the variable is taken by something called LINE, and LINE has the pattern, "The -1 takes a -2." So it concocts a provisional "FORM,"

The -1 takes a -2
The -1 takes a -2
Heigh ho the merry o
The -1 takes a -2

Into this, at a second stage, "farmer" and "wife" are inserted to fill out the pattern "LINE"; and with no more to be done stanza two is typed.

In the same way, working down the list, the machine compiles and executes each stanza in turn; and if it makes no mistakes that is not thanks to luck or miracle, but because *the program and the output are exactly equivalent.* The program, with its list of variables and its unambiguous instructions about their treatment—unambiguous because specified by the conventions of the programming language—is simply *a compact way of writing the output.*

Whereupon much mystery vanishes, for this is generally true. Think of the computer as a machine to print what for some reason we want printed: "The Farmer in the Dell," or thirty-five thousand utility bills, or all the words W. B. Yeats used in his poems, arranged in alphabetical order. It differs from the typewriter at which I sit in only one respect, that instead of typing in what you want to get out, you type in instructions for generating what you want to get out.

The discipline of devising these instructions is justified only by the time it saves in the long run. The arithmetic of utility bills is trivial, but there are so many of them; it is easier to state the rules, supply the meter readings, and leave the rest to busy hardware. Or we may want a result, 3.141592653589793, which takes seconds to type but took even Leonhard Euler an hour to arrive at, involving as it does the formation of many terms in a series and the addition of these; better state a rule and let the machine obey it, over and over and over.[2]

Over and over and over is the most general principle; it is quicker to write a program than to arrive at and write out the result only when the problem is such that the instructions can specify simple operations that get done many times. Why, at this phase of human history, we confront so many such problems is a question for another occasion, though no study of Higher Level Languages will permit us to stray from it very far.

These languages have a number of interesting peculiarities, beginning with the fact that nobody speaks them. Walter Ong has reminded us repeatedly that Medieval Latin was peculiar in being first learned at a writing desk and then spoken, a fact which encouraged certain geometric criteria of style: a sentence was elegant when its diagram was. Still, once learned, Latin *was* spoken. Programming languages are never spoken at all. Even in context, a fragment of FORTRAN conveys nothing to the most expert ear:

```
READ (5, 100) N, MAXIT, EPSILON, BIGGST
NPLUS 1 = N + 1
```

while this PL/I horror, where every mark is significant, is utterly unpronounceable:[3]

```
ANGLES(I)=2*ATAND(SQRT((S-A(IND(I,1)))*(S-A(IND(I,2))))/(S*(S-A
        (IND(I,3))))));
```

Both are intelligible to the practiced *eye,* but being eye language they stay obdurately "out there," in the eye's external domain, remote from tongue and ear, guarding their inviolate distance from the human psyche (Ψῡχή, breath, spirit) and pedantic about minute differentiations.

Eye languages? *Lingua* means "tongue." Why it is plausible to call such things languages at all is an interesting story. Late in the seventeenth century, and for complex reasons deriving partly from the emergence of printing, partly from missionaries' reports of the Chinese ideograph, it had become plausible to accord the written primacy over the spoken. In written syntax, it seemed, lay the logic of the language. A "word" was an entity existing in space like a chair, and its spatial existence was identical with the way it was spelled. (Spelling grew standardized.) Linguistic skill got called "literacy"; the literate were cautioned against writing the kind of thing they spoke. Mere speakers were improvisers, mispronouncers, corrupters. So language was removed from the tongue, and came to connote some orderly system of signs and of rules for combining them, impossible to master without pencil and paper. There ensued a craze for devising "philosophical" languages, purged of ambiguity, rational in mapping the taxonomies of creation, capable of effecting their syntactic transactions in accordance with the movement of reason and in no other lawful way. (Mathematicize "reason," and you are close to the computer.) These were written languages, equipped with systems of phonemes as if by afterthought. It is among the "philosophical" languages of the seventeenth century that we must seek precursors for the programming languages of the twentieth, in which "words" are quite explicitly mnemonics (the flesh is weak), and programmers are enjoined to make them pronounceable: POINT and POUND, not PQRST and PQSRT on which a machine won't stumble but a human will.[4] Speakability seems a regrettable afterthought.

If saying PQSRT is hard, remembering it is hard too, because it is a list and not a story, space-bound, not time-bound. Lists, it seems, forced the development of writing itself. If we are to trust its current decipherment, Linear B was devised to record inventories, not to preserve speech. An inventory is a string of nouns, so chirographically controlled systems tend to be noun-oriented and have trouble with the verb, the part of speech that affirms. Thus the "philosophical" languages were better at taxonomizing than at affirming anything save the logical relationships inherent in the taxonomy.

For a taxonomy is a diagram like an inverted tree, down which we travel, alert at the branching-points, to arrive at the place of some entity in the scheme of things. To devise a philosophical language you have only to arrange that the phoneme structure of each term shall indicate its location on the tree. When you do this you are, true, assigning names; but with this important difference from Adam's activity that you are not *calling* the thing by its name, but *using* the name as a mnemonic for the thing's location. "Rainbow" for John Wilkins (1668) was "Det*a*," *De* signifying the Genus *Element; t* its Fifth Difference, Meteor, a brightness in the air; *a* the first Species of the Difference and pronounced like the *o* in *cot*.[5] To name an arch of colors "Det*a*" is to guide someone's finger down a diagram, designating branches left and right. To name it "Rainbow" is to affirm its selfhood in something like a trumpet's tongue. This matters, and not only because "rainbow" records the centuries-old consensus of the English-speaking peoples, but because when we hear "rainbow" we hear affirmed an arching colored shining ("that is its name": our naivete is profound) whereas when we read "Det*a*" we think of the system wherein "Det*a*" marks a place. The system alone is real.

In the programming languages likewise names are arbitrary, bestowed ad hoc by the programmer to the end that the Central Processing Unit (CPU) shall allocate memory spaces consistently. The only real referent of a name is a location. Thus in our program for "The Farmer in the Dell" the entry "DEF, VERSE" in seeming to define "verse" in effect instructs the CPU to allocate a sequence of locations to which any further call of "VERSE" will refer it. Instead of "VERSE" we might have used "RATS" or "SQZX," anything at all so long as we kept the usage consistent. The machine cares only for consistency, and "VERSE" does prompt fallible humans.

Similarly with the sentence: the salient event is not a predication but a branch: not an impingement on affirmed substantiality but a choice of *this* course, hence a rejection of *that*. Branches correspond to natural-language words like *if* and *then* and *as* and *for*, even *a* and *the* (any member of an array? or a specified member?). Such structures have been probed by numerous twentieth-century writers. William Carlos Williams fifty years ago wrote a poem (called "Poem") with the structure:

As the . . . over the . . . of the . . .
first the . . .
then the . . .
. . . . .

It pertains to a cat. And, "not consequent on the cat but precedent to the cat," I wrote of this poem some years ago; "a pattern proffered and conceivable as pure syntax, but a pattern which the cat renders substantial."[6] The poem's tension is that of a cat against a verbal cat's cradle. Likewise Sam Beckett in 1944:

> Mrs Gorman called every Thursday, except when she was indisposed. Then she did not call, but stayed at home, in bed, or in a comfortable chair, before the fire if the weather was cold, and by the open window if the weather was warm, and, if the weather was neither cold nor warm, by the closed window or before the empty hearth.[7]

Computer folk will intuit how this can be flowcharted (see the accompanying chart). This mirrors the structure of most nontrivial programs. All happenings are choices among options, in a field defined without ambiguity, and closed.

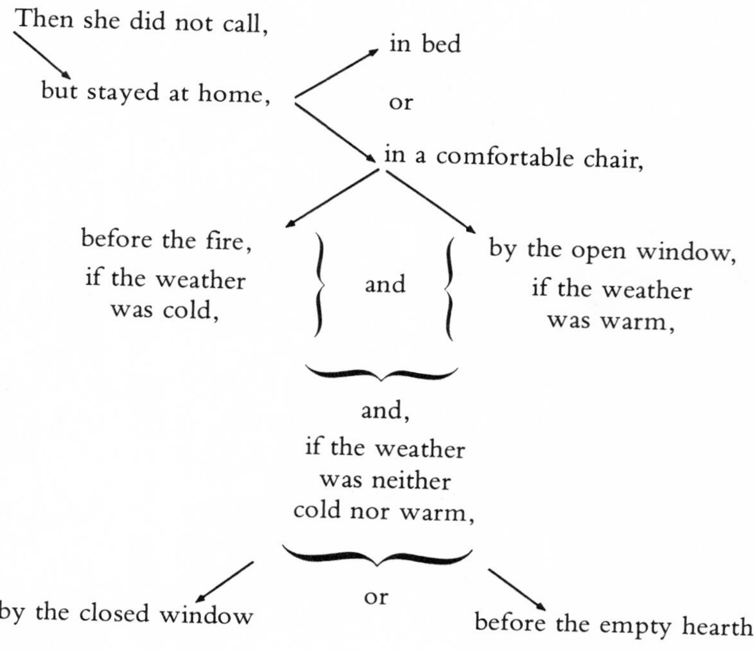

With nouns reduced to taxonomic arbitrariness, with sentences arranged as branching systems, the classic declarative gesture, affirmation, grew problematic as long ago as the seventeenth century. To affirm, what might that mean? It soon grew dubious. Affirmation was apt to connote opinion, something not scientific. (*Scientific* means "trust nobody.") What might one still say? One might narrate one's procedure and one's observations, implying that they could be repeated; one was then not asking to have one's judgment trusted but one's result verified. Or one might assert, in the Boolean algebra of classes, that sets were, or were not, or were only partially, subsets of other sets, as anyone might verify by retracing the reasoning. But these seem debilitated literary forms, despite Wordsworth's success with the former and Beckett's with the latter. The programming languages supply a new incentive for composition. In them, having just conceived something to be done, one can devise instructions for an executant who will promptly do it. Beckett's fans will empathize with this fulfillment of the fantasies of the blind immobile Hamm; and will note how ever more tightly his playscripts bind the actors, *Waiting for Godot* recognizably a play, but *Play* a program.

The programming languages are thus unique in having only one mood, the imperative. Despite appearances, they permit no affirmations. What looks like an algebraic statement, $a = b$, is in fact an instruction ("*b* belongs in box *a;* put it there"). Into an affirmation the psyche flows. Having affirmed that—affirmed anything—I am committed; there is a meaning to "I," and to commitment, and to the terms of the affirmation, which I underwrite. I say it is so, having seen that it is so. But to move things in and out of boxes is mere filing, mere efficiency, proper to a domain where you do nothing but give trivial orders.

> HAMM: I feel a little too far to the left.
> *(Clov moves chair slightly.)*
> Now I feel a little too far to the right.
> *(Clov moves chair slightly.)*
> I feel a little too far forward.
> *(Clov moves chair slightly.)*
> Now I feel a little too far back.
> *(Clov moves chair slightly.)*
> Don't stay there,
> *(i.e. behind the chair)*
> You give me the shivers.
> *(Clov returns to his place beside the chair.)*

> CLOV: If I could kill him I'd die happy.
> *(Pause.)*[8]

Happy! The voice of INTEL 8080, the Central Processing Unit. The orders that we now give to computers are the same we once gave to meek men in shirtsleeves. "Farrington?" cried a voice in James Joyce's story "Counterparts," a voice out of a head "like a large egg,"

> —Farrington? What is the meaning of this? Why have I always to complain of you? May I ask you why you haven't made a copy of that contract between Bodley and Kirwan? I told you it must be ready by four o'clock.

Farrington, c. 1904, was a human Xerox machine; nowadays the voice from the egg screams for a Xerox repairman. And in advanced societies microcircuitry has supplanted Clov, with feedback loops to obviate Hamm's finickiness and center his chair. All rolls on wheels toward certain liberations. Still, mapped by Higher Level Languages, certain habits remain, purged of *Endgame*'s melodrama but not of dubiousness.

> A precise definition of language is an elusive thing, but we come fairly close to one if we say that a language consists of a set of objects called its vocabulary, which can be combined into linear strings in accordance with certain rules known as its grammar, for communication to a recipient with the intention of inducing activity in the recipient relative to certain specific features abstracted from a general situation.[9]

Such a statement, it seems fair to say, could only have been formulated late in the twentieth century. A vocabulary is "a set of objects"; sentences are "linear strings"; and the purpose of "inducing activity" specifies the imperative as the normal mood. (A later sentence permits the indicative as a special case, when the activity to be induced is "a mere 'awareness.'") It describes the Machine Languages with studied exactness. If it seems an acceptable statement about language in general, that is because the machine and its languages epitomize what men have come to think of language during humanity's three most recent centuries. Men's technology images what they really believe, embodying deep decisions made long prior to "the state of the art." Scrutinized like our poems, our machines have similar things to disclose to us: in this instance, that during the years between Descartes and Chomsky we have fallen imperceptibly into the habit of regarding one another, much of the time, as machines.

Notes

1. Based on an example in Bryan Higman, *A Comparative Study of Programming Languages,* 2nd. ed. (London, 1977), p. 81. MACROGENERATOR was invented by C. Strachey in 1965.

2. The number, of course, is *pi* to fifteen places. Euler in fact got twenty places in that eventful hour, but since he was one of the three greatest mathematicians in history a 25 percent handicap seems fair.

3. The PL/I example is from Gerald M. Weinberg, *The Psychology of Computer Programming* (New York, 1971), p. 29.

4. This kind of point gets made routinely in books on programming style, the emergence of which in the 1970s suggests that the art is regarded by its practitioners as emerging from barbarism. It is no longer enough that programs merely *work.*

5. John Wilkins, *Essay Towards a Real Character and a Philosophical Language* (London, 1668), p. 415.

6. Hugh Kenner, *The Pound Era* (Berkeley and Los Angeles, 1971), p. 400. For the poem, see Williams's *Collected Earlier Poems* (Norfolk, 1951), p. 340.

7. Samuel Beckett, *Watt* (Paris, 1953), p. 139.

8. Samuel Beckett, *Endgame* (New York, 1958), p. 27.

9. Higman, *A Comparative Study,* p. 7.

D. A. MILLER

Language of Detective Fiction: Fiction of Detective Language

OF THE CONTEST represented in detective fiction between crime and detection, hiding and seeking, it may be asked: which side is taken by the *language* of the representation? Perhaps a case might be made that language plays accomplice to the criminal, whose secret it preserves virtually to the point of its own abolition. Do we not typically encounter this language in the act of *resisting* our demands for definite, definitive truth? Irritatingly dilatory, disingenuously dumb, it stays one or several steps behind where our desire for knowledge would be. Treacherous and evasive, all but perjured, it continually equivocates about the truth it professes to be disclosing. Such language would seem never able to "come clean," since as soon as its foul play is arrested, it has little else to say.

If it is true, then, that the language of detective fiction covers up for crime, it is only able to do so on the basis of a criminality of its own, a specifically linguistic delinquency. What threatens the readers of the detective story—threatens them, I mean, *as readers*—is the danger of a criminal language which would subject the truth to such extreme deferments, dispersions, equivocations, and oscillations that it could never be found whole and in one piece. The crime, therefore, whose effects are most in evidence in detective fiction has not to do with murder, but with meaning:

with the dissociation of signifier from signified, sign from meaning. "The principal difficulty of your case," Sherlock Holmes tells a client, "lay in the fact of there being too much evidence" (Arthur Conan Doyle, "The Naval Treaty"). At the scene of the crime, in place of the crime, we find a clutter of clues, signs dauntingly in excess of a meaning which would order and account for them. At the same time, Holmes can also declare in another case, "We are suffering from a plethora of surmise, conjecture and hypothesis" ("Silver Blaze"). Just as the excess of clues always points to a *lack* of evidence, the dearth of meaning is also manifest as a proliferation of meanings: arbitrary, unverified, competing speculations that threaten to remain forever in the air. Whether one has an overabundance of signs, or an excess of unattached meanings, the easy equatability of sign and meaning has been troubled. In the text generated and sustained by that troubling, the very prospect of an ultimate, authoritative meaning seems menaced. Worse than criminal, the language of detective fiction risks becoming criminally insane: distracted, de-tracked, always pulling back (suspense) or away (false leads) from the truth it will not fully predicate.

So sidling a language necessarily sides with criminality. Yet how, in the last analysis, is criminality characterized in detective fiction? From Hercule Poirot: "We are confronted here with an unknown personage. He is in the dark and seeks to remain in the dark. But in the very nature of things *he cannot help throwing light upon himself*. . . . Crime is terribly revealing. Try and vary your methods as you will, your tastes, your habits, your attitude of mind, and your soul is revealed by your actions" (Agatha Christie, *The ABC Murders*). From Sherlock Holmes, having driven a poisonous snake to return fatally upon its owner: "Violence does, in truth, recoil upon the violent, and the schemer falls into the pit which he digs for another" ("The Adventure of the Speckled Band"). (In his conception of crime thus recoiling, Holmes's own murderous part in the action scarcely matters.) "Crime never pays," then, except, to be sure, for the ideological dividends consequent on the notion itself. Far more important than the obvious moral caution carried in it is the ontological destiny it implies, whereby crime is bound by the nature of things to disclose its own secrets, punish its own wickedness. In the long run, the criminal is merely one who takes the law into his own hands: the unknown murderer proves an unwitting suicide. His apparent evasion of the policed regime of the law becomes finally no more than a circuitous, merely *perverse* return to its jurisdiction. For not only the law, but also its policing force have been installed *inside* crime: in the logic of criminal activity (the snake that bites its owner, the gang that exterminates itself), within the exigencies of the criminal mind ("tell-tale" guilt, nerves, overreaching).

The criminal language of detective fiction is subject to the same liability to backfire as crime itself. For all its deviancy, this language ultimately "plays" into the hands of the law: pointing, even aspiring, to its own rehabilitation. The signifiers of this language may appear to drift away from an ultimate signified, but their drift is always already anchored by it. Just as the question of a riddle is spoken and heard from the foreknowledge of its own answerability, the solution here presides over the very posing of the mystery, and the distractedness of language is read under the guarantee of its ultimate propriety and directedness. Although the text richly "stammers," such stammering serves the aperitive function of making the reader hungry for the ultimate meaning it teases him by hiding. "'I will reveal everything.' But he had presumed too much upon his strength. When he again tried to speak, he could not" (Emile Gaboriau, *Monsieur Lecoq*); "There was something else she would fain have said . . . but a fresh convulsion seized her and choked her words" ("Speckled Band"); "Her distended eyes saw—she understood—her lips seemed to form a word, but nobody made it out, and she fell back insensible" (Gaston Leroux, *The Mystery of the Yellow Room*). By seeming to subvert the already decided prospect of truth, this suspenseful, suspensive language produces the counter-effect of enhancing its value.

Insofar as the detective story dramatizes no more than the difficulties of *access* to the truth, it presupposes—and predisposes of—a truth to which one may accede: one, whole, universal, and merely *held back* for the duration of the text. We read through the language of detective fiction in order to get to this final truth—that is to say, more blatantly, we read this language in order *to put an end to it.* The notable amounts of tobacco and other drugs consumed by the great detectives assist in glamorizing a reading that is itself drugged and addictive: able to account for its pleasure only in terms of sheer compulsiveness ("I couldn't put it down," "I had to finish it"). From the distractedness which is the language of the text, we are in turn distracted, by the promise of the "fix" which is fixed meaning.

It is no exaggeration to say that the truth we pursue across the text is the detective's *reading* of it. For if the exemplary tool of classical detection, the magnifying glass, belongs as much to a technique of reading manuscripts and uncovering palimpsests as to criminology, this is because detective stories conceive reading and detection as fully analogous, often overlapping, at times perfectly identical activities. The crime will frequently come in the initial form of a verbal account of it, proferred by the client or reported in the newspapers, and the detective's ingenuity is commonly exercised on verbal puzzles, whether frankly cryptographic ("The Moabite Cipher," "The Gold Bug," "The Dancing Men"), or concealing semantic ambiguities he brings to light by way of adjudicating between them. (The *band* in "Speckled Band" is first thought to mean "band of gypsies," later "band formed by a snake.") The great detective is frequently said to "read" a character's appearance, or the ground about the crime frequently seen as a "blank page" signed by criminal footprints. Even when we are not dealing with explicit references to texts, language, or reading, a vocabulary of "trace," "sign," "clue," "indication," continues to refer us to a readerly rite of passage from signifier to signified.

Inevitably, the detective's reading consists in a *depletion* of the signifiers generated by the crime and accumulated in the course of inquest. If his final summing-up offers "the whole truth," it also contains "nothing but the truth," and there has always been more to tell, more to telling, than that. "Between what matters and what seems to matter, how should the world we know judge wisely?" (E. C. Bentley, *Trent's Last Case*). Thus begins a famous detective story, describing exactly the position in which it places a reader; but the story ends, like every other detective story, with the ability to sift wheat from chaff fully acquired and successfully exercised. As such-and-such is pronounced irrelevant, so-and-so a red herring, a large body of textual signifiers is exiled to a state of no status. It is no doubt paradoxical that our distracted, nerve-wracked, stupefied reading always reads about its "other": the attentive, cool, brilliant reading of the detective. The reading that places fewest demands on us curiously takes for its subject the representation of the most strenuous, meticulous, even "scientific" reading that can be imagined. Yet the more interesting paradox comes in the fact that, reading about the detective's apparently opposite reading, our reading always reads about itself. The de-tracked language *we* race through, *he* rectifies, with the same effect of cancelling it out. The censorship of the signifier involved in our state of distraction is mirrored—and, what is better, rationalized—in his act of dismissal.

The detective reads, as the detective story is read, under the assumption that only one reading of the matter at hand is correct—indeed, only one reading is possible. As detectives are fond of insisting, "There are no two ways of reasoning about the case." Qualified by the text as the *truth,* as (because at) the end of all the guessing, the detective's reading lays irrefutable claim to absolute validity. Did it not do so, it is likely that one would be more struck with the *distortion* invariably characterizing this reading, with the ways it fragments, edits, and reorders the continuum of the text. One item in a series is elevated to prime importance, minor event turns into major episode, figure yields to ground, as all the text's original hierarchies of presentation are overthrown. The name of truth is all that keeps the detective's fully valid reading from resembling its enemy: the "wild," "irresponsible" speculation that it is supposed to make henceforward impossible. *"Truth" is the alibi of detective fiction,* the ultimate signified that exculpates its language from the sin of being merely a sign. Truth licenses the dismissal of the sign under the pretense of being most faithful to it, at the same time as it arrests the multiplication of meanings by uniquely privileging one of them. Neither the detective story nor its readers can enjoy the "polysemicity" of language except as part of a project of subduing it into univocality—can enjoy even that univocality unless assured that it is more or less than interpretation: the truth.

The detective story only raises the possibility that language will never disburden itself of what it apparently "wants to say" for one reason: to lay it to rest. Like the criminal, the order of the signifier is eventually compelled "in the very nature of things" to surrender: to be converted into an order of the signified, sponsoring single, clear meanings. The ritual thus enacted, it must be added, affirms as well as represses, and celebrates as well as censors. For, moving from the order of the signifier to that of the signified, language dramatizes and reconfirms its own unrelenting truthfulness. Language cannot deceive, at least for long; nor, more importantly, can it ever remove the bar of the antithesis that keeps truth and falsehood apart. Inasmuch as the detective's final summation is the language of truth, it attests to no less than the truth of language: its irresistible orientation towards a truth with which it is finally identified. We began by asking: between crime and the police, how does the language of the detective story side? Its siding with crime, we see, shows finally for a masterful preemptive move whereby crime may be brought to justice. As such it recalls the tactics of every detective who operates, since Edgar Allan Poe, through "an identification of [his] intellect with that of his opponent" ("The Purloined Letter"). What the detective story finally describes, performs and exalts is a *detective language* which would be its own police force, infallibly designating and disciplining all "internal corruption."

Policing itself, the language of detective fiction polices the world which uses it. Whether in the urbane interviews of the "classical" kind or in the tough interrogations of the "hard-boiled" variety, *talk* is the detective's chief weapon in the conquest of criminal disorder. It is not hard to see why this should be so. If language is intrinsically truthful, then the detective's task is clearly to facilitate its production. Thus, the hard-boiled detective is required to get people to "talk" (or "sing" or "spill"), while the gangsters he is up against are usually occupied in buttoning lips. And the seemingly more genteel conversations solicited by the classical detective are charged with a similar policing function: "There is nothing so dangerous *for any one who has something to hide* as conversation! . . . A human being, Hastings, cannot resist the opportunity to reveal himself and express his personality which conversation gives him" *(ABC Murders).* The criminal cannot speak without incriminating himself in "telling" slips. Part of the proof against him at the end often consists in the fact that his language breaks down—or as it is sometimes put, "words fail him." Through talk, the detective story links together language, truth, and justice, and never more spectacularly than in the detective's final speech. Here vocality functions to attest a language fully present to meaning, as though the truth of what was said lay at least in part in the ritualized *act of saying it.* At the same time, with almost thaumaturgic powers, this speech also *enforces* the truth it comes to disclose. How else to explain why the detective story completely dispenses with the criminal's arrest, trial, and execution, except to say that these are so thoroughly *implied* in the detective's final utterance that they literally may go without saying?

Despite the many "histories" of detective fiction, there is in one sense no history to write, only a record of the venues in which a single ritual has been repeated. Or such at least would be the case were it not for the development of the now dominant hard-boiled form. For our purposes, the specificity of this American mutant lies in the heavy emphasis it places on violence—not on violence per se (whatever that is), but on violence as that which promotes and curtails the linguistic production of truth. In the classical detective story, what we have called the language of truth is freely volunteered by witnesses or teased out by the detective's logically irresistible cross-questionings. Language moves *automatically* toward truth, sorting out inconsistencies and excesses, gathering momentum from its own intrinsic veridicity. By contrast, the language in the American detective story must be extorted, coerced by muscle or at the point of a gun. Utterance is always entangled in a violent power which supervises it. This power finds its logical extreme in the frequent scenes depicting an assault on the vocal chords. For example, in a story by Raymond Chandler, a detective loops a wire around his interlocutor's throat, then jerks it taut: "You want to talk to me, spig. Maybe not right away, maybe not even soon. But after a while you want to talk to me" ("Spanish Blood"). No doubt the defensively "tight" mouth typical of the hard-boiled detective anticipates similar acts of violence against *his* vocal organs. There is now the danger that the voice of truth may be stopped in the detective's throat. One of Chandler's detectives displays a bullet-scar on his throat "close to his windpipe," as though for an emblem of the nearly perfect coincidence obtaining between the organ of speech and the object of violence. The slang and the solecisms of American detective fiction (Chandler's Marlow is archly made to remark that he "can still speak English if there's any demand for it") should not mislead us into thinking that language is debunked therein, or that it plays a weak second to "action." On the contrary, the violent power investing language dramatizes its extreme importance, as what is most at stake in the contest between the law and criminality. No less than it is the means to end the contest, language is *the very object of the struggle.*

In relation to its classical predecessor, the American detective story seems a blunt and disenchanted "critique of pure reason." It derisively places the once almighty word in a world of violent appropriations, where nonlinguistic forces of power safeguard or suppress every disclosure. Divested in the name of realism of its magical power to police the world, language is now demonstrated to require police protection itself. Despite its apparent contamination by power-relations, however, language continues to be idealized as the carrier of truth. Violence may help or hinder the production of language, but it cannot affect the nature of that production. Truthfulness remains the inalienable property of language, even as the truth—still one and indivisible—remains its ultimate subject. Like the abducted maiden of melodrama, language may be easily, perhaps fatally imperilled, but its fundamental honesty can always be counted on.

It may seem puzzling that the American form retains the ideality of an intrinsically *truthful* language while it flamboyantly, cynically dismisses the ideality of an intrinsically *powerful* language. The puzzle becomes less odd, however, if we consider the advantages of such a set-up. Just as language is now vulnerable to the violent attempts to suppress it, it also justifies the policing power which comes to compensate for its frailty. Contrary to what is sometimes thought, violence is not unleashed in this arrangement, so much as it is *licensed,* commissioned to let truth speak, to remove from the maiden her gag. Through the sheer obviousness of its justifications, a licensed violence—the violence of Order—tends to erase itself as an object of serious attention. As we see the detective moving in counter-attack or self-defense against the prior violence of the criminal "other," our perception of his violence as such is relatively neutralized. Of course, the detective story has always been an apology for Order, alarmingly disrupted by the initial crime, held in anxious suspense during the inquest, jubilantly restored by the apprehension of the criminal. The "repressed" that is "returned" at the moment of truth comprises really the existing police and para-policial systems of repression. The detective story forwards the power of these systems, not just by familiarizing us with police corruption (as with a kind of fate), but also by idealizing them at another level. "Get out of here or I'll call the police," someone screams at Ross Macdonald's Lew Archer. To which the private detective replies, "I sort of am the police" ("Find the Woman"). Ultimately, the private detective is nothing but *an ideal policeman,* doing the same work as the official force, only "better": better in a moral sense ("Down these mean streets," Chandler insisted about his detective, "a man must go who is not himself mean, who is neither tarnished nor afraid"), and better in a very practical sense as well, for he can go places, and do things, not permitted to official agents.

So ideal is this policeman's power that, in one sense, it frequently ceases to be real at all. For although he gives utterance to the truth, the American detective is seldom able or willing to be listened to by a civic order. The truth is not allowed to have public consequences. In this seemingly cynical destiny, the truth is once more set free from power-relationships, to which everything is now subject *except* the truth seen by a private, privatized eye. The entanglement between language and power is disentangled, and though the language of truth is now powerless, it is also by the same token immune from a power which can contaminate everything else. To the extent that the truth takes refuge in the private realm, one might well argue that it becomes more purely the subject of a novel—that is, the subject of a reading read by individual subjects. To the extent that we treasure an ideality so consoling that we can bear with anything, so redemptive that it need never be called on to redeem, one might also argue that this subject is part of our subjection.

LEO BRAUDY

Succeeding in Language

Pedagogy is the queen of all the arts, but in teaching we unavoidably must use an enormous amount of words as go-betweens, which creates confusion, because those who listen must transform the words into concepts and ideas.

COMENIUS, as quoted by Roberto Rossellini

More words, and then nausea.

INGMAR BERGMAN. *Persona*

. . . Hello. Duffy's Tavern, where the elite meet to eat. Archie the manager speakin'. Duffy ain't here. . . . Oh, hi, Duffy, I didn't know it was you.

ED GARDNER on the radio show *Duffy's Tavern*

WHEN I WAS in graduate school studying English literature at Yale University from 1963 to 1967, I often thought of myself as a football player, huddled over my precious cargo, facing a line of granite-chested bruisers. Beyond them was not just the goal, but the outside, and I was determined to break through, taking the punishment on my head and shoulders, looking up every so often to check directions, preserving whatever it was I carried within my arms until I could set it free.

Since I never played football and rarely watched it, the image could itself run free, until it threatened to become lost in its flourishes. But in those years it was constructed from pure self-preservation. "Try to run, try to hide, / Break on through to the other side," sang the Doors, and all around me, in the faces of my friends and acquaintances, my colleagues in the calling of language and literature, I could see what I hoped to evade: the despair or bravado of failure, the shell-shocked look of those who would find jobs but no comfort, and, most disconcerting, the twitching signs of success disfiguring those who had before seemed quite different. We had all come to study English through a combination of inward conviction, the insistence of favorite teachers, and the evidence of talent. Success would arise from a special relation to language and its uses, validated by the imprimatur of a university that still awarded its degrees in Latin. We were at Yale to learn, to search, to compound insight and labor into a name that would get a job—whereupon we would teach and the cycle would begin again.

Every profession, I knew, has its particular techniques and its special language, and I thought those students naive who had been horrified to discover that the literature they had loved as undergraduates had in graduate school often turned into a matter of footnotes, research, and lengthy papers. I knew already that part of my professional responsibility would be to take up what has been called, without irony, a custodial relation to language. But I was hardly more than dimly aware of the particular difficulties of a profession that had evolved special critical languages in order to discuss equally special literary languages. Nor had I yet experienced that enhanced sense of self a professional language can give, when a normal adult discovers he is faced with an English teacher and reduces himself to an insecure child: "That was my worst subject."

As a graduate student, I had little time to appreciate this power to exact instant subjection, although the status in being able to speak, master, and even to teach English must not have been too far from my conscious mind, since my grandparents spoke Yiddish almost exclusively. My parents, both born in America, spoke it primarily when they wanted to talk about matters they didn't want my sister and me to understand. Far from being a childhood language, then, Yiddish to me was a language of ritualized adult control, even though the secrets it veiled were usually arguments over when we should be put to bed. But I did carry with me other languages, neither those of my parents nor those of my teachers, and, in the interpreting style at which Yale was making me expert, I identified my protected football with those solitary languages of feeling salvaged desperately from my youth, that were considered irrelevant to the struggle for professional mastery and unworthy of professional tribute: the visual-verbal language of films and the musical-verbal language of popular songs. I may have realized that *Middlemarch* meant more to me married at twenty-three than it did when I wrote a paper on its imagery as a sophomore of nineteen. But it would be some time before I could see how the language of emotional connection might supplement, correct, or contradict my new professional language. Marriage, like literature, would organize the potential disruptiveness of emotion into social and linguistic forms easily subordinated to the more pressing business of vocation. Meanwhile, alone in my room on Chapel Street, I sat at my typewriter, a plug in my ear attached to a small portable radio, Fr. Klaeber open before me, translating *Beowulf* with the Beatles singing in my head.

Once again, the image crystallizes a time of defensive self-containment, when a comforting solipsism both complemented and tried to allay the forced atomization of graduate school itself. Appropriately enough, Old English (required then) was the only class first-year students took in common, and therefore the only ground of cooperation and community. Otherwise, New Haven was a world of library carrels and tiny apartments. I have since been told that, whereas the typical scientist looks back on graduate study with fondness and warmth, the typical humanist remembers only isolation and anxiety. While the embryonic scientist can enjoy the camaraderie of the laboratory, where teachers and students may even work together to create a group product, the budding humanist, in a discipline celebrated for its ability to transmit history, tradition, and "shared values," discovers a world of sharp and fragmenting competition. But the only difference may be that scientists must face later what humanists find out almost immediately, unburdened by impractical longings for collegiality and intellectual openness.

Initiatory rituals are of course a feature of all professions and many occupations as well. But how seriously one takes them should be determined by the extent to which they advance or erode the ostensible values of the profession. In the nineteenth-century evolution of professions, the founding of professional societies aimed to define who was a member, who was not, and how the change in status was to be regulated. The raising of professional standards answered well to the Napoleonic formula of careers open to talent, even while it also allowed the policing of charlatans, the ostracizing of failures, and the restriction of titles. Somewhat earlier, Samuel Johnson may have spoken slightingly of "the shelter of academic bowers" in his preface to the *Dictionary*. But he did not reject the protection his honorary degree might give him from the anxiety of eighteenth-century intellectual free-lancing.

Anyone who spends even a small amount of time in professional training begins to learn how intimately the power of a special language to define, and thereby to cure or solve, connects with the power to intimidate, and the authority of professional knowledge acquires a social dimension, where vocabulary implies class as clearly as does any Back Bay or Main Line accent. The intimidation is enhanced by the extent to which the professional views his special language as a kind of superself, an authority beyond the frailties of the immediate, a costume of eternity the otherwise inadequate individual can don and thereby escape his unpremeditated and merely personal vocabulary. To dwell on a word, to invent a language for talking about words, is to insist first that your audience admit the deficiency of their language (and their reality) so that they might then begin to measure up to the transcendent standard that you have defined but which, you must imply, exists apart from you in some rarefied common room, where the Forms take tea.

Although I have been talking about professions in general, I have in the last sentence strayed again into the special problems of the profession of literature. It is of course the profession that I know the best. But also, by its special commitment to the study of language, it can provide a focus for the ways in which all professions fortify their borders and consolidate their social and economic positions by codifying their languages. Academic disciplines, like professions, are tribes in which everyone believes in the importance of the same set of terms, but insists on wrangling endlessly over their meaning. To the extent that the terms are literally the same, the field has an ethics or a theology; to the extent that they must be continually redefined, the field has a politics and a history. The language of the academic literary critic, like the language of most humanistic disciplines, contains a group of words to be endlessly vexed in the attempt to reconcile their ambiguities, in much the same way that Edmund Leach has described the genealogies of the Old Testament as a framework within which otherwise rigid definitions of who is Jewish and who isn't can be effectively qualified. The irreconcilable urges are toward comfort and toward adventure. New people are inducted less because they are perceived to be capable of treating the field or tribe politically or historically—and therefore capable of change—than because they are perceived as being innately of the same sensibility, speaking a birth-language rather than an acquired language. The manufacture of new terms is therefore always a political act.

Before World War II, in the humanities division of the most prestigious institutions (and many farther down the ladder), one either spoke some approximation of the birth-language or one couldn't get in the door. Those non-genealogical humanists whose origins were outside the university definition of the acceptable classes had therefore to tailor their manners, style, and speech to the traditional form. Later their ideas, their personal energy, and even a small portion of their new language might get a hearing, once an acceptable professional image had been established. But a process was beginning in the 1930s, then urged quickly forward by World War II, that was reminiscent of what happened in eighteenth-century England, when outsiders like the Catholic Alexander Pope, the Irish Jonathan Swift and Edmund Burke, the Scots Tobias Smollett and David Hume, the non-Londoners and nonaristocrats Laurence Sterne and Samuel Johnson, began to teach the English about their heritage, history, and values. Instead of justifying cultural authority through lineage or wealth, they in their different ways insisted on a continuity and community of cultural sensibility that owed little to economic or political power and might even be opposed to them. If this tradition were traced to its roots, one would also see parallels in the way men as different as Dryden and Richelieu helped create a cultural climate in which literary history could be considered an alternative source of values in the face of a declining aristocratic tradition. Already within its own history, literary studies in the 1920s and 1930s had responded somewhat petulantly to the sciences by asserting the possibility that its methods and conclusions could similarly be codified and therefore "objective." In a related effort that first gathered strength in the more socially conscious 1930s, professors of literature defined their mission less in terms of analysis and interpretation of specific texts than in terms of the values they were preserving and inculcating by the mere enterprise of teaching literature.

After World War II, this interlocking emphasis on linguistic analysis and moral interpretation, energized by the admission of new people from new classes to the American university system, helped raise a defense of literary studies against any charges of conceptual archaism, historical irrelevance, or slackening social authority. In great part the presiding Zeus of the transformation was Samuel Johnson, not the Johnson who said that no one but a blockhead writes except for money, but the Johnson who through both his life and work implied that writing, the control of language, could preserve the writer (and thereby help him preserve his culture) from the willfulness and self-indulgence of aristocratic culture. To rise in class through one's mastery of language meant first to identify with the language and concerns of those whom one was joining and of necessity with the ethics of interpretation that language implied. But birth was no longer a criterion for interpretive accuracy. The glory of the postwar period in literary criticism was its insistence that special knowledge and privileged background were insufficient and even irrelevant to the discovery of meaning in literature. Johnson had amassed his own *Dictionary,* and we all had the *OED*. Everyman his own interpreter was the message. All worked individually, but all also worked implicitly toward the common verifiable end of the "complete reading."

But how does one recognize and distinguish the authentic inheritor of a tradition from the con man? The public horrors and propagandistic verbiage of World War II had brought in their wake a revulsion against language pressed into either the service of the state or the interests of demagogic individuals. In a manner reminiscent of the period after the English civil wars of the seventeenth century, postwar literary criticism attempted at once a greater precision of language and a new affirmation of timeless literary values. Pedagogy, in the form of the spellbinder or "great teacher," had traditionally used the trappings of classical oratory, and the new rhetoricians just as traditionally dismissed the orators as manipulators without any convictions of their own, suspect because they used language to persuade rather than to clarify. So, in their classic essay of 1954, "The Affective Fallacy," William K. Wimsatt and Monroe C. Beardsley included in their gamut of villains both Hitler and William Lyon Phelps. The style of self as part of the content of presentation was ruled out for both author and critic. Only by deemphasizing the self in the classroom could the democratization implied by the New Criticism be effective. The enemy to truth was personality, the excrescence that American etiquette had always been out to cure in the rising new classes. Now that literary study had been effectively separated from its class roots, the new autonomy required an etiquette of interpretation as well. If intellectual ability were to be translated into social mobility, some separation from one's prior languages was still needed, a willingness to be molded at least visibly into the preexisting forms of the chosen profession. The most important postwar development in academic politics was therefore the increasingly strong allegiance of the professor to his field rather than to his university. Scientists had long had such connections; humanists, aided by their new professional self-definition, were learning how to assert them. But the assertion of profession required the submergence of self. Class was to be shed in the service of the classroom, and along with the costume of self-effacement went an insistence on the "purity" of the play of ideas, a turning away from politics and toward ethics. The only spellbinders who might be acceptable were those who cloaked their language in the rhetoric of objectivity, withdrew their presences, and implied that their results could be verified and vindicated in the carrel of any student who cared to try.

New Criticism especially made this detachment a principle of interpretation. The self-contained critic would contemplate the self-contained work. If, as Hobbes had argued, without language there would be no society, then the mastery of language might hold off the barbarians at home and abroad, as well as repress the untoward and antisocial impulses from within. For the best practitioners, of course, mastery of language and mastery of knowledge were twin ideals. But as the new ideology was disseminated, the pose of pseudo-anonymity and pseudo-objectivity became more pronounced. Verbal analysis, it seemed, could keep the text under a control that was impossible if one allowed affective responses. By making critical language more specific and dispensing with any ambiguity that could not be encased as "tension" or "irony," the linguistic pattern was praised at the expense of other, less specifiable, modes of connection. E. B. White has remarked that "a good many of the special words of business seem designated more to express the user's dreams than to express his precise meaning."[1] But for literary study in the postwar period the dream was often a dream of precision, in which linguistic power would replace social power, and the prerogatives of a class would be transformed into the privileges of a profession. Words clarified, specified, ordered, and arranged. Self-enclosed, "sufficient" formal interrogation could discover secrets emotion could not, because, while feelings were always the same and primitive, intelligence and language evolved. Johnson had said that he was so upset by the end of *King Lear* that he could not bring himself to read it a second time until he came to edit it. So too the New Critical faith in the superiority of the work to its fallible creator concealed a fear of the power of art and its ability to excite the imagination of the reader and upset his carefully composed sense of self. The validation of the power to determine the meaning of literary language had shifted decisively from social lineage to professional commitment. But the implications and paradoxes of that new power often remained unexamined.[2]

The democratic faith of New Criticism accorded well with the general postwar fascination with both documentary evidence and religious belief. "America is a political reading of the Bible," announced an article by Richard Nixon, while at the other end of the spectrum of public politics Edward R. Murrow created a series called *This I Believe,* in which a variety of Americans formulated their personal testaments. For the nonbelievers, empirical philosophy, with its positivistic and depersonalizing mode of analysis, emphasized verifiability of interpretation. Thinking and believing occupied their mutually exclusive and mutually dependent universes. In this Pyrrhonist world, only feeling had no coterie. In 1950 my fourth-grade teacher spent many classes explaining why we should avoid *I* in expository writing. In 1964 a graduate-school teacher corrected "Thomson feels that" to "Thomson thinks that" and commented in the margin, "Poor fellow. Doesn't he know how to think?" Together the encouragement toward the passive voice and the primacy of thought were meant to subdue the ego and bow the head before truths larger than the individual. But in retrospect they seem less pure, like the operations of those priests who know that levers behind the statue can make the god roar. E. E. Cummings was celebrated in the 1950s for his playful use of language and the small letters with which he wrote *i* and his own name. With similarly back-handed assertion, analytic and objective criticism was creating impersonality cults as elaborate as the belletristic charismas of the past.

Under the democratic marquee, where intelligence was the only price of entrance, stood an increasingly long line of aspiring professors. Once inside the precincts, however, they discovered that the proud claim of the purity of true knowledge barely veiled a competition for preeminence in areas of learning and literary theory that were increasingly opaque to all but the protoprofessional. The democratic impulse of the G. I. Bill was no match for the occupational mystique of the literary scholar, which "was calculated to appeal to a powerful scribal minority, for whom linguistics still had a strong tinge of exclusive magic, and the very fact of literacy alone symbolized knowledge, authority, power."[3] In the manner of late-arriving torchbearers, the new initiates often showed their commitment by elaborating the ritual. Power was defined as the influence over word usage and word interpretation. Language therefore became at once more sanctified and more remote. Like the scholar-pornographers of the nineteenth century, such critics claimed both the privilege of being closest to the sacred material and the burden of denaturing it for the faithful who would be unable to face it without screens of critical terminology and antiquarian learning. Like the elaborate system of pulleys by which technicians handled atomic material, the literary criticism spawned by the cold war maintained life by staying at a distance.

Once the study of literature takes on the trappings of religion, then the choice of critical language becomes a moral issue, with its cults and heresies. When the critic-teacher defines himself as the master of language, then the reader-student becomes a tentative, woefully unprepared novice in the mysteries. If he falters for a second, he will not only fail to understand, but also prove himself unworthy of the time taken to instruct him. Since the time of the democratic and deindividualizing etiquette of the New Criticism, the intellectual hegemony of American literary criticism has passed through many capitalized phases, including Archetypal Criticism, Structuralism, Semiotic Criticism, Reader Response Criticism, Deconstructive Criticism, and other poststructuralist hybrids. In an important sense the field of literary study has become more permeable to perspectives and terminology from a host of other disciplines: anthropology, linguistics, philosophy, economics, art. But with this seeming intellectual expansionism has come a narrowing of vision that preserves the old hierarchies and continues to recast new energies into the images of their adoptive forefathers. New Critical formal analysis, in its effort to release literary criticism from the socially restrictive sensibilities of the past, had set the stage for the professor of the humanities to reassume his emblematic social role as a representative of "Western civilization." By banning ideology and personality from the concerns of literary criticism, the investigators of literary language had created new ideologues of their own.

But, while the New Critics at least assumed that there was a writer who had presented them with the opportunity to create a critical language that excluded the writer's importance, later criticism would attack the "illegitimately privileged" text itself, complaining of a sanctity that was unearned and authoritarian. The only necessary person was the critic who, like Berkeley's God, validated what he saw because he saw it. Saying that a literary work was a "text" allowed such a critic to manipulate it for his own ends, to create from it his own text, more privileged because more detached—the iconoclast in his turn creating, or becoming, an icon. New Critics may have assumed the intelligibility and therefore the specifiability of literary language, while many of their descendants now assume its final unintelligibility. But they are only the optimistic and the pessimistic sides of the same well-rubbed coin, a critical solipsism that may indeed be the necessary first step away from the undue pressures of society and history, but should hardly be the last. Yet the secular priesthood Coleridge had called the "clerisy" clearly appealed to those who had grown up on movie-nurtured images of the professional as an isolated moral hero who faced alone a hostile or indifferent town. As French critics already knew, and American critics were ready to learn, those who wish to be part of a romantic outlaw group of the truly moral must first create an argot, which the leaders will recoin at ritual moments: woe to the counterfeiters, outer darkness for the uninitiated.

In the hierarchies of the anointed, success naturally implies succession. Although the postwar emphasis on critical depersonalization led the way, it does seem appropriate that the schools of the newer criticisms have arisen in the past ten years, at a time when the baby boom of the war years has passed through the university. With a newly contracting student population, the university itself was changing, the open field for academic jobs that characterized the period from about 1950 to 1970 was increasingly crowded, and the competition becoming more cutthroat. The possession of one of the new languages therefore offered to the graduate student an efficient passport to security. Although his own thoughts might be inchoate, and what he wanted to say or contribute uncertain, his sense of where the professional winds were blowing might accompany but hardly required intelligence, understanding, or accomplishment. Professional language, critical jargon, could supply the necessary stilts to get the ambitious student over otherwise baffling hurdles. The process may not substantially differ from the traditional way the apprentice entered a profession; yet the social mobility that previously had been the reward of talent and intelligence was now often bestowed for the possession of a hermetic and ritualized vocabulary into which the world could be processed. The student armed with such a language could sell himself as the newest product of a literary profession that seemed more akin to an industry or a business, in both its standards of analysis and the social behavior of its practitioners. Efficiency was the watchword: the efficiency of landing a job by an efficient method of interpretation that employed a preexisting terminological framework, to such separate but equal ends as teaching language by computer or analyzing literature by decoding.

The concept of profession, with its emphasis on merit and a coherent body of knowledge, has, since the beginning of the nineteenth century, had a key role in the creation of both the opportunities and the barriers of the modern world. But when professions define themselves as priesthoods interested primarily in their own perpetuation, they can irretrievably stunt both their social and their intellectual vitality. Much insight has come from the efforts of those who took the study of literature away from the sole possession of a genealogical elite, and revealed its mysteries through a language literature itself rarely spoke. But more damage results when critical and interpretive language becomes so self-adoring and self-perpetuating that it offers its audience few if any new ways to open up or expand the understanding of any particular author, work, or period. Still laboring under the imperatives of postwar retrenchment, American literary criticism has distinctly failed to help bring cultural insight up to the level of the political, social, or economic insight available in the worst popular magazines. The benefits that have come from the concentrated investigation of literary language and procedures have rigidified into a variety of competing authoritarianisms of interpretation. The specificity of literature and its potential to deal with ungeneralizable situations are faced and often defeated by the critic's desire to extract generalizations that testify to his moral nature and professional insight. The writer's desire to create a work that is unique and intense is faced and often defeated by the critic's desire to "raise" its importance by showing how similar it is to other works or to point out that its real subject is criticism and interpretation.

To the extent that contemporary literary criticism has replaced a social elite with a language elite, it has confirmed and extended the worst aspects of the old hierarchies, institutionalizing an exclusionary view of knowledge that brandishes sacerdotal metaphors of initiation, mystery, and the passing on of the flame. Generalization is an essential part of the humanistic enterprise. But it should not be forgotten that the very nature of humanistic culture is in its incompleteness, its basic unwillingness to come to an end in its attempt to describe and to understand the possibilities open to human nature and human understanding. Those professions who pride themselves on their sensitivity to language have an obligation to distinguish between the generalizations that intensify meaning and those that displace attention to their own systems of incantation. *Theory* originally means "to take a view of" and *theoroi* were at first tourists who traveled to view the local celebrations of another city. Later, it is true, they had become official sacred emissaries, although one might assume that they did not view disdainfully, whatever the provocation, unlike those acolytes of professional language who are now sent out from the great centers to bring the message to the barbarians.

To the more common proposition that professions combine a practical theory with an ideal of service, William J. Goode has added a third element: the necessary trust between "client" and professional.[4] In these terms, although medicine is considered by sociologists to be the model profession, it is teaching that relies much less catastrophically and therefore more pervasively on bonds of social trust. The teaching of literature intensifies even that situation by its preoccupation with the way emotions and personal energies have been shaped by language and embodied in a variety of verbal forms. While the scientist may rule emotion out of his studies by definition, and the social scientist include emotion in order to quantify it, the student of literature considers it his prime subject matter—the emotions and thoughts of the past as they have been preserved for us by language. Lawyers connect us with social norms, doctors with the demands of nature, and clergymen with the realm of the spirit. But teaching—including the teaching of law, medicine, and theology—tends to deal with the variety of human languages and how to understand them and their relation to each other.

Of all the academic professions, literary criticism especially labors to steer between a flexible and an authoritarian use of its special language, between an open and a coercive attitude toward its subject matter. When the demands of professionalization create not teachers but salesmen for special languages that will supposedly unlock the doors of employment, the atomization process I first experienced in graduate school will have become the norm. The sensitivity to language will not have made teachers of literature like Odysseus—able to speak to anyone in their own language—but like hermits, each desperately peering from his professional enclave.

Authoritarianisms of all sorts flourish on the isolation of their subjects. It has been a phenomenon of twentieth-century life that the increasing professionalization of work has created a society in which economic and psychic hardships are freely visited on those outside the pale. But democracy in our world seems less and less to be the flatly egalitarian order that so many of its proponents and its detractors claim than a vital context in which a growing number of groups display their languages and make their demands. Since, in each of us, a good many of those groups overlap, is it possible that autonomy and interdependence, like Duffy the forever absent owner and Archie the garrulous manager, need each other for definition?

Language is the prime tool by which we understand the world, and the process of statement, correction, and adjustment is endless. Since it is an essential part of the social role of language specialists to teach how language unexamined becomes language as authoritarian truth, it seems hardly worthy that so many critics and scholars merchandise their own languages as stencils for the world. The privileges of the literary text are less dangerous than the privileges of the text about the text. Literary criticism needs as much replenishment by experience as does literature itself. Those who follow the profession of language should be less concerned with mandarin restrictions and distinctions than with creating a situation in which all languages might have equal entry and be subject to equal scrutiny. Otherwise the teaching of language and literature will have taken up a somewhat shorter place in social history than that of manciple. The learning of language, as Odysseus knew, is both an exploration of self and a journey through the world, a series of successive releases from the authority of static gurus and self-important oligarchies. The way in which, since World War II, special languages have first helped to insulate and then to stifle literary criticism may show us what elite learning in a democracy might be, rather than what it has been: not a self-protective professional group with little sense of its relation to the rest of society and its languages, but a special group among many special groups, each with its training and its goals—ours both to show the struggle of language to articulate without controlling and to foster a creative uncertainty amid competing truths. But when the categories of literary criticism ignore the emotions without which their patterns do not work, they create a self-contained process in which the critic discovers only the pattern of his own confinement. Writing, even writing about language, can be as much a response as a purification, for discrimination hardly requires the invocation of absolute hierarchies of moral and aesthetic value. Too often the fate of warriors has been to become inseparable from their armor, frozen in the stances of battle. Professional and personal defensiveness may make it difficult to unhunch one's shoulders, even after the ball has long since been carried across the line.

Notes

1. William Strunk, Jr., and E. B. White, *The Elements of Style,* 3rd ed. (New York, 1979), p. 83.

2. Compare, for example, Arthur Engel's remarks about the effort of the Tractarians in nineteenth-century Oxford to establish teaching as a lifetime career rather than merely a prelude to the clergy: "They saw that power was in the hands of a tight oligarchy of heads of houses, most of whom were hostile to their ideas. The Tractarians therefore wished to undermine the power of the present rulers of the university, while still preserving its autonomy" ("Emerging Concepts of the Academic Profession at Oxford, 1800–1854," in Lawrence Stone, ed., *The University in Society,* vol. 1 [Princeton, 1974], p. 319).

3. So Peter Green, in an article about classical studies, describes the survival of humanistic education in rhetoric and linguistics from the late Roman Empire through the Middle Ages and into the Renaissance ("The Humanities Today," in Peter Green, *Essays in Antiquity* [London, 1960], p. 4).

4. For a concise statement of Goode's views, see "The Professionalizing Occupations," in *Professionalism and Humane Values,* Columbia University General Education Seminar Reports, vol. 4 (Fall 1975): 97–104.

Societies

DAVID LODGE

Where It's At: California Language

IF YOU DRIVE northwards out of San Francisco by the Golden Gate bridge you will find yourself entering an idyllic landscape known as Marin County. It has hills and valleys crammed with redwoods and eucalyptus, a spectacular Pacific coastline and, on its lee shore, looking across the Bay, sheltered coves, marinas and the picturesque Italianate harbor town of Sausalito. In this immensely desirable location live the affluent, progressive, trend-haunted and fad-obsessed Californians who are the object of Cyra McFadden's wickedly knowing satire, *The Serial: A Year in the Life of Marin County.*[1]

At the center of its story are the Holroyds, a not-so-young couple whose income and energies are severely strained by their efforts to keep up with the Marin County Joneses. As one of their friends says, "Marin's this high-energy trip with all these happening people" and what these people are "into" is "the human potential movement" in all its ramifications (one character alone has tried, over the years, "Gurdjieff, Silva Mind Control, actualism, analytical tracking, parapsychology, Human Life Styling, postural integration, the Fischer-Hoffman process, hatha and raja yoga, integral massage, orgonomy, palmistry, Neo-Reichian Bodywork

---

This essay was originally published in a slightly different form in *Encounter* magazine under the title, "Where It's At: The Poetry of Psychobabble."

and Feldenkrais functional integration"), physical fitness, ecology and the cultivation of everything ethnically exotic in dress, food and design. Kate Holroyd herself is heavily into women's liberation and macramé, while her husband Harvey, who works in a San Francisco bank and cycles home from the Sausalito ferry every evening on his ten-speed Motobecane, is all too susceptible to other liberated ladies in the area. In the course of the chronicled year the Holroyds have a trial separation, and experiment unsuccessfully with alternative partners and life styles before, in the final chapter, renewing their marriage vows at a totally laid-back party where the Reverend Spike Thurston of the Radical Unitarian Church pronounces them conjoined persons and the guests shower them with brown rice.

The peculiar *frisson* enjoyed by a reader of *The Serial* derives from the narration of what is essentially a suburban soap opera in a style borrowed from the characters themselves, who are constantly asserting their membership of a sophisticated, liberated, trend-setting elite. The book is therefore an invaluable guide to the dialect of the Bay Area, "the consciousness-raising capital of the western world" as Cyra McFadden has justly called it, a golden treasury of the slang that is spoken there by the educated middle classes, and carried, by a kind of cultural gulf-stream, to every part of the world where English is spoken. The linguistic ingredients of this dialect are varied and sometimes difficult to discriminate. The Counter Culture of the 1960s, black ghetto slang, jazz and rock jargon, sporting terminology, are certainly key sources, and it tends to be adopted and disseminated around the world most readily by pop musicians, disc jockeys, top athletes and "alternative" artists. But what this language is applied to by the cultured, progressive middle classes is human relationships and states of mind. It is essentially a language of psychological description and negotiation.

For example, Kate's friend Martha feels that she has learned after five marriages that "marriage was this dynamic process. You had to stay in touch with yourself if you were going to relate to the other person's feelings instead of just ego-tripping"; but she hesitates to get involved in counselling Kate because "after all, she and Bill were still getting inside each other's heads, a high-energy trip that didn't leave a lot of space for outside interaction." Kate herself puts off an intrusive acquaintance by saying, "Harvey and I are going through this *dynamic* right now, and it's kinda where I'm at. I haven't got a lot of psychic energy left over for social interaction. So whatever it is, maybe you should just run it by me right here. Off the wall."

All the published comment on *The Serial* that I have read has assumed that this idiom is self-evidently absurd and vicious, and that by merely exhibiting its intensive use in cold print Cyra McFadden has destroyed its potency and performed a valuable act of linguistic hygiene. The author herself has given considerable support to this view by her comments in interviews and articles. A former college teacher of "bonehead English," she has presented her book as a polemic against sloppy and automatized speech, and has endorsed, as a generic term for the idiom her characters use, *psychobabble,* a word coined by R. D. Rosen in a critique of do-it-yourself ego-psychology entitled *Psychobabble: Fast Talk and Quick Cure in the Era of Feeling,* published in 1977, not long after *The Serial.* According to Rosen, psychobabble is

> a set of repetitive verbal formalities that kills off the very spontaneity, candour and understanding it pretends to promote. It's an idiom that reduces psychological insight to a collection of standardized observations, that provides a frozen lexicon to deal with an infinite variety of problems.

Cyra McFadden agrees. Conversations conducted in psychobabble, she says, "make any exchange of ideas impossible; block any attempt at true communication; substitute what Orwell called 'prefabricated words and phrases' for thought."[2] British commentators, always prone to fits of linguistic chauvinism, have eagerly concurred. In a long article in *The Guardian* heralding the English edition of *The Serial* and referring to Rosen's book, Christopher Reed declared that psychobabble is "the Newspeak of our age—puerile pap, specious speech, yet a dangerously pretentious nonsense talk which one day could engulf us all."[3]

I regard this consensus of opinion as simplistic and unduly alarmist, for several reasons.

(*1*) Any language is necessarily a finite system applied with different degrees of creativity to an infinite variety of situations, and most of the words and phrases we use are "prefabricated" in the sense that we don't coin new ones every time we speak. Spoken (as distinct from written) discourse is especially dependent upon verbal formulae because we can't take in more than a certain density of information through the ear and because speech is not always primarily referential in function, but also phatic, affective, expressive, etc., and formulaic repetition may be useful for these purposes.

(*2*) Slang (of which psychobabble is an example) is generated precisely to relieve the inevitable monotony and deadening familiarity of ordinary speech by providing an alternative lexicon which is both novel and yet easily acquired and widely applicable. It also serves to define membership of a particular social or cultural subgroup, and to this end may be made deliberately mystifying to the uninitiated (e.g., criminal argot), but most slang, and certainly psychobabble, is not deliberately exclusive in this way. Slang is the poetry of ordinary speech in a precise linguistic sense; it draws attention to itself *qua* language, by deviating from accepted linguistic norms, substituting figurative expressions for literal ones, and thus "defamiliarizes" the concepts it signifies. Once slang becomes so common and familiar that it is no longer foregrounded in this way against the background of more orthodox usage, its days are numbered and it either disappears or is absorbed into the standard language.

(*3*) The very success of psychobabble (for the sake of consistency I will adopt this heavily pejorative term)—the way it has spread across America and begun to penetrate English English[4]—suggests that it must answer some genuine linguistic need and possess some distinctive rhetorical appeal, which it would be worth trying to analyze and understand.

This brings me back to *The Serial,* which I found pleased and fascinated me to a degree that could not be accounted for solely in terms of satirical effect, or the author's stated intentions, but derived in large part from the purely aesthetic appeal of its dialect. Probably the English reader will react to this differently from an American—certainly from a Californian. What is no doubt familiar to the latter is still to a large extent novel to us, and its "poetic" dimension consequently more perceptible. That is my justification for venturing a rhetorical analysis of psychobabble. I write in the spirit of an anthropologist who once did some field work in the area,[5] but is a little rusty and subject to correction by the natives. The general descriptive points I would make about psychobabble are these. It is a predominantly metaphorical type of discourse, and the metaphors are usually drawn from *the movement or organization of matter in space,* though the vehicle[6] of a given metaphor is often extremely vague (this is what makes it both attractively flexible in application and vulnerable to criticism as lacking precision). Psychobabble is predominantly verbal rather than nominal in emphasis, and relies heavily upon the deviant use of adverbs and prepositions to give commonplace verbs a new, figurative force.

Now for examples from *The Serial,* beginning with some words and phrases that are already well established in English English.

For instance, *into,* as in the reference to "an artist who was heavily into belt-buckle casting," or the description of a former banking colleague of Harvey's who has "dropped out" (itself a spatial-dynamic metaphor) and is "into bonsai trees, meditation and Zen jogging." In standard English, *into* is a preposition qualifying verbs of motion and investigation like *go, come, run, look.* As a qualifier of the verb *to be,* which expresses a steady state, it is anomalous, and it is only figuratively that *into* may be applied to activities which have no precise location in space, such as belt-buckle casting, the cultivation of bonsai trees, meditation and Zen jogging. Used in this way, *into* becomes a metaphorical substitute for participles like *interested in, absorbed by.*

Another deviant combination of the verb *to be* + preposition is the phrase *where* [pronoun] *is at,* as in "Harvey and I are going through this dynamic right now and it's kinda where I'm at." This use of *at* is redundant in standard English, since the sense is adequately expressed by "where I am." However, by adding the tautological *at* in the emphatic position at the closure of the clause, the speaker implies that a position has been reached in a process of change which has been going on and is (by implication) likely to continue. Kate feels the need of a friend who knew "where she was coming from and where she was at." There is a kind of contradiction here, and in the previous example, in that Kate seems to see herself as both stationary and moving; and this illustrates one of Cyra McFadden's most effective devices for ridiculing psychobabble, namely to make its exponents mix their metaphors.

Where you're/I'm/he's/she's/coming from is a metaphor of movement in space particularly favored by the Marin set, used to denote the values or philosophy of life or personal experience that motivates behavior and speech. "I know where you're coming from" is roughly translatable as "I understand what you mean," but additionally connotes that the addressee is undergoing a process of change and has in some sense *moved* towards an encounter with the addresser. Another popular phrase, again a metaphor of movement in space, is *get behind,* meaning to accept, support, identify with. "Weddings were much less conformist now that people were getting behind marriage again," Kate reflects; and, told that one of her friends has become a Lesbian, exclaims, "How does she *feel* about it? I mean, can she get behind it?" When the two tropes are combined, the effect is comical. "So you see, Harvey," says Kate in the course of one of their matrimonial rap-sessions, "I can't exactly get behind where you're coming from."

Another, related, satirical device of Cyra McFadden's is

abruptly to expose the metaphorical nature of a psychobabble phrase by unexpectedly bringing into play its literal meaning and application. Kate's friend Martha insists on sending her husband's shirts to the laundry because she "couldn't get behind ironing boards." Harvey's daughter Joan refuses to wash her father's socks because "I'm not into that laundry bag." (*Bag* is of course another spatial metaphor in the same dialect, meaning matrix of interests, concerns.) These are unintended collisions of the metaphorical and the literal; but sometimes Harvey, who has a thin core of resistance to psychobabble and the life-style it articulates, will make conscious play with the same device. One evening he arrives home from work to find his wife and mistress lying in wait for him with a jury of feminist sisters. "I know where you're coming from," he acknowledges as they accuse him of being a male chauvinist pig.

> "So what are you going to do, Harvey? Where are *you* coming from?" "I'm coming from the bank," Harvey said. Nobody laughed.

Later, Kate refuses to tell him who she is meeting for a lunch date, on the grounds that she is entitled to her privacy. "Oh, sure," says Harvey. "Listen, I know where you're coming from. I just wondered where you're going."

As well as *coming from,* there is *coming down* (possibly a weather metaphor deriving from the sea-fog that suddenly descends upon the Bay Area in summer), meaning "happening" and usually applied to something unpleasant or serious or worrying. "Hey, look, what's coming down here anyway?" says Harvey, when he finds himself ambushed by the women's libbers. And there is *come on,* meaning "behave," but connoting movement again, as if the person to whom it is applied is advancing upon the addresser with offensive intent. "Stop coming on with all that incredible crap," says Kate to Harvey at the beginning of the same scene, when he defensively addresses the women as "Ladies." Then there is, of course, *coming out,* which used to be done by debs and is now done by gays.

But the verb that is subject to the greatest variety of mutation in psychobabble is undoubtedly *get.* In addition to *get behind,* already mentioned, there is *get centered, get down, get it on, get* [noun or pronoun] *together, get off on,* and *get to.* (I didn't notice *get with it* in *The Serial,* so perhaps that is now out, as distinct from far out, like Kate's Danish Modern extendable dining table.)

Get centered is self-explanatory ("What did matter was being true to yourself, getting centered . . . "). *Get down* is more elusive, but seems to be a contraction of *get down to* (a task), as in "That's why we're here [at a male-female consciousness-raising session], you know. To really get down and relate." But it can be applied to more hedonistic pursuits. For example, a party that is "getting down" is evidently becoming mildly orgiastic.

Get it on with has a specifically sexual meaning and is equivalent to the English colloquialism "have it off with," though I am unable to unpack this particular metaphor. The Reverend Spike Thurston presides at Martha's fifth marriage wearing a purple Marvin Gaye teeshirt inscribed, "Let's Get It On"—a witty play on literal and metaphorical meanings. *Get off on* is a doubly metaphorical expression, denoting the achievement of sexual excitement or climax of a masturbatory or fetichistic kind, but usually applied in *The Serial* to nonsexual gratifications. The following example brings out the distinction nicely:

> It sent Kate really into the pits when she learned from her "friend" Martha, who seemed to get off on laying bad trips on people, that Harvey was getting it on with Carol.

Note the other characteristic spatial-dynamic metaphors here—*into the pits* (= depression), *lay* (= inflict) and *trip* (= experience). Variants on *get it together* include *get my head together* and *get my act together,* all metaphors of assembling and integrating something fragmented and disorganized. *Get to* means to hurt, annoy or disturb. "When the news of Kate's and Harvey's separation reached Martha . . . it really got to her"—a metaphor of penetration.

Another key verb in psychobabble is *hang,* meaning to act, behave, comport oneself. The injunction to "hang loose" is familiar and expressive, conveying a quintessentially Californian state of relaxed readiness for new experience. *Hang in* seems to mean something like the English colloquialisms *hang on* and *hold on,* but without the connotations of strenuous effort those phrases have. "Now listen, Harv," his secretary counsels him when he is suffering from jealousy, "you gotta stay loose, you know? Hang in there; go with it. . . ." And Kate tells Harvey later: "So if you want me to hang in there any longer, you're gonna have to bring your energies to reconstituting this marriage entirely." It has been plausibly suggested to me by two independent correspondents[7] that the metaphorical vehicle in this phrase derives from surfing. To "hang ten" in surfing jargon is to cling to the front of the board with your ten toes while travelling at perilous speed down the face of a big wave. Presumably the preposition *in* originally evoked the concave shape of the cresting wave. *Hang in there* is however a phrase popular with all kinds of athletes—the "in there" being readily applicable to stadia, arenas, etc.

Some other characteristic spatial-dynamic tropes of psychobabble: *To blow away*=to surprise, astonish, as in "Martha's last wedding had just blown Kate away, so she was looking forward to this one too." This seems to be a pastoral mutation of the 1960s' psychedelic idiom, *to blow one's mind,* with its connotations of electric overload.

To dump on (intransitive)=to inflict one's worries upon, as when Kate says to a psychiatrist friend, "Leonard, I'm sorry to dump on you like this, but I'm on a really heavy trip right now."

Flash on=notice, realize, think of, an image of an object suddenly illuminated, as in this fragment of gallery talk: "symbolism's really heavy; did you flash on how all of her phalluses have these terrific mushroom clouds on top?"

Heavy=serious, grave, important, powerful, oppressive (see two preceding examples). The adverb *heavily* is frequently used as an emphatic of *into,* as in "Julie had been the only other woman on the block who was heavily into macramé."

Interface=relationship, as in "she and Harry hadn't finalized the parameters of their own interface." Sometimes used as a verb meaning to have a dialogue, as in "we've got to interface about the menu."

Off the wall=spontaneously, as in "She had decided to play the whole scene off the wall, to just go with the flow" (Kate preparing to confront Harvey's girl friend for the first time). Presumably this is a sporting metaphor, an image of a ball bouncing. (There is an older, Eastern application of this phrase to mean "mad, crazy, bizarre.")

Run [*it*] *by*=show, explain, as in " 'Martha,' he said when she'd finished, 'run that one by me again slowly, will you?' " (Bill to Martha, when she proposes a mixed consciousness-raising group). An image of exhibiting a mobile object.

Swing with=accept, tolerate, as in "minor annoyances Kate could have swung with had it not been for other, more oppressive problems."

Upfront=honest, honestly, as in "Harvey told everyone that living with Marlene was fantastic, but if he'd been really upfront, their relationship wasn't really a waterbed of roses."

As I remarked earlier, adverbs and prepositions are particularly important in psychobabble, and the use of *out* illustrates this very clearly. It qualifies a great many words, both literal and metaphorical, usually connoting the breaking of some conventional limit or boundary, a dangerous but exhilarating excess, e.g., to *munch out* (to gorge oneself), to *mellow out* (relax as a result of taking dope), to *wig out* (to get very excited, a variant of the older "flip one's wig"), to *freak out* (to go or cause to become very excited), to *gross out* (to disgust) and to *luck out,* which means not to run out of luck, but to find permanent good fortune. And of course anything admirably original or daring is *far out* or *outasight.*

Finally, I would note the metaphorical use of the word *space* itself, meaning, well, where a person's at. "Kate wasn't really high on chest hair . . . but Leonard had a lot going for him otherwise, and Kate liked the space he was in." "I hear you, babe," says Martha's husband, Bill, "I just can't figure out what space you're in. Like, I'm just not in the same place, you know what I mean?" Used as a participle, *spaced out,* or adjective, *spacey,* the word refers to the slowing down of perception and loss of control of motor functions as a result of taking drugs.

This glossary is by no means exhaustive, but I hope it supports the generalizations I advanced earlier, that psychobabble is a predominantly verbal and metaphorical type of slang, which presents experience primarily in terms of the movement and organization of matter in space. It thus has a kind of systematic coherence which lends itself to "poetic" patterning in a literary text like *The Serial,* and also expresses a definable ideology or world view, which might be summed up in Martha's words of counsel to Kate Holroyd: "'Kate,' said Martha soothingly, 'it's all process, okay?'"

Human existence is seen as a process of incessant change, readjustment and discovery—no one's condition is static or fixed. This is ultimately a very optimistic world view of a characteristically American kind, since it banishes ennui and promises that no evil will be permanent. The rhetoric of psychobabble also tacitly allays the fear of death by avoiding metaphors drawn from organic life, in which change means eventual decay; its model of experience is drawn from physics, not biology—the individual is pictured in terms of energy and mass, moving about in a curiously timeless psychological space.

It is significant that psychobabble is verbal rather than nominal, abstract rather than concrete, in its emphasis, and hardly impinges at all on the world of material objects. Indeed, the characters in *The Serial* are almost obsessively literal in their allusions to concrete objects—everything is very precisely ticketed according to its brand name or technical specification or place of origin, and the reason for this is not far to seek: these material objects, consumed and possessed, confer status and define identity in the subculture, and their indexical function in this respect would be blurred by "poetic" language. Cyra McFadden's cataloguing of such objects is as observant as her ear for speech is finely tuned:

> Harvey made a lot more money now . . . but they spent it on things they hadn't known existed ten years ago: Rossignol Startos and season lift tickets at Squaw; twin Motobecane ten-speeds; Kate's Cuisinart, which did *everything* but put the pâté in the oven; Stine graphics; Gumpoldskirchner and St. Émilion (Harvey had "put down" a case in the vacuum cleaner closet); Klip speakers and the top-of-the-line Pioneer receiver; Brown Jordan patio furniture; Dansk stainless and Rosenthal china; long-stemmed strawberries and walnut oil from the Mill Valley Market; Birkenstock sandals and Adidas (Kate didn't actually jog yet, but she was reading *The Ultimate Athlete*). . . .

The basic structural irony of *The Serial* is indeed the spectacle of people allegedly dedicated to "process," spontaneity, freedom and liberation, in fact being trammelled and subjugated by static, finite objects and possessions. Still, there are worse human fates, and, just as I cannot agree with the wholesale condemnation of psychobabble, so I wouldn't trust any middle-class, educated reader of *The Serial* who claimed not to feel even a twinge of envy for the life-style of its characters. As one of them says:

> "Yeah, but who would live anywhere else? . . . Like, I went to this garage sale last weekend: live music, hot *hors d'oeuvres,* Parducci Vineyards Gamay Beaujolais. *Wow,* I said to myself, *only* in Marin. This is where it's at, you know?"

Notes

1. *The Serial* is published in Great Britain by Picador and in the United States by Knopf.

2. Cyra McFadden, "Psychobabble," *Harpers Queen,* February 1978.

3. Christopher Reed, "The Psychobabble Enigma," *The Guardian,* 14 January 1978.

4. I recently had personal experience of the contagiousness of this idiom in the perhaps surprising situation of a university English department's examiners' meeting. When a rather disappointing result was being discussed, I remarked (no doubt as a result of reading *The Serial* in bed the night before) that the candidate, though with a good record in course work, hadn't been able "to get it together" in the final examinations. Within half an hour, two of my colleagues, including a

senior lecturer in Anglo-Saxon and historical philology, had used the same expression in similar contexts, though I had never heard it pass their lips before.

5. See my novel *Changing Places* (Secker & Warburg, 1975; Penguin, 1978).

6. I. A. Richards distinguished the two elements of a metaphor as the "tenor" and the "vehicle." Thus in "the ship ploughed the waves," the movement of the ship is the tenor and *ploughed* is the vehicle.

7. John Blackwell and Jocelyn Harris.

❧ GAVIN EWART

More Is Better—Or Is It?

NOBODY CONFRONTED WITH America could say anything but
'What a nation!'
What a genius for overdoing it, for overkill! Transport is
'transportation',
a house is never burgled any more, it has to be 'burglarized'
and instead of being buggered the boys (and girls) get 'sodomized'.
They never *shorten* anything—that would make it less important—
they inflate the English language in a way they certainly oughtn't
to, indeed everything goes into officialese, a kind of
gobbledygook
invented by the sort of people who never open a (hardcover)
book.
And they're prudish with it. A cock gets to be a 'rooster',
a bull is 'a male cow'. We're back in Cranford. What a
confidence-booster
to think that the Fate of the Western World, subject to every kind
of delay, difficulty and technical hitch
is in the hands of fellows who can't bring themselves to call a
hound a bitch!

'As of now', 'at this moment in time' and that dream word
'situation'—

surely such phrases as these have sodomized communication?
But in this ghastly patois 'meet up with' is most gooey—
in those innocent far-off days they said 'Meet me in St. Louis!'
and it was always 'meet me' in those old-fashioned conditions,
but communal self-importance has added two needless
prepositions.

I don't so much mind 'talk with' instead of 'talk to', but no
colloquial myth
is going to be established by saying 'I gave him a good
talking-with'.

But most terrible of all is how stupidly and dopefully
they use (and we use) that ubiquitous 'hopefully'.
Two birds with one stone are said to be killable
but they've done the reverse—by adding an extra syllable
to the 'I hope' or 'We hope'. And without getting into digressions
or sermons
I can tell you that *hoffentlich* is not used so much, in this way, even
by the Germans.
It's a wounded language—with transplants, amputation, suture—
when we've made a nonsense of a sentence like 'He looked
forward hopefully to the Future'.

Perhaps it *is* more logical to say 'on the street', not 'in the street'—
which suggests people under manhole covers and other people's
feet—
and another thing that I myself haven't any doubt of
is that it's neater to say 'out the window' than 'out of',
and 'gobbledygook' itself is a wonderful word—but when you've
said *that* you've said it,
that's about all that can be chalked up to America's credit.

ANDRÉ KUKLA

The Modern Language of Consciousness

IN THE LAST fifteen or twenty years a deepening introspective mood has descended upon Americans, promising to transform the world's extraverts into seekers of inner illumination. The result, in the realm of the mind, is a fabulous proliferation of new consumer goods. Just as we have deodorants in the form of sprays, sticks, pads, and roll-ons, we also have new and improved systems of self-analysis. Scientology, Transactional Analysis, Primal Therapy, Reality Therapy, Rational Therapy, Psychosynthesis, Arica, est (whose graduates, I cannot resist mentioning, call themselves estholes), and Eckankar (which produces ecks)—these are some of the brand names in this new market.

There also now exists a sizeable American following for every religious sect in the world, not excluding denominations which were thought to be extinct, like Druidism and the worship of Pan. I recall the amazement of a scholar from India who, returning to America in 1970 after several years' absence, found that the Vaishnavaite devotees of Krishna, with their painted foreheads, shaven pates, cymbals and drums, whom he had been studying in remote Indian villages, had arrived before him and were dancing in the streets of Cleveland and Chicago! By now, the average downtown shopper has ceased to find their presence at all remarkable. Even the Balinese fire-walkers elicit no more than a raised eyebrow. As the seventies come to a close, the number of Hindu, Buddhist, and Sufi teachers residing in America is beyond tallying; and it is a commonplace among them that Americans are more ardent, if also more naive, in their pursuit of inner experience than are their own countrymen. Perhaps we will soon see the children of Japanese industrialists and Arab oil magnates, unfulfilled by the materialism of their elders, setting off on holy pilgrimages to the West in search of enlightenment. They will no doubt collect native American trinkets, marvelling at how cheap everything is.

This inward turn of the American psyche is surely related to the general decay of Western civilization, but a specific cause may be found in the large-scale experiment with mind-altering drugs which began to occupy American society in the sixties, and which ultimately led to a reappraisal of the nature of consciousness. Until recently, the popular conception of consciousness did not permit of qualitative variation—either one was conscious, or one was unconscious—but the experience of marijuana, lysergic acid, and amphetamines introduced us to the idea of qualitative differences. In the long run, it scarcely mattered what these differences were, or whether the drugs were considered to be "psychedelic," "hallucinogenic," or "psychotomimetic." The main lesson was that ordinary consciousness is alterable; and the immediate corollary is that altered states of consciousness are more satisfactory than the dismal ordinary one. In this way, the door was opened to any teacher or system that promised to effect a radical psychic improvement. Thus the drug culture of the sixties generated the American yogis, Buddhists, and estholes of today. Of course the contemporary situation was anticipated by the English and French Romantics, who were also interested in mind-altering drugs; and an experience with nitrous oxide led William James to conclude, as far back as 1902, that "our normal waking consciousness . . . is but one special type of consciousness, whilst all about it . . . there lie potential forms of consciousness entirely different." But these were avant-garde ideas. What is new in our time is the movement of these ideas from literary salons to the living rooms and laundromats of America, from symbolist poems to network television and the newspapers.

This brand-new mass interest created the need for a new vernacular, and one might have expected it to derive from the languages of psychology, philosophy, or religion. But in fact the modern language of consciousness is almost wholly a grass-roots creation. If it lacks exquisite refinement and subtle discriminations, it still captures certain aspects of inner experience which, like microwave ovens and ecological crises, are now everyday subjects of conversation in America.

Standard English lacks any familiar word for the general concept of a state of consciousness; at least there is none comparable to the recent slang invention, in contemporary American speech, of the word *head.* One inquires about what sort of a head a person is in (more properly, "where his head is at"), whether it is a good or bad head, and so on. A more resonant, general alternative is *space. Heads* are states of consciousness from the perspective of the philosophical realist, with his presumption that subjective experience can change, while objective reality remains the same. But heads become *spaces* from the viewpoint of the idealist, for whom external reality is a construct built up out of experience. The compromise *head-space* is not infrequently heard.

To be in the ordinary state of consciousness is to be *straight.* Any other state is a *trip.* For example, one might hear:

A: Are you straight enough to go to the store?
B: Not yet, dear. I'm still tripping.

Trip retains the flavor of its drug-cultural origins in the suggestion of a temporally bounded episode which is discontinuous with the usual course of life. But meditation can also put you on a trip. A *head trip,* however, refers to mere intellectualizing as opposed to experiencing, as in:

A: He was really on a weird trip last night.
B: Nah. All that crazy talk was just a head trip.

The most readily made discrimination among trips is whether the experience is pleasant or unpleasant. Good trips are *highs* and bad trips are *bummers. High* perpetuates a synaesthetic relationship between positivity and upward direction which is well entrenched in our language. We are better for being uplifted. Heaven is above.

Bummer and *high,* like *trip,* found their first sphere of application in describing drug-induced states of consciousness. The phrase *righteous high* is sometimes used to specify a high that occurs spontaneously or is produced by such nonchemical means as meditation, fasting, chanting, austerities, etc. I know of no corresponding expression for nonchemical bummers.

A *contact high* is produced by sheer physical proximity to someone who is on a good trip. When highs were mostly drug-induced, it was often speculated that contact highs were due to the actual ingestion or inhalation of minute ambient particles of the drug. But the same phenomenon has been noted with righteous highs. The most popular explanation these days is contained in the disreputable theory of *vibes* (vibrations). These are said to be psychic emanations which everyone broadcasts involuntarily, and which color the experience of anyone within their range. Variations in signal strength and receiver sensitivity are assumed by the theory, although an explicit analogy to radio is not particularly favored. A person in an altered state of consciousness is supposed to be broadcasting exceptionally strong vibes. Hence contact highs. Trippers of the kind who prefer *head* to *space* often feel impelled to reduce vibes to the ordinary perception of small visual and auditory cues such as facial expressions and tones of voice. But the more prevalent view is that vibes are irreducibly real. There is even a fairly common belief that the existence of vibes has been established by "science."

It is recognized that bummers communicate themselves to others as readily as highs. But the expression *contact bummer* is rarely, if ever, encountered. Ordinarily, one hears only something like this:

> A: She got on such a bummer that she started to break all the furniture.
> B: What did you do?
> A: Well, it put me on a bummer too.

When a person's state of consciousness involves a loss of the distinction between subjective and objective experience, he is said to be *spaced out.* In the ordinary state of consciousness, our sense perceptions form a unified structure which stands out as a figure against the background of our feelings and thoughts. The figure constitutes the external world; the ground is what we take to be our inner self. Any drastic modification of the boundary between world and self counts as being spaced out. This concept, therefore, includes a veritable potpourri of experiential states. For example, we are spaced out if our inner fantasies are projected onto the world as hallucinations; or if objective sense perception takes on a dreamlike unreality; or if the boundary between self and world disintegrates, leaving fragments of sensory, imaginative, and emotional experience which do not come together in any sort of coherent entity; or if self and world are swallowed up in a mystic unification of opposites. The popular language of consciousness does not draw distinctions among these experiences. Instead, space-outs are categorized as: (1) those which are bummers, and (2) those which are highs. Spaced-out bummers are *freak-outs;* spaced-out highs are *bliss-outs.* In this language, the difference between Meister Eckhard or St. Theresa and a schizophrenic is that the former is blissed out while the latter is freaked out. The particle *out,* a nice touch, is inspired by the single feature shared by all such experiences: the experiencer himself is no longer around, "there is nobody home."

The condition of straight consciousness requires not only that there be a cleavage between inner and outer experience, but also that the outer world be the focal point of awareness. Being *stoned* is a reversal of this perspective. Subjective experience becomes an absorbing figure in the center of consciousness, while the objective world recedes to the periphery. The division of experience into two realms remains more or less intact; but a psychic inertia holds the stoned head fast within the boundaries of the inner. Try as he might, he cannot bring the outside world into clear focus. Like spacing out, being stoned entails a loss of contact with ordinary reality. Here, however, reality does not so much present a different aspect as it simply fades into inaccessibility. It is natural that the expression *stoned out* is never heard, for being stoned is the state of being totally *in*—not only are we at home, but the doors and windows are all shut. Like stones themselves, stoned heads are in a state of extreme contraction. It is difficult to move about in this condition, since movement through space and time is a form of relatedness to the world. When a person gets stoned, he takes up a stable position (e.g., lying down) from which he can contemplate the mysteries of phosphenes, stomach gurgles, or the sensation of dizziness without distress.

The difference between being stoned and being spaced out is illustrated in a story about two men who arrive at the closed gates of a city at night. One has taken lysergic acid, which is the spacer-outer *par excellence;* the other has smoked marijuana, which usually gets you stoned. "Let's sprout golden wings and *fly* over the gates into the city!" suggests the acidhead. The pothead, after a *very* long pause, replies, "Why don't we just sit down and wait till they open up in the morning?"

The popular language of consciousness also employs several terms for movement between one state of consciousness and another. Leaving the ordinary state for any other is *getting off.* Returning to the ordinary state is *coming down;* and being the agent of such a return is *bringing down.* Inelegantly, one comes down or is brought down from a bummer as well as a high. Getting off rapidly is a *rush.* Coming down rapidly is *crashing.* Crashing has an unpleasant connotation, whether the point of departure is a bummer or a high.

A: Did you get off on that acid you took last night?
B: Yeah, man, it was a real rush. But just as I start tripping, the kid next door comes in and asks me to help him with his arithmetic homework.
A: Wow, what a bring-down!

There is little more to be said about the truly popular language of consciousness. All of its ideas are projections of familiar American interests: pleasure (*high* versus *bummer, bliss out* versus *freak out*), novelty (*straight* versus *tripping*), movement (*getting off, coming down*), and speed (*rush, crash*). Evidently, the native genius of English is not remarkable for introspective psychology, any more than it is for gastronomy. Deficiencies of this kind have been traditionally overcome by loan words. Our culinary articulacy, for example, was substantially improved by the importation from the French of *hors d'oeuvres, soufflés, pâtés,* and *crêpes.* Perhaps the languages of the Orient can perform the same service in the realm of consciousness. Certainly the terminologies for states of consciousness in Sanskrit, Chinese, Japanese, and Tibetan are as meticulous and variegated as the language of Gallic cuisine. Consider, for example, the levels of concentrative absorption, or *jhanas,* described in the Buddhist *Visuddhimaga.* These levels of increasingly difficult attainment are preceded by a state known as "access," in which the mind attends one-pointedly to a single idea. At this level, one continues to be aware of sensory and bodily stimuli, and even to have wandering thoughts; but these thoughts and stimuli are unable to deflect attention from its single focus. At the level of the first *jhana,* all accompanying thoughts and stimuli fall away, resulting in the perfection of one-pointedness. This experience gives rise to feelings of "rapture" and "bliss," and even between these feelings a distinction is made. In the second *jhana,* the object of concentration itself falls away, leaving a contentless awareness colored only by rapture and bliss. In the third *jhana,* rapture, which is a form of excitement, is replaced by equanimity. In the fourth *jhana,* bliss also ceases, leaving an awareness which is both contentless and devoid of emotional coloration. There are also fifth, sixth, seventh, and eighth *jhanas,* the description of which requires an elaborate technical vocabulary. In contemporary American, all eight *jhanas,* as well as the level of access, translate into being stoned.

There are indications that the Orientalization of English may have already begun. There now exists a core vocabulary of several dozen terms, derived mainly from Buddhism and Hinduism, which is shared by all Oriental religious sects in America. This vocabulary includes words directly describing states of consciousness (*samadhi, nirvana, satori, moksha,* etc.); terms for techniques of consciousness alteration (*zazen, yoga, mantra, mandala, bhakti,* etc.); and concepts drawn from Eastern theoretical accounts of the nature of consciousness (*chakra, kundalini, prana,* etc.) Users of these terms are neither more nor less inclined to the scholarly investigation of cultures than are other Americans. *Mantra* and *chakra* are part of their everyday speech, springing to the lips as spontaneously as *hors d'oeuvres.* However, this kind of talk is far from being understood by the average American who uses it. The language of *mantras* and *chakras* is presently a jargon.

Like hi-fi enthusiasts, sportsmen, and other groups with intense special interests, the Orientalized subculture in America supports a quasi-official periodical—the *East West Journal*—in which its jargon is freely employed, without the encumbrance of definitions, quotation marks, or italics. Alex Jack, a staff member of the *East West Journal,* has also compiled *The New Age Dictionary* (Brookline, Mass., 1976), which the unprepared reader will find indispensable. Both central and peripheral interests of the regular readership are delineated on the title page:

> *The New Age Dictionary:* Acupuncture. Africa. Alchemy. Art & Archaeology. Buddhism. Christian Mysticism. Comic Books. Consciousness. Ecology. Education. Egypt. Gurus. Healing. Hinduism. Human Potential. Indians of North America. Judaism. Kabbalah. Literature & Poetry. Lost Continents and Tribes. Macrobiotics. Martial Arts. Meditation. Mother Goddesses. Music. Mythology. Natural Foods. New Communities. Nonviolence. Organic Farming. Parapsychology. Pre-Columbian Contact. Pyramid Energy. Quantum Physics. Radionics. Science Fiction. Sikhism. Solar Energy. Space-Time. Sufism. Synchronicity. Taoism. Tibet. UFOs. Utopias. Vegetarianism. Women. Yoga. Zen.

The unifying thread here is evidently heterodoxy—alternative belief systems and values which befit an altered consciousness. Indeed, *alternative* has become a catchword in this social group (as well as in the closely allied society of estholes and ecks which adheres to a Western therapeutic model of the inner search). *Alternative education, alternative technology, alternative community, alternative life-style, alternative health care,* and of course *altered state of consciousness* are standard locutions.

It remains to be seen whether the publication of *The New Age*

Dictionary foreshadows an extensive change in our linguistic habits. For the present, if we wish to communicate widely about exotic states of mind, we have no choice but to employ the indigenous American language of consciousness. Perhaps some day, when a stranger inquires about the smiling countenance and immobility of our friend in the corner, we may be able to explain that he has arrived at the level of the second *jhana*. But for now we must be content to say that he is stoned. At least this conveys something of his state. Not very long ago it would have been impossible to say even this much without elaborate circumlocution.

SEAN McCONVILLE

Prison Language

ASIDE FROM a tiny and pathetic group of broken-down and displaced persons, nobody likes to be in prison. The intensity of disliking varies considerably. Some regard it as an occupational hazard, others as a stage in their upside-down careers, which so surely progress through childrens' homes, young offender establishments, and the various grades of prison. For yet others—bank managers, treasurers of charitable organizations, spouses who let sincerity go too far in family quarrels, maybe even politicians—imprisonment appears to be the end of the world. All—even the rawest and most shell-shocked recruit—will adjust, adapt, and accommodate themselves surprisingly well to life after sentence. Despite their irritation, dislike, fear, or hatred, most will find that prisons do not seal them off from chances to enjoy wealth, power, status, companionship, fantasy, sex, and even inebriation. To a large extent prisoners will find it in their own hands as to whether they experience their sentence as a *hard time, a good time,* or a *short time.* Skills and social arrangements have been developed which allow many of the desires and concerns of life to be met in a scaled-down form, thus soothing some of the pains and discomforts of incarceration. Sociologists and psychologists rather humorlessly and ponderously describe and dispute these arrangements, which they call a "subculture." Despite their disagreements, however, all the professional commentators agree that the distinctive argot of inmates gives an insight into the institutions, preoccupations, and style of prison life. The color, hint of conspiratorial excitement, assertion of common values, and solidarity which the use of a special vocabulary brings are perhaps more attractive and rewarding to prisoners than to any other group.

Prison itself may be called *the nick,* or one may speak of "being in stir," doing *time, bird* (rhyming slang *bird lime* = time). Attitudes toward one's imprisonment may be expressed thus: "I just want to be left alone to do my bird quietly" or "This bird has really dragged out." Officially, prison is intended to be a severe form of deprivation and there are many basic possessions and activities which are missed there for the first time. A lot of these can be supplied on the black market. In British prisons tobacco still remains the gold standard which is made to back every transaction and promise. The official allowance is barely sufficient for individual smoking needs, but tobacco may expensively be borrowed or bought from a *baron,* possibly through his *runner.* It is referred to as a *burn* or as *snout* or *weed,* and is smoked in a *roll-up* or *spliff,* the paper of which is called a *skin.* Tobacco may be traded for goods bought legitimately at the prisoners' shop—the *canteen;* it may also be bet, in which case care must be taken to avoid making a bet with a *knocker* or defaulter. Exchanges of small gifts of tobacco are part of the everyday relationship of *chinas* (*china plate* = mate or friend).

In the last twenty or so years tobacco and illicitly brewed alcohol have been supplemented with several different types of drugs. These have, in turn, brought with them the liturgical and obsessive terminology of drug users. The most frequently used drugs are probably the various forms of *cannabis indica.* This might be smoked in an *African Woodbine, drag, reefer, stick,* or *sausage,* or, as *bhang,* taken orally. Cannabis is also known to prisoners by the names given to it in the different places in which it is cultivated: *charas* (India), *mataby* (Congo), *dagga* (South Africa), *ganga* (West Indies), and *kief* (North Africa). Other names include *Mary Jane, tampi, rope, muggles,* and *gage,* besides the familiar *pot, dope, tea,* and *weed.* A smoker of cannabis may be called a *pothead* or a *weedhead.*

Other drugs which are used in prison include the easily concealed LSD, and cocaine, heroin, barbiturates, and amphetamines, most of the terms associated with which are fairly widely known. Amphetamine-barbiturate mixtures seem to have spawned a particularly vivid range of nicknames and images, often arising from the appearance or color of capsules in which they are taken. These include *black and tans, black and white minstrel, bluey, double-blue, French-blue, purple heart, Christmas tree, nigger minstrel,* and *black bomber.* Librium capsules are known as *green and blacks,* benzedrine as *jolly beans.* Heroin, possibly because it is recognized as a hard taskmaster, has acquired strange and somewhat bitter nicknames. *Horse* or *H* are well known, but there are also *jack, shmock* and *shit.* The hypodermic is known as a *machine gun, works, business,* or possibly, *gear.* An injection is *cooked up* by dissolving a tablet or powder in a heated spoon. Injection may be described as a *deck, cranking up, jacking up,* a *jag,* or a *jimmy.* For example, it might be said, "He cranked up with a deck of heroin."

Disagreeable though some of these terms may sound, drug use offers even more unpleasant activities and experiences. There is the *croaker*—the doctor who prescribes for addicts. *Cold turkey,* the sudden stopping of narcotics consumption, can lead to the *horrors* or to feeling *sprung out.* A person may be *bugged*—suffering from many abscesses caused by unclean injections. When cash runs short and a *teahead* cannot make a *connection* or *get through,* he may have to search through his old butt-ends in the hope of finding one which could be completely consumed by using a *crutch,* or split match, as a holder. If all else fails, a *buzz* may be obtained by the down and out's standby, the *corporation cocktail,* which is coal gas inhaled through milk. Progress, in the shape of North Sea natural gas, has severely limited supplies of this intoxicant, which was formerly so plentifully accessible to the inmate who knew his way around a prison.

Sexual activity or sexual reverie is no less important in prison than outside. Masturbation is obviously the most accessible and common form of outlet, and is sometimes referred to as *blowing.* One might dream of a *jump* with a *chick* (girl), *tom* or *brass* (prostitute), or even a *queen* (effeminate homosexual), but never with a *nonce.* The sexual offence of the *nonce* usually involves children and this makes him one of the most despised people in prison. Women prisoners, it has been discovered, are more likely than men to give open sexual affection a place in their everyday institutional life. *Playing* (homosexual flirtation and involvement) seems to attract no great stigma in women's prisons, although the too-obvious *butch* or *femme* may be looked on as something of an oddity.

Musings about crime, the police and courts are very popular alternatives to sexual meditations. *Blagging* is the term for robbery, for which one might be *tooled up* (armed). A *blag job* might be to get money, or it may be in pursuit of *tomfoolery* (jewelry). For the less brave, the same objective might be attained by *flying a kite* (passing a dud check). The police, an experienced criminal might claim, only obtained his conviction because they *verballed* him (attributed incriminating statements to him). Despite the protestations of his *brief* (counsel), the jury convicted and the *beak* (judge) gave him a *lagging* (three years imprisonment). To this the offender might have observed, "Hang on guv, you're *strongin'* it a bit" (the sentence is too heavy). The judge, however, may not agree: "Don't come the *acid.* Have *six moon* for being *flash*" (six months is added to the sentence for being cheeky).

Prisons, more than most other institutions, have a clearly marked social hierarchy. At the bottom end there is a good deal of scapegoating. It is a great consolation, it would seem, the further beyond the pale you are yourself, to find someone upon whom to look down. The *nonces, nutters, fairies,* or *sex-cases* provide this valuable service in British prisons and can be guaranteed to fill the honest burglar, fraudman, or footpad with much warming and self-righteous indignation. A much subscribed to (and much broken) prison commandment is that one does not inform. The *grass* (*grasshopper* = shopper) or informer is in theory, therefore, only a shade above the nonce at the bottom of the social heap, although unlike the sexual offender, being a *grass* is not an absolute—there are degrees of grassing (or *shopping*) and a fairly large proportion of prisoners do some informing at some time. Women inform quite a lot on each other and are much more tolerant of this breach of etiquette, which in American prisons may earn one the childish sobriquet of *snitcher.* Also low in esteem is the *sap, joe, div,* or *slag.* A *cowboy* is disliked as a show-off or know-all, but a *daddy* or *chap* is likely to rank above a *baron,* as he has plenty of *bottle* (courage, daring) but is not mercenary or exploitative. *Bottle* is also used as a verb—"He was challenged and he *bottled out*" (backed down).

The police and prison staff are fateful parts of the environment rather than the social system of prisoners. Names for the police have changed slowly over the years from *coppers, peelers,* and *bull* to the *fuzz, old Bill, blue, bogey, law,* or (especially detectives) *filth.* The uniformed prison staff have various uncomplimentary individual names (though I have come across more than one *cripplecock* and *poison dwarf*); *boss* may be used in face-to-face contact, especially if the prisoner is a supplicant, *uniform* has a slightly hostile tone, but the venerable *screw* still seems to be almost universally preferred as a general term—sometimes slipping into the conversation of staff themselves. Although nowadays the term has a sexual meaning, in prisons *screw* goes back as far as the last century, when cranks—machines which produced nothing and were used simply as a form of hard labor—were installed in many prisons. Staff adjusted the machines to the varying strengths of prisoners by means of a *screw,* which increased or lessened the resistance of the handle. A principal officer, who is a type of foreman or noncommissioned officer, is called a *screwdriver;* and a chief officer, the senior uniformed rank, is called in rhyming slang, a *bully beef.* The affectionate regard with which borstal matrons are held (and which was so well expressed in Brendan Behan's *Borstal Boy*) comes through clearly in *maggies.*

Disciplinary and release procedures and everyday routine also have a place in prison language. A prisoner will normally be delivered to the nick in *bracelets* or *cuffs* in a *meat waggon* (black maria). After reception, an *eleven-fifty* (the stationery code number for a dossier cover) will be opened on him. He will then be *banged-up* or *screwed up* in a *peter* or *flowery* (*dell* = cell, thus, locked in a cell). This might be on the *ones, twos,* or *threes* (ground, first, or second floors), and will not have a *kharsie, cawsie,* or *cassey* (lavatory), but use will instead be made of a communal *recess.* Because of current overcrowding in British prisons, it is likely that a newly arrived prisoner will have to be *two'd up* or *three'd up,* that is, he will have to share a single cell with one or two other people. If he is an *old lag* he will be used to such conditions. If not he may become disturbed and *smash up* or barricade his cell. The *heavies* or *batter squad* (supposedly a special group of staff) may be called in, and the prisoner removed to the *block, cooler, chokey* or *rose garden* (punishment cells). Here, should he be especially violent, he might be placed in a *strip cell*—a room with built in, immovable furniture. Alternatively he may be taken to the *pads* (padded cells) in the hospital wing. If the outbreak is thought to be deliberate, the offender will be *booked* or *nicked.* He will be given a *white sheet,* which will state the charge against him and upon which he may write his defence. He may claim that he has been *fitted up* (unjustly accused). Rather confusingly, he will be *fitted* (certified as fit) by the doctor before the adjudication. Should the charge against him be *stitched up* or *fixed* (proved) he may say that his *weighting off* (sentence) is unjust.

As he progresses through his sentence such a prisoner may acquire a reputation as a trouble-maker, in which case the governor may decide to have him *ghosted* (moved without notice to another establishment). Staff may observe him *doing a moody* (behaving suspiciously) and may assume that he has *itchy feet* and is likely to *have it away* (escape), in which case he would be put on the *E* (scape) *list* and compelled to wear an easily distinguishable uniform; this is known as *being in patches.*

There are other ways in which a prisoner may get himself into trouble or *in stook.* He may be *at it* (fiddling in some way) and acquire forbidden goods such as drugs, money, or a *chiv* (knife). These may be found in his cell by a *scratcher* or *burglar* (an expert searcher) or be discovered in the course of a *rub-down,* a form of search in which the hands of the searcher are passed over the clothes. If this produces nothing, an inmate may be *strip-searched*—his clothes taken from him and his body closely inspected. Such searches are often initiated as the result of a fellow inmate *busting* (informing), an omnipresent possibility, no matter how *stoome* (*to stay stoome* = remain silent) or *cagey* (guarded) one is. A misfortune of this kind might be described so: "This nonce case grassed to the screws that I was holding snout in my peter, so the burglars turned me over. I was nipped bang to rights and copped three days chokey."

The language of prison officials is shaped by different needs from those which produce prisoners' argot. Convenience in the processing of large numbers of prisoners and the frequent repetition of certain operations lead to a superabundance of initials. These range from designations of the crimes and characteristics of the prisoners to the routines of institutional life. *ABH* stands for actual bodily harm, which is to be distinguished from *GBH*—grievous bodily harm. *EPD* is the earliest date on which a person may be paroled; *EDR* his earliest date of release. The various functionaries of the prison are known by initials—*AG* (assistant governor), *MO* (medical officer), *PO* (principal officer), *AO* (administrative officer). A person serving a long sentence is known as an *LTI* (long term inmate), and may even in conversation so describe himself. There are a number of insane prisoners in the English system, who are sometimes known as *sections,* after the various sections of the Mental Health Act under which they have been committed. A *star* is a person serving his first prison sentence, an *ordinary* one who has been inside before, and an *SW* is someone under special watch, usually because of a suicide attempt.

From time to time certain prisoners have to be held apart from others. These prisoners are known as *forty-threes,* because of the rule under which they have been segregated. If their removal from general circulation is at their own request, because, for example, they owe a debt which they cannot pay, or because as sexual offenders they are liable to attack, they are known as *ORs* (own requests) or *protections.* If segregation is because the authorities believe them to be trouble-makers they may be known as *Governor's forty-threes* or as being separated for *GOD* or *GOAD* (good order and discipline). Other punishments are known by their initials, such as *FOE* (forfeiture of earnings) or *SOE* (stoppage of earnings).

Another source of official prison language is the need, common to many organizations which process people, to protect staff dignity and feelings of self-importance, and perhaps to claim a professional or even scientific standing for their occupation. One way in which this can be done is by neutralizing or enhancing what might otherwise appear to be trivial or sordid or haphazard. This verbal inflation starts with the basics. Prisons are sometimes called *establishments* (not as bad as the U.S. *correctional facilities* or *institutions*), prisoners *inmates* or (if young offenders) *trainees*. Some prisoners take euphemism a good deal further—a white-collar criminal in an open prison once in a letter to me referred quite seriously to his prison as "the campus." Disciplinary hearings are called *adjudications* and punishments somewhat perversely *awards*. The routine of settling a person into prison is called *induction,* and ritualistic (and largely ineffective) letters to the home secretary are known as *petitions*. Straitjackets are said no longer to be used, but it would be hard for the nonexpert to distinguish them from *restraints,* which are used. An escape is known officially as an *abscond,* and unofficially as *scarpering*. Which word more vividly expresses the excitement, urgency, and anxiety involved?

For many prison staff it is personally and occupationally important to identify with kindred groups in the outside world. This can partly be achieved by keeping abreast of the latest fashions in social work, psychological and managerial terminology. By contrast, prisoners' argot remains relatively inert. There have been some changes, such as the relatively recent introduction of the drug-users' language. To a large extent this is probably due to the fairly new emergence in Britain of a significant number of drug-connected offenses. But drug takers and pushers are still only uneasily accepted as part of the traditional criminal world, which continues to flourish mainly on the proceeds of theft. Another source of change is an instance of nature imitating art. Prisoners watch a lot of television. Crime and prison programs are great favorites and often the subject of expert technical appraisal. The writers of such programs take a conspicuous pride in their familiarity with criminal and police language, but sometimes also slip in terms of their own to obtain a desired effect. If this is successful, these words gain currency and popularity in the real world. Such is the possible origin of the term *filth*. It seems too neat, humorless and explosive to have emerged from the existing pattern of criminal and prison language.

The conservatism of prisoners' social and political attitudes and habits has frequently been commented upon. Throughout the Western world social hierarchies are becoming more attenuated, but prisoners still sort themselves into the traditional pyramid. Straight society's extensive changes in approaches to sexuality have made virtually no difference to (male) prisoners' adherence to rigid sexual formulas and stereotypes. The rhyming slang which is still so vivid and rigorous in prison language is taken from the settled urban working class, even the most law-abiding members of which are probably familiar with or benefit at some time from the activities of neighborhood criminals. That the language of the poorer sections of city dwellers is slow to change can be seen, for example, by comparing Jack London's *People of the Abyss,* describing the *spikes* (workhouses) of 1902 with Orwell's account in *Down and Out in Paris and London* some thirty years on. Going back even further, would not some of Dickens's characters by their attitudes and slang establish their bona fides in a modern equivalent to a rookery or in a prison? And surely the death of the footpad (or as we would say, mugger) Tom, at the hands of Byron's Don Juan, would evoke sympathetic comment from prisoners and criminals today, for by his language is it not clear that he is one of them?

> Poor Tom was once a kiddy upon town,
> A thorough *varmint* and a real swell,
> Full flash, all fancy, until fairly diddled,
> His pockets first and then his body riddled.

The settled communities of the poor which contributed so generously to crime and to the prisons have been breaking up. It is true that to the chagrin of our town planners and social engineers there are some signs that the mere translation of populations to handsome new housing projects will not prevent the old ways from reestablishing themselves. On the other hand, the social, economic and demographic upheavals that have been with us since the forties may not yet have worked themselves out. A way of life and a variant language may be passing. We might, in this event, expect to see the catchphrases and fashions of the popular media of entertainment displacing tradition within the terminology of prisoners. But then there is the imponderable of the entry of large numbers of blacks into our prisons. Living, in the main, in declining inner-city areas, and occupying the bottom places in the economic hierarchy, the West Indians and Asians may already have taken the place of the indigenous slum and near-slum dwellers of past years. Should that be so, an essay of this kind twenty or so years hence will have to deal with a very different prison language indeed.

SIMON KARLINSKY

"More Piercing than a Whistle": Notes on English Sounds in Russian Ears

EVOKING DICKENSIAN LONDON in his 1913 poem "Dombey and Son," Osip Mandelstam begins: "When I hear English spoken, / More piercing than a whistle —." Those shrill English sounds conjure up for Mandelstam the atmosphere of a depressing nineteenth-century office, with its bookkeeping ledgers, bankruptcies, and exploited clerks, among whom we are surprised to find Oliver Twist. A whistling or hissing or birdsong-like texture associated with the sound of English is one of three recurrent notions about it in the Russian literary tradition. Two others are that English is really French (or, occasionally, German) in disguise, and that English signifies instant elegance, often tinged with snobbery. These notions were current in the early nineteenth century and they are very much alive today.

No account of Russian literary history of the past two centuries could hope to be complete without taking cognizance of the impact of Shakespeare, Scott, Byron, Whitman, and Hemingway. Yet, as Vladimir Nabokov lengthily points out in his commentary to his translation of Pushkin's *Eugene Onegin,* a Russian literary figure able to read English writers in the original is a rarity. Near-native command of French or German (or both) was the rule, rather than the exception among nineteenth and early twentieth-century literary Russians. But if we set up as an arbitrary criterion of fluency in English the ability to read Shakespeare in the original and to write a letter in idiomatic English, only four major Russian writers would qualify: Tolstoy, Pasternak, Nabokov, and Joseph Brodsky.

While French or German words may have been perceived as foreign in an understandable, predictable way, English was and often still is heard as foreign in an *alien* way by Russians who have had little exposure to it. Mandelstam's singling out of shrillness as the most striking feature of spoken English is probably as surprising to native English speakers as the typical English description of German as guttural is to Germans. What Mandelstam here offers is his own variant of an observation made by several earlier writers. In *Dead Souls* Gogol made fun of those Russians who strive to reproduce English sounds "which only a bird could manage" and who furthermore "make a birdlike face" in order to pronounce those sounds properly. Gogol was speaking of the sonorities of English words, rather than of their meaning. In the same novel he qualified the "speech of the Britisher" as distinguished by a "keen understanding of the human heart (*serdcevedenie*) and a wise comprehension of life." The content may be profound, but the sound is not quite human.

The epitome of this Russian idea of English sounds as not entirely human occurs in Anton Chekhov's early sketch "The Daughter of Albion" (1883). The title character is an English governess ("with crayfish eyes" and with a "nose like a hawk's beak") unable to communicate with her employer because she refuses to learn any Russian. The employer, a crude provincial landowner, uses profane language and takes a nude swim in her presence, something he would never have permitted himself with Russian women of his own class. She responds with aloof disdain, convinced that she is among savages from whom civilized behavior is not to be expected. The comical name Chekhov gives this woman conveys the oddity of English names to Russians. She is called Miss Wilka Charlesovna Twice. The Russian patronymic *Charlesovna,* devised by her employer out of her father's first name, Charles, makes her name and her person a bit more understandable within his Russian reality. (The alien and alienated Miss Twice was probably an early study for Chekhov's much more profound later portrayal of a foreign governess as a freak and an outsider in the character of Charlotte in *The Cherry Orchard.*)

Numerous loan words were taken from English into Russian over the centuries. This process has shown signs of acceleration in recent decades. Unlike the borrowed French, German, and Italian words, which are usually transcribed into Cyrillic letters, English words often enter Russian after undergoing alterations in accordance with Russian ideas of what English ought to sound like. From the French, the Russians have acquired a preference for ending English words with the participial suffix *-ing*. Like French, Russian also has *smoking* (a dinner jacket or tuxedo), *spinning* (a fishing rod equipped with a spinning reel), and *kemping* (a camping site). The trickiest representative of this large category is probably the Russian word for shampoo. English borrowed *shampoo* from Hindi, and when the French borrowed it in turn, they insisted on pinning their favorite suffix on it. The result, *shampooing,* designates in French the liquid rather than the action. Russians inherited this word with a French pronunciation, which led them to transcribe it with a palatalized final *n,* as *shampun'*, which in Russian sounds suspiciously Chinese.

Many other English words entered Russian in their plural forms. The final *s* of the English plurals satisfies the Russian supposition that English words ought to sibilate or whistle. But at the same time, those plurals are perceived as singulars in Russian, requiring the addition of the Russian pluralizing suffixes *-i* or *-y* in order to form plurals. Some of these words ended up as Russian masculine nouns (*turneps,* "rutabaga," pl. *turnepsy*); some got an additional final *a* to become feminine nouns (*rel'sa,* "rail," pl. *rel'sy* which, however, later changed its gender to masculine and became *rel's*); some exist in almost exclusively plural form (*butsy,* "soccer boots"); and some have become collective singulars, lacking a plural (*barbaris,* "barberries"). One of the more recent additions to this ever-growing category is *dzhinsy,* "blue jeans." A delightful instance of a Russian adding both the *-ing* and the *-s* to an English word which he felt was not authentically English without them is found in a letter Nikolai Gogol wrote to a friend in the 1840s about a vacation at a seaside resort in England he was contemplating. Gogol was enthusiastic about an inexpensive boarding house recommended to him, which served a typical English breakfast complete with *muffingsy.*

Because of its geographical position, France has often served as an intermediary between the Russian and English cultures. This has occasioned a blurring of sorts, when Russians seem to assume that English literature was actually written in French. The sentimentalist writer Prince Shalikov, extolling the novels of Ann Radcliffe to his compatriots at the beginning of the nineteenth century, urged them to read "her famous novel *La Forêt.*" More than a century later, Marina Tsvetaeva, in her memoir about her passionate infatuation with a half-English actress Sophia Holliday, "The Tale of Sonechka," compared her friend with various heroines of Dickens, among them "that strange little girl from *Our Mutual Friend,* who lures the old Jew up on the roof, inviting him to cease to exist: Montez! Montez! Soyez mort!" Obviously, Tsvetaeva felt that Jenny Wren's words to the old Riah "Come up and be dead!" are somehow more authentic in French.

Even Russian writers with some reading knowledge of English often confuse English words with similar looking French or German ones. Reading Byron with the aid of a dictionary, Pushkin jotted down beside "the Athenian's grave" his understanding of the phrase: "la grève d'Athènes," i.e., "the strand of Athens." The Romantic prose writer Alexander Bestuzhev-Marlinsky, whose command of English was better than that of most of his contemporaries, attempted a bit of English dialogue in his adventure yarn "Nikitin the Seafarer" (1834), where he used the word *barbed* in the sense of "bearded," assuming that it still had that meaning in modern English because of its similarity to the French *barbu*. Mikhail Lermontov, whose command of German was excellent, derived the meaning of the English word *kindly* from the German word for child, *das Kind,* when he rendered a line of Robert Burns, "Had we never loved so kindly," as "Had we not been children, / Had we not loved blindly."

The blurring of English with French continues in the work of present-day Soviet poets, who, unlike their nineteenth-century predecessors, know neither English nor French. In their case it is more a matter of imagery than of vocabulary. In his oft-translated poem "Striptease," Andrei Voznesensky has the stripper he meets in a sleazy New York strip joint ask him, "Order me a martini with absinthe." Even though the poem purports to reflect Voznesensky's actual experiences in America, the unlikely absinthe must come from the French Symbolist poets or else from an early painting by Picasso. (The English translations of the poem gallantly render the line as "Make mine a double martini.") Yevgeny Yevtushenko, for his part, accusing the French bourgeoisie of murdering Paul Verlaine (in his poem "Verlaine"), throws in two English words, *gin* and *juice,* the better to indict the hypocritical bourgeois who takes a swig of this combination as a nightcap (*vypiv dzhinu s dzhusom*) after having hounded Verlaine to death for alcoholism. Had the two Soviet poets pooled their respective experiences with foreign countries, they might have achieved greater verisimilitude by switching around the drinks they have served the nineteenth-century French bourgeois and the present-day American stripper.

The phenomenon of Russians unthinkingly substituting the more familiar French or German words for the unfamiliar English ones may help explain the reverse phenomenon of people in English-speaking countries assuming that Russian meanings are somehow better conveyed in French and also the related, seldom verbalized but now and then encountered equating of things Russian with things Jewish. Until very recently, it was considered bad form in England to translate the titles of Russian ballets and operas into English—they were supposed to be known by their French names. I remember an English acquaintance upbraiding me in the 1950s for referring to the Tchaikovsky ballet and the Borodin opera we were discussing as *Swan Lake* and *Prince Igor.* Their correct titles, he informed me, were *Le Lac aux Cygnes* and *Le Prince Igor* (the latter stressed on the last syllable). I did not have the heart to inform him that *Lebedinoe ozero* and *Kniaz' Igor'* (with a first-syllable stress) are their real names.

As for the Jewish connection, it could be observed in Lee Strasberg's production of Chekhov's *Three Sisters* on Broadway in the early 1960s, where the actor who played Andrei, the brother of the sisters, indulged in typically Jewish gesticulation and affected a Yiddish accent in the apparent belief he was achieving Russian authenticity. A commercially available British-made tape of Gogol's *Inspector-General* has the merchants who argue with the town's mayor speak in recognizably Jewish accents, even though Jews were barred from residing in Central Russia at the time and though the typical nineteenth-century Russian merchant was of Russian peasant descent. Other similar examples could easily be cited.

To return to the sound of English in Russian ears: while it can seem alien and shrill, it can also be perceived as elegant, exclusivistic, and even aristocratic. In the nineteenth century, this was at times achieved by contrasting English, spoken then by only a small number of Russian aristocrats and scholars, with the far more widely current French. The two talking and corresponding dogs in Gogol's fantastic tale "Diary of a Madman" are differentiated socially by their names in a way that might escape a non-Russian reader. The little lap dog Madgie whose witty letters are essential for the story's plot (and whom a student of mine has recently qualified as "the Madame de Sévigné of dogdom") has an English name, in keeping with the aristocratic milieu in which her owner moves. But Madgie's canine friend and correspondent, whose owners live in a modest apartment house, has the French name of Fidèle.

In *Anna Karenina,* English is regularly associated with Anna's aristocratic and somewhat snobbish lover Vronsky. In the chapters that describe the visit of Anna's sister-in-law Dolly Oblonskaya to Vronsky's English-style country estate, we find English words embedded in French phrases exchanged by other guests. (*On se réunit le matin au breakfast et puis on se sépare* and *une partie de lawn tennis* are found within one page.) While Tolstoy habitually inserted bits of French dialogue when recording the speech of his upper-class characters, the inclusion of English within the French indicated to Dolly that she was in both more elegant and more sterile surroundings than the ones to which she was accustomed.

For twentieth-century Russian writers, English acquired different associations than it had for Gogol and Tolstoy. For Vladimir Mayakovsky, it was the language of technology and industrial progress, which he equated with the future salvation of mankind. The sounds of American English fascinated Mayakovsky during his tour of the United States in 1925. His poems and memoirs about that trip are replete with bits of English. In a macaronic poem "American Russians," Mayakovsky ridiculed Russian immigrants who speak a grotesque mixture of English and Russian. Yet his own English phrases in the poem "The Young Lady and Woolworth" ("Drugs soda great and famous company-national") and in the memoir "How I Made Her Laugh" ("Yes white please double arm strong"), transcribed phonetically in Cyrillic characters in both cases, are strings of exotic sounds whose meaning he doesn't quite grasp and which he employs for conveying *couleur locale*.

In "The Young Lady and Woolworth," Mayakovsky found it necessary to introduce a new letter, nonexistent in the Russian alphabet, an *o* with a dieresis in order to reproduce the sound of *i* in the English word *girl,* transcribing it as *görl.* In this, he was following the earlier precedent set by Alexander Blok, who in his 1912 poem "It Was an Autumn Evening" transcribed *sir* as *sör.* How Blok imagined the English pronunciation of *sir* can be guessed from the fact that he rhymed it with *vzor* ("glance") and *kovyor* ("carpet").

An additional attraction of English, for Mayakovsky, was as a universal vehicle for the popular music of his day—jazz—the rhythms of which he sought to capture and express in some of his poetry. In his polemical essay "How Verses Are Made"

Mayakovsky quoted a popular song he had heard in America, whose haunting rhythm he intended to russify and utilize. As quoted by Mayakovsky, the song went:

Hat Hardet Hena
Di vemp of sovena
Di vemp of sovena
Dzhi-èy.

It takes a leap of imagination to decipher these words as Milton Ager's hit song of 1924, later popularized by numerous vocalists ranging from Bessie Smith to Ella Fitzgerald: "Hard-hearted Hannah, the vamp of Savannah, Ga."

Whether Russian writers heard English as harsh or as pleasing, the constant factor in their perception was its alien quality. By the time the history of Russian literature today is written, this is likely to have changed, because the four most important Russian writers now living reside in America: the poets Nikolai Morshen and Joseph Brodsky and the prose writers Alexander Solzhenitsyn and Alla Ktorova. Less significant but widely known Russian literary figures, such as Andrei Voznesensky and Yevgeny Yevtushenko, visit English-speaking countries on a regular basis. None of them is likely to mistake spoken English for a bird call or for French or German in disguise. The Russian poets residing in the West (and they are sure to loom large in any history of Russian poetry of our time) would never think of throwing in an English word for snob appeal or for decorative reasons, as Mayakovsky used to do, and as Yevtushenko still does today. At the present time, English is about to assume the position of *the* most familiar and indispensable foreign language for Russian literature, the position that French used to occupy for Pushkin, for Tolstoy, or for Tsvetaeva. But this is a phenomenon which cannot yet be described.

DENIS DONOGHUE

Radio Talk

THE BBC has a series of radio programs called "Words." The speaker is invited to give six talks, one every week: each talk is broadcast on Sunday afternoon and repeated the following Thursday. The talk must not exceed five minutes and the theme should have some reasonable bearing upon "the English language and the way we use it." As the rubric implies, the BBC assumes that language is available: we are deemed to be masters rather than slaves of language. The current assertion that we are merely programmed to utter a language that has its own mind and a stronger character in grammar, syntax, and diction than anything the most determined speaker can offer is not banned from the BBC, it is simply not entertained. It is assumed that if you speak in one way rather than another and say something rather than something else, the reason is that you have made that choice. Also, the BBC does not conspire with Michel Foucault and others to suppress the empirical character of the speaker: if the same voice is audible twelve times over a period of six weeks, his personal existence seems to be asserted. I shall transcribe five of my six talks and add a few comments on each. But I should report at once that I found the talks difficult to write: problems of tone kept cropping up. My brief was to write certain discursive material which I would speak on radio to an audience deemed to be listening: a listener would hear the words, would not be in a position to read them or consult them later, and would be unable to reply to any point raised. I was not writing sentences to be printed, so the decorum of print was not available. But equally I was not taking part in a conversation. The situation was a one-sided affair, at best: it had something to do with communication, indeed, but not enough for comfort and ease.

I

Robert Frost once wrote:

> No memory of having starred
> Atones for later disregard,
> Or keeps the end from being hard.

How would you feel if you were a word and got a starring role once and were never heard of again? Suppose you were the word *incarnadine* and Shakespeare used you once in a big part and you never got over the thrill of it and wasted away when the curtain came down. The dictionaries are full of such words, stars for one night. The supplement to the *Oxford English Dictionary* tried to do the word *findrinny* a good turn, rescuing it from its Irish form *findruine,* which means a kind of white bronze used to decorate the rims of shields and bracelets. Yeats evidently came across the word in Eugene O'Curry's book *Manners and Customs in Ancient Ireland* and he jammed it into "The Wanderings of Oisin" not once but thrice: "on a horse with bridle of findrinny"; "with hoofs of the pale findrinny"; and "with hoofs of the ruddy findrinny". But under any color it failed to take, and Yeats gave it up. But it had two more outings. On 16 October 1934 Joyce wrote to his son Giorgio and said, among other things, "a thirty-year wedding should be called a 'findrinny' one. Findrinny is a kind of white gold mixed with silver." Go back thirty years from 1934 and you come upon 1904, the year in which Joyce met Nora Barnacle and consummated what he regarded as his marriage. So between a silver and a golden wedding anniversary he thought to mark a findrinny one at thirty years. Like nearly everything else in his head, Joyce put *findrinny* into *Finnegans Wake,* and again set it between silver and gold. To the consolation that it's an ill wind blows nobody good he added:

> It's an allavalonche that blows nopussy food. If you only were there to explain the meaning, best of men, and talk to her nice of gulden-

> selver. The lips would moisten once again. As when you drove with her to Findrinny Fair.

Well, *Finnegans Wake* was published in 1939 and so far as I know we've heard the last of *findrinny*. It's a bit dismal to come upon it in the great dictionary between *finding* and *fine*, two words in good health. There must be some kind of Darwinism in language.

Still, a word from a dying language like Irish that found itself taken up by Yeats and Joyce is bound to feel that it failed under spectacular auspices. Think of all the words that survive only because rascals need them. Or, worse still, think of words which survive only in form rather than in truth and substance, words which live on shop fronts, for instance, and are never spoken. Suppose you thought of yourself as a victualler, sustaining an honorable trade going back to Chaucer and Langland; and suppose people called you a butcher. You often see butchers advertising, at least in Ireland, the sale of prime beef, but *prime* is a word you rarely hear in that sense. Still, there are minds which keep it alive. A few weeks ago, in Dublin, a friend of mine, Oliver Edwards, was praising a meal we had just consumed in a splendid restaurant. He went through the several courses, making appropriate tokens of appreciation, and then he said, "And the pineapple was prime." It would not have occurred to me to apply that word to the pineapple, though it was indeed a succulent slice. But I was pleased to find that a word I thought only nominally alive had come forth on a proper occasion. Some words may not be as lost as we fear. *Findrinny* may still have life in it.

II

I suppose you've noticed that something very odd has been happening to verbs: or rather, that the rule about plural subjects taking a plural verb is breaking down. The rule has been that if the subject of a sentence is A and B, the verb must follow in the plural form. John and James are good athletes. Nobody would get away with saying that John and James is good athletes. I was taught that sentences in which the subject is A and B have to take a plural verb, and I have never broken the rule. But it is widely broken in respectable newspapers, and in some cases with a show of reason.

A few weeks ago the *Sunday Times* had an editorial proposing that Britain and other countries should boycott the Olympic Games to be held in Moscow in 1980. The main reason given was the trial of Dr. Orlov. The *Sunday Times* said that the trial exhibited yet again the bad faith and intolerance of the Soviet regime: "intolerance, because the Orlov trial and sentence shows once again that the leadership in the Kremlin will not suffer any internal public criticism whatever of their system." My English teacher would have insisted that *trial and sentence* must be followed by *show* rather than *shows*—a plural subject, a plural verb—and while he would have appreciated the ironic use of the verb *suffer* in the sense of "allow" and registered the nice point that the Kremlin does not propose to suffer in any sense, he would have enforced his position on *show* and *shows*. The *Sunday Times* leader writer would presumably defend his honor by saying that he considers *trial and sentence* as one thing, one event, and that he is justified in emphasizing its horrible unity by giving it a singular verb. Later in the same editorial, when he argues that countries in which the Olympic Games are held tend to take them seriously and regard them as occasions for putting their better national foot forward, the leader writer says: "Both prestige and enhancement of national status is looked for by the host country to these great four-yearly gatherings." This is a far more daring violation, if it violates the rule at all. The writer insists on plurality by saying "both prestige and enhancement of national status," but then he follows with *is* instead of *are*. Can he be allowed to do this? My teacher would say: No. And if the leader writer retorted that prestige is really the same as enhancement of national status, the teacher would find him guilty of redundancy and tell him to choose one and get rid of the other. My own feeling is that if he would agree to a plural verb, I would settle for the touch of pomp and circumstance in the double subject.

My adversary could of course take the issue to a higher authority by asserting that such school rules are only a recent thing and that Shakespeare regularly (or rather irregularly) combined a plural subject with a singular verb. In *Measure for Measure* the Duke says to Friar Thomas:

> My holy sir, none better knows than you
> How I have ever lov'd the life removed,
> And held in idle price to haunt assemblies
> Where youth, and cost, witless bravery keeps.

My teacher, stricter with grammar than with Shakespeare, would try to change *keeps* to *keep*. And indeed, apart from any other consideration, it would sound better, because it would reduce by one the flurry of *s*-words which make such a fuss between *price, assemblies, cost, witless,* and *keeps*. Marianne Moore once remarked that it is hard to write anything in English without setting up a hiss of *s*'s all over the page.

Sixteenth-century writers were preoccupied with the patriotic duty of making English as eloquent as Italian and French, and as weighty as Latin, so that it would bear the whole range of experience, private and public. Seventeenth and eighteenth-century writers decided that enough was enough, it was time to put the house of English in order; hence the steadiness embodied in grammars and dictionaries. Only a few pedants really wanted to fix the language, but nearly everybody wanted to see it settled for long enough to have its temper domesticated. So plural subjects were required to take plural verbs, Shakespeare notwithstanding. But things are running loose again. For all I know, the *Sunday Times* may have deep plans in preferring singular verbs to plurals. The leader writer may be saying, as Isabella says to Angelo:

> Gentle my lord,
> Let me entreat you speak the former language.

III

There is a famous moment in Hemingway's novel *A Farewell to Arms* when the hero, Frederic Henry, is talking to Gino, who says, "What has been done this summer cannot have been done in vain." The next paragraph gives Frederic's response:

> I did not say anything. I was always embarrassed by the words sacred, glorious, and sacrifice and the expression in vain. We had heard them, sometimes standing in the rain almost out of earshot, so that only the shouted words came through, and had read them, on proclamations that were slapped up by billposters over other proclamations, now for a long time, and I had seen nothing sacred, and the things that were glorious had no glory and the sacrifices were like the stockyards at Chicago if nothing was done with the meat except to bury it. There were many words that you could not stand to hear and finally only the names of places had dignity. Certain numbers were the same way and certain dates and these with the names of the places were all you could say and have them mean anything. Abstract words such as glory, honor, courage, or hallow were obscene beside the concrete names of villages, the number of roads, the names of rivers, the numbers of regiments and the dates.

It sounds like Humphrey Bogart in *Casablanca,* but in the end

Bogart is braver than anyone else; he just doesn't put his courage into official words. His actions speak better than words. Abstract words have been getting a bad press for many years now partly because they've been associated with the rhetoric of war and sacrifice. When you hear an abstract word you're supposed to think that someone is putting something across on you; maybe he wants you to die for him. Frederic Henry's mood is weary disillusion: he wants to rid himself of abstract words so that he may rid himself of loose emotions and grand desires. It's not that he despises ideals. He wants to replace one value, War, by another, Love, but not by any theory or rhetoric of love. He loves Catherine: it's specific and therefore good. He thinks the official words obscene and wants to speak his own true words to Catherine.

But it's odd that the word *abstract* has become so tarnished. If you find dignity in numbers and the names of places it's because they don't make any demands on you. They merely name the thing; they don't propose any other relation than that of naming, affixing a label to the thing. Abstract words such as *courage, honor, glory,* and *loyalty* are empty or merely virtual until you fill them with your response to their demand. If you rise to their occasion, well and good: if not, your refusal or failure turns into resentment against the demand made by the words and the whole structure of values they endorse. In any case you resent the moral pressure they exert upon you.

One of the discoveries of this century is that you don't need to use the big, abstract, demanding words, you can use visual images instead. If Frederic Henry were fighting a war now, he would not hear the words *sacred, glorious,* and *sacrifice* while fighting in the rain: instead, his mind would be suffused with correspondingly silent images, pictures of other people being courageous, doing courageous things. Patriotism is now elicited by photographs rather than by verbal exhortations. Values are transmitted by images and counter-images; not by ways of saying but by ways of being (or rather, ways of appearing). Captions are still added to photographs in newspapers, but they are usually neutral, disinterested. They can afford to be neutral, because the message is contained, without the offensiveness of a verbal appeal, in the picture. This is bound to make a difference to language. Susan Sontag remarks in her book *On Photography* that the camera transforms history into spectacle. It may be one of the responsibilities of language—I mean, of the people who use language—to prevent that transformation from being too easy or too complete. The camera has an interest in turning history into spectacle, but none in reversing the process. At best, the picture leaves a vague blur in the observer's mind; strong enough to send him into battle, perhaps, but not to have him understand why he is going.

IV

Do you ever find yourself reading sentences you know you couldn't have written? Not because they're too profound or beautiful to be compatible with your limitations; there are indeed such sentences, but they're not what I have in view. I mean sentences which seem to issue from a form of life you've never lived and couldn't imagine living. I came across a passage of that kind recently in Dame Helen Gardner's book on T. S. Eliot's *Four Quartets*. She's describing the house and garden at Burnt Norton, the place of the first Quartet:

> Near the house, overlooking the garden, is a huge tree with 'figured leaves' on which, as Eliot did, one can watch the light at play. Passing through the rose-garden, down some steps, one comes upon a clipped hedge surrounding a large expanse of grass. Coming out of this, through a gap in the hedge, one finds oneself standing above a grassy bank and looking down on a big rectangular drained pool.

I find it hard to read that passage. I couldn't have written it. Hard to read, because I can't concentrate on the garden while that flotilla of *ones* is passing: "one finds oneself standing above a grassy bank." Well I don't, I find myself bemused by those *ones*. To write that passage you probably have to be an Oxford don and to think that you are addressing if not a colleague than at worst someone who can imagine what it's like to be an Oxford don. Some people say that the difference between "one finds oneself" and "you find yourself" is merely a difference of intimacy: if you want to keep the atmosphere fairly formal, with a hint of distance which you feel disposed to maintain, you say "one finds oneself." I'm not convinced. In some ways *one* is more intimate than *you,* because it invites the reader into the enjoyment of wide and superior experience. Either he is supposed to share that experience already and therefore he has only to be reminded of it; or he is being admitted to it, having shown himself worthy of admission. There's always an implied "of course" at the end of such sentences. The reader doesn't have to have the point explained, a nod will do, and he's expected to be pleased by the implication that he's worth this attention. So the sentence has the inflection of a glance, a nod to the qualified reader. It helps if the writer is an Oxford don; better still if he or she gives the impression of being such by birth, class, nature, and nurture, as well as by academic achievement and the publication of such a distinguished work as the one the reader is now reading. Then you can appeal to a tradition of shared values, good taste, fine discernment, which makes communication a privileged experience.

But why couldn't I have written Dame Helen's sentences if I had visited Burnt Norton with Eliot's poem in my head? The real reason is that English as spoken in Ireland doesn't allow the locution, "one finds oneself standing above a grassy bank." If you were to say or write that in Ireland, you would be taken as parodying Dame Helen Gardner or some other exalted citizen of England who writes in that style. There are grassy banks in Ireland still, but one doesn't find oneself standing above them. If an Irish traveller were to write of a visit to Burnt Norton, he would have to say "I found myself" or "you would find yourself" or, better still, "you find yourself standing above a grassy bank." There is no Oxford in Ireland, no institution which supposes itself to be the center of the literate universe. For well-known historical reasons, Irish experience is fractured: different languages, although Irish is nearly a lost cause; different religious traditions, conventions, allegiances. No Irishman can assume that he is at the center of any universe or that he and his reader share attitudes and values so deeply that they can be invoked by an unspoken "of course" or called into life by a raised eyebrow.

V

In 1961 Vivian Nicholson and her husband Keith won the football pools and collected a check for £152,319. When asked what she intended doing with the money, Vivian answered, "I'm going to spend, spend, spend." And she did. Her autobiography tells the story, and it has been told again in Jack Rosenthal's play for television, *Spend, Spend, Spend.* One of the telling features of the play is the poverty of speech which it ascribes to Vivian and Keith. Most of the feelings in the play are violent, but the violence never finds an original form for itself, it's always vented in the same few ways. The expression is belated, a continuous cliché. Some of the forms of expression are physical, the two bodies are shown going through the standard motions. When the violence is verbal, it runs along the same few stereotypes, repeated throughout the play. The word *bugger* is shouted hundreds of times, as verb, noun, adjective, and adverb. We have been schooled to expect a direct relation between poverty of feeling and poverty of speech. And the touching thing about the play is that the new life provided by winning the money is not new at all: the money makes no difference to the Nicholsons. They drink, buy two cars, a fancy bungalow, holidays in Las Vegas and Marbella, but their speech remains as it was, and their range of feeling remains what it was. Leisure hasn't changed their lives, except that they have more time to declare themselves unhappy. At one point Keith is quarreling with Vivian. "Why *aren't* you happy?" he shouts, and Vivian shouts back, "Why aren't *you?*" It may be true, as Marxists assert, that if you change the environment you change the structure of feeling; but such a change takes time, evidently. I think there's another explanation.

In the play, the structure of Vivian's feeling, such as it is, is what it has always been, apparently. We say that she is the sum of her experiences or, in a loftier version, the product of her environment. Until the early days of her first marriage, she was what her conditions of life had conspired to make her: the conditions were mostly father, mother, poverty, violence, sex, and unwanted pregnancy. If the structure of her feeling doesn't change when she comes into big money, the reason is that nothing that happens to her thereafter amounts to an experience: it never reaches the state of being an experience. Vivian is locked in her feeling as she is locked in her language. Critics talk glibly about a supposed relation between feeling and language, maintaining that the words we use testify to the nature of the feelings that provoke them. Literary criticism is largely justified by that supposition. But critics often forget that many events which we call experience are not experience at all, they are merely happenings. The test of an experience is that it indeed alters the structure of our feeling: if it doesn't, it hasn't been an experience, merely a circumstance. The moral of Rosenthal's play is not that you shouldn't do the pools because you might win and then you'd be in trouble, it's that many news-making events are not experiences at all. Walter Benjamin has a famous essay on storytelling in which he says that many soldiers who fought in the Great War came home in 1918 with nothing to say, no stories to tell. The reason is that their experiences in the trenches never became real in the sense of altering their structures of feelings, or were such as to overwhelm those structures, rendering the soldiers numb. The reason good war fiction is written only several years after the events is that the events come to the stage of being experience only with time, distance, memory, and imagination. At that point they are incorporated, for the first time, in the person who, surviving them, has been changed by them. That's why Jack Rosenthal's sense of life was acute in keeping the Nicholsons in the same prison of language all the way through; they were incapable of breaking away from themselves. Everything that happened to them was belated, already immobilized, a stereotype in the form in which they received it. They never had an original experience in their lives.

VI

A few comments on these talks.

On I, the one about *findrinny.* Note how anxious I was to put the word *you* in immediately, to conjure a listener into staying with me. Linguists since Jesperson call such words *shifters,* words understood only in their contexts; such words as *I, you, now, here, tomorrow.* In my talk the shifter was used at once in an effort to establish a context, that is, an audience. I was embarrassingly aware that I was talking to an unknown audience, talking rather than writing, and that I should be communicating in some positive way. The insecurity of tone comes through in the frantic conceit of imagining yourself as a word. I suppose I wanted to start by giving words a personality, lest I sound like some pedant bemoaning the fact that English isn't what it used to be. I was attending to the theme and hoping that someone out there who happened to be listening would catch the signs of attention and perhaps feel a certain mild pleasure upon hearing something he hadn't known before. I was pretty safe with *findrinny,* but the tone of the talk remained insecure. I didn't know whether the information would be interesting enough to hold the listener's attention or would have to be embellished with some kind of charm. I was wrong about *incarnadine,* by the way. Precisely because it has not been accepted into Standard English, it is bound to stick out from its setting wherever it's used, so if used at all it has to star. In the *Rubaiyat* it sounds like an aria:

> And David's lips are lockt; but in divine
> High-piping Pehlevi, with "Wine! Wine! Wine!
> Red Wine!"—the Nightingale cries to the Rose
> That sallow cheek of hers to incarnadine.

In *Far from the Madding Crowd* it needs a bit of poetry to share the color of Bathsheba's face, at the end, with Oak:

> Yet, though so plainly dressed, there was a certain rejuvenated appearance about her:
>
> *As though a rose should shut and be a bud again.*
>
> Repose had again incarnadined her cheeks.

I suppose the nice thing about *prime* is that the unexpectedness comes like a metaphor to prove that our speech isn't totally stereotyped.

On II, about singulars and plurals. The *you* comes in again with the first breath, but the tone settles down rather better to the schoolmaster's note of patience. I suppose I wanted the listener to ask himself whether it's fair to apply to language the morally charged terms we apply to conduct. To say that some linguistic habit is loose is to let an air of general looseness suffuse the occasion. Eliot did this regularly, not just in *Four Quartets;* he made no effort to keep implications of purity and health away from his descriptions of the use of language. Of course this has a long history, as in references to vices of style, a vicious diction: everyone refers to the corruption of language as if the corruption of youth were a similar outrage. Rules of grammar, rules of law, rules of conduct: that's the question I wanted to raise, but in a disarming way. I wanted the listener to find it odd that I was talking about language rather than about the trial of Dr. Orlov or the wisdom of boycotting the Olympic Games; and, finding it odd, go on to wonder why I was doing this.

About III, Hemingway on abstractions. The attack on abstractions comes from several directions; in modern literature, much of it is tied up with Imagism and the notion that images are somehow cleaner than concepts. There's also a notion that concretions are good and abstractions bad because the first stay close to the event and the second run off to the mind's self-indulgence. But it's not clear. I understand why Robbe-Grillet wants to ban words which imply a cosy relation between people and the planet on which we live; he thinks it leads to sloppiness, sentimentality, nostalgia, and spending too much time in Abraham's bosom. Still, the modern idea that concretions are innocent and abstractions guilty is very strange. Coleridge is the only critic I know who sets his mind against it, because he has an interest in keeping us free from the glamor of surfaces and appearances: he valued etymology because it leads the mind from surface to depth and history. He wanted to be free to consider any object according not only to its appearance but to its "idea," its theoretic form. Modern critics, on the whole, share Frederic Henry's embarrassment: they are embarrassed by the unlimited claims the moral abstractions seem to make. Even John Crowe Ransom, who wanted to defend abstractions, thought them easier to defend when they were accompanied by images which somehow corresponded to them and cleaned them up. About images replacing messages: I was thinking of Roland Barthes's analysis of the Algerian soldier saluting the French flag, and of advertising generally. It may be that most of human experience is now processed by visual images and appearances. We are told that politicians are elected not on policies but on their presented images, that a smile gets votes more effectively than a legislative program. Probably the best use we can make of words is to force images to subject themselves to discourse, to prevent historical meaning from being turned into a snap: hence my reference to Sontag's book.

About IV, Dame Helen and *one.* This was the most tendentious of the six talks, and it now seems tediously brash. My wife tells me I was wrong about Oxford and dons: *one* is used in this way by upper-class English people generally. Even so, it's still a form that takes for granted the shared possession of superiority. I'm sometimes irritated by English friends who put a complacent note into their praise of the English language. Randolph Quirk had an article in the *Sunday Times* claiming that English is better than, say, French and German because of its informality and urbanity. Unlike French and German, English uses the same *you* for friends and strangers alike, there is no need to insist upon different degrees of intimacy or rank. This doesn't mean that distinctions are not made, but that they can be made easily and without the grammatical fuss observed in French and German. Quirk's meaning was perfectly clear: in English, as in England, you live a congenial, unfussy life without insisting upon the niceties of decorum or pulling rank on your colleagues. I thought the article mildly offensive. I've often had the same feeling about other English references to English. One of Empson's early reviews, quoted in Christopher Norris's *William Empson and the Philosophy of Criticism,* talks about "the English way of thinking" and maintains that a decent English style "gives great resilience to the thinker, never blurs a point by too wide a focus, is itself a confession of how much always must be left undealt with, and is beautifully free from verbiage: to an enemy it looks like sheer cheating." It is not clear who the enemy is, unless Empson means someone who has to work with an allegedly primitive language while watching his English opponent run away with the spoils. Imperialism is never very far from

Empson's style, which has a way of dividing people into English and Others. I suppose it was this tone which made me give Dame Helen a bit of cheek. But there was another reason I hadn't time to mention. In Irish it is impossible to say, "one finds oneself standing above a grassy bank." Equally, Irish has no passive voice, in the strict sense. In Irish you can't have the sentence form which says "*Cartesian Linguistics* was written by Chomsky, not by McCawley." You have to say "It was Chomsky, and not McCawley, who wrote *Cartesian Linguistics*." Also, in Irish you can't say "I have been informed that. . . ." If you say "Deirtear," you mean that some unnamed and unlocated people are saying something, it's like "Rumor has it. . . ."If your lore comes from specific people, you say "Deir said"; they, those people, tell me. . . . *One,* in Dame Helen's usage, can't be translated into Irish. There is a theory that when Language A is supplanted by Language B, the native speaker of A who learns B for his need or advancement uses only those forms of B which are grammatically compatible with A. Or if he uses the remaining forms, he does so to ape his masters or to make fun of them. In time, his masters may find it charming if he retains some of the old forms of defeated A, translated more or less directly into B, as Synge did in his plays. Synge was not a native speaker of Irish, but he picked up enough Irish to see that its idioms, literally translated into English, would have a special flavor, as of an older culture. These phrases are charming to English visitors, provided they are assured that they have nothing to fear from the natives.

This is even more offensive, I'm afraid, than my original talk, but most Irishmen revert occasionally to this resentment against English, the conqueror's tongue. Stephen Dedalus's feeling about English words makes a touching chapter in *A Portrait of the Artist as a Young Man* and complicates the way we interpret the last forty pages of that book. And in general I suppose I resent the gunboat linguistics still audible in Helen Gardner and William Empson.

Finally, on V, *Spend, Spend, Spend.* I found it impossible to avoid sounding smug and superior to the Nicholsons. I've never been happy with the Leavis-like argument that the quality of a man's sensibility must be assessed on the evidence provided by his language, and I was probably trying to go as far as I could toward that argument without really giving in to it. Surely more evidence is required: language is not enough. I can see that critics find Leavis's argument a blessing because it makes criticism serious and far-reaching; it gives our activities a moral bearing if we can read books on the understanding that "by his words ye shall know him." I tried to avoid snobbery by concentrating on the definition of an experience; on a hint from Hans-Georg Gadamer who has an entire chapter in *Truth and Method* on the subject and argues that intentionality is an essential factor in any experience worth the name. It seems necessary to have some theory about the relation between the things that happen to us and what, if anything, we make of them with full intent and consciousness. Gadamer's argument seemed to me more persuasive then than now. If you say that your intention must reach out to the occasion before it can become an experience, you find yourself with at least two problems; how to define an intention or the state of intentionality; and the probability that the association of intention with consciousness divides our lives too neatly into two parts. If consciousness, intentionality, and experience go together, everything else, including the unconscious, dreams, fantasy, circumstance, coincidence, is thrown into the cellar of our lives. It's nearly impossible to make these arrangements without arrogance. Saul Bellow once wrote, with T. S. Eliot's work in view, that consciousness is the most available form of virtue. Precisely; and that is the problem. A theory of experience as consciousness quickly becomes a theory of consciousness as virtue.

Again, very little of this was clarified in my talk. This time, the problem was not to put implications into the talk but to keep the nasty implications out. I recalled the snobbery which Eliot couldn't avoid in *The Family Reunion* once he had committed himself to making Harry the only intelligent brother in the family. Setting him beside Agatha helped a little but didn't get over the difficulty that Harry is a prig in precisely the degree of his superior consciousness. I couldn't manage to say what I wanted to say about the Nicholsons without accusing them of being too stupid to have an experience. But it still sounds unpleasant to pursue the logic to the point of saying that to be worth a place on earth you have to be highly conscious. For this reason, *Spend, Spend, Spend* seems to me the most nagging of my talks. I found myself saying things that in conversation I would not say, or would certainly have to qualify if not withdraw; adopting positions which seemed valid until I thought about them in more reasonable, informal terms. In a genuine conversation I would have been forced into the give-and-take which results in greater precision as well as more tolerance. One-way communication certainly threw me into a specious logic; it would not have survived a genuine argument. In turn, this logic commanded a tone which seemed correctly rigorous at the time and now seems merely insecure.

JOHN DILLON

Antaeus and Hercules: Some Notes on the Irish Predicament

I SUPPOSE every Irishman sooner or later has his moment of confrontation with the English language. Mine occurred quite early in life, when I was sent, at the age of fourteen, to an English public school. The school was Downside Abbey, near Bath in Somerset, a Benedictine foundation of the previous century, which had spent its first fifty years or so assiduously becoming "the Catholic Eton," and the next fifty attempting to live down that reputation.

Looking back on it now, I think it was not at all a bad place to be, in spite of the aggressively imperialist attitudes it fostered, but for a fourteen-year-old from "the colonies" (the fact that Ireland had successfully revolted some thirty years previously did not make it an independent country, just an ungrateful colony), it was daunting. The British do not on the whole much like the Irish (Franz Fanon could explain why better than I can), and English public schoolboys have no inhibitions about expressing their distaste directly. As for me, I had decided in advance that I was not going to be typecast or pigeonholed; if I was to be disliked, I intended to be disliked as an individual, not as an ethnic minority.

I had not long to wait. Before I had been in the place more than a few hours, one of those fat, sad characters who try to compensate for their various inadequacies by bullying new boys lurched up to me. He had found out who the Irish were.

"Arrah now, sure and begorrah," he yammered, "do we have someone here from ould Oireland? And what might your name be, Paddy?"

This plainly had to be nipped in the bud. I drew myself up to my full four feet nine inches.

"I beg your pardon," I said icily, in my best BBC accent. "I don't think I quite caught that. Could you repeat it again slowly?"

The shock value of this simple rejoinder persisted long after the immediate discomfiture of my would-be persecutor. I was not bothered by sallies in dialect after that.

This was a victory at the time, but it is plain to me now that it was a Pyrrhic victory. I developed very quickly a more or less impeccable British accent, which I found impossible, in later years, to shake off. Having put the brandishers of false brogues to rout, one could hardly turn round later and try to develop one oneself.

So I joined the English language. My conscious confrontation with it, however, was only beginning. For the Irish, learning English has always been part of an effort to beat the conquerors at their own game. As I understand it, the Gaelic language received what was substantially its deathblow when Daniel O'Connell, "the Liberator," in the early decades of the last century, decided that the only way the Irish people would break out their state of hopeless serfdom would be to abandon Gaelic for English, and take with both hands all the opportunities for advancement, educational and otherwise, which the British were, grudgingly or incautiously, prepared to give them. That was, after all, what he himself had done, as a young lawyer from Kerry, with brilliant success. His influence was paramount, and a resolve to learn English swept the land. By the census of 1851, only 15 percent of the population admitted to being "Irish-speaking"—a ridiculously low figure, but one which shows the attitudes of the people very well—even as the ridiculously high figures for Irish speakers in recent censuses show our aspirations at present.

Of course, "beating the British at their own game" necessitates not just using their language, but using it more effectively. This, I would say, is the chief driving force behind the alleged fluency of the Irish race. There is much mental confusion on this question. No doubt the Celts of old were a very voluble class of men, but I do not see what that has to do with Goldsmith, Sheridan, Wilde, Shaw, Yeats, George Moore, or even Joyce. Synge, of course, profited greatly from the richness of Irish peasant speech, but he himself was using it as a sympathetic outsider—indeed, it might be said unkindly, as an 1890s Paris aesthete in search of new experiences. No, it seems to me that the immediate stimulus to linguistic exuberance is the one that I am conscious of in myself, the resolve to take the language of the British and do more with it than they can.

In a way, though, praising an Irishman for his eloquence is like felicitating a black on his sense of rhythm. Eloquent we may be, but this eloquence was acquired at the price of our own language, and, to some extent, of our soul.

But what does all this Anglo-Irish business amount to, as a living literary tradition, in 1979? A survey of my literary friends and acquaintances suggests to me that for them writing Anglo-Irish is not an issue, except insofar as one strives to keep out of the shadow of Yeats, if a poet; Joyce, if a novelist; or O'Casey, if a playwright. That is the problem weighing most heavily upon the present generation, I would say—that, and wondering where the next square meal is coming from. As writers, they write English. A novelist, of course, must strive to represent real people and their speech patterns, if he wishes to give any degree of life to his creations, and this will frequently necessitate presenting the idiom and accent of Dublin, Cork, Kerry, or Belfast, but otherwise one strives, I think, for basic English, without any Irish mist about it. If one considers, for instance, John McGahern, who is probably our most distinguished current novelist, one sees him writing, in *The Barracks*, *The Dark*, or *The Leavetaking*, on Irish themes—naturally—but without any special effort to be Anglo-Irish. He is concerned with the close dissection of the world he knows (an Irish country police barracks, for instance), not with the forging of a special Irish idiom. And such, I feel, is the case with our other leading prose writers, Aidan Higgins, John Banville, William Trevor, and so on. If an idiom emerges, it will be a natural product, not the result of special striving.

For a playwright, things are more difficult. Brian Friel or Tom Kilroy must write in "dialect," in deference to their characters, whether Ulstermen or Dublin jackeens; in each case they merely represent what they know. But neither of them, I think, is striving for regionalism.

The poets, it would seem, have the greatest freedom of idiom, but on the other hand poets are most liable to think deeply about language and the national mind, so it is in that quarter one would most expect to find agonizing, if agonizing were going on. I must say, however, that I have not noticed much of this happening. It is a touchy subject, but I would regard our major poets at the moment as being, perhaps, Thomas Kinsella, John Montague, Eavan Boland, Michael Hartnett, Seamus Deane, and Seamus Heaney (a nonexclusive list). As far as I can observe, they go about their business of being poets without worrying explicitly about whether or not they are being Anglo-Irish poets—with the interesting exception of Hartnett, to whom I shall revert in a moment. Of course they reflect upon the Irish predicament in various ways, but not on the *linguistic* predicament. Let us take an example, the first stanza of a poem of Seamus Heaney's, from his recent collection *North,* called "Act of Union":

> Tonight, a first movement, a pulse,
> As if the rain in bogland gathered head
> To slip and flood: a bog-burst,
> A gash breaking open the ferny bed.
> Your back is a firm line of eastern coast
> And arms and legs are thrown
> Beyond your gradual hills. I caress
> The heaving province where our past has grown.
> I am the tall kingdom over your shoulder
> That you would neither cajole nor ignore.
> Conquest is a lie. I grow older
> Conceding your half-independent shore
> Within whose borders now my legacy
> Culminates inexorably.

Now this is thoroughly Irish in its reference—apart from the more obvious one—to the infamous Act of Union of 1801, and the imagery of the greater island at one's back. There is also some play with bogland, a substance of great fascination for Heaney; but otherwise, what is here that is Irish? Not the language. The sensibility, you say, perhaps, the way of looking at things. But is that not the characteristic of a great poet in any language? I will return to Heaney, however, and to *North*, since elsewhere he provides me with a theme for this essay; for Heaney does in fact think deeply and creatively about the Irish problem in its many forms.

I have been referring to the "Irish predicament." For this term I am indebted to Conor Cruise O'Brien, himself a connoisseur both of the English language and of Irish sensibility. In the course of a review of Vivian Mercier's *The Irish Comic Tradition* entitled "Our Wits about Us," published in the *New Statesman* of February 1963 and reprinted in his collection of essays *Writers and Politics,* he says (p. 140): "There is probably no continuous and distinctive 'Irish mind', but there has been, since the seventeenth century at least, an Irish predicament, a predicament which has produced common characteristics in a number of those who have been involved in it." He identifies the main characteristic as an "ironical mode of expression, sometimes achieving wit." The predicament, I presume, is what to do about England and the English, first politically, then culturally. The first problem was largely solved some time ago, at least for twenty-six counties (though I may note that we only achieved an independent currency in January 1979); the second remains. Our cultural predicament, after all, is only a variation on the basic postcolonial one: how to achieve some semblance of autonomy from the "mother country" without throwing out the baby with the bathwater. One possible reaction—an extreme one, though tempting—is to reject the English language altogether for purposes of serious composition—a course taken by, among others, Conor Cruise O'Brien's own wife, Máire MacEntee, who has become one of our most distinguished Gaelic poets. One younger poet already mentioned, Michael Hartnett, already successful in English, has now turned to Gaelic, he swears, for all future work. We shall see. On the other hand, Samuel Beckett has escaped into French, though whether this move has any ideological significance I couldn't say. Joyce, of course, in the *Wake*, is triumphantly transcending the English language, together with all others, but this can hardly be denominated a cultural *retreat*.

Except for this notionally ancestral language of ours, however, to which some adventurous souls can turn for new inspiration, our position is more or less that of the other English-speaking "colonies," Canada, Australia, New Zealand, even the West Indies (I exempt the United States from this list; it has been around long enough to look after itself). Our writers have the choice either of becoming aggressively "regional," or of declining to recognize that there is a problem. It is this latter course, as I have suggested above, that they are taking. We have no Hugh MacDiarmids about, composing fiercely in an Irish Lallans.

I find the Irish predicament reflected very well, in fact, in the works of the brilliant West Indian V. S. Naipaul. Like an Irish writer, though to a more acute degree, Naipaul has a problem of identity and roots. He is both a master of Trinidadian idiom, black and Indian, and a superb manipulator of English prose; and in his most serious, reflective works, such as *The Mimic Men,* he agonizes deeply about the problem of national identity. Is one

Indian, British, or Trinidadian? Only recently did the older generation of his own family, I believe, begin to support the West Indian cricket team rather than the Indian, in a test match (the game itself, of course, being quintessentially British).

We do not have quite the problems of a Naipaul. For one thing, the fate of the Irish cricket team (there is one!) leaves us generally unmoved. And yet there is a problem for the English-speaking Irishman, even if we do not let it cramp our literary style. I for one tend to cherish jealously the few regionalisms to which I can lay claim—and precious few they are—in the interest of the preservation of distinctness, of roots: "Amn't I just after giving you one?" (to a child, wheedling another chocolate); "Herself is inside in the house"; "He had a right to help me" (in the sense of "he had a *duty*"); "He did *so*" (opposite of "he did *not*"); some distinctive uses of the "dative," such as "That fella has a fine stomach on him!", "He went and sold it on me" (to be distinguished from the American "He sold me on it"), and "She went and died on him"; and a handful of distinctive words. A few rags and tatters, but without them I would feel quite deracinated. Antaeus-like, one loses vital force if entirely parted from the home ground. (Indeed I feel that that, perhaps, is what has happened to some good Irish writers, such as Edna O'Brien or Brian Moore, whom circumstances have parted from their native haunts for too long.) The image of Antaeus pleases me. It has pleased also, I am glad to discover, others for whom I have respect. Yeats used it, near the end of his life, in a stanza of his retrospective poem "The Municipal Gallery Revisited." He is brooding on the portraits of dead friends:

> John Synge, I, and Augusta Gregory thought
> All that we did, all that we said or sang
> Must come from contact with the soil, from that
> Contact everything Antaeus-like grew strong.
> We three alone in modern times had brought
> Everything down to that sole test again,
> Dream of the noble and the beggarman.

This image Seamus Heaney, *doctus poeta* that he is, picks up and develops in two fine poems included in *North*, "Antaeus" and "Hercules and Antaeus," in the latter of which I choose to take Hercules to be, broadly, the English language and culture. I will end with quotations from each of these:

> . . . I cannot be weaned
> Off the earth's long contour, her river-veins.
> Down here in my cave

Girdered with root and rock
I am cradled in every artery
Like a small hillock.

One of Heaney's favorite images here, the womblike, knotted recesses of the earth, that "native dark" of which Yeats speaks elsewhere. And here is Hercules:

Sky-born and royal
snake-choker, dung-heaver,
his mind big with golden apples,
his future hung with trophies,

Hercules has the measure
of resistance and black powers
feeding off the territory.
Antaeus, the mould-hugger,

is weaned at last.

Sky-born and royal, the English language. Perhaps it will beat us in the end. But we will continue to wrestle, staying as close to the earth as we can.

PETER PORTER

Sonata Form: The Australian Magpie

IT MAKES A preliminary statement
with its head to one side and an eye
far too large to be seemly.

It is no relation to the English magpie
yet is decently black and white,
upstaging its cousin the kurrawong.

Its opening theme is predation.
What it scavenges is old cake
soaked in dew, but might be eyes.

Such alighting and strutting
across the mown grass of the Ladies' College!
Siege machines are rolling near.

Bustle in a baking tin,
a feast of burnt porridge—
the children are growing on their way to school.

You can upbraid the magpie
saying, 'What do you know of Kant?'
It might shift a claw an inch or two.

This poem originally appeared in *Vole* (Fall 1978) and is reprinted by permission of the author.

It can tell when an overlord is unhappy.
When one sweeps out in tears to clatter
the petrol mower, magpie flies off.

But never flies far. Big feet
are moving to their place in dreams—
a little delay in the sun won't count.

Are these the cries of love, or of magpies
sighting food? Some things about desire
call for explicit modern novels.

Magpie talk: Nation, National, Nationalist!
In this tongue its name is legion.
We speak English ourselves, with a glossary.

We have certainly heard this theme before,
the sound of homecoming. Anticipation
needs a roof, plus a verandah for magpies.

The coda, alas. It can be Brucknerian.
We say the end is coming. The magpie
has found its picture in an encyclopaedia.

Where can there be nature enough
to do without art? In despair, the poet
flies to the top of a camphor laurel.

Girl and magpie leave him in the tree.
Tomorrow a trip down the coast for her
and spaghetti rings left out for the bird.

QUENTIN SKINNER

Language and Social Change

THE QUESTION I wish to consider is less concerned with the state of our language in itself than with a separate though closely related theme: the state of current thinking about language in general and our own language in particular. This is obviously an immense topic, and I only propose to examine one small corner of it. I want to offer some reflections about the relationship between our social world and the changing vocabulary we use to describe and appraise it. Even this is of course a vast subject, and in order to make it manageable I shall concentrate on one particular study which has recently sought to analyze the connections between linguistic and social change. The book I have in mind—which I intend to use as a stalking horse in what follows—is Raymond Williams's *Keywords.*[1]

The specific question I want to ask—the question that Williams is also concerned with in *Keywords*—is this: what can we hope to learn about our culture and society through studying the changing meanings of words? Williams argues that a study of "variations and confusions of meaning" may help us to understand matters of "historical and contemporary substance" (p. 21).[2] If we take "certain words at the level at which they are generally used," he suggests, and scrutinize their developing "structures of meaning," we may be able "to contribute certain kinds of awareness" to existing social debates, and in particular an "extra edge of consciousness" (pp. 20–21). But what precise kinds of "awareness" can we expect to acquire if we study the history of key words? And how should we conduct our investigations in order to ensure that this awareness is duly acquired? These are the questions I should like to examine at somewhat greater length.

I

Before proceeding, however, we need if possible to neutralize one serious doubt. It might be objected that, in singling out "a shared body of words," we are focusing on the wrong unit of analysis altogether (p. 13). Williams's aim, he tells us, is to illuminate "ways not only of discussing but of seeing many of our central experiences" (pp. 12–13). But if we wish to grasp how someone sees the world—what distinctions he draws, what classifications he accepts—what we need to know is not what words he uses but rather what concepts he possesses.

It is true that this objection may appear a purely verbal one. For it might be replied—and the claim has often been made—that possessing a concept is equivalently a matter of knowing the meaning of a word. This certainly seems to be Williams's own view, for in discussing the term *nature* he equates "the word and the concept," and in speaking of *democracy* he explains how the "concept" is "embodied" in the word (pp. 84, 189).

However, to argue for any such equivalence is undoubtedly a mistake. First of all, it cannot be a necessary condition of my possessing a concept that I need to understand the correct application of a corresponding term. Suppose, for example, that I am studying Milton's thought, and want to know whether Milton considered it important that a poet should display a high degree of originality. The answer seems to be that he felt it to be of the greatest importance. For when he spoke of his own aspirations at the beginning of *Paradise Lost,* what he particularly emphasized was his decision to deal with "things unattempted yet in prose or rhyme." But I could never have arrived at this conclusion by examining Milton's use of the word *originality.* For while the concept is clearly central to his thought, the word did not enter the language until a century or more after his death. Although a history of the word *originality* and its various uses could undoubtedly be written, such a survey would by no means be the same as a history of the concept of originality—a consideration often ignored in practice by historians of ideas.

Moreover, it cannot be a sufficient condition of my possessing a concept that I understand the correct application of a corresponding term. There is still the possibility (explored by Wittgenstein as well as Kant) that I may believe myself to be in possession of a concept when this belief is in fact mistaken. Consider for example the difficulties raised by certain highly general terms such as *being* or *infinity.* A whole community of language users may be capable of applying these terms with perfect consistency. Yet it might be possible to show that there is simply no concept which answers to any of their agreed usages.

What then is the relationship between concepts and words? We can scarcely hope to capture the answer in a single formula, but I think we can at least say this: the surest sign that a group or society has entered into the self-conscious possession of a new concept is that a corresponding vocabulary will be developed, a vocabulary which can then be used to pick out and discuss the concept with consistency. This suggests that, while we certainly need to exercise more caution than Williams does in making inferences from the use of words to the understanding of concepts and back again, there is nevertheless a systematic relationship between words and concepts to be explored. For the possession of a concept will at least *standardly* be signalled by the employment of a corresponding term. As long as we bear in mind that "standardly" means neither necessarily nor sufficiently, I think we may legitimately proceed.

II

If our aim is to illuminate ideological disputes through the study of linguistic disagreements, the first issue we need to clarify—as Williams acknowledges—is obviously this: what exactly are we debating about a word when we find ourselves debating whether or not it ought to be applied as a description of a particular action or state of affairs?

Unfortunately Williams's answer is confusingly vague. "What is really happening in such encounters," he claims, is a "process" whereby "meanings are offered" and are then "confirmed, qualified, changed" (p. 9). All such debates are thus taken to be about "meanings"; about the "available and developing meanings" of the words involved (pp. 13, 19, 20).

This question-begging tendency to speak without further explication about "changes of meaning" is due, I believe, to the fact that Williams at no point tries to isolate and describe the class of terms in which he is chiefly interested—the class of what he calls the "strong" or "persuasive" words, the words which "involve ideas and values" (pp. 12, 15). No consistent account of how certain words come to "involve values" is ever presented. But it seems clear that, if any further progress is to be made in discussing the phenomenon of meaning change in ideological debates, the provision of such an analysis will have to be treated as a crucial preliminary step. As it happens, this is a less Herculean task than might be supposed. For a great deal of attention has lately been paid by theorists of language as well as moral philosophers to isolating and commenting on precisely these terms.[3] Drawing on their accounts, we may say, I think, that three main requirements need to be met if such terms are to be understood and correctly applied.

First, it is necessary to know the nature and range of the criteria in virtue of which the word or expression is standardly employed. Suppose, for example, that I am unaware of the meaning of the appraisive term *courageous,* and ask someone to explain to me how to use the word properly. He will most naturally reply by mentioning various criteria that serve to mark off the word from similar and contrasting adjectives, and so provide it with its distinctive role in our language of social description and appraisal. When listing these criteria, he will surely have to include at least the following: that the word can only be used in the context of voluntary actions; that the actor involved must have faced some danger; that he must have faced it with some consciousness of its nature; and he must have faced it heedfully, with some sense of the probable consequences of the action involved. Summarizing these criteria (in what is only apparently a tautology), we may say that the conditions under which the term *courageous* can be applied are such that the action involved must have been a courageous one.

Next, to apply an appraisive term correctly I also need to know its range of reference. I need, that is, to have a clear sense of the nature of the circumstances in which the word can properly be used to designate particular actions or states of affairs. Now the concept of reference has often been taken to be an aspect or feature of the meaning of a word. But it is perhaps more helpful to treat the understanding of the reference of a word as a consequence of understanding the criteria for applying it correctly. To grasp these criteria is to understand the sense of a word, its role in the language, and thus its correct use. Once I have acquired this understanding, I may expect in consequence to be able to exercise the further and more mysterious skill of relating the word to the world. I may expect, for example, to be able to pick out just those actions which are properly to be called courageous, and to discuss the sort of circumstances in which we might wish to apply that particular description, or might wonder whether we ought to apply it rather than another one. For instance, someone might call it courageous if I faced a painful death with cheerfulness. However, it might be objected that strictly speaking no danger is involved in such circumstances, and thus that we ought not to speak of courage but rather of fortitude. Or again, someone might call it courageous if I stepped up from the circus audience to deputize for the lion tamer. But it might be countered that this is such a heedless action that it ought not to be viewed as courage but rather as sheer recklessness. Both these arguments are about the reference (but not the meaning) of *courageous:* both are concerned with whether a given set of circumstances—what a lawyer would call the facts of the case—are such as to yield the agreed criteria for the application of the given appraisive term.

To apply any word to the world, we need to have a clear grasp of both its sense and its reference. But in the case of appraisive terms a further element of understanding is also required. We need in addition to know what exact range of attitudes the term can standardly be used to express. (To adopt J. L. Austin's jargon: it is necessary to know what type of speech acts the word can be used to perform). For example, no one can be said to have grasped the correct application of the adjective *courageous* if he is unaware that it is standardly used to commend, to express approval, and especially to express (and solicit) admiration for any action it is used to describe. To call an action courageous is at once to describe it and to place it in a specific moral light. Thus I can praise or rejoice at an action by calling it courageous, but I cannot condemn or sneer at it by describing it in this way.

If these are the three main things we need to know in order to isolate the class of appraisive terms and apply them correctly, we can now return to the question raised at the beginning of this section. I asked what we might be debating about a "keyword" if we found ourselves asking whether or not it ought to be applied in a particular case. As we have seen, Williams's answer is that such arguments must be about the senses or meanings of the words involved. As I have sought to show, however, we might be disagreeing about one of at least three different things, not all of which are self-evidently disagreements about meaning: we might be arguing about the criteria for applying the word; or about whether the agreed criteria are present in a given set of circumstances; or about what range of speech acts the word can be used to perform.

III

So far I have tried to isolate the main debates that arise over the application of our appraisive vocabulary to our social world. I now turn to what I take to be the crucial question: in what sense are these linguistic disagreements also disagreements about our social world itself?

I have suggested that one type of argument over appraisive terms centers on the criteria for applying them. Now this is certainly a substantive social debate as well as a linguistic one. For it can equally well be characterized as an argument between two rival social theories and their attendant methods of classifying social reality.

As an illustration of such a dispute, recall the way in which Marcel Duchamp liked to designate certain familiar objects (coat-pegs, lavatory bowls) as works of art, thereby causing them to be framed and hung on the walls of galleries. Some critics have accepted that these are indeed significant works of art, on the grounds that they help us to sharpen and extend our awareness of everyday things. Others have insisted that they are not works of art at all, on the grounds that we cannot simply *call* something a work of art, since works of art have to be deliberately created.

This disagreement arises at the linguistic level. It centers on whether or not a certain criterion (the exercise of skill) should or should not be regarded as a necessary condition for the correct application of a particular appraisive term (*a work of art*). But this is certainly a substantive social dispute as well. For what is at issue is whether or not a certain range of objects ought or ought not to be treated as having a rather elevated status and significance. And it is obvious that a great deal may depend on how this question is answered.

A number of the arguments in *Keywords* are primarily of this character. For example, the essays on "literature" and "science" largely fit this analysis, as does the useful discussion of "the unconscious," where Williams actually points out that "different theories" have generated "confusions between different senses" of the term (p. 272). Moreover, Williams is surely right to claim that in these cases the argument is in fact about the senses or meanings of the words involved. It is true that powerful voices have lately been raised against the contention that, if we introduce a new theory relating to a given subject matter (for example, what constitutes a work of art) this will inevitably give rise to changes in the meanings of the constitutive terms.[4] And there is little doubt that Paul Feyerabend and other post-empiricists have tended to employ this assumption with an altogther excessive enthusiasm. Certainly we cannot readily say that every change of theory brings about a change in the meaning of all the words involved (if only because nouns and adjectives shift in meaning so much more readily than, say, conjunctions). Moreover, it seems unduly anarchistic to claim that the meaning of a word must have changed if we simply change our beliefs about whatever the word is customarily used to denote (although it is admittedly very hard to think of clear cases in which meanings have in fact remained constant in the face of changing beliefs).[5] However, it does seem that if someone is mistaken about the criteria for applying a term, then he cannot be said to know its current meaning. And since I have argued that the question of whether Duchamp's coat-peg is a work of art is (at one level) an argument about the criteria for applying the term *a work of art,* I agree with Williams that in this type of argument about "keywords" the disagreement really is about the meaning of the word concerned.

What Williams misses, however, in his account of these disputes is their almost paralyzingly radical character. He remains content to suppose that in all discussions about "meaning" we can "pick out a word of a problematical kind" and consider only "its own internal structure" (p. 20). This fails to recognize the implications of the fact that a term such as *art* gains its meaning from the place it occupies within an entire conceptual scheme. To change the criteria for applying it will thus be to change a vast deal else besides. Traditionally, the concept of art has been connected with an ideal of workmanship, has been opposed to the "merely useful," has been employed as an antonym for *nature,* and so on. If we now endorse the suggestion that an *objet trouvé* or a manufactured article can count as a work of art, we at once sever all these and many other conceptual links. So an argument over the application of the term *art* is potentially nothing less than an argument over two rival (though not of course incommensurable)[6] ways of approaching and dividing up a large tract of our cultural experience. Williams appears in short to have overlooked the strongly holistic implications of the fact that, when a word changes its meaning, it also changes its relationship to an entire vocabulary.[7] What this tells us about such changes is that we must be prepared to focus not on the "internal structure" of particular words, but rather on their role in upholding complete social philosophies.

IV

Even if we agree about the criteria for applying an appraisive term, I have suggested that a second type of dispute can arise over its use: a dispute about whether a given set of circumstances can be claimed to yield the criteria in virtue of which the term is normally employed. Again, such a disagreement will certainly be a substantive social one, not merely linguistic in character. For what is being contended in effect is that a refusal to apply the term in a certain situation may constitute an act of social insensitivity or a failure of social awareness.

As an illustration of this second type of argument, consider the claim — being advanced with increasing frequency — that wives in ordinary middle-class families can properly be described as suffering exploitation, as being an exploited class. The social argument underlying this linguistic move might be characterized as follows: that it ought to be evident to all persons of goodwill that the circumstances of modern family life are such that this strongly condemnatory term does indeed (if you think about it) fit the facts of the case; and conversely, that if we fail to acknowledge that the application of the term *exploitation*—in virtue of its agreed criteria—is indeed appropriate in the circumstances, then we are willfully refusing to perceive the institution of the family in its true and baleful light.

Many of the arguments Williams cites appear to be of this general type. But he crucially misdescribes what is at stake when he lumps these cases together with those in which "new meanings" are "offered" and are then "qualified" or "confirmed" (see p. 13 and cf. pp. 99, 109, 143, etc.). For it is of course essential to the success of the social argument underlying this form of linguistic debate that the appraisive word in question should be offered in virtue of its *accepted* meaning as an apt way of describing a situation which has not hitherto been described in such terms.

It is true that, as a consequence of such arguments, new meanings are often generated. But the process by which this happens is the opposite of the one Williams describes. When an argument of this nature is successful, the outcome will not be the emergence of new meanings, save that the application of a term with a new range of reference may eventually put pressure on the criteria for applying it. The basic outcome will rather be the acceptance of new social perceptions, as a result of which the relevant appraisive terms will then be applied with unchanged meanings to new circumstances. It is only when such arguments fail that new meanings tend to arise.

This contention can readily be supported if we consider some of the ways in which a failure in this type of argument is capable of leaving its traces on the language. It may be that, when a social group seeks to insist that the ordinary criteria for applying a particular appraisive term are present in a wider range of circumstances than has commonly been allowed, the other users of the language—not sharing the underlying social perceptions of the first group—may simply assume in good faith that a "new meaning" has indeed been "offered," and may then accept it. The history of our culture (and in consequence our language) has been punctuated with many such misunderstandings. One fruitful source has been the continuing efforts of the proponents of commercial society to legitimate their undertakings by reference to the most highly approved moral and spiritual values. Consider, for example, the special use of the term *religious* that first emerged in the later sixteenth century as a way of commending punctual, strict, and conscientious forms of behavior.[8] The aim was clearly to suggest that the ordinary criteria for applying the strongly commendatory term *religious* could be found in such actions, and thus that the actions themselves should be seen essentially as acts of piety and not merely as instances of administrative competence. The failure of this move was quickly reflected in the emergence of a new meaning for the term *religious* in the course of the seventeenth century—the meaning we still invoke when we say things like "I attend the meetings of my faculty religiously." It seems clear that the need for this new lexical entry originally arose out of the incapacity of most language users to see that the ordinary criteria for *religious* (including the notion of piety) were in fact present in all the circumstances in which the term was by then beginning to be used.

There are many recent instances of the same phenomenon, some of which are cited in *Keywords*. For example, many industrial firms like to claim—with reference to their own business strategies—that they have a certain *philosophy;* and firms regularly promise to send their *literature* (meaning only their advertising brochures) to prospective customers. Again a crude attempt is clearly being made to link the activities of commercial society with a range of "higher" values. And again the failure of such efforts often gives rise to genuine polysemy. Hearing that a firm has a certain philosophy, most language users have assumed that a new meaning must be involved, and have gone on to use the term accordingly; they have not in general come to feel that corporations can indeed be said to have philosophies in the traditional sense of the term.

The language also supplies us with evidence of such ideological failures in a second and more decisive way. After a period of confusion about the criteria for applying a disputed term, the final outcome may not be polysemy, but rather a reversion to the employment of the original criteria, together with a corresponding obsolescence of the newer usages. This can be observed, for example, in the history of the word *patriot*. During the eighteenth century, the enemies of the ruling oligarchy in England sought to legitimate their attacks on the government by insisting that they were motivated entirely by their reverence for the constitution, and thus that their actions deserved to be commended as patriotic rather than condemned as factious. This at first bred such extreme uncertainty that the word *patriot* eventually came to *mean* (according to one of Dr. Johnson's definitions) "a factious disturber of the government." With the gradual acceptance of party politics, however, this condemnatory usage gradually atrophied, and the word reverted to its original meaning and its standard application as a term of praise.[9]

Finally, the same form of argument can also have a more equivocal outcome, one which the language will again reveal. It may be that, after a similar period of semantic confusion, the original rather than the newer usage becomes obsolete. At first sight this may seem to indicate a success in the underlying campaign to change people's social perceptions. For this certainly makes it harder to invoke the primitive meaning of the word in order to insist that its newer applications may be nothing more than a deformation of its basic sense. But in fact such changes again tend to be indexes of ideological failure. For the standardization of a new set of criteria will inevitably carry with it an alteration of the term's appraisive force. Sometimes the power of the word to evaluate what it is used to describe may be retained in a different (and usually weaker) form, as in the well-known case of the word *naughty*. But often the process of acquiring a new meaning goes with a total loss of appraisive force. A good example is provided by the history of the word *commodity*. Before the advent of commercial society, to speak of something as a commodity was to praise it, and in particular to affirm that it answered to one's desires, and could thus be seen as beneficial, convenient, a source of advantage. Later an attempt was made to suggest that an article produced for sale ought to be seen as a source of benefit or advantage to its purchaser, and ought in consequence to be described and commended as a commodity. For a time the outcome of this further effort by the earliest English capitalists to legitimate their activities was that *commodity* became a polysemic word. But eventually the original applications withered away, leaving us with nothing more than the current and purely descriptive meaning of *commodity* as an object of trade. Although the capitalists inherited the earth, and with it much of the English language, they were unable in this case to persuade their fellow language users to endorse their attempted eulogy of their own commercial practices.

V

Even if we agree about the criteria for applying an appraisive term, and also agree that a given set of circumstances can properly be said to answer to those criteria, I have suggested that still a third type of dispute can arise: a dispute about the direction of the term's evaluative force—a dispute, that is, about the nature and range of the speech acts it can be used to perform. Once again this can certainly be characterized as a substantive social dispute and not merely a linguistic one. For in this case what is at issue is the possibility that a group of language users may be open to the charge of having a mistaken or an undesirable social attitude.

We can distinguish two main routes by which an argument of this kind will be likely to issue in a contentious use of evaluative language. First, we may dissent from an orthodox social attitude by employing an appraisive term in such a way that its standard speech-act potential is weakened or even abolished. This can in turn be achieved in one of two ways. If we do not share the accepted evaluation of some particular action or state of affairs, we may indicate our dissent simply by dropping the corresponding term from our vocabulary altogether. There are many instances of this move in current social debate. Among terms which have hitherto been used to commend what they describe, this seems to be happening in the case of *gentleman.* Among terms previously used to express an element of condescension or patronage, this already seems to have happened with *native,* at least when used as a noun.

The other method of registering the same form of protest is more challenging. While continuing to employ an accepted term of social description and appraisal, we may make it contextually clear that we are using it merely to describe, and not at the same time to evaluate what is thereby described. Again, there are many contemporary instances of this move. Among terms previously used to evince condescension or even hatred, the classic example is provided by the word *black* (used as the description of a person), whether employed as an adjective or a noun. Among terms previously used to commend, we may note the new and carefully neutral applications of such words as *culture* and *civilization*. As Williams himself observes (pp. 50, 80), these latter usages appear to have originated within the discipline of social anthropology, but have now come to be very generally accepted by those who wish to disavow any suggestion that one particular civilization may be more deserving of study than another.

The other main way in which we can use our evaluative language to signal our social attitudes is more dramatic in its implications. It is possible to indicate, simply through our use of appraisive terms, not that we dissent from the idea of evaluating what they describe, but rather that we disagree with the direction of the evaluation and wish to see it reversed.

Again there are obviously two possibilities here. We may use a term normally employed to condemn what it describes in such a way as to make it contextually clear that, in our view, the relevant action or state of affairs ought in fact to be commended. As Williams points out, one interesting example of this reversal can be seen in the history of the word *myth*. In a more confidently rationalist age, to describe an explanation as mythological was to dismiss it. But in recent discussions the term has often been used to extol the mythological "version of reality" as "truer" and "deeper" than more mundane accounts (pp. 176–178). Conversely, we may dislike a form of behavior now regarded as praiseworthy, and indicate our disapproval by making it contextually clear that, although the term we are using is standardly employed to commend, we are employing it to condemn what is being described. Once again, there are many instances of this kind of struggle in current ideological debates. One only has to think of those politicians who are regularly praised by one group of commentators as *liberal* while others employ the same term in order to denounce them.

Williams surveys a large number of disagreements that fall within this third general category, and in many cases his comments on them are extremely interesting and shrewd. But his discussion suffers throughout from a failure to distinguish this type of argument from the first type we considered, in which the primary point at issue was the proper sense or meaning of the terms involved. Indeed Williams not only fails but refuses to distinguish between these two types of argument. For example, he insists that the change involved in the move from condemning myths to commending them must be construed as a change in the "sense" of the word *myth* (p. 177).

It would be perfectly possible, however, for both the sense and the reference of *myth* to remain stable in the face of the sort of changes in the use of the word that Williams is concerned to point out. It may be that all (and only) those theories and explanations which used to be called mythological are still called mythological, and that the *only* change involved in the use of the term derives from the shift from condemning myths to commending them. It is true that such a variation of speech-act potential will be very likely in due course to affect the sense (and in consequence the reference) of the word. But it is a mistake to suppose that this type of argument is primarily (or even necessarily) concerned with sense. What is changing—at least initially—is nothing to do with sense; what is changing is simply a social or intellectual attitude on the part of those who use the language.[10]

VI

I have now tried to furnish at least a preliminary response to the very large question I raised at the outset. I asked what kinds of knowledge and awareness we can hope to acquire about our social world through studying the vocabulary we use to describe and appraise it. I have answered that there are three main types of insight we can hope to gain: insights into changing social beliefs and theories; into changing social perceptions and awareness; and into changing social values and attitudes. I have thus attempted to supply at least a sketch of what seems to me most seriously lacking in Williams's book: an account of the sort of methodology we need to develop in order to use the evidence of our social vocabulary as a clue to the improved understanding of our social world.[11]

This in turn suggests a further and even more vertiginous question: are we now in a position to say anything about the nature of the role played by our appraisive vocabulary in the process (and hence in the explanation) of social change?

Williams clearly thinks that we are, and conveys this sense by alluding repeatedly to the image of language as a mirror of social reality. The process of social change is treated as the primary cause of developments in our vocabulary; conversely, such developments are treated as reflections of the process of social change.

Describing the emergence of capitalism as "a distinct economic system," for example, Williams remarks that this gave rise to "interesting consequent uses of language" (p. 43). And in commenting more specifically on "the economic changes of the Industrial Revolution," he notes that these produced a "greatly sharpened" and extended "vocabulary of class" (p. 53).

There is no doubt that this image serves to remind us of an important point. Where we encounter a wide measure of agreement about the application of key social terms, we must be dealing with a strikingly homogeneous social and moral world; where there is no such agreement, we can expect chaos. But it is arguable that the metaphor is also misleading in one crucial respect. It encourages us to assume that we are dealing with two distinct and contingently related domains: that of the social world itself, and that of the language we then apply in an attempt to delineate its character. This certainly seems to be the assumption underlying Williams's account. He sees a complete disjunction between "the words" he discusses and "the real issues" in the social world. And he sometimes speaks as if the gap between the two is one we can barely hope to bridge. "However complete the analysis" we offer at the linguistic level, he maintains, we cannot expect that "the real issues" will be fundamentally affected (pp. 13–14).

To speak in this way is to forget something that Williams emphasizes at other points in *Keywords* with striking force: the fact that one of the most important uses of evaluative language is that of legitimating as well as describing the activities and attitudes of dominant social groups. The significance of this consideration can be brought out if we revert for a moment to an example already cited—the entrepreneurs of Elizabethan England who were anxious to persuade their contemporaries that, although their commercial enterprises might appear to be morally doubtful, they were in fact deserving of respect. One device they adopted was to argue, as we have seen, that their characteristically punctual and conscientious behavior could properly be seen as religious in character, and hence as motivated by pious and not merely self-seeking principles. Their underlying purpose was of course to legitimate their apparently untoward behavior by insisting on the propriety of describing it in these highly commendatory terms.

Now it may seem—and this is evidently Williams's view—that this sort of example precisely fits the metaphor of language as a mirror of a more basic reality. The merchant is perceived to be engaged in a more or less dubious way of life which he has a strong motive for wishing to exhibit as legitimate. So he professes just those principles, and offers just those descriptions, that serve to present what he is doing in a morally acceptable light. And since the selection of the principles and their accompanying descriptions both relate to his behavior in an obviously *ex post facto* way, it hardly seems that an explanation of his behavior need depend in the least on studying the moral language he may elect to use. For his choice of vocabulary appears to be entirely determined by his prior social needs.

As I have tried to hint, however, this is to misunderstand the role of the normative vocabulary which any society employs for the description and appraisal of its social life. The merchant cannot hope to describe *any* action he may choose to perform as being "religious" in character, but only those which can be claimed with some show of plausibility to meet such agreed criteria as there may be for the application of the term. It follows that if he is anxious to have his conduct appraised as that of a genuinely religious man, he will find himself restricted to the performance of only a certain range of actions. Thus the problem facing the merchant who wishes to be seen as pious rather than self-interested cannot simply be the instrumental one of tailoring his account of his principles in order to fit his projects; it must in part be the problem of tailoring his projects in order to make them answer to the preexisting language of moral principles.[12]

The story of the merchant suggests two morals. One is that it must be a mistake to portray the relationship between our social vocabulary and our social world as a purely external and contingent one. It is true that our social practices help to bestow meaning on our social vocabulary. But it is equally true that our social vocabulary helps to constitute the character of those practices. To see the role of our evaluative language in helping to legitimate social action is to see the point at which our social vocabulary and our social fabric mutually prop each other up. As Charles Taylor has remarked, "we can speak of mutual dependence if we like, but what this really points up is the artificiality of the distinction between social reality and the language of description of that social reality."[13]

The other moral is that, if there are indeed causal linkages between social language and social reality, to speak of the one as mirroring the other may be to envisage the causal arrows pointing in the wrong direction. As the example of the Elizabethan merchant suggests, to recover the nature of the normative vocabulary available to an agent for the description and appraisal of his conduct is at the same time to indicate one of the constraints on his conduct itself. This in turn suggests that, if we wish to explain why our merchant chose to concentrate on certain courses of action while avoiding others, we are bound to make some reference to the prevailing moral language of the society in which he was acting. For this, it now appears, must have figured not as an epiphenomenon of his projects, but as one of the determinants of his actions.

To conclude with these morals is to issue a warning to literary critics and social historians alike to avoid a prevalent but impoverishing form of reductionism. But it is also to suggest that the special techniques of the literary critic have—or ought to have—a central place in the business of cultural criticism which a book like Williams's *Keywords* has scarcely begun to recognize.

Notes

1. This is a slightly altered version of an article which originally appeared (under the title "The Idea of a Cultural Lexicon") in *Essays in Criticism,* July 1979. I am very grateful to John Dunn, Susan James, Jonathan Lear and Richard Rorty for many valuable comments on earlier drafts.

2. All page references in the text are to the Fontana (paperback) edition of Raymond Williams, *Keywords: A Vocabulary of Culture and Society* (London, 1976).

3. Among moral philosophers I am most indebted to Philippa Foot, "Moral Arguments," *Mind* 67 (1958): 502–513. Among theorists of language, my approach owes most to the writings of J. L. Austin and the later Wittgenstein, and to the analysis of Gottlob Frege's views presented in Michael Dummett, *Frege: Philosophy of Language* (London, 1973), esp. pp. 81–109.

4. For an attack on this line of thought, see Hilary Putnam, "How Not to Talk about Meaning," in *Mind, Language and Reality,* Philosophical Papers, vol. 2 (Cambridge, 1975), pp. 117–131.

5. Even Putnam's examples are unconvincing. In "How Not to Talk about Meaning," he takes the case of *gold* (pp. 127–128), and argues that the meaning of the word would not be affected if we found gold rusting, and were thus obliged to change our beliefs about the substance. This seems dogmatic. Would we really go on saying things like "as good as gold"? And if not, would we not have to concede that the meaning of *gold* had changed?

6. Otherwise it is hard to see how the disputants could be *arguing*.

7. See Michael Dummett, "The Justification of Deduction," *The Proceedings of the British Academy* 59 (1973): 201–232.

8. Here I offer a different—a corrected—account of an example I originally mentioned in my article "Some Problems in the Analysis of Political Thought and Action," *Political Theory* 2 (1974): 277–303, at pp. 298–299.

9. For a full analysis of this example, see my article "The Principles and Practice of Opposition: The Case of Bolingbroke versus Walpole," in Neil McKendrick, ed., *Historical Perspectives* (London, 1974), pp. 93–128.

10. In this paragraph I draw on John R. Searle, "Meaning and Speech Acts," *The Philosophical Review* 71 (1962): 423–432. However, Searle does not I think

succeed in showing that meaning and speech acts are wholly separate. All he shows is that sense and reference are capable of remaining stable while speech-act potential is undergoing a change. But we might still want to insist that speech-act potential is a part of meaning, even if it is separate from both sense and reference.

11. I have also (though incidentally) tried to supply what I take to be the sort of typology one would need to construct in order to investigate the class of so-called essentially contested concepts in a satisfactory way. In the growing literature on this topic the discussion has tended to center on the analysis of the concepts in themselves. This seems insensitive to the fact that concepts are the possessions of particular groups. In order to understand a dispute about a contested concept we need to understand why certain groups may wish to employ it in certain ways while others do not. Strictly speaking, there is no analysis to be given of contests about concepts in themselves, but only of their uses in argument.

12. In this and the previous paragraph I am drawing heavily on the preface to my book *The Foundations of Modern Political Thought,* 2 vols. (Cambridge, 1978).

13. Charles Taylor, "Interpretation and the Sciences of Man," *The Review of Metaphysics* 24 (1971): 3–51, at p. 24.

ROBERT M. ADAMS

Authenticity-Codes and Sincerity-Formulas

EROSION-PROBLEMS always have a long history, at which it's probably worth glancing, even though knowing the history may lead one to despair of ever solving the problem. The problem of dwindling authentication for a modern wordsman is acute because it is ancient. In primitive society, when the writer appeared before his contemporaries as a rarely talented member of a specially appointed caste, his words were vouched for, by the mere fact of his using written letters, as carrying special authority. Egyptian priests were not only spokesmen for Thoth, but atavars of Thoth himself, Thothlets, so to speak: a few words of their copying, however carelessly done, however meaningless the phrases copied, could serve as an ignorant man's passport to eternity. Hebrew prophets were understood to enjoy privileged access to the thoughts of the deity, which they formulated and transmitted—though how they established that privilege is not clear, and sheer numbers must on occasion have provoked scepticism. Ahab, king of Israel, once assembled 401 prophets to give him military advice (1 Kings 22)—they spoke with a single voice, and were absolutely wrong, but as the king died following their orders, he had no effective comeback. Prophecy was originally a collective function, and it may be that admission to the society or guild of prophets conferred authority; in a larger context, the prophets exercised special influence within a community suffering from oppression yet convinced to begin with that they enjoyed the special favor and protection of Yahweh. Already in Israel we find them competing with one another—a process which the medieval church in its wisdom early recognized as destructive of all clerkly authority. By establishing a canon of scriptures, a body of written dogma within which future interpreters and prophets must confine their thinking, the church consolidated and formalized the power of the written word, not only over the laity, but over the society of clerks as well. Medieval clerks owned their books in a special monopolistic sense (only the clerk could read, only the clerk could write); but they were owned by them too. They spoke with unquestioned authority because they spoke the language of one common faith rooted in a single revelation explained by a united army of saints, doctors, martyrs, and confessors—and sustained, in cases of incipient schism, by a strong secular arm. Whether one views such an arrangement with horror or nostalgia, it certainly imposed on the writer within the bounds of orthodoxy few burdens involving the establishment of his authenticity.

Obviously in a democratic, or at least pluralist, society, where nearly everybody can read, write, and hold an opinion (after a fashion), the writer cannot take his acceptance for granted, even by proposing himself as the spokesman of a commonly recognized source of authenticity. In various forms, the problem is obviously a very old one; every persuader who has had to deal with critical or independently recalcitrant minds has had to face it. When he has no *a priori* authority to command belief, what accent shall he use, what device of language or strategy of thought to convince his audience that of all the competing voices declaring themselves voices of truth, his is the authentic one?

Phrasing the problem this way, one sees at once that self-verification is an absurdity; the fact that I need to be vouched for instantly disqualifies me as one who can vouch. If there were any verbal device for establishing authenticity, it would promptly be turned to contradictory ends, and so self-destruct. As things are, a man who raises the question of his honesty, like a girl who makes noises about her "virtue," can only be suspected of talking up the product in order to dispose of it at a better price. The fact that a dealer in secondhand cars has to label himself "Honest John" is *prima facie* evidence that nobody else will give him that character. As a matter of fact, giving oneself a character of any sort implies presumption and duplicity: the basic thought is, "It's not for you to say." Like Saint Augustine, Rousseau is not exempt from the suspicion of assigning himself a much worse character than he deserved, so that he could have something really juicy to confess, and at the same time give proof of his total integrity in confessing it. The minute we start talking about ourselves and assessing our veracity, we are entangled in confusion and self-contradiction. A man who calls himself a liar is either telling the truth, in which case his statement is a lie, or else lying, in which case his statement is so far true. The wheeze is ancient in itself (it was known to the pre-Socratics as the paradox of the Cretan liar); it's also curious because, while in form it's an exposure of inevitable duplicity, in content it's an act of duplicity itself. Even in asserting, as I do, that there's no way for a man to characterize himself honestly, I am advertising my superiority to self-advertisers, and following the timeworn formula of the confidence man, who demonstrates his superiority to the maker of glib promises by refusing to make any promises at all. Not only so, he invites your suspicion as the ultimate proof of his good faith. Would he arouse all your suspicions, would he urge you to test his integrity in every possible way, if he were out to trick you? He implies that he wouldn't, we know of course that he would. The denunciation of other impostors, the demonstration that there are no cards up his sleeve, are all part of his flash, his indirection—they direct your attention away from the six aces concealed in his shirt-front. And even here as I write, explaining the tricks of confidence men, I advertise my own superior integrity—which is exactly what any con man would like you to believe in, as he goes about his next trick.

How to eliminate, or seem to have eliminated, the manipulative element in language and the many thickets of mental reservation and duplicity that lie behind it? A mere listing of the various strategies employed over the past century or so might easily fill a volume: one of their common characters, and a "deep" one, is the abdication of authorial responsibility for that arrangement (of episodes, motives, appeals for sympathy) by which a reader's responses are manipulated. The old objection to rhetoric, that it advances on us like a bold thief and pushes its hand shamelessly into our pants pocket, is here expanded to all writing. Multivalent or polysemous language, very frequent nowadays, is capable of several or many interpretations, choice among which is the responsibility of the reader. The very tone of a work can be left so indefinite that the reader's most intense response is anguish at conflicting impulses to guffaw and to moan: as we all know, tragicomedy is very much a mode of the day. Insoluble enigmas may be scattered through a work, or the insolubility of the work as a problem of interpretation may itself become the work's major theme. The pattern of entities as distinct as *Rashomon, The Ring and the Book,* and the *Alexandria Quartet* involves relating the same story several times over from several different, and mutually destructive, points of view, one potential conclusion being that nobody possesses more than a fraction of the truth, and that the next recension of the story may cast doubt even on that. The process, frequent now in prose as well as poetry, of scattering enigmatic symbols about and inviting the reader to give them what weight he will, to see what interconnections among them he can establish, implies a kind of authorial abdication. Beckett often pretends that the "voices" attached to his characters are outside his control, he is as bewildered by the story they compound as the reader is, and in fact the story is mere babble, talk for the sake of the talker. If literature is not to be any more a "teaching of lessons" or a "criticism of life" (those assumptions involving intolerable presumptions), one consequence will be the reduction of character to a set of mannerisms, tropisms, or outlines, and the substantial elimination of backgrounds in the shape of social complexes. Representation itself is questionable as involving either aesthetic fraud, an insidious anthropomorphizing of the world, or covert ideologies; since Ibsen, it has not been infrequent to find an attack on the falsity of aesthetic existence at the heart of an aesthetic performance. We note, perhaps with a shade of irony, that authenticity used to be vouched for by associating oneself with an authoritative caste claiming a special position; now it's vouched for by dissociating oneself from elites, conventions, positive assertions of all sorts. The closer one approaches to a nihilistic postion, the less one can be criticized as insincere, self-seeking, or manipulative. It goes without saying that the literary devices described have other functions as well; but an important element in their use is to authenticate the voice of the writer, to indicate that he is other than a contriver, making use of language to seduce his victim into unexamined and unjustified complacencies.

The anxieties perhaps seem excessive: yet it's really true that a major function of *belles lettres* over the earlier centuries was to flatter and comfort a reading, that is, a fantasy-prone and self-important, public. It is the discovery of the late nineteenth century that the reader need not be accepted as a judicious, fair-minded fellow, comfortably sustained in his easy chair by the operation of an ideal society, and demanding nothing more of the book in his hands than a discreet mixture of instruction and entertainment. The great writers of the last hundred years have been, *exceptis exceptandis,* great disquieters, who found one of their major functions in representing to humanity the value of an Ideal which has as its ultimate reality a deadly and destructive side. "Anywhere," Baudelaire wants to go, on his only true voyage, "anywhere, anywhere out of this world!" Beyond the *Idéal,* for Mallarmé, is the higher achievement of *Néant;* after a lifetime of running after his self, Peer Gynt learns from the Button Moulder that "to be oneself is to slay oneself." For Beckett even a definitive ending is often too much: "Well, shall we go?" says Vladimir; "Yes, let's go," replies Estragon. They do not move. As they represent the weakness and incapacity of man, these figures also represent a kind of passive mental heroism; they are secular, sceptical, and often unbelieving saints. In their presence common sense and the compromises linked with common sense do not have to be renounced or denounced; they are simply out of the heroic character's range, so that in their presence he registers a total blank, like Beckett's personage Molloy when faced by a policeman asking what his name is and what he is doing. Often enough, the exemplary character is not far from a sacred idiot, his mind fixed on a something or a vacancy so remote from the observances of this world that the gap speaks for itself. So with the always frustrated, never defeated exegetes serving as Kafka's protagonists, who lead us inexorably toward, hardly ever to, the blank conclusion that interpretation is inherently impossible. All the puzzles posed in those orphic leaves lead merely to other puzzles, and only in an unpublished fragment of parable whose application is completely indefinite does Kafka advise us to "Give it up!"

That imaginative literature can thrive on such a limited and negative diet is a new discovery of our age, made perhaps in reaction to the thick and thingly literary atmosphere of the nineteenth century, perhaps in response to the prevalence of journalism and advertising, perhaps out of a genuine sense of literary exhaustion, of language being "used up" as a system of references. Whatever the cause or combination of causes, the new labyrinth-makers burrow, not into themselves, but into their language, establishing by deliberate contradictions and absurdities its independence of anything but its own inner arrangements and inner tensions. One of the most fruitful of these tensions is that between the reader's desire to "understand" and the author's desire to tantalize. And since this forces the reader to act as at least partial creator, it absolves the author in some measure from the guilt of creation, the responsibility of imposing on anyone an ideological seduction.

In the larger world such fineline negative cobwebs are not much spun, and would not be well understood if they were, but some of the same principles apply, and they point in the same general direction, toward the downgrading of discursive or persuasive language. The fact itself doesn't need a great deal of documentation; the prevalence of social groups based on sex or sexual preference, on race or skin color or a particular sort of surname, on youth or age, indicates a kind of general usurpation of raw biological fact on areas that used to be described as "of the mind," that is, available to rational discourse by persons of different genetic stock and differing social outlook. It's not unlikely that the recurrent use of an idiotic phrase like *y'know* would have, if spelled out, some such meaning as the following:

> I'm not one of those phoney verbal types who can go blah blah blah all day trying to tell you what they think and just confusing you because you're not a verbal person either. You and I know what things are like, and trying to put it in words would just confuse both of us because either we understand each other or we don't, and if we don't it's no use trying to explain, so—y'know, or don'cha know? And that's it.

The coincidence of vulgar with erudite deconstructionism is a circumstance worth remarking; whether the devaluation of language that's implied in both derives from too lofty demands or too little readiness to credit language with those common advantages it has always enjoyed and still enjoys (such as context, social convention, a kind of complicity in the attunement of reader to writer), the result in both cases is much the same. It's an old story that language communicates most completely between those who already know and agree with what it purports to say—but increasingly, these days, that agreement is determined by, and limited to, biological or other nonverbal functions. Whatever a male says or pretends to say, it is assumed that he cannot effectively represent females in political gatherings, and vice versa. People whose skins are black or yellow, or who have Spanish surnames, are supposed to be entitled to lawyers or doctors whose skins are black or yellow or who have Spanish surnames; and this link is presumed so strong that many of those who agitate for reform are clearly indifferent whether they get good doctors or competent lawyers, as long as they are doctors, lawyers, or for that matter airline pilots and brain surgeons, who are of the right color, the right sex, or have the right surnames. That which is merely learned, which consists simply of words and technical skills and mental discipline, is widely assumed to be less important than that which is biologically determined. It's a point of view that leads, it seems to me, directly toward race warfare, of which the advancing signs are everywhere too prevalent to be enumerated. One of the more striking apparent in my home state of New Mexico is for legal trials to consist almost entirely of jury selection. A jury of "Spanish" citizens, it is understood, will not convict a "Spanish" defendant; an "Anglo" judge or jury will not convict one of their own sort. And both will be ruthless—so it is expected and understood—with "the others." A neat legal point was recently made when an Anglo and a Spanish crook went on trial for conspiracy to cheat the state government. A jury, whose composition may be guessed, found the "Spanish" defendant innocent, and the "Anglo" guilty—making him one of the few solo conspirators on record. The failure of judicial authentication here, or rather its reduction to a simple matter of group loyalty (not "race," for there is no Spanish race, not national, for both defendants were ostensibly alike and equal Americans) suggests obviously far-reaching consequences for the codes formulated in language and dependent on belief in language.

The self-analysis and self-consciousness which are so much a part of the modern style also lead directly to an acute sense of verbal inadequacy—words being, after all, common counters and so inadequate to express the full inwardness of individual experience. By the same token, and in the same context, language is obviously inadequate to convey the mental states created by mind-altering drugs. We have a peculiar half-awareness of the forces of subliminal persuasion which assail us daily—we know about them, but don't very often know them directly—as a result of which we tend to suspect them behind what is often felt as the facade of language. Knowing ourselves to be undermined from within by the powerful, conflicting, and only partly accessible currents of the subconscious (as Freud and the Freudianizing novelists have taught us to see ourselves), we are automatically suspicious of language which seems to go against our intuitions or manipulate our sympathies by too overt an inwardness. From these perils and suspicions, one common and easy refuge, akin to that noted above, is declining expression entirely and seeking refuge in inarticulateness.

Modern athletes, heroes, and lovers are none of them expected to use much language, and some evidently cultivate taciturnity on purpose as an accepted signal of manly sincerity. Hemingway used to present abrupt and laconic protagonists like Jake Barnes and

Lady Brett, whose reluctance to verbalize was carefully contrasted with the explanatory loquacity of a jerk like Robert Cohn. Philip Marlowe, modelled after these severe Stoics, makes a point of saying nothing a great deal of the time, and is especially good at turning off insults by saying nothing whatever in response. The implication is that the words don't touch him, the topic is a bore, the speaker so obviously expressing simply his own hangups, that a big, secure man doesn't have to notice him. And, since Wordsworth's time at least, there has been a function for the completely silent character who by saying nothing whatever stands outside of time as the passive butt of nature, just existing like a stone in a stream. Such characters are found in Conrad *(The Nigger of the Narcissus)* and in Faulkner *(Soldier's Pay, The Sound and the Fury);* by acting as a lump in the "plot" by refusing to participate in the "action," the character sets himself outside contrivance, against entertainment and ingratiation. There is probably no direct connection here, but the very strong Buddhist streak in much modern writing of the avant-garde persuasion suggests an effort to get off the inauthentic wheel of life, and to achieve perfection through total renunciation. But obviously there's likely to be an element of self-advertisement here as well; lecturers on Buddhism, like voluble exponents of total Trappist self-denial, are bound to carry less conviction the more they seem to care what the rest of us think. If the phrases mean anything like what they say, getting off the wheel of life and unchaining oneself from the world of desire have to mean something different from a career of preaching, public relations, and ideological persuasion. But the high value of silence as a hallmark of authenticity is evident from the fact that lack of it can cast doubt even on those who preach its value most loudly.

An alternative to saying nothing at all (which always carries with it the serious risk that nobody will notice or care that you're saying nothing at all) is to use many words but use them to fulfill a purely formal and nonsignificant pattern. An early instance of this is the catechism chapter, "Ithaca," in Joyce's *Ulysses,* where every question has its answer, and every answer is severely factual, paralyzingly detailed, and wholly insignificant. Lists of conspicuous irrelevance, or attempts to exhaust the ways of arranging a fixed number of counters establish the authenticity of the language by conspicuously declining its relevance to anything but itself. Beckett describes the maneuvers of Watt in his bedchamber:

> Here he moved, to and fro, from the door to the window, from the window to the door; from the window to the door, from the door

> to the window; from the fire to the bed, from the bed to the fire; from the bed to the fire, from the fire to the bed; from the door to the fire, from the fire to the door—

and so on through a full page of permutations mechanically varied. This is a way of establishing the absolute authenticity and absolute meaninglessness of the mind making verbal patterns in the void—just as on another occasion it exercises itself by arranging sixteen sucking-stones in an endlessly elaborate, purely arbitrary pattern. An agnostic anchorite, intensely doubtful even of his own doubts, Beckett defines himself repeatedly as a backward schoolboy struggling mechanically to fulfill an assigned but incomprehensible task, or a deliberate retrograde performing one idiot operation to numb the pain of the other, bigger one going on outside him.

To write about the act of writing itself is to minimize one's claims by another, closely analogous technique; it is to reduce one's presence in every respect except the absolutely inescapable one. Of course it smacks of buffoonery, which as double-mindedness offends in one way against authenticity, but in another way preempts it by playing into the hands of its own criticism—who can complain of deception when the deception was advertised in advance by the deceiver? John Barth does a good many of these illusionistic calisthenic exercises, compounding the sense of vacancy by proclaiming that he's unspeakably weary of writing about the act of writing. His compulsion to do it remains either tacit or unanalyzed, but coincides conveniently with a current critical tenet that the writer does not write his language but is himself written by it. There's an element of truth behind this paradox; but the sense in which we are passive agents of our language is very indefinite (if a prison, it is one with thousands of rooms, windows, courtyards, gardens), and most people seem better able than John Barth to resist the impulse to write books when they have nothing to say except (in various ways) that they have nothing to say. I think we are most aware of our language controlling our thoughts when we encounter someone versed in a different language which controls his thoughts into different patterns. Very likely if we were all members of one cultural unit, we should all be passive agents of the common tongue, and as unconscious of its influence on us as we now commonly are unaware of the air we breathe and the universal pressure of gravity. This isn't to say that we shouldn't, under those unlikely circumstances, be just as subject to influence from our language as now, or more so. But as there is no dialect that does not have its buried restrictions and directives, there is hardly any way to transcend the limitations of one speech, even by using several simultaneously or protesting the inadequacy of all—since the protest, if understood, carries its own refutation, and if not, well. . . .

Overcoming obstacles, real or apparent, is a way of seeming to guarantee authenticity, and the more persuasive as it seems to involve not only language, which is always subject to discount, but personal behavior which is subject to manipulative penalties. One notes that even writers like Joyce and Eliot, who in their theoretical writings deplore the confessional mode, are drawn into it. It isn't simply a negative matter, as Baudelaire complained in his poem "Au Lecteur," of the writer feeding his garbage-laden soul to the yawning, insatiable reader. By confessing to transgressions which his readers have themselves committed in thought or deed, the confessor establishes bonds of sympathy with them; if, in addition, he invites or challenges punishment in their stead, he offers them the agreeable experience of vicarious atonement. The mechanisms are simple, easily divisible, and of infinite application. After-dinner speakers tell jokes and vulgar stories to establish rapport, in the form of a shared, faintly illicit experience, with their hearers. Certain simple but carefully selected obscenities establish instant complicity with groups which think themselves more authentic than the polite conventions they make a point of despising. The thief who has spent years in jail as evidence of his authentic vocation is acclaimed as a saint; the adventurer in evil may be hailed as a hero of humanity, a widener of spiritual horizons. The madman is an ultimate truthteller; what we are doing outside the padded cell is made a legitimate question only by one who's inside it. And at another level altogether, two men who want to be sure of one another—a briber and the recipient of a bribe, for example—will often seal their understanding by jointly violating a conventional code of some sort. One man may buy the other a girl, or the two may get disgustingly drunk together. It's a bond, a giving of oneself into the hands of the other: I'm no better than you, and we're both in league against the squares out there. Authentication, instead of meaning that one party is higher, better, purer of intent than the other, means that they are rascals together, *arcades ambo.*

Without endorsing either the sensationalism or the sentimentality that have accompanied public representation of the Mafia, one can see a lot of reasons why the bonds of that organization should be particularly deep and authentic. They are based on close family ties, a blood brotherhood, reinforced by centuries of historical tradition and fierce pride; punishment of the traitor is cruel and inevitable, rewards for the faithful are magnificent, and the tightness of the bonds is strengthened by the sense of being linguistic and social outsiders in an alien community. It's of course hard to know how much of their intimacy comes from this kind of linguistic occlusion, but as cause or effect it's an apparent fact. What mafiosi do is something they can talk about only with one another, and even then they are notably tightlipped. "Cosa nostra," our thing—if you know what it is, you'll know what I'm saying, if you don't, nobody's going to tell you.

Black authenticity may indeed be more authentic than white because less expansive, less directly self-aggrandizing; but for all that, it is not to pass unquestioned. Not every great sinner is an authentic sinner; there are just as many exhibitionists in that line of work as in any other, and considering simply the verbal strategies of persuasion involved, there's not much difference between this problem and that. In fact, one needn't be a hardboiled sceptic to sense that authenticity is a state of mind in the hearer, quite as much as a condition of what's being said. It is provisional complicity, a moment or more of assent; and assent, it goes without saying, is generally given on the basis of evidence much more complex than the verbal strategy of the propounder. Still, that's no unimportant matter, above all in an age of suspicion and anxiety. When nowadays we try to define in traditional terms an authentic and fair-minded man, we are in curious danger of producing the portrait of a pompous impostor. Hardly any claim to disinterested judgment based on evidence can be made without an obligation to recognize that this too is a *parti pris;* hardly any effort to explain what one means without a preliminary statement of what one is—already an act of crude presumption, with obvious overtones of deceit. Acting natural, the minute the question has been raised of what is natural, is simply acting. And yet in most discourse there is nothing else to do; we write or speak for those who are sympathetic to begin with or can be lured into sympathy by the apparent frankness of our approach, our readiness to get down to business, our lack of self-protective machinery. On one level at any rate, the best defence seems to be very close to no defence at all; one writes or speaks one's thoughts, and those who want to come along do. Of course nobody runs for public office on a program of unaffected frankness, but under those circumstances nobody expects authenticity anyway. The situation is structured against it, as abattoirs are structured against sensitivity, or pneumatic drills against concerts on the violin.

Obscenity may establish one's credibility with certain groups (not, I'm afraid, very critical groups), as after the war it was almost imperative, when teaching veterans, to establish that you were one of them by a few well-chosen words. A symbolic gesture of wider application though less general availability is getting out of an educated or bookish dialect and into one smacking more of the "real world." In countries like England and France, where there's a striking contrast between the polite and the vulgar tongues, one finds writers like Céline and D. H. Lawrence having resort to the dialect to express the fullness of a personal commitment. Mellors talks broad to Lady Chatterley on the same principle that Paul Morel talks broad to an old blind pit-pony; Shaw makes the point dramatically enough, in *Mrs. Warren's Profession,* when Vivie outtalks her mother easily in the educated dialect, but is badly beaten when the argument turns to street talk. Talking bad grammar deliberately, as a means of classing oneself with one's hearers, is a device almost as effective as talking a foreign language badly to a linguistic minority. (Talking it well gives no credit at all, is indeed suspect, as showing that one's had too good an education; but blurting out a few ill-formed phrases is understood to imply that one is making an imaginative effort to transcend one's limitations.) Failing such resources, the sincere often turn to very simple devices such as repetition and vociferation. A triple invocation ("Friends, Romans, countrymen") or a triple repetition (as when the Bellman in "The Hunting of the Snark" assures his crew that what he tells them three times is true) will add rhythmic and incantatory qualities to a simple assertion. Observers of battlefield rhetoric, including some as acute as Stendhal, tell us that absolute nonsense bellowed at the top of one's voice is more effective under those circumstances than the cool enunciation of good sense. Hammerlike repetition, violent vociferation, and strong, simple rhythms are the core of revivalist preaching, as of rock music; and in both instances coherent syntax and good sense are not to be looked for, they are impediments to the sort of communication being sought. Jean Louis David once delivered to the Assembly a violent, incoherent defence of Marat, which made not a shred of sense but seems to have been perfectly understood by those who heard it. The cheers at football games consist very largely of nonsense syllables, but nobody is in the slightest doubt about what they mean. Yet there is a contrary maneuver: a man who has been shouting will make more of an effect by suddenly speaking softly, directly, and with what is called "deadly seriousness," than he will by shouting still louder. The fact of a shift in tone, rather than the direction of the shift, creates emphasis—which I suppose is one element entering into the impression of sincerity, which is itself an element building toward a conviction of authenticity. Or may be. Violating a speech norm, frustrating a created expectation, breaking a syntactical commitment is such an ancient rhetorical device that the Greeks had a word for it, *anacoluthon*.

The basic conservatism of all devices of intensification is as natural as it is evident: inventive originality would simply call attention to the speaker's persuasive efforts, and distract from the point being made; it could even be interpreted as evasion and equivocation. One sees this in oaths when used, not as expletives or insults, but as a form of verbal reinforcement. (The double function of the oath, like the double reference of the word, tells its own story of the alliance between the sacred and the unholy.) A rational mind would complain that an everyday formula like "so held me God" is an idle form in these days when only simpletons expect God to help the truth-teller or rebuke the liar. Of course that's true, but the literal sense of the phrase is hardly in question, and in fact no verbal formula exists which will guarantee that a witness will even try to tell the truth—far less that ridiculous impossibility which we daily undertake to perform, telling "the whole truth." Still, there's some point to putting people on their guard that truth is expected of them and that penalties of some vaguely menacing sort are attached, under certain formal circumstances, to not telling it.

To attack others for complacency is a standard flash way of proving, if only to oneself, that one isn't smug. By decrying the pedantry of others, one implies one's superiority to that failing; and by electing oneself spokesperson for an entire generation, it's possible to advertise one's up-to-dateness without committing oneself to any specific intellectual position or process. "We today" think thus and so, and don't accept any longer the (presumably outdated) views of some earlier commentator. To write such contorted jargon that any critic can promptly be told he has absolutely misunderstood one is to achieve a sort of facile safety, if not total authenticity: such a gambit may be made to carry with it the implication of a thought so subtle and intricate that the coarse web of language altogether fails to catch it. When half a dozen people get together and agree they understand one another, though nobody else can, the privileged position becomes even more privileged, especially when it consists overtly of an attack on privileged positions. And there are many combinations of these various modes of charlatanry, not the least of which is to place oneself in the superior role of a taxonomist of charlatans. This is in miniature the spiral of words sucking down words, the vortex where all language is self-defeating and only mockery of the language process as such retains a meager quantum of authenticity. From this total self-isolation springs ultimate self-division; and it's been argued, by those who haven't tried it, that the schizoid or psychotic personality represents final freedom from the various tyrannies imposed by socialization. It's like an inevitable fulfillment that absolute freedom and absolute authenticity are discovered only in a mental state that we cannot reach and that cannot reach us. An ironist might express it that catatonia is the modern equivalent of the peace that passeth understanding. I don't think this terminus is often reached by the pathway of linguistic analysis, but that linguistic analysis often points toward this general outcome—if only by setting too high a standard for successful communication, by demanding too much of unaided language—is also apparent. In the simplest terms, any time that words are used to authenticate other words, they call into inevitable question not only the first words, but themselves. We began with that thought, we end with it; words authenticate other words only insofar as they define formal relationships between words—which is to say, when they call attention to a linguistic structure within which they themselves exist and by which they are inescapably conditioned. Trying to gain a critical perspective on language by means of language is like trying to cut butter with a knife made of butter. Fortunately, the whole authentication gambit is optional, and can be declined without penalty—when, to our agreeable surprise, we find that language, with all its constraints, buried assumptions, and built-in falsities can be made to serve remarkably well many of the limited purposes for which we want it. The clock strikes ten, but we all know it's three hours slow and understand by a habitual, almost instinctive translation, that it must be about one o'clock.

ROBERT MEZEY

Words

WE THOUGHT a day and a night of steady rain
was plenty, but it's falling again, downright tireless.
I like it well enough, the mild crackle
In the alleyway, lulling or minatory, either way
Full of the freshness of life. Much like words.
But words don't fall exactly; they hang in there
In the heaven of language, immune to gravity
If not to time, entering your mind
From no direction, travelling no distance at all,
And with rainy persistence tease from the spread earth
So many wonderful scents. And they recur,
Delicious to nose and throat. The word cunt
Particularly recurs, the word more than the thing,
Perhaps because I came to it relatively late.
Ocean recurs, maybe for the same reason, and egg,
Horseman and horse manure, bridal, sap,
And lap with its childish and charming delight in rhyme,
And denial describes its orbit, and blight, and transfigure.
And (though I argue that those smells of earth
Under the rain's long kneading hands
Are sweeter and more ambiguous than any words),
Darkness, one word that does seem to fall,
Falls, and we're back where we started from.

LEONARD MICHAELS

Legible Death

IN THE SEVENTEENTH CENTURY, when the word *sentence* implied much more than it does today, Hobbes could write: "To hear a young man speak sentences is ridiculous." The word meant "moral truth," "wisdom," "pithy saying," even something like "numinous utterance." (*The Book of Sentences,* for example: a compilation of sayings of the Church Fathers.) *Sentence* also meant "legal decision" or "prevailing opinion of a population" as in "It is the common sentence of the people." The word could distinguish valuable substance from mechanical form—"What you say is full of good sentence"—but it might mean either substance or form: "The brainless boy read every sentence in the book."

In the nineteenth century, a philosopher makes these two meanings equivalent: "What a logician calls a proposition a grammarian calls a sentence." In effect, substance is surrendered to one sort of analyst, form to another. As for the old dignity, authority, wisdom, experience, learning, pith, numinousness—it no longer declares itself. *Sentence* has become silent as a corpse submitted to the analytical knife.[1]

A similar literary devolution, says Michel Foucault, occurred in the nineteenth-century medical clinic, where the individual patient was now being described in a language that rested upon "the stable, visible, legible basis of death." He was seen, in relation to his disease, as "only an external fact."[2] This new medical language was inconceivable earlier, because individuals were seen as mysterious incarnations of a vital principle, mediations of eternity, uniquely feeling beings, voices, persons. Foucault's idea of this linguistic innovation, inspired by Nietzsche, issues through the grin of a modern skull exhilarated by its own finitude. In any case, what happened to the way people saw one another also happened to the way they saw their sentences.

In our own time, Wittgenstein, a Father of the logical church, who is great for his compilations of agonized sentences, writes:

> My only difficulty is an—enormous—difficulty of expression.

His reasons are implicit in many other sentences, but this one is dramatically revealing. "Enormous" swells in the middle and hangs by its dashes, and the word "difficulty" is repeated on the left and right of the dashes like arms. Between them the body, "enormous," pulls ponderously down. The problematic passion is within Wittgenstein, it seems, not history. He sounds lonely, crucified by his mind.

Though *sentence* is still used to mean decision—as in "The judge sentenced him to deadly labor at propositions"—its familiar modern application is to a unit of speech or writing. To be exceedingly precise, *sentence* now means "a series of words beginning with a capital letter and ending with a period, between which a subject and predicate are juggled, thereby signalling a thought." A young man speaking these will not be considered comical, only artificial. While we write sentences, nobody usually speaks them.

Indeed the modern idea of a sentence, though it includes many rhetorical possibilities, has no crucial connection with a voice, certainly not in the large sense of authority or origin. When President Nixon was told he contradicted himself, his press secretary announced that the president's earlier remarks were "inoperative." There is really no such thing as a liar anymore. Modern sentences are generated in motions of the infinite gas, what some call "discourse," or the mumblings of depersonalized millions.[3] "I am not a Marxist," cried Marx too late.

A definition, then, of the voiceless modern sentence should emphasize its structural-visual character: "It is manufactured by alienated beings who know some words, the rudiments of punctuation, and are capable of what *looks like* a thought." *Sentence* must not also be considered an auditory phenomenon, something that necessarily must be heard—even through one's eyes—for the fullness of its occasion. Here, for example, Coleridge talks about listening, and thus hearing, through one's eyes:

> The eyes quietly and steadfastly dwelling on an object not as if looking at it or as seeing anything in it, or as if exerting an act of sight upon it, but as if the whole attention were listening to what the heart was feeling and saying about it / As when A. is talking to B. of C.—and B. deeply interested listens intensely to A., the eye yet steadfastly fixed on C. as the subject of the communication—

This is comparable to reading a sentence; the old kind; the old way.

Finally, then, *sentence* has not only fallen from its antique implications, it no longer has the slightest residual connection with *sentire. Sentence* is insensate. It bears no scent of presence, human or divine. A clean corpse. It is to be looked at, like modern glass and steel constructions, by nobody. It is wrought in the feelings, experience, learning of nobody. It is inspired by nobody. Furthermore, many modern nobodies insist that sentences are essentially meaningless, they have nothing to say.

To suppose any vanished implication or application of *sentence* might be revived, even if we all consented to try, would be nonsensical. Too much has changed. Even the poor word *sententious* which, to Samuel Johnson, meant "a lot of sentences," had already come to mean in his day an expression of scorn. Today, the mere sight of a lot of sentences may strike some people as an affront to sense, not to mention sensibility. Still, there remains an innocent, if melancholy, pleasure in reconsidering what we valued before we achieved modernity in legible death. To begin, please consider this sentence about the sentient body, by Martin Luther:

> Faith resides under the left nipple.

We notice he does not say "heart," but substitutes a medical reality, "left nipple," for the pathetic banality, and thus, in a few particular words, makes his point terrific, his implication awesome.[4] A power—somewhat reminiscent of the power of God, residing neither in what we see nor literally hear—rings in these word things. The sentence does not signal to its readers, as if it were written for dogs. Nothing is signalled. Everything is, for Luther and for us, in the sense of this sentence. One might even say, in the desperate contemporary formula, "I hear you, Luther."

The comic drama of this next sentence, by Bertolt Brecht, also achieves great force of implication by playing with the relative proportions of a man and something hugely, ominously other:

> The man who is laughing has not heard the news.

Compared to the looming, unspecified news, risibility is ridiculous, but, more impressive, the unidentified laughing man appears suddenly identified, naked as a nipple, so to speak.

Whereas Luther's sentence expands immensely by concentrating its focus, Brecht's sentence concentrates—showing us an idiot—by expanding its focus. They operate in verbal sound, or in the dynamics of voice, the way photo-receptive cells operate in the eye, seeking exact degrees of resolution through contrasts. (Background/foreground, dark/light, big/little, etc.)

These might be called sentences of visionary authority. If neither Luther nor Brecht says the very thing, what they say is nothing else. Therefore we "hear" it or "see" it. *It* is like a shadow, what Coleridge defines as subsisting in "shaped and definite nonentity." Derrida calls it a "trace." The difference is between absence and presence or everything and nothing. Tranströmer, the great Swedish poet, says, speaking of life these days, ". . . often the shadow seems more real than the body."[5]

Less stunning than either Luther or Brecht, but more exquisite, is this sentence by Wallace Stevens which also does not say what it says so that we may hear it:

> It is the word *pejorative* that hurts.

This isn't one of his famous or lovely observations, but it is supposed to seem less remarkable than it is. The sentence contains no hurtful word, only the category of such words, in *italics,* but—and this is its beauty—the sentence feels complete. It says all it has to say, even to our shrivelled ears, without saying all. The feeling of completion comes mainly through the rime of "hurts" and "word." Auditory sensation carries a sense, the effect of closure, the effect of a hurtful word. Stevens avoids the possible vulgarity of a too particular word so that we may feel the pure impact of pejoration without the punch of a pejorative. ("It is the word *ratface* that hurts.") His sentence is the *sentio* of experience. Of course it is also a line, or what used to be called a "period," and therefore implicated in kinaesthetic feeling as well as sound.

Now please consider a famous sentence by La Rochefoucauld, which is also about pain, and, like Stevens's sentence, also faintly precious, reluctant to specify, to touch:

> There is something in the misfortunes of our friends that does not entirely displease us.

The vagueness of "something" is vaguely turned and refined by "not entirely," thus making the brutal sentiment nice, suitable or sayable in society, and yet it is the kind of remark that might offend socialists. Swift, who approved of La Rochefoucauld, nevertheless makes such vagueness vicious:

> Last week I saw a woman flayed and you will hardly believe how much it altered her person for the worse.

"Last week" is a journalistic *frisson.* It introduces lust for immediacy in looks and effects. The grotesque urgency of "how much" deepens the depravity in the voice of the sentence. You cannot read it simply with your eyes, the very instruments of abstraction responsible for "how much." Again, this great sentence by Jane Austen requires you to hear its voice and the voice behind its voice, its genius:

> It is a truth universally acknowledged that a single man in possession of a good fortune must be in want of a wife.

She says a man in "possession" must be in "want," and her "universally" applies muscle to "single," tumbling it down the path to the anticlimactic "wife." The speaker seems, as if against her will, to suggest that being in want of a wife is the cause of good fortune. The same invincible willy-nilly marries that single man at the stop. The voice is officious, vigorous, funny, maybe a little depressed, and, in its push from exceeding generality through impotent individuality, gobbling up a world in words, finally thrilling.

For the sake of contrast with all of the above, here is a sentence by a young modern writer who would say the very thing, the thing itself, and not one word more:

> I leaped to my knees.

Near the exit of our sentence museum stand two sentences like sentinels. They are a splendid contemporaneous pair, from Hegel and Blake, saying opposite things, with equivalent cogency, in different ways. First Hegel:

> The animal is the other in its agony.

Blake answers:

> How do you know but ev'ry bird that cuts the airy way,
> Is an immense world of delight, clos'd by your senses five?

These sentences speak beyond the language in which they are written. "She sang," says Wallace Stevens, "beyond the genius of the sea." The internal rime makes the echo that is his meaning, and, while it might be imitated, the line cannot be easily explicated. Because the sentences from Hegel and Blake also have a form in which their intuitions are realized, and preserved against rational analysis, it is not easy to explain them without letting their energy and pleasure bleed away.

However, Hegel's idea of "the other" and "the animal" is given concrete elaboration by Ortega y Gasset. First he considers the monkey in the zoo—the way its nervous, fearful attention to the environment never ceases—and then he says:

> objects and events in its surroundings . . . govern the animal's life, . . . pull it and push it about like a marionette. It does not rule its own life, it does not live from within *itself,* but is always alert to what is going on outside it, to what is *other* than itself. . . . [This] is equivalent to saying that the animal always lives in estrangement, is beside itself, that its life is essential *alteración.* ("Otheration.")[6]

Hegel means consciousness without self-consciousness—"the animal"—is how we perceive "the other" in its distinction from ourselves, beings with an inner life, a self, capable of meditation, of ideas. The animal is imprisoned by sheer existence, or the forces of blind selfless existence. Agony.

Blake says self-consciousness is agony sufficient unto itself. The question form leaves Blake's sentence yearning, as if beyond the "five," though it is stopped hard at that word. Each sense, because it is countable and therefore definitively limited, is a prison bar. There is more to explain, but Kafka says our time is up. He concludes the Hegel-Blake exchange with a minuscule narrative sentence:

> A cage went in search of a bird.

If we surrendered the substance of Kafka's sentence to a logician and the form to a grammarian, their analyses might discover the paranoic dynamism of our contemporary chemistry. It is, I think, the perfect modern sentence. Heavy with ancient resonance, and yet, in its radical form, immediate as this instant.

The sentence recalls Wallace Stevens's line about the motive for metaphor—"The vital, arrogant, fatal, dominant X"—being death. But Kafka's "bird" (freedom, life, art), like Blake's, seems to invoke its strange antithesis, rather than to be motivated by it.

Neither of them is so concerned as Stevens to crush sentimentality; and Kafka's "bird," because it has less respect for logic, flies farther than Blake's. Literally preposterous, Kafka's whole sentence mimics the action of life, as if there were no other way to seize a certain weird, ultimately inexplicable, intuition: "The meaning of life is that it stops."

Notes

1. The first and second paragraphs are based, in a very general way, on definitions of *sentence* given in the *Oxford English Dictionary.* Only its quotations from Hobbes and the philosopher are reproduced. "The brainless boy" is invented. C. S. Lewis's *Studies in Words* (Cambridge, 1960), chapter 6, "Sense," treats *sentence* among several semantically related words, illuminating the historical net of nuance in which they lie. Most of the exemplary sentences quoted later are translations. The original languages might not have greatly obscured the meaning of these sentences, but, in any event, what they gain in English is indispensable.

2. Michel Foucault, *The Birth of the Clinic* (Pantheon, 1973).

3. W. K. Wimsatt uses the phrase "infinite gas" in his book *The Verbal Icon.* The idea of iconicity is implicit in the discussion above, especially in the passage on Luther.

4. Stanley Cavell refers to this quotation in his very brilliant essay on *King Lear,* collected in *Must We Mean What We Say?* (Cambridge, 1969).

5. The quotation is from "After A Death," by Tomas Tranströmer, included in *Friends, You Drank Some Darkness: Three Swedish Poets,* trans. Robert Bly (Beacon Press, 1975). The stanza from which the quotation comes is:

> It is still beautiful to feel the heart beat
> but often the shadow seems more real than the body.
> The samurai looks insignificant
> beside his armour of black dragon scales.

The poem is much more complicated than my comment above suggests. It is about the effect of death in life or on life.

6. "The Self and the Other," trans. Willard R. Trask, in *The Dehumanization of Art,* by Jose Ortega y Gasset (Princeton, 1968). Ortega does not say the following: The idea of Otherness is made into a noun that feels more concrete, "the Other." This noun is made to feel yet more concrete by identifying it with another noun, "the Animal." Passing back through degrees of concretion we return to the idea of Otherness, which is anything that is not anything else, or, most particularly, anything not the self. "The Animal," then, is the most interesting concretion of the life of the not-self, the living not-selfness which is "the Other." To be all this and conscious, but not to know it is all this, not even to know it is conscious, is the agony of the animal. (But animals dream. Dogs twitch, whine, and snarl in their sleep, as if they were running and fighting in an inner wilderness. This means they have an inner life? They are subjects or selves, perhaps even capable of meditation, like us? No; the way animals dream is the way we make sentences these days.)

NOTES ON CONTRIBUTORS

ROBERT M. ADAMS is Emeritus Professor of English at the University of California, Los Angeles, and author of a book on the dark side of language, *Bad Mouth* (1977), and a study of vanished works of art, *The Lost Museum* (1980).

KINGSLEY AMIS is a poet, novelist, essayist, honorary fellow of St. John's College, Oxford, and former teacher of English literature at two British and American universities. He has published many articles on the language, and in 1974 he gave a series of talks on the subject on BBC radio.

DWIGHT BOLINGER is Emeritus Professor of Romance Languages and Literatures, Harvard University, and author of *Forms of English* (1965), *Aspects of Language* (1965), *Degree Words* (1972), *Meaning and Form* (1977), and a book tentatively entitled *The Words Will Get You If You Don't Watch Out,* to be published in 1980.

LEON BOTSTEIN, president of Bard College and Simon's Rock Early College, was educated in the fields of history and music. He is a violinist and has made numerous appearances as an orchestral conductor. His articles have appeared frequently in *New Republic, Partisan Review, Change Magazine, Harper's, New York Times Magazine,* and other journals.

JULIAN BOYD teaches English at the University of California,

Berkeley, and ZELDA BOYD teaches English at California State University, Hayward. They have written several articles on language and literature.

LEO BRAUDY, Professor of English at Johns Hopkins University, is the author of *Narrative Form in History and Fiction* (1970), *Jean Renoir* (1972 National Book Award nominee), and *The World in a Frame* (1977); he has also edited anthologies on Norman Mailer and on François Truffaut's *Shoot the Piano Player* and has co-edited *Great Film Directors* (1978).

ROBERT BURCHFIELD is chief editor of the Oxford English Dictionaries at Oxford University Press, and editor of the first two volumes of *A Supplement to the Oxford English Dictionary.* Since 1963 he has been a fellow and tutor of English language at St. Peter's College, Oxford, and he lectures all over the world on various aspects of lexicography.

ANTHONY BURGESS is a novelist and critic. His novel *A Clockwork Orange* (1962) was filmed in 1971. His recent publications include *Joysprick: An Introduction to the Language of James Joyce* (1973), *Napoleon Symphony* (1974), *The Clockwork Testament* (1974), *Moses* (1976), *A Long Trip to Teatime* (1976), *Beard's Roman Women* (1977) *New York* (1977) *Ernest Hemingway and His World* (1978), and *1985* (1978). He wrote the scripts for the television series *Moses the Lawgiver* and *Jesus of Nazareth* and is a frequent contributor to the *Times Literary Supplement* and other journals.

ANGELA CARTER is a writer of fiction (seven novels and two volumes of short stories) who lives in South London. She has also written a feminist monograph on the Marquis de Sade, *The Sadeian Woman* (1979).

BASIL COTTLE is Reader in Mediaeval Studies of English at the University of Bristol, and author of *The Penguin Dictionary of Surnames* (1967, enlarged 1978), *The Triumph of English: 1350–1400* (1969), and *The Plight of English* (1975). From 1943 to 1945 he worked as a cryptoanalyst in the "Enigma" team at Bletchley Park.

JOHN DILLON, born of Irish political stock and educated in Ireland and England, is Professor of Classics, University of California, Berkeley, and author of *Iamblichus: The Platonic Fragments* (1973), *The Middle Platonists* (1977), and (with Brendan O'Hehir) *A Classical Lexicon to Finnegans Wake* (1977).

DENIS DONOGHUE is Professor of Modern English and American Literature, University College, Dublin. His books include *The*

Third Voice: Modern British and American Verse Drama (1959), *Connoisseurs of Chaos* (1966), *The Ordinary Universe* (1968), *Jonathan Swift* (1971), *Yeats* (1971), *Thieves of Fire* (1974), and *Sovereign Ghosts: Studies in Imagination* (1977).

MARGARET A. DOODY, Associate Professor of English at Berkeley, is author of *A Natural Passion: A Study of the Novels of Samuel Richardson* and a novel, *Aristotle Detective.* She is an Anglican (Episcopalian) and the daughter of a minister of the Anglican Church of Canada.

JUDY DUNN is assistant director of the Medical Research Council Unit on the Development and Integration of Behaviour, University of Cambridge, Madingley, and a fellow of King's College, Cambridge University. She studies child development, has three children, and is the author of (with Martin Shaffer) *Your Child's First Five Years* (1974); *Distress and Comfort* (1977); and (with David Shaffer) *The First Year of Life* (1979).

D. J. ENRIGHT, director of Chatto and Windus, has written many books of poetry and fiction, including several for children, and is a contributor to *Scrutiny, Encounter,* and *Listener.* His most recent publications include *Daughters of Earth* (1972), *The Terrible Shears* (1973), *Sad Ires* (1975), and *Paradise Illustrated* (1978); and he has edited *A Choice of Milton's Verse* (1975) and Samuel Johnson's *The History of Rasselas, Prince of Abissinia* (1976).

GAVIN EWART has taught English language and literature. His books of verse include *No Fool Like an Old Fool* (1976), *Or Where a Young Penguin Lies Screaming* (1977), and *All My Little Ones* (1978).

FRANCES FERGUSON is Associate Professor of English at the University of California, Berkeley. She is author of *Wordsworth: Language as Counter-Spirit* (1977) and is currently working on a book on the relation between literacy and literature (and the ideologies of education) in the eighteenth and nineteenth centuries.

M. F. K. FISHER published *Serve It Forth* in 1937, and since then thirteen more books, as well as stories, articles, and poems. She writes regularly for the *New Yorker.* The daughter of a newspaper editor, she was raised with *Webster's International Dictionary* beside the dining room table.

RONALD HARWOOD is a novelist, dramatist, scriptwriter, and television chairman. He has written a biography of the actor Sir Donald Wolfit. Among his recent works is a dramatic adaptation of Evelyn Waugh's *The Ordeal of Gilbert Pinfold.*

KATHRYN HELLERSTEIN is translating Moishe Leib Halpern's Yiddish poems as part of a study of American modernism in the Yiddish voice. Her poems, essays, and translations have appeared in *Poetry, Kenyon Review,* and other journals and anthologies.

LIAM HUDSON is Professor of Psychology at Brunel University. Among his recent books are *The Cult of the Fact* (1972), *Human Beings* (1975), and a novel, *The Nympholepts* (1978).

DIANE JOHNSON is Professor of English at the University of California, Davis. Her biography of Mary Ellen Peacock, *Lesser Lives* (1972), was nominated for the National Book Award in biography; and her recent novel *Lying Low* was a 1979 nominee. Her other novels include *Burning* (1970) and *The Shadow Knows* (1974). Her critical articles appear in the *New York Times* and the *New York Review of Books.* She is married to a professor of medicine.

SIMON KARLINSKY is Professor of Slavic Languages and Literatures at the University of California, Berkeley. His most recent books are *The Sexual Labyrinth of Nikolai Gogol* (1976) and *The Nabokov-Wilson Letters, 1940–1971* (1979).

HUGH KENNER is Andrew W. Mellon Professor in the Humanities at Johns Hopkins University. His books include *The Pound Era* (1971), *The Stoic Comedians: Flaubert, Joyce, and Beckett* (1975), *A Homemade World: The American Modernist Writers* (1975), *Geodesic Math and How to Use It* (1976), and *Joyce's Voices* (1978).

MAXINE HONG KINGSTON wrote *The Woman Warrior: Memoirs of a Girlhood among Ghosts* (1976), which won the National Book Critics Circle Award for general nonfiction. Her next book, *Gold Mountain Heroes,* will be completed at the end of 1979 and will be published by Knopf.

ANDRÉ KUKLA, Associate Professor of Psychology at the University of Toronto, has published psychological and philosophical articles in *Psychological Review, Philosophy of Science,* and other journals. He is currently on a leave of absence from the university to study Oriental psychologies of consciousness with several Eastern teachers.

KARLA KUSKIN is the author and illustrator of over thirty children's books, and she has written criticism and reviews for *Saturday Review, New Republic, New York Magazine,* and the *New York Times,* among others. She has recently won the National Council of Teachers of English Award for Poetry for Children.

ROBIN TOLMACH LAKOFF teaches in the Linguistics Department at the University of California, Berkeley. Her principal publications include *Abstract Syntax and Latin Complementation* (1968) and *Language and Woman's Place* (1975).

DAVID S. LEVINE received his law degree from Boalt Hall School of Law, University of California, Berkeley. He is associated with a large law firm in Oakland, California, doing commercial and general litigation, and between 1969 and 1978 he worked as a stringer with *Time* magazine.

DAVID LODGE, Professor of Modern English Literature at Birmingham University, is a novelist and critic. His most recent novel, *Changing Places,* was awarded the Hawthornden Prize. His works of criticism include *Language of Fiction* (1966) and *The Modes of Modern Writing* (1977).

LOUIS B. LUNDBORG retired as chairman of the board of the Bank of America and of BankAmerica Corporation in 1971. In more than twenty-eight years of business experience, he has also been general manager of the San Francisco Chamber of Commerce, vice president in charge of university development at Stanford, and director and vice chairman of the Stanford Research Institute. His recent books are *Future Without Shock* (1974) and *Up to Now* (1978). He is a contributing editor of and writes the column "Executive Survival Kit" for *Industry Week.*

SEAN MCCONVILLE, who lectures in social administration at the University of Sussex, has published numerous essays and articles on penal policy and administration and has recently completed a major historical study of English prisons. He has worked in a prison and now serves as specialist advisor on penal policy to the House of Commons Expenditure Committee, and as a member of the Board of Visitors at Lewes Prison.

ROBERT MEZEY, who teaches at Pomona College, California, has over the past thirty years published his poems in the *New Yorker, Kenyon Review, Poetry, Partisan, Harper's,* and others. His books of poetry include *The Lovemaker* (winner of the Lamont Award), *White Blossoms, A Book of Dying, The Door Standing Open, New and Selected Poems,* and *Couplets.* He has also edited several anthologies, including (with Stephen Berg) *Naked Poetry.*

LEONARD MICHAELS is Professor of English at the University of California at Berkeley, author of *Going Places* (1969, nominated for the National Book Award in fiction) and *I Would Have Saved Them If I Could* (1975), and editor of *University Publishing.*

WALTER BENN MICHAELS teaches English at the University of California, Berkeley, and is writing a book on the philosophical background of American literary criticism.

JOSEPHINE MILES is a poet, critic, and Professor of English at the University of California, Berkeley. Her works of criticism include *The Vocabulary of Poetry, The Continuity of Poetic Language, Eras and Modes in English Poetry, Style and Proportion,* and *Poetry and Change*. She is also the author of a number of books of poetry, from *Lines at Intersection* (1939) to *Poems, 1930–60, Kinds of Affection* (1967), *To All Appearances* (1975), and *Coming to Terms* (1979).

D. A. MILLER teaches English and comparative literature at the University of California, Berkeley.

JANE MILLER, Lecturer at the University of London Institute of Education, has taught English for many years in London schools. She is currently involved in research into the educational implications of language diversity, and she writes regularly for the *Times Literary Supplement*.

LISEL MUELLER is the author of *Dependencies, Life of a Queen, The Private Life* (the 1975 Lamont Poetry Selection), and *Voices from the Forest.* She was the recipient of the Emily Clark Balch Prize of the *Virginia Quarterly Review.* She teaches at Lake Forest College.

ALICIA OSTRIKER is Professor of English at Rutgers, author of *Vision and Verse in William Blake* (1965), and editor of the Penguin edition *William Blake: The Complete Poems* (1978). She has published three books of poetry, most recently *A Dream of Springtime* (1979), and has written articles and reviews on women's poetry.

J. R. POLE is Rhodes Professor of American History and Institutions at Oxford University and Fellow of St. Catherine's College. He was a guest scholar at the Woodrow Wilson International Center for Scholars in Washington, D.C., during 1978–1979. His books include *Political Representation in England and the Origins of the American Republic* (1966), *Foundations of American Independence* (1971), and *The Pursuit of Equality in American History* (1978).

FELIX POLLAK, former Curator of Rare Books at the University of Wisconsin and now retired, is the author of four collections of poetry—*The Castle and the Flaw* (1963), *Say When* (1969), *Ginkgo* (1973), and *Subject to Change* (1978)—and twice winner of the poetry award from the Council for Wisconsin Writers.

PETER PORTER is a poet, journalist, reviewer, and broadcaster. His books include *The Last of England* (1970), *Preaching to the Converted* (1972), *Living in a Calm Country* (1975), and *The Cost of Seriousness* (1978).

RT. HON. J. ENOCH POWELL is a Member of Parliament (Ulster Unionist) for South Down. He was formerly a professor of Greek and Minister of Health in a Conservative government. Among his recent books are *No Easy Answers* (1973) and *Wrestling with the Angel* (1977).

RANDOLPH QUIRK is Quain Professor of English Language and Literature at University College, London, and director of the Survey of English Usage, the resource base from which—with his colleagues and co-authors—he has derived many of his chief publications, notably *A Grammar of Contemporary English* (1972). He is a fellow of the British Academy and chief academic adviser on English studies to the British Council.

FREDERIC RAPHAEL is the author of fourteen novels, including *The Limits of Love, Lindmann, Like Men Betrayed,* and *California Time,* as well as a collection of short stories, *Sleeps Six,* and a number of screenplays. For his sequence of six television plays, *The Glittering Prizes,* he received the Royal Television Society's award as Writer of the Year in 1976. He is a fellow of the Royal Society of Literature and a frequent contributor to the literary columns of the *Sunday Times* (London) and other publications.

ISHMAEL REED is a novelist, poet, and essayist. His books include *The Free-Lance Pallbearers* (1967), *Yellow Back Radio Broke-Down* (1969), *The Last Days of Louisiana Red* (1974), *A Secretary to the Spirits* (1977), and *Shrovetide in New Orleans* (1978), among others. He has been nominated for the National Book Award in both the poetry and fiction categories.

DAVID REID is Contributing Editor of *University Publishing.* He is working on a book about secret history.

CHRISTOPHER RICKS is Professor of English Literature at Christ's College, Cambridge University, and author of *Milton's Grand Style* (1963); a critical biography, *Tennyson* (1972); and *Keats and Embarrassment* (1974). He edited *The Poems of Tennyson* (1969) and is an editor of *Essays in Criticism* and a reviewer for the *New York Review of Books,* the *Sunday Times* (London), and the *Times Literary Supplement.*

IAN ROBINSON is Senior Lecturer in English at University College of Swansea; secretary of the Brynmill Press; former editor of *The Human World*; and author of *Chaucer and the English Tradition* (1972), *The Survival of English* (1973), and *The New Grammarian's Funeral* (1975).

RICHARD RODRIGUEZ has published essays on education, literature, and politics. His essay in this collection is from his forthcoming autobiography, *Toward Words*—a description of a life experienced through language.

VERNON SCANNELL is a poet and novelist, and at one time was a professional boxer. Among his recent books of poetry are *Selected Poems* (1971) and *The Loving Game* (1975).

NATHAN SILVER, head of the William Morris School of Architectural Studies, North East London Polytechnic, also runs his own architectural practice. American born and trained, he has taught at Columbia and Cambridge universities and for several years was regular architecture critic for *New Statesman*. His books are *Lost New York* (1967), nominated for the National Book Award; (with Charles Jencks) *Adhocism: The Case for Improvisation* (1972); and a forthcoming critical history of the Centre Pompidou in Paris.

JOHN SIMON, drama critic for *New York Magazine* and *Hudson Review* and film critic for *National Review,* also writes the language column for *Esquire*. His books include *Movies into Film* (1971), *Ingmar Bergman Directs* (1972), *Uneasy Stages* (1976), and *Singularities* (1976).

QUENTIN SKINNER is Professor of Political Science at Cambridge University and author of numerous articles in the history of ideas and the logic of the human sciences. His most recent book is a two-volume study, *The Foundations of Modern Political Thought* (1978).

GENEVA SMITHERMAN is Director of Black Studies and Professor of Communications at Wayne State University and has taught in the Afro-American Studies Department at Harvard University. Her books include *Black Language and Culture: Sounds of Soul* (1975) and *Talkin and Testifyin: The Language of Black America* (1977).

MONROE K. SPEARS is Libbie Shearn Moody Professor of English at Rice University. His books include *The Poetry of W. H. Auden* (1963), *Hart Crane* (1965), and *Dionysus and the City* (1970).

MICHAEL TANNER is a fellow of Corpus Christi College, Cambridge University, and University Lecturer in Philosophy.

CHARLES TOMLINSON is Reader in English Poetry at the University of Bristol. His most recent publications are *Selected Poems, 1951–1974* and *The Shaft*, and he has also edited *The Oxford Book of Verse in English Translation*.

MARINA VAIZEY, a critic, essayist, and frequent broadcaster, is art critic for the *Sunday Times* (London), and a member of the History of Art Board, Council for National Academic Awards. Lady Vaizey is a past member of the Arts Council of Great Britain and a former art critic for the *Financial Times*, as well as the author of *One Hundred Masterpieces of Art*.

JANET WHITCUT is associate editor ine dictionary and reference book department of Longman Hou. She is co-author of the *Longman Dictionary of Contemporary glish* (1978) and has done research for the Survey of English Uge at University College, London.

EDMUND WHITE is the author of two rvels, *Forgetting Elena* (1976) and *Nocturnes for the King of Naples* (19). With Charles Silverstein he wrote *The Joy of Gay Sex* (1978).Iis latest book of essays is *Travels in Gay America.* He has taughtreative writing at Yale and Johns Hopkins.

MARY-KAY WILMERS is fiction edir of the *Times Literary Supplement*.

DESIGNER: Eric Jungerman
COMPOSITOR: Viking Typographics

TEXT: VIP Bembo
CLOTH: Holliston Roxite A 49275
Permalin Oriental Gold
PAPER: 50 lb. P&S Offset Regular